Engendering Latin America

A Culture of Everyday Credit

Housekeeping, Pawnbroking, and Governance in Mexico City, 1750–1920

MARIE EILEEN FRANCOIS

UNIVERSITY OF NEBRASKA PRESS
LINCOLN & LONDON

Manufactured in the United States of America
♾

Portions of chapters 1 and 3 were previously published in "Cloth and Silver: Pawning and Material Life in Mexico City at the Turn of the Nineteenth Century," *The Americas* 60.3 (January 2004): 325–62. Reprinted with permission.

Portions of chapter 2 were previously published in "Prendas and Pulperías: The Fabric of the Neighborhood Credit Business in Mexico City, 1780s–1830s," *Estudios de Historia Novohispana* 20 (1999): 67–110. Reprinted with permission.

Table I in appendix 1 has been translated and augmented from a table published in "Vivir de prestado: El empeño en la ciudad de México" in *Bienes y Vivencias: El Siglo XIX Mexicano*, vol. 4 of *Historia de la vida cotidiana en México*, ed. Ann Staples, series ed. Pilar Gonzalbo (México: El Colegio de México / Fondo de Cultura Económica, 2005).

Library of Congress Cataloging-in-Publication Data
Francois, Marie Eileen, 1963–
A culture of everyday credit : housekeeping, pawnbroking, and governance in Mexico City, 1750–1920 / Marie Eileen Francois.
p. cm. — (Engendering Latin America)
Includes bibliographical references and index.
ISBN-13: 978-0-8032-6923-1 (pbk. : alk. paper)
ISBN-10: 0-8032-6923-4 (pbk. : alk. paper)
1. Pawnbroking—Mexico—Mexico City—History. 2. Home economics—Mexico—Mexico City—History. 3. Pawnbroking—Government policy—Mexico—Mexico City. I. Title. II. Engendering Latin America (Unnumbered)
HG2106.M63M494 2006
332.3'40972530903—dc22
2006004735

CONTENTS

List of Illustrations vi

List of Tables vii

Acknowledgments xi

Abbreviations xiv

Introduction 1

1. Hocking the Private in Public: Credit Policy, Housekeeping, and Status, 1750–1840 17

2. Collateral Lending: Pulperías and the Monte de Piedad, 1750–1840 48

3. Collateral Living: Consumption, Anxious Liberals, and Daily Life, 1830–80 78

4. Brokering Interests: Casas de Empeño and an Expanded Monte de Piedad, 1830–75 114

5. Positivist Housekeeping: Domesticity, Work, and Consumer Credit, 1880–1910 150

6. Porfirian Paradoxes: Profit versus Regulation, Capital versus Welfare 189

7. A Material Revolution: Militancy, Policy, and Housekeeping, 1911–20 224

Conclusion: Housekeeping, Pawnbroking, and Politics 258

Epilogue: Still A Culture of Everyday Credit 268

Appendix 1 273

Appendix 2 293

Appendix 3 317

Notes 337

Index 411

ILLUSTRATIONS

1. "El Camino del Curato o sea La Oca de la Orquesta, 1869" 2

2. "La Molendera" 89

3. "La Planchadora" 106

4. "La Lavandera" 109

5. "Camarera Mexicana" 166

6. "Las Lavanderas" 170

7. "Cargadores" 180

8. "Venta de Prendas, Monte de Piedad, and New Home Sewing Machine" 186

9. "En el Empeño" 238

TABLES

1.1. Female Household Heads in Cuartel 9 Sample, Mexico City, 1811 Census 33
1.2. Household Goods in Pawning Transactions, 1787–1830 39
2.1. Principal Balance of Monte de Piedad, 1802 71
2.2. Type, Average Sale Price, and Customer Gender of Auctioned Goods at Monte de Piedad, 1802 74
3.1. Dowries Provided to Women, Mexico City, 1838–55 97
3.2. Household Goods in Pawn, 1867–80 105
4.1. Transition from Retail to Empeño on the Corner of Peredo Bridge and Plazuela de San Juan 117
4.2. New Empeños Established and Bonded, 1842–43 119
4.3. Interest Rate on One-Peso Loan, Based on Schedule in 1842 Empeño Law 125
4.4. Municipal Contributions Payable by Class of Empeño, 1867 129
4.5. Changes in Ownership of Casas de Empeño, 1842–79 135
4.6. Loan Average, Total Lent, and Total Appraisal for Pawned Goods 137
4.7. Operations in the Monte de Piedad, January 1875 146
5.1. Population by Civil Status, Federal District, 1895 and 1910 157
5.2. Distribution of Middle-Class and Working-Class Occupations, Federal District Censuses, 1895 and 1910 158
5.3. Housekeeping in the Federal District, 1895 and 1910 Census 168
5.4. Household Goods in Pawn, 1902–9 178
6.1. Multiple Pawnshop Ownership during Porfiriato 194
6.2. Longevity of Pawnshop Ownership 197
6.3. Longevity of Empeño Business Location 199
6.4. Taxation on Empeño Business Volume in Pesos, December 1901 200
6.5. Vergara Empeño Daily Business Volume, May 1902 201

6.6. Volume of Business at Cartagena Casa de Empeño, Adela Noriega, Owner, 1908 204

6.7. Capital Balance at Monte de Piedad 207

6.8. Volume of Business at Monte de Piedad, 1875–1904 210

6.9. Volume of Business at Montepío Luz Saviñón, December 1908–June 1909 212

7.1. Household Goods in Pawn, 1914–21 249

Appendix 1. Collateral Transactions Data

A. Breakdown of Pawned-Good Database from Inventories by Business, 1787–1921 274

B. Categories of Goods in Pawning Transactions, 1787–1830 277

C. Categories of Goods in Pawning Transactions, 1867–80 280

D. Categories of Goods in Pawning Transactions, 1902–9 283

E. Categories of Goods in Pawning Transactions, 1915–21 285

F. Categories of Pawned Goods in Samples Compared 288

G. Collateral Values of Goods in Retail Pawnshops, 1787–1825 289

H. Repeat Pawning Customers by Gender 290

I. Comparative Collateral Loans, 1818–1915 291

Appendix 2. Pawnbroker Data

A. Store Profits, Net Worth, and Active Pawn Investment, 1785–1823 294

B. Retail Stores in Continuous Operation with Continuous or Changing Ownership, 1781–1843 296

C. Census Stores with Continuous Ownership in the Family 297

D. Salary Increase, Monte de Piedad Employees, 1826 298

E. Volume of Pawning and Redeeming at Monte de Piedad, 1775–1887 299

F. Limosnas and Loans at the Monte de Piedad, 1802 301

G. Disposition of *Prendas Cumplidas* at the Monte de Piedad, 1802 302

H. Casas de Empeño in Locations Formerly Retail, 1840–78 303

I. Casa de Empeño Database, 1836–1915 304

J. Retail Establishments Complying with the 1842 Casa de Empeño Bond Requirement 305

K. Entrepreneurs in Both Retail and Pawning, 1854 305

L. National Monte de Piedad Directors, 1775–1924 306

M. Porfirian Empeños in Traditional Retail or Pawning Locations 307

N. New Empeño Locations, 1870s–1910 308

O. Changes in Ownership of Porfirian Pawnshops 310

P. *Demasías* Deposited by Pawnbrokers, 1877–79 315

Q. Collateral-Credit Interest Rates Compared, 1758–1920 316

Appendix 3. Census Data

A. Mexico City's Population 318

B. Cuartel 9, Mexico City, 1811 Census 318

C. Cuartel 9 Sample, Mexico City, 1811 Census 319

D. Widows in Cuartel 9 Sample, Mexico City, 1811 Census 319

E. Household Heads in Cuartel 9 Sample 320

F. Servants Living in Cuartel 9 Sample Households, Mexico City, 1811 Census 321

G. Households with Servants in Cuartel 9 Sample, Mexico City, 1811 Census 322

H. Ethnicity and Marital Status of Male Merchants, Mexico City, 1811 Census 323

I. Distribution of Middle-Class Occupations, Federal District, 1895 Census 324

J. Distribution of Middle-Class Occupations, Federal District, 1910 Census 325

K. Distribution of Working-Class Occupations, Federal District, 1895 Census 326

L. Distribution of Working-Class Occupations, Federal District, 1910 Census 328

M. Females in Federal District, 1895 Census 330

N. Females in Federal District, 1910 Census 333

ACKNOWLEDGMENTS

A decade is a long time, even to write a book about almost a century and a half of Mexican history. I incurred innumerable debts in the process of producing this book and surely will spend decades more repaying them. Many scholars have shaped questions I asked in this project, going back to my college days at Virginia with William Taylor and Joseph Miller, then on to Master's years in Santa Cruz with David Sweet and Sonia Alvarez. A summer at the Programa Interdisciplinario de Estudios de la Mujer (PIEM) at the Colegio de México and then doctoral training at the University of Arizona with Michael Meyer, Donna Guy, Kevin Gosner, Bert Barickman, Karen Anderson, Nancy Hunt, and Doug Weiner introduced me to historiography and feminist theory, which continue to rattle around in my head. Keeping up with the likes of *compañeros* Bianca Premo, Michael Brescia, Sharon Bailey-Glasco, Jeff Shumway, Osvaldo Berreneche, Wendy Waters, Helen Wheatley, and Andrew Sessions challenged my intellect. This book would have been impossible without the archival expertise of Juan Rodríguez Buendía, especially in uncovering pawnshop inventories and combing nineteenth-century newspapers for pawning references.

Michael Meyer, Kevin Gosner, and Donna Guy on my dissertation committee, as well as Doug Cope and John Kicza, gave me valuable feedback on my dissertation and helped transform that project into this more ambitious book. María del Pilar Martínez López-Cano, Anne Staples, and Judy Ewell gave me much to think about in editing articles that came out of the project. I cannot thank Donna Guy and Kevin Gosner enough for reading the manuscript on short notice before it went off in search of a publisher. Silvia Arrom and two anonymous readers for the University of Nebraska Press contributed more than they know with their comments. Others who have offered suggestions about conference papers and chapters over the years include Rodney Anderson, Jay Kinsbruner, Edith Couturier, Bill Beezley, Jane Mangan, Jurgen Buchenau, Victor Macías, Katherine Bliss, John Lear, Rob Buffington, Phyllis Smith, and Patience Schell. I have tried to heed all their sage advice, and any blame for inconsistencies or a lack of clarity that remain rest solely with me.

My decade of research took me into numerous archives in Mexico, and I thank the staff at the Archivo de la Nación, Archivo Histórico de la Ciudad de México, Archivo General de Notarías de la Ciudad de México, and Nacional Monte de Piedad for their generous and expert assistance. Pilar Gonzalbo and Anne Staples secured my access over the years to the stacks at the Biblioteca Daniel Cosío Villegas at El Colegio de México, and the staffs of the Biblioteca de México at the Ciudadela, Hemerotéca Nacional, Fototeca Nacional, Biblioteca Miguel Lerdo de Tejada, and Biblioteca Nacional were very helpful. I thank the staff at the Bancroft Library in Berkeley, and especially the Inter-library Loan personnel at the University of Arizona and Auburn University for keeping up with my constant requests for rare books and microfilm. The staff at the Latin American Library at Tulane University offered expert assistance in my search for illustrations for the book, as did the staff of Artes de México.

Generous funding from numerous sources over the years facilitated my research and allowed me time to write. At the University of Arizona, a Sybil E. J. Pierce Scholarship in 1995 and an Edwin S. Turville Scholarship from the History Department; a WOSAC Travel Stipend from the Women's Studies Program in 1995; and a Social and Behavioral Sciences Research Institute Graduate Research Grant in 1996 funded dissertation research. I was honored to receive an Albert J. Beveridge Grant for Research in the History of the Western Hemisphere from the American Historical Association in 1996 and a Dissertation Fellowship from the Western Association of Women Historians in 1997. From Auburn University a Competitive Research Grant in 1999, Humanities Development Grants in 2001, and a Marguerite Scharnagel Award for Research in 2002 allowed me to undertake the second phase of research and to write the book. My colleagues in the History Department and my students at Auburn continually make me thankful for having chosen this line of work.

My family, those under my roof and those scattered about the globe, have been supportive and understanding of my preoccupation with cloth and silver goods revolving in and out of pawnshops in Mexico City. As an infant, my daughter Eileen stayed up late with me while I worked out the dissertation, and my daughter Elizabeth's last words to me at night as she drifts off are still "Are you going to work for awhile?" I come out of this decade sane and happy because of my girls and their father, Juan—husband, research partner, household partner, and guide to the rich Mexican culture. My brothers and sisters are always there for me, as are so many friends in Maryland, California, Alaska, Oaxaca, Nezahuacoyotl, Coacalco, and everywhere else. I want to thank my brother Michael for extraordinary support. I am indebted to my parents, Frank and Eileen Francois, and my mother-in-law, Delfina Buendía Arrieta, for the stories about their lives and their interest in mine. I dedicate this book to my mother, who died shortly after it found a home in Nebraska. You are my inspiration and a hard act to follow.

ABBREVIATIONS

AGN Archivo General de la Nación

AGNCM Archivo General de Notarías de la Ciudad de México

AHCM Archivo Histórico de la Ciudad de México

AHNMP Archivo Histórico de la Nacional Monte de Piedad

BN Biblioteca Nacional

CONDUMEX Centro de Estudios de Historia de México

A CULTURE OF EVERYDAY CREDIT

Introduction

In 1802 an embroidered shawl sat in hock for six months in Mexico City. Its owner, Gertrudis Castillo, a white fifteen-year-old woman from Guadalajara, pawned it for a loan of four pesos at the Monte de Piedad, a public charitable pawnshop. A century later in a private neighborhood pawnshop, a customer listed as "Morena" hocked a string of corals and a silver thimble for a loan of twenty-five centavos, while another identified as "Perez" pawned two pairs of irons for loans of eighty-seven centavos and one peso respectively.[1] Regular small-scale collateral-credit relationships constituted a fundamental continuity in the material history of Mexico City for hundreds of years. This book examines popular credit and the material culture in which it was embedded from the late eighteenth to the early twentieth centuries.[2] Since at least the 1600s, the most common way for middling as well as poor residents to raise cash in the specie-starved economy of Mexico City was to pawn material possessions such as clothing, tools, and jewels.[3] The regularity of pawning was so much a part of the city's material culture—so everyday—that a pawnshop found its way onto a popular board game in the middle of the nineteenth century.[4]

Figure 1 reproduces an 1869 version of the popular Juego de la Oca (Goose Game) called "El Camino del Curato o Sea La Oca de la Orquesta" (The Road to the Rectory or It Could Be the Goose of the Orchestra), in which players would advance and backtrack with throws of the dice on thirty-four squares around the game board.[5] The squares of this particular version of the game depict different aspects of political and material culture in Mexico City at midcentury, and the "Montepío" (Pawnshop) in square twenty-one represents a crucial intersection of economy, politics,

Fig. 1. "El Camino del Curato o sea La Oca de la Orquesta, 1869." Santiago Hernández. Used with permission from *Artes de México: El arte de la suerte* 13 (1991): 42.

and culture. While highlighting through satire an emergent male, public middle-class milieu amidst other male working-class imagery, the creators of the game virtually ignore middle- and working-class women. Yet the households run by those women both produced and reproduced liberal citizens and the Mexican culture in which the Juego de la Oca was played. Creoleness and middle-class respectability were about social class, as were working-class identities. Women across economic and social hierarchies created public personas through creative financing with private household resources in public and privately owned businesses in the marketplace of pawnbroking. The montepío and other squares on our game board are windows on Mexico City a half-century into republican rule and a half-century away from revolution, windows on a culture of everyday credit. The liberal subjects of the games' squares, along with subjects that remain invisible—behind the curtains, so to speak—are the subjects of this book.

Class, Collateral Credit, and Housekeeping

The historical literature on Mexico as well as on Latin American cities generally emphasized a society of two classes until the twentieth century—an upper one of *gente decente* (decent people) or *gente de bien* (people of property) or even *gente de razón* (people of reason) and a lower one supposedly without those defining characteristics, that is, not decent, without property, not able to reason.[6] Our Juego de la Oca squares depict mostly middle-class symbols: male clothing styles of top hats and frock coats, a bearded orchestra musician, a natural history museum, a dance (at which men are dancing with men in an anticlerical jab at the homosocial *curato*, or parish rectory), and the Tivoli de San Cosme café. The board game privileges an emerging middle-class culture embedded in political and economic liberalism at a time when, demographically, "the middle" of society was relatively small. Colonial Mexico City, as the capital of the Viceroyalty of New Spain, was whiter than the rest of Mexico, where indigenous populations were more important.[7] About half of the city's residents in 1811 identified as either Spanish or Creole (i.e., American-born white), with virtually all the white women born locally. In the early 1800s most people in the city were poor, with four-fifths of the population plebeians suffering from low wages, high grain prices, underemployment, cramped housing, and epidemics. This majority, the so-called *léperos* of contemporary literature, was "largely mestizo, mulatto or Indian who earned their living from begging or from sporadic employment."[8] Poorer whites lived and worked amidst mestizos and Indians who shared their economic lot. To the extent that there was a middle class in the early part of the century, it was whiter, though increasingly ethnically mixed.[9] As the city expanded from about one hundred thousand in 1811 to over six hundred thousand in 1921, it went from a white to a mestizo majority and the middle class grew to about a third of the population.[10]

At the time of our 1869 Juego de la Oca, arguably two-thirds of the capital's population made up the lower socioeconomic sector, most "readily identifiable as mestizos."[11] This majority is present but underrepresented on the game board. Men from popular classes wearing jackets and caps appear as subordinates, facing interrogation by frocked men in squares labeled "Califaciones" (Quality Judgments, presumably to determine suffrage eligibility) and "Elecciones" (Elections). Other "ordinary" men appear as participants in Lancasterian vocational education and patriotic juntas. A solitary park bench in square seven titled "Arbolitos" (Little Trees) conjures two images: one of those without shelter but with a poncho that could double as a blanket taking a quick nap or even retiring for the night, and the other of an exhibitionist middle-class culture, with benches in public parks like the Alameda, places where gente decente sit in their sumptuous outfits.

A central argument of this book is that the Montepío occupying square twenty-one—with pawned clothing hanging behind the counter on which a pawned table clock sits—was crucial to economic life for both the small middle class and the majority working class. By the late eighteenth century, a two-tier institutional pawning framework existed in Mexico City. As the city grew, steady demand for collateral credit meant that both pawning tiers expanded lending over time. The first tier consisted of corner store retailers who doubled as pawnbrokers. By the 1830s freestanding pawnshops emerged, making higher-interest collateral loans that averaged one peso. These businesses were called *casas de empeño* in legislation and montepíos in popular usage, as in the case of the board game. Were the owner of the pawnshop in square twenty-one present, we would likely see a caricature of a *gachupín* businessman. The collateral-credit business was dominated by middle-class immigrant Spanish men throughout the century despite political independence from Spain, and these entrepreneurs suffered a poor public image. On the second tier is the public Monte de Piedad, offering low-interest loans that averaged ten pesos, or ten times the average loan in the private sector, throughout the first half of the nineteenth century. Established as part of the Bourbon reforms, the Monte de Piedad constituted a charity for the middle ranks, especially women who lived in the city without male breadwinners contributing to housekeeping expenses. The Monte's founding in 1775 was featured in a later Juego de la Oca in 1907 entitled "Ciclo Histórico" (Historical Cycle), which commemorated watershed years in Mexican history.[12]

Women made up half of the city's population in the nineteenth century. And women, especially needy widows, stand out as the most visible pawning customers in literary and legal discourses on pawning. Women's clothing such as *enaguas* (petticoats) and *rebozos* (shawls) were the goods most commonly found on pawnshop shelves, along with goods used largely by women in housekeeping work. Yet the only women to appear on our Juego de la Oca board are those in square three, labeled "Viudas" (widows). Here, three women draped in rebozos are walking through a door marked "Treasury." These are middle-class women, as only widows of government bureaucrats were eligible to collect pensions from the government. In the course of everyday life in Mexico City in the 1860s, the widows' next stop could be the Montepío in square twenty-one, where they would use some of their pensions to redeem the collateral goods they had hocked as part of regular strategies to finance household consumption. Respectable middle-class widows as well as poorer ones used this strategy to buy food, a mundane yet necessary household expense for comfortably situated as well as poorer housekeepers. Square thirteen features a fat man in an apron and a caricatured Chinese-style hat, cooking on the grill at "La Cocina de Palacio." While reflecting regular habits of middling and poorer folks who obtained meals outside the home, this stop on the game board obscures the women—ever present in literary portraits of the nineteenth century—selling enchiladas and other fare on the streets. And the windows of the board game are closed completely to the goings-on inside poor and middling households in the city, where this type of game was played in family settings.

Throughout the long nineteenth century, one way to define "the middle" has been in terms of who did household chores.[13] Part of being gente decente was having a staff of domestic servants, a measure adopted by the emergent middle class.[14] Housekeeping is one of the processes at work in the creation of social class. Crucial social distinctions such as honor, respectability, whiteness, decency, and so forth, are products of housekeeping just as are subsistence, washed sheets, or mended clothing. As part of housekeeping, both consumption and pawning linked the production and reproduction involved in securing a livelihood for people across the social-status spectrum in Mexico City.[15] Engaging some theory about what else constitutes and creates class is helpful in deciphering the cultural history of Mexico City. Pierre Bourdieu's concepts of "habitus" (defined by him as "a structured and structuring structure" and by Ann Farnsworth-Alvear as "the everyday, interpersonal terrain," not unlike our board game), social class, class fractions, and "constructed class," taken together, suggest that distinctions between and among individuals and groups are variable—dependent on and determinate of structure, culture, and agency. Bourdieu sees credit as maintaining distinctions between class "conditions" and fending off the process of "declassing," an idea easily applied to the way pawning played out in Mexico.[16] Equally useful is E. P. Thompson's understanding of class "as something which in fact happens (and can be shown to have happened) in human relationships."[17] Recent studies of Latin America suggest that class definition is about material struggles, language, and identity while "making do." Using a model of both structure and discourse, D. S. Parker finds a middle class in Lima only in the twentieth century.[18] Contradictory and complementary, these fluid conceptualizations of social class push beyond simple measures such as occupation or income level to include ethnic and gendered identities, material manifestations, physical and social spaces—in short, cultural reproduction.

When can we talk about a middle class of significant size for Mexico City? Observers during the Porfiriato (1876–1910) emphasized the development of both a proletarianized working class and a professional and consumption-oriented (if fractioned) middle class in the last two decades of the nineteenth century.[19] In a short story entitled "Historia de un Peso Falso" (History of a False Peso) published in 1883, the modernist Manuel Gutierrez Najera described a counterfeit peso coin that the protagonist received from a "respectable merchant" in change for a five-peso bill. The true pesos are represented as "aristocracy," while the false peso was "of unknown parents" and "the poor thing [*el pobretón*], that of the middle class, neither a centavo nor a decent person." Thus this mock lament about an orphaned middle-class identity dependent on counterfeit money shows that "clase media" was a meaningful term in the early Porfiriato, but also suggests that decency and respectability were sought but not yet achieved by those in the middle.[20] In contrast to this sad portrayal, Irene Elena Motts, a science teacher born as the nineteenth century came to a close, described her parents as "belonging to the comfortable middle class and very cultured, especially my father who had been educated in Europe: he was an accountant by profession and also multi-lingual; and he as much as my mother, [were] great enthusiasts of music and lovers of the Fine Arts." As a child, the Mott family's status meant that she had "no lack of diversions" with regular outings in the city and its surroundings, museum and circus trips, as well as attendance at "all the events and places where one can acquire culture"—cinema, opera, comedy, and concerts.[21] Judging by our Juego de la Oca, some of these middle-class cultural markers—orchestras and museums—were in place before the Porfiriato. By the time of the Mexican Revolution, some in this middle class had both high expectations and high consumption levels, but also economic and political frustrations that they shared with the working class and the truly poor. Their frustrations were exacerbated when their privileged pawning arena, the Monte de Piedad, shut down as the revolution hit the streets of Mexico City. The revolution disrupted the fundamental collateral-credit household financing apparatus, and hence brought middle-class and working-class residents into the revolutionary fray.[22]

Household Credit in Comparative Perspective

On the Juego de la Oca gameboard from 1869, the National Treasury appears twice—once as the destination of the widows and once in its own square (no. 27), with an open door and bags of money piled on a counter.

This, too, was money secured by credit. What little strength the newly independent Mexican state mustered depended on its relationship with *agiotistas*, or private lenders who financed the treasury.[23] The Monte de Piedad itself lent to the government on many occasions. Central in the political, economic, and cultural history of the modern world, credit has been tied to imperialism, the growth of capitalism, and modern state formation. Legend has it that Queen Isabella pawned the crown jewels to finance Columbus's voyage to the New World, paving the way for the Spanish conquest of Mexico.[24] Silver from the Americas provided the Spanish crown with credit to pay for military campaigns and a bloated bureaucracy, allowing Spain to "live beyond its means."[25]

Essential on the macro level of empire and nation, credit was also vital at the local level of household, community, and small business. Arguably the most common credit transaction in Mexico City was a pawning transaction.[26] Each month for two hundred years, thousands of city residents have borrowed money by converting household goods into collateral. Pawning credit differed from some other forms of popular credit—like the *tienda de raya* (company store)—in that no debt was incurred because loans were secured with collateral goods. Yet the pawning process and the company store linked households to the political economy of Mexico. From medieval times to the present, "preindustrial forms and networks of credit usually provided a vital and important place for women," who were involved in both consumption and productive lending and borrowing.[27] For colonial Mexico, married and widowed elite women were often lenders.[28] Many of those living off of rental property in Mexico City throughout the nineteenth century were women, putting capital in a few thousand female hands for lending. By the 1920s the importance of female lending may have diminished as women lost ground in the real-estate market.[29] A study of late twentieth-century rotating credit systems among Mexicans finds women central to petty lending networks as representatives of their households, but it misses the continued centrality of pawning strategies in Mexico.[30]

A key difference between Mexican pawning and pawning in Europe and the United States is the regular use of pawnshops by middle sectors in addition to the traditional poorer clientele in Mexico.[31] In late colonial Mexico, the reality that middling groups and the bottom tier of the elite needed small collateral loans was recognized by the state when it established the Monte de Piedad, but pawning by the well off was nonetheless disguised in rhetoric about the charitable institutions' mission to help needy women and the poor in general. By the end of the nineteenth century in a period of rising consumerism, collateral-credit practices of middle sectors in republican Mexico City may still have been disguised through pseudonyms; the record of patrons at a provincial Monte de Piedad in the late 1870s shows a "list of pseudonyms such as Carlos III, Fernando VII, and Agustín de Iturbide."[32] Liberal policy makers as well as novelists nonetheless recognized middle-class pawning.

As in other places in the nineteenth century, most of the goods pawned in Mexico were recovered by their owners and not abandoned, as is common in pawning in the United States today. A borrower did not necessarily need liquid cash for redemption but instead might pawn another piece of collateral to get the first one out.[33] Also as in other settings, the clients (or their representatives) who passed through the doors of pawning establishments were more often women than men.[34] The preponderance of women among pawning clientele is not surprising, as pawning fit in with other economic and consumptive housekeeping activities such as marketing. Studies of contemporary housework in Mexico have shown pawning to be of "enormous importance" for the reproduction of popular households, especially during times of economic crisis.[35] Mediation work done by women in the household—especially mediating between income and needs—led to pawning activities to stretch the family budget.[36] In this sense Mexico had much in common with England, where, in the working-classes, "women were disproportionately responsible for household functions, including the management of small-scale household credit," and women's access to credit shaped "the interrelationship of the household with the market."[37] But the economic function of housework was not limited to "just squeaking by" during economic crisis. Women as managers and consumers were "creators as well as the bearers of status."[38] And it is not only conspicuous consumption that was important, but also the mundane but essential patterns of *inconspicuous* consumption managed by women of all classes.[39]

Mexican women from middle sectors used pawning to facilitate their housekeeping and consumption, as did poorer women, and that consumption constituted work for housekeepers in the lower ranks of Mexican society, not just in "comfortable" households. The intersecting and central roles of women as housekeepers, managers of consumption, and pawning clientele in the Mexican capital reflects the demographic reality of a third of the city's households headed by women in the first half of the nineteenth century and over 40 percent of the female population widowed throughout the century.[40] Pawning is a partial answer to the question of how this demographic reality shaped daily life in Mexico City and how women heading households coped with a gendered labor market, with lower wages for females than males and ideological contexts that cast female employment as dishonorable and glorified a domestic role for women. Whether households were headed by women or men, one of the functions of a household was to ensure the physical and cultural survival of its members, and pawning household goods facilitated this survival. Female household heads were a diverse group—the majority widows, some single mothers, some living alone or with a servant, others living with sisters or friends. Both female heads of households and partners of male household heads regularly turned to pawning to facilitate their housekeeping work, whether they visited the pawnbroker themselves or sent someone out to pawn for them.[41]

Social class, pawnbroking, consumption, and housekeeping are intertwined in this book as they were in the material history of Mexico City. If our Juego de la Oca had a square depicting the interior of the typical middle-class household, it might mirror this description by Mexican social critic Guillermo Prieto:

> A steep stairway led to a corridor paved with red varnished millstones. The corridor was embellished with cages filled with stuffed birds, squirrels, wind chimes, and earthen crocks packed with stored foods and vegetables. Landscapes . . . adorned the walls. Comfortable chairs and couches . . . furnished the principal chamber. Cuspidors occupied its corners, and a large brazier for cigarettes and heat stood on the floor. In the bedroom were a large bed of fine wood, easy chairs, and wardrobes. . . . The dining room contained a washstand holding towels, soap, straw, and a scouring stone for scrubbing. Colored vegetables, pots, and pans, and jars lined the kitchen walls . . . with strips of garlic and pepper for a festive air. A huge barrel of water stood at its center.[42]

There were, of course, more elements in the construction of this middle-class home—servants, the clothing people wore, the status of the people who came to visit. Middle-class families in the capital were engaged in inconspicuous day-to-day consumption when sitting on those chairs, taking turns reading novels aloud, as the educator Motts recalls. Washing up for dinner after the servant brought the warmed water in the silver pitcher, eating meals, sleeping in their beds—all of this was inconspicuous consumption relative to the circumstances when the family dressed for theater, threw a dinner party, or attended a ball in the latest fashions. Thousands of people daily managed these levels of consumption through the use of collateral credit, converting easy chairs and wardrobes, even pots and pans, into cash when expenses outran cash in hand. Imported furnishings were staples for middle-class households.[43] Housekeeping goods had "the status of near money" because of their collateral value, the popular and middling classes cashing in their domestic and imported goods throughout the nineteenth century as a liberal economy developed in Mexico.[44]

Liberalism

Liberal governance was unstable in nineteenth-century Mexico until the defeat of the French occupation in 1867. Our 1869 Juego de la Oca is celebratory of the liberal triumph: Men in frock coats and top hats populate the squares of the game board, depicting liberal institutions such as the city council, the Congress, and the Supreme Court. The police appear, symbolizing order and good governance, as does an air balloon, symbolizing technological advancement. Most of the squares picture liberal heroes: "Don Benito" Juárez is in square twenty-two next to the montepío; his secretary of war, General Ignacio Mejía, marches on the other side of the board; and the diplomat Matías Romero, the politician Sebastián Lerdo de Tejada, and Nacional Monte de Piedad director (1868–76) Francisco de Paula Cendejas occupy other squares. Additional featured liberal institutions are the Junta Patriótica and a polling table. All in all, the liberal symbols on our board game exhibit a public male *political* liberalism, yet people in Mexico lived through liberalism in many ways. Popular economic practices and relations between business people and other residents of Mexico City intersected with policies of an evolving liberal state. Introduced in Mexico by the Bourbons through their economic and social reforms and then further elaborated to include political rights and representation for a limited citizenship beginning with the Cortes and on through the independence struggle and the nineteenth century, liberalism "happened" in the city in particular ways. Recent work on Peru has revealed the importance of "liberalism in the bedroom." This book considers liberalism in the rest of the Mexican household, too, and highlights the way in which liberalism played out in the small businesses and on the streets, where the daily routines of men and women who headed households were linked to the city's liberal political economy.[45]

The study of material life reveals important continuities in the city's history through traditional political-period breaks. During the Bourbon era, the short-lived first empire, the tumultuous early republican era ending with the Reform, the French intervention, the Restored Republic, the

Porfiriato, and the Mexican Revolution, women were most often the ones seeking collateral loans in the capital. The Enlightenment and the development of liberalism throughout the century, nonetheless, brought changes to households. While women benefited to a greater extent from the promises of economic liberalism in terms of paid employment by the end of the century, their formal political participation as full citizens was kept at bay as their domesticity was lionized.[46] The nineteenth century brought restricted access to property for some women. Under Spanish law, a widow inherited half of the communal property (as well as being entitled to her dowry and whatever property she might have owned separately), and daughters and sons received equal portions. Women of means went into marriages with dowries consisting of clothing, jewelry, and furniture, both to contribute to the needs of the family and to assure that the woman would be provided for in widowhood. While the husband had the right to administer his wife's dowry, he pledged not to alienate, gamble, or otherwise lose her property.[47] In colonial Puebla and Guadalajara, clothes, linen, jewels, furniture, and silverware were the most numerous items that went with women into their marriages. The value of these movable goods was between one-quarter and three-quarters of the total value of most dowries. It is precisely these personal and household goods that most often constituted the collateral "mortgaged" with pawnbrokers in Mexico City for cash loans. Less valuable housekeeping goods such as *ollas, trapos, canastos* (pots, cloth, baskets), omitted from late colonial dowries, also appear in the pawnshop inventories and, indeed, constituted the goods available for collateral purposes for poorer households where dowries were absent.[48] The practice of endowing daughters waned in the nineteenth century, and liberal legislation in the late nineteenth century brought the potential for other changes in the relationship of Mexican women to property. Married couples were able to choose between communal and separate regimes, daughters were no longer guaranteed an inheritance equal to sons, and testators were free to leave their property to anyone. Over time, Mexican women lost some of their guaranteed property rights, and their continued access to movable property such as household goods became increasingly important in their decision making and management of household economies.

On our game board, only the cook in square thirteen represents economic activities beyond the liberal professional middle class. Yet in the laissez-faire economy, the range of popular commercial activities in nineteenth-century Mexico City was vast, including anything to do with sales, purchases, investments, and exchanges. The sale of services such as brokerage or legal defense; the labor of maids, laundresses, chauffeurs, and apprentices; the sale of merchandise such as groceries, petticoats, and pocket watches—all were commercial activities involving the exchange of cash. So, too, were the purchase of lottery tickets, cab rides, liquor, and sex. Many aspects of popular commerce are touched upon in this book, with the focus on consumption work and pawnbroking.

The regulation of the pawning business prompted brokers to fight for their rights as businessmen, while statesmen weighed in on "the public good." A study of the pawning business reveals tensions between state formation and liberalism. Taxation and regulation made the state interventionist, while liberal theory held that the state was to leave the economy to entrepreneurs. Interactions between pawnbrokers and their clientele in neighborhood households, where few of the former and many of the latter were women, also structured economic relations at the local level. Male middle-class pawnbrokers were part of the story of capitalist expansion, and they engaged the state in negotiating the course of Mexican capitalism through the discourse of liberalism.[49]

Governance was part of the everyday "relations of forces," "bundles of relationships," and a "multiplicity of force relations" that shaped political, economic, and material culture. The pawning process constituted relations between and among tiers of state and society—brokers, clients, servants, housewives, tax collectors, inspectors, regulators, government ministers, generals, newspaper editors, social critics, and so on.[50] The Mexican state attempted to assert itself in the pawning process at multiple levels, encountering both clients and brokers. In building hegemony both the colonial and national states regulated pawning as part of welfare policies. In the transition to the liberal state, governance of pawnbroking passed to a growing bureaucracy. The state included employees of the Monte de Piedad, as well as the bureaucrats of the ministry of Gobernación charged with keeping tabs on private and public pawnbrokers.[51] Though the state was embedded in the bundles of relationships between and among brokers, clients, bureaucrats, and others, both pawnbrokers and clients often failed to comply with pawning regulations. Through petitions and other discursive mechanisms, brokers and clients resisted and shaped pawning legislation.[52]

Evidence of Culture

On square thirty-three of the Juego de la Oca sits a trunk labeled "The Archive." Most evidence of the culture of everyday credit was found in city and national archives, as well as in the archive of the Nacional Monte de

Piedad. This book basically draws on three kinds of primary materials. The first are archival documents: government oversight memoranda, laws, censuses, court documents, police records, business records, tax records, letters, petitions, and so forth. The second are newspapers, memoirs, novels, and other literary sources. The reader will notice the steady use of quotations from this second group of sources, as well as from petitions and memoranda from the first group, to provide a sense of the tone of dialogues and word choices made in discussions of pawning policy and pawning practice. Testimonies, editorials, and literary portrayals constitute verbal snapshots of material circumstances, as well as recordings of public opinion and information about actual behaviors of participants in the collateral-credit market. Middle-class men—journalists, short-story writers, and novelists—generated much of the discourse about pawning, and they stress pawning as a strategy of the desperately poor and/or as vice.[53] Despite biases, these discursive sources are a window on hegemonic process, a way to measure the influence of ideology on political economy and cultural behaviors and to determine the degree to which pawning practitioners on both sides of the collateral transaction consent to or resist the plans of policy makers. Culture is a contested terrain, and looking at the discourse about pawning alongside pawning practices and policies allows us to examine how the contest played out in households, in pawnshops, and on the streets of Mexico City.[54]

The third kind of source consists of inventories from pawnshops found mostly in archives, but also published in newspapers. How useful are inventories of pawned goods (*prendas*) for getting a picture of the nature of household goods and personal possessions that city residents regularly acquired and consumed in everyday life? The idea of anthropologists Mary Douglas and Baron Isherwood that consumption of goods "has a double role in providing subsistence and in drawing lines of social relationships" is useful here. So, too, are Bourdieu's concept of "economic capital," the "social life of things" and "sex of things" explored by recent scholarship, and conceptualizing consumption as both inconspicuous and conspicuous.[55] Throughout the book, comparisons are made to assess changes in material culture across time, as well as identification of levels of material culture related to status, class, and gender. This kind of information can be obtained through estate records such as wills, dowries, and probate, but only for those who leave such records, generally members of middle ranks and the elite. Pawnshop inventories have the potential of providing consumption information for a broader sector of society, and they offer more detailed information about mundane or inconspicuous goods that generally are not specified in estate inventories.[56] Indeed, a growing and changing cast of ordinary and sophisticated housekeeping goods pass in and out of the pawnshops' revolving doors.[57]

Pairing the study of household consumption with a detailed study of the rise of private and public pawnbroking sectors reveals the fundamental role that credit and small business played in everyday lives in Mexico City. The book offers an analysis of the cultural practices of people who borrowed money using personal belongings, household goods, and tools. The book is also an exercise in policy analysis in a long-term historical context —policy affecting households and small businesses, policy hotly debated in the print media.

Chapters 1, 3, and 5 highlight pawning customers and develop the political and socioeconomic contexts in which pawning became and remained a regular part of everyday routines for managing household consumption and shaping identities. Clothing and household linens constitute the vast majority of the more than eight thousand *prendas* (collateral goods) in a database compiled from pawnshop inventories from 1787 to 1920, with silver spoons and plates as well as jewelry also important early on, especially in the Monte de Piedad. Each of the housekeeping chapters provides an analysis of a time block from the pawned-goods database. The collateral data, which have been organized into analytic tables in appendix 1, are referred to throughout these chapters. The housekeeping chapters are built on the material base of goods found in pawnshops, with the discursive picture in the narrative sources filling in the context. Full contextualization of the material evidence would have been impossible without the very rich monographic literature on Mexico City and the broader Latin American literature on material culture, ethnicity, and gendered honor. My debt to these scholars, especially the Mexicanists, is enormous.[58]

Interspersed chronologically between the housekeeping discussions, chapters 2, 4, and 6 highlight the middle-class Spanish men who staffed the Monte de Piedad and owned the private pawnshops (only a small minority of brokers were female). Using a second database of over two thousand individual businesses engaged in collateral lending from 1787 to 1916 that was culled from business records of the Monte de Piedad, retail outlets that engaged in pawning, and the casas de empeño, these chapters trace the development of the private pawning sector and the changes in administration of the public charity during different political periods. Tables in appendix 2, which compile pawnbroker data, are referred to throughout the business chapters. Business volumes and profit margins, the longevity of particular business locations, and the longevity and volatility of business ownership are considered in these chapters. Pawnbrokers engaged liberal and conservative Mexican statesmen in negotiating the regulation of their trade and asserting their rights as businessmen in a liberal capitalist economy while facing recurring anti-Spanish sentiments among policy makers and in public opinion.

Chapter 7 examines the response of housekeepers to the practices of pawnbrokers in the context of social revolution in the second decade of the twentieth century. The reign of Porfirio Díaz (1876–1910) saw interest rates in the private sector skyrocket to 40 percent a month. Mobilizations led by women from popular and middle-class households challenged Spanish pawnbrokers when they rejected revolutionary decrees severely limiting interest rates to the Monte de Piedad rate of 5 percent a month.

Statistical tables of census data in appendix 3 are referred to throughout the book. I sampled the manuscript from the 1811 census for a downtown neighborhood, while I analyzed the published occupational summaries for Porfirian censuses from 1895 and 1910.

Interpreting the evidence of pawning policy and practice has meant understanding that material life consists of "material objects, their symbolic and emotional meanings, and the social relationships in which they were embedded."[59] While the symbolic and emotional meanings of the objects found on pawnshop shelves remain elusive, some of the social relationships involved come alive in novels and archival documents from the period. Goods, including collateral goods, "are part of a live information system."[60] Goods on the pawnshop shelves, which secured access to a line of credit, divulge something about their owners. Pawning practices were embedded in the material culture of Mexico City, contested as brokers and clients negotiated values for their goods, as husbands wrestled dowry goods from their wives to convert to cash, as housekeepers decided which household item was both dispensable and valuable enough to secure a loan, and as brokers and clients resisted or ignored attempts by the state to regulate their business activity. The social relations involved in hocking items such as clothes, furniture, and jewels reflected and shaped ethnic, class, and gender relations in the large urban center that was (and is) Mexico City.[61]

It was big news in 1997 when the Monte de Piedad shut down. The charitable pawnshop, providing consumer credit in a dozen branches throughout Mexico City, closed for almost six months due to a strike of its employees' union in the midst of a structural adjustment crisis in the Mexican economy. The recent strike made headlines because Mexican working- and middle-class families have long depended on pawnbroking services to keep their households afloat. We pick up the story of the culture of everyday credit back in the eighteenth century . . .

ONE

Hocking the Private in Public

Credit Policy, Housekeeping, and Status, 1750–1840

In a downtown neighborhood of Mexico City in 1811, Ygnacia Ruiz pawned a cotton jacket for six reales at the *pulpería* (corner grocery store) a block and a half from her house near the Parque del Conde. A fifty-year-old Creole widow, Ygnacia lived in the household headed by her son *licenciado* Don Francisco Alvarez, with her other adult children (two daughters and another son) and an indigenous woman who was a live-in servant. Her young Creole neighbor María Rosales, whose husband, José Trinidad Paz, was unemployed, had enaguas and a rebozo in hock for one peso three reales with the same storekeeper, Don Miguel Domínguez. These two Creole women might have encountered fellow Domínguez customers who were servants in middling and elite homes, such as Ygnacia Excorcia, a twenty-seven-year-old Indian widow, or Doña María Gertrudis, a forty-year-old Creole widow. Ygnacia Excorcia worked as a servant in the household of an immigrant merchant from Rioja and his Creole wife and had a petticoat in hock for four reales, or half a peso. Doña María Gertrúdis and her five-year-old daughter lived with the extended family of a Creole attorney, for whom she worked as a domestic servant. She pawned a rebozo with Domínguez for four reales.[1] Women such as these—wives, widows, and servants of Creole, indigenous, and mixed-race heritage—regularly pawned personal and household goods, especially cloth, for very small cash loans with grocers. Corner-store owners, the most well-known personages in city neighborhoods, had many "very personal" relationships with neighborhood residents.[2] Women with more valuable material goods to convert into cash turned to the Monte de Piedad, which gave cash loans of at least two pesos for silver jewelry and table service and for silk skirts, linen petticoats, and other luxurious cloth goods.

This chapter explores the neighborhood experience of women and men in households such as those run by Ignacia Ruiz and María Gertrúdis, assessing the policies of colonial governors that affected household economies and the financial practices of household managers from the middle of the eighteenth century into the decades after Mexican Independence. Urban housekeeping patterns included the pawning strategies women used in managing budgets along a spectrum from subsistence levels to conspicuous consumption. Housekeeping work entailed the reproduction of people and of status, the production and preparation of food and clothing for household consumption, and the creation of culture. Three sets of evidence shape this discussion. First, in concert with other social legislation, Bourbon-era laws regulated pawning practices in corner stores and the Monte de Piedad. The gendered dimensions of the impact of regulatory and institutional policies on urban households illustrate how intersections of social class and ethnicity shaped material life. Second, census data offer a demographic picture of the largely white neighborhoods in the city center, where at least a third of the households were headed by women. Third, pawnshop inventories, court records, and colonial literature reveal what city residents actually pawned in the Monte de Piedad and retail pawnshops—mostly cloth and silver that women owned personally or used in housekeeping—and what those goods tell us about the daily lives of their owners.

Larger contexts for this discussion include the intersections of race, class, and gender in the formation of discourses about honor, respectability, and patriarchy, as well as the development of Enlightenment ideas and liberalism in reshaping political economy and culture in Mexico City in ways that challenged the livelihoods of city residents.[3] There was a tension in discourse regarding the behavior of honorable women: They were to maintain virtue by restricting activities outside the home while at the same time being responsible for provisioning the home, which took them into the streets and public business arenas. Enlightenment and emerging liberal ideologies about motherhood and women generally incorporated an older ideological complex of honor while expanding some female roles and rights and restricting others. Policies that regulated public urban spaces such as pawnshops and policed ostensibly private urban spaces such as homes incorporated gendered understandings of honor. In the colonial setting of New Spain, eighteenth-century economic and political reforms underscored the importance of "whiteness" for the achievement or maintenance of status and power. When metropolitan charitable institutions such as the Monte de Piedad and royal marriage edicts arrived in New Spain, colonial administrators and subjects transformed them to serve the needs of the existing and aspiring colonial elite, including downwardly mobile Creole families, some headed by widows.

Two Tiers in Bourbon Policies

At the end of 1758 in Mexico City, the Bourbon viceroy Marqués de las Amarillas ordered that there be no loitering on street corners in front of grocery stores or in the doorways or around the counter, no "ambushing of the Persons who come to shop." Neighborhood women acquired foodstuffs as well as household goods at the corner stores. The colonial governor warned against "provoking the Women who come to these offices in order to take necessary provisions to their home" and against "saying dishonest words to them," upon penalty of jail time or a fine, depending on the color of the perpetrator's skin. The law also charged the *pulperos* (storekeepers) themselves with honorable comportment: they were to be "courteous in word and deed [in their transactions] with the Women who go to shop, without impure actions, or provocative, indecent, or dishonest words."[4]

The pulpería was a daily stop for women in the city, where they acquired household supplies either with cash or through pawning a piece of clothing, a bedspread, or jewelry. The 1758 regulations limited the amount a storekeeper could give in silver for a pawned good to two reales, the amount deemed sufficient to help a poor person even for an urgent medical need. The retailer could sell against a pawning account "that which he judged was enough supplies for one day." Thus, while a household might be cash poor, the material possessions in that house guaranteed the members' access to daily provisions for meals. The 1810 legislation stated that pulperos could not refuse "new or used clothing, and some silver jewelry of little value, that which the Monte Pio will not take" from "poor neighbors," because pawning collateral goods was "the only legitimate means to relieve their urgent needs." This mandatory provision in pawning policy, made explicit in a decree by Viceroy Revillagigedo in 1790, represents a royal social-welfare policy that recognized the socioeconomic function of the pawning process in the capital. Another welfare aspect of the 1790 decree was the limitation of the cost to the customer of the lending services to one-quarter of a real per peso loaned, effectively mandating a lower interest than the Monte de Piedad. This policy was temporary (if ever heeded at all by pawnbrokers), however, as the 1810 regulations omitted any recommendation as to what interest, fees, or costs customers could be charged.[5] Showing more ambivalence on the part of the Bourbon state in guaranteeing pawning as a social-welfare policy, colonial state discourses characterized pawning as a vice encouraging idleness when work tools were pawned and leading to increased "nudity," as people pawned scarce clothing.

In the thirteenth-century Spanish Siete Partidas laws that governed the colonial world, women's honor was tied to their not "mingling publicly with men."[6] Five centuries later, honor was still bound up in the public behavior of men and women. With the 1758 *ordenanza*, the state recognized the need many women had to go out into public every day to provision their families and regulated the public space so such shopping trips would not jeopardize their honor. In the new grocery-store regulations in 1810, the repeating of the prohibition against loitering in the doorway suggests that the honor of female retail-pawning customers continued to be in jeopardy. The state further instructed storekeepers to admonish "provocative and idle subjects" hanging about their stores and impede their unruly behavior toward the women who had to venture into public to provision their families.[7] A pamphleteer in 1820 featured honorable married and unmarried women in this portrayal of retail pawning clientele:

> honorable *casados* [married men and women] whose personal labors do not provide enough to complete their subsistence or even the primary needs of the families, that surrounded by their tender luxuries, with tears in the critical hours of sustenance, they ask for the bread that they have been unable to acquire with any other remedy; virtuous widows who in the last abandonment feel the effects of hunger; honest *doncellas* [young unmarried virtuous women], justly wanting to conserve their modesty, search for help, and now without *padres* [fathers; parents], with all their hard work not enough some days to alleviate hunger, they beg for relief; all the poor of all the classes, because of their misery they seek sustenance.[8]

For "modest" and "honorable" women "of all the classes" and of any civil status at the end of the colonial period, retail pawning arenas were still of fundamental importance to daily life. The title of this pamphlet, *Dolores del parto* (Pains of Giving Birth), echoes the central role that pawning played in the reproduction of families.[9] The metaphor ties this everyday activity to women and suggests that pawnbrokers made the collateral-credit process as difficult as giving birth. Under the Siete Partidas, only widows and emancipated single women, not wives and daughters, could engage in public business transactions without permission from a male relative. Presumably daily provisioning errands did not require formal permission each time women with patriarchs at home went out on the streets. In any case the 1758 and 1810 corner-store ordinances incorporated the ideal that the public business of women, perhaps especially women without patriarchal protectors, be handled honorably and safely, and pamphleteer literature on the eve of Independence also reflected this ideal.

The state concern about providing honorable credit arenas took another form in 1775 when the colonial government opened the Monte de Piedad, a charitable institution initially funded with a pious donation from Pedro Romero de Terreros, the Count of Regla.[10] While ostensibly charged by Viceroy Antonio María de Bucareli with helping "the public" in general by offering interest-free consumer credit, the institution restricted its clientele to only those who had relatively valuable collateral goods.[11] Even with an administrative fee of one-fourth a peso per peso loaned, securing collateral loans at the Monte de Piedad was generally less expensive than it was in the retail sector, where there were no limits set on service charges or interest (except while the 1790 decree was in effect). Women constituted two-thirds of the clientele making use of the low-cost collateral lending service at the Monte de Piedad in the early nineteenth century, many of them Creole widows.[12]

Both of these policy initiatives—regulating pawning in corner stores and establishing a charitable pawnshop—continued a tradition of legal protection, if not vigilance, of women, including Creole wives, widows, and mothers. They also were part of a larger program of Enlightenment-influenced and liberal reforms in the Bourbon era that attempted to integrate women into the colonial political economy.[13] Most reforms aimed specifically at Mexico arose from a *visita* (general inspection) by José de Gálvez (1765–71). This visitation was part of a larger process by which principles and ideas of liberalism made their way into New Spain, including political ideas that would lead first to republican government in Spain and its empire and then to movements of independence in the Americas.[14] The story of household credit is part of the larger picture framed by emerging liberal policies that affected the daily lives of people in Mexico City differently depending on their class and ethnicity and by persistent codes of honor that called for the protection of certain women.

In eighteenth-century America the Spanish elite used honor codes to set themselves apart from other colonial groups, and nonelite mixed-race men and women also deployed understandings of honor. The colonial state arbitrated honor, especially that of white men and women. The honor of women was tied up with the honor of their families, especially male relatives, and was defended by fathers, husbands, and brothers. White men maintained vigilance over wives and daughters, demanding fidelity from the former and virginity from the latter. At the crux of elite and state concerns about honor was the sexual behavior of female relatives who could produce heirs, as claims to elite status depended on one's *calidad* (quality). Institutions for "depositing" women to safeguard honor stood in for absent patriarchs but were on the wane in the eighteenth century; yet male state authorities continued to be concerned about elite honor. Statesmen expected honorable men to police the sexuality of female relatives and servants and stepped in to protect worthy, "decent," and "honest" women themselves, as seen in the pulpería ordinance language.[15]

A number of Bourbon initiatives concerned the status of elite white women. The 1776 Royal Pragmatic on Marriage aimed to shore up the differences between Spaniards and the rest of colonial society and to socially reproduce a white elite untainted by the poor, both white and nonwhite.[16] The Montepíos provided pensions for a few hundred respectable widows of government officials in New Spain. The royal state in Mexico protected promiscuous elite women through the court system, where they could sue to keep their identity as mothers secret but at the same time guarantee their children an elite social position. The Casa de Niños Expósitos facilitated the abandonment of thousands of white infants by single and widowed "women from good families" in order to protect the honor of the women and their families.[17] The Bourbon state also charged the Monte de Piedad, and even pulperías under ideal conditions, with protecting white women as they provided them access to pawning credit. Some of these women had patriarchs at home, others were unwed mothers, still others widows. The state took an active role in shaping public pawning arenas used by these women in order to protect them and the honor of their families.

While protecting at least some women, the eighteenth-century Bourbons also sought to redefine women as mothers and as workers.[18] In terms of motherhood, the state placed new emphasis on a mother's role as moral compass for the family, efficient manager of household economies, and educator of children of the empire. As was true for other Enlightenment thinkers, the Spanish liberal Benito Gerónimo Feijóo y Montenegro pushed for expansion of women's education in order to enhance this modern motherhood. In Mexico City in the 1760s, a few hundred elite girls entered new academies where they studied academic and domestic subjects and about a hundred Indian women were schooled in housekeeping skills by nuns from the Company of Mary.[19] While these schools expanded female education, they reinforced class and ethnic differences among women and the patriarchal social order.

The Bourbon state also attempted to expand female job opportunities. Women owned half of the small cigar-making enterprises in the city, and a third of the cigar labor force was female, before the crown established a monopoly on tobacco growing and product manufacturing. Opened in 1770, the royal cigar factory was the single largest employer in Mexico City, employing mostly women and girls, which allowed the factory to reduce wages over time.[20] As for other manufacturing enterprises, Viceroy Miguel Joseph de Azanza permitted women to work as cobblers. The decree argued that women and girls needed income, either to enhance their dowries or "as assistance to maintain their houses and obligations."[21] Nonguild artisan businesses challenged most of the guilds by the turn of the nineteenth century. Many of these renegade artisans were widows or daughters of deceased master craftsmen who continued the trade and could not afford to pay a nonrelative master to administer the shop as the guild required.[22]

In opening guilds to women and employing thousands of working-class women in its factory, the crown recognized the economic needs of women charged with housekeeping and motherhood roles. Educational policy also incorporated this recognition, as the public-school curriculum included vocational training such as sewing and embroidery. The state recognized class differences among females: some needed income to enhance dowries, an elite convention on the wane in the late eighteenth century as families had fewer resources to endow marriageable daughters, while working women needed regular income to run their poorer households. The two-tiered pawning policies of the Bourbon state as well as educational and employment policies reflected both the provisioning roles women across classes played in urban households and the complex ethnic and class power relations rooted in the material base of households in colonial Mexico City.

Reforms Hit the City: High Costs, Anxiety, Downward Mobility

A volatile economy dogged New Spain in the eighteenth century. Bourbon reforms sought to strengthen the economy through freer trade policies and more efficient governing institutions, but those same reforms hit the pockets of colonial subjects hard. Taxes on basic commodities increased sharply, as did other revenue-generating mechanisms such as license fees and forced loans to the Spanish crown in need of money for European wars. Subjects in the colonies bore the brunt of the crown's revenue initiatives more than did people in Spain.[23] Adding to the economic squeeze, inflation in the second half of the eighteenth century meant that prices for corn, wheat, and beans doubled between 1750 and 1800. By the first decade of the nineteenth century, staple prices had tripled.[24]

Low wages and chronic underemployment exacerbated this increasing cost of living for colonial subjects. To support a family of five in the 1790s, a household would have needed to collectively earn at least five reales daily. An unmarried woman working at the royal cigarette factory or as a live-in maid could have survived on her wages, but a widow with even one child would have had a harder time. Generally, skilled workers earned between four reales and a peso a day, with unskilled workers receiving between two and four reales daily.[25] Workers' incomes would have been further taxed when dress codes for the tobacco-factory workers were extended by Viceroy Azanza to guilds, to religious brotherhoods, and during civic and religious processions. Residents were to be decently dressed at all times, "according to their class." Appearing in public in just a sheet or sarape (poncho) could result in eight days in jail. Those unemployed might take to stealing in order to comply with the viceroy's order.[26] Conditions at the bottom of the socioeconomic ladder did not improve following Independence in 1821. In the 1820s and 1830s most people were poor, 98 percent had no real estate, and only 30 percent had a steady job. Domestic servants—the majority of people with jobs—had to pay the equivalent of three days' salary in income tax after 1823. Salaries in the 1830s were eroded because many were paid in copper, which suffered devaluations.[27]

The state's discourse about pawning suggested that it was the city's poorest who needed the collateral credit services the most. Pulperías had from 25 to 70 percent of their loans secured by *prendas menudas* (collateral goods of little value) worth less than four reales (see appendix 1, table G).[28] Echoing Revillagigedo's decrees of 1790, the 1810 pulpería regulations recognized the indigent clientele in Article 12 and protected their access to collateral credit. In the 1820 pamphlet chastising storekeepers, people literally pawn the clothes off their backs: "needy sufferers who in the hours of greatest common need, remove the poor clothing that covers them, and approach your counters presenting to you with these clothes a most irrefutable testimony that should excite your due compassion."[29]

Despite this public image of the desperately poor collateral borrower, archival evidence about who used pawnshops and what they pawned suggests that those with a life-style supported by a more stable income, as well as the poorest of the poor, made regular use of the pawning process. Corner-store customers included *gallineras* (female chicken vendors), *mandaderas* (female errand runners), and *coheteros* (male fireworks makers). These clients were employed, known to the broker for their occupation, and were not an undifferentiated mass of *léperos*. The consumer goods they and others (whose full or last names are documented) pawned prove that their level of material possessions did not put them among the most destitute. After independence these middling folk might have considered themselves on different levels than dependent laborers, though both groups availed themselves of collateral-credit services.[30]

Strategies for managing day-to-day lives in the volatile and inflationary economy of the late colony included informal and illegal ways of generating income.[31] Pawnshop inventories show that another strategy to "make do" amid economic crisis, one that continued throughout the republican era, was the everyday practice of converting material goods into cash loans with neighborhood pawnbrokers. The average loan for prendas listed individually in pulperías was six and one-half reales, enough to meet one day's subsistence needs for a family of five (see appendix 1, table G).[32]

Bourbon social policies addressed the precarious economy, with state-run charitable institutions established to shield the "better" groups in society from the vagaries of the economy. Arguably the Bourbon institution with the widest reach into city households, the Monte de Piedad made loans averaging ten pesos to over twenty thousand people a year, more than two thousand people monthly.[33] The Monte de Piedad—along with the pensions, the poor house, the foundling home, and the tobacco enterprise—continued operations into the national era. When the Monte de Piedad crossed the Atlantic in the 1770s, it was transformed from a charity for the poor into a charity for downwardly mobile elites. Viceroy Bucareli told Charles III that while the Madrid Monte de Piedad, established to serve the lending needs of the metropolitan poor, would be the model for the colonial Monte de Piedad, the Mexican Monte would make some changes "to account for the circumstances in New Spain and the customs of the 'naturales.'" Bucareli expected that some of the loans would be for more than a thousand pesos. The local "circumstances" included the relative impoverishment of colonial elites who needed sizable infusions of capital for business or life-style needs.[34] Indeed, a major difference between the two Montes de Piedad illustrates their distinct clientele: the Madrid institution set a maximum with no minimum loan amount, while the Mexico City Monte established a minimum loan of two pesos with no maximum.[35] One reason people might have wanted to pawn their possessions at the Monte de Piedad instead of their local corner store or with some other lender was the low interest rate charged. But because the Monte only took collateral worth at least three pesos, those who could least afford to pay the higher private-sector rates were denied access to the public charitable institution until the 1860s, when it expanded into branch offices that gave smaller loans. Nonetheless, colonial administrators of the Monte de Piedad, as well as the clergy, continued to characterize the institution's clientele as indigent.[36] In an exchange of documents in 1815—in the midst of the Independence wars—Monte officials and the archbishop's office described the "poor and common people," the "indigent public," and "the miserable ones [whom the institution] assisted." Real Hacienda officials recognized that some users of the Monte in 1815 were better off and were seeking loans to mitigate "present calamitous circumstances" that left so many with "a scarcity of the capital that they needed" to remedy "their pitiful downfall."[37]

In the late colonial era a middle group was predominantly Creole and often educated. It included members of formerly elite families who had fallen on hard times, Creoles and peninsular merchants, and bureaucrats.[38] In the last three decades of the eighteenth century, government annual salaries ranged from about 200 pesos for doormen and scribes to 6,000 pesos for directors of the Dirección General de Rentas and the Casa de Moneda and 4,000 pesos for the postal director.[39] At the end of the second decade after independence, a military commander earned an annual salary of 3,000 pesos, while the chief superior of the ministry of Hacienda earned 2,000 pesos.[40] For Creole wives facing long periods during which their bureaucrat husbands were not paid or were only partially paid, regular visits to the Monte de Piedad, from which they walked away with 10 or 20 pesos at a time, surely allowed them to maintain their standard of living.[41] How much income was needed to live a middle-class Creole life-style? Echoing the amount Bucareli believed would be commonly sought for Monte collateral loans, historian D. S. Chandler found that "if one did not need to uphold the dignity of high office and consume imported goods, an annual income of 1,000 pesos would have been quite adequate in late eighteenth-century Mexico."[42] One transaction from the Monte de Piedad ledgers approximates the annual income needed for a middle-class life-style in one loan. On February 22, 1802, Manuel Gonzalez took out a loan from the Monte de Piedad using a very expensive set of jewels described as "*pichoas, paxaritos, y pulseras*." These crowns, "little birds," and bracelets secured a loan of 1,170 pesos. The recorded appraisal of the jewelry set was 2,514 pesos, so Manuel's loan constituted 46 percent of the value of his collateral. It took him sixteen months to get the money together, but on June 7, 1803, he redeemed the jewels.[43] While we do not know if Manuel's wife displayed the family's status by regularly wearing these jewels, or if they were his own property acquired through inheritance or perhaps inventory from his business, this transaction shows that elites used the Monte de Piedad.

Life-styles—expressed through jewelry and clothing as well as what one ate—were constructed and then had to be maintained, which was hard for some consumers to do in the Bourbon era. Elaborate jewels were worn at public events, mass, and the theater, as well as when entertaining at home.[44] Members of the upper and middle ranks used worked silver and fancy clothing to adorn and thus define their public personas, marking their economic and cultural status in society, advertising that one had attained or could maintain a high standard of living. These same goods provided women and men in the middle station a means to maintain that status in more lean times, converting them into collateral for loans in pawning establishments.[45] Social critic and novelist José Joaquín Fernández de Lizardi suggested in his satiric novel *El periquillo sarniento* that the precarious status of some Creoles would have them associated either with poor or rich classes depending on their ability to dress. Clearly for this commentator on material culture in the city, clothes made the man, and though Lizardi does not mention them here, they also made the woman: "With a cape or woolen frock . . . , I was associated with the rogues that wore this attire, and when I could only muster a sheet I had to accompany those that wore sheets."[46] The downward mobility of Creole middling and upper-class residents of the city was featured in a debate among bakers, storekeepers, and the city government in 1793 about where fine wheat bread could be sold for two reales a loaf, as opposed to the common loaf sold for half a real. Not only the poor shopped with storekeepers, but also those "born in the womb of opulent families, taught since the crib to enjoy the best, [and] afterwards even in misery they maintain the same conduct and [seek the] consolation that their taste for superior bread gives them."[47]

While establishing the Monte de Piedad to cushion or prevent the fall down the economic ladder by white subjects, colonial officials nonetheless blamed those sliding down for their economic demise. In 1800 Viceroy

Felix Berrenguer de Marquina blamed the "ruin of families" on a conspicuous consumption of "excessive luxury in suits and dresses."[48] This echoed an Enlightenment critique of luxury in Spain that centered on overspending *petimetras*, single and married women whose consumption was seen as counterproductive not only because it was a waste of time and money, but because they antipatriotically consumed imports.[49] By using the pawnshop, Creole families living off bureaucratic or private-sector incomes could keep their high standard of living and still avoid financial ruin, whether or not they conspicuously consumed luxury imports. Displaying wealth, eating wheat bread, and securing legitimation certificates were all strategies that, like pawning, were used in the formation and maintenance of Creole identities and in the defense of honor and status in the taxing late colonial period. The early republican political economy continued to be volatile, and life-styles of "bankrupt sectors of the upper classes" remained a challenge to finance.[50]

In official discourse about the Monte de Piedad's mission, the reality that access to its services was restricted to those who had relatively expensive collateral goods was masked by language concerning the indigence of the women who constituted the charitable institution's clientele. After Independence Monte employees continued to argue that most people pawned with them for subsistence needs. In a proposal in 1829 employees called for the Monte to open earlier in the morning so that customer families "did not have to go hungry until the afternoon." In other documents the administration identified clients as "especially poor" women.[51] This hedging about the real aim of the Monte de Piedad—to shore up the financially strapped middle sectors and elite—also reflected a reluctance to recognize that men had legitimate needs for pawnshop services just as women did. The characterization of collateral credit seekers as "especially women" was also clear in the colonial legislation on retail pawning. The view that it was mostly women seeking assistance from retail pawnbrokers because it was their job to provision their families carried over into the discourse of government ministers when talking about the Monte.

While statesmen saw a female household-provisioning motive for pawning as legitimate, the ascribed motives for men who visited pawnbrokers were linked to vice.[52] A 1771 Bando regulating pawning in retail and liquor stores claimed that many men only pawned to fund their "laziness and drunkenness."[53] The 150,000 pawned goods found in taverns in Mexico City during a crackdown in the 1760s, enough for at least one item per city resident, indicates the frequency of this type of pawning activity.[54]

Whether or not pawns-for-drink inventories were consistently so heavy, the *pulquería* (tavern serving fermented juice from the maguey cactus, associated with indigenous culture) was seen by the colonial state as an illegitimate pawning arena, due to illegitimate pawning motives, and not to be encouraged by poor relief. Drinking was understood to be a habit of the "undeserving," usually male, poor.[55] Viceroy Bucareli accused tavern keepers of increasing unemployment by accepting collateral items that were needed to make a living and for causing poor women to go around half naked, as men pawned their wives' things, depriving them "of the little clothing they have."[56]

In the late colonial period the "nudity" of Indians and mestizos and other *castas* (mixed-race people) was widely commented on and linked both to pawning and to vices. Clothing was expensive, and many plebeians could not afford "anything more than some rags or a beat-up sheet stolen or bought with the proceeds from the occasional job or from begging." The colonial police claimed that the pawning of clothes by gamblers left the lower classes walking about nude.[57] This picture frequently appears in Lizardi's *El periquillo sarniento*, written in the last years of the colony. Many times the protagonist, a poor Creole, pawned his clothing and bedding to secure money for his own subsistence or that of his domestic partner. He also frequented the broker for gambling money or hoped to redeem his goods with gambling winnings.[58] Does this portrayal reflect a top-down stereotype, mirroring the view of government authorities who would have been Lizardi's peers, or is the novelist commenting, albeit with exaggeration, on a prevalent social practice? In any case some men pawned not only to get drunk or place bets. Men reported that they frequented pawnshops to meet family needs. Unemployment in 1812 led the former sacristan Lucas González to pawn all of his clothes in order to provide for his wife and children.[59] Yet male pawnshop clients with legitimate household credit needs remained outside the official gendered discourse about honorable pawning, which emphasized housekeeping women and protected their access to petty credit arenas.

The retail pawning decrees that called for the protection of honorable women as they went about their provisioning duties also aimed to protect elite property and domestic space. Article 11 of the 1758 pulpería regulations stated: "No Storekeeper should accept as collateral any jewel or other object that is not likely to belong to the person pawning it, such as Holy jewels, and those of Saints, Books, Plates, Cups, Goblets [*Bernegales*], and Spoons, Forks, and silver jewelry, Keys, Locks, Bridles, Livery, Saddles,

Coach Adornments [*Guarniciones*], and all types of Cordage, and that pertaining to the Literas, and everything else that might be suspicious." This list of "forbidden collateral goods" consisted of those items easily stolen in service: silver trays used by the maids of the comfortable homes when serving meals; silver spoons, plates, and goblets used by the members of the household and their guests, which servants cleared from the table, washed, and polished; and door handles and cushions of carriages in the care of doormen and drivers. The list did not include other goods such as clothing and linens, also easily stolen in service (or from a neighbor's clothesline). Successive legislation clarified what constituted forbidden collateral, suggesting that it continued to turn up in pawnshops. In 1781 artisans' tools were added to the list, ostensibly in order to keep workers from idleness and the poor from further misery, but certainly also in order to protect the production property of master artisans. The 1810 regulations specified that individual pieces from silver tableware sets easily secreted out of elite households were not legitimate collateral, though sets of silverware were. They also repeated the prohibition against horse and carriage accessories as collateral, explaining that "the drivers and footmen steal them and pawn them."[60] Regulatory language about goods that might be stolen in service reflects the anxiety of statesmen and Creole householders concerning their precarious social position in the late colonial period as much as any proclivity of servants to steal small items of private property.[61] Statesmen from Europe as well as Creole ministers and council members protected their locally born women, their material goods, their access to collateral credit, and hence their own elite status through regulation and provision of credit arenas.

The evidence from pawning inventories suggests that the portrait of the desperately poor, vice-ridden, or dishonest pawning clientele in the discourse of Spanish statesmen was overdrawn, while the image of the typical pawning customer as a woman was more on the mark. Yet the emphasis in the rhetoric on women as pawning clientele perhaps served the state in making pawning and state policy regarding pawning more acceptable. If women were seen as the chief beneficiaries, the government policy was cast in a positive light, protecting the population as a good patriarch should. This material study of everyday credit in Mexico City mirrors the official discourse to the extent that women are highlighted as the majority of both the pawning customers and the city's population. But this emphasis on the female gender is also due to the links between pawning and housekeeping and to a relatively high level of female household headship. The gender, ethnic, and class-based Bourbon policies and discourses regarding pawning are better understood through consideration of a demographic portrait of the population at whom they were aimed.

The Demography of Daily Life

In Mexico City, whiter and richer than the rest of New Spain, a majority of residents were female.[62] The divisions among groups along gender, race, and class lines evident in Bourbon social policies and discourses reflected the demographic picture in the capital city. Throughout the eighteenth century there were about 100,000 people in the city, and by 1811 the population had increased to about 140,000. Widows outnumbered widowers three to one. A third of households were headed by women, a marked increase from a quarter of households in the 1753 census.[63] This picture of the households in the central neighborhoods of Mexico City in the early nineteenth century draws on data from the 1811 census for a downtown section, Cuartel 9, with details about a subsection of households. One of the smaller demarcations in terms of population, Cuartel 9 was made up of an area two blocks wide and six blocks long going south from the Zócalo, the central plaza where the cathedral, government buildings, principal market, and Monte de Piedad were located. There were pulperías or other retail establishments at virtually every street intersection in the residential neighborhood.[64] This section was mostly white in 1811, with 71 percent of the residents either born in Spain or Creole. Among white women, almost all of them Creole, 20 percent were widows (see appendix 3, table B). The census category "casta" referred to those with different combinations of mixed racial heritage, most commonly mestizo, *castizo* (mestizo and European), or mulatto. Twelve percent of the section's population was identified as castas, with 27 percent of casta women widowed. Seventeen percent of the population was Indian, with 23 percent of Indian women widowed. Of the total female population, widows constituted 22 percent. This cuartel housed a mix of wealthy Spanish merchants and high-ranking bureaucrats in large homes with full domestic staffs and more humble Creole artisans in the multiple dwellings of the *casas de vecindad* (rooming houses) alongside casta or Indian neighbors, some of the latter in trades, most in some kind of service occupation (see appendix 3, table F).

Most households were headed by fathers and husbands, with sons, wives, and daughters subject to the authority of the patriarch, at least in theory. The significant minority of household heads that were women could escape this system, though other male relatives might exert authority. Wives were to engage in economic activity only with the permission of husbands, though in fact more than half of the women living in the city were employed outside the home.[65] The conditions of life in Mexico City in the late eighteenth century made some women independent—even defiant. Especially among plebeians, the diverse network of employers and acquaintances meant that women in the city had more physical mobility and could escape from male surveillance more easily than in rural areas.[66]

Widows, whatever their ethnicity, were often, though not always, household heads in 1811. The sample suggests that Creole widows were just as likely to be taken into the house of a relative or friend (see appendix 3, table D). Casta and Indian widows were more likely to work as live-in domestic servants in someone else's house. The likelihood of a woman's heading a household was greatest in the white population, which "commanded the most resources."[67] For the sample of Cuartel 9, 65 percent of all widows were Creole, 37 percent of all widows were also household heads, 45 percent of Creole widows were household heads, and 78 percent of all widowed household heads were Creole. Colonial elite society opposed the idea of women living outside of patriarchal relationships, or as Lizardi put it, "free and without masters."[68] Widows and single adult females had considerably more rights than married women under Spanish law. Some widows lived alone. Some continued managing their husbands' businesses and ran large households. Some, especially elite widows, enjoyed the freedom of their new status and experienced productive and prosperous twilight years. Others were quite vulnerable to dishonest business partners or hounded by creditors, "forced to sell their belongings, search garbage heaps for food, or beg for a living."[69]

Women headed 33 percent of the 183 households in the sample, with widows making up 70 percent of the female household heads (see appendix 3, table E). Half of the female household heads were unemployed Creoles without the income of other household members, as shown in table 1.1. This demographic picture of so many Creole women as the household authority but without an official occupation is part of the context in which the viceroys shaped regulatory policy for the grocery and pawning trades. The Bourbon effort to increase the female work force was unsuccessful; women were the same one-third of the labor force in 1811 as they had been in 1753, though the earlier concentration in domestic service and seamstress work had expanded to other opportunities for women who worked.[70] Of course many of the women for whom no occupation was recorded in census data may have been employed in a combination of part-time jobs—

TABLE 1.1

Female Household Heads in Cuartel 9 Sample, Mexico City, 1811 Census

	Creole	Casta	Indian	Total
Employed				
Living alone	2	2	1	5
With other female	2			2
With dependent/s	2	2	1	5
With other female/servant/s	1			1
Total employed	6	4	2	12 (21%)
With employed dependents	11	2	0	13 (21%)
Unemployed				
Living alone	8	1		9
With other female	5	1		6
With other female and servants	1			1
With dependents	14	1		15
With servants	2			2
With dependents and servants	2			2
Total unemployed	32	3	0	35 (57%)
Total	49	10	2	60

Source: AGN, Padrones, vol. 55.

housekeeping skills such as laundry and cooking done for pay, street vending, money lending, teaching, and so forth—but on an informal basis not reflected in the census. Some women also may not have stated occupations because of perceptions of dishonor for those working outside the home. A case from 1809 illustrates the multiple employment strategies that might have escaped census data. Women in a household on Arco headed by Manuela Gonzalez were accused of running a house of prostitution. Testimony in court from Manuela, her daughter, and neighbors argued that she was not in fact a madam and that she instead made a living as a go-between (*corredora*) in the buying and selling of jewels and clothing, working in contact with both men and women (which explained why they visited her house frequently) who had businesses in the Parián market. When the errand-running business was insufficient to live on, Manuela worked as a seamstress.[71] Which occupation would Manuela have given the census taker when he canvased two years later?

Where and whether a female worked depended to some extent on her ethnic background; in the late colonial period the majority of white females worked as *costureras* (seamstresses), many mestizas worked in the tobacco factory, and most Indians and mulattas worked as servants.[72] Women of all ethnicities in the middle and lower business classes operated small retail establishments such as grocery stores, liquor stores, and a few pawnshops, as well as restaurants and bars. Women in the middle socioeconomic group also ran informal *amiga* schools, opened *fábricas de rebozos* (workshops producing shawls) in their homes, or sold sweets from their kitchens. Some upper-class women engaged in business activities. Many women working for wages were single female household heads, but married women were also among them, especially in mestizo and Indian populations.[73] Though legally under the control of husbands, married women might control their wages.[74] Whatever the nature of wives' relationships with their husbands, the material evidence provided by pawnshop inventories suggests that married women did more than make do with their husband's salaries as they went about the work of housekeeping. As did female household heads, married women also included the collateral value of housekeeping and personal goods in their household budget capital.

Opening the doors to residences in Cuartel 9 reveals how these demographic and occupational patterns looked on the ground in the city center in 1811. In an upstairs apartment in a casa de vecindad on Calle Tacuba, thirty-two-year-old Creole Doña Juana Francisca Samano managed her household, made up of herself, her tailor husband Don Manuel Flores, a forty-three-year-old Creole, and their two children. Also living in the household of Doña Juana and Don Manuel were Doña Josefa Samano and Simón Samano, Creoles of thirty and sixteen years of age respectively, who were probably either sister and brother of Juana Francisca or perhaps sister and nephew. Downstairs from the tailor a thirty-six-year-old Creole widow, Doña Ana Gertrudis Arellano, lived alone in one room. Down the street, Creole Doña María Josefa Saldana managed a merchant household living in a single-family home, responsible for the comfort of her husband, Don Domingo Martínez, twenty-seven-years-old and born in Castilla in Spain, as well as Don Martín Menchaca, a forty-year-old Spaniard from Rioja, who was in the same line of business as her husband. Doña María Josefa supervised four mestizo servants, three female and one male, and five Indian servants, two female and three male. Four of the servants were couples, one mestizo-Indian, the other Indian-Indian. Only one of the servants had been born in the city, the rest having come from nearby towns such as Cuernavaca and Pachuca. At an address on the second block of Mesones, a household made up of four single women rented a room in another casa de vecindad. Three Creole seamstresses, Doña María Ana Ruiz, Doña Vicenta Ruiz, and Doña María Negrin, aged fifty-five, fifty, and fifty-seven respectively, shared a room with Carlota Mascareñas, a fourteen-year-old mestiza who worked as a cigar maker. Doñas María Ana and Vicenta may have been spinster sisters and the others friends or relatives.[75]

Though no longer virtually the only option, domestic service was the main occupation of women working for wages in Mexico City at the turn of the century, especially casta and Indian women, as seen in the examples above. In 1753 a full 77 percent of female workers were identified as servants. By 1811 the number was down to 54 percent of females in service. While domestics represent only 17 percent of the females in the sample population, 40 percent of the casta females and 49 percent of the Indian females in the sample were live-in servants (see appendix 3, table F). Among the servants in the sample, two-thirds were female and half were Indian. Seventy-five of the 183 households in the sample from Cuartel 9 had servants, or 41 percent (see appendix 3, table G). Of the households with servants, 53 percent were headed by Spanish immigrant men; 44 percent were headed by Creoles, 27 percent of them female. In one household from the 1811 sample, a tailor from Valladolid, married to a Creole woman from Mexico City, lived with four tailor sons, two daughters, three Indian servant women, and one nine-year-old Creole boy apprentice. Around the corner, two merchant bachelors from Viscaya lived with a Creole merchant bachelor, two Creole servants (a man and a woman), a mestiza cook, and a castizo servant. On Calle Venero Doña Ana María Frenero, a forty-nine-year-old single Creole woman from Puebla, lived with María Merced, a sixteen-year-old Indian servant from Xochimilco.[76]

The Bourbon state responded to the demographic reality of a notable number of Creole women without patriarchs at home to defend their honor, attempting to protect their honor when developing pawning regulations and institutional policies. Those few who were widows of government officials might avoid going out in public to work because they were eligible for a small pension from the new pension system. Other Creole women (married, widowed, and single mothers) could turn their dowry goods—whether jewelry with precious stones, silver service sets, or fine household linens—into cash, and the pawning legislation protected them as they did so. It was now against the law to accost "worthy" women as they went about their provisioning business. This same legislation also protected women with husbands who nonetheless left the privacy and protection of the home on a daily basis in order to go into public shops to secure provisions for the family. The state, staffed by white men from the upper middle and elite groups, protected their own luxury goods from the vagaries of servant stealing, just as they protected the access of relatively comfortable Creole families to credit arenas, where women could take advantage of their relative material wealth to maintain an honorable Creole life-style in the absence of a male breadwinner. Nonwhite women, too, such as the Indian servant Ygnacia Excorcia who frequented the Domínguez pulpería mentioned at the beginning of this chapter, might benefit from the protection against "dishonest words" and harassment if the pawnbroker did not accuse her of stealing from her employer whatever it was that she brought as collateral.

Skirts, Sheets, Silver: Housekeeping and Pawning

Work done in the household by servants, mothers, wives, and widows shaped the identities of the city residents featured in the demographic portrait above in the lives they lived beyond the household. In their housekeeping endeavors and facing economic challenges brought about by Bourbon policies or perhaps the loss of a spouse, Creole women used the material stock of fine cloth and silver goods in their households as collateral for loans to maintain the "gente decente" or "*hombres y mujeres de bien*" life-style with which they distinguished themselves from the nonwhite and/or nonwealthy in colonial New Spain.[77] Pawning was a coping strategy of elites to deal with lean times, high taxes, low wages, or the absence of wage earners and the need to keep up appearances. Poorer Creole women, as well as mestizo and Indian women in the city, used their more humble stocks of household linens and petticoats to ensure the livelihood of their households in a context of chronically low incomes and high costs of living.[78]

Some city households used the silver jewelry or fine clothing that family members wore in public to enhance their reputations or to resist being labeled or stuck on a wrung of the socioeconomic ladder.[79] Turning to the Monte de Piedad for loans when the transaction costs were low, pawning those same jewels or garments allowed second (or more) rounds of use of the items in maintaining social positions, as the loan secured by those goods financed further consumption and/or acquisition of new goods, which in turn completed a conventional-collateral use cycle. This was not a strategy limited to Creole elite women. The well-dressed mestiza at the end of the colonial period wore "white cotton petticoats, a cotton blouse colored a sober blue, brown, or gray; and a small, equally sober rebozo, or shawl, which passed over the arch of a hair comb perched atop her head."[80] Once the garments passed out of fashion, the wearers of these typical petticoats and rebozos converted them into collateral, as attested to by the large numbers of them on the pawnshop shelves. In this sense pawning was the culmination of an investment strategy, in which housekeepers deliberately chose to purchase certain goods as an investment to draw upon in the future. Pawned goods were commonly redeemed, after which they would be incorporated back into the household routine or repawned for another loan.[81]

Investing in material goods for their collateral value as a household finance strategy would have been most effective in the first years of the Monte de Piedad's operation, when there was no charge for its services and people instead left a donation. By 1780 the donation became mandatory, and by 1782 the rate was fixed at one-quarter of a real per peso loaned over the six-month pledge period, or 6 percent annually. For those on the bottom of the economic ladder with goods of little value that were relegated to the usually higher-interest private lending sector, repeated pawning of the same humble household good as collateral would constitute a loss on the initial investment, as cumulative transaction costs would soon outstrip the price originally paid for the item.[82] Following the 1790 decree that may have been in effect until 1810, however, private-sector pawning clientele would have been better able to use the invest-in-collateral-goods strategy if they left their goods in hock for the full pledge period of six months, as interest limits of one-eighth of a real per peso loaned were established, effectively undercutting even the Monte de Piedad rates.

The inventories analyzed from private pawning enterprises as well as from the Monte de Piedad for this study yield a database of more than three thousand transactions from the late colonial period, in which the pawned goods are identified, often with a detailed description.[83] Seventy-eight percent of these goods were clothing or other cloth goods, and only 24 percent of those were pawned in the Monte de Piedad.[84] The cloth goods pawned most often with retail brokers and the Monte de Piedad were enaguas, petticoats often worn in layers under a skirt, though the petticoat alone could serve as a skirt. These petticoats were more or less evenly distributed between the pawning arenas, with 293 of them found in the store inventories and 313 in the Monte de Piedad ledger, though it was more common at the Monte de Piedad for the enaguas to be pawned in a bundle of two or perhaps one with a rebozo or some other garment. In both locations the maximum loans that individual enaguas secured was ten pesos, but most petticoat loans in the retail outlets ranged from four reales to one peso, while most petticoat loans at the Monte de Piedad ranged from two to five pesos. The most common fabric of these collateral petticoats at the Monte was *indianilla* (cotton fabric printed on one side in the manner of South Asian textiles), representing a third of enaguas. The other favorite fabrics for the Monte de Piedad patrons' petticoats were, in order of occurrence, *cavo* (imported coarse cotton weave), linen, *quimon* (Japanese-style stamped and painted fabric), *gasa* (gauze), and *muselina* (muslin). Silk was not common among the petticoats at the Monte, though most of the dozen *sayas*, or skirts worn over petticoats, were silk.[85] The next most common good found in the database were rebozos, another garment worn by women. Indeed women's clothing was pawned much more often than men's clothing.[86] This pattern suggests that the observation that "for most of the poor, their wardrobe served as a line of credit" is true especially for women's clothing, and the statement holds for the more affluent as well.[87]

Linens and other household goods also acquired, embroidered, cleaned, and used by women in households could be pawned by housewives or female household heads or by servants in homes that had them. *Colchones* (feather mattresses) "gave a measure of comfort accessible to families in the middle position" in society, who might use "two, one on top of the other." Given the relatively high cost of bed linens and the enhanced value through the embroidery work done on them by family women, bedding easily surpassed the value of "the modest wood structure" that they covered.[88] The usefulness of these household goods went beyond their utilitarian function to yield cash for basic provisions, being used for the acquisition of new status items or for items for special occasions. Including clothing, the percentage of goods related to housekeeping would be 81 percent of the database. Because of the complicated nature of clothing (at once personal attire, finished good, and work "tool" for those who wash it, iron it, and so forth), table 1.2, which outlines the housekeeping goods in the database for 1787–1830, excludes clothing. Women made up 65 percent of those pawning nonclothing household goods in the database for 1787–1830 for whom the gender is given. (This number is an underestimation of women's pawning patterns, as the "unknown" category of clients is so large for the retail arenas.) More housekeeping goods were pawned in the private shops than in the Monte de Piedad. Not surprisingly, most of the silver tableware was hocked at the middle-class charitable institution, while most of the cloth found its way to the private pawning outlets. While this reflects a more humble material base of the households that were

TABLE 1.2

Household Goods in Pawning Transactions, 1787–1830
(730 transactions out of 3,135, or 23 percent)

	Customers							
	Monte de Piedad			Retail				
Category	Female	Male	All	Female	Male	?	All	Total
Fabric	31	27	58	45	31	142	218	276
Household Linens								
sheets	2	1	3	20	15	45	80	83
blankets				12	17	33	62	62
mattresses				5	5	35	45	45
bedspreads	2	1	3	2		1	3	6
curtains	6		6			1	1	7
tablecloths	2	3	5	1		4	5	10
napkins	1		1			3	3	4
aprons				2		1	3	3
other					1	4	5	5
Subtotal	13	5	18	42	38	127	207	225
Table Service								
eating utensils	34	28	62	6	7	13	26	88
plates	41	33	74			1	1	75
saltshakers	3		3			1	1	4
serving platters	19	18	37					37
cups	1	2	3					3
pitchers	4	3	7			1	1	8
Subtotal	102	84	186	6	7	16	29	215
Kitchen Utensils								
braziers	3		3		1		1	4
cooking pots/pans					1	2	3	3
coffeepots	1	1	2					2
colanders	1		1					1
grills					1		1	1
Subtotal	5	1	6		3	2	5	11
Furniture					1	2	3	3
Total	151	117	268	93	82	289	461	730

Source: AHNMP, Libros de Empeños, 1802; AGN, Consulado, vol. 11, exp. 43, fs. 388–93; vol. 24, exp. 13, fs. 302–6; vol. 25, exp. 13, fs. 310–12v; vol. 28, exp. 5, fs. 231–41; vol. 38, exp. 2, fs. 21–25v, 35–38; exp. 5, fs. 292–48v; exp. 6, fs. 271–74; vol. 47, exp. 5, fs. 298–301; vol. 53, exp. 12, fs. 365–71; vol. 67, exp. 10, fs. 129–32; vol. 292, exp. 3, no. 3, fs. 1–4; no. 8, fs. 1–7; exp. 4, no. 3, fs. 1–6v; no. 5, 1–4; no. 7, fs. 2–5; CONDUMEX, Fondo CDLV–2.

Note: Totals by category include housekeeping goods that were bundled with clothing or jewelry, and therefore the totals are greater than those given in the breakdown in appendix 1, table B, which counts each transaction and not each individual good that might be in a bundle.

regular pawning clients of the pulperías compared to the wealthier households with banks of silverware, the fact that these retail pawning customers had so many feather mattresses, sheets, and blankets shows that some had beds, a measure of a middling material level, and were not always sleeping on the ubiquitous *petates*, or straw mats, of the city's poor. Notably, the retail-loan recipients also used as many tablecloths as collateral as did the Monte de Piedad patrons. While lacking in silver with which to serve meals, these households of working people and those on the lower rungs of the middle sector did have tables that they covered with cloth for dining occasions (at least when the tablecloth was not in hock).

Women and men from middling and elite households took silver table-service items to the Monte de Piedad. Silver and the servants to deploy it were markers of the status associated with Creole respectability, and when pawned, those items further contributed to the maintenance of that status. Silver items also made excellent collateral for petty mortgage loans, as their value was determined by their weight, "independent of their use value and the merit of the craftsmanship."[89] To be fully outfitted with silver service for the necessary entertaining at the elite level was quite expensive.[90]

The loans that silverware secured at the Monte de Piedad in 1802 ranged from 2 pesos for a single silver spoon to 150 pesos for four serving platters. While a pair of forks or several spoons were sometimes bundled into one collateral package, other examples from the Monte database show that whole sets of silverware could yield sizable loans. It might be the man of the house instead of the housewife who took the household table silver to the pawnshop, whether for his own reasons, to secure cash for his wife to supplement the housekeeping budget, or to meet the expenses of a holiday season. On January 4, 1802, Antonio Suarez hocked eighteen spoons and eighteen forks for a loan of 85 pesos, redeeming the eating utensils in June 1802.[91] More common silverware transactions in the Monte de Piedad ledger were smaller sets of forks and spoons. In five cases where sets of six of each utensil were pawned from January 1802, three women and two men secured loans of between 32 and 48 pesos. Only one of these five Monte de Piedad patrons in the sample was unable to redeem her silverware: Felipa Gomez instead received 2 pesos 2 reales from the sale of her silver in September of that year.[92] While females were slightly more likely than males to pawn silver table-service items, females pawned small numbers of eating utensils much more frequently than males. Females made twenty-four of the thirty transactions where from one to ten eating utensils were pawned, and in every case (eleven total) where only one eating utensil was pawned, the patron was female. Of the collateral made up of single or small sets of eating utensils, only two went unredeemed. Clearly silver household goods were reliable collateral that held their monetary value and could be used again and again to secure the low-cost loans of the Monte de Piedad. If the women taking one spoon or two forks in for loans were female household heads, this pattern may reflect the thinner material base of their households. It could also be that some of these female patrons were servants sneaking the spoons and forks out of their employers' houses in their pockets, thus supplementing their low wages with (repeated?) loans of a few pesos using the stolen collateral.

The household property and social position of peninsular and Creole whites who could afford live-in servants, whether in households with female or male heads, were protected by the colonial pawning legislation. In the seventeenth century, King Philip IV prohibited merchants from accepting goods as collateral from servants, assistants, or store clerks in order to curb theft by employees.[93] It is clear from the pawned-goods database that single silver tableware items were pawned in retail stores, regardless of their prohibition, since 1758. And servants could still easily pawn goods not on the forbidden list such as linens, clothing, and jewelry stolen from their employers. In 1794 María Josefa de la Trinidad Jiménez allegedly stole ladies' bloomers and some white silk stockings from her employer and pawned them at a corner store on Frayle Street for 6 reales. With those 6 reales she could have purchased two packets of sewing needles, three *arrobas* of *chile ancho*, or three yards of yellow muslin at a corner store.[94] A year later, domestic servant Máxima López allegedly stole her employer's clothes instead of washing them and pawned them in a store for a considerable 13 pesos. She defended herself by saying she did it for money to feed her children, echoing a common refrain.[95] A jail and stocks were put in at the Monte a few years after its opening "to exact swift justice on those who pawned stolen articles."[96]

The corner-store legislation aimed at protecting the mobile property of well-to-do households such as silver forks and plates limited the access to credit for poorer women, including Creole women, from households without full silver-service sets to pawn for a few months to finance household provisioning. While the majority of residents in Cuartel 9 were white, they were not all elite. Most Creole female household heads had no steady income, and only a few could afford even one servant (see table 1.1 above and appendix 3, table G). The poorer or downwardly mobile Creole woman did have protected access to the Monte de Piedad as long as she had jewels, fine clothing, or linen, and she was supposed to be safe from harassment as she took her less valuable household goods such as aprons, featherbeds, and coffeepots to pawnbrokers. But if there came the day when she had no cash and only two or three silver forks or plates to pawn, she could not legally secure daily supplies with that collateral. By the 1790s work tools were added to the forbidden list, suggesting that the poor economy was prompting artisans to pawn the tools of their trade, which inventory lists show they continued to do after it was illegal, though tools do not constitute a large portion of the transactions sample (see appendix 1, table B).[97] Most of the artisans in Cuartel 9 were Creoles and were married. For housewives in these largely Creole households, not being able to legally take either their few silver forks or a shoemaker's awl or weaver's shuttle to the pawnbroker was an added barrier to the credit arena. In these cases the royal policy's interest in protecting elite property trumped any intent to prop up poorer Creoles on the decline.

Women comprised two-thirds of the pulpería clients in the database for whom gender can be determined.[98] Elsewhere, I have analyzed the repeated pawning by individual female pawning clients. One, named Eusevia, had at least eleven items in pawn in one month in 1788 at the same pulpería for loans between four reales and two pesos two reales. Another, "La Robago," over a six-month period in 1795–96 pawned more valuable cloth items at least twenty-one times for between one and three pesos.[99] For the Creole and mestizo women who headed households, investing in collateral goods helped insure their dependents against periods of hardship. For a married woman, the loss of her wages to her husband's control might be mitigated by control over property she brought into the marriage through her dowry or through access to goods she acquired once married, whether personal items from her wardrobe or jewelry box, items from her children's wardrobes (such as a girl's petticoat Eusevia pawned), or the forks and spoons from the table service.[100] For women who worked in clothing production or selling clothes, the inventory of finished goods or even garments in progress could be converted into cash through pawning to finance more production in the workshop or more inventory or could be converted into groceries at the corner store on the way home. "La Robago" may have been in the clothing trade. Thirteen of her prendas were petticoats, four were shirts, three were sheets, and one was a shawl.[101] Whether from wardrobes, from household linen closets, or from seamstress inventories, clearly textiles doubled as both clothing and linens on the one hand and convertible investments on the other for many women in the city.

Neither Eusevia nor "La Robago" was as poor as those numerous city residents who pawned goods worth less than four reales (see appendix 1, table G). The average loan of Eusevia's eleven transactions (one peso one and one-half real) are well above the average loan for those customers in the inventories whose goods are listed individually (six and one-half reales). If Eusevia was married with children, this pawning strategy could have kept her at home more often with her children instead of having to work to supplement her husband's wages; were she widowed or a single mother, these goods would have helped provision the household she headed whether she worked for wages or not. Part of the housekeeping role of women in the middle was building and maintaining ethnic identities required for their social position. In Mexico City, where the material base of household goods, wardrobes, and fashion accessories was arguably higher than in other places in Mexico and Spanish America, men and women could cushion downward mobility and prolong the benefits of their social positions for as long as possible.[102] The goods Eusevia pawned ranged from relatively high-quality clothing items to relatively valuable gold jewelry and table settings, and while we do not know specifically what she did with the money on any of these occasions, the conversion of these goods into cash loans likely financed consumption beyond basic subsistence. But only one of these prendas would have allowed Eusevia access to the Monte de Piedad, where the minimum loan was two pesos.

At the Monte de Piedad some customers were regulars, and their average loans were ten times that in the retail arenas.[103] Fifteen percent of customers in the sample were listed more than once, and among those whose visits to the Monte de Piedad are recorded three or more times, 70 percent in 1802 and 65 percent in 1823–26 were female (see appendix 1, table H).[104]

One regular during 1802, Mariana Ruiz, apparently repawned goods immediately after she redeemed them.[105] Her diamond ring, pawned on April 7 for twenty-five pesos and redeemed on October 5 at the end of the six-month pledge period, again yielded a loan for the same amount on October 6 and was redeemed in April of the next year.[106] How many loans was Mariana able to secure with this single investment in its lifetime, a more secure investment than cloth goods, which would deteriorate easily over time? She redeemed other goods a few weeks after pawning them, such as a large shawl pawned in January. She was not among the richest Monte de Piedad customers. The loan value of her jewelry was well below the forty-two-peso average for pawned jewelry in the 1802 Monte de Piedad sample. Whatever her identity, the conversion of her material wealth into cash loans certainly would have afforded her about the equivalent of the typical pension of three hundred pesos per year drawn by widows of low-level bureaucratic officials in 1799.[107] This access to low-cost credit could keep respectable Creole women in economic need out of the public labor sector, a potential source of dishonor.

The presence of widows among the Monte de Piedad clients fits "the feminization of poverty" identified by historians, as female-headed households among the lower middle sector held disadvantaged positions in the employment structures of the city, earning less and thus needing the services of the Monte de Piedad more.[108] But clearly many repeat Monte de Piedad customers were not poor; instead, as in the case of Mariana Ruiz, they were converting their material investments in fine cloth and silver—up to then their cultural currency in the world of fashion and respectability—into real currency. In this way these Monte de Piedad patrons, mostly women, used the institution to nurture their own Creole ethnicity and social status and that of their families. Effectively wielding a public identity rooted in Creole ethnicity depended on a material minimum, and once one had invested in the "stuff" of Creoleness, it could be milked for a long time.

This examination of pawning policy and practice as a function of housekeeping in Mexico City suggests a number of conclusions about patriarchy and about Spanish and Creole hegemony beginning in the 1750s in Mexico. It has been more than fifteen years since Silvia Arrom cautioned us to examine the differences between women under Spanish patriarchy—especially between widows and wives. Both widows and wives had property rights that women in other societies did not have, but widows had rights and authority denied wives in eighteenth- and nineteenth-century Mexico. Looking at household structures and patterns of pawning activities in Mexico City allows us to see how these differences among women played out, as well as differences among Creole women and among women of different classes and ethnicities. But we also see what many women had in common—at least some access to material goods. For those widows and wives with some means—expressed through silver jewelry, silver service sets, and fine fabric clothing and linens—regular visits to the Monte de Piedad allowed them to mitigate patriarchal labor structures in the city, which limited their access to well-paid work opportunities. Pawning also let them take advantage of inheritance and property laws that allowed their male and female relatives to endow their futures and gave them some control over dowry goods and other personal property. Perhaps the majority of women with access to only more humble possessions, and without steady incomes as their access to jobs remained restricted, could not as easily mitigate the patriarchal relations in their lives. Their access to credit through pawning household goods was more limited because of policy concerns about servants and stolen goods. The pawning relationship in the Monte de Piedad and the corner pawnshops remained patriarchal nonetheless, in that the vast majority of formal pawnbrokers were men with a largely female clientele. The state buttressed patriarchal honor codes as they safeguarded public places such as pawnshops that women—both wives and widows—frequented.

Though some aspects of legislation concern regulating retail and pawnshop culture as part of a gendered poor relief, the Bourbon state was more interested in preventing poverty than in relieving it. Prevention was the aim of institutionalized charity, which for pawning was the Monte de Piedad. In New Spain this institution was aimed at the middle sector with a material culture well beyond the poverty level, not at the poor as in Europe. While couching the mission of the Monte de Piedad in a discourse about helping needy women, in fact its mission seems to have been keeping "proper" women such as the Creole widows in the Monte record books from sinking into the ranks of the poor, allowing them to keep up some semblance of a life-style befitting white widows by pawning heirlooms and fine linens and protecting their honor while they did so. Toward this end the Monte de Piedad can be seen as an institution through which the state played the role of patriarch, providing for women of a particular ethnic and class background. Public patriarchy also underpinned the call for private brokers to protect the honor of their female customers while they were on business premises. The state's concern for widows among the pawning clientele reflected patriarchy in crisis, with so many households headed by women. Prevention of poverty can be seen in other ways in pawning legislation. Lawmakers hoped to prevent male idleness that might lead to poverty and therefore prohibited the pawning of work tools. The state also wanted to prevent theft, which could push victims into poverty. It tried to prevent pawnbrokers from accepting stolen property, as the ease of fencing stolen goods encouraged those struggling near the poverty line to steal instead of working.

Bourbon policies of the eighteenth century generally modified "traditional" patriarchal relations and expectations. Part of the Enlightenment Bourbon package was to get more out of women—to educate them so they could be more efficient housekeepers, raise more productive children, and raise the consumption level of their households to fuel the economy. But women's relegation to the home was never a reality for poor women, who had to work for others as well as themselves in order to maintain families whether they had a male partner or not. Another part of the reform program was to get women working outside the home in more lucrative occupations, especially in artisan occupations that supposedly suited their talents, such as textile and tobacco production. Both of these reforms modified patriarchy in New Spain, empowering women as mothers and household managers and to some extent as breadwinners, but still within a rubric of male governance and vigilance of female sexuality by the state and by fathers and husbands.

Pawning policies and practices had both gendered and ethnic motivations and implications that shaped social class in Mexico City at the turn of the nineteenth century. The economic volatility in the capital in the Bourbon period meant the downward mobility of Creoles, a slide that continued after Independence. The protection of private property with the list of forbidden collateral goods included in colonial pawning laws shows that male state officials used policy to protect white material culture and private space as part of a larger effort to shore up the position of whites in Mexican society. Their numerical strength in the city was no longer enough to guarantee prominence and high status. Enlightened royal policy protected the privileges and status of Creole ethnicity. Like the Royal Pragmatic on Marriage, pawning policy fostered the social reproduction of Creole elite culture. It continued to protect elite material culture and white women, whether married, widowed, or single. The Bourbon state understood that housekeeping women went into public to provision their families and respectable women needed an honorable place to pawn goods. If a line of credit works as a metaphor for interpreting the evidence about collateral goods, this maximization of the value of material possessions through pawning also suggests that goods served as savings accounts or investments managed by housekeepers across the economic and ethnic spectrum. After "depositing" a garment or a piece of silver jewelry with a broker or the Monte de Piedad, one could then withdraw between a few reales and many pesos, money that went a long way toward stretching household budgets on a day-to-day basis, whether for subsistence or conspicuous consumption. This financial strategy was commonplace and repeatedly used by city residents, especially women.

Housekeeping and provisioning had different meanings in different households—the differences between life-style and subsistence. Those who were more well-off materially hocked private personal possessions and household goods in public institutions to keep the family in Creole style when times were tough, including times when there was no breadwinning male at home. Creole widows such as Doña Juana Olivares, who pawned her diamond earrings for six pesos cash at the Monte de Piedad in 1802, had a deep stock of collateral to draw on to keep up appearances. Their poorer counterparts, such as the Creole widow Ygnacia Ruiz as well as the neighborhood maids Ygnacia Excorcia and María Gertrudis portrayed at the beginning of this chapter, could only turn to corner stores with their cotton clothing for credit of half a peso. The collateral of Indian, mestiza, and Creole servants working in white households might be viewed with suspicion no matter what it was. Access to the banks of valuable material collateral goods—the silver and silk in Creole homes—was protected by antifencing policies that impacted poorer Creole, mixed-race, and Indian households. María Rosales, the young Creole wife whose husband was unemployed in 1811, might have been hurt by the forbidden collateral goods list if she had run out of dispensable clothes and had to turn to her silverware drawer for one or two spoons for collateral. She may have been grateful that policy makers tried to make her pawning experience one free of challenges to her honor, having no "provocative, indecent, or dishonest words" to deal with. But she may not have appreciated the fact that white hegemony was privileged over dinner for her family.

TWO

Collateral Lending

Pulperías and the Monte de Piedad, 1750–1840

A satirical pamphlet addressing Mexican storekeepers in 1820 strongly rebuked them: "Not content with the customary earning of one real per peso, maliciously you weave the net that traps the incautious, lending them six and demanding from them seven, and making a web between *tlacos*, *pilones* and other effects, finding the account always in your favor."[1] A pamphlet in response to the first urged detractors not to generalize about a few bad examples and stressed that "there are many who have been compassionate with humanity . . . to the benefit of many people."[2] Corner-store owners such as Don Miguel Domínguez, whose customers Ygnacia Ruiz and María Rosales opened the previous chapter, were indeed fundamental resources for the subsistence and life-styles of people living in Mexico City's neighborhoods in the late colonial period, as were the clerks in the depository of the Monte de Piedad. Nonetheless, the businessman who made a living from giving loans secured with collateral goods, sometimes very small loans, suffered from a poor public image. The officials running the Monte de Piedad, too, suffered a bad reputation in public opinion, with its directors lamenting the "voces vagos" that besmirched their image as charitable benefactors. Both pawnbrokers and those staffing the Monte de Piedad also faced steady criticism from government ministers.

Beginning in the 1750s, regulation of the pawning trade in pulperías and the Monte de Piedad shaped the state's policy toward household credit in the late colonial period and into the first decades of the national era. The state anticipated a transition toward the separation of pawning from retail, establishing the Monte de Piedad as part of the Bourbon reforms. While a charitable institution, the Monte de Piedad was also a business employing dozens of people that aimed to operate in the black. Though not directly seeking profits in the sense that entrepreneurial pawnbrokers did, the Monte de Piedad nonetheless tried to make more than it spent in its operations, if only to guarantee its charitable mission of providing low-cost collateral loans to the exclusive middle tier of society. Using business records from pulperías and the Monte de Piedad, government oversight documents of both private and institutional pawning, and a series of retail censuses, this chapter focuses on the business of pawning from the 1750s through the 1830s.

Like other storekeepers, pawnbrokers were mostly immigrant men from Spain occupying the bottom tier of the middle class, though those running smaller businesses had incomes more comparable to the top tier of the working class. Virtually all pulperos were also pawnbrokers, while pawnbroking might complement the wine shop, tavern, and bakery businesses.[3] The pawning business could be profitable, but it also could be burdensome. Brokers were not free to turn away poor customers from the neighborhoods around their shops, and they had to endure reputations as usurers, gougers, and dishonest men whether they were or not. Private brokers and Monte de Piedad employees alike faced government oversight of their day-to-day operations, and as was true for other small businesspeople, they often did not heed government regulations.

Retail Culture and the State

Pawning and retail were linked through centuries of colonial rule. Pulperías, wine shops, pulquerías, general stores, bakeries—all these commercial retailing enterprises accepted pawns in lieu of cash payment for merchandise.[4] The Spanish state brought a tradition of regulating retail to their American colonies, including stipulations that stores be well lit so customers knew what they were buying, that cloth be measured properly, and that damaged goods not be sold. In the early eighteenth century, laws on bookkeeping detailed four different kinds of books to be kept by merchants at all levels, with notes made in Castilian Spanish. If a businessman did not know how to read and write, he was to employ someone who did. Pulperos were under the jurisdiction of the city government, and their business practices were governed by the Consulado, or merchants' guild, which registered and monitored retail merchants as well as large wholesalers, and by a council of twelve peers responsible for regular inspections.[5] In 1812–13 and again in 1820–21 when the Spanish Constitution of 1812 was in effect, storekeepers would have participated in governance (along with many of their customers, as this early suffrage was broad among the male populace) through voting for electors, who then chose representatives to the city council and the Cortes in Cadíz.[6] After Independence in 1821 the Creole-dominated elected city government assumed oversight of the retail trade, including audits and inspections, though it was not until 1824 that the Consulado itself was dissolved and its duties fully absorbed by various branches of the new republican government.[7] Retail pawnbrokers came into contact with bureaucrats when they failed to follow the rules, but also when their business underwent some change that was documented by a notary employed by the Consulado. Viceroys repeatedly expressed dismay at "frauds, swindles and other moral turpitude" committed by dishonest auditors who charged high fees for their services.[8]

The struggle for control of the physical arena of petty commerce is seen in the 1758 regulations for pulperías, according to which a corner-store owner was to prevent the congregation of customers at his counter, in his doorway, or on his street corner who might harass the women coming to shop and pawn. In a decree published by Viceroy Carlos Francisco de Croix in 1779, the state characterized retail merchants as delinquents who denigrated "the good credit and fame of the city" by their poor treatment of needy customers. Legislation in 1810 again charged storekeepers with supervising the behavior of their customers, as well as their own behavior toward their largely female clientele.[9] The fact that references to crowds accosting customers appear in subsequent store regulations suggests that state efforts to insulate store transactions and participants in the market economy were unsuccessful.[10]

Pulquerías were legally excluded from accepting pawns at least since the late eighteenth century, yet their owners regularly contravened the law into the national era.[11] It was not just pulque tavern owners that defied regulation of the liquor trade; other retailers disobeyed rules about hours of operation and what they could sell. The state concern with keeping drinking out of retail outlets was part of a larger public-order package that combated vagrancy and crime. It was also due to the majority of retail customers' being women provisioning households, needing protection from drunkards. Laws regulating drinking were repeatedly renewed, but neighborhood residents continued to patronize pulquerías and *viñaterías* (wine stores) through the 1830s and 1840s in rowdy fashion, and the owners of these establishments continued to violate repeated regulations about behavior, hours, and brokering pawns.[12]

The prefaces to late colonial as well as republican pawning legislation lamented habitual noncompliance with regulations.[13] Among the pawned goods on pawnbrokers' shelves were weapons from the government's arsenal and artisans' tools, both goods forbidden as loan collateral.[14] Revillagigedo issued a decree whose single topic was the banning of military uniforms pledged in corner stores.[15]

There were various ways that pawnbrokers attempted to increase their profits. While they were allowed to give part of the prenda-secured loan in store credit, they were not to deliver the other portion in *tlacos* (tokens issued by the retailers themselves), the value of which they could manipulate, but instead were to give silver.[16] Repeated decrees were published condemning this practice, suggesting that storekeepers circumvented regulations and used tokens as a means to increase their profits. The 1810 Reglamento recognized this custom, as Article 9 prohibited storekeepers from valuing a media real at five *tlacos* instead of the legal and customary four.

Regulation of the private pawning business aimed in part to guarantee access to small loans through pawning for those with subsistence needs. A change in the law reflected the need of city residents to get their hands on cash and not just groceries. By 1810 the law called for the storekeeper to give half the loan in cash (instead of only two reales in silver, as the 1758 law imposed) and half in credit at the store, lending up to two-thirds of the value of the good.[17] Social welfare trends are evident in colonial pawning legislation that remained in force in the national era until the 1840s. The terms set for the redemption and sale of pawned goods were established to benefit the poor, not to maximize the profits of the businessmen. The colonial state characterized retail merchants as delinquents who denigrated "the good credit and fame of the city" by their poor treatment of needy customers, in the words of Viceroy Carlos Francisco de Croix in 1779.[18] The state recognized that customers needed not only the immediate loan to stretch their budgets, but also the return of their collateral good or a portion of its value upon sale, as they provided mechanisms to return profits above costs and interest to pawning customers. Pawned goods had to be held for a fixed term.[19] After the pledge term, the good could be sold only after informing the owner that it was going up for sale. The storekeeper had to post a list of *prendas cumplidas* (goods for which the pledge period had expired) on the door of the business in plain view of customers, announcing that the goods would be auctioned. An official from the Consulado would then make a list of goods and determine their values for the auction. If a good sold for more at auction than the total of the loan plus "corresponding costs," then the *sobrante* (the difference, also known as *demasías*) would be held by the storekeeper, who was to turn it over to the original owner of the good. If the owner did not appear for the difference within a month of the auction, the storekeeper was to post another notice on the door. Owners of collateral goods that were sold had a year to claim the profit from the sale. In the 1758 Ordinance, the unclaimed *sobrantes* could be kept by the storekeeper-pawnbroker. In a 1781 Bando and the 1810 regulations, the state claimed this windfall, which would be applied to public works and charity aimed at the deserving poor, denying this source of profit to pawnbrokers.[20]

Even if the pawning regulations did not favor profit-seeking brokers, storekeepers still had advantages over their pawning customers. Despite regulations, it was brokers who decided what value to assign prendas, as well as how much of that value to lend, perhaps after haggling with the customer.[21] Storekeeper-pawnbrokers decided if and how to apply laws that regulated their activity. For example, both the 1757 and 1810 regulations stated that storekeepers could not accept in pawn "anything that prudently could be presumed not to belong to the subject, or that would impede the exercise of an art or trade." Therefore, brokers had to make a decision as to whether or not goods were stolen or essential for work and then perhaps another decision as to whether or not to make the transaction anyway.[22]

Storekeepers could indirectly influence legislation regarding their trade, as common practices previously prohibited by law became sanctioned in new laws. For example, the 1758 Ordinance stated that pulperías had to be on corners and not at midblock. Those that were already at midblock could not be sold and were to close instead. There were many stores with the notation "media quadra" (midblock) in the 1781 census. In 1785 Viceroy José de Gálvez recognized this reality and permitted businessmen to set up shop anywhere on a block.[23] Colonial pawning legislation remained the law of the land until 1842.

Profile of Pawnbrokers and the Reputation of *Gachupines*

Storekeepers by virtue of their economic position were considered *españoles*, pejoratively reffered to as *gachupines*, regardless of actual genetic backgrounds. They were all certainly referred to as *dons* in Consulado documentation and referred to themselves as *vecinos*.[24] In addition to the *peninsulares* engaged in colonial businesses, Creoles commonly engaged in commercial activities. The 1758 Ordinance specified that nonwhites could be pulperos, but not those of African heritage: "Spaniards, Indians, mestizos and castizos, and women of said quality," even if illiterate, could operate stores.[25]

Most merchants listed in the 1811 population census sample were immigrant Spaniards, and most were single men (see appendix 3, table H).[26] The pamphlet in defense of *tenderos* suggested that some were cautious lenders, because they had to "maintain their business and even their family when the capital was not very large."[27] Don Felix Garrido, a forty-two-year-old married *peninsular* from La Rioja listed in the 1811 residential census as a "comerciante," was listed as owner of a pulpería on Flamenco in the 1806 and 1815 retail census. And Don Manuel Rivera, a guest in the home of Don Vicente Montes de Oca, listed in the residential census as a single twenty-eight-year-old *comerciante* from San Angel, operated a general store on Portaceli in 1811.[28] It was not unusual for more than one merchant to live in a household.[29] In the late colonial period small business owners would often live in rooms attached to or above their stores and shops, and their employees often lived with them. Don Antonio García Jurado's household was contiguous with his liquor store, in the third block of the second Calle de Santo Domingo.[30]

Some small entrepreneurs operated more than one retail establishment, with merchants higher up in the commercial hierarchy often owning several retail outlets, which they provisioned from wholesale operations. Another characteristic of the retail trade was the formation of many partnerships, sometimes outright full partnerships, at other times percentage and salary arrangements with administrators.[31]

Most retail pawnbrokers who have made it into official records were men. While women were not barred from retail, in 1781 they were reported as owning only 11 percent of the small grocery stores in Mexico City, a much lower percentage than was found in other settings.[32] According to the government, women owned 6 percent of the pulperías in 1806, and by 1815 they owned less than 1 percent of retail businesses in Mexico City. Women were more likely to own businesses on a smaller scale. The underrepresentation of women and the scale of their enterprise may have had to do with their being less likely to have the opportunities to earn investment capital or the contacts necessary for a capital loan to get started in business. The pulpero regulations recognized that women might need income-generating opportunities. Article 3 stated that only "women and the poor" could run *acesorias* (small outlets for the sale of firewood, carbon, lime powder, and fruit and vegetables, often located in downstairs, outward-facing rooms of boardinghouses). This change is consistent with the movement in royal social policy that opened up artisan guilds and tobacco dispensary jobs to women. That women continued to run small-scale stores is apparent in the 1843 industrial census, which lists 123 women as owners of *tendajones* (small stores, perhaps equivalent to the *acesorias* of an earlier time), or 25 percent. Women also operated 17 of the 36 *velerías* (candle shops). Female entrepreneurs also continued to operate pulque stalls and street-market stands. Wives invested in their husbands' businesses. For example, in the 1820s Don Juan Compis and Don Juan de la Serna expanded their viñatería business using capital raised when their wives, Doña María Francisca Cepeda and Doña María Teresa Campuzano, pawned their jewels at the Monte de Piedad. When the company went bankrupt, the women sued to protect their property from creditors, as the jewels had been part of dowries and as such were protected by law. The viñatería was worth 5,847 pesos; Doña Cepeda had loaned 2,312 pesos in pawned jewels and cash and Doña Campuzano 1,228 pesos, again in pawned jewels and cash. Together, the wives loaned the store 60 percent of its worth.[33]

Embedded in class, ethnic, and gender understandings, relations between storekeepers and customers were certainly acrimonious at times. Echoed in the sentiments that opened this chapter, grocers throughout the Americas had poor reputations.[34] In tight economic times in 1808–10, with population pressures and droughts, many nonelites were "shopkeepers' dependent debtors."[35] When money was hard to come by, retailers increasingly turned to using *tlacos*, whose value they manipulated, and this angered customers, including poorer Creoles. Storekeepers and their stores were targeted by Miguel Hidalgo's movement. By 1810 José María Tornel y Mendívil, close colleague of Santa Ana in the national period and son of a Spanish grocer—along with other other middle-class Creole statesmen such as Carlos María Bustamante, Ignacio Allende, Juan de Aladama, and Miguel Domínguez—came to develop a hatred of Spaniards and wished to banish them from Mexico once they came to power.[36] In the Bourbon era peninsular immigrants acquired a bad name among the American-born, because they "grabbed positions as merchants, shopkeepers, and local administrators—the petty bureaucrats who abused their posts to intrude upon lands, water rights, trading patterns, and other traditional privileges."[37] Spanish merchants could be loyal subjects even while flexing their muscle, as seen in an 1808 coup that overthrew Viceroy José de Iturrigaray, led by a small group of gachupín merchants and their militia. The popular image of the ruthless Spanish merchant taking advantage of his hungry clientele is seen in the pamphlet *Dolores del parto*: "But, o lamentable disgrace! . . . the poor of all the classes will only find their sustenance . . . with those that get fat on the common hunger: with those that harvest distant miseries, and with those that eat people like *un bocado con pan* [i.e., a typical Spanish-style snack]."[38]

After Independence many gachupines retained their commercial and managerial positions and, hence, control over choice civil, military, and ecclesiastical offices. Anti-gachupín sentiments in republican Mexico were held both among Creole elites, who wrote and voted on bills to expel Spaniards, and among barrio residents, who resented the local economic elite made up primarily of Spaniards. In 1824 both confederalist and Iturbidista plans included the elimination of Spanish employees from the government. In the Constituent Congress in 1824, the issue of the status of resident Spaniards came up at least seven times. Many of them held commercial and managerial positions, "which made them visible agents of an encroaching capitalism."[39] They were an ethnic and cultural minority with key positions in the civil, military, and ecclesiastical structures that did not seek assimilation, and in the postcolonial era they became targets of popular racism. The most serious attempt at expulsion came in April 1824, when the targets were former Spanish soldiers who had remained in Mexico, most of whom had become civilians in lower-class occupations. There is debate about the expulsions. Between 1827 and 1829 the Republic expelled several thousand Spaniards, though many who were technically expelled avoided leaving, so it is difficult to know how many actually left.[40] The Spaniards in small business were the most hated by the populace, perhaps because of direct competition for better jobs in the lower class or because of their daily contact with the non-Spanish populace as clientele. Spanish merchants were famously targets of the Parián riot in 1828.

Perhaps the most notorious image of Spanish pawnbrokers was that of usurer, in both the public mind and official discourse. Catholic prohibition of usury was long-standing. After 1786 the Spanish crown imposed a limit of 5 percent to be charged by moneylenders and merchants, with anything above that defined as usurious. Laws against usury were revoked during the Liberal administration of 1833–34 but were reinstated in 1839 by President Anastasio Bustamante (only to be repealed by liberals in the late 1850s, reinstated again by Maximilian in the 1860s, and repealed again early in the Restored Republic).[41] The eighteenth-century legislation for the corner stores generally did not specifically limit the amount of interest a storekeeper could charge. The 1758 regulations identified but did not limit "corresponding costs" that would be deducted from the sale price of an unredeemed pawned good upon its sale. Presumably, these costs were left to the discretion of the broker, whose greed would be tempered by the usury ban. In a January 1790 decree, Viceroy Revillagigedo limited the amount that storekeepers could gain upon redemption or sale of a prenda to one-eighth of a real for each peso loaned over a six-month period, or just over 3 percent annually if the collateral was redeemed in the sixth month. The rate went up incrementally if the good was redeemed early.[42] It is not clear how long the 1790 limits were in effect or if retail pawnbrokers heeded them; the 1810 regulations for corner stores again made no mention of limits on interest or costs being passed on to customers. A look at business records of individual pulperías suggests that the profits of these businessmen were not high, whether or not they were charging "usurious" interest to their pawning clientele.

The Business of Retail Pawning

At the beginning of the nineteenth century, the city had a bustling business sector. The retail business was volatile. In the colonial period and well into the republican era, pulperías sold "everything necessary for the supply and feeding of the public." There were also *tiendas mixtas* (general stores), which offered cotton and linen cloth, other woven fabrics, paper, and spices. In the early nineteenth century "no street was without two or more stores . . . that contributed to commerce and gave impulse to daily industry."[43] The life of any particular establishment was short-lived, ownership changed hands frequently, and profits were limited.[44] The retail establishments that were also pawning business had to face a spectrum of business issues. The obligations for active prendas by law were assumed by new store owners upon sale of the business, as reflected in the inventories.[45] These documents are silent about goods that were pledged and then quickly redeemed. The pawning transactions that did appear in inventories were those that reached four reales, while the average loan certainly could be much smaller (see appendix 1, table G).

Inventories suggest that profits were not especially high in the pulpería business, but it was not a uniformly depressed business either (see appendix 2, table A). Another factor that appears to have affected the health of the business, perhaps more than the amount tied up in prendas, was the amount of noncollateral cash loans that were outstanding versus the sum of the debts owed by the storekeeper.[46] We have no way of knowing whether interest rates were as "usurious" as popular discourse claimed, as they were hidden in the "corresponding costs" of the pawning process and not itemized in inventories. We also do not know how often pawnbrokers were saddled with unsellable *prendas cumplidas*. Pawnbroking could be a burden for storekeepers, because so much capital was tied up in pawned goods.[47] Most of the inventories studied here, however, do not reflect this situation. Out of eighty-eight inventories that list active prendas, pawned goods represent an average of 17 percent of the net worth of the business.[48]

The inventory data suggest a wide range of capital invested in the retail business. The least valuable store had a net worth of 263 pesos, while the most valuable had 8,076 pesos. The volume of business also clearly varied from store to store.[49] By 1810 pulperías were to operate by law on at least 1,000 pesos capital, though it is clear from the inventories that this was often not the case.[50] Determining the profitability of the pawn business is tricky. Interest rates are unknown, and records of sales of unredeemable goods—a potential area of high profit—are also unavailable. In the Monte de Piedad in this period, the redemption rate was as high as 92 percent.[51] Evidence from sale inventories of retail establishments suggests that redemption was also a regular part of the private pawning process.[52] There is other evidence that goods remained in the same stores when businesses were sold (as required by the Ordinances), as the redemption period was not yet expired.[53] Storekeeper-pawnbrokers would probably prefer that goods be redeemed, the surest way for them to profit from the transaction, as whatever interest a broker charged and costs would be part of the redemption sum. If interest rates were a flat rate per peso loaned (as laid out by Revillagigedo in 1790), brokers would prefer that a collateral good be redeemed just before the end of the pledge period to charge higher rates.

There was a greater continuity of businesses than of ownerships in the retail trade of the 1780s to 1840.[54] Over the years there were more stores in the same locations and with the same names than there were owners of the same name running the same store. A few business owners did experience remarkable longevity. A number of locations had continuous store operation even when ownership changed (see appendix 2, table B). One hundred and fifty stores in business between 1781 and 1843 had a lifetime of over twenty-five years, usually in the same location.

A few family enterprises stayed in business for many years, with more general stores than other stores in this category. Wives and in-laws who may have taken over a business would be missed because of different last names.[55] While it appears that most retail establishments were not handed down from parent to son, daughter, or some other relative repeatedly, some long-term owner families were clearly well embedded in the neighborhood credit fabric (see appendix 2, table C).

Changes are also apparent. Storekeepers moved from store to store frequently, selling one store and buying another; administrators, too, moved around. The ownership of many stores changed often.[56] There is a trend of tiendas mixtas increasingly turning to the viñatería business over the long term.

Certain streets had clusters of stores, especially pulperías. A few streets were central to the neighborhood credit fabric, with many stores, and not just at every block corner but also in between. Competition must have been tough for these stores, as neighborhood residents could decide which shops to patronize. It might be that pawning terms were more favorable in stores in such clusters, as clients could have shopped around for the most favorable terms, with businesses failing to compete shutting their doors.[57] The business records of pulperías show that while pawning could be profitable, it was a risky business. Those working behind the counter at the Monte de Piedad knew this all too well.

Governance of the "Most Beneficial Establishment"

The culture of everyday credit in Mexico City had two tiers. While the pulperos catered to the working poor, the Monte de Piedad served as the collateral credit arena for those more well-off. The Monte was in effect a not-for-profit state business, quite different from the retail pawning outlets. The traffic of goods was also distinct, with limited hours and a careful definition of what was suitable collateral. Despite these differences, the pawning business at the Monte de Piedad could be just as volatile as it was in the neighborhoods.

The institution was open for business every day except Sunday and holidays, from eight o'clock in the morning until noon and again from three o'clock to five o'clock in the afternoon. Monday, Wednesday, and Friday were pawning days and Tuesdays and Thursdays redemption days, "so as not to confuse the two operations."[58] The pledge period was originally six months. Able professionals, that is, tailors and silversmiths in the employ of the institution, were to inspect the goods brought in as collateral, which were to be "of the species of gold, silver, and precious stones, such as diamonds, pearls, emeralds, and others." Clothes made of woven silk and wool and their mixtures or of threads of gold or silver were to be admitted as pledges as long as they were not in poor condition, which could inhibit their sale. Cotton or linen manufactured items, such as "tablecloths, towels, *camisolas* [men's dress shirts] and *camisas* [women's chemises], mattresses or sheets, shawls, handkerchiefs, muslins, capes, *quimónes* [swathes of fine Japanese cotton cloth], and other goods from China" were also accepted, as long as they were not wet or contaminated and they were worth more than a "muy corta cantidad" (very small amount).[59]

The 1775 Bando stated that the institution was to exact no "lucro, ó interés alguno" (profit, or interest of any type), but rather the loans should be given charitably and without usury. The Monte could accept *limosnas* (alms) given upon redemption of pledges by clients that "want to give *very much on their own free will*."[60] If the six-month pledge period expired without the owner bringing in the printed redemption ticket and claiming the good, then it was to be sold in public auction. The institution recovered the loan amount and held anything over that for the owner, to be paid when he or she asked for it. Here, the Monte de Piedad and the private pawning outlet regulations converged. The Monte was also to function as a deposit bank, accepting quantities of money as "confidential deposits," which would be returned to the interested party promptly whenever his or her ticket was presented. And finally, the Monte de Piedad was to maintain a chapel on its property, where a sufficient number of masses would be celebrated daily to beseech mercy for the souls of the dead relatives of donors, with an annual Novenario for the souls in purgatory in general.

The Monte de Piedad in Mexico City was based on institutions dating from the fifteenth century in Italy and later in Spain. The aim of the Italian institutions was not just to fulfill urgent social needs, "but also to free the Christian poor from economic dependence on the Jews, and to eliminate the sin of usury committed by nominal Christians."[61] By the fifteenth century in Spain public-welfare institutions such as the grain *pósitos* and *arcas de misericordia* (mercy funds) were established, and Montes de Piedad "de Crédito en Especie" (giving credit in kind, such as grain) emerged out of those institutions. Other Spanish institutions, founded beginning in 1626, were based on the Italian model, which gave credit in cash with pawned goods as collateral, usually with a maximum loan limit. These Italian and Spanish antecedents were founded in contexts of high-interest lending by moneylenders and pawnbrokers. The main divergence of the institution from the European model when it was transferred to the colonial world was that it was a middling and even elite clientele that were being saved from usury, not the poor.[62]

As a public institution, the Monte and its employees' allegiances were expected to follow the political currents. By order of Viceroy Francisco Javier Lizana y Beaumont in 1810, the royal army set up a munitions factory in the patio and warehouse area of the Monte de Piedad. In 1812 Viceroy Javier Venegas ordered that all public employees, including those at the Monte de Pieded, swear allegiance to the Constitution passed by the Cortes de Cádiz. In return for loyalty, the Monte management expected the crown to provide security for the institution. In November of 1816 the director, Don Antonio Manuel Cuoto, asked Viceroy Juan Ruiz de Apodaca for better security measures, as the adjacent buildings were now empty and troops that used to be quartered nearby were no longer there.[63] In June 1820 Apodaca repeated the order to swear allegiance to the newly restored Constitution of 1812. After the royal government collapsed in 1821, the provisional government ordered that the employees of the Monte swear allegiance to the Plan de Iguala and recognize the Treaties of Córdoba and Mexico's Independence from Spain. In 1824 employees had to publicly support the Republican Constitution.[64]

In addition to being a loyal resource to governments, the Monte de Piedad and its staff were engaged in daily intrastate relations with the colonial and then the national state. The colonial Hacienda and national Gobernación ministries had jurisdiction over the Monte and its employees. Their relations were not always cordial, as oversight included prosecuting for graft and docking pay for poor management. The Monte survived Independence in both name and substance, and it continued to survive changing national governments. Bureaucrats from different parts of government sat on the institution's governing boards. Viceroys and presidents approved and made appointments to vacancies in the staff. Oversight by the ministries of Hacienda and then Gobernación included reviewing accounting records, handling complaints from patrons, and prosecuting fraud and embezzlement.

The institutional pawnshop had four sections—Contaduría (Administration and Controller), Depositaría (Depository), Almoneda (Auction), and Tesorería (Treasury)—and two governing boards, or juntas, the Junta General and Junta Particular.[65] With Independence in 1821 the Monte de Piedad's governing structure changed along with that of the nation. The president had administrative oversight and the Congress legislative authority.[66] The Consulado, the governing institution of large merchants in the capital as well as smaller pulperos and *viñateros*, had representation on the Junta General of the Monte de Piedad, highlighting the connections between public and private sectors of the colonial political economy. Hacienda officials believed that the health of the Monte de Piedad was of great interest to the Consulado due to the Monte's function as "no different than a Bank lending on collateral goods *con premio* [with interest]." Statesmen recognized that the Consulado had a vested interest in the Monte de Piedad because it provided cash loans to residents of the city, who would then spend the money in their stores. The Monte de Piedad was not to be in direct competition with small merchants represented by the Consulado, as the laws regulating pawning in pulperías specifically stated that the corner stores were to accept new and old clothing and jewels of little value that "would not be accepted in the Monte Pío."[67] The Monte was not supposed to give loans for under two pesos and, as is evident from the 1802 ledgers, generally kept to this rule. While the inclusion of the Consulado in the governing of the Monte suggests a positive relationship between the private and public sectors of the pawning trade, viceroys and royal legislators also expressed a negative one: the Monte was to counter usurious lenders, many of them the same small merchants represented and governed by the Consulado. Viceroy Bucareli first made this connection in 1775, and successive directors of the establishment in the republican era noted that the only alternative to their institution was the "enormous usury" of storekeepers.[68]

The Monte de Piedad moved from its original home in the San Pedro and San Pablo Convent to the Convent of Santa Brígida in 1821 because of crowded and poor storage conditions in the former location.[69] In 1836 the Monte moved again, this time to buildings known as the Casas de Moctezuma on the Empadrillo fronting the Zócalo, which remain the headquarters of the institution today. In each of its homes the Monte de Piedad was an arena in which residents of the city brought household goods to be appraised by the institution's employees, the context for broker-client relationships with cultural and economic contours that were part of the daily rhythm of life in the city.

The Staff of the Monte de Piedad and Its Troubled Management

The individual men who sat on the boards and managerial positions of the Monte de Piedad came from the ranks of the gente decente in the colonial period and then the republican hombres de bien.[70] When director of the Monte de Piedad Don Vicente Tresbuestos died in 1796, the appointment of his replacement fell to the viceroy, who considered the recommendations of both juntas. The list of candidates included six men, one of them the treasurer of the institution, and other royal bureaucrats. The chosen successor was Don Manuel de Gamboa, previously an auditor on the Royal

Tribunal of Accounts. It was not only the director's position that was appointed by the viceroy, but also other administrative posts such as Colocador (personnel director) and Contador. Even midlevel positions such as auction judges, bookkeepers, and appraisers had to be confirmed by the viceroy.[71] The statutes called for persons of good character and ability to man the various administrative levels of the institution, stating that standards should include "*limpieza de sangre*, moral customs and judicious conduct, and also, that in addition to being hard-working, they should have the ability to write, count and *inteligencia en papeles* [ability to do paper work]."[72] Young single Spanish men were among those who ran the day-to-day activities at the Monte de Piedad, especially in its first fifty years. Don Luis Cerna, twenty-five years old and single, was named as personnel director for the depository in 1806 because of his "good conduct, health, and application" in his two-year career with the Monte. The other two candidates for this position were single and in their early twenties as well. There were also more mature employees, many of whom had come up in the ranks throughout their careers. Don José Palacios, a forty-year-old widower in March 1805, had entered into service at the Monte at the ground level as a *meritorio* (employee without salary) in January 1783, had moved up to Depository official in 1788, and then in February 1805 was promoted to interventor (controller) in the same section. He was the top candidate for the position of Depository section head in March 1805, when Don Rafael Cadena retired. Other employees were married, some middle-aged and others younger. Don Juan Antonio Laspita, a fifty-five-year-old "español" married to Doña María Bárbara González, was the Monte's Contador in the 1800s, and Don Tomás García, a fifty-year-old "español" married to Doña Josefa Serrano, was the treasurer of the Monte in the same years. In 1816 Don José María García Figueroa, a Creole tailor from Toluca, worked in the Depository. He was twenty-nine years old and married to Francisca Torres, a twenty-eight-year-old Creole from Mexico City.[73] Some Monte employees were provided with lodging in the Monte de Piedad building. Such was the case for auction judge Don Juan Centenac and his wife, Doña Francisca Antonia Catalán. When Doña Francisca Antonia petitioned to have her dowry goods freed from the embargo against her husband in 1805, one reason given was that she wanted to move them from "the room that we have had up to now in the Monte" to another room "on the street." The room she was forced to take was devoid of any furniture, which she argued was detrimental to her small children, as were their dire financial straits due to her husband's five-year imprisonment.[74]

The Monte statutes called for candidates for lower and mid-level positions to be sought among those already employed by the institution and whose service had been meritorious. When lists of candidates did not contain enough employees, they might be sent back for reformulation. In one instance the Junta Particular wanted to go outside the institution because of the "ineptitude" of the employee pool, and they washed their hands of any problems that might arise from choosing among them. Loyal employees climbed the ladder at the Monte, as seen by the example of Don José Antonio Casela, who was promoted to auction judge in April 1805. This opened up the job of auction bookkeeper, for which two employees and one outsider were candidates. Earlier that year, Don José Palacios had moved up from the position of bookkeeper in the Depository to interventor, responsible in his new job for ensuring that the Monte's operations met the letter of the law.[75]

It was important that administrators actually perform their duties. When Don Pedro Martínez, jewelry appraiser, missed work for two weeks due to illness in 1793, the public suffered because, according to the statutes, the Monte could not accept jewels in his absence (although subaltern employees seem to have taken in some jewels anyway). The institution suffered when unqualified employees engaged in pawning transactions in Martínez's absence. Overvaluing goods meant that if the Monte were stuck with the jewel and had to sell it in auction, the institution would take a loss. The Monte management supported Don José Manuel Ynfante as jewelry appraiser in April 1802, but Ynfante was unable to obtain a *fiador* (bondsman) for the one-thousand-peso bond required by the Monte statutes. The appraisers only worked on Mondays, Wednesdays, and Fridays, which were days of empeño, so Martínez's continual absences were seen as inexcusable since he did not have to go in every day. Martínez was finally replaced in January 1804 by Don Sebastián Rodríguez, with the approval of Viceroy Iturrigaray.[76]

Employee absenteeism seems to have been a recurring problem for the Monte. In 1825 Director Couto reported to the president of the new republic, Guadalupe Victoria, that Don Manuel Nagera, on the Treasury staff at the Monte, had missed work on October 31 and therefore clients had been unable to redeem the goods they needed for the Day of the Dead holiday in a timely manner.[77] On other occasions other duties of employees kept them from their posts. In August 1829 jewelry appraiser Don Antonio Sausedo was called out of the city by the Civic Battalion of the militia, in which he was a captain. Director Couto asked the minister of Gobernación to reassign Sausedo to some other militia activity that would not take him out of the city. Couto argued that finding another silversmith to stand in for him, properly bonding him, and training him in the procedures at the Monte would be time consuming, and meanwhile "the large part of the population of this City that find assistance in this pious establishment" would suffer, as operations for the pawning of jewels would have to be suspended.[78] Upon retirement administrators continued to receive their full salaries as pensions, a practice that certainly drained the principal. When Don Rafael María Velásquez was granted retirement from his position as head of the Depository by the viceroy in March 1805, he was to continue to receive his twelve-hundred-peso annual salary, with nine hundred pesos coming out of the institutions' treasury and the remaining three hundred coming from his replacement. This practice reflects the fact that government jobs were considered property, "plaza en propiedad."[79]

With the Monte de Piedad under royal patronage, the behavior outside of work, marital relations, and life-style of its employees were investigated by the government on occasion, records of which give us a glimpse into personal lives. In 1804 Don Estéban Enciso, who worked in the Treasury Department of the Monte, unsuccessfully petitioned the viceroy to rescind a court order that he give half of his four-hundred-peso annual salary to his estranged wife, Doña Apolonia Gutiérrez de Rosas, for her maintenance and that of their children, because she refused to settle in a *casa de recogimiento* of his choice and instead was living with her mother and uncle, coming and going at will. A third of his salary was also tagged for repayment of a debt he owed to the Marquesa de Sierra Nevada. As a result of his petition, the government looked further into Enciso's social habits, discovering that he maintained an ostentatiously appointed vehicle that was well beyond the means of his salary as a Treasury official in the Monte de Piedad. Witnesses in the investigation included other employees of the institution such as Laspita, who testified that Enciso was a man of "good conduct," though he was a little negligent in meeting his obligations, and that it was true he had a fancy car that he was rumored to have financed through gambling. Other witness-employees claimed that Enciso gambled nightly, winning up to one hundred pesos at a time. By March 1805 Enciso had served over nineteen years at the Monte, but his climb was slowed by his reputation as an "insubordinate and daily gambler." In 1827 Enciso left the Monte de Piedad, victim to legislation that barred Spaniards from the civil service in response to plans to reimpose Spanish authority over newly independent Mexico.[80]

The statutes dictated how the employees were to present themselves: they were not to wear hats or "indecent suits," and they were not to smoke in the offices or introduce any other type of disorder.[81] The authors of a recent institutional history argue that when, in May 1822, the institution established a uniform for all employees with no exceptions, the move was influenced by nationalist and anti-Spanish sentiments and meant that staff could no longer use their clothing to show that it "pertained to an elevated social status."[82]

Relations between employees and clients concerned regulators from time to time. In 1816 Judge Protector José Mexia noted that the job of the Monte personnel was tough, as it was impossible to keep up with the "incessant work" and equally impossible "to satisfy the demands of the Public, who by shouting sought to speed up the service." A few months earlier, the Royal Tribunal of Accounts argued that Monte managers had enough to do ensuring that their employees did not engage in fraud through the course of their daily operations or that clients did not defraud the institution, without having to deal with women who complained about the service.[83] There is evidence that the Monte employees looked for better ways to serve the public. A petition in March 1828 argued for longer morning hours without a lunch break, because customers were most desperate in the morning and needed sufficient time to get through the lines so their families did not have to fast until the afternoon or endure the abuses of storekeepers. The employees also argued that in the afternoon it was often raining or foggy and therefore the lighting in the dispatch room was bad, slowing work and making it impossible to attend to all waiting customers, and that more goods were misplaced at that time. A third reason for changing the hours was related to the mood of the staff: "Employees would have a better disposition if they did not have the distraction of leaving to eat and then having to come back to work."[84]

The Junta Particular undertook a review of procedures and accounts in the Monte in December 1805 in order to quiet "las voces vagos" (vagabond voices) that criticized its operations and its employees' honesty. It found that Director Gamboa could go very far in correcting the public image if he himself set a good example and stepped up the supervision and vigilance of his staff. The Auction section was deemed in need of the closest supervision, as its cache of long-held and unsold goods was the biggest temptation for dishonest employees. Still a problem area a few decades later, the auction hall was the source of various complaints from the public in 1834. Employees were selling goods without putting them up for bid, instead taking the first offer and often leaving the owner with neither proceeds nor his or her possession. This loss was "so unjust, so illegal and so worthy of avoiding" that the minister of Gobernación ordered the director to ensure that abuses like this did not occur.[85]

If public opinion of the Monte and its staff was at times unfavorable, the bureaucrats charged with oversight of the institution were no more forgiving. The fiscal of the Real Hacienda and the judge protector of the institution regularly accused the employees of inefficiency and even dishonest behavior. Conversely, employees of the Monte repeatedly characterized the institution as something special. In the words of the director in 1823, "One could justifiably call it the most beneficial establishment of its kind." The Monte's managers considered the cash in the Treasury "sacred funds."[86] On several occasions the director or other officials asserted that the institution was different from private pawnshops and therefore should be treated differently. In 1832, when the national government wanted the Monte de Piedad to begin paying taxes, the director claimed that it should not have to pay them because of its status as a state-sponsored charity. Yet in many ways the Monte was like private pawnshops, sharing some of the same business practices and facing some of the same decisions.

Royal oversight of the Monte fell to the viceregal secretariat, who aggressively prosecuted frauds and embezzlements and attempted to correct less nefarious irregularities. Financial troubles plagued the institution from its inception. In 1776, shortly after it opened, it already had a negative balance of 17,368 pesos. In the 1780s the king sought an explanation for the declining health of the institution, sending examiners from the Royal Tribunal of Accounts charged with solving the administrative problems. While investigators expected to find evidence of large amounts of graft, Don José de Echeverría y Urquinaona was only found guilty of embezzling 2,152 pesos. Other amounts—as small as 4 pesos—were taken out of the salaries of other officials to cover losses from the sale of goods in auction.[87] In January 1804 the viceroy ordered a full inventory and audit. Director Gamboa informed him that in the Depository, where goods were received and stored until they were redeemed or passed on to the Auction section after the redemption period, an inventory had never been done because it would have been "an extremely laborious and lengthy operation." He said it was impossible to track transactions on days when clients come in to redeem goods, and the monthly traffic of unredeemed goods going to the Auction section would also be difficult to monitor. In the Treasury Department, however, in addition to monthly accounting, Gamboa reported that a complete account reconciliation and inventory occurred at the end of every year under his direction, a practice that had begun under his predecessor, Tresbuestos, in 1782. In the auction hall daily records of sales and redemptions were done, and every year the accounting staff completed an account balance, at which he was present.[88]

In an effort to shore up the lending principal, Monte administrators asked the viceroy to authorize a raffle similar to the Royal Lottery, selling tickets for four pesos and awarding up to twenty thousand pesos in prizes. Ten years earlier, the royal government had entertained the idea of depositing Royal Lottery monies not claimed in the Monte de Piedad. Neither of these measures was undertaken.[89] In a review of administrative procedures ordered by the Hacienda ministry in September 1815 to see if the staff could be reduced to save money, the management of the Monte argued that the nature of transactions, accounting, and administrative processes in the institution was quite complex and that the personnel structure was already insufficient to ensure efficiency and honesty. Officials overseeing the pledge and redemption end of the business were too busy to also supervise the auction proceedings, which meant that careful accounting and audit procedures were not routinely implemented. If the staff was reduced, management argued, the public would suffer slow service, as certain transactions would have to be put on hold while others were underway.[90]

When there were irregularities in the operations of the institution, the officials in charge were held accountable. In 1797 Don Vicente Candamo, Depository official, faced an investigation by the crown's solicitor for having abused his authority and for poor conduct. That same year Don Antonio Esquivel, the clothing appraiser, was prosecuted for "mala versación" (poor judgment) in the use of his authority.[91] When money was missing, the government embargoed the responsible Monte employees' goods to meet the sum, even after death. When the treasurer Don Pedro Ossoro died in July 1794, his estate was frozen until accounts could be settled in the department that he oversaw. When the court suspended the salary of the interventor Don Mariano Gerardi in October 1800 because of the discovery of irregularities in the Auction side of the business, his wife, Doña María de los Rios, argued that it was not his fault, as he had not been in to the office in five years due to a paralytic illness. Gerardi had left daily operations to the Marqués de Valleano and Don Juan Pinto, two "qualified fellows." Doña María's plea was granted, and Gerardi did not lose his salary despite being incapacitated, but only because Don Juan Centenac, the Auction judge, declared that the robbery had occurred on his watch. Five years later, Don Pedro Martínez, the jewelry appraiser, was not as lucky as Don Gerardi. In November 1805 the judge protector had him jailed and his goods embargoed because he was held responsible for a shortage of over 6,300 pesos that had occurred while he was employed at the Monte, which prompted his wife to ask the Monte employees in her husband's old department for help in meeting her daily subsistence needs. Don Juan Centenac was prosecuted for shortages totaling 3,422 pesos that were discovered in the 1800 audit and inventory, and in 1804 he was still in jail, though his poor health meant that he was also in and out of the Hospital de Jesús Nazareno while his case was under review. In the middle of 1805 Centenac's goods had been embargoed, and his wife, Doña Francisca Antonia Catalán, sued to get back seized property that she argued was part of her dowry and therefore protected by law. Doña Francisca Antonia also petitioned the courts to reconsider her husband's case, arguing that he was not guilty, or at least not the only guilty party. She claimed that the accusations against Centenac had arisen from poor administrative practices of the directors, Tresbuestos and then Gamboa, as they did not perform inventories as directed, and that when Gamboa finally did so in 1800, the goods and money missing could have been the responsibility of "many judges and clerks that had managed the office" over the years.[92]

The problem of *descubiertos* (shortages) continually plagued the Monte de Piedad. When the viceroy ordered an audit in August 1814, Don Ramon Otañez was held responsible for 3,552 pesos missing from the Depository and 683 pesos missing from the Auction section, while Don Manuel Carrion was held responsible for 2,223 pesos. Also found guilty at this time, the auction judge, Don José Antonio Casela, pleaded with the government not to jail him for shortages because of his advanced age and poor health and instead to free him on the bond of Don Mariano Santa María. It is not clear how much of this was outright robbery and how much poor management.[93] In 1816 the institution established new accounting procedures, but there were other ways that employees committed fraud.[94] In May 1823 management accused accountant Don José García of using a fraudulent ticket to claim the difference between the pawn and sale prices of a prenda. The fake ticket had allegedly been created with the assistance of the *meritorio* Don Pedro Castro Virgen, whose initials were on the ticket. The pair were punished in the interest of "a numerous public very susceptible to fraud."[95]

By 1815 the institution was in dire financial straits. The volume of daily ministrations in loans to clients, combined with poor administration, meant that the institution was operating at a deficit.[96] Hopes of getting further charitable contributions were dim, or so believed the fiscal from the Real Hacienda, because "who would undertake putting their capital in a foundation that, because of the poor management by its employees and for the current dangerous system of administration, has seen its own capital disappear." Judging by the relative volumes of loans made and repaid, the year 1815 was indeed the worst for the institution since its first year (when twice as many loans were made as were repaid). With more than 8,500 more loans than redemptions in 1815, it may be that solvency was beyond the control of the institution's managers (see appendix 2, table E). Nonetheless, in 1816 the crown's solicitor suggested that operating costs be cut and deficits covered by cutting salaries. The judge protector rejected the idea, as he felt that employees were barely getting by on what they were making. Salary cuts would only encourage dishonesty and "the prostitution of duties, which would in turn increase the discredit and ruin of the Monte."[97] Employees themselves rejected the idea, arguing that when they were hired they were not told their salaries would be discounted in the event of a deficit in the Treasury. Already their wages were so low that "with them we do not eat, dress ourselves or pay for our houses, much less other remedial needs of life." Lower salaries would only invite fraud. Officials in the Real Hacienda in turn accused Monte employees of being inefficient and unworthy of their salaries, suggesting that docking their pay for operating deficits would make them do a better job.[98] In the end all royal employees earning over 500 pesos annually suffered a discount in their salaries by order of Viceroy Félix María Calleja.[99]

Even without discounts, employees at the Monte de Piedad considered their salaries to be low. Perhaps when Don Manuel Garzon Varela sought permission in November 1800 to procure for himself one or two reales from pawning transactions for his own subsistence "due to his having served meritoriously 11 years" at the Monte de Piedad, it was to make up for his low salary. His request was denied by the governing junta, as it was against Article 34 of the statutes of the establishment.[100] Employees from all levels of the Monte petitioned the minister of Gobernación in 1826 for an increase in their salaries. They claimed that the low wages of employees at its founding were supposed to increase as the lending principal grew and that this promise was never kept. According to the employees' petition, business was brisk at the Monte de Piedad. Because of the multitude of people that came in, jewels were lost, and the responsible employee would have to pay its value out of his salary so as not to bother his bondholder nor arouse complaints from the public.[101] While under "the immediate protection of the government," employees did not earn the kind of salaries that those in government ministries such as Hacienda did. They asked the government to increase their salaries, as they had been loyal employees all those years, waiting for the promise to be kept that in better times they would make more. The salary petition was passed to the director of the Monte, who was charged with justifying an increase in salaries so that the administration, in turn, could justify it to Congress. Director Couto reported that the employees deserved a raise. He had witnessed their hard work, and while the funds were sufficient to cover raising salaries, the government should authorize the increase. The director opined that for men handling such large sums of money, Monte employees were paid far too little, and instead of going the route of dishonesty, they honorably suffered the "misery" of low pay. After checking the statutes to make sure there was no impediment, and because the move would not cost the public treasury anything as the salaries came out of the institution's own principal, the minister of Gobernación recommended to the Congress that the salaries be increased, with the director going from 2,000 to 3,000 pesos annually and the doorman from 250 to 400 pesos (see appendix 2, table D). In 1829 and 1848 the Congress again reformed the salary schedule of the Monte.[102]

The Business of Institutional Pawning

The operating capital of the Monte de Piedad fluctuated, affected by ebb and flow in the volume of business, the state of the economy, and efficient or sloppy management. From its founding in 1775 until the middle of August 1805, over a million pawning transactions took place at the Monte de Piedad, for a combined loan value of 17,452,299 pesos. The employees of the Monte de Piedad served over two thousand customers a month, sometimes two hundred people a day, in the late Bourbon era. They continued to serve increasing numbers of the city's middle class through the tumultuous politics of the Independence and early national periods.[103] The 1802 ledgers show balance fluctuation for one year, as summarized in table 2.1, while the comparative volumes of lending and redemption transactions demonstrate fluctuations from year to year (see appendix 2, table E). Reporting in 1823 on the forty thousand persons a year that came to the institution for help, the director said that the numbers "had increased extraordinarily in these last years" because the early years of Independence were difficult economically for city residents.[104] Some years there were

TABLE 2.1

Principal Balance of Monte de Piedad, 1802

Month	Amount	
	Pesos	Reales
January	4,363	2 3/4
February	4,798	3 3/4
March	1,840	3 3/4
April	1,557	5 3/4
May	1,796	2 1/4
June	2,165	7
July	17,573	2 3/4
August	6,717	5 1/2
September	10,346	4
October	7,496	7 3/4
November	6,267	
December	10,091	

Source: AHNMP, Libros de Empeños, 1802.

more redemptions—that is, loans paid back—than loans made, complicating the director's view on the impact of national Independence. In 1821, the very year Independence was achieved, there were more people who had enough money to pay back loans than people who sought them.[105]

The type of currency with which the Monte did business was as much a source of consternation for managers and clients as it was for retail. In 1823 the government of Emperor Iturbide wanted the Monte to switch from metal to paper money, but the director resisted, claiming it would hurt the institution and the clients. He argued that "more than half of the four or five hundred people who come daily" pawned goods for three-peso loans, an impossible sum to give in paper money. The change called for the institution to accept paper currency in the repayment of loans that were made in pesos and reales of silver. The director opposed accepting paper from clients redeeming their goods, because there would be insufficient coinage on hand for the many daily transactions too small to be paid in paper currency. He feared the move would push clients back into the "bitterness of days gone by," when they had to turn to some store to secure food at the cost of "enormous usury." The government relented and exempted the institution from the paper-currency policy. Two years later, clients complained to the new Federal District government that employees at the Monte would not let them redeem their goods with coins because of their unstable value. The Monte administration again argued that the institution needed smaller fractions of money to conduct its business. President Guadalupe Victoria ordered the Monte to accept gold coins at the intrinsic value of eighteen pesos per ounce, reprimanding the institution for scandalizing and discrediting the nation.[106]

The statutes of the Monte de Piedad withstood the succession of governments in Mexico, though its leadership did alternate between liberal and conservative as the national leadership changed.[107] Yet operations did change over the years, as management and boards adapted to a changing business and political climate throughout the nineteenth century. In 1810 the repawning of pledges was limited to one day a week. In 1814 the governing board banned repawning, deemed responsible for the depletion of funds as loans were not paid back but extended. The board revisited the issue in 1842, when repawning of items was again allowed as long as customers paid the interest due from the first pledge period. As the Monte de Piedad could (and sometimes did) lose money in auctioning goods, this option of extending pledge periods would give clients more time to put together the money they owed and redeem their good.[108]

Because of long-standing prohibitions against usury and the stated aim of combating it, clients of the institution were not charged interest in its early years. Instead, the institution encouraged customers to leave a *limosna* (voluntary contribution). In 1780 the board decided that to cover losses the limosnas should be given at the time goods were left in pawn and not when the goods were redeemed. Two years later the board ordered Monte managers to post a notice telling clients that limosnas would now be obligatory and should be calculated at a quarter real per peso loaned. This flat fee translated into a 6.25 percent annual interest rate for Monte customers if they left collateral deposited for six months (double the short-lived legal limits for corner-store pawnbrokers set in 1790). In 1786 the Monte management again charged the limosnas at the time of redemption. However, a decade later the limosnas were still not sufficient to cover the costs of daily operations.[109] Throughout the year 1802 the percentage of donation per peso loaned out was steady at 2.5 percent until August, when it began to fluctuate (see appendix 2, table F). Only in three months (August, November, and December) was the obligatory 6.25 percent annually met. In 1815 the Junta General revisited the question of whether or not the institution could charge interest without breaking prohibitions against usury. Junta members were worried that the "popular intelligence" of their supposedly "needy, poor and vulgar" clients would consider any fee "sinful and usurious," and any such perception was to be avoided. In the end the government approved a rate hike only for those clients whose goods were sold at auction, and beginning October 1, 1815, deducted a half real for each peso loaned (equal to a 12.5 percent annual interest rate) from the sale price, reducing the amount the original owner of the collateral could collect. The limited fee increase was to cover the costs of storing the pledges and maintaining them in good condition beyond the six-month pledge time until they sold. This fee allowed the establishment to cover operating costs and even yielded a small surplus, which was applied to the principal used to give loans—a timely windfall, as the institution was again on the verge of bankruptcy.[110]

While the redemption rate was quite high at the public pawnshop, the volume of business meant that some abandoned collateral accumulated on the shelves. The statutes called for an inventory of all goods whose pledge period expired every month, which were to be appraised before being put up for bidding at an auction. The proceeds above loan amount and costs would go to the owner. In 1800 the viceroy ordered that jewels of extreme ("quantiosísimo") value were to be scrupulously appraised to ensure that the best price was received for them at sale.[111] In the sample from January through March 1802, 28 percent of goods sold at auction sold for the loan amount and no more (see appendix 2, table G, for examples). A third of the goods that sold for more than the value of the secured loan garnered windfalls of under five pesos.[112] As for the expensive items that had concerned the viceroy two years before, five items sold for between fifteen and fifty pesos above the loan amount. There was no interest charged to customers in 1802, so the entire difference was to go to the owner of the good. For most of the items in the sample this was done, especially for goods of high value. On a few occasions customers did not appear to receive the difference for a year or two after the sale. Only seventy-four items, or 7 percent of the over one thousand in the sample for 1802, were *prendas cumplidas* offered for sale. The average length of time for sale of the goods after the six-month period was two months, with only six items sitting in the auction room for more than four months and two of those for over six months. Table 2.2 summarizes the gender breakdown of the owners of goods sold at auction in the first quarter of 1802. The average sale price was twenty-four pesos. Females pawned 62 percent of these goods and their average sale price was ten pesos, while males pawned 38 percent with an average sale price of forty-six pesos. This suggests that although men

TABLE 2.2

Type, Average Sale Price, and Customer Gender of Auctioned Goods at Monte de Piedad, 1802

			Male		Female	
Good	% of Sample	Average Sale Price	%	Average price (in pesos)	%	Average price (in pesos)
Jewelry	24	42	44	79	56	12
Silver Service	22	39	38	61	62	25
Clothing	43	8	31	7	69	8
Pieces Cloth	8	2	40	6	60	5
Accessories	3	32	0	—	100	32

Source: AHNMP, Libros de Empeños, 1802.

pawned fewer of the items sold overall, they pawned more of the more expensive goods, especially jewelry and silver table-service items.

All pledge items in the sample were either redeemed or sold, suggesting that at least in 1802 there was not a large stockpile of unsellable items. In 1823, shortly after Independence, the director of the Monte claimed that the number of unredeemed goods that the Monte could sell was "infinite." While likely an exaggeration, this assessment suggests that the economic hardships of the period meant that people were less likely to repay their loans and get their goods back and that the Monte had trouble unloading them at auction.[113] Indeed, the data on the volumes of loans and redemptions shows that the instance of higher redemptions already noted for 1821 was not a permanent trend, with both 1822 and 1823 years in which substantially fewer people were able to redeem goods than people who sought loans (see appendix 2, table E). Rafael Castro experienced such hardship in 1836, when he explained that times were particularly difficult for him financially and he was unable to redeem several pieces of jewelry he had pawned at the public pawnshop. Castro's goods were sold for low prices, yielding small profits, which he had a hard time getting from the institution.[114]

While the 1802 ledgers show few items sold at auction relative to the number pawned, none in the sample were sold at a loss, suggesting perhaps that the appraisers fixed reasonable values for goods offered at auction that year. This was not always the case, however. Losses incurred upon the sale of unredeemed goods were not swallowed by the institution (unlike the situation for the private retail pawnbrokers). In 1805 the jewelry appraiser Don Pedro Martínez had his goods and his silversmith shop embargoed to meet the cost of over six thousand pesos of such losses. The shortage arose from Martínez's overvaluing of jewels at the time of pawning transactions, giving customers more in loans than the jewels sold for on the auction market.[115] The statutes outlined the appraisal process: for jewelry, the intrinsic values of metal and precious stones were to be considered, as well as design and manufacture of the piece. For clothing, the appraiser was to consider whether or not the item would sell well at auction, expected deterioration in storage, and fabric and construction. Loans were to be for no more than seven-eighths the value of jewels and two-thirds the value of clothes.[116] In 1823, Monte director Don Antonio Manuel Couto complained that more often than not the amount received upon sale of an unredeemed good did not even cover the loan amount, constituting a loss and contributing to further depletion of the principal because the Monte did not receive the 12.5 percent fee. In 1834 customers complained to the government about low sale prices for their goods. Monte administrators were not the only ones concerned with getting fair prices for auctioned goods.[117]

As this was an institution for "beneficencia pública" (public charity), the stated aim was not turning a profit. Nonetheless, administrators did squeeze money out of the institution, with various methods of embezzlement and fraud. But the preoccupation of bureaucrats in the Hacienda ministry and on the institution's boards was not with profits, but rather deficits. The thwarted move in 1815 to charge a half real per peso loaned across the board was an effort to meet operating costs. The crown's solicitor noted that many *restos sobrantes* (the difference between the loan amount plus fees and the sale price) went unclaimed, which was good for the institution, as the money would be held in the Treasury and considered operating capital until claimed. In fact increasing *restos sobrantes* by selling goods was encouraged by the Fiscal (as opposed to holding on to them for a longer period of time, providing clients more opportunity to get their belongings back), as it would generate these funds. Even if clients claimed their portion of the profit from the sale of their goods, selling stockpiled goods benefited the Monte, as the Treasury would receive the half real per peso loaned, capital that went ungenerated when pledges sat on the shelves beyond the contingent six-month term.[118]

The face of the pawning business in Mexico City in the last decades of the eighteenth and first decades of the nineteenth century was white and male.

The Spaniards occupying the middle business tier in the city's pulperías and those staffing the Monte de Piedad ran credit operations largely on their own terms, despite government attempts to structure their trade. Though there were certainly changing rhythms of business in both the private and institutional sectors, the business of pawning was a constant feature of material life in the capital city in the transition from colony to independent nation. The reputation of Spanish pawnbrokers as usurers and gougers, criticism by politicians and clients of the flawed service at the Monte de Piedad, and demand for collateral-credit services in a cash-strapped economy continued to shape the popular culture in this Catholic city as Mexico worked through its separation from Spain.

The pulperías and other retail businesses that doubled as pawnshops for locals in neighborhoods were complex enterprises. While stores were closely watched by the state, the reality of daily transactions did not always correspond to official prescriptions, and in fact small businessmen were often in open defiance of government regulations. The pawning business was volatile and competitive, profitable for some but not for all. Customers had multiple pawnshops to choose from, with some becoming regulars in specific stores even when ownership changed. Establishments that engaged in pawning were an integral part of the cultural, economic, and political fabric of the city, with many corners and particular streets continuously home to pawning businesses, some run by the same families for long periods of time. The perceived abuses of private pawnbroking prompted the founding of the Monte de Piedad. Retail pawnbroking continued side by side with the Monte, with each mandated by law to accept goods the other did not.

Staffed by Spanish men of "pure blood," the governing structure of the Monte de Piedad was paternalistic, with the institution under the patronage first of the crown then of the republican government. The position on the governing board held by the Count of Regla's family (which they still hold today) is called a *patronato*, setting up the Romero de Terreros men as patrons of the institution and its clients. At times the government's attitude toward Monte employees was patronizing, chastising them for being dishonest and incompetent. The institution, not set up to turn a profit, originally had no interest mechanism to ensure coffer replenishment. Inefficient operation often obtained at various levels of bureaucratic hierarchy, and the institution was seldom free of financial worries. While certainly not always the case, some appraisers overvalued goods so that upon auction the institution lost lending capital. Directors and managers were responsible for depletion of the principal through malfeasance, and the pension system was a further drain. The paternalistic chain of command meant that the minister of Hacienda or ultimately the viceroy and then the secretary of Gobernación or ultimately the president had to grapple with these structural and behavioral problems, just as they were responsible for personnel decisions. There were patron-client relationships within the public institution between ranked state agents, and not just between the institution and its clientele. While the character of internal relations was paternalistic, relations between the Monte's men and the public were more patriarchal; the lines streaming in and out of the Depository were full of household women turning to male bureaucrats for cash collateral loans.

While the state and the Count of Regla founded the Monte de Piedad ostensibly to aid the poorest classes, its clients were middle class, including pulperos. The collateral goods in the Monte were generally more valuable than those in retail establishments, with more silver jewelry and table-service items, and men pawned more valuable goods than women. At the beginning only whites comprised the employee pool, and the staff continued to come from the elite after Independence. An enduring characteristic of the behavior of many Monte employees was widespread noncompliance with the regulatory statutes. Though a public institution, the Monte de Piedad had to face many of the same business issues that framed the private sector. Now we return to the city's neighborhoods as housekeepers navigated the volatile decades of the 1840s to the 1870s, extending their pawning practices further into the nineteenth century.

THREE

Collateral Living

Consumption, Anxious Liberals, and Daily Life, 1830–80

During the first half of 1868, just after Mexican statesmen reclaimed the national government from the Austrian Maximilian, who ruled Mexico for the French, María Robledo repeatedly visited the pawnshop of Don Agapito Cortés in Portal de Cartagena in Tacubaya on the outskirts of Mexico City. In nine visits María secured loans of two or three reales at a time by pawning three used sheets, a "no. 6" iron, a tablecloth, two scarves, a coffee-colored petticoat, and a woven silk shawl.[1] Residents of Mexico City and Federal District municipalities under early republican and then imperial governments lived with a continued scarcity of cash as a consequence of low salaries and lack of circulating specie. To manage household budgets or small businesses, working- and middle-class residents pawned personal items such as clothing and jewelry or household goods such as sheets, spoons, or irons. With less frequency, they pawned work tools and finished products of their labor.

This chapter analyzes household economies and material cultures in the middle of the nineteenth century. Laws that governed pawning and households, portrayals of collateral-credit customers and daily life in contemporary literature, and inventories of collateral in private pawnshops and the Monte de Piedad from the 1860s and 1870s show that people continued to turn to both pawnbrokers and the Monte de Piedad, depending on what they were going to pawn. Identifying clear patterns of governance over the material world of housekeeping, lifeways, and collateral credit is difficult in the first fifty years after Independence. During this period in which hombres de bien maintained political hegemony in the new context of republican politics, they apparently had little concern for expanding social-welfare policy to guarantee access to low-cost small collateral loans in Mexico City. Instead, statesmen took more steps to protect the movable property of the well-to-do and the downwardly mobile; they continued and expanded forbidden goods lists and servant vigilance measures.

This protection of material goods and reputations of families "de bien" paralleled protection of patriarchal rights as liberal governance evolved following Independence. Seamstresses, female household heads, and others, including working people and thieves, continued to employ pawning as a housekeeping strategy, with less valuable collateral goods pawned in private businesses. Women in middle ranks—*mujeres de bien*—still made regular visits to the state-supported Monte de Piedad, thus living on family material investments, some inherited, some acquired in better times. The "stuff" of daily life continued throughout the nineteenth century to be dominated by cloth and silver, though fashionable presentations of those goods changed. Indeed, a third of the goods in the pawning sample for midcentury are household goods, more than the quarter of the Bourbon sample.

Governance and Households

Life in nineteenth-century Mexico City often happened amidst a state of emergency, with innumerable conspiracies and foreign occupations that might force businesses to close and make it risky to go about one's business in the streets. The Monte de Piedad continued to operate almost uninterrupted during American occupation of the city in 1848, though stores did close periodically.[2] While on the face of it politics were volatile, power changed hands back and forth between a relatively small number of men with similar socioeconomic backgrounds. An assessment of laws passed by those men concerning property, pawning, domestic service, and gender relations reveals that postcolonial governance in Mexico followed a general liberalizing trend. Government policy had a direct impact on working- and middle-class households. In short, politicians were anxious about liberalism, worried about sharing power with poorer folks, and concerned about protecting their patrimonies of movable property, all the while readjusting patriarchy to keep wives subordinate but empower the widows next door. There were contradictions within liberalism between ideas of free trade and laissez-faire economies on the one hand and government activism in terms of social reform, regulation of commerce, and the maintenance of public order (including the protection of private property) on the other.[3]

Hombres de bien dominated governance in postcolonial Mexico, with government positions limited to either male property owners or males with a certain level of income. Though earlier male suffrage had less stringent requirements, by 1835 the citizenry was defined as men with yearly incomes of at least one hundred pesos. The definition of citizenship excluded the illiterate, domestic servants, the unemployed, and vagabonds, not to mention all women, effectively disenfranchising 80 percent of the city's population. The conservative statesmen Mariano Paredes y Arrillaga argued in 1843 that there were "only two estates" in Mexico: the first, which he represented, and the second, which "we call *chaquetilla*." Thus Paredes identified day laborers and other working people whom he wished to exclude from republican life by the most common item of clothing—the jacket—worn by men of the group, the very same attire on "popular" characters on the 1869 Juego de la Oca game.[4] Also called *hombres de orden* ("men of order"), gente decente ("decent people"), and *gente de frac* ("people of the frock"), the ruling cohort was not defined by its political persuasion. It consisted of conservatives, liberals, moderates, *puros*, freemasons, centralists, and federalists alike. Instead it was identified by material contours. Michael Costeloe paints this portrait of an hombre de bien: "He was a believer in the Roman Catholic faith, with a strong sense of honour and morality, and of sufficient financial means to maintain a certain life-style."[5] These were men of property (indeed, the term "bien" can be interpreted as "property" or even as "good," as in a material item, and not just as the opposite of the adjective "bad"), but their wealth did not have to be in real estate (*bienes raices*). As liberal statesman José María Luis Mora put it, wealth in this social class could derive from "a job which provides him with the necessities of life," or approximately one thousand pesos annually. Remarkably, in this volatile political economy, this is the same income that a respectable family needed at the end of the eighteenth century.[6]

As long as one acquired and maintained the material goods "necessary" to gente decente status, one and one's family would be counted among the power elite of republican Mexico. It is unclear to what extent this class of *gente de bien* corresponds to Creole middle groups and elite of the Bourbon period and how many were from the growing mixed ethnic population, some of them passing into the "white" crowd. Mexico City's population grew to 170,000 by 1850, and municipalities on the outskirts of the Federal District grew as well. But because after Independence census takers did not record ethnicity again until 1921, the ethnic makeup of the population at midcentury is not clear.[7] The still small middle groups as well as the elite grew in the first decades after Independence, though there was little change in occupational structure. By 1849 there were 23 percent unskilled worker households, 38 percent skilled worker households, and 26 percent upper middle-class households, leaving 13 percent elite.[8] This reality of a sizable working class and growing middling population undermines efforts to see the city residents as either poor or rich at midcentury.

The Mexican ruling class absorbed more nonwhites after Independence, but women remained absent among those holding state power. Racial prejudice was still important in early republican years in defining status, but mestizos could become hombres de bien if they had enough wealth and status. Part of the status requirements involved appearing properly turned out in public, which was accomplished through daily work generally overseen by women in the family and done by domestic staffs: shopping for wardrobes and groceries; doing laundry and ironing; and grooming themselves, the children, and the men for public presentation. While women were excluded from statesmanship, their provisioning roles were crucial for reproducing the ruling elite.[9]

Republican statesmen generally protected their personal property—real estate or movable goods stored and displayed in the home, acquired by women at Parián shops or through inheritance—as part of governance strategies. Radical liberals had smaller households and fewer servants than either moderates or conservatives, yet they paid higher rents than either group. These statesmen were most concerned with changing property relations. While radicals, during their brief control of national government in 1833, talked of class warfare and redistribution of property, they apparently did not pass any legislation that changed colonial pawning laws. The more conservative hombres de bien in power in 1835, led by Lucas Alamán, were effectively guaranteed a monopoly of elected office by the Siete Leyes, a position from which they could protect their property interests.[10] Conservative republicans did not alter colonial pawning laws either.

Regardless of which faction of whatever party was in power, from the 1830s onward the state remained on the brink of bankruptcy, unable to meet payrolls, including obligations to "pensioners, widows and many others dependent on the public purse." In the decades after Independence, state employees and their dependents were strapped for cash, which increased the importance of material investments in household and personal goods. Compounding cash-flow problems for bureaucrats as well as other residents were repeated failed minting of copper coins, which generally only benefited counterfeiters. In general the late 1830s were a time of unpaid salaries, rising prices in shops, a scarcity of basic foodstuffs, higher taxes, and devalued currencies—all of which hit the working poor as well as the middle classes hard.[11] In 1836 the Monte de Piedad even suspended the time-honored payment of "restos," affecting those who relied on consignment of goods with the charitable institution for eventual sale.[12] In July 1840 the downtown neighborhoods of Mexico City endured a twelve-day siege, as the conservative centralist Bustamante government defended itself against a liberal federalist coup, during which daily life was disrupted with shop closings, cut-off food and water supplies, and random looting. A similar scene took place downtown a year later in September, with the Bustamante government exchanging cannon fire with rebels backing Generals Paredes and Santa Anna and shops and businesses closed. Neighborhood retailers only resumed business in October 1841 after the government ordered them to do so. Another copper currency crisis occurred in 1841, with riots outside food shops that refused to accept copper, and women working at the tobacco factory protested violently when the factory tried to pay them in copper.[13] No doubt visits to pawnshops (at least those that were out of the line of fire) picked up in these times of economic crisis.

In January 1842 the Santa Anna administration enacted a new empeño law that was as much about the caudillo's attack on copper-coin counterfeiters and Spanish businessmen as a concern for social welfare. In terms of direct impact on household credit strategies, on the one hand the law limited the interest that pawnbrokers could charge. Given the regularity of pawning strategies for city residents, this was a big deal. On the other hand the 1842 law continued to list goods that were forbidden as collateral, thus extending into the republican state Bourbon anxiety about safeguarding movable property from pilfer.[14] In January the same year, the Monte's governing board, chaired by the minister of Gobernación, eased the collateral-loan process for the middle class. In February the Monte de Piedad's directors decided that any collateral good could be repawned upon payment of interest due for the original pledge period. This measure benefited those who might otherwise lose their collateral, in effect protecting private property of middling Monte patrons.[15]

In 1852 provisions of another law, the Reglamento para criados domésticos enacted by Federal District governor Miguel María de Azcarate under President Mariano Arista, intensified the state's protection of private property in households. While the percentage of working people who were domestic servants had decreased by midcentury, enough city residents still employed one or two of the over five thousand *criadas* and *criados* in the city that the state promulgated the 1852 Reglamento. Four out of five domestic servants were female. The law codified the registration, hiring, mobility, and behavior of servants, broadly defined beyond household staffs to include, among other people, waitpersons, truck drivers, and cowboys.[16] The law imposed vigilance over hiring and firing of "servants," requiring these workers to obtain an official *libreta*, or notebook, from local police and in it have recorded all work arrangements with employers as well as reasons for dismissal. Lack of a *libreta* carried a penalty of fine or prison, and pawning notebooks was prohibited "under any circumstances." The regulations also specified where a servant could live and store clothing, a continuance of antitheft policies.[17] Servants were not supposed to rent living spaces without permission from employers. Landlords were not supposed to rent rooms to servants without notifying the police. Servants could not "keep or deposit clothing, trunks, boxes or dresses" anywhere but in houses of employers without permission. Anyone with an unauthorized storage place could be prosecuted as "ocultadores."[18] The republican state was clearly still concerned to protect personal property of middling and elite households (many if not most of whom were Creole) from pilfer by maids, carriage drivers, stable hands, and pages. The first decades after Independence were times of recession and high male unemployment. The state helped middle and upper groups keep the goods with which they had built their households and their reputations in this context. Servant regulations for the city were renewed in 1879.[19]

Consumption and other taxes increased steadily as successive liberal and conservative republican governments were unable to meet their budgets. The Bustamante government in June 1838 levied taxes on a wide array of categories, including urban and rural property, business enterprises, professions and trades, wages and salaries, invested capital, and luxury goods. In December 1838 a monthly poll tax was levied on heads of households, ranging between one and one hundred pesos a month. While the other taxes affected the working population, the tax on household heads hit the middle class, as a minimum income of twelve reales a day exempted most of the working class and poor. Another round of taxes came under Bustamante in 1841, the most controversial being a "personal tax" of between one real and two pesos levied on all males over age eighteen who either owned property or were able to work. Santa Anna levied similar taxes in April 1842, a few months after retaking power, though "due to the paternal consideration of the supreme government for the miserable condition in which day laborers and domestic servants find themselves today," the working poor were again largely excluded from head taxes.[20] In the next two years Santa Anna's fiscal policies emptied middle-class pockets, with increased property and business taxes, forced loans, reduced government salaries, and import tariffs raised by 20 percent. To what extent did city residents evade these taxes? Did paying them mean hocking household goods or borrowing from moneylenders whose interest rates rose? In any case government taxation efforts did not alleviate chronic problems of the National Treasury, which meant that government salaries and widow pensions often went unpaid.[21]

Government policies also had an impact on household rents. In 1835, under the conservative government facing the war in Texas, all urban property owners faced a forced loan through a 1 percent tax on the purchase price of their properties and then a direct tax on property value at the rate of two pesos per one thousand. When even higher property taxes were included in 1838 decrees and later under Santa Anna from 1842 to 1844, private landlords raised their rents. A hallmark of the liberal program in Mexico was the ideal of a secular state and economy. Partly driven by the financial difficulties of republican governments, those in power transferred property from church institutions to lessen their dependence on high-interest lenders. The privatization of ecclesiastical property meant higher rents in the city.[22] The church, while owning half the property in Mexico City until the middle of the nineteenth century and thus holding a monopoly in the residential rental market, charged low rents and went easy on poor tenants, especially during epidemic or famine. Carlos Bustamante reported in 1837 that honorable men were turned out of their homes when they could not meet higher secular rents. This situation intensified after the liberal Reform, as new secular landlords took delinquent renters to court in 1861 when they could not pay higher rent, sometimes four times what ecclesiastical landlords had charged.[23] By the end of the century a majority of those living off of rental properties in the city were female, up from a third of property owners at the end of the colonial period. It is not clear to what extent women acquired more property in the anticlerical privatization process at midcentury.[24]

Interestingly, the famed late 1850s Reform period saw few legal changes pertaining directly to collateral goods in pawnshops and households. Instead, it was the government of Maximilian who opened three branches of the Monte de Piedad in popular neighborhoods where pawnshops were concentrated; neighborhood residents could pawn clothing and furniture for loans of between twenty-five centavos and twenty pesos.[25] Under the

Restored Republic in 1871, pawnshop regulations were revisited and the Monte's main branch added a new department where the city's comfortable middle and upper class could convert knickknacks and crystal wine decanters as well as furniture that they used for entertaining at home into cash loans.

Liberalism, similar to Spanish imperialism and other governing principles, was rooted in patriarchal households.[26] The new state retained colonial methods of control over family formation among those actively involved in ruling. The Constituent Congress in 1824 voted 6–69 against allowing public employees to marry without prior permission.[27] In other ways the republican system departed from tradition, rejecting corporate structures such as church and guilds in favor of rights of individual men; but there was no parallel rejection of the patriarchal family for rights of individual women. Liberal thinkers debating the merits of expanding civil rights for women agreed that wives would remain the most restricted category of women. Sexual propriety still constituted necessary behavior for "honorable" women, and now was a prerequisite for claiming new rights as widows or mothers over property and children. The Constitution of 1857 defined subordinate obligations of wives to husbands and the household division of labor.[28] Liberal laws such as the 1859 Law on Civil Matrimony reaffirmed patriarchal definitions of proper gender roles and requisites for legal separations. The only change was that marriage was removed from church jurisdiction. The 1870 Civil Codes likewise incorporated most colonial laws concerning women and excluded women from voting or holding political posts. Married women and daughters in republican legislation remained under patriarchal authority, and women were punished for sexual transgressions under a double standard. Within this liberal patriarchy, the ideal of enlightened domesticity continued to shape the state's mission for female education, as postcolonial governments saw the proper instruction of women in motherhood and housekeeping as central to nation building. The Bourbon agenda to expand employment options for women was largely abandoned in the first decades of republican rule. By 1840 the state assumed the obligation to provide for primary education and theoretically supported secondary schools for females. Yet in Mexico City, where they first appeared, secondary schools for girls were not available until 1869. When women in the growing middle ranks who could acquire an education took jobs, they generally moved into the public sector as educators of children, an extension of enlightened motherhood that sheltered them from dishonor despite their working in public.[29]

Mid-nineteenth-century data reveal large numbers of women still heading households, many of them widows. The 1844 census found 27 percent of all matrifocal households in the barrio of San Salvador and 31 percent in the barrio of Necatitlán were females living together. In 1848, 36 percent of city household heads were women (up 3 percent from 1811), with 68 percent of those widows. Thus at midcentury there were more female household heads and more widows who had to support themselves than there had been in 1811. Widows constituted a quarter of all household heads and 41 percent of the city's adult female population. Most widows worked in producing and selling food, with others employed in craft production or domestic service. Prospects in widowhood were dramatically different for poor women than for those who were well off. Elite widows were more likely to be businesswomen and to hold onto their estates instead of passing them on to daughters as dowry declined in importance. Those middling women who had been recipients of pensions earned by their husbands' service in managerial positions in the tobacco factory or from government Montepíos had a harder time collecting them in the 1830s and 1840s, when pension funds were strapped for cash. Most working-class women would not have even the hope of a delayed pension payment.[30]

The liberal 1870 and 1884 Civil Codes, while drawing on colonial law as well as innovations of the Imperial Civil Code of 1866, began to reconcile individual rights with the subordinate status of women, at least for single women.[31] Patriarchs yielded authority to state courts and schools, undermining the cohesiveness of extended families, over which fathers had had control. By the end of the nineteenth century, Mexican fathers had firm control only over their wives and minor children. As the power of individual patriarchs was weakening, the Civil Codes continued the Bourbon posture of the state as patriarch in laws that affected daily life.

Widows, legally separated mothers, and single mothers who legally recognized children were granted *patria potestad*, which only fathers had had up to 1870, as long as they lived "honestly" as single women. However, widowed mothers would lose new rights to control their children, their property, and any income from that property if they remarried or "lived scandalously." Only single and widowed women who adhered to statesmen's notions of sexual propriety could exercise the new rights of motherhood. Traditional honor codes continued to shape the bounds of legality under liberalism, with statesmen in the role of patriarch, replacing absent husbands and fathers, limiting the sexual activity of single women. New rules granting single mothers *patria potestad* brought them into the governance structure and gave them new legal standing. Having parental rights empowered some women, and this "challenged the basic principle of patriarchal society: that only men rule."[32] The panorama of choices and opportunities for empowered single mothers was in contrast to that of their married sisters and female neighbors, who remained under their husbands' control and still needed permission to engage in most legal activities or to work for wages. Yet even these married women controlled aspects of their daily lives, inheriting, investing in, and taking control of household assets such as table settings and bedspreads, which were regularly converted into cash at the pawnshop to provide family income.

Costs of Consumption, Everyday Credit, and Working People

In the chronic context of low wages and high costs of living in the city, investing in durable small goods proved to be an effective creative-financing strategy. Indeed, durable material goods of a given household constituted a savings account, all the more important in a specie-starved economy in which there were no banks where men and women could save earnings. Household finance through repeated pawning of small collateral goods such as pearls and wool capes filled a niche in the nineteenth-century Mexican economy, which offered few petty-credit alternatives. Workers could ask employers for loans, with the usual mercantile loan rate of 12 to 24 percent interest a month. Professional moneylenders lent to the poor at high weekly interest rates.[33] When casas de empeño emerged as collateral-credit arenas, city residents turned to them even when interest rates were high, as they had turned previously to retail merchants, because there were no other institutions to lend them money.[34] Despite the absence of credit banks, credit continued to be fundamentally important to commercial activity at all levels in the republican era, including housekeeping.[35]

The utility of some cloth and jewelry items might be measured more in their collateral value and expendability than in their function as clothing or adornments. Residents believed that investing in small articles of jewelry that they could convert into cash when necessary was a safe bet in the tumultuous situation of early republican Mexico. In his memoirs Waddy Thompson, the U.S. Ambassador to Mexico in the 1830s, told the tale of an elderly Indian woman he knew who sold vegetables door to door. While her garments were humble, no more than a blouse and a rebozo, she wore a string of genuine pearls around her neck. When Thompson asked why she did not invest in something more "useful" such as a house, the vendor replied that a house could be destroyed in a revolution and would be taxed by the government. With the pearls, she was "secure against whatever suffering, when sick or very old, I can pawn these at the Monte Pío or sell them one by one, as I bought them."[36] Jewelry and silver-service items especially, both more durable than cloth goods and of more stable value, could still serve as investments through the collateral-loan process. But to make this strategy work in the 1840s and 1850s, pawning clients had to be careful about when they redeemed their goods, as the same graduated interest schedule was in place in both the Monte de Piedad and casas de empeño, depending on how long the good was in pawn. If goods were redeemed in odd-numbered months, customers effectively paid higher interest than in even-numbered months.[37]

Just how much income did workers have to run their households and maintain their status from the 1830s through the 1860s? What impact would loans of three reales or three pesos have on subsistence and low-consumption budgets? In general many in the city lived in poverty, as separation from Spain meant deterioration of already inadequate living conditions. Outside observers considered the poor a majority, labeling them "léperos" and "vagos," although many claimed occupations and were employed at least part time.[38]

Wages for working women were lower than men's throughout the nineteenth century, even when they were doing the same work. According to the industrial census of 1849, the average female among servants, laborers, and artisans earned less than one peso a month, while the average working-class male earned nearly three pesos a month. Female servants earned between one and six pesos monthly. At midcentury one-third of working single women were employed in this sector in which indigenous women were concentrated. Male servants earned from one and a half to eight pesos. The wide range for each gender reflects both the fact that some servants received lodging and meals as part of their job and a hierarchy of household jobs. Other evidence suggests that servants could earn more: Fanny Calderón de la Barca (the wife of the Spanish ambassador to Mexico) reportedly paid her chief housekeeper twelve to fifteen pesos a month, while her coachman earned forty pesos. Like the *molendera* (corn grinder) photographed circa 1860 in figure 2, Indian and mestiza maids employed in middle- and upper-class houses wore their hair in long braids to the waist, muslin blouses, and long full skirts, which they usually had to purchase themselves. Those serving in wealthier households had to wear uniforms, sometimes provided by their employers; coachmen apparently pawned these uniforms when in need of cash, as their constant appearance

Fig. 2. "La Molendera." Courtesy of the Latin American Library, Tulane University, Cruces y Campa Collection of Mexican Occupationals.

in lists of forbidden collateral goods in pawning legislation attests. Skilled artisans such as tailors, carpenters, weavers, and smiths—some of whom might be considered more middle class than working class—earned from a few pesos to thirty-six pesos a month. *Maestros* (male supervisors) in the tobacco factory made up to fifty pesos a month in 1849, while *maestras* only made twenty-nine to thirty-eight pesos a month. The highest wage for male cigar makers in 1849 was twelve pesos a month, while the high for females was only five and a half. Women making cigars or sewing at home who were paid by the piece would have earned even less, with work interrupted by demands of housekeeping and child rearing. Seamstresses, a sector that Creole women had dominated early in the century, earned from two to six pesos a month, and washerwomen, a job without a male equivalent, earned four to twelve pesos a month. The seamstresses depicted in *Los mexicanos pintados por sí mismos* lamented that "for a pair of paints that takes one an entire day to sew, they don't even pay a real and a half; for a shirt, the same amount, and for the rest of the items proportionately less depending on the amount of time they take to make; we're lucky to earn barely enough to eat poorly and to pay the rent on this uncomfortable room."[39]

If women's employment opportunities broadened somewhat under the Bourbon state, in the republican era the situation changed. The number of female artisans did not increase, and even the number of working women employed as domestic servants declined from 54 percent in 1811 to 30 percent in 1848 as middle-class households found it harder to employ them.[40] Prostitution continued as an employment sector for women, still illegal in the 1830s and then regulated after 1865.[41]

Beyond daily costs of food, clothing, and shelter and the growing array of taxes, other expenses exceeded budgets of the working poor at midcentury. For example, marriage at the church of Santa Catarina Mártir cost six pesos six centavos; a supervised childbirth, fifteen pesos; burial in a cemetery on the outskirts of town, eight pesos; and a shoemaker's tool kit, eight pesos. As Frederick John Shaw suggests, "Any one expense would have exhausted [a] couple's life savings. Two or more would have driven them into debt." The earlier Bourbon concern about rationalizing economic roles of working women was not paramount among republican liberals; neither was the need for poor relief, despite the reality of many poor women with dependents.[42]

At midcentury lower- and middle-income households still lived side by side in Mexico City's neighborhoods. Upstairs apartments of casas de vecindad remained more exclusive, while downstairs dwellings were quite crowded: three upstairs apartments of a rooming house in 1848 rented for six and a half pesos each, with fourteen people living upstairs; downstairs, fifteen rooms went for two pesos each, with a total of forty-four people living downstairs.[43] The rooming house depicted in *Los mexicanos pintados por sí mismos* housed people of different economic resources. In upstairs rooms lived an office clerk, an artist, an artisan, and an instructor of piano and dance. In downstairs rooms lived a tortilla maker with her water-carrier husband, an elderly woman with two daughters who were seamstresses, laundresses, and bricklayers. A single room might simultaneously serve as "tortilla factory, common kitchen, closet, living room, dining room and everything else."[44] Single men as well as multiple families joined together in one living space to save rent. In 1849 carpenters, carbon sellers, load bearers, and water carriers paid an average of one peso two reales in rent, while carpenters and shoemakers paid between one peso six reales and two pesos. For those months when earnings were not sufficient to pay rent, people turned to pawning. In the account books of a casa de vecindad owned by a *cofradía* (religious brotherhood) in 1838, a female weaver satisfied an accumulated rent debt of eighteen pesos in part by pawning her loom for fifteen pesos.[45]

The official colonial portrayal of pawnshop clientele as "the unfortunate class" and "destitute" carried on into the nineteenth century, and government regulators, social workers, pawnbrokers, and clients themselves shaped this discourse. In 1849 Ygnacio María de la Barrera, a government accountant, considered the 1842 law regulating the pawning business a "gift" to a "very considerable part of the population" in need of pawnshops to relieve their poverty. Reformer Francisco Ramírez y Rojas, who successfully lobbied for expansion of the Monte de Piedad in the 1860s, identified the principal private pawning clientele as the "proletarian class," reflecting changes in the economy at midcentury. In communications with the government, brokers identified their clients as the "needy class," whom poverty brought to them to meet the "most urgent need of sustaining their families."[46] Broker portrayals of their clientele should be taken with a grain of salt; it is difficult to distinguish genuine concern on the part of brokers for their poor clients from self-serving attempts to get the government off their backs. In the early 1870s pawnbrokers continued to argue that workers and the "absolutely poor" made up the majority of their customers. They said "unhappy ones who pawn daily" visited pawnshops just before mealtimes for cash to feed their families, when the Monte's branch offices were closed. The pawnbrokers asked rhetorically: who among them had not faced "the painful cry of the unhappy widow who has nothing more to pawn than a tattered tunic to slake the urgent needs of her family and herself, a tunic so worn that they should not even take it (the Monte would not), not even good enough for cleaning windows?" Nonetheless, pawnbrokers also recognized that it was not just the poor but "all classes of society" that came through their doors, including "employees, artisans, military men, and the industrious" who brought cheap goods for small loans to supplement budgets of housekeepers to relieve "the necessities of the moment."[47] This pawnbroker sketch echoed long-standing rhetoric about pawning and the poor. But it also fit a context in which wages seldom supported the requisite living standards for working and middling families. Securing basic necessities such as food, clothing, and shelter as well as maintaining more affluent life-styles were constant challenges, and pawning continued to be a financing strategy for running households across the city.

For some householders who sought collateral credit, the difference was between eating or not. In a report addressing why poor children so irregularly attended school, the Society of Charity in 1850 painted this picture of everyday needs of poor artisans, illustrating the interconnections between production and reproduction: "[Poor children] present themselves at school at eleven or twelve o'clock because, being extremely needy people, their parents cannot send their children to school until they give them their first meal of the day, which they cannot do unless they complete a product that they can sell or pawn some garment."[48] Angel de Campo's story shows that pawning clients continued to use the discourse of consumption for subsistence when they were portraying pawning motives. When a golden cross inlaid with gemstones was stolen from the Monte de Piedad branch where Angel had pawned it in 1868, he tried to recover seventy-two pesos, claiming that was what it was worth. When asked why he secured a loan for only twelve pesos (not even one quarter the cross's supposed value) if it was really worth that much, Angel responded that he borrowed so little because that was what he needed "to feed his family" in the "emergencies of the moment."[49] We cannot, of course, know if Angel framed his activities this way deliberately to elicit more sympathy in the belief that using the official discourse would serve him best, whether or not his reasons for pawning were actually due to these "acceptable" subsistence motives. In addition to subsistence, special occasions (weddings, holidays) provided other motives for working people to make trips to the pawnshop. In the 1840s water carriers who marched in a group as Nazarenos in Holy Week processions customarily pawned their large jugs in order to outfit themselves in costumes. Prieto noted that Corpus Christi was a time of increased traffic in clothing stores and workshops, restaurants, and guesthouses.[50] Would pawnshop traffic pick up, too, during these festivities?

The everyday nature of pawning activity continued to hold a prominent place in literary works. In Lizardi's 1832 novela *Noches triste y día alegre*, when seamstresses did not have enough work to meet household budgets, they would pawn a tunic or blouse "which they had made at the cost of a thousand million pin pricks, at the cost of illnesses and sleeplessness," only to be in need and hungry again in two days time.[51] In Vicente Riva Palacio's 1868 novel *Calvario y tabor*, a mother and daughter have to wait for their reunion with their long-lost husband and father, "because [they] do not have anything to wear out on the street: having pawned even their *rebozos* in order to eat." Inés, an actress portrayed in the same story, is a regular pawning customer, as her "poor jewels came and went from the *casas de empeño*."[52]

In addition to their function as collateral-credit arenas, pawnshops also served as retail outlets for those searching for inexpensive consumer goods. In the midcentury *costumbrista* work *Los mexicanos pintados por si mismo*, "La china" regularly went to the pawnshop on Saturdays to pick out a silk scarf to wear for the weekend, only to return it the following Monday or Tuesday. The young women who worked in the tobacco shops were also reported to buy their outfits at the pawnshops, as did young men looking for frock coats to wear when they went dancing.[53] Those in the middle ranks visited the Monte's auction rooms to recycle aristocratic fashions.

Sites at which to acquire material goods abounded, with wealthy and popular shopping areas mixed together. The Portales to the west and south of the Zócalo, "seemed like the arcades of Babylon" to one observer.[54] Also in the city center was the Plaza del Volador—the principal meat and vegetable market as well as a place to buy *mantas* (cuts of muslin cloth), rebozos, belts, and hats—until 1863, when it was replaced by La Merced market further south of the Zócalo. In contrast to *cajones*, where middle and upper classes bought clothing and accessories, the poor frequented used-goods markets called *baratillas*. Located in the Plaza del Factor was the city's principal such market, where small merchants sold secondhand clothing as well as fenced stolen goods to popular classes. The elite complained repeatedly to the Ayuntamiento about secondhand markets in proximity to their fancy shops, unhappy with foot traffic and the tendency for *pulqueros* and viñateros (both purveyors of liquor) to set up shop nearby. In 1842 the council considered relocating El Baratillo to a plaza further away from the center. In response a committee of forty petty *comerciantes* (merchants) who sold in the Baratillo, five of them women, defended the existence of the used-goods market and showed an awareness of its necessary function in provisioning, as they put it, *la clase ínfima*: "It is there where they find a multitude of objects, which are necessities, and without it they would never obtain these goods because of the excessive price that such objects have . . . when they are new." These merchants emphasized that "the upper and middle classes would lose nothing with the extinction of the Baratillo, but that [an] infinitely more numerous class would become extinct, as would the first groups with the extinction of *cajones de ropa* and notions stores."[55]

Working-class earnings often were insufficient to pay for rent and food, much less clothing and other goods available in these various shopping arenas. Clothing made by a tailor, fashionable dressmaker (*modista*), or seamstress was expensive. Among popular classes in the 1840s, "*jerguetilla* [coarsely woven fabric] was for working, and beaver cloth for provocation and luxury." But for the poorest, fashion was unattainable luxury. For the wife of a cigar maker in 1845 purchasing new *paño* (tightly woven fabric) trousers, vests, and jackets to outfit her husband, the clothing cost would soon surpass his income, with each item costing two pesos or more. Used clothing was not much cheaper: a pair of old cotton trousers cost five reales, an old sarape two pesos, a used cotton blanket twelve reales, and four used petticoats seventeen reales.[56] In order that breadwinners could appear as respectable as possible in public, women and children might forego new clothes. Women and children's clothing was preferred collateral, because those items were less indispensable to the production and reproduction of the family's public image. The typical *tortillera* living and working in rooming houses in the 1870s wore only a poor shirt and petticoats of ordinary fabric and was almost always barefoot. These poor working-class women could replace their petticoats with better though still used ones, such as the dozen or so on the shelves of the pawnshop at the Portal de Magdalena in Tacubaya pawned for between twenty-five and fifty centavos. Someone shopping at pawnshops for something used with which to dress up a bit could choose among jackets of cashmere "del pais" (made locally as opposed to imported) for between two reales and two pesos in the pawnshop at the Plaza de la Constitución in Tlalpan in March 1879.[57]

Other costs had to be met daily. The majority of rooms in casas de vecindad, where most people lived, did not have kitchens, and many people ate daily at street stalls, in markets, or in *fondas* (small restaurants). In 1852, in the *fonda* El Moro de Venecia on Tlaperos Street, lunch could be gotten for two reales and a full meal cost three reales: "broth, a choice of bread, rice or *masa*, a serving of veal or mutton [*puchero de ternera o carnero*], a dish cooked in sauce [*un guisado*], grilled steak with salad and *pastas de dulce*."[58]

Consumption by "Hombres y Mujeres de Bien"

By the middle of the nineteenth century, families who occupied upstairs apartments in rooming houses comprised a small but growing middle group of shopkeepers, merchants, small entrepreneurs, professionals, and office clerks. By the end of the century the middle was larger and more defined as a class, set apart from both upper and lower classes, especially those employed in "white-collar" capacities—bureaucrats, professionals, and businessmen and their families.[59]

In 1849 *gente de bien* paid an average of 24 pesos a month in rent, or 288 pesos a year. The range was wide, reflecting diverse life-styles at lower and higher ends of the middle sector. The average rent that merchants paid for their residence was 8 pesos a month, government clerks paid on average 12 pesos, and attorneys paid on average 35 pesos. Rents paid by those men in positions of power in the government in the late 1840s ranged from 7 pesos to 125 pesos a month, with those politicians coming from the provinces generally paying higher average rents (54 pesos a month) than those native to the city and better connected to landlords (34 pesos a month).[60] Some statesmen lived quite well, such as José Bernardo Couto, who represented his home state of Veracruz in Congress. Couto's wife managed a large house at Acequia No. 7 in the 1840s, where she, Couto, and their four children were attended by fourteen servants. Unusually for the time, the Coutos owned their residence, worth 22,500 pesos. Other statesmen lived more humbly. Miguel María Arrioja, a low-level bureaucrat in 1848 who later would serve as a minister of foreign relations, and his wife lived for about five years with their daughter and three sons in quarters at Santa Brígida y Letrán No. 1. The housekeeping in the Arrioja family was no doubt done by Miguel's wife and daughter, as there were no servants. They rented from the convent of Santa Brígida for 90 pesos a month. Most people continued to rent their homes as opposed to owning them in the nineteenth century, even those among the elite. Renting an appropriate home was part of maintaining status.[61]

Government bureaucrats earned from 500 pesos per year for a scribe to 2,000 per year for a chief accountant, with an office boy earning 100 pesos if he was paid at all. The range of remuneration in the office hierarchy is a reminder that income is tricky as a class barometer—the scribe or store clerk might hope to and would be expected to live "better" than the average city resident, even though his paycheck would not be sufficient for his wife to meet expenses requisite for that level. In the 1830s a young Guillermo Prieto earned 16 pesos monthly as a *meritorio* in the customs house, and with this salary he had to pay rent on a small downstairs room in a rooming house (maybe somewhere near the 6 pesos a month that those rooms could go for in 1849), care for his sick mother, and still manage to dress like an hombre de bien, which in his day meant a not-inexpensive *indiana* jacket, the preferred uniform for public employees.[62] A commercial clerk with experience might earn 100 pesos a year by midcentury—not much with which to clothe and feed oneself, much less a family.[63] In 1855 an administrative clerk at the Monte de Piedad earned an annual salary of 600 pesos (or 50 pesos monthly), while the clothing appraiser at the same institution, probably a professional tailor, earned 750 pesos annually (or 63 pesos a month). A printer contracted to earn 1,400 pesos a year (or 117 pesos a month), while the contract of a "machine inventor" called for remuneration of 350 pesos monthly. Two male company managers signed contracts for annual salaries of 3,000 pesos (or 250 pesos a month) and 4,200 pesos (350 pesos a month).[64]

Women married to these professional men managed households on these incomes, perhaps adding their own income from working outside the home. Some women in the middle class who did not work outside the family nonetheless made financial contributions to the household through dowries and inheritances. Table 3.1 represents all dowry documents for given years in the notary archives of the city, confirming that this kind of endowment of daughters had greatly declined since the colonial period.[65] While only representing the financial and material situation of a handful of women, these figures nonetheless are helpful in assessing what at least some women might have taken into their marriages, and therefore what goods (jewelry, furniture, clothing) they might have turned into collateral to contribute to household budgets. The thirty-nine dowries in the 1855 notary index total up to 113,400 pesos, which is an average value of 2,973 pesos for each dowry. But this average distorts the situation. Three dowries

TABLE 3.1

Dowries Provided to Women, Mexico City, 1838–55

Pesos	1838	1839	1841	1853	1855
280–999	27	10	24	9	30
1,000–2,999	2	2[a]	3	0	
3,000–9,999	4[b]	7		2	6
10,000–50,000	3	2	1[c]		3
120,000				1	
Total	36	21	28	12	39

Source: Josefina Zoraida Vázquez and Pilar Gonzalbo Aizpuru, eds., *Guía de protocolos, Archivo General de Notarías de la Ciudad de México; año de 1838* (México: El Colegio de México, 1986), 352, 395; *Guía de protocolos, 1839* (1987); 324–25, 330; *Guía de protocolos, 1841* (1989); *Guía de protocolos, 1853* (1998), 295; *Guía de protocolos, 1855* (2000), 307.

[a] These two dowries consisted of jewels, the first for 1,200 pesos described simply as "alhajas," the second described as "gold earrings and a coral rosary" for 2,190 pesos.

[b] One of these is described as being made up of "jewels, clothing and furniture" worth 6,744 pesos.

[c] This dowry is described as being made up of "various jewels" worth 9,228 pesos.

were clearly for very wealthy women: one worth 50,000 pesos and two worth 16,000 pesos. Six documents represent a larger subset of dowries of between 3,000 and 6,500 pesos. The remaining thirty dowries ranged from 300 pesos to 900 pesos, with an average of 310 pesos.[66]

At midcentury the middle-class life-style of an hombre de bien consisted of numerous expenses for which his wife might not have sufficient cash on hand, despite her husband's yearly income of 500 or 1,000 pesos or the contribution of her dowry. Funding her pastimes would tax the family budget even more. As Costeloe summarizes: "[The] gentleman would have had domestic servants to cater to his daily needs and possibly a carriage, which he could have purchased or rented from one of several suppliers in the city. Always keen to adopt the latest in European fashion, he would have bought his best clothes from one of several French tailors, his frock coat costing 34 to 42 pesos, his trousers, 14 to 16, and a good quality pair of boots, seven to eight. He would have subscribed to a newspaper, possibly *El Siglo XIX*, costing 20 reales a month."[67] How many middle-class wives scrambled to make up for gambling losses at popular cockfights at San Agustín de las Cuevas that affected household budgets? In addition transportation expenses could be incurred multiple times in a day for middle-class residents without a carriage and driver of their own as they moved about, though some cabs could be hired hourly. In November 1867 the official rate for a *coche del sitio* (a carriage for hire or taxi associated with a particular stand) fluctuated between 25 centavos and 1 peso depending on distance traveled.[68] Clearly, life among the middle class entailed regular everyday expenses beyond basic consumption.

In order to keep up appearances with the latest European fashion, wealthy families "de bien" continued to shop at fashionable markets on and near the Zócalo, as they had done in the Bourbon era. The Parián market was famous for imported goods, especially from the Philippines. After it was sacked during the Revolution of the Acordada in 1828, more goods produced locally were sold there, as looting hit merchants hard. Until it was demolished in 1843, the Parián had two floors, with shops on the bottom and warehouses on top.[69] Clients in these *cajones* were mostly women, and many enjoyed credit in the form of long-term payment schedules. When elite women shopped indoors, they were accompanied by female maids and male *cargadores* to carry bulky packages home.[70] The elite shopped in other establishments, often buying cloth and linens right from their carriages as clerks brought goods outside for their perusal. Expensive watch and jewelry shops were clustered under the Portales de los Mercadores and on Calle de Plateros nearby. Plateros had many stores "with the most luxurious objects and the latest French fashions, showing them in beautiful crystal showcases to tempt the elegant ladies."[71] Consumers purchased shoes, clothes, jewels, and furniture at the site of their production in artisan shops, though artisans were losing their direct market to encroaching middlemen. In 1865 there were 988 artisan shops and 377 small factories in the city where household provisions and personal effects used in shaping public reputations could be purchased. In addition to stores and markets with stalls, ambulatory vendors provisioned residents of the capital throughout the nineteenth century. In the 1830s Fanny Calderón remembered being awakened at dawn by cries of "Carbon, Señor?" and "Mantequilla! lard! at one real and a half," with different wares such as cheese, honey, and sweets sold at midday and at dusk. She went on to describe a peddler selling notions in her neighborhood: "He enters the house, and is quickly surrounded by the women, young and old, offering him the tenth part of what he asks, which, after much haggling, he accepts." And the fruit vendor called out the names of his bananas, oranges, and *granaditas* "till the cook or housekeeper can resist no longer" and purchased them to accompany her middle-class employers' meal.[72]

Maintaining fashionable wardrobes was as much part of keeping up appearances as it had been a century earlier, especially for those in the middle sector or aspiring to higher status. Generally, after Independence people continued in the same garb they had worn in the past, but there were some changes as foreign goods were more readily available. Prieto remembered that in the 1840s, women wore a lot of Barron and English prints, rebozos and *paliacates* (large handkerchiefs used as belts). By 1850 a "truly elegant young man" wore cashmere pants, a broad tie, pleated shirt, and a velvet waistcoat, topped off with a large Spanish cape with a beaver collar and laced half-boots or full riding boots.[73]

Outfitting the middle-class men, women, and children in the household meant that housekeepers had to adapt to tariffs and changing costs. In the Sastrería Frances in February 1842, men could acquire cashmere trousers for between fourteen and sixteen pesos, about half the monthly salary of a merchant or almost the entire monthly salary of a cashier. Wives who did not work outside the home would have counted on husbands' salaries or loans secured with collateral goods from their dowries or inherited goods when shopping for their own clothing. For a special occasion in 1854, a well-to-do woman could buy a velvet dress for ninety pesos at the Cajón Últimas Modas or a Scottish suit of pure silk for sixteen pesos.[74] Announcements in the 1875 *Guías de forasteros* for shops selling "ropa hecha" (ready-made clothing) suggest that mechanization of clothing construction brought prices down generally and also that clothing made from domestic cloth could be cheaper than that made from foreign cloth.[75]

Elite fashions changed. In the late eighteenth century "simple tunics replaced the ample dresses" of earlier times. A dress of Genoa velvet, a black mantilla, and of course diamond earrings constituted female formal attire by 1840. At the theater elite women filled upper boxes "presenting an endless succession of China crepe shawls of every colour and variety, and a monotony of diamond earrings." Those with lesser economic resources "exerted their imagination to appear merely fanciful," combining a blue satin dress with a purple satin skirt, both trimmed in yellow. Even more humble women in attendance managed to wear diamonds and pearls. By midcentury, elite women seem to have been dressing lavishly again, with "high-bodiced, tight-waisted, and full-skirted dresses that dropped to the floor," calling for corsets, hoops, and many *enaguas*.[76] How did women manage this, given the high cost of living and intermittent professional salaries of their husbands? Maintaining standards of dress requisite to middling and elite status was accomplished through pawning strategies, whether turning to Monte de Piedad or private pawnbrokers.

In Mexico City the middle sectors continued to avail themselves of access to the Monte, though an increased demand for collateral credit prompted by reforms could have pushed more middle-class residents through the doors of *empeñeros* as well.[77] Indeed, the differentiation of empeñeros into various classes based on the capital of the enterprise suggests that more middling residents were turning to those venues to hock small durable goods. There is even a story about Porfirio Díaz, a war hero after defeating the French but penniless, with nothing to his name but the jeweled sword that the City of Mexico had presented to him, which "he was forced to take to a usurer in the Capital."[78]

These impressionistic portraits of different costs of daily consumption and incomes show that a loan of ten pesos or even a few reales or centavos could help a bureaucrat's wife or a seamstress find housing, acquire clothing, or purchase a meal. Again, what was "necessary" for a family that was relatively well off was not the same as for a family of more humble means; a comfortable family had more goods with which to secure cash for necessities and luxuries that they might lack at a given time. Working people managed to live at a sufficient material level because they could convert personal and household objects that they had acquired into cash when need be to meet daily expenses, just as some of the more accommodated maintained their higher standard of living. Well-off widows, wives, and spinsters still pawned valuable objects at the Monte de Piedad to maintain the life-style requisite for their social status, while they took their more used clothing and linens to the corner pawnbroker if they began sliding down the socioeconomic ladder. Witness the case of the downwardly mobile *casera* (boarding-house manager) depicted in *Los mexicanos pintados por sí mismos*:

> Our house manager, after having shined at the side of a bizarre official or dignified employee as she was brought up to do, passed into a more precarious life once her beloved partner died or retired. Frequently visiting the Monte de Piedad and at other times grocery stores, she secured a third of the value of some item, cash which would be an insufficient quantity to keep up luxurious spending of the past. She was reduced to almost always presenting herself in the same dresses, whose use and worn shine revealed the decadence of her fortune. She lived this way for some time, until she was accosted by scarcity, and she needed to sell her dresses to some used clothing vendor, or pawn her clothing one by one to pay rent for the humble house to which she retired. But finally exhausting all her resources, with a poor shawl the only thing remaining from all she

> had had before, once colorful, she had dyed it black to hide the stains and its age, [the shawl is] her final recourse. Thanks to her many relations and by using the name of some former acquaintance, in the end she is able to find a job as a rooming house manager. They show her to her new home, a small humid room, above which is a sign with big letters: Casera.[79]

The principal clientele at the main branch of the Monte de Piedad continued to come from the small middle sector and likely those such as this *casera* slipping out of the middle, pawning personal and household goods, whether utilitarian or decorative, for loans of between ten and two hundred pesos. In the 1870s pawned objects at the flagship Monte branch were jewels 72 percent of the time, "various objects" (furniture and other house wares) 22 percent, and cloth only 2 percent.[80] For the many clients of casas de empeño at midcentury who rented downstairs rooms in casas de vecindad in the city's neighborhoods, however, cloth was overwhelmingly the favorite collateral good.

Cloth, Silver, and Housekeeping after Midcentury

Neighborhood pawnshops and the Monte de Piedad were steady everyday resources for women in the city. As was true earlier, most goods pawned at midcentury either belonged to women or were associated with housekeeping work. Returning to María Robledo's goods mentioned at the beginning of this chapter as pawned at Agapito Cortés's casa de empeño, over half were housekeeping goods: used linen sheet, used *hamburgo* (unbleached cotton) sheet, cotton muslin sheet, tablecloth, and iron. The remaining four items were articles of clothing: two scarves, a coffee-colored petticoat, and a woven silk shawl.[81] Female clothing as well as feminine jewelry were still pawned more often than their masculine counterparts. Women were also the clients most often pawning housekeeping goods such as bed and table linens, silver spoons, cookware, and irons.

Housewives and the women heading a third of the city's households who left home to do the work of provisioning in the grocery stores and markets first found it necessary to drop in at pawnshops, where they would secure coins to buy food for their families or clothes to dress their children. As María Robledo's pawning record and the data in six inventories from the Cartagena pawnshop in the 1860s suggest, pawning continued to be an everyday, even habitual, practice, with frequent visits of neighborhood women to the same pawnbroker. Out in Tacubaya Inéz Inostroza passed through the Cartagena pawnshop door twice in one day in 1866. The first time she brought a tablecloth and a piece of fabric for a loan of one peso; on the second visit she hocked another tablecloth and a calico sheet for another one-peso loan. Ramona Gútierrez made visits two days in a row to Don Agapito's shop; the first day she pawned a cut of flowered cloth for three reales and the next a petticoat of *hamburgo* for two reales. Ana Sanchez also was at the Cartegena shop two days in a row, the first time pawning fabric cut for a silk petticoat for a loan of six reales, and the next day taking a piece of boy's attire in for the same size loan.[82]

The public institution, too, had its share of regular customers, and the pace of business at the Monte remained brisk throughout the decades of the midcentury (see appendix 2, table E).[83] The average loan secured with collateral at the Monte de Piedad was at least five times the minimum of two pesos virtually every year until the establishment of the branch offices in the 1860s. These patterns confirm that those with a relatively high level of material wealth frequently converted their possessions into cash.

Cloth and clothing continued to claim the most space on neighborhood pawnshop shelves (see appendix 1, tables B, C, and F), even as cloth became less valuable with industrial production. Clothing had represented more than 80 percent of the collateral goods held by the pulpería Cacahuate in 1818. Fifty years later in the Cartagena pawnshop, clothing, bed linens, and swaths of fabric represented the same percentage of the inventory of goods that were unredeemed.[84] Three criminal cases from 1852 highlight the importance and value of clothing, even that worn by women, in this urban society. In early January Doña Ygnacia Aguilar had allowed Francisco Hernández, a thirty-year-old married tailor with "no place to stay," to live in her house. Hernández proceeded to abuse Doña Ygnacia's confidence, stealing petticoats made of *jerguilla* and pawning them. Although they were made of coarse fabric and nothing fancy, Doña Ygnacia cared enough about the petticoats to have her boarder arrested. In another case of stolen petticoats, Josefa Peres was accused of stealing muslin petticoats off of a bed in her stepson José Felipe Ytar's lodgings. She was in his room because she went to retrieve a bedspread that she had lent him but that he had failed to return, and while she was there "it seemed convenient to also take the *enaguas de manta* to make him pay for not having taken one step to return the bedspread to her." The close living quarters of casas de vecindad made stealing a neighbor's goods easy. In October 1852 Tiburina Velázquez accused her neighbor María Fernández of taking her sheet off the common clothesline at their boardinghouse on San Antonio Abad.

María, a twenty-six-year-old widow native to the city, denied the charge.[85] In all of these cases, although petticoats and sheets were relatively inexpensive and made of common fabrics, they were nonetheless of sufficient value to their owners that they sought prosecution of thieves.[86]

Of clothing headed for auction at the Cartagena pawnshop, 58 percent were feminine articles (mostly petticoats, shawls, and dresses), while 21 percent were masculine items (coats, trousers, knee britches, and ponchos), the same percentage as clothing that could be worn by either sex (sashes, blouses, shirts, jackets, vests, belts, capes, scarves, and stockings).[87] As was true in the Bourbon era, petticoats were the goods most often pawned, with sheets in second place. Perhaps it is this function of petticoats that brought our two skirt thieves to face criminal charges. Individual petticoats still served as skirts for women of few resources, while middle-class women wore them in layers underneath a crinoline dress.[88] In the past petticoats were the most common collateral in part because they were the article of clothing that women had the most of in wardrobes. A historian of clothing has suggested that this custom of layered petticoats had passed out of fashion by the mid-nineteenth century. In that case there would have been more incentive to pawn these clothing items instead of other ones that were in fashion. Other commentaries suggest that some women were still using petticoats. It was Prieto's opinion that at dances, "there was a complete division [of those in attendance], accentuated with the petticoats, jackets, and knee britches on one side, and the tunics, headbands, and gloves on the other."[89]

Many notations describing clothing in inventories describe items as "old," "used," or "tattered." It was commonplace for old sheets to be used to make underpants and undershirts, which then could find themselves among collateral for very small loans. Outer clothing, too, was often made from used items. When the boarding-house manager in *Los mexicanos pintados por sí mismos* removed "degenerated *faldones* [ruffle or skirt]" from her old jacket, its aristocratic traces were still evident, but so were the "comings-and-goings [*vaivenes*] of changing fortune."[90] A piece of fabric could have many lives, witness many changes, and pass numerous times through pawnshop doors. In this way goods were like their owners.

Judging by the large number of pawned articles of clothing-in-the-making or swaths of cloth and other clothing construction items such as spools of thread and thimbles, the Cartagena pawnshop may have been in a garment district. An example of a probable clothing worker is Carmen Delgado. In early 1866 she pawned a white petticoat for four reales, and then a few months later she pawned one and a third varas of common linen for two reales. Sometime during the next year, she again turned to Don Agapito Cortes's lending service, this time bringing in half a dozen half-silver buttons for a loan of five reales.[91] Another way to read unfinished cloth as collateral might be that more people were sewing their own clothes at home and their economic situation was such that they had to pawn cut cloth before they could finish sewing.

Goods used in housekeeping chores in the mid-nineteenth century sample constitute 9 percent more than they did in the sample from the late eighteenth and early nineteenth centuries (compare table 1.2 with table 3.2). If indeed there were fewer servants at midcentury because some in the middle ranks could no longer afford them, then the same economic pinch may have led more people of lower-middle status to pawn their housekeeping goods.[92] Although nineteenth-century liberal discourse promoted ideas of separate public and private spheres, labor done at home or "in private" by housewives, daughters, and maids—chores such as cleaning, cooking, and embroidering bedspreads and tablecloths—often produced goods that were taken into the commercial or "public" world of finance as they were temporarily converted into cash loans to supplement family budgets.[93] In inventories from the Cartagena pawnshop, embroidered cloth items such as vests, shirts, curtains, and napkins appear, as well as items adorned with lace.[94] Some women of middling status left household cooking, cleaning, and laundry to servants, while they dedicated themselves "to embroidering handkerchiefs, *carpetas* (furniture runners), monograms in clothing, etc. . . . For this reason their houses are full of decoration: *carpetas* for tables and other furniture, napkins with which to hold hot casseroles, bed spreads, pillow cases and sheets that make an embroidered set, etc."[95] Prieto recalled the Virgin of Guadalupe in corner alcoves in homes with "her blue and white dress embroidered in the home with special devotion." The decoration of clothing was also the work of embroiders who lived as servants in well-to-do homes, as well as ubiquitous women living in neighborhood boarding houses who embroidered and sewed items to sell.[96]

Nearly a third of pawned goods up for auction in the 1860s to 1880s sample were household goods, as summarized in table 3.2.[97] Collateral from the kitchen include frying pans, bronze, copper and iron pots, and large water bottles. An illustration of the kitchen of the typical middle-class woman, *La China*, drawn by Manuel Verrúa, shows some of these household goods.[98] The photograph of the *molendera* from the 1860s Cruces y

TABLE 3.2

Household Goods in Pawn, 1867–80
(965 transactions out of 3,055, or 32%)

Category	Empeños 1867–80	Monte de Piedad Branches 1867–73	Total
Household linens	459	2	461
Whole fabric	226	4	230
Irons	86	0	86
Table service	58	14	72
Fabric cut for clothing	56	0	56
Kitchen utensils	32	2	34
Sewing utensils	7	6	13
Furnishings[a]	9	4	13
Total	933	32	965

Source: AGN, Gobernación, leg. 2187 (1), exp. 1, no. 9(2), fs. 4–6; leg. 1517, exp. 1, no. 1, fs. 1–33v; leg. 1517, exp. 1, no. 5, fs. 1–12; leg. 1296(1), exp. 5, no. 7; AGN, Gobernación, Section 4–A, leg. 873(7), exp. 1, fs. 6–73; AHCM, Inventario General de la Municipalidad de Tacubaya, no. 120, exps. 3, 5, and 7; AHCM, Inventario General de la Municipalidad de Tlalpan, no. 69, exps. 11 and 71.

[a] Includes tables, chairs, beds, chests of drawers, mirrors, and table clocks.

Campa collection shows the interior of a kitchen with a dozen plates on shelves and an altar behind the woman at work on her grinding stone, or *metate* (see fig. 2). Cooking utensils identified with Indian women (though certainly also used by other women, or at least in their kitchens, as in the photograph)—such as metates for grinding corn for tortillas, ceramic *comales* for heating tortillas, or *molcahetes* for making chile sauces—are not listed individually in pawnshop records, reflecting their low monetary value.[99] The pawned goods sample includes a large variety of table-service items: soup tureens, serving trays, and entrée platters; plates and cups, both silver and ceramic; silver forks, knives, and especially spoons; tablecloths (most commonly in a style called *alemanisco*), coffeepots, and water jugs. Most table-service items in Monte de Piedad branches were silver goods, while tablecloths, pitchers, single silver spoons, and all of the ceramic plates were found in neighborhood pawnshops. Having silver-service items continued to be a sign of a comfortable standard of living,

Fig. 3. "La Planchadora." Courtesy of the Latin American Library, Tulane University, Cruces y Campa Collection of Mexican Occupationals.

and for families experiencing a decline in their fortunes, table silver and the servants that carried the tureens and platters continued to be a source of pride. In sharp contrast more humble midcentury homes had "no more chair or table than the hard floor, no knife or fork other than their hands, no spoon other than the tortilla, with which the soup and beans were eaten."[100]

Household linens in pawn in the 1860s and 1870s consist of bedclothes such as comforters, sheets, blankets, bedspreads, and pillowcases as well as towels. These goods, along with jewelry made with gold, silver, and precious stones, might still come into a marriage as dowry. Fine linens and sets of silverware passed from the hands of women to relatives, friends, and servants through wills. Even pawn tickets were passed on, with wills specifying the name of the good, with whom it was pawned, and the value of the loan it secured.[101] For wealthier homes, household linens constituted the work tools of chambermaids and laundresses. The "daily exercises" of chambermaids consisted of "getting up at seven, washing out the chamber pots, making the beds, sweeping the house, and washing the towels." In more humble homes, making the bed meant no more than rolling up the palm bed mat, since "it was common to sleep dressed so there was no need for a comforter."[102] María Robledo's three different sheets in pawn indicate that her household had a material comfort level somewhere between those with a cadre of servants and the bedless poor. For the third of households in the city headed by women, the collateral value of these household goods mitigated chronically low incomes for working women, insufficient widow pensions, or dwindling inheritances.

Among irons in the database, a well-worn one might be the property of a middling married woman who did not use it herself but instead depended on her maid to do so after receiving clean clothes washed by the widow next door. Another iron might belong to a woman dedicated to housework in her own home. Either circumstance might correspond to the woman in the 1860s photograph "La Planchadora," reproduced in figure 3. A pair of irons might be tools of the trade for a laundress whose workload doing laundry for multiple client households in a given day fell short of earning the capital needed to meet her own household expenses. Laundresses differed from other women who did housework for a living, such as chambermaids and cooks, as they did not usually live with employers. Many washerwomen maintained their own homes, which were also their workplaces when they used washboards and sinks in patios of casas de vecindad to wash, communal clotheslines to dry, and their floor, or perhaps kitchen tables, to iron clothes and linens. Some laundresses worked at public fountains, carrying their baskets of dirty dry laundry on their heads or on one hip like the laundress photographed in the 1860s and reproduced in figure 4, then carrying wet clean laundry back through the streets to patios where they would hang it out to dry.[103] Wherever laundresses worked, their labor facilitated the continued consumption of clothing by their clients, and any care taken with cloth items contributed to their potential as collateral.

There were times, of course, when the person pawning the housekeeping good was not actually its owner. When on a pawning errand, the maid was supposed to tell the pawnshop clerk the name of the good's owner, "as was customary."[104] The practice of sending household servants to do the family pawning favored dishonest servants. Republican-era pawnshop regulations expanded the colonial "forbidden collateral goods" list. Adherence to these lists would have continued to legally bar access to pawning for those who only had artisan's tools, work uniforms, or a few silver spoons to use as loan collateral.[105] With the servant law of 1852, Mexican statesmen policed the service work force, inserting law-enforcement officers into the relationship between employer and employee for the entire service sector of the city. But for most *criados*, the workplace was also a middling or elite household, space long under vigilant protection by the state. The 1871 pawnshop regulations eliminated single silver table-service items from the forbidden list. In inventories from the Monte neighborhood branches from the 1860s, much of the tableware is listed as silver, with a side notation "it is copper," suggesting that valuable cutlery was on the wane. It could also be that the 1852 regulations of servants forcing a record keeping of one's service history and run-ins with employers was successful in curbing theft by servants. There were still cases, nonetheless, when silver table-service items were stolen and then pawned, such as a stolen silver spoon that was recovered from Branch No. 1 of the Monte de Piedad in 1868. Were any of nine individual spoons and two forks on the shelves at the empeño at the Plaza de Constitución in 1879 down in Tlalpan stolen?[106]

The formal regulation of domestic servants was a response to the need of gente decente to protect their private property.[107] But servants also came to be owners of luxury goods legitimately, including goods that had once belonged to their employers. In August 1836 Doña Manuela Valdivieso, owner of a boardinghouse and a single mother, in her will left to her maid Mariana Bolaños her bed, three used *paja* (straw) chairs, household linens,

Fig. 4. "La Lavandera." Courtesy of the Latin American Library, Tulane University. Cruces y Campa Collection of Mexican Occupationals.

a ceramic table, and cookware "for the love with which she has attended me."[108] And there were domestic servants who had once "belonged to decent and rich families, but upon finding themselves in ruin, wander wealthy neighborhoods looking for employment in service," who might have guarded in their trunks goods that represented their past glory and could serve to finance their present.[109]

Although it was women who most frequently hocked household goods in pawnshops at midcentury, men did too, whether on their own or for cash to hand over to wives managing household consumption. Many men working as servants were doormen and carriage drivers, and the same sections of pawning regulations that prohibited table service as loan collateral also prohibited items that pertained to carriage service. Men also pawned linens, especially sheets and blankets. The literature of the late colonial period and especially of the nineteenth century is full of images of *léperos* wrapped in sheets as their only clothing. These *ensabanados* were ubiquitous until the 1860s.[110] How many of the numerous sheets and blankets on pawnshop shelves were clothing of the poor and how many were from the linen closets of the well off?

The Monte de Piedad clientele were from upper-middle ranks as well as perhaps those whom management defined as "comfortable poor." Private pawnbrokers insisted that it was they who succored the needs of the destitute and that the Monte had "clients who have worked silver and jewels and other effects that are valuable, not the ones that do not have enough to feed their families."[111] In a small sample of 290 goods in Monte branches between 1868 and 1872, the average loan was twelve pesos, half that at the main Monte de Piedad, but still five times the average loan in the branch office in 1875 and more than ten times the average loan for the few jewels pawned in neighborhood pawnshops (five reales in 1868 and one peso two centavos in 1879).[112] Most goods in this small sample were those that made it onto lists of goods stolen from branches and are not representative of more inexpensive goods that thieves chose not to take. Most goods whose owner is identifiable are men, contrary to the general gendered pattern of pawning transactions; it may be that many of these male customers, especially those appearing multiple times with big-ticket jewels, were in the jewelry or pawning business.

Judging by average loans in private and public pawning arenas, collateral-credit clients with more material resources continued to visit certain pawning arenas, while the poor visited others. Two Monte de Piedad branches and private pawnshops such as the one on the corner of Ancha and San

Antonio in the south of the city made average loans of over ten pesos, while the Cartagena and Cacahuate pawnshops averaged loans of only half a peso (see appendix 1, table I). The notable number of weapons, watches, and silver jewelry items in the limited sample from Monte branches and the relative absence of those same goods in the larger empeño sample confirm a class difference in clientele between respective pawning arenas (see appendix 1, table C). Clearly some in the lower middle class patronized new Monte branches instead of or in addition to private pawnbrokers in their neighborhoods. In 1871 the main Monte branch continued its tradition of succoring to financially strapped elites when it opened a "various objects" division with its own salesroom. This new division afforded the downwardly mobile a line of credit while simultaneously creating consumption opportunities for those on the rise, "in consideration of the decaying fortunes of those with aristocratic social status who, quite glued to custom and tradition, gave up their family jewels with difficulty, first preferring to pawn their furniture and other types of articles acquired in times of bonanza. Those in the ascendant middle class frequented the auctions of these articles with great interest."[113]

A quick scrutiny of a photograph of a section of five-story shelves along a very long wall in the new "various objects" department reveals dozens of statues that appear to be mostly bronze or some other metal; a great many crystal decanter sets and other silver, ceramic, and glass candy dishes and desert trays; dozens of blown-glass and ceramic vases; silver and crystal lamps, shades, and candlesticks; a few small wooden boxes with worked silver hinges and inlaid panel detail; and an indeterminate number of small figurines and other decorative items. The Monte governing board pressed for the expansion of acceptable collateral to include these goods "invented by artisans and industry that have been used among civilized families of good taste."[114]

Republican liberal policy was more explicitly concerned with middle- and upper-class hegemony than with guaranteeing collateral arenas as part of social-welfare policy. Continued low wages, rising costs of living, increased taxation, new pawning regulations, and policies defining gender relations all affected household finance decisions revolving around both subsistence and consumption needs in homes that were increasingly headed by women. Yet the newly independent state dominated by Santa Anna, the imperial state of Maximilian, and the liberal state that reemerged in 1867 did not withdraw from limited poor relief through the regulation of the pawning process that had begun under the Bourbons. Statesmen continued to implement mechanisms that returned some profits from the sale of pawned goods to their owners. They also continued to limit access to small collateral credit to what the colonial state had termed the "deserving" poor through forbidden collateral lists. And they still used welfare discourse that identified most pawning customers as poor widows who needed help in order to take care of their families, discourse that cast the state in the role of a patriarch protecting and providing for "good" women while disciplining the unruly poor, and discourse that continued to ignore the pawning clientele from the middle sector even as it grew.

Through regulation, republican statesmen protected property rights of owners of pawned goods, effectively making pawning a safer option for financing housekeeping efforts. Santa Anna's administration in the early 1840s issued the first new pawning regulations of the republican era, adding explicit interest regulations to protect neighborhood households from usury and keeping restrictions on collateral goods designed to curb petty theft in households and workshops. Generally throughout the first two-thirds of the liberal nineteenth century, the right of pawning clients (many of them not poor) to property trumped the pawnbrokers' right to profit. The hombres de bien dominating politics from the 1830s to the 1870s were anxious to protect their middle-class interests against the "rabble" that had participated in political mobilizations as well as those on their domestic-service staffs. The much-heralded reform period of 1857–58 was really a nonperiod in this material history of household collateral credit, with few laws affecting household pawning practices.

The colonial Creole elite were now republican hombres de bien, with petty property so important to their social position that it needed protection. The problem was that servants were also important to their social position, part of the "making it" package; because servants might steal, hombres and mujeres de bien were vulnerable. Especially in times of economic instability and stagnation, when money was not coming in, they needed to maintain appearances, and they depended on material possessions to do that. The servant laws are best understood in this light. They were part of a general trend toward social order and the containment and/or prevention of crime, but also had to do with protecting the material goods that status, image, and reputation rested on. The number of relatively valuable goods on shelves in the city's pawnshops in the 1860s and 1870s—especially elaborate silver jewelry and tableware in the Monte de Piedad main and branch offices—and laws protecting small private-property items in regulations on domestic service suggest that policy makers served their own class interests when privileging pawnshop customers over brokers. Housekeeping through pawning continued to facilitate the reproduction of status, the promise of upward mobility, or the mitigation of downward mobility. The protection in pawning legislation of the material culture of those in the middle and at the top of the economic ladder allowed higher-status households, managed by mujeres de bien and many headed by white widows, to continue living the life-style to which they were accustomed, at least for awhile. Whether or not it was the intent of lawmakers, the same laws also benefited poorer pawnshop clients, of whom there were a great many, the majority of customers hocking personal, household, and production goods. They too could collect the consolation prize of the windfall sale profit or extend the pledge period when they unhappily had been unable to put money together to get their skirt or sewing kit out of hock, with redemption of goods arguably harder as the century marched on. Economic scarcity or ambition prompted some pawnshop clients to assess what was necessary for survival or success, and their solutions, including stealing and pawning "forbidden" collateral, were often out of step with official rules for city living and business transactions.

From at least the eighteenth century, everyday credit regenerated material life. Evidence from the middle decades of the nineteenth century shows that cloth and silver continued to be valuable collateral goods for working- and middle-class housekeepers, who continued to incorporate pawning into their daily provisioning regimens even as they converted new consumption goods such as watches and statues into cash for daily consumption needs and perhaps for purchasing new collateral goods. Indeed, pawning activity intensified and household goods increasingly doubled as collateral in the face of changing production systems, trade policies, and political regimes that characterized the nineteenth century.

FOUR

Brokering Interests

Casas de Empeño and an Expanded Monte de Piedad, 1830–75

Don Juan Acosta represented fellow pawnbrokers in a petition in 1842 to change a new law regulating their trade. He highlighted the social welfare and paternal role of brokers who assisted city residents with the "most urgent need of sustaining their families." In his proposal to Emperor Maximilian to expand the Monte de Piedad in 1865 to accommodate city residents with low-value collateral goods, reformer Don Francisco Ramírez y Rojas renewed familiar charges against private pawnbrokers for "usurious" interest rates. He estimated them to be between 25 and 100 percent annually, a "black cancer" on society. In 1872 pawnbroker María José Galindez defended himself for disregarding new laws regulating the pawning trade, as he believed they contradicted liberal laissez-faire principles. Galindez argued that "the pawning contract is a contract like any other" and as such was due the "absolute freedom of commerce" of other business relations.[1] While these broker and reformer views of profit-seeking collateral lending services could not have been farther apart, they nonetheless represent tenets of liberal philosophies that were transforming Mexico in the nineteenth century. Social-welfare concerns and laissez-faire ideologies were part of the weave of liberal governance in Mexico, as were strands of political liberalism expressed through republican electoral politics and the exercise and protection of rights. Statesmen, businessmen, and reformers negotiated contradictory tenets of liberal philosophy as they developed policy for the emerging nation. The biggest sticking points in economic relations between the private pawning-business sector and the state were whether or not pawnbrokers had the right to charge interest and whether or not the amount of that interest should be regulated.

The "doctrinaire" economic liberalism of Adam Smith and Jean Baptiste Say, which favored commerce free from government intervention, was slow to take root in republican Mexico, with a "pragmatic" liberal approach instead dominating until 1847, especially in terms of tariff policy.[2] In the republican era pawnbrokers like Galindez pushed for their own freedom of commerce, resenting what they saw as over-regulation of their business activities and restrictions on the interests they could charge. While industrial liberal development did not come into its own until late in the nineteenth century, entrepreneurial liberalism in the form of profit-seeking pawning businesses developed much sooner. By the 1870s this postcolonial business form developed without the constraints of usury prohibition, as pawnbrokers took full advantage of their freedom to compete for profits. Yet pawnbroking still faced government regulation and was not completely a "free" enterprise. The postcolonial state continued to oversee pawning in both the private and public sectors and attempted to shape pawning-business operations in new ways. Pawnbrokers also engaged in political liberalism when they joined together as an interest group to negotiate with the state regarding their own governance. Some would have voted in municipal and national elections as well. The welfare discourse of reformer Ramírez y Rojas and broker Acosta represent a different thread of liberal governance. Ramírez y Rojas's social-welfare concerns reflected secularizing trends in social services that had been developing since the Bourbon era and became more or less consolidated under the rubric of public "beneficencia" by various republican statesmen as well as Emperor Maximilian.[3]

Private institutions dedicated exclusively to pawning flourished, and the Monte de Piedad expanded its services in the mid-nineteenth century, changing the face of the petty collateral-loan business. Drawing on legislation for private and public pawning arenas, petitions by brokers regarding that legislation, commercial census material, notary documents, pawnshop inventories, and editorials and announcements in newspapers such as *Diario Oficial* and *El Siglo XIX*, this chapter traces these developments. The transition to casa de empeño was not abrupt. Both retail establishments and empeños provided everyday credit into the 1860s.[4] The state, at both national and municipal levels, continued to regulate pawning with new laws beginning in 1842, taxation measures, and classification of pawnshops. When casas de empeño emerged as freestanding business enterprises, they met the growing demand for outright cash, not just hocking a skirt for groceries or drinks, reflecting capitalization of the economy. To meet increased demand for collateral credit and come closer to a mission to help the poor, the Monte de Piedad opened branches in Mexico City during the reign of Maximilian in 1866, a move that was confirmed by the restored liberal government after 1867. While government at the national level changed hands often in the mid-nineteenth century, both the private empeñeros and employees of the Monte remained under the jurisdiction of the ministry of Gobernación, which punished brokers who circumvented regulations on interest and redemption practices. The Ayuntamiento and the Federal District government also had jurisdiction at different times, a source of confusion for brokers in dealings with the state.

From Retail to Empeño

Beginning in the 1830s the pawning business was breaking out of retail, where it had been a sideline driven by the demand of clients for basic food, household supplies, and alcohol, which were sold in corner stores and drinking outlets in a context of specie scarcity. Empeñeros were in the exclusive business of lending cash with interest against collateral, and their only direct relation with retail was in the sale of unredeemed goods at public auction. The year 1842 marked a legislative watershed. Santa Anna's regulation of pawnshops reflected the fact that the empeños business was distinct from other businesses. Many retailers identified themselves as empeñeros and came into compliance with the new regulations, especially those concerning *fianzas* (bonds) to guarantee the value of goods in pawn. The 1842 legislation also apparently prompted more people to establish new casas de empeño. Nonetheless, classification of an establishment as a pawnshop or a retail store was not always clear over a decade later, suggesting a long and fluid transition to nonretail pawnbroking.[5]

It is possible to follow the transition of some retail establishments into casas de empeño by using a database of 552 pawning-business ownerships from 1836 to 1875.[6] Some pawnshops took over retail locations, some of which were long-standing (see appendix 2, table H). For example, the retail store at the corner of Monzón Bridge and Regina, owned by Don Pedro Blanco and administered by Don Diego Fernández in 1781, was a casa de empeño a hundred years later, owned by Trinidad de Villar.[7] Table 4.1 chronicles the life cycle of a business location on the corner of Peredo bridge and Plazuela of San Juan, clearly illustrating the transition from retail outlet to pawnshop. It was not just locations that went through transition; individuals themselves underwent the transition from retailer to empeñero at different locations. Don Fernando Portones, who in 1843 owned a combined general and wine store on Portaceli, by 1854 operated a

TABLE 4.1

Transition from Retail to Empeño on the Corner of Peredo Bridge and Plazuela de San Juan

Year	Owner	Business Type
1806	José Gordillo	Viñatería
1815	Don Agustín Munguia	Not specified
1846	Doña Catarina Rivas	Tienda, viñatería
1858	Not specified	Casa de empeño
1879–82	Mateo Mejia and Co.	Casa de empeño

Source: AGN, Consulado, vol. 267, exp. 8, fs. 1–18; AGN, Padrones, vol. 54, f. 326; AHCM, Empeños, exps. 27, 46, 57, 58; *El Siglo XIX*, July 28, 1858.

casa de empeño on the corner at Vergara and San Francisco.[8] Sometimes the transition of a particular store took place under one owner, who phased out the retail side of the business, as happened to Don Carlos Domínguez. His business at the corner of Amargura and Papas was a general store in April 1842, but by October 1854 it was a casa de empeño with no retail operations.[9]

Not all empeñeros left retail behind. At the corner known as Cruz Verde, there had been a retail establishment since at least 1781, when Don Josef Escobedo was the owner. In 1868 the retailer was G. Cortes, who complied with empeño regulations on publishing announcements about the sale of goods whose pledge time had expired. Another example is Maximiana Zayas de Velasco, who in 1877 operated a combination retail *tienda* (shop) and casa de empeño on Plazuela de Santa María, where there had been a corner store for a hundred years.[10] Some existing retail establishments complied with the 1842 legislation calling for bondholders to secure collateral goods (see appendix 2, table J).[11] At least 5 percent of pawnshops in the sample were opened by men and women who already had retail establishments and embarked on new ventures with the empeños. Don Ignacio Domínguez had two retail establishments listed in the 1843 retail census, one a general store in the third block of Rastro and the other a combination tienda and wine store attached to house no. 8 on San Pedro y San Pablo. In September 1842 he had added a casa de empeño to his portfolio and was bonded for prenda loans for up to two hundred pesos by Don Gregorio Ruiz.[12]

Whether a particular empeño business was new or part of an existing retail establishment, the 1842 law held that pawnbrokers had to secure bondholders to guarantee goods held in pawn.[13] Some bonds may have been holdovers, as retail legislation had long called for bonding business owners. Judging by ninety-seven bond contracts from the notary archive for 1842–44, pawnbrokers knew each other well enough to stand up for each other as bondsmen. For example, Don Gregorio Ruiz guaranteed up to 50 pesos so that Don Eligio Cadena could continue accepting pawns at his tienda on the corner known as Santísima, and Don Eligio returned the favor, guaranteeing up to 50 pesos for Don Gregorio. And Dons Florencio Vázquez and José Perez traded *fianzas*, for 200 and 156 pesos respectively.[14] Sometimes the bondsman was a family member, as in the case of Don Basilio Ortiz, who had a general store on the corner of Alcaicería and Arquillo de Plateros in 1843. Don Basilio served as *fiador* for 300 pesos for his son Don Ramón Ortiz Cosio in June 1842, so that he could establish a new casa de empeño capitalized at 900 pesos. Some bondsmen guaranteed the value of pawned goods in multiple establishments. Don Juan Acosta served as bondsman for Dons Vicente Alvaro, Ignacio Alvarez, José María Medrano, Antonio Rosas, and Bartolomé Zelaya. In only one case in the sample was the bond held by a woman, when Doña Agustina Montenegro guaranteed up to 2,000 pesos so that Don Jacinto González could establish a pawnshop in July 1842. Doña Agustina's guarantee was one of the largest *fianzas* in the documentation, which averaged 454 pesos. Many (37 percent) of bondholders for pawnbrokers listed in the 1842–44 notary documents can be matched with owners of retail establishments in the 1843 census. Bondsman Don Juan Acosta, the spokesman for pawnbrokers mentioned at the beginning of this chapter, had two combined general and wine stores as well as a new empeño in 1843.[15]

In April 1842 authorities in different districts of the city reported lists of the existing casas de empeño in preparation for visits to ensure compliance with the new legislation. Some of these were operating without a license of any kind.[16] The June and July bond contracts drawn for Don Manuel Labarreta and Don Ramón Cosio both indicated that they were for casas de empeño "to continue" their operations.[17] Other pawnshops had just been established. Table 4.2 lists brand new casas de empeño identified in notary documents in the early 1840s.[18]

The transition from retail to pawnshop was not a simple one. In 1843 Santa Anna barred foreigners from retail (except those who were naturalized, those married to "Mexicanas," and those whose business also

TABLE 4.2

New Empeños Established and Bonded, 1842–43

Address	Owner	Bondholder
Cuervo Bridge	D. Francisco Carrillo	D. José María Rendón
Gallas & Montón	Obregón y Sanchez	D. Joaquín Gonzalez
Garrote	D. José Gutiérrez	D. Camilo Colmenero
Plazuela de Jardín	D. Mariano Plata	D. José María de la Torre
La Alamedita	D. Mariano Rivero	D. José María Hermosa
Molino Bridge	D. Mario Arrellano	D. Clemente León
Nahuatlato & Ratas	D. Telesforo Alegre	D. Mauricio Pacheco
Parque del Conde	D. Clemente León	D. Isidro Cartagena
Quiquistengo	D. Gregorio Sigles	D. José María Manrique
San Ramón	D. Pedro Corona	D. Ignacio Peña

Source: AGNCM, Calapiz, vol. 1053, fs. 23, 68, 69v, 83, 94v, 115–16; vol. 1054, fs. 1v–2.

constituted the family residence).[19] Despite this attempt to nationalize retail, many Spaniards apparently continued business as usual in their corner stores in the 1850s while opening separate pawnshops elsewhere. It is possible that Santa Anna's decree prompted retailers to transform themselves into empeñeros, a branch of business not mentioned in the September 1843 decree. (Foreigners were allowed to have industrial shops and sell artisanal production on site, as long as they had "some Mexican apprentices and journeymen.") In any case the 1854 *Guía de forasteros* listed eleven businessmen who had separate pawnshop and retail businesses at different addresses (see appendix 2, table K). The same guidebook listed twenty-one businessmen's addresses as both retail store and pawnshop. The dual retail-pawnbroker character of colonial brokers seems to have carried well into postcolonial economic culture.[20] Other colonial patterns that continued included the family nature of at least some business enterprises and the predominance of Spanish men among those making collateral loans.

A Profile of Pawnbrokers at Midcentury

Most retail-pawnbrokers in the Bourbon period were Spaniards, and while republican policies in the 1820s and 1830s aimed to expel Spaniards from Mexico, many Spanish businessmen remained. After Spain recognized Mexican Independence in 1836, the flow of Spanish immigration resumed.[21] While only a few names can be matched in the 1838 and 1841 notary data with the pawnbroker database, Spanish pawnbrokers were prevalent in the 1850s. Possible family ties between Spanish residents in the late 1830s with known pawnbrokers in the 1840s and 1850s emerge in the documentation. For example, the Eulogio de Villaurrutia who made his will in April 1838 may have had ties to the Manuel Villaurrutia who opened a new pawnshop in September 1843.[22] Clearer connections can be made between individual Spaniards in the notary index from 1841 and the pawnbroker database. Manuel Gonzales de Salceda, Antonia Sanchez Iglésias, Domingo José Velázquez, and José Antonio Villar all appear in the 1841 notary documents and pawnbroker documents. Clemente Martínez del Campo and José de la Peña are two pawnbrokers who have the same surnames as Spanish businessmen in the 1841 notary index.[23]

Moving into the 1850s after American occupation forces had left the city at the conclusion of the Mexican-American War, the Spanish face of the pawnbroker comes into clearer focus. In July 1850 Spaniard Teodoro Aranguren completed paperwork concerning his marriage with a notary, while the *Guía de forasteros* for 1854 lists him as owner of the casa de empeño on San Juan de Dios.[24] Emeterio Alvear, Francisco Bustillos, Francisco Calleja, Pedro Diego Collado, Vicente Fernández de Perega, Juan de la Fuente, Luis Gallopín, Ramón García Pelayo, Luis Gómez, José Gómez de la Cortina, José Hernández, Francisco Herrería, Francisco Lejarza, José Lopéz Bustamante, Josefa Lozano, Narciso Pedraza, Manuel Peña, Francisco Perez Fernández, and José Perez de Arce are all pawnbrokers identified as Spaniards in notary documents from 1853 and 1855. Doña María Rincon had two pawnshops in 1854, one on Zapo and the other on Ancha. Was she the daughter or sister of Luís Rincon, listed as "foreigner" in documents setting up a company in 1855?[25] Spanish ethnicity continued to distinguish the city's pawnbrokers in the years following the French intervention. Both José Lezameta and Joaquím Poo are Spaniards who appear in records in the early 1870s and go on into the Porfirian years owning multiple pawnshops. By the time he died in 1886, Lezameta owned five, with at least two in the first-class category.[26]

Some sectors of the commercial economy were dominated by non-Spanish foreign businessmen. By 1833 there were at least 21 wholesale and 438 retail businesses owned by French immigrants, representing a value of 30 million francs. Over half the businesses indexed in the 1832 *Guía de forasteros* were in the hands of Europeans and Americans. A number of pawnbrokers had non-Spanish last names. The broker identified most clearly as foreign is "Mademoiselle Maria Gongues," who opened a new empeño in the second block of Plateros in 1845.[27] While a few names ring as somehow "Mexican" (such as José María Montes de Oca with a pawnshop in 1846, Manuel Moctezuma with one in 1842, and Ramón Moctezuma with one shop on Palma in 1854 and another at Alegria No. 6 from at least 1866 until 1877), it is difficult to judge to what extent locally born businessmen were engaged in the formal pawning sector.[28]

In some ways pawnbroking did not change much from the eighteenth to mid-nineteenth centuries: most pawnbrokers continued to be Spanish immigrants with few women among them, and the earlier trend of pawning businesses staying within families continued. One example of a family business was located on a corner of San Francisco Bridge. In 1815 Don Pedro Caso operated a pulpería, which in 1840 was a wine store that accepted prendas, now owned by Don Pedro, Doña Rafaela Caso, and Don Luis Rojas. Doña Rafaela was probably Pedro's daughter, with Don Luis likely her husband or a hired store administrator.[29] Doña Rafaela was among only a few female pawnshop owners. Female ownership constituted from 7 to 15 percent of the portion of pawnbrokers listed in archival sources from 1840 to 1880 for which owner gender is known.[30] These numbers approximate the percentage of female pulpería owners at the turn of the century, which was 11 percent. In general, employment opportunities for women decreased as patriarchal culture and structures became reinforced after Independence. Fewer businesswomen appeared in commercial censuses and lists in *Guías de forasteros*. This continuity may reflect the "domesticity" of women among the middle class in Mexico City, as working outside the home became even less respectable than it had been in the colonial era.[31] It is likely that more women were working as pawnbrokers than is statistically evident, as most wives and sisters assisting in family businesses would go unrecorded. And women who gave cash loans for pawned goods informally through neighborhood networks throughout the nineteenth century are not counted in the data at all.

Pawning was not the only masculine business enterprise. Men dominated most of the formal small-business sector throughout the nineteenth century. No doubt the sources undercount businesswomen, as they would have been more likely to operate smaller businesses whose owners were not mentioned by name. A woman is listed as one of five owners of *fondas* classified as "first class," while the female presence may be more prevalent among the 128 "fifth class" *fonderos* whose names are not listed in the guide published in 1874. Judging by published city guidebooks, women owned more businesses in 1854 than they did twenty years later, and businesswomen were concentrated in a few sectors.[32]

Auctioneering is an area dominated by foreign businesswomen at mid-century.[33] While it is difficult to determine from available documentation, pawnbrokers and auctioneers might have had business relationships. The auction houses in the 1854 guidebook are concentrated on Plateros (with six) and Zuleta (with five) downtown, with two-thirds of them at addresses on streets that also had pawnshops. By 1874 another business category appears in the guidebook, that of "bazares," with twenty-two listed, owned by nineteen different men, many of them also appearing in notary documents as Spaniards. The extent to which these bazaars were a variety of pawnshop would be debated heatedly in the Porfiriato. Three addresses listed as bazaars in the 1874 guidebook are also listed as empeños in the same book; in one case the owners of the bazaar and empeño businesses at the address are different. Other 1874 bazaar addresses appear in the empeño database for other years, three with the same owners and two with different owners. Spaniard Joaquín Poo owned two "bazares" in 1874 in the first block of the Merced, one of them with the same address as one of his pawnshops five years later.[34]

While domination by male Spanish immigrants of the small-business sector was tempered after Independence with other European faces taking their place behind the counters of some shops, the bad image of the *gachupín* continued in urban popular culture. Pawnbrokers petitioning for changes in the 1842 law identified themselves as good, honest, and compassionate businessmen, as opposed to a class of "opulent" brokers who bled the city's poor with high interest rates. They described relations between these latter lenders and their clients as "anguishing." The brokers took it upon themselves to speak for pawning clients, stating, "If the 'low people' had the means to bring their grievances to you, you would hear thousands and thousands of times that the pawnshops are absolutely necessary for them, and that the justice system should reform the most notorious abuses." The frequent abuses committed by the few brokers who gave the rest a bad name included keeping all auction profits for themselves, closing without notice and taking collateral goods with them, charging up to 70 percent annual interest and thereby "getting rich off orphans, widows, employees, artisans, and even the merchant." Brokers most in need of reform were those who did not document transactions, operating under clandestine contracts that stipulated that if the pledge period was extended the client could lose his or her possession. In contrast to these nefarious characters were responsible brokers: "In our stores and pawnshops there is no clandestine activity, no darkness or mystery. Everything is done publicly face to face with clients and the authorities." These "good" brokers kept records, issued complete tickets, and treated their customers with respect.[35] In 1852 Don Francisco Canseco announced in the *Guía de forasteros* that he was opening an "establecimiento benefico," or charitable establishment, in which he would "receive pawned goods, offering [rates] that would be considered equitable as the circumstances demanded."[36] That this pawnbroker described his trade as charitable work echoes the petitioning brokers a decade earlier who argued that some of their peers played positive roles in the city economy, regularly and charitably heeding "the painful cry of the unhappy widow" bringing in a tattered tunic as collateral for a loan to feed her family. In the 1870s newspapers published by Spaniards in Mexico also editorialized about benefits that pawnbrokers provided to society.[37]

Negotiating Liberalism and Regulating Business

In the mid-nineteenth century pawnbrokers, governors, Monte de Piedad administrators, and social reformers engaged in an evolving discourse about the proper role of state in society, many drawing on economic liberal theory and debating its application to business operations in Mexico. Debate among middle-class businessmen, politicians, and other bureaucrats centered on rights of businessmen, limits of state authority in business affairs, and development of laissez-faire capitalism. This discourse reveals the negotiation of governance. Brokers asked the president to quash parts of a law issued by the Federal District governor and generally argued that pawnbrokers, like any other businessmen, had the right to earn profits unencumbered by state regulation. Conservatives in national power renewed colonial restrictions on usury and expanded services at the public pawnshop founded to counter usurious practices. While liberal views on the right to make profits through interest prevailed as the nineteenth century progressed, even when liberals were in power the state continued to support the Monte de Piedad as a public charity that provided an alternative to "usurious" lenders. Brokers defended their business rights against regulatory efforts of both liberal and conservative rulers.

Legislation of the private pawning trade was repeatedly reworked by changing governments beginning in the 1840s. The process of making legislation and its implementation allows us to examine broker-state relations and the aims of the state. Santa Anna, Maximilian, Benito Juárez, and Sebastían Lerdo de Tejada all enacted comprehensive pawning legislation. Brokers working in association with each other attempted to influence changes in legislation. They made their views regarding new laws known through the petition process, and their objections were sometimes heeded. Brokers and the state negotiated terms of regulation employing the discourse of economic liberalism.[38]

Efforts to regulate casas de empeño began with their emergence. In 1831 Don Francisco Fagoaga put forth a plan to reform the empeño business. Fagoaga developed his project for the Juzgado Constitucional, concerned with the "enormous abuses" pawnbrokers committed against "the unfortunate people who have the disgrace of falling in their hands."[39] Fagoaga's plan apparently did not make its way into legislation. Instead, it was Santa Anna's administration that promulgated the first law to regulate casas de empeño (which also extended regulation of pawning in retail establishments) in January 1842. The preamble to the law stated that its purpose was to counter high interest rates and the insecurity of pledge items that sat on brokers' shelves. This law was in the company of other new taxes that alternating liberal and conservative governments (with Santa Anna representing one or the other at different times) levied in order to support large armies and the large civilian bureaucracies that had developed since Independence. The law is also consistent with Santa Anna's efforts to clip the wings of Spanish merchants, which culminated in closing and razing the Parián market in 1843.[40] Four articles comprised the new law. Article 1 confirmed the customary six-month pledge term and set an interest schedule that depended on when the good was redeemed.[41] As shown in table 4.3, the interest rate in annual terms was fixed at just over 9 percent if the good was redeemed in even months but would be higher if the good was redeemed within the first month of each two-month block in the schedule. The interest schedule would encourage pawning customers to wait until even-numbered months to redeem their goods in order to get the best interest rate. This article also specified that upon sale of an unredeemed item, any difference over the sum of the amount of the loan and the corresponding interest was to go to the owner of the item, as had been the case with retail pawning. Article 2 called for the sale of goods whose six-month redemption time had expired to be announced to the public, continuing colonial practice. Article 3 concerned the bonding of casas de empeño, "those existing as well as those to be newly established." The language about the size of bonds was vague, stating that it had to be a quantity

TABLE 4.3

Interest Rate on One-Peso Loan, Based on Schedule in 1842 Empeño Law

Repaid Within (months)	Charge (in real/peso)	Repayment Amount (in reals)	Difference (Loan/Repayment) %	Annual Interest Rate[a] %
1	1/8	8.125	1.56	18.75
2	1/8	8.125	1.56	9.34
3	1/4	8.25	3.13	12.50
4	1/4	8.25	3.13	9.34
5	3/8	8.375	4.69	11.25
6	3/8	8.375	4.69	9.34
7	1/2	8.50	6.25	10.71
8	1/2	8.50	6.25	9.34

[a] Annual interest rate calculated by dividing the difference between the loan amount and repayment amount by the number of months in pawn and then multiplying by 12 months.

"believed to be sufficient for the security of the pawned goods." Article 4 stated that pawnbrokers not in compliance with this law would be punished, and in the case of repeated infractions their shops would be closed and they would be barred from trade. The "forbidden collateral goods" list from the 1790 colonial decree was retained, and the minimum amount of money loaned relative to the worth of the pledged item, the obligation of brokers to keep the collateral items safely stored, and the requirement that brokers note installments paid on the redemption ticket were all colonial holdovers.[42]

Brokers responded quickly to Santa Anna's regulations, especially the provision regarding interest rates. Represented by Don Juan Acosta, the empeñeros wanted permission to charge a flat one real per peso loaned regardless of the time in pawn, instead of the fractions outlined in Article 1. Had brokers got their wish, a customer paying back a one-peso loan in one month would pay what would have amounted to 150 percent annual interest, while a customer redeeming his or her collateral in the sixth month would have paid 24 percent. While the government did not agree to this (in fact Santa Anna banned the one real per peso rate throughout the Republic, calling it "usury"), authorities did amend the law to account for loans smaller than a peso. Brokers could charge an eighth of a real on loans of from one to seven reales, as long as the value of the prenda did not exceed twelve reales (or a peso and a half). Brokers had asked for this provision, saying that it would mean less of an interest burden for clients pawning the cheapest goods, the bulk of their business. Even at these low values, the flat fee meant varying rates, low only for those waiting six months to redeem their property.[43]

Pawnbrokers petitioned the government as a group to change specific provisions of the new law a second time. Thirty-two brokers began by agreeing that reform of the empeño sector was needed so that those who had "the disgrace of needing to pawn can count on a guarantee that their goods will not be lost, that when the pledge time is up the good will be available to redeem, or at least that the owner will profit from its sale." The petitioning pawnbrokers also believed that all pawning contracts should be public. But brokers thought the law as written went too far. Again, Article 1 and its interest schedule were of grave concern. Brokers now called for the interest limit to be set at 18 percent annually for all goods over twelve reales, regardless of the month redeemed. They believed that this rate was necessary to cover costs and safeguard against bankruptcy. The limits as stated would simply force more brokers to operate clandestinely. While legislators might be counting on reason, brokers felt that only they had the experience of the neighborhoods. This was especially true when it came to applying provisions from the 1790 law to 1842. Article 4 of the earlier law, requiring brokers to lend two-thirds of the value on clothes, was not applicable to current times. The pawnbrokers recognized that their success in business was tied closely to the stamina of goods and the vagaries of passing fashions that characterized material culture. They argued that in 1790 one could lend two-thirds of the value on clothes, because fashions did not change repeatedly before the good was redeemed, and if an item went unclaimed, one could sell it and break even or even make a profit for the owner. But in 1842 the fashions changed weekly, devaluing cloth goods in only one month. Article 8 of the 1790 regulation, which called for making note of installment payments on pawn tickets, became part of the new law. Brokers again argued that customs had changed, just as had demands of fashion, and that in 1842 committing frauds with pawn tickets was easier. In the old days there were few pawned goods in stores, business was done at a relaxed pace, there was time to let clients pay installments on their loans, and one could trust them. "Today what a difference," the clients mark up their tickets to defraud the broker, which leads to lawsuits to get the goods back. Another problem with marking installments on pawn tickets was that if the ticket were lost, the client would have to get someone to swear to its value, and the broker might demand the full value recorded in his transaction book, as payments already made would be hard to prove.[44]

That pawnbrokers regularly circumvented regulations on licensing, maintaining proper books, issuing pawn tickets with proper information, and charging interest only within the allowable range is evident from a sampling of a popular daily newspaper, *El Siglo XIX*. In January 1855 the paper informed the public that two pawnbrokers—Don José Correa of the shop at No. 2 Las Ratas and Don Gabriel Cortés from the pawnshop at the corner of Plazuela de Covacho and Niño Perdido—were charging higher interest than the law allowed. The next week another empeñero, Don Pedro Arillaud of the pawnshop at the corner of Relox and Monte Alegre, was accused of the same infraction. Don Luis Gómez, owner of the pawnshop on the corner of Puente del Fierro and Puerta Falsa de la Merced, found himself in trouble with local police for operating without a license.[45] And Don Antonio Briviesda, owner of the shop at No. 12 San Hipólito, and Doña Joaquina Vega, who owned the shop on the corner of the Plazuela de Ave María and Ave María, were ordered to reform their bookkeeping procedures to comply with the law. They were also forced to return pawned goods in stock and to stop charging high interest rates, or each "would be treated as a criminal of illegal usury."[46] In a petition from pawning customers to Empress Carlotta in 1864, "usurious" pawnbrokers were accused of charging from 25 to 100 percent annual interest.[47]

Other continued abuses by private brokers included selling pawned goods before the pledge time was up and fencing stolen goods. In July 1866, the same month that the expansion of the Monte de Piedad was approved by the imperial government, the Ayuntamiento published an announcement in the *Diario del Imperio* that at the pawnshop La Reforma, located at Escalerillas No. 7, goods whose redemption period had expired would be sold. There was an additional line in the announcement that "in no way would goods whose pledge period had not lapsed be sold." The qualification suggests that this broker, or brokers generally, had a reputation among the public for selling goods before he should.[48] The fencing of stolen goods continued to be a common occurrence in pawnshops. The next law to regulate the trade lamented the frequency with which owners of pawnshops had to be obliged to return stolen merchandise from their shops, suggesting that brokers "generally do no not listen" to the government's concerns about fencing, resulting in "unjust violations [against the rights of] property."[49]

The 1842 legislation survived Santa Anna's last ouster in 1855. Indeed, it governed the pawning trade through American occupation later in the 1840s, the Reform era of the late 1850s, and Maximilian's rule in the late 1860s. The restored liberal government of Juárez did not issue new pawning regulations until four years after regaining power. But as soon as they had power again, liberal statesmen did clarify the tax burden and licensing of commercial enterprises; the tax schedule by class for pawnshops is laid out in table 4.4. Owners of casas de empeño had to pay the Ayuntamiento every three months, with levies depending on which of the six classes individual shops were in. In addition to paying taxes, the state expected brokers to have their books stamped by municipal accountants, purchase a license, and register their business with the government. Fines for not complying with the license requirement ranged from 10 to 120 pesos, not to be less than the value of three months of tax contributions. Offending pawnshops were closed until licenses were obtained and fines paid. If operating capital was more than the value of the license, brokers paid another fine, with shops closed until the fine was paid and a new license obtained. Any retail store or other commercial establishment in the pawn business was supposed to comply with the tax law.[50] Pawnbrokers resisted this intervention in their business affairs and ignored regulations by not paying taxes.[51]

Alfredo Chavero, Federal District governor under the Restored Republic, published new regulations for private pawnshops in 1871. Pawnbrokers were to seek permission before establishing casas de empeño so "the inspections that political authorities should exercise will be effective." This time the law specified that the amount of the pawnbroker's bond be "equal to the capital that they manage," which apparently meant the capitalization or worth of the store. This law, much longer than the 1842 legislation, had forty-five articles, with a number of them mandating the type and number of books to be kept by brokers and others detailing the duties of state regulators.[52] Colonial prescriptions against accepting military weapons, church jewels, uniforms, horse bridles, artisan's tools, locks, and keys as collateral were repeated, with the addition of "all class of goods that pertain to the nation." Brokers were to make loans in cash only, to store goods safely, and to help authorities recover stolen goods. Regulations regarding the sale of goods whose redemption time had expired were more detailed in 1871 than in earlier legislation. Articles 13, 15, 22, and 23 involved appraisal of these "prendas cumplidas" by an expert designated by the government of the Federal District. The sale of said goods was to be an-

TABLE 4.4

Municipal Contributions Payable by Class of Empeño, 1867

Class	Operating Capital (in pesos)	Monthly Tax (in pesos)
First	More than 3,000	40
Second	2,001 to 3,000	20
Third	1,001 to 2,000	15
Fourth	501 to 1,000	8
Fifth	101 to 500	4
Sixth	Less than 101	2

Source: Diario Oficial, December 4, 1867, 1.

nounced fifteen days prior to auction, with notice posted on the door of the establishment as well as announced in newspapers of the capital. Government inspectors were to be present at auctions, which were to be public, with goods going to the highest bidder. The new law also regulated the sale of casas de empeño, to be announced two months in advance. Bankruptcy was an issue in this legislation, suggesting that the pawning business was volatile and that many pawnshops were disappearing. The state stepped in to protect the property rights of pawning customers when brokers went out of business. Upon closure of pawnshops brokers had to turn over record books and inventory to authorities, from whom clients could recover their goods. The 1871 law also included provisions to prosecute appraisal frauds committed by brokers at the time of credit transactions. The state appointed appraisers to price unredeemed inventory, and pawnbrokers had to pay them a fee equal to 6 percent of the total value of goods.

Unlike the 1842 legislation, the 1871 law said nothing specific about interest rates, leaving credit entrepreneurs open to charge whatever interest they could get from customers. The law did, however, limit pawnbrokers' profits in the time-honored manner of having auction profits returned to owners of goods, with a new provision for the city's Administración de Rentas to hold on to windfalls for six months so owners could claim the money upon presentation of their pawn ticket. The new law further stipulated that unclaimed auction profits would go to charities, distributed by the Ayuntamiento as it saw fit, and not to the pawnbroker.

Brokers again participated in the governing process, petitioning as a group to seek changes in the 1871 law soon after it was published. Among other things, pawnbrokers objected that the honorarium brokers had to pay appraisers for their work increased from 4 percent of the value of clothing and 3 percent for jewels to "the enormous quantity of 6 percent."[53] They argued that this increase would hurt the pawning clientele, as brokers would simply pass it on to them.[54] Brokers also felt that government appraisers had too much leeway—some would value goods too low, thus making it difficult for brokers to break even when they sold at auction, while others would value goods too high in order to push up the honorarium. While the law provided for a third party to settle disputes between brokers and state agents, this third party would also charge brokers an honorarium. This cost, too, would be passed on to clients, along with interest charged (brokers cited 12 percent in this document), the 6 percent for the government appraiser, the costs for the printing of announcements of auctions, the officially sealed paper needed for documentation, and the municipal licensing tax. All together, clients would have to swallow 43 percent in costs (over and above any interest) for the pawning service. The requirement to secure multiple copies of documents also displeased these brokers, who saw it as both unnecessary and costly, as they had to pay scribes to make all the copies. The provision that a government representative had to be present at all auctions was unfeasible according to brokers, as transactions were not concluded in just a few days. In larger establishments pawned goods offered at auction might remain on the premises for four months or more, and according to the law, "all this time the inspectors should remain in the establishments." This introduction of outsiders into shops would intimidate regular customers and generally turn daily operations upside down.[55]

Six months after the 1871 law, new Federal District governor Tuburcio Montiel issued another regulation clarifying sticking points. Pawnbrokers again engaged the state in conversation about laissez-faire economics, presenting pleas for freedom from government intervention, rebellion against needless bureaucracy, and the sanctity of property relationships and contracts. The first twenty-two articles of the 1872 law were identical to those in the 1871 regulation. Article 23, which involved settlement of disputes regarding the value of goods between state-appointed appraisers and brokers, was changed, perhaps because of brokers' concerns. While in 1871 a third appraiser was to settle the dispute, the 1872 law called for the state agent's and broker's estimates to be averaged. A new provision called for inspectors to return to noncompliant shops every fifteen days.[56] The main change in the new law involved disposition of goods whose redemption time had passed. The brokers' concerns about government agents camping out in their shops were solved by the state in a way probably not anticipated by lenders. The auction could not continue more than three days, with goods that went unsold in that time to be held over for the next auction, which could not take place for another month. Pawned goods that were not sold in the first or second auction were to become property of the lender.[57]

Pawnbroker José María Galindez, mentioned at the beginning of this chapter, disregarded the new regulations. In 1871 Galindez had been fined for operating an establishment with capital beyond the amount in his license and for not turning over auction profits (minus costs and interest) that were due to his customers to the government for dispersal.[58] In 1872 he auctioned goods in his pawnshop at Puente de la Leña whose pledge time had lapsed without having them appraised by a government agent. He then sold them for the same amount as the loan, thus depriving customers of the chance to profit. The pawn tickets he issued did not contain loan amounts or interest charged.[59] We cannot know how representative Galindez's behavior was of the rest of the pawnbrokers in the city. It is likely that most were not such scofflaws, but enough were that the popular reputation of brokers remained generally unfavorable. An item in an August 1874 edition of *El Distrito Federal* noted "constant complaints of the public" that goods were sold for less than they were worth at pawnshop auctions and that *sobrante* profits were not delivered to customers.[60]

Galindez's confrontation with the government of the Federal District provides a fascinating window on interpretations of economic liberalism in the Restored Republic. The government fined Galindez for writing pawning contracts with illegal provisions. He responded with the claim that under civil law, he had the right to make contracts with any conditions he wanted, and that the pawning regulations violated his rights as a businessman. Galindez claimed that while the 1842 laws promulgated by the Santa Anna government limited business rights, the laws of the Reform era had declared "that money was a merchandise like any other, and that therefore the owner of money was free to set terms as he pleased." From that time, he believed, casas de empeño were considered commercial businesses like any other. It was the governor's opinion that most pawning clients did not know their rights, that in times of need people would subject themselves to poor and even illegal terms to get the money they needed, and that therefore clients' liberty needed the protection of the state.[61] Galindez was certainly armed with eighteenth-century liberal economic theory. He insisted that the parties to a contract knew better what was in their interests than any third party, even if that be the state. The state did not agree. He had argued that he set terms similar to those of a real-estate mortgage, while the state held that the pawning contract was different. As for civil law, the governor informed Galindez that the laws he claimed gave him freedom of commerce were superseded by other civil laws regarding the pawning process as well as by regulations specific to the pawning trade. The governor also told Galindez that he was free to set interest rates to cover his costs and to profit from his service that way.[62]

It was not just brokers who shared their views on pawning legislation with the government. In March 1873 inspector of empeños Epifigenio Cumplido noted that it was a "very rare case" when owners of goods received their share of proceeds from auctions in private pawnshops. For their part pawnbrokers had asked to keep proceeds of sales for six months and then pass them on, so that they could make at least temporary use of these profits. Trying to sway the state to their view, brokers argued that their clients had to make two trips to redeem sale profits: one to the broker to find out if their good was sold and for how much, and another to the government to actually get the money. They claimed that this was too much effort to receive a pittance, and that that was why clients did not receive what was due them.[63] The governor of the Federal District clarified the 1872 law, ordering that brokers turn over money due to clients to the government inspector on the day of the auction so that it could be held in the municipal treasury until the owner appeared to claim it. Another change made by Montiel responded to earlier concerns of brokers that there was not a sufficient number of appraisers. The governor increased that staff from four to six.

The regulatory role of the government colored relations between brokers and bureaucrats, and brokers on occasion accused government inspectors of abusive behavior. Whether in public or private pawnshops, daily operations were increasingly watched by the state as the nineteenth century progressed. In private shops, state agents undertook inspections to ensure compliance. Just who did the inspecting changed over time.[64] When the pawning business became concentrated in casas de empeño, the authority for inspection remained with the Ayuntamiento.[65] In early 1862 President Juárez issued a regulation for pawnshop inspectors in the city, jurisdiction of the audits now sitting with the government of the Federal District. The law called for inspections to be made from January to March, and for the inspector to take an assistant and a neighbor of the shop as witness. The interaction between the state agent and the pawnbroker entailed the broker's showing his license and the inspector's checking to see that the capital of the store matched the amount licensed and that all pawned goods were listed in the proper books. The books had to have the government seal, which indicated that they had been taken to tax authorities. The inspector was also to look for forbidden goods. If there were any fines for infractions, one-third would go to the inspector, which could invite abuse of authority. The pawnbroker being audited had to pay the agent for the inspection, the amount depending on the class of the establishment.[66]

Apparently some government inspectors were in the habit of charging pawnbrokers fees on the side and demanding loans for themselves, as the 1871 law had an article that specifically forbade these practices. Brokers certainly complained to authorities about abuses, including drunk inspectors.[67] The governor of the Federal District had to order an investigation of cases of someone impersonating an inspector.[68] One case allows us to examine the interaction of a pawnbroker, an inspector, a client, and a judge. In March 1873 Don José Lezameta, who owned the pawnshop at Sepulcros de Santo Domingo No. 6, complained that inspector Epifegenio Cumplido forced him to sell a gold ring at auction. This sale was despite the fact that the owner of the ring, Don Aurelio Velasco, had arranged with the broker that it would not go to auction, since he was putting together the money to redeem it. Lezameta accused Cumplido of having bought the ring himself at auction through a third party. When Velasco, the owner of the ring, sued Lezameta for having broken his contract, Lezameta protested that it was not his fault. The broker said the inspector forced him to sell it, and that the inspector should pay damages to the owner and return the ring, which the broker believed was in the inspector's possession. The inspector expressed outrage at the broker's accusations, claiming he was only following regulations: if a good's pledge period had passed, it was to be auctioned publicly. The item in question had already been appraised and listed in the book listing goods whose pledge period had passed so that they would go to auction. Cumplido admitted that there was precedent for owners holding back goods at the owners' request, but that it had to be done with the previous acknowledgment of authorities, which had not happened in this case. Since the ring had been listed in the account books as ready for sale at auction, and because there was no proof that the inspector had paid for the ring himself at the auction, the judge decided against Lezameta and held that inspector Cumplido was not responsible for satisfying the demands of the client.[69]

The Business of Pawning at Midcentury

The amount of operating capital of pawnshops at midcentury varied widely. The 1842 legislation did not specify how much money a bond had to be (that is, a percentage of the amount of capitalization or more than capitalization). The bond agreement between Don Basilio Ortiz and his son, who opened a pawnshop at the end of May 1842, specified that the bond was for nine hundred pesos, three times the stated capital of the store. In other instances that year the bonds equaled the amount of capitalization.[70] Out of eighty-four pawnshops in the database from 1842 to 1844 for which the bond amount is known, 21 percent were under fifty pesos, 33 percent were under one hundred pesos, 73 percent were under two hundred pesos, and 79 percent were under five hundred pesos. Only 10 percent of these businesses operated with more than one thousand pesos. The biggest, owned by Don Manuel Ruiz at letter A on the first block of San Juan, was bonded for four thousand pesos by Don Pablo Córdova. The pawnshop established by Don Nicolás Aros and bonded by Don Trinidad Gutiérrez at the end of September 1842 only had capital of twenty-five pesos, one of the smallest amounts in the sample. This range of capital investment foreshadows the classification of pawnshops in the 1860s.[71]

A number of casas de empeño closed before they could come into compliance with the January 1842 law.[72] This may indicate continued volatility of the trade, especially in the early post-Independence years, when retail establishments still offered formidable competition. Like the pulpería trade earlier, some casas de empeño turned over ownership frequently, though the businesses themselves often continued at the same locations. Some patterns of spatial distribution of business in the city continued as well in the transition from retail to pawnshop. Clusters of pulperías on streets such as Santo Domingo and Plateros at the beginning of the nineteenth century were replaced by the end of the century by clusters of casas de empeño. New street clusters emerged, such as four shops on Relox in the 1850s and four in the first block of Merced in the 1870s. Some neighborhoods had no empeños.[73] Of course some pawnshops operated outside the law and therefore escape documentation.

Table 4.5 lists pawnshops in the sample that changed ownership. In contrast to this volatility of ownership, a few empeños had the same owner for over ten years. Don José Ortiz operated his pawnshop at the corner of Lagunilla and Vaquita at least from July 1842 to May 1854. The Hoacalco pawnshop persevered for at least twenty years. It was in the hands of Don Vicente Chávarri in January 1854 and was then listed among the first-class

TABLE 4.5

Changes in Ownership of Casas de Empeño, 1842–79

Business Address	Owners	Date
Amaya & Misericordia	D. Felix Cabaños	Apr. 23, 1842
	Gutiérrez and Zaro	May 11, 1854
Esclavo & El Aguila	Da. María Nestora Hernández	Dec. 15, 1840
	D. Miguel Azcarate	Apr. 23, 1842
Jardín Plaza & Pila de Habana	D. Mariano Plato	Jan. 15, 1844
	D. Dionicio Gonzalez	May 11, 1854
	H. Moreno	unknown
	Guadalupe Cortés	Feb. 12, 1878
Sapo Street No. 22	Pedro Diego Collado	Jun. 4, 1858
	Margarita Santieste	Jan. 9, 1868
Pila Seca & Medinas	D. Ygnacio Romero	Jun. 1, 1842
	D. Luis Gallopín	Oct. 16, 1854
	Cirilio Manrique	Jan. 29, 1878
	Esteban Becerril	Jun. 16, 1879

Source: AGN, Gobernación, leg. 2167(1), exp. 2. no. 20(1), fs. 5–7; *El Siglo XIX*, May 5, 1954, October 16, 1854, June 4, 1858, January 9, 1868; AGNCM, Ferriz, vol. 1477, f. 108; AHCM, Empeños, exps. 35, 37.

pawnshops capitalized with between seven and fifteen thousand pesos in 1874, owned by J. Chávarri. Some brokers had multiple pawnshops. Don José María Andrade owned one on a corner of Salto de Agua in April 1842 and another in the middle of the block of Misericordia in June of that year.[74]

The pawnshop inventories from 1867 to 1880 allow further analysis of the volume of business, average loans given, and degree to which particular pawnbrokers might have faced the problem of shouldering large inventories of unredeemed and unsold goods. For the Cartagena pawnshop located in Tacubaya, a series of five inventories from January 1867, May and August 1868, and February and June 1869 list *prendas cumplidas* that were up for sale at auction, the amount of loans secured, and official appraised values of collateral. This pawnshop in a western suburb of Mexico City saw an average of 326 pawning transactions per month over the first six months in 1866, while in the next two years business volume more than doubled. For February through November 1867 the average was 876 transactions per month; in March through December 1868 it was 862 transactions per month. In the southern municipality of Tlalpan, the pawnshop Del Portal de la Magdalena had only an average of 178 transactions per month from January to May 1870. The pawnshop on Plaza de la Constitución in Tlalpan averaged 535 transactions per month from April to September 1879.[75]

These pawnbrokers were not left with large numbers of unredeemed goods. The June 1869 inventory for the Cartagena pawnshop lists only one of the 346 goods going to auction as having been more than two years old. These 346 goods represent only 7 percent of the 4,874 pledge goods that we know passed through the establishments' doors in the six months covered by the inventory. And comparison of inventories from the same establishments that are only a few months apart shows no overlap of specific goods still for sale from one inventory to the next. The clientele of the Plaza de Constitución pawnshop in Tlalpan in 1879 appear much more likely to be unable to redeem their collateral before the pledge period expired than those at the Cartegena shop in Tacubaya a decade earlier. The former had a smaller volume, judging by the item numbers in the inventories, but a higher number of collateral goods going to auction than the latter.

Table 4.6 suggests that in peripheral pawnshops the average loans were small, from under half a peso to over a peso and a half. All inventories represented in this table are of *prendas cumplidas*, with the exception of the inventory of 72 goods in the Magdalena shop, which represents active collateral that moved with the shop when Don José Carreras sold it to Don Vicente Espinosa. When he was left with unredeemed goods to sell, the broker's chance of recovering the loan amount depended on a number of factors, some beyond his control. If the item was one that had little resale appeal, whether due to wear and tear or the rules of fashion, it might be written off as a loss or perhaps repawned with another broker. One factor suggested by the inventories at hand is the interplay between what the pawnbroker judged to be the loan value (ideally and customarily two-thirds the real value of the object, or 66 percent, with the remaining third to make up for the lost interest should loans not be repaid) and what a government appraiser deemed to be its value. While the documents at hand do not tell us whether these *prendas cumplidas* actually sold or at what price, the appraisal value was to serve as guide when goods were auctioned under government supervision. The data allow an approximation of the ability of pawnbrokers and their employees as appraisers, and therefore of the likelihood that they would get their capital back upon sale of that good. Mario

TABLE 4.6

Loan Average, Total Lent, and Total Appraisal for Pawned Goods

Inventory Date	Average Loan	Total Loans	Total Appraisal
Cartagena (Tacubaya)			
January 7, 1867	4 rs.	89 ps. 4 rs.	144 ps. 6 1/2 rs.
May 14, 1868	3 1/2 rs.	122 ps. 4 rs.	189 ps. 3 1/4 rs.
August 15, 1868	3 4/5 rs.	119 ps. 4 rs.	174 ps. 7 3/4 rs.
February 27, 1869	45 cs.	125 ps. 7 cs.	199 ps. 38 cs.
June 18, 1869	3 3/5 rs.	156 ps. 3 rs.	227 ps. 5 1/2 rs.
Magdalena (Tacubaya)			
September 28, 1871	80 cs.	58 ps. 11 cs.	
Plaza de la Constitución (Tlalpan)			
March 3, 1879	1 p. 3/4 r.	643 ps.	776 ps. 4 rs.
April 27, 1880	1 p. 25 cs.	991 ps. 29 cs.	

Source: AHCM, Inventario General de la Municipalidad de Tacubaya, no. 120, exps. 3, 5, 7 and 11; AHCM, Inventario General de la Municipalidad de Tlalpan, no. 69, exp. 11 and exp. 71.

Note: Except for the Magdalena pawnshop, this accounting includes only goods going to auction and does not include the vast majority of goods that were redeemed before the pledge period expired.

de Guzmán, the appraiser charged with valuing unredeemed goods in the Cartagena pawnshop in June 1869, described his job this way: "We the experts signing this appraisal declare that with the exception of various goods, all of the goods that have been 'justipreciado' are used, old, broken and some useless; and that in appraising their value we have had in mind their quality, state of use and value that similar new goods have, and therefore the appraisal has been just and without any harm according to our loyal knowledge and understanding."[76]

Collateral owners and more often pawnbrokers complained that appraisers erred in the valuation of goods, whether arriving at too low a number or too high. The 1871 law considered that appraisers might make faulty appraisals and provided avenues of recourse for brokers and owners of collateral goods. In table 4.6, if one assumes that the two-thirds rule still approximated business reality and takes Mario de Guzmán at his word that appraisers were "just" in their appraisals, then Adolfo Fernández, owner of the Constitución pawnshop, was the least likely to profit from the sale of unredeemed goods, as the total amount of loans secured with these goods was 82 percent of the appraisal value. Agapito Cortés, in contrast, came under the 66 percent in three out of five inventories, and he came within three percentage points in the remaining two.[77]

A closer look at loans secured by and appraisals of specific goods in Fernández's shop suggests that he was better at appraising some goods than others. The March 1879 inventory is broken into four categories: 45 goods are classified as "alhajas" and include pocket watches (one of which was pawned along with a broken *bandalón*, or string musical instrument), silverware, and jewelry; 18 goods are categorized as "armas"; 149 objects are listed as "varios objetos"; and 376 objects are grouped as "lanas," mostly women's and some men's clothing, sheets, and blankets.[78] Of the six watches in Fernández's shop, three had appraisals that exactly matched the loan amount (two for two and a half pesos and one for five pesos), one had an appraisal for half a peso less than the two and a half pesos loaned, and one had an appraisal a half peso higher than the three pesos loaned. Only one watch, the most valuable, had an appraisal that might yield the broker a profit upon resale. A gold watch with diamonds belonging to a client named Retana secured a loan of twelve pesos and was appraised at fifteen pesos.[79] Fernández lent customer Aguilar seven pesos against a broken "American" alarm table clock in a wooden box, but the expert opinion was that it was only worth four pesos. Perhaps Fernández or his clerk had trouble judging the value of pocket watches and table clocks as they were relative newcomers among collateral. But the differential between loan amount and appraisal was also narrow or nonexistent for many of the jewelry items, weapons, and "various objects." In one case customer Castillo had pawned a pair of gold earrings for a loan of two pesos two reales, while the appraisal reached only one peso. In another case customer Nava pawned a bit, harness plate, and small chain that the broker must have thought were made of silver but which the appraisal inventory lists as "todo falso." This riding gear secured a loan of three pesos but was appraised at only half that. Fernández's judgment was much more on the mark when it came to silver spoons and forks, collateral arguably more familiar to those behind the counter. Seven loans of between one and a half pesos and five pesos were secured with individual pieces or pairs of silverware, and in each case the appraisal was at least one and a half pesos higher than the loan amount. As for the goods most often pawned, Fernández only undervalued 2 of 376 cloth goods, with the vast majority of appraised values for cloth items just one or two reales above the loan amount. In the rare case of a cloth good worth more than a few pesos, Fernández's appraisals seemed to have followed the two-thirds rule fairly well. The difficulty in appraising changing collateral goods that customers brought in was also a challenge employees at the Monte de Piedad faced.

Expansion of the Institutional Pawnshop

The colonial state linked public and private branches of the pawning business when they established the Monte de Piedad to counter high private interest rates, and connections between the two sectors continued in the nineteenth century. Brokers in the public institution and private empeñeros recognized that there was a dynamic between them, though often making contradictory claims. Pawnbrokers commenting on the 1842 law welcomed the legislation as part of much-needed order and progress, though they tried to modify the interest structure. They argued that they differed from the Monte de Piedad, which they believed had abundant funds and therefore could afford to lend at the low interest of one and a half percent every two months. They justified higher interest rates in private shops by arguing that empeños were more convenient to the pawning clientele because they could be visited at any hour of day, and even some hours at night, without the wait of two or three hours in line found at the Monte.[80] For their part Monte administrators tried to set themselves apart from private brokers, who "appeared philanthropic and disinterested, but really were motivated by the interest they charged."[81] The Monte director in the 1860s believed his institution was preferable because Monte employees were responsible and did not mistreat or lose pawned goods, did not charge interest (although they did charge a "service fee"), and always had someone available to take pawns during business hours (unlike private shops, where customers often had to return several times before finding the broker in the shop). The relationship between the two types of establishments was not always oppositional. Monte de Piedad tickets were legally accepted in private shops as pawnable items, and private shops deposited their tax contributions to Beneficencia Pública (required by law) in Monte coffers. As had been true for the main branch earlier, some customers listed in neighborhood branches of the Monte de Piedad were pawnbrokers in this middle period. For example, Manuel González pawned a watch at Branch No. 3 for twenty pesos in 1873. He owned an empeño at Relox No. 1 in the late 1870s.[82]

Employees at the charitable pawnshop continued to pay the price for their status as public employees even as that status was sometimes ambiguous. They had to swear allegiance in 1841 to the Plan de Tacubaya and in

1843 to the Bases Orgánicas. When Mexico faced rebellion in Texas in 1836, the government turned to the Monte de Piedad for help in meeting costs of the war. The pawnshop was unable to loan money to the government in this instance, as its capital was tied up in the purchase of its third home, on the Zócalo. Sometimes the connection to the government could be a boon for employees. In 1848 pensions were extended to subaltern employees of the Monte.[83] In 1857 President Ignacio Comonfort declared that employees of the Monte de Piedad did not have to swear allegiance to the new liberal federal constitution, because employees of charitable establishments were determined not to be government employees. Nonetheless, the federal Secretaría de Relaciones Exteriores y Gobernación continued to sit on the governing board and the president continued to set employment policy for the establishment, suspending the right to retirement pensions for Monte employees.

In May 1860, in the midst of civil war between liberals and conservatives, the conservative government of Miguel Miramón, which had control of Mexico City, demanded a three-thousand-peso forced loan from the institution. A third of the loan had to be raised among the staff, the contributions proportionate to salaries, with the director, department heads, controllers, secretary, seven *oficiales*, two appraisers, and three scribes all contributing. In August the president ordered that the Monte board meet to consider a twenty-five-thousand-peso loan to the city government, which would be secured with jewels belonging to the city. When liberal forces retook the city in 1861, President Benito Juárez again declared that Monte de Piedad employees were not government employees and therefore were exempt from the now secular oath to the Constitution (which replaced the religious one). Juárez also included the Monte de Piedad under the Dirección General de Fondos de Beneficencia and exempted the institution from paying taxes due to its character as a public charity. On Juárez's way out of town as the French were occupying Mexico City, the Monte loaned his government-in-internal-exile fifty thousand pesos.[84]

Considering the frequent turnovers of national political leadership, occupation of Mexico City by American troops in 1848, and civil war in the late 1850s, the Monte de Piedad's day-to-day business continued with remarkable persistence. There was a more steady increase in the average loan value given by the Monte into the 1840s, even as the numbers of transactions diminished. Though the relationship between the two is not clear, it is interesting that the remarkable near doubling of the number of transactions and a significant drop in loan values from 1841 to 1842 occurred as the first law regulating casas de empeño was promulgated (see appendix 2, table E), also the year that interest rates increased. The average loan amount was highest in 1840 at 18 pesos, came down to 17 pesos in 1841, and dropped significantly to 10 pesos in 1842. Then the average hovered around 12 pesos for the rest of the decade. Judging by the overall decrease in average loan amount, the Monte de Piedad staff in the "Age of Santa Anna" might have seen more people from the lower middle class, who had less expensive goods that they could leave as collateral for loans. A comparison of the relative amounts of money going out and coming back to the establishment's coffers in the 1840s shows that in eight out of nine years in the 1840s between 20,000 and 70,000 more pesos were lent than recovered, and in each year except for 1847 between 38,000 and 45,000 people took out collateral loans totaling between over 400,000 to over 500,000 pesos. Only in 1847 was more money repaid through redemption of collateral than money lent, with 245,426 pesos being lent out in 35,448 transactions, while 26,788 customers repaid 256,767 pesos. Was this balance related to the temporary closing of the establishment after the American occupation of the city and a portion of the Monte de Piedad's building in September 1847? In January 1848, after reopening the institution for lending services, the new director, Manuel Gómez Pedraza, a former president of Mexico, complained of the American troops still occupying a portion of the Monte de Piedad building.[85] Presumably, were private pawnshop records available for the five months that the Monte de Piedad was closed, we would see regular Monte customers turning to casas de empeño in their neighborhoods instead. In 1850 the average loan at the Monte increased 2 pesos from that of 1849 to reach 12 pesos, and the next year it rose to 14 pesos. The number of transactions and total capital loaned also rose, almost 5,000 more people in 1850 than 1849 and 2,500 more people in 1851 then 1850, when more than 50,000 collateral loans were made for over 670,000 pesos (see appendix 2, table E).

While the hum of collateral lending remained basically steady in the tumultuous middle decades of the nineteenth century, the public pawnshop continued to suffer from financial shortfalls, certainly exacerbated by repeated forced loans to different governments. Santa Anna tried various schemes to keep the institution solvent.[86] The institution attempted other strategies to improve its capital holdings. In July 1849 the directors of the Monte de Piedad established a *caja de ahorros* (savings bank), paying 4 percent annual interest for deposits over five pesos. Deposits of between one and four pesos would not earn interest. Two years later, the savings-bank operations were fused with pawning operations in the Depository. In 1855 the savings bank was separated from the Monte's accounting, and interest was fixed at 6 percent annually.[87] The government justified continuing the savings bank, saying that the working poor could save small amounts that they could put together, and maybe they could even move up to "la clase mas acomodada" (the more comfortable class).[88] When the Monte was founded in the 1770s, its fees were to be voluntary and limited to 6 percent, after which interest became "usurious." The flat service charge of 12 percent annually remained from 1815 until 1841, when the governing board established a sliding scale that was exactly the same as that in the 1842 empeño legislation. The fee of between just over 9 and almost 19 percent, depending on the month redeemed (see table 4.3 above), was to be charged at the time of redemption of sale of the pawned item; the earlier flat fee had been paid at the time of the original transaction. After more tinkering with fees, by the beginning of 1874, the establishment settled again on a flat interest rate of one centavo per peso loaned per month, or 12 percent annually.[89]

During Santa Anna's last administration of 1853–55, a plan for branch offices of the Monte de Piedad did not come to fruition, as the Monte did not have sufficient liquid funds to finance new outlets. When Maximilian investigated the possibility of doing the same in 1864, director Antonio María Lazpita responded that the Monte's capital was tied up in lending to the needy, and contrary to what Don Francisco Ramírez y Rojas (author of a proposal to expand the Monte) posited, there was no huge treasury available, as the capital rose and fell with the volume of loans and rhythm of redemptions.[90] Reformer Ramírez y Rojas directed his proposal to Empress Carlota, framing it with maternal imagery. Using mother-son images in a deferential apology for his daring to address the empress, he called upon her "paternal goodness" for protection of the poorest of the city's pawning clientele. Ramírez y Rojas outlined how the Monte de Piedad abandoned the poor. First, it did not lend under one peso, effectively shutting out the working class, as it was "notorious that *jornaleros* (workers paid weekly) and *menestrales* (workers paid monthly) never have objects of high value." Second, the Monte had limited hours when workers were on the job. And third, there was only one pious establishment for so many needy people. Private empeños had problems, too, and lent credence to the reformer's call for the Monte's expansion. They often lacked funds for lending, despite the high interest they charged, and he said that they lent half in cash and half in kind of some sort. Ramírez y Rojas believed that the

Monte de Piedad had over one hundred thousand pesos that could be used to fund additional branches to save the poor from "the habit of usury." Director Lazpita did not agree that the Monte de Piedad had sufficient funds to expand on its own.[91]

In July 1866, on orders from Emperor Maximilian, the Monte did open branch offices in outlying neighborhoods of the city.[92] Maximilian characterized the expansion of the public institution as a response to "criminal abuses committed in the majority of casas de empeño against the unfortunate class."[93] After the French were ousted from Mexico in 1867, the liberal government of Benito Juárez confirmed Maximilian's effort in 1868. In keeping with other anticlerical reforms, liberals secularized the Monte after the French left, removing the archbishop and the cathedral's representative from the governing board.[94] The expansion of the Monte de Piedad confirms Silvia Arrom's argument that it is the Second Empire and not the Restored Republic that "deserves the credit" for expanding social-welfare services. Nonetheless, the relatively high interest rates in branch offices put in question how much the charity might benefit those with only very humble goods to pawn.[95]

The minimum loan at the new branches was twenty-five centavos. Ramírez y Rojas had called for a maximum loan of five pesos so that more people could be served, but the imperial government set the maximum at twenty pesos.[96] Maximilian ordered that service fees be "as low as possible." The interest schedule was as follows. For goods pawned for less than four reales, the client would pay one centavo for up to six months. For a loan of twenty-five centavos, the twenty-six centavos paid back would represent a 48 percent annual interest rate if redeemed in the first month and an 8 percent annual interest rate if redeemed in the sixth month. For loans over four reales (or the equivalent of fifty centavos), the interest rate paid would be 24 percent annually regardless of the month paid back.[97] The pledge period for jewels could be extended for a fee in the first two weeks of the seventh month, but clothing could not be repawned. As in the main branch of the Monte de Piedad, cloth and jewels whose pledge period had expired were to be auctioned on separate days. This separation of auction goods perhaps reflected a class division between buyers of used cloth goods and buyers of used jewelry. Loans had to be paid back in the same currency that they were given in, except that those worth less than four centavos could be paid in copper.[98]

Hours of the branch services were to be from eight o'clock in the morning until one o'clock in the afternoon and then from three o'clock to five o'clock. They would also open from eight o'clock to twelve noon on holidays. The contents of the pawn ticket were spelled out, as in statutes for the main Monte and regulations for the private shops. After eight months goods would go up for sale under the same rules as those at the main branch. If upon sale of the good the loan, interest, and corresponding fees were met, the client had rights to the remaining profit. Under Maximilian there were no restrictions on what could be pawned in the Monte branches, except that they "have a realizable positive value," which suggests that clients would try to pawn goods in poor condition or of very low value that would not sell at a profit.[99] Later legislation modified options for clients. The poor were expected to pawn clothing and household furniture. They were not allowed to pawn paintings, sculptures, or books.[100] Might these limits reflect continued anxiety about the provenance of luxury goods in the hands of poorer city residents?

The first two new offices opened in September 1866 in neighborhoods where private pawning had brisk business: No. 28 in the second block of Mesones and No. 6 of the Acequia. The third opened in October at Montealegre No. 9. By the time the restored Juárez government approved the expansion plan, four branches were in operation and funded by the Monte's Treasury, with new locations to be opened when circumstances dictated the need. The staff in each branch—appointed by the director of the main office in consultation with and with approval from the governing junta—included an administrator (earning an annual salary of 1,300 pesos), an appraiser (salary, 800 pesos), two scribes (salary, 500 each), a clerk (salary, 144 pesos), and a doorman (salary, 240 pesos). The first three officials had to be bonded. In addition an inspector and an assistant were to be appointed for each branch. The law charged the main office's chief accountant with checking the books of branches.[101]

Reformer Ramírez y Rojas had argued in 1864 that the Monte de Piedad was one of the few institutions to survive the many revolutions of the period, and that maybe it was the only institution that served as a model of morality and order.[102] Director Lazpita agreed that residents of the city had confidence in the Monte. Because of the volume of business every day, Monte employees did not generally know their customers by name. The volume of more than three hundred people seeking aid every day meant that from the director down to the doorman, all employees "worked triple" hours.[103] Such exemplary behavior in the Monte was not always evident. In January 1868 the minister of Gobernación charged that the Monte branch offices opened with a staff that was not carefully chosen. Appraisers had been overvaluing goods, giving bigger loans than the sale of an unredeemed good could cover. Some appraisers had disappeared and could not be held accountable. President Lerdo agreed that two former appraisers, Agustín Martínez and Florencio Maya, would be charged for losses close to 300 pesos incurred in 1866. The first had moved on to be an employee of the national Congress and the other of the national Treasury, where their salaries were discounted by one-third to pay for the shortages in the Monte branches. The two men succeeded in petitioning to cancel the dock in pay a year later. The director of the main branch was faulted for not keeping a close supervision of the establishment's offspring.[104]

The director of the Monte de Piedad, while himself under the authority of the minister of Gobernación, represented the state's authority through oversight of the main and branch offices of the public institution. In October, 1872, Agustín Olmeda, the administrator of Branch No. 2, complained to the minister of Gobernación that the director had severely reprimanded him in front of his customers for not balancing the books on time. Olmeda was fined twenty pesos by the director. A few years later, inspector Juan Butrón y Pereda complained that the director had unjustly fined him ten pesos for signing in "with anticipation," or before the opening hour. In both Olmeda's and Butrón y Pereda's cases, the employee appealed the fine to the president of the Republic. Olmeda had his fine reduced by half, and Butrón y Pereda was exempted altogether.[105]

While the state empowered the director of the Monte to discipline his staff, when poor management problems resurfaced it was the director himself who faced disciplinary measures, along with his guilty employees, as in the 1866 case against the appraisers. The director was reproached again when the government investigated operations at the Monte in 1872. Inspectors found that the auction judge, Manuel de los Cobos, pawned a good that had been offered for sale at auction. Don Yldefonso Velasco had pawned the silver jewelry originally for 750 pesos on August 3, 1871. The jewelry passed to the auction room in March 1872, where it was appraised at 1,000 pesos. On the last day of May, De los Cobos took it out of the auction room and over to the Depository and pawned it himself for 800 pesos. Meanwhile, the account books reflected that the jewel had sold and the owner had received 77 pesos and 50 centavos at the end of June. How was this fraud possible when the regulations of the Monte had many checks and balances? Those responsible for reviewing De los Cobos's books had not checked them against the receipts of auction sales. In the end De los Cobos lost his job, the appraiser who had taken in the jewel as a

TABLE 4.7

Operations in the Monte de Piedad, January 1875

	Number Clients Pawning	Amount Loaned (in pesos)	Average Loan (in pesos)	Number Clients Redeeming	Amount Repaid (in pesos)	Average Repaid (in pesos)
Main	3,308	77,923	24	3,104	67,562	22
Branch No. 1	6,685	19,390	3	5,992	16,453	3
Branch No. 2	6,926	15,009	2	6,244	13,489	2
Branch No. 3	5,596	13,513	2	5,004	11,848	2
Branch No. 4	4,696	12,394	3	2,806	10,693	4
Total	27,211	138,229	5	24,153	120,045	5

Source: AGN, Gobernación, 4th section, leg. 875(1), exp. 1, no. 30.

new pledge was suspended without pay, and the director was reprimanded by the minister of Gobernación. The director retorted that the new responsibilities to supervise operations in four branch offices as well as the headquarters meant that he was away from his office and his primary duties much of the day.[106]

To what extent did the Monte de Piedad's expansion meet the stated goals of expanding collateral-credit services to more of the city's population? The sample of pawned goods from the 1860s and 1870s suggests that customers coming to the new branch offices were still pawning goods of greater value than those in pawnshops, at least those on the outskirts of the city in Tacubaya and Tlalpan. As can be seen in table 4.7, nine years after the public institution's 1867 expansion into working-class neighborhoods, the Casa Matriz had half as many pawning operations as each branch but six times the capital of any one branch. This suggests that the institution's stated aim to serve the poor was now closer to reality, and that indeed there were a great many more people in need of the lower-level services of the branches than the original institution had offered to assist. The evidence illustrates clear class divisions in the city in the 1870s, with the fewer middle-class customers at the main branch of the public institution having a material life-style sufficient to generate almost 78,000 pesos in loans in January alone, more than what the poorer clients of the four branches combined could muster. Yet the average loan of two and a half pesos at the branches of the institutional pawnshop in 1875 was still considerably higher than the half a peso average for the Cartagena pawnshop from 1868 or the just over one peso at the Constitución pawnshop in 1879. Thus, while the Monte de Piedad indeed expanded its services, it was still not an institution aimed at the poorest of those seeking collateral credit.

The growth of the pawning-business sector proceeded at a fast pace throughout the nineteenth century. There were some continuities from colonial times in locations and ownership of businesses in transition from retail to pawnshop. There were fewer women in the new business structure. The mostly Spanish male brokers knew each other, stood for each other as bondsmen, and engaged the state as a group in debate about the regulation of their industry. In identifying their clients as "needy women" and widows, pawnbrokers petitioning to lift interest-rate limits from the 1842 empeño law and to lower the tax rates of the 1871 laws positioned themselves in a patriarchal role, arguing that they made a social contribution catering to the needs of these vulnerable women.[107] State hegemony in the mid-nineteenth century was built in part in Mexico through negotiation among pawnbrokers and state agents in a political economy that was at once patriarchal and liberal, with overlapping understandings of public and private arenas. The patriarchal structures and cultures, reinforced as liberalism developed in this period, kept the collateral-lending sector of the economy male dominated. These male pawnbrokers were private entrepreneurs engaging in a public business arena, where they used patriarchal rhetoric emphasizing the help they gave to needy women. Thus, pawnbrokers legitimized their business enterprise and tried to imbue their private capitalist efforts with an air of public good.

The evolution of pawning legislation through a succession of governments from the 1840s to the mid-1870s is instructive on a number of levels. State regulators replaced the self-policing of retail pawning done by the colonial Consulado. The republican state no longer obligated brokers to accept pawns from regular customers and neighbors. Continuities with the colonial period can be found as well. The client's right to receive her share of the proceeds from the sale of goods was a requirement of both old and new legislation. The lists of "forbidden collateral" from 1790s legislation was incorporated in all the laws of the nineteenth century, with some additions. And the responsibility of local government (either city or Federal District) in supervising inspections continued.

It has been argued that the secret to the colonial state's stability was its mediating role among all sectors of society.[108] The requirement that corner-store owners provide pawning services for regular customers and neighbors fit this mediating role. With the fall of the colonial government, a new state was built slowly, as it had to gain legitimacy and build a revenue-generating system. John Tutino has argued that instead of mediating social relations, the new national state took sides with property holders.[109] This allegiance reflected the rise of liberalism as a guiding philosophy of state building. The tendency to protect private property can be seen in pawning legislation in urban areas in the republican era. But, as is apparent in the government's position in the case of José María Galindez, there were also state-welfare tendencies in pawning regulations that contradicted freedom-of-commerce tenets of liberalism in Mexico. The state consistently saw its role in the pawning process as defending the public interest, that is, protecting pawnshop customers from many potential abuses of pawnbrokers. The Monte de Piedad expanded its services in the 1860s and was later secularized by liberal governments, but liberal governors apparently never considered closing the public establishment, which would in effect have gotten the state out of the pawning business and more in line with "doctrinaire" liberalism.

The pawning legislation reflected liberal principles as it protected private property. The law protected the property of clients, the owners of pawned goods, with rules about how goods should be stored and about chances for owners to redeem them before they were sold. The law consistently held that any profit on the sale of a good (beyond the loan amount and the costs and interest) must go to the owner or to public charity. The law protected private property of the victims of theft, as fenced items were to go back to rightful owners, with brokers charged with avoiding the problem by determining the ownership of goods before accepting them. The list of "forbidden collateral" contained many items that were easily stolen—knives and forks, uniforms, production tools—by working-class employees from middle-class employers.

The early republican legislation limited brokers in determining the profits they would gain from the interest they charged. The liberal laws in the 1870s, in contrast, made no mention of interest rates, and when the matter was taken up by the courts, brokers were declared to be free in this aspect of their business. In other matters the state most definitely intervened in the supposedly private business concerns of brokers. Taxation and regulation were part of the state-building process, and their implementation produced large bureaucracies of tax collectors and inspectors, creating tensions between state building and liberalism. Taxing power was one measure of a strong state.[110] Perhaps the new state hoped to earn legitimacy through its brokering of these daily popular economic operations by playing ombudsman and protecting the public.

The poor continued to be the majority of clients in private pawnshops. The Monte continued to favor its middle-class clientele at the expense of poorer people. By the 1860s the official establishment recognized this class division in clientele and established branch offices to broaden its mission. The private shops had to compete with Monte branches for customers, adding a new dimension to the long-standing relationship between the private and public institutions. Even with the branch offices, however, the Monte de Piedad clientele was still better off than most of those taking collateral goods to private pawnshops. Social relations among brokers, clients, and state agents often were not cordial, with accusations and mistrust built in. Pawnbrokers had an unsavory popular reputation, while popular opinion and the state's official view characterized pawnshop clients as both needy and worthy. Although some brokers saw the need to cleanse their ranks of those most notoriously abusive of peoples' need for small cash loans, brokers on the whole challenged the state's right to interfere in their "honest" business dealings. The biggest change for brokers was the freedom in the 1870s to charge whatever interest the market would bear. In the next stage in the evolution of the pawning business and state regulation, clients repeatedly turned to the state to protect them from Porfirian brokers, who increased both their interest rates and their disrespect for those whose everyday credit needs made them richer.

FIVE

Positivist Housekeeping

Domesticity, Work, and Consumer Credit, 1880–1910

In her 1887 memoir *Face to Face with the Mexicans*, American visitor Fanny Gooch Chambers commented on numerous "public charitable institutions" in Mexico City. Her opinion of the Monte de Piedad was high; she thought it "one of the noblest benefactions, enabling those whom misfortune has visited to realize or receive advances upon valuables without the risk of losing them. These pawnshops exist all over the country, and all classes can avail themselves of their advantages."[1] In contrast Spanish resident Julio Sesto lamented the sight for sore eyes that casas de empeño owned by his compatriots presented to visitors in 1909, with "dirty clothes, above all, which makes one sick (*da asco*) to see hanging in the view of the public. Clearly this obeys the general needs of the moment in an unequal society, where each person pawns what they have; but if the pawnbroker was not [himself] dirty, accepting, in his quest for profit, unattractive collateral (*prendas indecorosas*), the ugly aspect of these establishments could be avoided along with the danger of contagion that these infernal caverns enclose."[2] Visitors to Mexico City during the reign of Porfirio Díaz (1876-1910) regularly commented on both the wonderful service provided by the Monte de Piedad and the seedy character of neighborhood pawnshops. Most commentators on collateral-credit practices emphasized the poor and illicit character of pawning, although—as Fanny noted—people of all classes benefited from temporarily hocking private possessions in the public world of commerce and charity. Indeed, as levels of consumption by individuals and within households kept pace with the modernizing and scientific emphasis of the Porfirian years, consumer credit continued to be an everyday need in proletarian neighborhoods and middle-class suburbs across the expanding city.

This chapter picks up the demand side of the collateral-credit story during the positivist liberal reign of Díaz. Drawing on inventories from casas de empeño and branch offices of the Monte de Piedad as well as extensive travel and memoir literature, fiction, and newspapers, it considers the degree to which the material culture of the city changed, including an increasing attention to household decoration; changing clothing fashions, with clothing itself losing collateral value; and the adaptation of modern appliances. Empeños and Monte branches in the city center and in new middle-class neighborhoods served a clientele who lived comfortably, while those on the outskirts lent against more humble collateral. The dynamics of housekeeping, especially the roles played by domestic servants and "commercial housekeepers" such as laundresses, seamstresses, and food vendors, continued to shape the material lives and public identities of the working class and an emergent middle class.[3] The chronic need for collateral lending continued among housekeepers despite political stability. The heralded liberal development of Porfirian capitalism did not alleviate pocketbooks of most city residents, though it did alter the gendered labor market somewhat. Long accustomed to shaping material life in the city, household women saw legal frameworks for and discourse about gender relations changing, while material goods that were "prime essentials of a well-arranged home . . . [placed] with the careful forethought of the housewife" also changed. Perhaps those who saw the least change were poorer women depending on collateral-credit services to provision families, the typical "unfortunate woman" of newspaper editorials turning to the Monte de Piedad branches or facing humiliation exacted by pawnbrokers in order to get more for her collateral, "representing all of her hopes."[4]

Liberalism and Domesticity

After a tumultuous fifty years of republican rule, Mexican politics settled down under the firm rule of Díaz, military hero of the resistance to the French intervention turned liberal statesman. Since the Reform of midcentury, liberal legislation had been expanding individual liberties, especially in economic terms. Protection of "private property" went further during the Porfiriato, with the amount of property in the hands of some individuals increasing substantially. As part of this protection, the double standard on adultery safeguarded the inheritance system based on legitimate heirs. Other changes in family law served to disinvest some women of means of their property.

The Civil Codes of 1870 and 1884 allowed couples to choose whether to marry under separate or community-property systems. The statesmen writing the 1870 Civil Code offered the separate-property regime as an improvement for the married woman, who could administer her own property and retain any interest it earned, as long as she renounced her half share of community property.[5] But for middle-class and elite married women, most of whom did not hold salaried jobs, foregoing a share of the husband's earnings might mean a less secure future than rights to dowry and inherited property had provided.[6] Changes in Civil Codes led to insecurity for daughters of propertied classes.[7] The testamentary freedom introduced in the 1884 Civil Code reveals tensions in patriarchal liberalism.[8] Testamentary freedom could mean that a widow, who in the past would have received half of the communal property when her husband died, might now inherit her husband's entire estate, improving her financial status at the expense of her children. Or a favorite daughter might inherit everything at the expense of other siblings. This may be the way in which some of the women who make up 68 percent of landlords in the city in 1910 acquired their property.[9] But the chances of empowering women through inheritance of entire estates depended on the good will of husbands and parents and certainly represented long odds.[10] The new property laws further restricted access to real property for some married women and for daughters. This, together with a doubling of the ranks of unmarried women over the years 1895–1910, meant that continued access to movable personal property, such as that used to outfit homes and wardrobes, became more important for women in the middle sectors managing daily household expenses or dealing with an exceptional time of financial distress.

In addition to reform of civil legal codes, the Porfiriato witnessed sustained economic development following a positivist emphasis on scientific rationality, hygiene, and technological advancement that changed the face of Mexico City. Intensified gendered ideologies about proper roles for men and women in modernizing Mexico proliferated in print media, while female economic participation expanded throughout different sectors. As had been true since the Bourbon-era state employed thousands of women rolling cigarettes, women were channeled into work supposedly "appropriate for their sex." For women of the working classes, this typically meant work in the textile sector, one of the first to industrialize and an alternative to the still dominant domestic-service sector. Women working for wages faced mixed messages about their economic roles. The positivist position glorified women in the domestic sphere, where they should provide a sanctuary for husbands from the public sphere or wage labor. *Científicos*, as positivist intellectuals were known, argued that women were biologically, spiritually, and socially different from men.[11] Despite the reality that many women were forced to work to meet family subsistence needs and that other women chose to work beyond the housekeeping labor required of them within their home, social-scientific ideology held that woman's role in society, based on her biological function, was that of a home-based caretaker and socializer of working men and children.[12]

Views on the role of women in a modernizing Mexico were found in a number of venues. A few female journalists promoted rights for women, among them Juana Gutiérrez de Mendoza, Dolores Jimenez y Muro, and Elisa Acuña y Rosette. Positivist academics such as Horacio Barreda taught the philosophy of gendered difference, cemented in a simultaneous practical submission by and spiritual elevation of women. The labor lawyer M. A. Sanz and elite Porfirian L. Josefina Reyes elaborated on the benefits of the domestic role of women for society in popular books.[13] Several women's periodicals circulated among elite and middle classes in the 1880s.[14] Much of the material in these publications promoted a cult of domesticity. In the first issue of a monthly published by Mariano de Jesús Torres entitled *La Mujer Mexicana*, with the subtitle "dedicated to the beautiful sex," articles celebrating famous virtuous women alternated with "useful recipes" for washing silk stockings and lace garments, diminishing freckles, and making fish croquettes. The next installment had a column expounding on the "sacred rights of women" to "always open their soul to purify hearts where evil has germinated, the right to console, to nurture, to love." The article urged a woman to exercise her "right to forget about herself, to live and die for that person which she loves, to beautify for them this material life with her smile and her love songs."[15] Women of a certain material level and education were the intended audience for this domesticity discourse.

Another article on "domestic accounting" provided as a "gift for our kind readers" a table for easy calculation of servant wages.[16] This recognition of the role of servants in maintaining middle-class homes reflects the fact that more females were still employed in domestic service in Mexico City than in any other sector. The census data clearly identify an economically active female population, especially in commercialized housekeeping roles. The press opined on the need to work among many mothers, wives, and daughters while lamenting their loss of gentility: "In the industrial cities, the woman works in the factories in order to feed her children, and she performs mechanical tasks throughout the day, leaving only the night for resting and for straightening the household and caring for the family . . . her health deteriorates, her strength breaks, she suffers until her customs are broken and she is degraded."[17] Work outside the home thus tainted innocent girls and women in public opinion, bringing them into illicit contact with men. This stigma was attached to occupations such as those of servants, laundresses, and seamstresses—jobs in which most women in fact worked—as well as the ultimate degradation of prostitution.[18] The choice to go out to work in public would have been more difficult in this ideological climate, but nonetheless it was a choice that many women made, while others had no choice but to work.[19] Indeed, a study of the 1882 municipal census for Mexico City found that married women were more active in the work force than single men, single women, or widows.[20]

For women of sufficient means to afford formal study, better paying work was available but limited. Graduation from secondary schools led to a career path in education, with female teachers concentrated in primary schools. The few women graduating from college after 1880 were channeled into gendered professional tracks. María Sandoval del Zarco, the first female lawyer, was restricted to civil law. In 1884 the weekly *La Familia* argued that it was necessary to improve education for women so that they could be more effective in society.[21] In 1897 positivist Jesús Galindo y Villa argued against education, because Mexican men do not need "a wife that can solve a mathematical problem or that can illustrate a historical thesis, but rather one who cares diligently for the domestic home . . . , that sacred mystery left to the woman to undertake as the tender and loving collaborator of the man." Galindo felt that education would make women less attractive, as any man who tried to be with her would be justly afraid that his wife was more educated than he, and "just imagine the situation of the husband perennially corrected by his companion." Galindo concurred with others of his generation that women should be educated only to the degree that the education of children was not left in the hands of "vulgar intelligence."[22]

Not all liberal statesmen supported limiting women's public activities. Genaro García felt that laws of his day regarding women violated the Constitution.[23] Despite a few proponents of expanding political rights to women, positivist opposition to female suffrage was firm, based in the idea of Herbert Spencer that women should not vote because they were too religious and impulsive.[24] While denied political rights, some Porfirian women nevertheless extended their gender roles into society, taking on reform projects of "conspicuous benevolence."[25] While educational and work opportunities opened up for some women under Porfirian liberalism, political rights were still a half century away.

By the end of Díaz's reign the ideological emphasis on women's domestic role was evident in statistics. In the past, while women hired as household servants dominated employment data, housewives were invisible to census takers. Women involved in "domestic chores" (*quehaceres domésticos*) were given a census category in the last of three Porfirian censuses, done in 1910, with 59 percent of adult women in the Federal District counted as being employed as housekeepers in their own homes. Many of these women likely were married and middle class. This sudden statistical inclusion of unpaid housekeeping has largely escaped analysis by historians. Scientific governance concerned with measuring production and work to maximize economic development and profit was carried into the household, where labors of women were recognized as a necessary component for modernization. Statistically including these women certainly fit the ideology of domesticity. If women were encouraged through print media and cultural pressures to devote themselves "diligently to the domestic home," why not reinforce discourse and positivist hegemony through the census process? Certainly, housekeepers continued to be charged with managing household budgets in the positivist era; in literary stories from the period, we see gentlemen's wives "waiting for these twenty pesos."[26] When wages and salaries were insufficient to finance their distinct standards of living, women running worker and white-collar households continued to rely on collateral credit.

The Demography and Economy of "Progress"

The much-heralded economic "progress" that went alongside political "order" in positivist governing ideology brought a population boom to Mexico City in the last decades of the nineteenth century. The city in which rich and poor had lived in close proximity was transformed into one with new neighborhoods settled by distinct classes: to the northeast and west proletarian neighborhoods such as Guerrero sprung up, while the middle class concentrated in Santa María de la Ribera to the northeast, and the wealthiest moved into new exclusive neighborhoods to the south of the Zócalo such as San Rafael, Cuauhtémoc, Juárez, and Roma.[27] By the first decade of the new century, all outlying suburbs and municipalities (except Xochimilco) were connected with the city center by electric trains.[28]

Census gathering in the positivist era tells us more about class and gender than ethnicity. There are no breakdowns by ethnicity in the published censuses. Presumably, much of the population was mestizo. While no doubt indigenous migration from the countryside picked up, only eleven thousand residents (with females and males about equal) were reported to speak a native language in 1910, about the only measure of indigenous ethnicity discernable in data. Generally, foreigners were twice as likely to be male as female. Most of the foreign residents were engaged in commercial endeavors.[29]

Census data reveal gendered patterns of property ownership and civil status that provide context for gauging housekeeping strategies. Females make up two-thirds of those who lived on rents paid by others living on their property, with the number of landlords overall almost doubling from 1895 to 1910.[30] How many owned valuable properties on which they earned sizable incomes, and how many owned humble dwellings or a store that they rented out for not very much? According to the census, these female landlords "lived off their rents." How many also lived off their movable property, converting goods into collateral loans when the rents were not sufficient for spending needs?

As seen in table 5.1, the Federal District population increased 54 percent in the last fifteen years of the Porfiriato. In 1895 there were nearly five times more widows than widowers, and there were four times as many widows in 1910. In both 1895 and 1910 there were more married men than married women. Perhaps the most remarkable statistic in this table is the doubling of the single adult population, both male and female, compared to only 11 percent increase in the married population. There are more females in widowed and unmarried populations in both censuses and more males than females in the minor and married populations.[31] In 1882 female household headship ranged from 14 to 25 percent depending on the neighborhood.[32] Later in the period, a significant number of women continued to live outside formal patriarchal authority, especially as population increased. In 1895, 60 percent of adult women did not have husbands; in 1910, 70 percent. Even if about half the single females were "hijas de família" and not out on their own or in informal unions, there would still have been 40 percent of adult women without patriarchs at home.[33]

Employment data reveal that the city underwent many changes. The white-collar and professional sectors grew, especially for women, as did the factory sector. Table 5.2 presents the population according to approximations of class using occupation as indicator. The city had a smaller middle sector and slightly larger popular sector compared to the national

TABLE 5.1

Population by Civil Status, Federal District, 1895 and 1910

	1895			1910		
	Female	Male	Total	Female	Male	Total
Minors[a]	65,902	70,760	136,662	97,575	103,424	200,999
Single	75,542	70,333	145,875	153,380	143,821	297,201
Married	70,886	72,015	142,901	79,245	79,688	158,933
Widowed	33,186	8,527	41,713	44,092	10,158	54,250
Unknown	836	718	1,554	4,903	4,467	9,370
Total	246,352	222,353	468,705	379,195	341,588	720,753

Source: México, Ministerio de Fomento, Dirección General de Estadistica, *Censo general de la Republica Mexicana verificado el 20 de octubre de 1895: Censo del Distrito Federal* (México: Oficina Tip. de la Secretaria de Fomento, 1898); México, Secretaria de Agricultura y Fomento, Dirección de Estadistica, *Tercer censo de población de los Estados Unidos Mexicanos: Verificado el 27 de octubre de 1910*, vol. 3 (México: Departamento de Aprovisionamientos Generales, 1918), 4–5.

[a] Comparing the numbers by age group with the total for "minors" suggests the age of majority was 15 years of age. For 1910, 244,284 individuals between the ages of 0 and 15 are listed. The discrepancy with the "minor" civil status likely means that some under 15 were married.

pattern for 1895.[34] The overall population of the Federal District grew 54 percent, from over 450,000 in 1895 to over 700,000 in 1910.[35] The adult population in the Federal District increased by 41 percent from 1895 to 1910, and the percentage of the employed population engaged in middle-class occupations increased over fifteen years almost to the same degree that the percentage of those in the working class decreased (6 percent and 5 percent respectively).[36] While females were a minority of those with white-collar jobs, the percentage of employed females in middle-class jobs increased much faster (46 percent more) relative to employed males in that sector (27 percent more). Almost twice as many males as females were employed in working-class occupations throughout the period, but the percentage of women increased by 11 percent, while the percentage of men decreased by 14 percent. Some of these industrial workers were children. After 1907 children seven years old and older could work in factories with parental permission.

Industrial growth in the second half of the nineteenth century, especially during the Porfiriato, displaced many artisans while expanding white-collar jobs.[37] The wages of men and women working in factories were generally higher than they were for other employment sectors, but were

TABLE 5.2

Distribution of Middle-Class and Working-Class Occupations, Federal District Censuses, 1895 and 1910

	Middle-Class Occupations[a]						Working-Class Occupations[a]					
	1895			1910			1895			1910		
Municipality	Female	Male	Total	Female	Male	Total	Female	Male	Total	Female	Male	Total
Mexico City	9,033	36,081	46,039	20,142	59,666	79,808	47,734	72,423	120,157	59,598	85,528	145,126
Atzcapotzalco				396	1,025	1,421				702	3,412	4,114
Coyoacán				195	963	1,158				828	2,862	3,690
Cuajimalpa					26	132	158			43	1,398	1,441
Gpe. Hidalgo	226	1,021	1,247	602	1,574	2,176	852	3,949	4,801	1,087	3,712	4,799
Ixtapalapa				178	656	834				492	6,813	7,305
Mixcoac				635	1,647	2,282				1,786	4,339	6,125
Milpa Alta				248	510	758				702	4,313	5,015
San Angel				212	662	874				919	4,504	5,423
Tacubaya	563	2,658	3,221	1,309	3,424	4,733	2,506	6,810	9,316	4,188	6,565	10,753

Tacuba				800	2,800	3,600				2,564	7,619	10,183
Tlálpan	36	1,598	1,962	143	979	1,122	1,390	12,336	13,726	688	4,179	4,867
Xóchimilco	113	951	1,064	237	841	1,078	513	11,218	11,731	275	8,546	8,821
Total	10,299	42,309	53,533	25,123	74,879	100,002	52,995	106,736	159,731	73,872	143,790	217,662
% of Adults[b]	6	28	16	11	32	22	30	71	49	27	61	47
% of Employed[c]	13	29	24	24	33	30	65	73	70	72	63	65

Source: Censo general . . . 1895; *Tercer censo*, tomo 2, 387–428.

[a] See appendix 3, tables I-L, for categories of middle-class occupations: commerce, public administration/police/military officers, and professionals; and categories of working-class occupations: agriculture/mining/fishing, petty commerce, artisan/crafts, factory work, and service sector.

[b] Female adults 1895: 177,317. Male adults 1895: 150,593. Total adults 1895 in Federal District: 327,910. Female adults 1910: 277,436. Male adults 1910: 235,047. Total adults in Federal District 1910: 462,483. This calculation does not include categories "escolares," "estudiantes," or "sin ocupación por menores de edad." It does include women employed in unpaid "quehaceres domésticos" for 1910 (150,998), adult unemployed, and unknown occupation.

[c] Females employed 1895: 81,474. Males employed 1895: 145,673. Total employed 1895: 227,147. Females employed 1910: 103,027. Males employed 1910: 229,667. Total employed 1910: 332,694. This calculation does not include categories "escolares," "estudiantes," "sin ocupacion por menores de edad," unpaid "quehaceres domésticos" (1910 only), or adult unemployed. It does include unknown occupation.

eroded by fines for broken machinery, arriving late, or "disorderly" behavior.[38] Other artisans in the Federal District joined the already large numbers of domestic servants and others paid for providing services as employment surged 31 percent in the service sector, from over 60,500 in 1895 to about 79,000 in 1910. Females increasingly dominated services, representing 61 percent of those so employed in 1895 and 67 percent in 1910 (compare appendix 3, table K, with appendix 3, table L).

Reports on what working people earned in the city toward the end of the nineteenth century are conflicting. A worker newspaper claimed that factory workers in 1894 were lucky if they earned five pesos a week. In contrast Charles F. Lummis, an American visitor, reported in 1899: "The average Mexican workman gets about three bits [thirty-seven and a half cents] a day. On the haciendas it is often less; in the factories and on the railroads it is generally more."[39] A list of daily wages from an 1896 study by Matías Romero spans from fifty centavos for a seamstress to five pesos for mechanics.[40]

Despite economic growth, worker living conditions deteriorated in the last Porfirian decades while prices climbed. Throughout the Porfiriato years, at least twice the daily wage was needed to maintain a family of four. Most households with only one wage earner depended on a male head of household, though many others were headed by females, whose wages were generally lower. In a short story from 1883, Gutierrez Najera depicted the political economy of a young newspaper vendor. When sales were slow, the boy was afraid to return home to his mother because he had not even one centavo in his pocket, afraid "because he did not want to afflict his mother." The author ruminates with the boy on what he and his mother would do with just one peso, an amount he had never had all at once: manta for his sister to make a shirt ("The poor little one complains so much about being cold!"), breakfast for one centavo, a tamale with *atole de chocolate* for another centavo and a half, another centavo for a glass of tequila for the mother, one centavo for a lottery ticket, various centavos to pay his mother's debts at the bakery and the corner store.[41] In 1885 twenty-five centavos daily would provide food and drink for a single laborer. Single-room dwellings rented for one to five pesos monthly, and the annual cost for men's clothing was five pesos. At these prices a wage of a peso a day would be needed "just to eat and pay rent," much less pay for clothing or other regular expenses such as transportation costs.[42] Though modern streetcar lines were increasingly another option, getting around in the city in the 1880s was still done by carriage if one could afford it, with hires costing between fifty centavos and one peso an hour depending on the class of the line.[43]

For 1903 the salary average was thirty-eight centavos a day in the countryside, which pushed many to cities; at the same time urban wages were kept artificially low by a steadily growing labor pool.[44] Increasing inflation exacerbated low wages to produce a marked deterioration for working-class households after 1900. Domestic inflation averaged 0.7 percent a year in the 1890s and 4 percent a year for the decade 1900–1910.[45] The plight of many worker households was difficult, as they faced frequent illness and scarcities of food, medicine, clothing, and fuel. To mitigate the impact of development on the lower classes, the Díaz regime maintained a network of charitable institutions, public and private, including a public dormitory that in 1898 served more than eighty thousand people, public baths, and laundries. But monetary reforms during an economic depression in 1905 meant the buying power of both workers' wages and middle-class *empleados'* (white-collar employees') salaries decreased, with an estimated 200 percent increase in the cost of living. Lenders—often men and women who supervised workers—operated inside factories and large artisan shops at the end of the century, charging between 5 and 25 percent interest weekly.[46] As an alternative, those with available collateral continued to turn to pawnshops, where interest could be comparable but was generally lower than the high end of interest charged by workplace moneylenders. As seen in novels depicting daily life in the changing Porfirian city, "the firm conviction that mothers had to mortgage life in favor of her offspring" played out in the hocking of everyday goods to meet everyday needs. Women continued to be the typical pawning clients portrayed in newspaper editorials—"las victimas" of both greedy brokers and inefficient employees of the Monte de Piedad, regularly "mortgaging" goods for cash.[47]

The urban lower classes were long defined by interrelated constructions of Creole, mestizo, or indigenous ethnic identity and life-style. Increasingly, economic means became more important in determining middle status. By the early twentieth century this middling sector had a clearer class identity, wielded collectively through associational activities such as those of the National Center for Business Employees, which celebrated its anniversary in June 1906 with an event in the Renaissance Theater with music, drama, speeches, and poems.[48] While business sectors absorbed some of the growing professional class, it was work in the public sector—"empleomanía"—that was the bastion of "Porfirian peace" as the politically inclined were incorporated into government in the early years of the regime.[49] Over the thirty-odd-year rule of Díaz, however, new talent from the growing middle class was increasingly shut out, and many came to resent what liberal critic Andrés Molina Enríquez called "a minority of new Creoles closely tied to foreign interests" who came to dominate government ministries.[50]

Novels such as Rafael Delgado's *Los parientes ricos* and *Angelina* portrayed both the expanding middle class and the slide of some down the economic ladder. In the first novel Doña Dolores Collantes, widow of an old liberal, struggles to support her five children at a level commensurate with her social connections and reputation while watching the ascent of opportunistic family members in the commercial Porfirian world.[51] In *Angelina* spinster daughters of a military hero can no longer count on his pension, because "the government says they are not in the position to pay." The elderly sisters slowly sell off their inheritance and work at multiple home-based jobs. They take in sewing, make food to sell, roll cigarettes at home, make artificial flowers, and "give reading and catechism lessons to a group of twenty children," all so that their orphaned nephew can continue to study at the university in Mexico City.[52] The white-collar jobs at the entry level for those just out of college paid little. Delgado reflected on the limits of education in terms of guaranteeing sufficient income to live a middle-class life-style. Quintin Porras, the provincial scribe in *Angelina*, laments that there is "little future for the youth" in late nineteenth-century Mexico: "Twenty pesos a month, do you think one can live on this? . . . Would this be enough for food, clothing, housing, and family necessities? No, clearly not! This twenty pesos, or fifteen, or ten, or less that some will earn . . . is not enough to buy a pair of boots, much less the luxury of ties."[53] For a rising office clerk, however, the tie would have been a necessity, not a luxury.

Many in the middle class continued to rent lodgings, with home ownership still not a hallmark of middle-class status. Fanny Gooch Chambers thought middle-class housing in Mexico City was expensive in the mid-1880s: inside apartments upstairs in casas de vecindad with five rooms facing the courtyard rented for forty pesos a month; those with windows facing the street rented for sixty to eighty pesos a month, depending on location. Fanny noted, "Many well-to-do families occupy apartments over business houses, and sometimes over pulque shops."[54] By the turn of the twentieth century, many neighborhood business owners moved out "into a larger and more comfortable apartment or home."[55] By the crisis years

1905–10, rents for middle-class dwellings had doubled and tripled, and rising prices for middle-class subsistence articles such as meat and rice outpaced more slowly rising salaries.[56] For those who could afford to rent a single-family home instead of rooms in a casa de vecindad, Motts reports large houses with "three or four bedrooms, living room, dining room, kitchen, bath and patio" in middle-class neighborhoods going for between twenty-five and sixty pesos monthly at the turn of the century. For those able to purchase their own modest middle-class home, it would set them back two thousand to four thousand five hundred pesos, depending on address and construction.[57]

While material circumstances improved generally for the middle class in the first decades of Díaz's rule, including their commute to work in downtown offices and their concentration in posh outlying neighborhoods, the cumulative effects of falling domestic demand and crisis in international markets after 1900 led to decreased exports from Mexico after 1905. This hit the professional classes in the city as well as the working class, especially during 1907–8. Bank reform limited middle-class access to credit. Novelists highlighted low salaries of entry-level middle-class *empleados*, such that "the mother and sisters of the poor *meritorio* work in order to clothe the young man."[58] The official press commented on the "inability of the middle class to save" in 1900 due to low salaries compared to high costs of living. The editors of *El Imparcial* counseled middle-class families to adjust their spending to their incomes and even to send their women out to work.[59] While by the end of the period most women were employed in domestic activities in their own or someone else's home, a growing number of women were moving into middle-class jobs such as teaching, public administration, and nursing (see appendix 3, table N).

While a tight economy, especially after 1905, meant that some middle-class households could no longer afford domestic staffs, this impact was not uniform, as municipalities in the Federal District with the largest number of domestic servants in 1910 (Mexico, Tacubaya, Tacuba, and Mixcoac, in that order) also had the most people in middle-class occupations. Guadalupe Hidalgo was the next municipality in terms of middle class, only slightly smaller than Mixcoac. The servant class of Guadalupe Hidalgo was about half the size of that of Mixcoac, however, while the number of women listed as employed in "domestic chores" at home in Guadalupe Hidalgo was 30 percent higher than in Mixcoac. Guadalupe Hidalgo and Mixcoac's commercial middle classes were about the same size, whereas

Guadalupe Hidalgo had almost three times as many people employed in government service as Mixcoac, and conversely, Mixcoac had a bigger private professional class than Guadalupe Hidalgo (see appendix 3, table J). Thus, professionals employed in private firms—a group more likely to include women, who would therefore need replacements for housekeeping services at home—were more likely than government employees, a sector overwhelmingly male, to have paid domestic staffs.

Increasing *numbers* of females went to work over the fifteen years covered by the censuses, though the *percentage* of adult females they represented decreased over the long term, while the percentage of females among all working adults remained about the same. More than half of adult females (54 percent) living in the Federal District were identified as employed, 45 percent for Mexico City (see appendix 3, table M).[60] Although employment statistics regarding women are problematic—they undercount those employed in multiple part-time jobs and those whose work outside the home was made invisible by concerns about honor and respectability—we can nonetheless gauge some changes in gendered work. In the 1910 count, different from 1895, the percentages of working women were slightly higher for Mexico City than for the Federal District as a whole: a little over 83,000 women represented 33 percent of the adult paid work force for the city, but about 103,000 in the Federal District represented only 31 percent. Some women stayed out of paid employment, perhaps reflecting the power of domesticity discourse, with 44 percent of adult women working beyond housekeeping in their own home, a 10 percent reduction from fifteen years earlier. For the Federal District as a whole, 37 percent of the adult female population worked for pay. While the structure of categories changed somewhat from 1895 to 1910, females still dominated certain sectors and were virtually absent from others (see appendix 3, table N). The 1910 "Domestic Work" category, which includes housewives and servants, was 93 percent female for Mexico City. Females made up 64 percent of those counted in "Clothing Manufacture and Toilette" (with nearly 6,000 laundresses, more than 7,000 seamstresses, and 2,000 modistes). Seamstresses had their own mutual-aid society, the Sociedad Fraternal de Costureras.[61] Surprisingly, females were only 35 percent of those recorded in the "Food Industry." While females still made up all tortilla makers and corn grinders, they were barely represented among bakers, biscuit makers, and cigar makers (females had dominated the last job a century earlier).[62] In the commercial sector females continued to constitute 26 percent, while their presence in "Arts and Sciences" was 37 percent, dominating instructor, actor, singer, and typist jobs. Two-thirds of telegraph operators in "Communications" were female but none of the electricians in "Miscellaneous." In other professional areas females made up 30 percent of the medical sector, monopolizing midwifery and nursing. There were fewer female clerks and public administrators and only one female attorney. As for craft categories, only a quarter of those in textiles were female (all embroiderers and most spinners), with barely a female presence among furniture makers, book binders, or those working with chemicals (virtually no soap makers or dyers, more matchmakers and wax makers). Finally, a third of the 1910 "Other Industrial" category—presumably factory workers —was female.

There are more people employed in domestic service than in any other single category, the vast majority female. Just as their presence was assumed in middle-class women's publications, servants are ever present in traveler descriptions of Mexican middle- and upper-class homes. House servants were featured on postcards travelers could send home chronicling their visit, as seen in figure 5. Fanny Gooch Chambers commented that poor relations "in many instances fill the places of housekeeper or upper servants." Formerly wealthy families who did not prosper in the new commercialized economy might still count on loyal servants, though fewer in number. This was the case for the downwardly mobile family in *Los parientes ricos*, whose maid, Filomena, stays with the family even when they can no longer pay her. Mrs. Alec Tweedie was surprised at the number of men employed in domestic service when she visited the city in 1900, and she observed that "domestics do not live luxuriously: they exist on tortillas and hot sauces, and generally sleep rolled up in a blanket on the floor."[63] In the 1890s servants reportedly received from four to twenty pesos monthly, depending on responsibilities and gender, plus a daily allowance for food and incidentals of up to twenty centavos. For the early 1900s Motts reports female servants earning from six to ten pesos monthly plus a twenty-five-centavo allowance.[64]

Table 5.3 compares the housekeeping population over the fifteen years between the 1895 and 1910 censuses. The 1895 portion represents a narrower measure of housekeeping than do the 1910 data, as 1895 census takers did not count women primarily occupied in housekeeping in their own homes.[65] For both 1895 and 1910, not all women who might be construed as engaged in housekeeping—given the broad conceptualization

Fig. 5. "Camarera Mexicana." Courtesy of the Latin American Library, Tulane University, Postcard Album (#6) of Mexican Views.

used throughout this book—are accounted for in table 5.3. Women selling food in the street that they prepared at home or on the spot sustained their customers much as housewives maintained their family or live-in cooks their employers.[66] Some males were employed as domestics as Mrs. Tweedie noted, but females dominated this sector. It was still common for those in the middle class to employ only one or two domestic servants, while those who could afford it would have a large domestic staff. In 1900 the majority of domestic servants were indigenous and mestiza women recently arrived from the countryside.[67]

In table 5.3 most striking is the sudden presence of women doing housekeeping work in their own homes in 1910. Interestingly, there were almost twice as many women listed as occupied in "quehaceres domésticos" as there were married women (see table 5.1 above). Even adding widows, perhaps more likely to head their own households than single women, there are still about 20 percent more unpaid housekeepers than there are wives and former wives. Some of these women likely lived with a wage-earning consort, friend, adult relative, or child. For those heading households and for wives, conversion of their work tools—household goods—into collateral was indispensable to their livelihood and that of their dependents.

Only counting females in table 5.3 who were paid to do housekeeping, there is a slight 6 percent increase in the percentage of employed females engaged in the domestic sector over fifteen years, while the actual number of individual females working in paid domestic work increased about 45 percent, slower than the rate at which population increased (54 percent). Do these statistics reflect that more women needing to work for wages were finding work in other sectors? Or was there a decrease in demand for servants as middle-class households' budgets dealt with high inflation? Looking at the commercial laundering sector, it remained overwhelmingly female and grew a moderate 20 percent from 1895 to 1910. Perhaps more care of clothing was done in house than farmed out to neighborhood washerwomen as costs of living outstripped incomes. There was also increased competition from Chinese laundering businesses.[68] Then again, the marked increase in single men by 1910 likely translated into more demand for washerwomen like those pictured in figure 6, a circa 1908 postcard of laundresses at work. The gendered structure of the housekeeping work force, as well as the labor market and class structure in general, shaped material life and everyday credit patterns of working- and middle-class households in the positivist era.

TABLE 5.3

Housekeeping in the Federal District, 1895 and 1910 Census

	Maids/Servants			Porteros[a]			"Quehaceres domésticos"	Washing/Ironing		
	Female	Male	Total	Female	Male	Total	Female	Female	Male	Total
1895										
Mexico City	25,129	8,883	34,012	1,431	994	2,425		5,673	112	5,786
Gpe. Hidalgo	618	198	816	1		1		72	3	75
Tacubaya	1,754	563	2,317	28	2	52		253	10	263
Tlálpan	1,044	340	1,384	5	10	15		117	16	133
Xóchimilco	737	354	737					63		63
Total	28,928	10,338	39,266	1,464	1,029	2,493		6,178	141	6,319
1910										
Mexico City	33,514	8,624	42,138	1,752	966	2,718	89,346	5,982	653	6,635
Atzcapotzalco	593	117	710	4	8	12	3,844	38		38
Coyoacán	591	160	751	4	6	10	3,249	59	8	67
Cuajimalpa	41	20	61				1,564	1		1
Gpe. Hidalgo	783	155	938	17	8	15	4,750	108	1	109

Ixtapalapa	289	66	355				6,846	26		26
Mixcoac	1,419	329	1,748	13	3	26	3,071	117	12	129
Milpa Alta	181	150	331				4,229	52	4	56
San Angel	535	123	658	4	7	11	4,394			
Tacubaya	2,982	549	3,531	58	22	80	7,399	419	19	438
Tacuba	1,864	531	2,395	25	19	44	9,604	306	9	315
Tlálpan	432	195	627	3	4	7	3,997	57		57
Xóchimilco	202	118	320	3		3	8,705	40	6	46
Total	43,426	11,137	54,563	1,883	1,043	2,926	150,998	7,166	751	7,917

Employed population paid for housekeeping (i.e., excluding "quehaceres dómesticos"):

	Female (%)	Male (%)	Total (%)
1895	45	8	21
1910	51	6	20

Source: Censo general . . . 1895, 62–64; *Tercer censo*, vol. 2, 387–428.

[a] These "doorpersons" likely include those employed on the domestic staff of elite homes and also the equivalent of the "casera" from the nineteenth century, in charge of opening and closing the door of tenements and rooming houses in the downtown neighborhoods.

Fig. 6. "Las Lavanderas." Courtesy of the Latin American Library, Tulane University, Postcard Album (#6) of Mexican Views.

Porfirian Pawning Scenarios

Generally ignoring consumption motives beyond basic survival, Mexican and foreign writers returned to themes of collateral credit for subsistence or vice again and again, though more "positive" motives such as financing artisanal production or special occasions also appear. Successive wives of the carpenter protagonist in Manuel Payno's *Bandidos del Río Frío* pawned clothing from one day to the next to purchase fixings for dinner. But he also pawned his poncho to finance his marriage and to buy tools at a Spanish-owned pawnshop. While working on a particularly intricate piece, work that lasted a year, he and his wife pawned everything valuable they owned until the piece was finished and ready for sale. After pawning a silver saber he had inherited, they were able to redeem most of their possessions from pawnshops, only to repawn the poncho, handkerchiefs, and underskirts again when sale of the prize furniture piece was delayed. This cycle of pawning, redeeming, and repawning was repeated four times before the piece sold.[69]

One of the only authors to explicitly tie collateral credit to middle-class livelihood is Angel del Campo. His 1894 "Una corista" is the story of Doña María, inflicted with rheumatism and no longer able to sew. She "lost the White sewing machine in the Pawnshop and I ask myself what she must be asking herself: and now where will she get the means to feed these four mouths . . . her children? This was an afflictive problem, difficult to resolve for a widow without opportunity in this country in which the conquest of bread, for women, is almost impossible."[70] In another Del Campo story the educated but unemployed Castroverde, from a middle-class family, hopes that with the salary from a business office job he can "extend the pawn tickets, eat, live, sleep, and above all, free my house of this sad seal, my poor wife, my daughters." He does not get the job, because he does not have sufficient skills in English and French. Yet the family does not miss a meal, as "there was a slow moving of furniture to the Pawnshop." They held onto five chairs, a commode, half an armoire, a table, beds, two dressers, dishes, pots, and pans. Despite their relative poverty, "the family had not forgotten their origins; they kept the memory alive of their grandparents' tradition [*abolengo*] and did not fall into the habits of the ordinary neighborhood nor adopt the customs of the 'gente sin verguenza y sin blanca' [shameless and nonwhite people]." Indeed, this family's way out of poverty and back up the socioeconomic ladder was through careful protection of their daughters' virtue and successful marketing of one of them, who married a wealthy man, "ugly, but with a good heart." Recovering their heirlooms and with additions brought by the son-in-law, "the Castroverde couple returned to the heights of distinction."[71]

The most frequent image in newspapers continued traditional discourse about pawning women "satisfying an urgent need" and the Monte de Piedad's mission as guaranteeing that "those who [are] in moments of anguish can be sure of alleviating it with the protection of the charitable establishment."[72] Sometimes journalists went further, using pawning as a vehicle to explore Mexican culture at large. In an 1887 front-page editorial decrying abusive pawnbrokers, *El Monitor Republicano* lamented that brokers preyed on bad habits of the Mexican poor: "In the majority of cases, the majority we said, not in all of them, pawning maintains—even makes robust—the bad habit of wasting money among the proletarian class. In effect, since it is known that the habit of saving money is unknown among even those of us good Mexicans, those that believe that tomorrow they can escape their urgencies sending a collateral good to the pawnshop spend excessively with greater ease." The editors surmised that urban diversions—great bullfights, festivals, visits to the Virgin of Guadalupe shrine in La Villa—prodigiously increased loan operations in pawnshops. "The people pawn to go out and enjoy themselves, not to calm some supreme necessity. . . . This forms part of our national character." In this vein reform of private pawning businesses, even eliminating them, was touted as a way to "moralize a great part of the poor and unprotected classes [*clases desvalidas*], turning them into useful citizens," which vice through pawning prevented.[73]

The discursive imagery of pawning continued to emphasize pawning for vices, echoing Viceroy Revillagigedo. In the early 1880s American traveler Frederick Ober believed the majority of pawnbrokers were "in league with thieves and pickpockets." According to Mrs. Tweedie, "A man will go out and pawn his coat for this drink [*pulque*], return and pawn his hat or knife, anything and everything, in order to obtain the soddening liquid." Later she comments that doormats "are chained to the floor," seats "are secured to the counter," and ink bottles in the post office are "sunk down into the tables so that they cannot possibly be removed. . . . Everything is done to try and prevent theft; yet innumerable pawn-shops groan beneath the weight of ill-gotten property, kodaks, opera glasses, and endless articles stolen from houses as well as travelers' trunks." She described an English servant traveling with his master who despaired at his inability to hold onto his sponges and currycombs: "Lor', sir, these people would pawn their own mother, and steal the teeth out of their sweetheart's head."[74] This association of pawning with fencing was continually conjured. The belief that fencing stolen goods was central to the pawning process continued to work against those who had come by their few valuable collateral goods honestly. A satirical poem published as the Porfiriato came to an end lamented that customers had to put up with such poor treatment by pawnbrokers who lent little dearly and who suspected that any valuable collateral was stolen:

Por cada objeto;	For each object
(No son habladas,)	(Which are not said aloud,)
Prestan peseta,	They lend a peseta
Tostón o nada;	*tostón or nothing*;
Para que un *duro*	In order for *a full peso*
Salga de casa,	To leave the business,
Se necesita	It is necessary
Que avaluada,	that the appraisal
Esté la prenda	Of the collateral
Por *cien* del águila;	Is for *one hundred* of the eagle [i.e., 100 pesos];
De otra manera,	Otherwise,

Insultan, hablan,	They insult, talk,
Y a los *marchantes*	And to the *male customers*
Y a las *marchantas*,	And to the *female customers*,
Les dicen cosas	They say things
Que hay que escucharlas	That one has to hear to believe
'*Refotre* chica,	"*Forget it* girl,
'No vale nada	That little watch
'El relojillo;	Is not worth anything;
'Lárgate a casa,	Get away, go home
'Y dile luego	And later on
'Allí a tu ama,	Tell your employer
'Que venga ella	That she should come
'Para empeñarla.'	To pawn it."[75]

Sending servants to do family pawning was still a common enough occurrence that one could pretend to be on such an errand when trying to fence stolen goods. In the poem the broker assumes the watch must be stolen. If the woman with the watch was in truth a servant on an errand or if the watch was actually hers, she not only walked away empty handed but had to deal with the pawnbroker's abusive attitude.

The poor did not have a monopoly on dishonest pawning. Ober reported: "An American dealer in hardware told me that he lost more through the pawn-shops than in any other way; for young men, of apparent respectability, have repeatedly bought revolvers, knives, etc. of him on credit, and had them in pawn-shops before the day had closed." This questionable practice was done "in order that the Mexican fop may keep up appearances." Middle-class people maintained the level of consumption commensurate with their status through credit secured with collateral that was also bought on credit, the equivalent of paying on one credit card with another today. Del Campo's story "El heredero" talks about a boy who inherits from a wealthy relative, only to sell off most of the estate and then turn to "pawning the crown, pen and watch of his father" to keep up his life of drinking and women.[76]

Another pathological reason for pawning with a hallowed place in lore is gambling. Witness this *El Monitor Republicano* editorial: "How many times, how many, [everything] down to the last shirt is pawned to go to the games. It is for this reason that so many pawning businesses are located right next door to gambling houses, in direct violation of the law." Mrs. Tweedie noted that it was not just the poor who gambled away money meant for other things. She described brisk business in casinos frequented by middle and upper classes: "See the bales groaning under the weight of silver dollars. One thousand pounds in silver is upon each of those tables, and more in the bank if needed. Men and, alas, sometimes women, with their books and their systems, will sit there all night." When a man loses after "another flirtation with Dame Fortune, . . . he must not pawn his things in the [casino] rooms, the law forbids that." While surely these well-off gamblers could find a pawning venue, it is the poor's gambling that Mrs. Tweedie explicitly connects with pawning: "Look at the religious feast of Guadalupe with its pilgrims, who pray on one side and gamble away their last cents on the other, and then pawn their blankets or hats in order to obtain more to fling away in like manner."[77]

Whatever motives led people to seek collateral credit, supply and demand for pawning outlets continued unabated.[78] *El Obrero Mexicano* noted in 1894 that "day by day the *casas de empeño* are full of individuals of all classes, most notable among them the proletarian who resorts to seeking a miserable loan backed by some good he leaves, only to be charged a high fee later."[79] But among the "individuals of all classes" were middle-class residents, who not only turned to the Monte de Piedad but also to the private pawnbrokers. During the Porfiriato the Monte expanded its services with more branch offices.[80] Ober described the Monte de Piedad as "the most beneficent institution in Mexico—[and] in the world" and its clientele as "poor people and worthy members of the shabby-genteel class, whose ancestors were once wealthy, and left them money which they have squandered and property they fain would realize upon."[81] Journalists disagreed in part with Ober, arguing that the poor were still not served by the charitable institution. Even though the Porfirian Monte charged 12 percent annual interest, much less than the more than 50 percent or more charged in casas de empeño, journalists noted that the poor continued to prefer the private pawnbrokers over Monte branches. The service in the latter was slow and the hours were restricted. In 1887 *El Monitor Republicano* called attention to the "disorder that poor people face" in Monte branches: "Not only is it difficult to even get to those who loan the money, but the quantities lent are scandalously insignificant. . . . The people pile up, push, scream, it is a mob scene [*batahola*]. And they only lend money for two hours [a day]."[82]

In a period of rising consumerism, it may be that visiting the pawnbroker and the Monte de Piedad became more of an issue for the rising middle class. In other settings than Mexico, public knowledge of the need for collateral credit could damage one's reputation, and euphemisms for the pawning process hid a family's need. Did "respectable" citizens in Mexico City try to disguise their participation in collateral-credit operations? Some patrons at the Monte de Piedad in the late 1870s gave fake names.[83] In *Bandidos del Río Frío* a count frequently asked his wife for jewels "which he promised to show to a friend," and she never saw them again.[84] Hidden, anonymous, or just ignored by society at large, the reality of middle-class credit needs was recognized by some. None other than Porfirio Díaz himself chastised the middle-class proclivity "to rise from bed late, to be public employees with influential godfathers, to arrive at work at any hour, to feign illness frequently and receive paid leaves, to never miss a bullfight . . . to marry young and have children in excess, to spend more than they earn, and enslave themselves to usurers to pay for their parties and social gatherings."[85]

Judging from the Porfirian portion of the collateral sample, casas de empeño downtown on Estampa de Jesús María and on Leguisamo Bridge in 1902 catered to clients with a higher material base than those farther from the center of town on Verónica. Acquiring the tandem bicycle left with broker Leon Alvarez for a loan of fifteen pesos or the typewriter securing a ten-peso loan would break the budget of a working-class household. The broken telephone that yielded a loan of three pesos, too, likely came from a middle-class home.[86] The gold watch pawned for forty-five pesos by "El Licenciado" at Venancio Dosal's pawnshop on Leguisamo bridge indicates a certain comfort level. Alvarez's shop on Estampa de Jesús María was located a block behind the National Palace, and Leguisamo passed in front of the Casa de Moneda; maybe clients there included government employees working in those institutions, many now living in outlying suburbs such as Tacuba and Tacubaya. Also close to the Casa de Moneda, between the National School of Medicine and the National Preparatory School north of the cathedral, the Monte de Piedad branch on Relox saw a lending volume that approximated that of casas de empeño nearby.[87] Ober noted "the family gods of the country—rich garments, saddles, swords, gold ornaments, diamonds, pearls, and rubies—were collected" in the Zócalo branch of the charitable institution, indicating that the Monte continued to cater to the more well off, or as Ober put it, those who "were once wealthy."[88] In sum, at the beginning of the twentieth century there were still distinctions between pawning arenas and the clientele who visited them, though the pattern became more complicated. As with persistent images of desperate and pathological pawning clients, pawnshop shelves suggest continuity with earlier patterns. Poor and middling residents alike relied on loans that their household goods could secure to finance different levels of consumption. What changed was the nature of those goods.

"Quehaceres Domésticos" in Modernizing Households

The American Fanny Gooch Chambers and the English Mrs. Tweedie, like Fanny Calderón de la Barca before them, had little to say about working-class homes and much to say about wealthy and middle sectors of society and their consumption and entertainment preferences, this being the world in which they circulated. In the 1880s Gooch Chambers believed that the Mexican middle class was growing, as more humble folk every year were "making giant strides to a nobler place in life through the fine educational advantages now afforded them." Their "taste for ceremonious display and profusion is natural, and enters into all arrangements, whether of house, dress or equipage, being limited only by the means for its indulgence."[89] The establishment of new pawnshops in poor neighborhoods as well as in wealthier neighborhoods and the prevalence of household goods among collateral indicate that housekeepers secured at least some of the means for daily consumption expenses through pawning consumer goods acquired earlier. By the end of the century, department stores such as El Palacio de Hierro, El Puerto de Veracruz, El Puerto de Liverpool, and El Centro Mercantil provided imported and locally produced household and luxury goods to middle and upper classes. Street vendors continued to hawk vegetables, household goods, and notions, "which they sold to the women, embroidered strips, combs, little mirrors and other such things, at prices double and triple the warehouse price."[90] Middle-class growth in the last decades of the nineteenth century and the first of the twentieth coincided with rising consumerism. Consumption patterns changed: "Elite women no longer pulled up to the curb outside a textile shop while the shopkeeper brought bolts of silk to the carriage for her perusal. Middle- and upper-class women entered into shops and markets, hesitantly rubbing elbows with their fellow shoppers." White-collar workers anxious to consume but without the budget to do so turned to the Monte de Piedad and casas de empeño for cash loans, secured with previous purchases such as fancy clocks and bicycles.[91]

Mrs. Tweedie noted that "many families possess beautiful silver, glass and china, brought from Spain by their ancestors." The Englishwoman also observed that large, wealthy families gathered regularly for celebrations such as feast days, birthdays, "name days" and that on these frequent festive occasions, "big luncheons and dinners" were the fashion, with servants attending needs of the family as usual. When outsiders were included in gatherings in upper-crust homes, "entertainments were costly and well done."[92] This emphasis on fine dining was not limited to the wealthiest, as middling households had long displayed their position through display of their level of material comfort.

A comparison of pawnshop inventories from the late nineteenth century with those from earlier periods (see appendix 1, tables B, C, D, and F) shows that household goods overtook clothing as the most pawned category, with more household decoration items and modern amenities such as timepieces and electric fans. Yet it is clear from the Monte de Piedad, Montepío Luz Sáviñon, and empeño records that pawning cloth as a household finance strategy did not abate.[93] A pawnshop just off Alameda Park owned by Adela Noriega made over eight thousand loans a month, with loans averaging under a peso, mostly secured with cloth.[94]

The late Porfirian household goods for which we have details are represented in table 5.4. Relative to earlier periods, the numbers of silver plates and forks, knives, and spoons and other silver-service items decrease. There is a marked increase in ceramic tableware as well as a few metal plates, along with copper, plaque, and steel eating utensils. Some "loza" ceramic items were porcelain, or "china."[95] In inventories from 1902–3 ceramic pieces pawned for twenty-five centavos—the vast majority of earthenware in empeños—must have been inexpensive items made in local factories. How much of the family silver that so impressed Mrs. Tweedie rotated in and out of middle-class households in this period is not known, but silver likely continued to serve as collateral, though perhaps not now the favored investment, as the worldwide price for silver had declined.

Irons were still among items of household collateral, though not as many as in the 1860s to 1880s. The abundance of irons in the second half of the century reflects the accessibility of these domestic appliances to middle-class housewives and women among the working poor, including those providing commercialized laundering services. In a poem published in 1905 in *La Mujer Mexicana* by Mariano de Jesús Torres, the "lavandera de mi vida" (washerwoman of my life) heats up her iron beside a fire that puts color in her cheeks.[96] Tablecloths and napkins for the dining room also continued to be important collateral for loans. New in the table-service sample are metal napkin holders, fetching loans for a peso and a half. Bedroom linen continued to serve as collateral, with the size of the loan depending on the fabric and condition of sheets, bedspreads, and feather

TABLE 5.4

Household Goods in Pawn, 1902–9
(228 transactions out of 851, or 27%)

Category	Empeños 1902–9	Monte de Piedad 1902	Total
Table service	101	2	102
Household linens	44		44
Furnishings[a]	28		28
Whole fabric	23	1	24
Irons	11		11
Sewing utensils	2	5	7
Kitchen utensils	6		6
Fabric cut for clothing	5		5
Total	220	8	228

Source: AHCM, Gobierno del Distrito, Empeños, vol. 1422, exp. 5, f. 17 and exp. 38; Empeños Ventas, vol. 162, exps. 1, 7, 9, 14, 15, 16, 17, and 20.

Note: Totals by category include housekeeping goods that were bundled with clothing or jewelry, and therefore the totals are greater than those given in the breakdown in appendix 1, table D, which counts each transaction and not each individual good that might be in a bundle.

[a] Includes furniture, table clocks, lamps, heavy fans, electric appliances, a commode, and decorative accessories.

mattresses. How much of the over twenty thousand collateral goods classified as "ropa" reported by the new charitable Montepío Luz Saviñón and the Cartagena pawnshop in 1908–9 was whole cloth, cloth cut for clothing, or bed and table linens, and how much was finished clothing? Judging by earlier trends, perhaps about a quarter (as was the case in the 1787–1830 sample) to even a third (as in the 1868–80 sample) of the undifferentiated cloth goods constituted household linens (see appendix 1, table F). Among collateral differentiated in the sample, manta sheets pawned in outlying pawnshops in working-class neighborhoods yielded twenty-five centavos, while wool bedclothes could fetch four pesos in upper-scale pawnshops downtown. One observer reported in 1887 that for housewives, "Great care is bestowed on the marking of household linen, the husband's initials or monogram being exquisitely embroidered on each article." Likewise, "Great pains are taken in the execution of elaborate embroideries, laces, tatting and crochet for [bed] coverings, those with drawn threads being the most distinctively national."[97] Tablecloths and napkins, too, were ornamented through embroidering by family women. Embroidery likely enhanced the collateral value of linen; branding linens perhaps made it more likely that they would be recovered.

Describing the modern transformation of interiors of upper- and middle-class households, Mrs. Tweedie noted that although they contained "rare old Spanish furniture, bric-a-brac, pictures, things that have been in the family for generations, [m]ost of them, alas! are stowed away in the nurseries or servants' quarters, while modern French furniture appears in the best rooms." Noting that the same thing occurred in England, she opined that old furnishings—"countless treasures"—were more valuable than "all the modern wardrobes put together."[98] If furnishings needed to be stored for a long time, they might find their way into "varios objetos" rooms of the Monte de Piedad, as José Juan Tablada tells us in his memoirs: "What to do with the beloved family furniture, the heavy tables, profound scented wardrobes, brocaded living room sets, almond chandeliers, and table service imported from China? In Mexico where there are no warehouses to speak of, families in this position could only send their household furnishings to the Monte Pio, pawning them for insignificant amounts and thus securing their safe-keeping and conservation."[99] Among database goods with relatively high loan values and likely from middle-class housekeeping stock, a wardrobe cabinet (*armario*) yielded 150 pesos at the downtown pawnshop on Estampa de Jesus, and "half of an old tapestried furniture set" was pawned for twenty pesos at a casa de empeño on Veronica, northeast of the city center.

Chandeliers and light fixtures not only had utilitarian functions, but those made of porcelain and steel in elaborate styles also served as "an element of decorative ostentation," announcing prestige. Less ostentatious lighting was also common, such as the *quinqué* (gas lamp) with a green shade that illuminated the cloth-covered table where spinster aunts and their servant manufactured artificial flowers in Delgado's *Angelina*.[100] Household furnishings associated with electricity fetched loans from only a few pesos to ten pesos—an electric bell, "Casey" electric fans, telephones, a "maquina para escuchar" (a phonograph?), lamps, and accessories for light fixtures.

Other household goods that served as collateral in the first years of the twentieth century are commodes, chairs, table and alarm clocks, desks, and paintings.[101] Gooch Chambers remarked that living rooms early in the Porfiriato had an "unusual number of chairs" alongside sofas, with "occasions of reunion as their *raison d'etre*." Mrs. Tweedie noted, "Furniture

Fig. 7. "Cargadores." Courtesy of the Latin American Library, Tulane University, Postcard Album (#6) of Mexican Views.

removing is another strange performance; there are no vans, so everything has to be carried to its destination. Four men, each holding the end of a pole, trot along with a heavy wardrobe suspended therefrom, and as the streets are not over wide, and the traffic considerably congested by tram-cars, the width of a wardrobe passing along does not tend to make matters less difficult."[102] Indeed, the circa 1908 postcard in figure 7 renders much the same scene. Might any of those furnishings have served as loan collateral?

Sewing machines are not included among household goods in table 5.4, as their owners could be housekeepers and commercial sewers such as seamstresses and tailors. Cloth cut for sewing is included, however, as the high cost of tailored clothing meant that many middle- and lower-class women continued to engage in clothing construction at home, whether or not they had access to machines. In Gutierrez Najera's 1883 story about the counterfeit peso, when the coin is passed off to a newsboy, his most urgent concern is to buy manta "so that the little sister can make a shirt." In Delgado's 1893 novel *Angelina*, the book's namesake works for and takes care of two downwardly mobile spinster sisters, spending much of her time making and adorning dress shirts and handkerchiefs for their nephew Rodolfo.[103]

Clothing construction done by women within the home, as well as women's management of wardrobes generally, constitute housekeeping as social reproduction. *Angelina* gives us an idea of how this played out in Porfirian Mexico. On his way out for a walk, Aunt Pepa stops Rodolfo with "You're going out in that suit?" Disapproving of his dusty and listless clothing, she indicates a trunk: "No, wear something better. . . . Dress yourself; go out for a walk, so that you are seen." The problem, noted Rodolfo, was that with the aunts' waning fortune, "the trunk did not come well provisioned, there was not much in it with which to gussy myself up [*engalanarme*]." Not to be dissuaded from their job of grooming the nephew the best they could, Aunt Pepa and Angelina make do sufficiently for Pepa to exclaim, "That's it, that way, like a decent person!" with what Delgado refers to as "maternal satisfaction."[104] It was not just the downtrodden or downwardly mobile who wore homemade clothing. Mrs. Tweedie commented that even society girls made their own dresses. Motts remembers that "ladies magazines" were popular in the first decades of the twentieth century. Her description of *El Hogar* highlights the textile chores of relatively well-off housekeeping women: "In addition to the interesting articles, it included patterns for making diverse articles of clothing, figures and drawings to work up in cross-stitch, embroidery patterns in white, lace, and crochet and knitting."[105]

A 1902 issue of *La Mujer Mexicana* published a poem entitled "La Aguja" (The Needle), which associated home sewing with the full life cycle of a woman who by the end is downwardly mobile. First, her needle "runs" to finish linens for the bassinet for the baby she is expecting. In the next verse the woman and her needle "must hurry to finish a white dress" and "embroider the transparent veils," because "tomorrow the girls make their first communion." In the third verse the needle helps with the wedding dress for a daughter, "so that she will shine and enchant her spouse." And finally, the last verse finds the woman in dire straits, with cloudy eyesight, suffering parents, and a child crying with hunger. One last time she implores "run, my needle," because "we need bread for everyone tomorrow." This time, instead of something for a special occasion, woman and needle make something that can be converted into cash to feed the family. A few years later the same periodical published a "little manual for the seamstress" outlining the skills a seamstress should have: taking measurements, drawing patterns, cutting and knowing about quality fabric, as well as which fashion publications to subscribe to and where to find out about the latest fashions (for the theater and elegant gatherings such as award ceremonies). Some readers of this middle-class women's magazine one day might have found themselves, too, making a living sewing beyond the family.[106]

In the sample of pawned goods for 1902 and 1903, there are many pieces of fabric and clothing cut for sewing, although less than had been true at midcentury. Some of this collateral would not have come from household stock but instead from stock of tailors, modistes, and seamstresses. Tailors complained to the Federal District that their employees pawned unfinished materials regularly.[107]

Though no longer dominating pawnshop shelves, clothing continued to serve as collateral, especially in empeños. The Spaniard Sesto commented on pawning of "dirty clothes, above all," but also said that artisans' tools worth five pesos "are pawned for brusque necessities." While the database for the late Porfiriato lists few tools, there is plenty of cloth. A comparison of data for categories of goods pawned in empeños (see appendix 1, table E) over time reveals that 30 percent of collateral was cloth at the turn of the twentieth century, down from 54 percent in the 1860s and 1870s. Most of the clothing in 1902 transactions from two pawnshops on Veronica to the northeast of downtown was listed as "viejo" and secured loans from twelve centavos to two pesos. The two pawnshops on Estampa de Jesús and Leguisamo in the city center gave loans of from two to ten pesos for silk petticoats, rebozos "de bola," and wool dresses. Even though some clothing collateral was high quality, pawnbrokers faced accusations that "in their quest for profit" they accepted worthless and unsanitary clothing. Concern about infection from piles of clothing in pawnshops surfaced now and again in newspapers, and in 1904 *El Imparcial* reported a plan to disinfect pawnshops.[108]

With industrialization, the value of clothing decreased. At midcentury seamstresses still took "their best dresses to the pawnshop."[109] Handmade clothing saved innumerable housewives and widows in difficult moments throughout the nineteenth century. Due to "propagation of the black suits, ready-made clothing, [and] steady imports," clothing at the end of the century no longer had the same significance. Yet inventories and other evidence suggest that clothing made by hand had not passed completely out of fashion and continued to have collateral value. Indeed, for middle-class professionals, being among the clientele of tailors, modistes, and seamstresses was a status symbol.[110] Factory-produced clothing was less expensive but also less prestigious.

While the value of clothing diminished, some styles continued to be popular even as new ones became fashionable. Foreign travelers reported that the wealthiest Porfirian families displayed status through European clothing, though elite women still wore traditional mantillas to morning mass. Mrs. Tweedie noted "the small boys are dressed in Jack Tar suits [and] many of the men get their clothes from London, as their wives do from Paris."[111] Motts credits the preference of imported clothing among even the middle class to the low exchange rate relative to the dollar (two pesos to one dollar) and low tarriffs. Ober associated the domestic rebozo at the end of the nineteenth century with mestiza women. Middle-class women and their servants in stories by Delgado, Del Campo, and Payno are seldom without one. Into the 1950s the rebozo held on "despite the strong influence of Spanish and French fashions."[112] This continuity is evident in the collateral-goods database, with the same number of rebozos in the 1902–3 portion as in the sample from 1868–80. Petticoats were still worn as slips by some and as skirts by others, such as *lavanderas* whose "stiff petticoats sound like a hurricane" when they walked by, and they still appeared on pawnshop shelves in the early twentieth century.[113] But enaguas were replaced by watches as the most common collateral goods.

Of clothing items in the data that we can identify with a gender, 70 percent of them are female items. Clothing belonging to women was pawned throughout the century far more frequently than men's attire. Clothing still "made the man" and was at the center of foppish acquisitiveness for upper-class men.[114] The public image of the man of the house continued to be paramount, and not only did women's labor power (shopping, washing, ironing, mending, grooming) go into maintaining that appearance, but so did the view that women's clothes were more expendable than men's when scaring up collateral for housekeeping credit. Echoing charges made by Viceroy Revillagigedo a century earlier, *El Monitor Republicano* lamented the "worker who pawns his wife's petticoats or the underclothes of his children" in order to get drunk, a reminder that not all capital from pawned women's clothing was reinvested in household budgets. The concern of Porfirian middle-class men to prove themselves through an ability to consume luxury accessories for public display taxed household economies managed by women, in effect impoverishing middle-class women and their households as the goods linked to them found their way to the pawnshop.

If data on pawned clothing show the persistence of gendered collateral patterns, it is also evident that Mexican styles (enaguas, rebozos, sarapes) were more dispensable (and more affordable?) than newer imported cuts of dresses and suits. Fabric preferences changed.[115] In the early Porfiriato most enaguas in pawnshops in Tlalpan in the south of the Federal District were made of domestic *indiana* and manta, with some made of *muselina* and *hamburgo* and only one or two each of *brillantina*, *cambaya*, *castor*, *percal*, *varé*, and silk. In the sample from the early twentieth century, the vast majority of petticoats are of *percal* and wool, with a few of *liga*, manta, silk, and *cambaya*. The *indiana* and *hamburgo* of earlier times had disappeared, while *varé*, *castor*, *brillantina*, and *gró* were scarce. Taking a long view, the most identified collateral fabrics for the nineteenth century were cotton, silk, *cambaya*, and wool.[116] Cotton occupied an important place in manufactured cloth and as collateral, with *muselina*, *percal*, *indiana*, and *manta* all made from cotton fibers.

Again, finished clothing is not included among household goods summarized in table 5.4 because of its complex nature as personal attire and housekeeping good. Nonetheless, as has been said, choosing, making, and caring for clothing was an integral part of the work of housekeeping. Clothing worn by household members projected image and status. The cleaning and ironing of a family's clothing and linens, especially, still consumed many of women's working hours, whether done by housewives, female household heads, and their daughters or by hired help. A sector of housework that had long been commercialized, laundering continued to employ thousands of women (see table 5.3 above). In Torres's homage to "la lavandera," the laundress was the one servant who knew all the dirt, so to speak, on her clientele or boss, and who therefore should be respected and "treated like the favorite girl in the house." She could reveal that the well-turned-out dandy in fact had "an undershirt that is full of patches." And the one with airs of an "archimillonario" in his double-breasted blazer and shiny boots in fact "has no more than one pair of socks, which is full of holes, one pair of torn underpants, and one undershirt that in the beginning was embroidered but later so patched with various colors that it looks like a street corner where all kinds of announcements are posted." And she could besmirch the image of the young woman with the fashionable haircut and wide hat, perfumed and fanning herself at the theater, because underneath her silk blouse and fancy skirt are a tattered undershirt, enaguas "that would disgust," and repeatedly darned stockings. In short the washerwoman could let the world know that: "This apparently opulent family, which attends all the elegant balls and the up-scale charity events, and which as the vulgar saying goes, eats beans but burps red snapper, [in reality] has no more than one change of clothes for sleeping, so worn out and dirty that the sheets look like 'geographic maps,' and that during the night they pile the *tápalo* or *enaguas* of the women and the cape and overcoat of the man [on the bed] because the blankets are threadbare and the bedspreads look like pulled apart chile peppers."[117] This satirist stresses how important it was that the washerwoman be "secret, quiet and prudent" to prevent the ruin of the family reputation. But reportedly this was not always the way laundresses behaved. The American Ober believed "[w]asherwomen of the *lépero* class pawn the clothes of unsuspecting and trusting Americans when given them to be washed, and more than one engineer has had to visit some *empeño* and pay down the cash for garments that were already his to get them out of pawn."[118]

Symbols of Modern Times

Some collateral goods provide clues about changing material circumstances in the modern city, both inside and outside of households. Although arriving in Mexico shortly after it was invented, the sewing machine took longer to debut in pawnshops.[119] In 1902 an "old manual machine" could only yield a loan of two and a half pesos, the same as a loom, while a "Singer" backed a loan for twenty-seven pesos. Some sewing machines held as collateral were stolen. In January 1903 Elpidio Luna, a student at the Industrial School for Orphans, was accused of pawning a "New Home" sewing machine (figure 8) for forty-five pesos in a pawnshop near Plaza Santo Domingo a few blocks north of the city center. The director of the school found the pawn ticket under the student's pillow.[120]

Other signs of the heralded Porfirian material progress and the accelerated pace of daily life include increasing numbers of watches and clocks in pawning data and the arrival of the bicycle. The "leopoldina" pocket watch had served as a sign of luxury since the Bourbon era. It appeared increasingly in the nineteenth century in empeños and the Monte de Piedad, alongside many stem-wound "Remontoir" pocket watches with double lids and the occasional clock.[121] In Monte branches beginning in the twentieth century, while jewelry was more often gold, watches were still mostly silver. Instruments for marking time seem to have been widely adopted in the city at the turn of the century, and they also came in handy as collateral. In 1903 in pawnshops along Verónica, there were seven alarm clocks and two parlor table clocks from inside credit customers' homes among over fifty pocket watches listed as made mostly of steel, though there were also nickel, silver, copper, and even gold watches. Most loans secured by the Verónica watches were for about one or two pesos, with alarm clocks securing loans of between fifty centavos and one and one-half pesos and more valuable furniture clocks securing six-peso loans.[122]

el Salón de Sorteos, 1.ª calle del Reloj núm. 8, á las tres de la tarde.

NACIONAL MONTE DE PIEDAD

AVISO.

Se participa al público que las prendas empeñadas en la Casa Matriz y sus sucursales, en el mes de Mayo de 1886, se rematarán el presente mes en el órden siguiente:

Casa Matriz. Ropa, sábado 11.

Idem idem. Objetos varios, sábado 18.

Idem idem. Alhajas, viernes 24.

Sucursal número 1. Segunda de Mesones, número 14, miércoles 29.

Sucursal número 2. Primera de la Merced, número 3, lunes 27.

Sucursal número 6. Esquina de las Moras y Sepulcros de Santo Domingo, jueves 28.

Las personas interesadas pueden ocurrir á desempeñarlas, refrendarlas ó á presenciar su venta conforme á lo estipulado en los billetes en concepto de que los remates comenzarán en la Casa Matriz á las diez y en las sucursales á las nueve de la mañana, con la concurrencia que hubiere, continuándose los dias siguientes á las horas de despacho.

México, 1.° de Diciembre de 1886.—*A. Villamil.* —V.° B.°, *Jesús Fuentes y Muñiz.*

6a—6

VENTA DE PRENDAS.

El dia 3 del próximo mes de Enero, se hará de las que existen cumplidas en el empeño de la calle de San Andrés núm. 8.

Lo que se avisa al público para que los interesados en ellas ocurran con tiempo hábil á sacarlas, refrendarlas ó presenciar su venta, la que se hará con arreglo al reglamento.

México, Diciembre 17 de 1886.—*J. Gutierrez*

Núm. 44. —2a—2

Interesante á los enfermos

En la Farmacia homeopática de J. GONZALEZ

AVENIDA DEL CINCO DE MAYO NUM. 17,

se dan consultas de 9 á 1 y de 2 á 5.

Las personas residentes fuera de la capital, pueden hacer sus consultas por escrito, enviando el importe de la medicina, la cual recibirán con contestación á vuelta de correo.

Fig. 8. "Venta de Prendas, Monte de Piedad, and New Home Sewing Machine." Detail from *Diario del Hogar*, December 21, 1885, 4.

In the pawned-goods database bicycles arrive in 1902, with their owners receiving loans for between forty and fifty pesos—more than sewing machines. The inventories where they are found most frequently are from the city center, whether Monte branches or private pawnshops. While horse transportation continues to be represented in the data with a few saddles and bits, another change that symbolizes the modern pace of city life is the appearance of the electric train. The Compañía Limitada de Tranvías Eléctricos de México had ordered special pins from abroad that were to be worn on the hats of employees so that the public could easily identify transit workers who conveyed middle-class employees into the center from the suburbs. The company pressured the Federal District to make it illegal to pawn these pins, as "in some pawnshops they give money for them to those who present them as collateral for loans."[123]

While most collateral goods can be tied to work done by women in the home, only a few are associated with work done outside the home. Only a handful of artisan tools is in the database.[124] Most goods that we might associate with the middle class have more to do with life-style (bicycles, field glasses) than work. In León Alvarez's pawnshop on the central Estampa de Jesús, two items for sale in 1902 are suggestive of white-collar work done by both men and women: a letter-copying apparatus pawned for two pesos and a typewriter pawned for ten.[125]

Housekeeping shaped material lives and public identities of residents working in new factories and the growing business sector in the Porfiriato just as it had for centuries, though the level of consumption feeding life-styles changed with the times. The chronic need for collateral lending among lower- and middle-class housekeepers continued throughout the era of positivist development, even as the ideological glorification of the domestic role intensified. A gendered discourse about the role of mothers and wives in national progress proliferated in print journals in the 1880s at the same time that more married women went to work outside their own homes, though by the end of the Porfirian era most women—whether married or not—were identified chiefly with domestic chores.

A distinctly middle class emerged amid "progress," but some people slid down the economic ladder, especially after 1900, when the economy stagnated. In neighborhoods where middle-class women put their education to work in offices and classrooms, perhaps in response to the slipping economy and despite a discourse pushing their own domesticity, servants continued to do housework in apartments and new single-family suburban homes. In working-class neighborhoods where those domestic servants lived, other women went to work in factories or as seamstresses, with a second shift of chores in their single-room homes. Evidence in pawnshops shows long-established pawning patterns continued amid the changing gendered labor market, the increased capitalization of the economy, and the intensified consumption necessary to maintain middle-class status or working-class standards of living.

The everydayness of pawning is clear in material evidence from pawnshops' shelves as well as in satirical poetry and fictional literature, despite "outsider" and journalistic views of Porfirian pawning clientele that continued earlier discourses about the degenerate poor. Daily life in the increasingly proletarianized popular culture contrasted sharply with the increasingly materialist middle-class culture, even as both cultures continued to depend on everyday credit. Material life changed, with more imported goods in living rooms and in laundry baskets. Furniture, clocks, bicycles, imported tablecloths, embroidered sheets, English suits, and French dresses—these goods in concert advertised one's middle-class status. Chairs and armoires continued to shape material life when converted to cash through collateral credit, as did embroidered linens. Fashions of yesterday might still contribute to one's middle-class image, as rebozos and enaguas remained common collateral. Material life changed least for those who could not afford to keep up with fashions. The working classes, nonetheless, consumed what they needed and converted used goods, and sometimes goods they had yet to consume, into cash for household budgets. Whatever class of household the collateral came from and whether women or men brought it to the pawnshop, collateral goods continued to be most often those owned by women or used by women in everyday housekeeping routines. As the city expanded, so did pawning and pawnbroking, to which we now turn our attention.

SIX

Porfirian Paradoxes

Profit versus Regulation, Capital versus Welfare

The Pearl of Saint Catherine. The Ideal of Art. The Rose of the Sea. Shower of Gold. In her memoir of her stay in Mexico City at the turn of the twentieth century, Mrs. Tweedie characterized these colorful pawnshop names, along with others for *pulquerías*, grocery stores, and butcher and barber shops, as "funny and extremely inappropriate."[1] As for appropriateness, perhaps the last name was closest to the mark. Indeed, the reign of President Porfirio Díaz witnessed a boom for pawning businesses. This period of political peace and economic development was also one of legislation and vigilance over private pawnshops, with laws in 1881, 1886, 1890, and 1895. The positivist political economy had an uneven impact on households in the city. One consequence of this was a continued demand for collateral credit. The Porfirian years were also a time in which the services of the Monte de Piedad were expanded further into new neighborhoods of the city, as it and other parts of the welfare system were reorganized and bureaucratized. It was the opinion of American traveler Frederick Ober that "the amount of good that [the Monte de Piedad] has done in the century and more of its existence is incalculable," while newspaper editors often expressed the idea that the Porfirian Monte was poorly run by ostentatious bureaucrats.[2] By the end of the Porfiriato the Monte de Piedad had become a more "private charity," and brokers publicly defied regulation of their private business practices.

As the daily exercise of taking household goods to pawnshops for quick cash remained central to everyday life for many working- and middle-class residents of Mexico City, relations between brokers and these clients became increasingly acrimonious, and brokers squeezed more profits out of their clientele at the end of the century. Relations between the state and brokers also went downhill, as the petitioning stance of earlier years did not always bear fruit, and organized brokers turned to more disruptive tactics to defend what they saw as their rights as businessmen. As the newspaper *El Partido Liberal* put it, in the Porfirian era two "antagonistic interests" clashed: the public interest and the empeñeros' interest.[3]

Profile of the Porfirian Pawnbroker

Pawnbrokers, corner storekeepers, and bar owners occupied the lower strata within the emergent middle class, though clearly some pawnbrokers made a better living. Right up until the Mexican Revolution of 1910, in complaints to state officials, customers refer to pawnbrokers and storekeepers as "españoles," or less kindly as "gachupines," suggesting that this sector of the middle class was or was perceived to be largely white and immigrant.[4] When brokers tried to circumvent 1886 regulations by converting to consignment business (discussed below), some residents called for application of Article 33 of the Federal Constitution in order to expel offending foreign-born brokers.[5]

Despite earlier attempts at expelling Spaniards and a sustained anti-gachupín strain in popular culture, Spaniards dominated the foreign population in the city, with more Spaniards at the end of the Porfiriato than all other nationalities combined. The numbers of Spanish immigrants living in the city increased over the years of Díaz rule, with around two thousand in the city in 1876 and over twelve thousand by 1910. Coming from throughout the Iberian peninsula, perhaps the largest contingent in the Porfirian years were the Catalans, who formed a subcolony and developed institutions separate from the colony at large. Concentrated in retail, baking, the cantina business, and banking, the Spanish colony remained a group apart, with its own social clubs such as the Casino Español, its own theater companies, its own charitable organizations such as the Sociedad Beneficencia Española, which provided health care to members of the colony, and even its own cemetery. The Spanish community also published its own newspapers, such as *La Colonia Española*, *El Pabellón Español*, *La Voz de España*, and *El Correo Español*, keeping up with events in Europe as well as local issues. Spanish journalists also wrote for Mexican papers.[6]

Certainly part of the Spaniards' poor reputation had to do with their dominance of retail. Spanish immigrants preferred this business sector, as it required only a small investment and the industrious could secure at least a modest success. To expand successful businesses depended on clerks who were mostly Spanish immigrant men—some family, others entering at this level to learn the ropes and eventually open their own small businesses. When the economy was sour or if a business was located in a poor neighborhood, grocers and other small businesses were scapegoats for rising prices. In public opinion small merchants were believed to cheat their customers in any way possible. In December 1886 the district government published an advisory to merchants to accept pesetas for the twenty-five centavos they were legally worth instead of discounting one centavo. The government also prohibited the use of anything as money other than official coinage, suggesting that merchants were renewing long-standing conventions from the days of *tlacos*, or soap and wooden coins issued by corner stores. Newspapers drew attention to their public service in publishing the news item: "The poor now know: merchants are required to receive pesetas for their real value."[7] In Gutierrez Najera's 1883 story about the counterfeit peso, the storekeeper who discovers the coin is false as it hits the cash-register drawer after the unknowing newsboy has turned it over to pay for all the things he never had before—the one responsible for bursting the boy's bubble—is of course identified as "gachupín."[8]

The seedy reputation of Spanish storekeepers continued to carry over to Spanish pawnbrokers. The press regularly identified pawnbrokers as "españoles," and historians agree that in the 1890s pawnbrokers were generally Spaniards but also Cubans. Spanish pawnbrokers certainly had public relations problems: "The colonia and Mexican society touched . . . on an individual level in these shops, and from this much bitterness ensued."[9] A clause in regulations for pawnbrokers suggests that relations between them and their customers was not always positive, and that there was something behind the reputation. Article 61 of the 1886 regulations stated: "Conceding to public action, any citizen can denounce before the Ministerio Público or before the Governor of the District the abuses of the owners of pawnshops, of appraisers and of auditors." There were also many articles outlining the punishment of pawnbrokers guilty of non-compliance with the very detailed regulations.[10] *El Monitor Republicano* characterized pawnbrokers as "adventurous peninsulars" and "the worst contingent of foreign immigration" motivated by greed and ambition, "who transplant themselves to American soil to extort a strange people, people that they think have no value, and against whom they let lose the full force of their rapacity." These unwelcome foreigners were indicted by the press for lending so little on goods worth five times as much or more and doing so with "brutal arrogance."[11] The Spanish press in turn defended pawnbrokers, arguing that Spanish enterprises such as pawnbroking benefited Mexicans, and that not all Spaniards were gouging grocers or pawnbrokers.[12] In 1895 links between the Spanish press and brokers were direct. José Porrua, who had come to Mexico as an unpaid representative of the government in Madrid to explore Hispano-American literary and commercial enterprises, bought *El Correo Español*, adding this enterprise to the pawnshops that he owned with his brother. The brothers also founded one of the longest-standing publishing houses in Mexico. Led by Porruá, *El Correo Español* continued to defend the Spanish commercial community and to serve as the voice of that community. Under Porrúa's leadership rivalries within the colony continued, but he used the paper to mediate between pawnbrokers and the public and between pawnbrokers and the revolutionary government after Díaz's demise.[13]

The Spanish writer Julio Sesto painted a very unflattering portrait of his compatriots among the city's pawnbrokers at the turn of the twentieth century in his memoir of ten years of residence: "Spaniards, that is to say, a degenerate part of the Spanish colony, exploit this ugly merchant trade. These *empeños* satisfy the necessities or needs of vice and not honest motives, such that the pawnbroker has a social function little envied, a species of vampire that draws sustenance from disgrace, a degenerate that, under the guise of protection, exploits another degenerate. The Spanish clerks of the pawnshops treat the public poorly; they throw money in a bad manner; they receive articles with an irritating analytic disdain; and, in a word, they mock the customer [*lo escarnecen*]."[14] Some of their peers felt the same way. When Tomás Gavidia petitioned in 1902 for a reduction of a fine imposed for failing to publish auction dates in the paper, he argued that it was an honest mistake and that he was "of Mexican nationality," not like other notorious brokers.[15] The dominance of Spanish immigrant men in this branch of small business represents a long continuity in the material history of Mexico City, even as the geography and pace of economic life changed.

The Porfirian Pawning Business

During the Porfiriato the pawning trade continued to expand, with the opening of new private businesses, new branches of the Monte de Piedad, and other establishments modeled on the public pawnshop. As empeños evolved out of retail establishments in midcentury, another transition in the evolution of this branch of small business was venturing into the sale of used goods through consignment or the accumulation of unredeemed pawned goods. Patterns of ownership and business longevity established early in the century continued through the end of the century, especially the prevalence of Spaniards among pawnbrokers. Freed from colonial and conservative government restrictions, Porfirian interest rates soared. At the same time the Porfirian state continued old taxation measures and added new ones.

In the 1840s and 1850s, there were at least 100 pawnshops in the city. Early in the Porfiriato in 1879, archival records show at least 107 pawnshops, about the same number as in the previous decades. The year with the most businesses in the data is 1902, near the end of the Porfiriato, with 137 pawnshops reportedly in operation in that year (see appendix 2, table I).[16] These data suggest a 25 percent increase in the number of pawnshops over sixty years, but with the population more than doubling from 1854 to 1910 (see appendix 3, table A), it represents a relative contraction of this business sector. The increase in the number of establishments in no way kept up with population growth.[17]

The growth of the city, which included rerouting and renaming of streets, hampers systematic tracking of the addresses of pawning establishments. Nonetheless, we can trace considerable longevity in pawning locations over the course of the nineteenth century (see appendix 2, table M).[18] As the city grew, however, new locations sprang up to meet the continued demand of residents for credit (see appendix 2, table N).[19] Pawnshops opened up next door to each other, with some streets housing a large number of prenda businesses. Some of these new locations, such as Guerrero (in the northwest quarter of the city), were located in new working-class neighborhoods that sprang up with population growth and real estate speculation. Most of Guerrero's residents were poor laborers, domestic servants, and *tortilleras* living in crowded casas de vecindad. But Guerrero was not only a workers' zone; respectable middle-class residents built homes there as well, especially in the southwest corner of the neighborhood. Most blocks of the north-south street named Guerrero had a pawnshop by the turn of the century, with another handful on Lerdo, the eastern border of the neighborhood. Along the northern edge of Alameda Park, home to pensioned widows of military men, new empeños opened on Portillo Santo Domingo and San Hipólito. Empeños also arose in new middle-class neighborhoods, such as the two along Rivera de San Cosme and the two along Santa María de Rivera, in the fashionable western San Rafael and Santa María neighborhoods.[20]

Historical patterns continued in the Porfirian era. Some owners had multiple businesses, as seen in table 6.1.[21] When some brokers expanded

TABLE 6.1

Multiple Pawnshop Ownership During Porfiriato

Owner	Locations	Date
Altuna & Co.	Manrique No. 22	Feb. 1879
	San Hipólito No. 19	Nov. 1886
	Vergara No. 9	Aug. 1880
	Vergara No. 10	Dec. 1895
Leon Alvarez	Jesús Estampa E	Jan. 1902
	Manzanares 2nd Block No. 5	Jan. 1902
Raymundo Alvarez	San Juan Plaza No. 6	May 1898
	Juan Carbonero No. 5	May 1898
	Aduana Vieja & San Gerónimo	Jan. 1902
A. Dosal	Santo Domingo Bridge No. 6	Dec. 1895
	Leguisimo Bridge No. 3	Dec. 1895
S. Dosal	Santa Catarina 2nd Block No. 3	Jan. 1885
	Leguisimo Bridge No. 3	Aug. 1898
V. Dosal	San Diego Portillo No. 10 1/2	Dec. 1901
	Leguisimo Bridge No. 3	Jan. 1902
	Jesús Bridge & Corazón No. 7	Jan. 1902
	Santo Domingo Sepulcros No. 10	Jan. 1902
Gregorio Fernández	Merced 1st Block No. 28	Jan. 1877
	Verde No. 28	Aug. 1880
Ramón Fernández	Trapana No. 1	Jan. 1902
	Leña Puente No. 83	Jan. 1907
Lucio Flores	Veronica & Armando Corner	Sep. 1874
	San Antonio Totatlán	Feb. 1878
Juan Perea	Alegria No. 2	Jan. 1878
	Estampa de Jesús	Jan. 1878
F. Pérez Fernández	Hoacalco & Pelota Corner	Feb. 1879
	Ancha & San Antonio Corner	Jun. 1879
Joaquin Poo	Merced 1st Block No. 31	Feb. 1878
	Indio Triste	Feb. 1882
Porrúa Hermanos	Guerrero 2nd Block No. 10	Jan. 1902
	San Pedro & San Pablo No. 14	Jan. 1903
Antonio Portillo	San Andrés No. 8	Jun. 1901
	Vergara No. 10	Jun. 1901
M. Posada y Porrúa	Victoria & Santísima Bridge	Dec. 1895
	San Pedro & San Pablo No. 11	Dec. 1901

TABLE 6.1

Continued

Owner	Locations	Date
	San Pedro & San Pablo No. 14	Jan. 1902
B. Quintana & Co.	Damas 2nd Block No. 5	Dec. 1895
	Damas 2nd Block No. 2	Jan. 1902
Camilo Rivera	Guerras Bridge	Jan. 1907
	Santa María Redonda Calzada	Apr. 1907
Margarita Santieste	Sapo No. 22	Jan. 1868
	Sapo No. 32	Jan. 1868
	Ortega No. 22	Feb. 1882
Pedro Gavito	San Juan & Madrid	Jan. 1902
	Merced & Jesús María Bridge	Jan. 1902
Gomez Hermanos	San Juan & Peredo Corner	Dec. 1895
	Hospital Real & Victoria	Jan. 1903
Wensceslao Goni	Alegría No. 2	Jan. 1878
	Alfaro No. 4	Oct. 1886
	Santa Clara & Manrique Corner	Jan. 1902
Manuel González	Relox 4th Block No. 1	Feb. 1879
	Santo Domingo, Sepulcros No. 6	Aug. 1880
	Damas 2nd Block No. 2	Dec. 1895
	Guerrero 3rd Block No. 49	Jan. 1903
J. Lezameta	San Diego Portillo No. 10 1/2	Dec. 1874
	Santo Domingo Sepulcros No. 6	Dec. 1874
	Santo Domingo No. 8	Mar. 1881
	Tezontlale 2nd Block No. 7	May 1886
Pedro Lobrado	Arquillo & Cazuela Corner	Jan. 1878
	Coliseo Viejo No. 16	Feb. 1878
Luengas Hermanos	Niño Perdido 1st Block No. 28	Dec. 1901
	Asención No. 4	Jan. 1903
	Niño Perdido 2nd Block No. 33	Jun. 1906
M. Molleda & Co.	Santo Domingo Sepulcros No. 10 1/2	Jan. 1885
	Paz Avenue No. 7	Jan. 1902
	San Pedro & San Pablo	Jan. 1902
M. & T. Sobrino	Santa María Bridge No. 4	Jan. 1902
	Lerdo & Moctezuma Corner	Jan. 1902
Taméz & López	Santísima Plaza No. 3	Jan. 1903
	Paz 1st Block No. 7	Jan. 1903

TABLE 6.1

Continued

Owner	Locations	Date
B. Trespalacios	Santo Domingo Bridge No. 6	Jul. 1898
	Santo Domingo 3rd Block No. 4	Dec. 1901
	Santa Catarina 3rd Block No. 4	Jan. 1902
Domingo Ugarte	Sapo No. 3	Dec. 1874
	Damas 2nd Block No. 6	Feb. 1878
	San Hipólito	Mar. 1881
Velar & Gonzalez	Veronica 2nd Block No. 6	Jan. 1902
	Veronica & Fraternidad	Jan. 1903
Yarto & Co.	San Hipólito No. 10	Dec. 1895
	San Hipólito No. 19	Aug. 1898

Source: AHCM, Empeños, vol. 885, exps. 10, 12, 14, 18, 19, 22, 23, 24, 35, 37, 39, 46, 57, 95, and 113; Gobierno del Distrito Empeños, vols. 8, 9, 1422, 1429, and 1430; Gobierno del Distrito Empeños Ventas, vol. 162; *El Siglo XIX*, 1885–95; *El Diario*, 1912–13; *El Imparcial*, June 22, 1906; *El Pueblo*, 1914–15; *El Demócrata*, 1915; Juan E. Pérez, *Almanaque estadístico de las oficinas y guía de forasteros y del comercio de la república para 1875* (México: Imprenta del Gobierno, 1874), 238–41; and AGN, Gobernación, 2nd section, vol. 811.

into a second business, they opened the new store on the same street as the original one: the Quintana company operated two stores on Damas, the Altuna company had two on Vergara, and the Trespalacios company had three on Santo Domingo. This pattern suggests a monopolization of neighborhood pawning services during the Porfiriato. Some businesses were family enterprises. The Bustillos family owned two stores on Colegio de Niñas between 1878 and 1882, alternately managed by Ramón, Diego, Francisco, and Felipe Bustillos.[22] The Campuzano family owned the pawnshop on Verdeja from 1854 until at least 1879, a twenty-five-year span. An increasing number of partnerships and companies outside of obvious family relationships ran pawning enterprises during this period.

The data in table 6.2, representing stores with the same owner for at least five years, suggest that the turnover rate increased during the Porfiriato, as only five stores in the sample were in the same hands more than ten years.[23] An example illustrates the volatility of the trade, as a stable and prosperous business was replaced by a short-lived, small-scale enterprise. In 1876, when the government investigated a pawnshop in connection with a lawsuit between Agustín Arellano and Ramón Moctezuma, the records

TABLE 6.2

Longevity of Pawnshop Ownership

Location	Owner	Documentation Earliest	Documentation Latest	Total Years
Santa Ana Bridge No. 15	Antonio Piedras	1871	1901	30
Santa Ana No. 4	Fidencio Cortez	1879	1902	21
Quemada & Gallos	Narciso Pedraza	1854	1871	17
Jesús Estampa	Juan Gutierrez	1881	1895	14
Santo Tomás	I. Trejo	1874	1887	13
Merced No. 4	José del Torno	1879	1886	9
San Lorenzo & Estampa	José Simon Alonso	1898	1907	9
Santo Domingo Bridge No. 6	B. Trespalacios	1898	1907	9
Aduana Vieja 2nd block	Juan Urrutia	1878	1886	8
Alfaro No. 12	Donesteve Brothers	1871	1879	8
Leña Bridge No. 3	Santiago Barquín	1871	1879	8
León No. 8	Juan Huerdo	1872	1879	7
Peredo & San Juan	Mateo Mejia & Co.	1879	1886	7
Vanegas 2nd Block No. 1	Emilio Fernández	1895	1902	6
Colegio de Niñas No. 2	Diego Bustillo	1877	1882	5
Coliseo No. 16	Pedro Lobrado	1875	1881	5
Damas 2nd Block No. 2	Benigno Quintana	1902	1905	5
Factor No. 1	Manuel Arratia	1877	1882	5
Palma No. 1	Teodoro Hermosa	1902	1907	5
Verdeja & Miguel López	Joaquín Alvarez	1895	1902	5

Source: AHCM, Empeños, vol. 885, exps. 10, 12, 14, 18, 19, 22, 23, 24, 35, 37, 39, 46, 57, 95, and 113; Gobierno del Distrito, Empeños, vols. 8, 9, 1422, 1429, and 1430; Gobierno del Distrito, Empeños Ventas, vol. 162; *El Siglo XIX*, 1885–95; *El Diario*, 1912–13; *El Imparcial*, June 22, 1906; *El Pueblo*, 1914–15; *El Demócrata*, 1915; Mariano Galvan Rivera, *Guía de forasteros en la Ciudad de México, para el año de 1854* (México: Imprenta de Santiago Perez y Cia., 1854), 330–32; Peréz, *Almanaque estadístico*, 238–41; and AGN, Gobernación, 2nd section, vol. 811.

showed that from 1866 until February 1875, Moctezuma had operated an empeño at Alegría No. 6 with a capital of 3,000 pesos. In February 1875 the business reopened in the name of Doña Dolores Ordaz with an operating capital of only 498 pesos. Doña Dolores was out of business the next year.[24] Other evidence suggests that female-owned pawnshops were among the more vulnerable businesses. The case of Maximiana Zayas de Velasco illustrates how family situations may have framed the business experience for women. A widow, Zayas de Velasco closed her prenda business once her son died, because she no longer had the resources to stay open.[25]

In January 1903 the city government noted the closure of seven pawnshops and the transfer of ownership of three others. Commenting on the difficulty of keeping track of openings and closings of shops, bureaucrat Francisco Moncada noted that matters were complicated by cases where a judge stepped in to run errant businesses. For example, the owner of the shop at the corner of Amargura and Altuna had abandoned his obligations to have goods appraised and auctions announced in the newspaper and on the shop door; a judge seized the shop. The business later reopened under the ownership of another broker.[26] This turnover in pawnshops continued through the Porfiriato, with nine establishments changing hands at least five times and a dozen shops changing owners at least four times between the 1870s and the 1910s (see appendix 2, table O). In marked contrast is the information presented in table 6.3, which shows that many addresses continued to be pawnshops for multiple decades while the owners changed, as had been true since the eighteenth century.

Archival documents allow a glimpse of day-to-day business dealings of brokers and quantitative changes over time. Business volumes increased, with high-end establishments operating with much larger amounts of capital than businesses at midcentury. Interest rates were higher, and profits increased. The tax burden on individual brokers was also higher. The Porfirian government, in liberal fashion, left brokers to charge whatever interest they wanted. But the state also generated more revenue on broker profits.

Pawnbrokers paid a variety of assessments on their businesses in the last decades of the nineteenth century. They had to deposit with the Monte de Piedad the *demasías*, or the difference remaining from the auction price after the loan amount, costs, and interest were deducted (see appendix 2, table P). Failure to meet this requirement could mean prosecution by the city government.[27] When the inspector José M. Machuca had to report to superiors that broker Juan Gutiérrez had not deposited the thirty-five pesos thirty-eight centavos he had from auction profits, he made sure to note that Gutiérrez cooperated completely with the government agent during the auction, that his tickets were in good order, and that he had not charged the 5 percent in transaction costs that he was allowed by law. The inspector believed this broker's noncompliance stemmed from ignorance, as it was the first time he had *demasías* to deposit.[28] Some brokers made deposits of auction profits collectively.[29] New regulations in 1886 called on the Monte

TABLE 6.3

Longevity of Empeño Business Location

Location	In Existence	Total Years
Nahuatlato & Ratas	1843–1902	59
Factor No. 5	1854–1912	58
Hospital Real & Victoria	1846–1903	57
Altuna & Amargura	1854–1901	47
Peredo & San Juan	1858–1902	44
San Antonio Totatlán	1878–1914	36
Ancha & San Antonio	1868–1902	34
Colegio de Niñas No. 2	1878–1907	29
Medinas & Pila Seca	1854–80	26
Factor No. 1	1878–1902	24
Jesús Estampa E.	1878–1902	24
Jesús Bridge & Corazón	1878–1902	24
Niño Perdido No. 28	1878–1902	24
San Diego Portilla No. 10 1/2	1879–1902	23
San Pedro & San Pablo No. 14	1879–1902	23
Santa Ana No. 4	1879–1902	23
Santo Domingo No. 6	1879–1902	23
San Andrés No. 8	1879–1901	22
San Hipolito No. 19	1886–1902	16
Tezontlale 2nd Block No. 7	1886–1902	16
Alfaro No. 4	1886–1901	15
Santísima & Victoria	1867–1902	15
Santísima Plaza No. 3	1887–1902	15
Colegio de Niñas No. 1	1874–86	12
Damas 2nd Block No. 2	1895–1907	12
Hidalgo & Galeana	1902–12	10
Indio Triste 2nd Block	1872–82	10
Alegría No. 6	1866–75	9
Juan Carbonero & San Juan N.	1872–81	9

Source: AHCM, Empeños, vol. 885, exps. 10, 12, 14, 18, 19, 22, 23, 24, 35, 37, 39, 46, 57, 95, and 113; Gobierno del Distrito Empeños, vols. 8, 9, 1422, 1429, and 1430; Gobierno del Distrito Empeños Ventas, vol. 162; *El Siglo XIX* 1885–95; *El Diario*, 1912–13; *El Imparcial*, June 22, 1906; *El Pueblo*, 1914–15; *El Demócrata*, 1915; Galvan Rivera, *Guía de forasteros*, 330–32; Peréz, *Almanaque estadístico*, 238–41; and AGN, Gobernación, 2nd section, vol. 811.

TABLE 6.4

Taxation on Empeño Business Volume in Pesos, December 1901

Shop	Owner	Loaned	Adjudication	Capital	2% Tax
Damas No. 2	B. Quintana & Co.	8,340.20	599.31	8,940.11	178.80
Santa Ana H	Fidencio Cortés	7,318.77	211.88	7,530.65	150.62
San Diego Portillo	V. Dosal (B. Villar)	7,155.35	287.30	7,442.65	148.85
Merced 1st Bl. No. 4	Santo Sobrino	6,106.28	421.20	6,527.48	130.54
Vergara No. 11	N. Mendiola	1,800.27	46.10	1,846.37	36.92
Ascensión No. 4	Tomás Gavidia	1,119.97	80.95	1,280.92	25.62
San Juan & Polilla	Farré & Co.	634.20	45.56	684.76	13.69

Source: AHCM, Gobierno del Distrito, Empeños, vol. 1422, exp. 21.

de Piedad to hold these windfalls for one year (in previous legislation the term was six months), during which time the owner could claim them and after which time the money went into public charity projects such as hospitals and hospices, not to brokers.[30]

Pawning businesses were also assessed a tax of 2 percent on the operating capital by the city. We can see from table 6.4 that brokers were taxed on goods that became their property through adjudication. This provision, not found in colonial or early republican legislation, suggests that brokers could in fact sell at least some of those goods, presumably closer to their market value than the loan amount. The acquisition of unredeemed goods that did not sell at auction appears to be one element in the transition of some empeños into businesses selling used goods, like the shop in the second block of Vanegas owned by the Fernández brothers that was identified in a 1902 document as "Empeño y Bazar."[31] Another element in this transition was taking goods on consignment, which began as a way to avoid new regulations in 1886. In 1878 the Monte de Piedad had anticipated this evolutionary trend of the pawning trade, as it accepted goods on consignment for auction in its halls.[32]

The range of capitalization of Porfirian pawnshops was wide, ranging from over 600 pesos to almost 9,000 pesos. The old classifications were no longer adequate, and shops capitalized with 3,000 pesos moved from the first to the second class by 1884.[33] Documents from four pawnshops for the year 1902 illustrate the range in the different classes of store. The Santa Ana and Merced pawnshops loaned between 5,000 and 8,000 pesos monthly, while the Vergara business loaned from 1,500 to 3,000 pesos, and

TABLE 6.5

Vergara Empeño Daily Business Volume, May 1902

Day	Pesos Loaned	Day	Pesos Loaned
May 1	70.69	May 16	47.72
May 2	19.49	May 17	58.99
May 3	119.49	May 18	20.50
May 4	93.99	May 19	95.84
May 5	140.15	May 20	52.72
May 6	55.50	May 21	33.00
May 7	25.71	May 22	69.98
May 8	59.22	May 23	75.47
May 9	72.23	May 24	164.75
May 10	60.97	May 25	32.00
May 11	52.70	May 26	67.97
May 12	75.73	May 27	50.49
May 13	52.96	May 28	152.47
May 14	30.98	May 29	18.20
May 15	185.94	May 30	29.48
		May 31	149.48
Total			2,242.28

Source: AHCM, Gobierno del Distrito, Empeños, vol. 1422, exps. 4, 21, and 48.

the San Juan and Polilla store loaned under 800 pesos a month.[34] At the pawnshop at Damas No. 2, owned by B. Quintana and Company, the volume of business was somewhat volatile. In January 1902 brokers loaned out 8,099 pesos, in April the amount increased to 11,095 pesos, and in October they only loaned 6,911 pesos.[35] Table 6.5 shows how volatile business volume could be from day to day. The empeño at Vergara No. 11 loaned 2,242.28 pesos in May 1902, with the daily volume ranging from 18 pesos to 185 pesos. In June the spread was extremely wide: the high loaned daily was 569.97 pesos, and the low was 15.48 pesos.

It is difficult to determine how much of a business's capital was profit (that is, over and above loan amounts and overhead costs) or to know exactly what went into pawnbrokers' calculations regarding how much interest to charge in order to make their businesses going enterprises. Out of 683 unredeemed goods from seven pawnshops sold between January and June 1902, only 22 were reported to have generated a "sobrante," with a total of six and a half pesos being deposited in the Monte de Piedad for collection by the twenty-two owners of the collateral.[36] The press argued that whether or not there was a windfall rightfully belonging to the owner of the good, when they were asked, pawnbrokers generally responded "No sobró nada," or there was nothing left over.[37]

Sixty-four pawnshops operating in the city in 1885 had a collective capitalization of 2.5 million pesos, lending at a "very high" interest rate. In 1895 common interest rates were 12 percent in the first month, 25 percent in the second month, and 35 percent in the third.[38] In an editorial *El Siglo XIX* suggested a fundamental difference between the Monte de Piedad and private pawnbrokers in addition to their charging different interest rates. The former lent less on an object so that the loan would be easier to repay. As a nonprofit business, it was important that the Monte recover capital lent out so that it could be used again. The latter, however, appraised goods that would likely sell higher at auction, therefore lending more, because they allegedly wanted to make it difficult for clients to come up with the redemption money, thus acquiring the object and "tripling the capital they invested" when it sold.[39] When debating tax rates and pawnbroking practices in 1900, the city council reported that over a six-month period, the city's pawnshops lent a total of 1,333,796.25 pesos, with interest rates between 4 percent and 16 percent a month and an average monthly interest of 10.92 percent. The council, however, believed that the "real average interest rate reached the enormous number of 21.84 percent a month." Other reports put interest rates at the end of the Porfiriato at 20 percent to 40 percent a month.[40]

Examples of pawn tickets found in archives show that interest rates were high in private Porfirian shops in comparison with those of earlier times and those of the Monte de Piedad, and that they varied from broker to broker (see appendix 2, table Q, for comparisons). The text from one such ticket reads:

> Santa Ana, No. 4. In the respective book of this shop, under the number ________ it states that a Don ________ was loaned in silver coins and should pay back in silver the quantity of ________ pesos for the goods that in his presence were appraised and with the following description ________ for the unextendable term of FOUR MONTHS under the following conditions: 1. For all class of goods that are redeemed within the first three months counting from the date of the pawning transaction, [the client] will pay 14 centavos for each peso loaned per month, and for loans less than one peso 16 percent will be paid. 2. In the fourth and last

> month of the pledge period, [the client] will pay 25 percent per month. 3. Once the pledge period passes, [the client] will suffer a charge of 45 percent and once the good has been appraised and goes up for sale, will be charged 5 centavos for each peso as called for by the current Regulations. The broker is not responsible for damage or accidental loss of goods deposited. For cases covered in part 6 of article 10 of the Regulations and in case of loss covered by article 17, the amount is fixed at 50 percent of the value of the good plus the amount loaned. While installment payments may be made, the contract cannot be altered. The client agrees to all these conditions. Goods will not be shown [upon demand]. Mexico. ________ de ________ 1901. Fidencio Cortéz."

The language in this ticket was fairly standard, with other brokers charging up to 80 percent under condition 3 and some allowing for extension of the pledge contract for a fee. How aware were clients of the interest rates? Many were illiterate and therefore unable to read the details on the pawn ticket.[41]

Pawnbrokers at the turn of the twentieth century continued to lend sometimes very small amounts of money on clothing, as their counterparts had done a century earlier, though clothing now made up a smaller percentage of collateral goods than it had in earlier times. Some brokers' business overwhelmingly constituted giving loans secured by cloth goods. For example, on May 1, 1907, the pawning company of Noruega y Corral reported to the city on their transactions for the month of April. A full 219 of the 257 transactions involved cloth collateral (89 percent), with the average loan for cloth items fifty-three centavos. Twenty-six of the goods were "objetos varios" (10 percent), with loans averaging seventy-nine centavos. Only one good each was in the furniture and jewelry categories. The average loan given for all 257 transactions in April at this pawnshop at No. 30 in the second block of Rivera de San Cosme was sixty-two centavos. As this shop was in an emerging middle-class neighborhood in the west of the city, such a low loan average is surprising. It may be that the shop was frequented by servants working in middle-class homes in the area.[42]

Considerably more data are available for another pawnshop in 1908, on Avenida de Juárez running along the downtown Alameda Park, as seen in table 6.6. The size of the loans given by Adela Noriega was small, averaging less than a peso, and the vast majority of collateral constituted clothing. Noriega apparently served a sizable poor and working-class clientele at her central location. The sale price of unredeemed goods cleared four times the amount of the average loan, though sales only accounted for less than

TABLE 6.6

Volume of Business at Cartagena Casa de Empeño, Adela Noriega, Owner, 1908

	Pawned			Renewed			Sold		
Date/Category	Pesos Lent	No. Loans	Avg. Loan	Pesos Received	No. Loans	Avg. Fee	Pesos Received	No. Sales	Avg. Sale
July 1908									
Clothing	5,025.52	6,622	0.76	60.87	360	0.17	108.00	25	4.32
Furniture/Objects	2,219.30	1,711	1.30	338.37	104	3.25	17.00	4	4.25
Jewels	1,044.88	360	2.90	114.87	47	2.44	134.00	32	4.19
Subtotal	8,289.70	8,693	0.95	514.11	511	1.01	259.00	61	4.25
August 1908									
Clothing	4,793.35	6,437	0.74	444.50	277	1.60	165.00	43	3.84
Furniture/Objects	2,212.35	1,473	1.50	175.50	71	2.47	16.50	2	8.25
Jewels	685.62	284	2.41	129.87	53	2.45	131.87	39	3.38
Subtotal	7,637.62	8,194	0.93	749.87	401	1.87	313.37	84	3.73
September 1908									
Clothing	5,123.38	6,231	0.82	217.07	164	1.32	90.50	19	4.76
Furniture/Objects	2,142.80	1,466	1.46	125.70	164	0.77	42.00	6	7.00
Jewels	948.34	201	4.72	61.33	13	4.72	56.00	17	3.29
Subtotal	8,214.42	7,898	1.04	404.10	341	1.19	188.50	42	4.48
December 1908									
Clothing	4,208.64	5,757	0.73				168.25	40	4.21
Furniture/Objects	2,242.46	1,568	1.43				9.00	5	1.80
Jewels	848.23	316	2.68				89.50	21	4.26
Subtotal	7,299.33	7,641	0.96				266.75	66	4.04
Total	31,441.07	32,436	0.97	1,668.08	1,253	1.33	1,027.62	253	4.06

Source: AHCM, Gobierno del Distrito, Empeños, vol. 1420, exp. 322.

1 percent of Noriega's 33,942 business transactions. She reported more money in fees collected from clients who paid to renew their pawn contract and keep it out of auction than she did in sales, suggesting that customers expected to recover their goods, whether to reincorporate them into their daily routines or to use again as collateral. *El Monitor Republicano* suggested in 1890 that more than half the goods pawned in the city went unredeemed, while the city council believed in 1900 that as a general rule, 75 percent of goods pawned were redeemed. In either case Adela Noriega likely had many more goods on hand for sale than actually sold. The council members also cautioned, however, that reports by pawnbrokers of their sale figures were suspiciously low, as some tax rates were pegged to the volume of sales, which therefore were underreported.[43]

Perhaps the most important point to take from Adela Noriega's data is that she represents only one of more than a hundred brokers, and she alone in 1908 made a remarkable eight thousand loans against collateral each month. The last years of Porfirio Diaz's rule were years of high inflation. Perhaps the volume in pawnshops picked up in response. The collateral-credit business continued at a brisk pace. While in the private pawning sector business was booming, the public institution faced a number of challenges in the "order and progress" years.

The Porfirian Monte de Piedad

Deposits in the Monte de Piedad increased in the Porfirian era, eventually pulling it out of the red, but only after a long period of continued instability combined with innovations. Loans from the 1860s and 1870s were not repaid, which contributed to a deficit of more than forty thousand pesos in 1874. Another reason for such a large deficit was renewed mismanagement.[44] The Díaz government expanded the institution to a total of eight branches and added a bank to its services. In 1879 director Mariano Riva Palacio issued bills (called "confidential deposit certificates") in denominations of five, ten, twenty, fifty, one hundred, and one thousand pesos, totaling 3 million pesos, with an additional 6 million issued in 1881. Expansion of the Monte also included real-estate mortgage operations at the main branch and new branches in Puebla, Oaxaca, and San Luis Potosí.[45]

The administration tinkered with what it charged for collateral-lending services (see interest comparisons in appendix 2, table Q). In four branch offices the minimum loan was lowered in 1881 from twenty-five centavos to twelve centavos, opening credit access to those with more humble collateral. The interest schedule differed depending on the branch at which one pawned collateral. In the original four branch offices (those established by Maximilian in 1866 and confirmed by Juárez), annual interest rates ranged from 12 to 48 percent, with interest highest for redemption in the first month and lowest for redemption in the fourth and eighth months. In the last four branches annual interest ranged from 16 to 48 percent, with interest lowest for redemption in the third and sixth months. What the rates in new branches meant was that potentially a customer could pay four times the flat 12 percent annual rate charged since 1873 by the Casa Matriz downtown. The explanation given by the adminstration for different rates was that although there were fewer operations in the main branch, they were for goods that were worth much more. Therefore, if the collateral was sold, it would be much more likely to cover the costs of the loan operation. When the branches used the same interest scale as the main branch, the institution suffered "considerable losses." The fee for patrons who wanted to keep their goods out of the auction hall in 1881 without actually redeeming was 1 percent of the amount loaned.[46]

The charitable institution continued to be a resource for the government as well as for those with valuable collateral to hock. President Manuel González forced a loan of three hundred thousand pesos, which brought the total outstanding loans owed to the Monte by the government to more than 1 million pesos. In 1881 the Monte de Piedad faced a financial crisis. Competition for banking services from the newly created Banco Nacional Mexicano (founded with French capital), the Banco Mercantil (founded with Spanish capital), and the Banco Hipotecario (also founded with French capital) also troubled the Monte. When patrons of the Monte bank began changing bills for *pesos fuertes* (silver pesos), the institution turned to the new banks for loans and to the government for repayment of its debt. Both efforts failed, forcing the Monte to sell real-estate holdings.[47] The Monte de Piedad continued to face crisis conditions until April 30, 1884, when new director José Fuentes Núñez called a special meeting of the governing board. At that time all operations except pawning were suspended, and all remaining property was either mortgaged or sold, except for the headquarters building. Three branches in the city, along with the Puebla branch, were closed, and a loan of one hundred thousand pesos was finally secured from the Banco Mercantil. Following these measures, the Monte was able to pay out when customers exchanged their Monte de Piedad bills.[48] Table 6.7 shows the ebb and flow of the Monte's efforts to stabilize its finances while exchanging its bills for cash.

TABLE 6.7

Capital Balance at Monte de Piedad

Date	Deficit (in pesos)	Surplus (in pesos)
1850		346,442.00
1874	40,000.00	
1875	676,584.00	
Dec. 1884	940,482.20	
Apr. 1885	621,913.17	
Nov. 1885	428,205.32	
Jan. 1886	390,055.60	
Nov. 1886	320,008.26	
May 1887	299,859.83	
Oct. 1887	269,426.75	
Jan. 1888	272,515.45	
Feb. 1888	270,797.55	
Mar. 1888	273,306.43	
Dec. 1888	277,191.02	
June 1888	297,712.03	
Oct. 1888	306,889.48	

Source: El Siglo XIX, January 16, 1885; May 20, 1885; March 8, 1886; December 7, 1886; June 10, 1887; November 9, 1887; January 10, 1888; February 10, 1888; March 9, 1888; April 10, 1888; July 8, 1888; November 13, 1888; Esperanza Cabrera Siles and Patricia Escandón, *Historia de Nacional Monte de Piedad, 1775–1993* (México: Nacional Monte de Piedad, 1993), 63, 73, 74.

When the Monte closed three city branches and all branches outside the city in late 1884, the goods in the auction sections of Branch No. 3 and Branch No. 5 (located at Chavarri No. 3 and Puente de Jesús No. 2, respectively) were moved to Branch No. 4 (San Andrés), where people could go to redeem them or seek sale profits. The remaining six branches open at the end of 1884 were: Casa Matriz; Branch No. 1, Mesones 2nd block, No. 4; Branch No. 2, Merced 1st block, No. 3; Branch No. 6, at the corner of Moras and Sepulcros de Santo Domingo; Branch No. 7, at the corner of León and San Lorenzo; and Branch No. 8, at the corner of Zapo and Ancha. By 1886 only No. 1, No. 2, and No. 6 and the main branch were open. Auctions were staggered across the month at different branches, with none occurring on the same day. At the headquarters, clothes, furniture, and jewels all had separate auction days. In 1888 operations were stable enough that branch services were again expanded, with the Chavarri and Puente de Jesús offices reopening.[49]

For those who did not make regular visits to the Monte de Piedad or private pawnshops, there were nonetheless daily reminders of their existence, as seen in figure 8, a detail from an 1886 edition of *Diario del Hogar*. Both the Monte and brokers published announcements of sales of unredeemed goods in the city's daily newspapers, as required by law. The auction announcements could fill an entire page of a twelve-page newspaper. They were so ubiquitous in print culture that their form could be adapted to social and political commentary. For example, *El Hijo del Ahuizote*, an opposition paper that did not regularly run Monte or pawnbroker ads, nonetheless ran a spoof of one in a December 1888 issue. Under the familiar banner "Venta de Prendas," the item read in the standard language: "Those interested are advised that on 31 February, the following prendas that have been pawned in the Monte and whose pledge period has expired will be put up for sale." Then follows the list of "collateral" up for auction, only a portion of which is reproduced here: the idea of no reelection and tax supression; the military draft and the "Ley Fuga," or practice of shooting prisoners in the back; the Constitution of 1821; "The free Suffrage . . . to the blessed Souls" (this a spoof on the Monte's name, which included "de Ánimas" when founded); (the need for) double, triple, and multiple jobs; the preference for foreigners in government concessions and jobs; and a long list of "the viceroylaty of," with some real names of Porfirians, such as Don Teodoro Dehesa, and some fictional names, such as Don Carlos Diez Periodos and Don Prospero Embotellado.[50] The political satire worked because either the middle-class readers of *El Hijo de Ahuizote* frequented the Monte de Piedad themselves, or they regularly came across the institution's ads when they read other newspapers.

Literate urban residents were well informed about the charitable lending institution, as the press kept up a running commentary on the goings-on at the Monte and regularly urged the institution to expand its social services. During the troubled 1880s Francisco W. González, editor of *El Monitor Republicano*, advised the Monte to call "a meeting of 'hombres de dinero' who have humanitarian sentiments . . . and ask them for two or three million pesos, offering them a rate of return of five or six percent."[51] A week later, in an editorial signed "Juvenal," the *Monitor* described the director of the Monte de Piedad as a wooden statue, sitting by while "poor classes" needed help. When pawnshops closed over regulation issues, the editor felt the Monte should step up its services. Instead, the anxious poor who flooded into the Monte's offices had to deal with haughty employees and people pushing their way through long lines. Rhetorically, the editorial puzzled over how so many employees in the Monte branches could do so little to satisfy the public's need: opening late in the morning at ten A.M. and closing soon thereafter, taking their time in attending people who had to wait a long time, lending little compared to the value of goods, and so forth.[52] A few years later in August 1890, after complimenting director Fuentes Nuñez on his honest shepherding and the staff for its efforts to put operations in order, the editors of *Diario del Hogar* called on the Monte to further expand its services: "The Monte de Piedad has arrived lately at a level of staying afloat sufficient to sustain its improved condition, and now it is time to extend its sphere of action, establishing more branches and improving those already in existence . . . to benefit the poor."[53] Responding to the press criticism, the Monte published figures showing that, indeed, they were expanding their services. To wit, in the first eight months of 1890 the institution had lent over 180,000 pesos more than in the first eight months of 1889, for a total of over 1 million pesos.[54] Neither the newspaper editors nor the administration commented on what impact such an infusion of capital would have on the economy. The editors instead focused on the increased misery of the city's population, in need of the social service of collateral lending.

In 1877 Díaz, newly in power, had federalized welfare establishments in the city under the oversight of a public charity board under Gobernacíon. When he came back to formal power in 1884 (after Manuel González sat in as head of state), Díaz declared that it was "indispensable to complete the [capitalist] system, and to help Public Charity." He acknowledged that the government had a role in providing the means to assist the indigent classes, though the Díaz regime also stressed that the state role should be limited. Instead, the state promoted the role of the private sector in charity for the poor.[55] By the end of the century the Díaz government took steps to privatize the financing of the Monte de Piedad. Laws in February 1898, November 1899, and August 1904 redefined the Monte de Piedad and formally recognized it as a charitable corporation with a "private" juridical identity. Instead of Gobernación, the oversight body for the Monte and the fledgling Montepío Luz Saviñón was a new state-appointed Junta de Beneficencia. As a "private charity" with legal ownership of its funds, the Monte de Piedad invested in real estate.[56]

It is clear from table 6.8 that the volume of business in the Monte de Piedad increased sharply during the Porfiriato. Comparing figures for 1875

TABLE 6.8

Volume of Business at Monte de Piedad, 1875–1904

Date	Number of Branches	Transactions	Pesos Lent
Year 1875	Main & 4 branches	27,211	138,227.75
May 1883–Apr. 1884	Main & 3 branches		1,732,975.00
Dec. 1884	Main & 5 branches		68,591.75
May 1884–Apr. 1885	Main & 3 branches		720,826.75
Jan. 1886	Main & 3 branches	17,607	99,217.25
Feb. 1886	Main & 3 branches	16,245	82,273.76
Nov. 1886	Main & 3 branches	15,668	92,092.50
Year 1886	Main & 3 branches	206,169	1,112,887.60
May 1887	Main & 3 branches	15,453	77,733.25
June 1887	Main & 3 branches	14,975	83,209.25
Year 1887	Main & 3 branches	193,122	1,021,813.60
June 1888	Main & 3 branches	16,309	121,393.75
Oct. 1888	Main & 3 branches	18,786	98,957.00
Aug. 1890	Main & 3 branches	23,650	178,961.00
Year 1904			2,500,000.00

Source: *El Siglo XIX*, January 16, 1885; May 20, 1885; February 10, 1886; March 8, 1886; December 7, 1886; January 12, 1887; June 10, 1887; January 10, 1888; July 7, 1888; AGN, Gobernacíon, 4th section, leg. 875(1), exp. 1, no. 30; Moisés González Navarro, *La pobreza en México* (México: El Colegío de México, 1985), 118; *El Monitor Republicano*, September 9, 1890, 3.

to those for 1886 and 1887, there were seven times the number of the 1875 transactions in each of the latter two years for eight times the amount of pesos loaned. The 1904 volume was almost double that of the late 1860s. Middle-class clients continued to use the establishment in the later years, as they were able to pawn various objects of household adornment—furniture, clocks, lamps, statuettes—that were more expendable luxuries than silver tableware and were not necessarily heirlooms like expensive jewelry. It is not clear how much of the increase in volume is from the branch offices, some in neighborhoods where the increasingly proletarian popular classes would have been regular customers, as it was common for even two-income working-class families to be short of cash to meet expenses.[57]

El Monitor Republicano argued in 1886 that the Monte de Piedad branches had "the same odious character" as empeños, in that seldom did the auction room produce any profit for the former owner of the good: "We have pawn tickets in our possession that show the truth in what we say. The auctioned goods have a higher intrinsic value than what they are sold for. We know well that the appraisers to be on the safe side, and supported by the reglamento, conveniently fail to appraise according to the intrinsic value of the goods that are going up for auction. But this practice is eminently prejudicial to the unhappy ones [*los infelices*], and the exaggerated use [of undervaluing goods] stamps the most odious character on this institution, which should instead be charitable." In June 1904 the charitable lending institution reported 38,020 loan operations for the month, for a total of 370,844 pesos. Here the average loan of 9 pesos 75 centavos was higher than the average loan had been since the middle of the nineteenth century (see appendix 2, table E, for comparisons). The data for this month also include 34,403 redemptions, for a total of 332,146 reincorporated into the Monte de Piedad's capital. The only 10 percent difference between the number of loans and redemptions suggests that the majority of goods pawned with the institution returned to their owners. In any case the Monte only sold 4,620 items in June 1904, for a capital of 76,626 pesos, and they paid out 15,710 pesos to 3,456 patrons whose goods had been sold (an average of 4 ½ pesos per good).[58]

The nonprofit collateral-lending sector expanded at the end of the Porfiriato under the rubric of "Beneficencia Privada." In 1902 the Montepío Luz Saviñón, a charitable pawnshop on the model of the Monte de Piedad, opened with a private donation of 300,000 pesos given by Señora Luz Saviñón.[59] The breakdown from the business data for December presented in table 6.9 suggests that the Luz Saviñón clientele were generally in the middle class, pawning more jewelry and furniture than clothing. Seventy-one percent of the 22,045 transactions over these six months at the Montepío Luz Saviñón constitute loans that were made, 19 percent of the transactions represent pledge renewals, and only 10 percent involve a sale of an undredeemed good. Customers were less likely to extend their pledge periods in December than in subsequent months; also, the more expensive goods were more likely to have their pledge period extended with a new loan. This could mean that loan customers were more willing to part with cheaper collateral when they could not redeem it, or that customers were more likely to redeem more inexpensive collateral. December was a boom time for jewelry and furniture sales in the charitable Montepío.[60] In a front-page editorial at the end of August 1904, the official *El Imparcial* crowed that the privatization of charity had already had "good effects," noting that private donations to the Montepío Luz Saviñón were up.[61]

TABLE 6.9

Volume of Business at Montepío Luz Saviñón, December 1908–June 1909

	Pawned			Renewed			Sold		
Date/Category	Pesos Lent	No. Loans	Avg. Loan	Pesos Received	No. Loans	Avg. Fee	Pesos Received	No. Sales	Avg. Sale
Dec. 1908									
Clothing	1,858.75	606	3.07	197.00	40	4.93	3.50	2	1.75
Furniture/Objects	6,553.25	807	24.91	1,296.50	137	9.46	4,772.50	302	15.80
Jewels	22,259.00	890	25.01	2,161.75	101	21.40	10,193.00	331	30.79
Subtotal	30,671.00	2,301	13.33	3,565.25	278	12.82	14,969.00	635	23.57
Jan. 1909	30,570.00	2,275	13.44	13,058.75	591	22.10	6,973.50	327	21.33
Feb. 1909	31,350.25	2,063	15.20	15,143.75	638	23.74	3,911.74	303	12.91
Mar. 1909	33,690.75	2,226	15.14	15,508.25	638	24.31	4,511.25	312	14.46
Apr. 1909	38,574.50	2,400	16.07	16,919.75	636	26.06	5,076.00	295	17.21
May 1909	33,942.75	2,242	15.14	15,589.75	629	24.78	5,261.25	324	16.24
June 1909	29,488.50	2,185	13.50	14,338.25	697	20.57	3,906.00	340	11.49
Total	228,287.75	15,692	14.55	94,123.75	4,107	22.92	44,608.74	2,246	19.86

Source: AHCM, Gobierno del Distrito, Empeños, vol. 1420, exp. 109.

When a new version of the board game Juego de la Oca came out in 1907, entitled "Ciclo Histórico" and designed by Andrés Oscoy, square 39 commemorated the year 1775 with the phrase "Beneficio a los Pobres" and a picture of the imposing main branch of the Monte de Piedad, which still sits today across from the cathedral off the Zócalo.[62] With the nation's economy in crisis by 1907 due to an international depression, demands on the Monte de Piedad increased as customers sought to stretch their budgets and fewer people were buying goods at auction. Both of these trends meant that the Monte, clearly embedded in the nation's historical narrative and culture, was again headed for bankruptcy. The precarious situation was exacerbated when, in celebration of the centennial of Mexican Independence, goods pawned for less than a peso in February 1910 were returned in September 1910 without payment of the loan amount or the interest. Such generosity cost the Monte more than two thousand pesos.[63]

Both the charitable and entrepreneurial sectors of the pawning trade underwent transformations in the Porfirian era. The Monte de Piedad stumbled after experiments with different services and expanded in the face of an increasing population, including both a pinched working class and a middle class with more household possessions to parlay into cash loans. While private brokers often owned more than one business and could earn large profits, the nature of the pawning business remained volatile. Porfirian pawnbrokers were free to earn whatever interest the market would bear on their pawning transactions, but in other ways their endeavors were hemmed in by the Porfirian state.

Paradox, Discourse, and Broker-State Relations

Collateral-credit entrepreneurs continued to engage in debate about the proper role of the state in the economy, or the discourse of liberalism. Newspaper editors and reformers also expressed their opinions, whether about the behavior of brokers, the needs of the public, or the regulatory efforts of governors. Engaged in liberal development projects where foreign and national capital had free reign and pushed laissez-faire views against government intervention in labor relations, the Porfirian state took an interventionist stance in the pawning trade. Pawnbrokers no longer cast themselves as benevolent patriarchs succoring needy women but instead emphasized their rights as liberal businessmen.

The ministry of Gobernación continued oversight of both the private pawning trade and the Monte de Piedad (until the Monte was privatized in 1898). Porfirian legislators fine tuned pawning regulations, adding more specific details of the pawning process and bookkeeping, codifying the practice in order to "bring order" to the system. As they had been doing since the 1840s, pawnbrokers either attempted to amend laws to their liking or invented ways to circumvent them. In 1877 a group of brokers sued the city government over its right to require license renewals in order to continue operation of their businesses. A judge had the protesting brokers deposit their taxes with the Monte de Piedad while the case was being considered.[64] In February 1881 the *Diario Oficial* noted that an aim of new regulations was to replace state agents with "others who inspire more confidence in meeting their obligations."[65]

Interaction between individual brokers and the state could stem from failure to follow the complicated letter of the law. In two separate cases Maximiniana Zayas de Velasco, owner of an "empeño y tienda" on the corner of Santa María Street and Ratón Alley, and Doña Manuela Bistrain, also owner of a pawnshop, asked the city government in July 1877 for exemptions from the business-operation tax, as they had not received collateral goods since January. The city investigated through the police commissary and found that, indeed, neither woman was any longer in the pawning business, but they were still liable for taxation because they had not followed the article of the 1864 law that called for owners to alert the government of the closure of a business within three days of that closure and return the business license.[66] Pawnbrokers continued to have problems complying with closure requirements after the turn of the century.[67] In other cases red tape frustrated brokers who were bounced from one state branch to another. This was the case for Joaquín Poo, Juan B. Pérez, Laureano Sarandona, and Pedro Lobrado, whose requests for license renewals were rejected by the Ayuntamiento on grounds that this process was out of their jurisdiction but instead was in the purview of the Federal District (though the promulgation of the law requiring the license renewal was apparently within the city's authority).[68] Broker resistance to state intervention in their business affairs could take the form of ignoring regulations. In 1878 fourteen brokers did not pay their tax obligation to the city treasury on time.[69]

The editors at *El Monitor Republicano* viewed the troubles at the Monte de Piedad in the 1880s as leading directly to new regulations in the private sector. When the charitable institution faltered, people had to turn to private collateral lenders, which, because of the poor treatment of customers and their goods, brought more complaints to the ears of the government.[70] The 1886 regulations had a total of sixty-six articles, many of them with multiple-part subsections; together with sections of the new commercial code, they applied to any type of business that made cash loans on goods held as collateral. Equally detailed regulations aimed at cleaning up the city's markets also focused on hygiene and on reshaping small-business culture. The new Porfirian collateral-credit legislation specified the manner in which pawned clothing should be folded and stored "one meter above floor level," the tagging of each prenda with one card inside and another outside, and the physical layout of shops, with an office "comfortable for the public" and with wood floors.[71] Newspapers debated the correctness of these physical requirements. *El Nacional* proposed that the government had no authority to make these demands on brokers, as it "invaded the prerogatives of the domestic home" and the right to privacy even in business dealings. *El Partido Liberal* pointed out that if one followed this logic, then nothing could be ordered by the government, including safe carriages, clean restaurants, or restricted hours for pulque bars. To *El Nacional*'s argument that the government can only step in when "public security" is at stake, *El Partido Liberal* argued that regulating the physical condition of pawnshops met that requirement.[72]

New regulations spelled out the appraisal process in greater detail, outlining how different considerations should be used to determine the value of furniture, jewelry, and clothing. The auction process also fell under review. The owner of the collateral good up for auction had the right to be present and to "push up the bid" on his or her possession, a measured response to abuses in which brokers often sold goods below their market value. New laws continued to incorporate sections of old laws, and other laws from earlier times continued to be in force.[73] In December 1886 empeñeros petitioned the minister of Gobernación to repeal some of the articles of the November regulations. In particular they took issue with section 10 of Article 10, which limited the operating costs that they could recover from customers to 5 percent of the value of the pawned good. The government refused to alter the law, saying that it was not prejudicial, because the brokers were free to charge whatever interest they wanted and could therefore recover any costs in excess of the 5 percent.[74]

In January 1887 brokers responded to the new 1886 regulations by drawing up contracts with their customers that they argued were qualitatively different from pawning contracts, documents that formalized consignment transactions in which brokers had already been engaging. The language in the contracts stated that the customer would receive an amount "in anticipation" of the sale of goods that were left with the broker "in commission," and that the customer would pay the broker 30 percent of the sale price as commission or 25 percent of the amount advanced if the good did not sell. The consignment broker would have four months to sell the good for at least the price agreed upon by the two parties; the broker could sell it for less only if the buyer was someone procured by the customer, in which case the sale price would at least have to cover costs. Sale profits above the 30 percent fee were the property of the customer. If the good was not sold at the agreed price in four months' time, the broker could sell it for less without being liable to the consignee. If the object still did not sell, it would be adjudicated to the broker at the value of the originally agreed upon sale price.[75]

The editors of *El Siglo XIX* publicized this new-style contract in order to "inform" the general public. Once there was public reaction, the paper came out against the subterfuge of brokers "that mocked the precepts" of public policy. An editorial portrayed pawnbroker-consigners as wanting to "fight power to power ['potencia a potencia'] with the Government." The newspaper decried the brokers' intransigence: "Why do all countries pass laws if not so that they are faithfully obeyed? From where comes the right of one *gremio* [guild or trade] to protest in order to erase them, whether in silence or with actions? And this is Mexico, where we do not consent to tutelage outside the constituted authorities, and at this time of order, of peace, of our solid and firmly rooted institutions! The national sentiment is stirred up against these resolutions of the owners of pawnshops, perhaps unconsciously, and for this the organs of the press in general attack them vigorously day by day."[76] Arguing in favor of regulating usury, the editorial noted that the nation had suffered enough at the hand of the *agiotistas*, who financed fledgling governments at high interest; that individual property owners had lost real estate to foreclosures; and that all kinds of businesses were hampered by onerous loan terms. Pawnshops, in turn, ate away at the salaries of public and private employees, day laborers, and artisans. Employing a positivist simile, the paper said the pawnshops were no more than "the pustules that denote the ill state of the social body."[77]

Pawnbrokers had long defended their right to earn profits unencumbered, arguing that they were commercial lending establishments like any other. The editors of *El Siglo XIX*, however, saw things differently. There were key differences between pawnshops and other lending enterprises. Pawnshops were physical establishments open to the general public, while other lenders "did not have fixed places of business" (presumably meaning that they worked out of their homes or offices of some other types of business) and dealt with individuals. Pawnshops issued identical tickets to multiple customers, with only the amount varying, while lenders issued unique documents, with the particulars fitting specific instances. The editors argued that pawnshops were "public institutions" and therefore subject to regulation by the government. "Just as the authorities have perfect right to close unsanitary establishments, and to prohibit the sale of poisonous substances, they have the right to impede all types of abuses in pawnshops," whether going under the name of *empeño* or some other disguise.[78]

Manuel Romero Rubio, the minister of Gobernación, foiled the brokers' attempt to circumvent pawning regulations. He informed the governor of the Federal District that "the new *casas de comisiones* [consignment shops] that have opened in manifest substitution for the old *casas de empeños*" were to be held to the same regulations as pawnshops, as their transactions implied a lending contract with interest secured by a collateral good.[79] Brokers responded with a more militant stance, closing their doors in protest on the day that the new law went into effect. *El Siglo XIX* reported that the businessmen assumed that even a one-day closure would send their clients into the streets, demanding that the government meet the brokers' demands so as to guarantee access to cash flow through loans. The people, however, reportedly sided with the government instead.

In the face of repeated militancy by private brokers, newspaper editors wondered rhetorically why the government did not expand the budget of the Monte de Piedad so that its branches could meet the needs of the poor during this crisis. The editors understood that the government had other financial obligations and that the Monte's impact would be minimal, given the limitations of hours and staff. Other reformist proposals surfaced in response to the stance of the private brokers, such as founding a private charitable society in which citizens would have shares that would open "*casas de empeño* with all the advantages that the ones that are today closed have, and with none of the dangers that owners of goods have found in them."[80]

A week after the pawnshop closures to protest new regulations, their reopening was announced on posters on street corners all over the city. The papers reported that while agreeing to comply with the regulations, the brokers exacted higher interest rates. *La Federación* reported that "now they no longer lend for one real [i.e., centavo] per peso for four months, but instead they calculate day by day. . . . Now they impose on the loan 50 percent interest for three months and however many days, plus charges for successive renewals. . . . Some brokers, though not all, are charging 20 percent interest a month, or 2 reales for each peso, such that someone asking for a loan of one peso . . . will end up paying two pesos [when they redeem their good]." *La Convención Radical* reported that pawnbrokers agreed to the new regulations but now charged 13 centavos per peso loaned in the first and second months, 23 centavos in the third and fourth month, and the fifth month after the good was appraised for auction, 100 centavos per peso loaned to keep the good from going up for sale. For its part *El Monitor Republicano* reported shortly after the pawnshops reopened in January 1887 that interest rates had increased to "inconceivable" amounts "of ninety, one hundred, and two hundred percent!"[81]

This series of editorials reveals the public debate about contradictory tenets of liberalism: the rights to profit on the one hand, and the rights to protection from abuse, even relief from poverty, on the other. The *Monitor* was not against usury per se, as it followed "economic science," but was against "this runaway usury [*desenfrenada usura*]." An editorial signed by "Juvenal" a few years later went further, calling on an expansion of and improved service in the Monte de Piedad to combat usury, because "Mexico, underneath its cape of brilliant colors woven by the new streets and modern buildings, is a city in which . . . misery reigns; this society, for the most part, is corroded by usury, and, what better way to combat this cancer than to fight against usury?"[82] Again, the *Monitor* took up the question of the legality of usury in a developing liberal state in an editorial signed "M.":

> Usury, as a form of credit, has social benefits, because it has the virtue of multiplying capital, and consequently increases the productive force of that capital. We do not believe that anyone condemns the freedom that the law has wanted to guarantee for contracts for interest loans, because this would put obstacles in the way of the circulation of one of the most important elements of production. But there are in Mexico, certain forms of usury that are certainly not those that we want to promote, but on the contrary, those that we want to eliminate. Certain forms that do not bring prosperity, neither in the field of the big speculators, the risky companies, nor in the industrious application of labor. This is not the usury that feeds the prosperity of budding businesses with the capital that they provide, but instead the usury of ruin, which builds itself up on the misery of the lower classes, and the needs of the middle class.[83]

In yet another editorial two days later, the same author went so far as to say "being this kind of lender" was unpatriotic.

Since Bourbon times reformers had hoped charitable institutions such as the Monte de Piedad would replace private pawnshops. This was apparently the result in the provincial capital of Guanajuato, where the closure of three empeños was attributed by journalists to the establishment of a Monte de Piedad in that city in 1888.[84] In Mexico City, however, "instead of the number of pawnshops diminishing, others were founded, and, surprisingly, right next to the pompous branches of the Montepío."[85] The editors decried the pawning clientele's "inexplicable preference" for private pawnshops, where they paid double and triple interest rates, losing their possession in the end without gaining even a profit from its auction. The reasons for such preference continued to be that the transactions were much faster (because private brokers were less concerned about the possibility of goods' having been stolen than the Monte was) and less complicated. And the access was better with the private shops' more ample hours of operation.[86]

Pawnbrokers continued to petition the minister of Gobernación to change laws or build in exemptions. In August 1890 they complained of a new municipal tax that levied a separate 2 percent tax on all goods adjudicated to the owners of pawnshops. Empeñeros took the government to court to push for an interpretation of the law that would tax them only for the difference between the loan amount and the good's adjudicated value, not on the entire value of the good. The courts eventually decided in favor of the brokers, who in November 1891 petitioned Gobernación to make the city treasury pay back 2,000 pesos that was wrongly collected from them.[87]

In September 1895 the city's Hacienda commission noted that tax revenues from pawnshops were low, while the number of establishments was growing. The city council appointed licenciado Mariano Sánchez to a new auditor's position, created to investigate whether the brokers were paying proper taxes. The brokers immediately complained of this new intrusion into their business affairs, questioning the jurisdiction of the Ayuntamiento and arguing that only the president of the Republic had the authority to alter the regulations.[88] The owners lost this case, as Gobernación ruled that the city council had the right to govern and appoint employees toward that end.[89] Sánchez found that brokers were, indeed, defrauding the city by withholding what amounted to 120,000 pesos in taxes. The auditor believed that if brokers received 2,000 pesos of collateral in a month, one-quarter of them would be redeemed, leaving brokers with approximately 1,500 pesos' worth of goods to auction. Instead of presenting all of these goods to auction appraisers and inspectors, he accused brokers of holding back 1,000 pesos' worth and therefore saving the 5 percent appraisal fee and the 2 percent adjudication fee payable to the city. Ultimately he called for reforming the regulations to demand a receipt from the broker proving that a good had been redeemed and therefore would not be auctioned off.[90]

At the end of 1895 licenciado Francisco Alfaro represented six brokers who were victims of a corrupt government employee who had collected one amount from brokers then recorded another amount in the city's treasury books; the government expected the brokers to pay the amount embezzled by the tax collector.[91] In January 1897 Gobernación clarified the tax obligations for private pawnshops. Owners were to pay 2 percent of the amount they loaned out, 2 percent of the value of goods adjudicated to them or acquired through consignment, and 5 percent on the value of goods up for auction. The owners petitioned to have these various taxes substituted for one of 3 percent over the amount loaned to customers, claiming that the government would actually earn more. The argument against this change was that a flat tax would open the door for brokers to reap profits on the bazaar business, buying and selling used goods without paying taxes. Also, since different brokers made more money from certain operations than others, they should be taxed separately. Brokers were unsuccessful in pushing a flat tax and continued to defy the government by holding back tax payments. In August 1898 twenty-one brokers paid fines of over 4,000 pesos for tax evasion.[92]

In 1900, debating whether to restructure the four different taxes charged under 1897 tax codes into a flat tax for pawnbrokers, city-council members articulated why regulation was important: "The authorities have the right to intervene in the pawning operations because there is a third party involved, the owner's rights need protection. In the case of bazaars, the owner of the good loses rights of possession upon sale." This argument reflects a change in liberalism during the Porfiriato "from an atomistic to an organic philosophy," with "organic liberalism" privileging the needs of society over those of the individual.[93] Council members characterized pawnbroking and the bazaar business with positivist imagery as "toxic for society and representing the same gangrene of certain social classes." But the councilmen also distinguished between the business types. Bazaars (of which it was noted there were only six according to 1900 license tax records) catered not to those with "true needs" but instead to those who had the intention of getting whatever price possible for the goods, perhaps hiding a crime. These folks avoided pawnshops, because the pawn ticket could be the thread by which the police would discover them and punish their crime. The city council believed that the reporting of business volume for taxation purposes by pawnbrokers was "perfectly unbelievable" and even "laughable," with brokers underreporting in order to diminish their tax base. Given the inability of a liberal government to interfere in interest rates, even "illegitimate interest," because of the "the principles of economic science," the city council settled for "imposing taxes in such a manner that meets the needs of public power and also limits the gouging of the needy classes."[94]

One exchange of documents from 1908 allows an examination of the positivist trend of collecting statistics from the perspectives of the pawnbrokers and the statesmen. In April 1907 the government of the Federal District required pawnbrokers to fill out daily reports that separated their business transactions by loan, repawning, and sale. After filing the first installment of such documents in May, brokers complained that the data collection was too time consuming and succeeded in having the reports due biweekly instead of daily, though the brokers' request to leave off the repawning and sales information was denied. Still seeking to rid themselves of the role of statistician, in September 1908 brokers representing two dozen businesses petitioned to alter a July 1907 addendum to the 1886 pawnshop regulations in order to ease their burden of compiling monthly statistics on the volume of pawning, extension of contracts, and sale of collateral goods.[95] If the government needed the data, they argued, then government employees should collect it:

> We are disposed, Mr. Governor, to provide to the authorities whatever data they ask for about the march of our business and we promptly offer to show the government inspectors and commissioners our books and documents each time we are required to do so in order that they acquire all the necessary information; but neither our aptitudes nor our labor allows us to comply with the requirements fixed by the addition to which we refer, as our contribution to this compulsory formation of statistics produces defective results, as we do not have the capacity that the work demands . . . and we are obliged to spend our time in a task that that is very much beyond our abilities, and the result does not serve the ends the government seeks.

In October, when their petition got bumped from the district government to the federal ministry of Gobernación, the brokers reiterated their request through two attorneys, Lorenzo Elízaga and Fernando Noriega. The renewed request went further than the earlier petition, criticizing the positivist penchant for collecting statistics: "We consider it of very little interest for the government to be ordering and classifying of the data contained in these lists, and we estimate that even in the impossible likelihood that the statistics are perfect, they will not serve the ends that are sought, that which is beyond our reach. Since the statistics do not include the Nacional Monte de Piedad, the Montepío Saviñón, and other similar establishments, there is no doubt that [the government] will never manage to obtain complete statistics without those from these establishments." The government defended its statistical mission: "Certainly the collection of statistical data, of whatever class it may be, can serve as a basis for the study of legislation or for other interesting and diverse questions." But the government also admitted that if the statistics were incomplete, conclusions based on them would be flawed. The solution found by the government was not to stop collecting statistics from private pawnbrokers but instead to add the charitable institutions to the project.[96]

Porfirian pawnbrokers continued to resist regulation of their trade, turning to long-standing petition strategies as well as more militant actions to effect legal changes. The identification of pawnbroking with Spanish ethnicity continued, as did the persistence of pawnshops at the same addresses and the steadiness of pawning clientele. Women continued to constitute only a small fraction of brokers, and their businesses may have been more vulnerable than those of men. Yet the nature of pawning businesses and institutions changed as the city grew under the Porfirian liberal development model. At the Monte de Piedad financial trouble stemmed from banking endeavors, and some branch offices had to close temporarily during the Porfiriato before it expanded further. As part of the Porfirian welfare apparatus, the Monte underwent a transformation from a public to a private institution under the liberal Díaz regime. Pawning establishments fanned out into new areas of the Porfirian city, though the increase in establishments did not keep up with the population explosion in the city. This narrowing of competition, also reflected in the ownership of multiple businesses by individual entrepreneurs as well as pawning companies, allowed pawnbrokers to charge higher interest rates for their services. The pawning business changed during the Porfiriato, with larger capitalization in private shops and higher interest rates and a transition into consignment shops.

The story of Mexican pawnbroking continued to concern links between entrepreneurship, class, and ethnicity at this tier of the economy. Spaniards had now dominated this niche in the economy for over a century. In the beginning the pulperos had been at the bottom rung of a retail hierarchy, as likely to go broke because of pawning trade as to make any money from it. With empeños, lending outright and not against a retail customer's account, brokers specialized their business. When usury restrictions fell away again under liberal governance, the trade developed into different classes depending on capitalization, with some Spanish brokers and firms making big profits and wielding sizable capital investments.

The Porfirian era saw a continuation of the role of the state as mediator between sectors of society as well as liberal paradoxes of regulation and intervention for public welfare alongside laissez-faire discourse and policies. The state increased regulation, with very specific laws and interventions in the pawning process. While stepping up taxation measures and prosecution of brokers' circumvention strategies, the Porfirian state was staunchly liberal in that profits and interest rates were left alone and therefore skyrocketed. It was also liberal in protecting property rights of clients up to the point of adjudication of goods. Concern with the well-being of the poor, especially the "deserving" poor, persisted in the Mexican political culture, though now carrying out the Monte de Piedad's task of helping the needy was up to "private" charity.

While newspaper editors, reformers, and bureaucrats pushed for stricter regulation and limits on the profits of pawnbrokers, they all stayed within the boundaries of liberal economic discourse, recognizing the sacred right of businessmen to enter into contracts and to earn interest in their commercial endeavors. Pawnbrokers continually employed this discourse in defense against what they judged to be a paradoxical acceleration of the regulation of their trade by a regime that in other ways was very liberal. The Díaz state was also a positivist state, and as such aimed to bring order to a rapidly expanding pawning business with continued ties to the fencing of stolen goods. It also needed tax revenues to maintain its power, and the pawnbrokers' increased tax burden can be seen in this light. The liberal state could not outlaw usury, as the lending contract was as inviolable as any other contract. Instead, the state continued to support the expansion of charitable collateral lending in order to dampen the effects of abusive pawnbrokers. There was much more conflict about business rights versus the public good on the horizon, however. The Díaz era came to an abrupt end in 1910, and in the revolutionary turmoil that followed, the culture of everyday credit brought people into the streets of Mexico City.

SEVEN

A Material Revolution

Militancy, Policy, and Housekeeping, 1911–20

In February 1915 neighborhood women amassing "strength from who knows where" removed sewing machines, desks, and dressers during pawnshop sackings and carried them down the streets, fighting off others who wanted the property for themselves. Pawnbrokers informed a reporter from *El Demócrata* (a newspaper siding with Venustiano Carranza's Constitutionalist cause) about the collective actions of these empowered "mujeres del pueblo." Their businesses were in eastern neighborhoods around San Antonio Tomatlán and Manuel Doblado, along Guerrero in the northwestern suburbs, along La Paz in the northeast, and along the new Avenida Netzahualcoyotl in the south. The pawnbrokers blamed the revolution for trouble in their neighborhoods. Small groups of supporters of revolutionary general Emiliano Zapata allegedly broke into their pawnshops after they resisted opening their doors. Once inside, the soldiers allegedly proceeded to pick among the goods for weapons, jewels, saddles, and hats that were to their liking. They then called on the crowd not to leave the pawnbrokers anything, "not even the clothes of the employees and the servants." The "rabble" emptied the businesses of collateral goods, also "carrying off even the wood from the counters and the shelves." When the "so-called conventionalist authorities" were alerted to the events, the reporter noted with irony, the very same troops who had fanned the fire were called in to put it down. Reportedly, the Zapatistas let their friends escape while selecting others for summary execution right there on the street.[1] Thus, the Mexican Revolution, with all its factional name-calling and tumultuous energy, played out in the neighborhoods and pawnshops of Mexico City.

Relations between pawnbrokers, city residents, and the state had been tense for some time. Pawnshop sackings like those in February 1915 also occurred during the Decena Trágica, or "ten tragic days" in February 1913, when counterrevolutionary forces assassinated President Francisco Madero, who had been elected after Díaz went into exile. Porfiristas laid siege to the city, bringing sustained revolutionary violence to the capital for the first time.[2] Now, "war polarized the politics of everyday life."[3]

The contradictions of the Porfirian liberal development program, including a growing but frustrated middle class, culminated in labor militancy and anti-foreign sentiments at the turn of the twentieth century. This combined with other factors to weaken the position of Díaz. The jailing of opposition journalists, the lack of turnover at the top echelons of government, and the political inflexibility in the face of democratic pressures all set the stage for Díaz's overthrow by Madero and his followers in 1911.[4] The revolution ushered in by Madero's call for democratic elections in 1910 resulted in a decade of civil war, but it eventually brought to power a new group of middle-class statesmen who embarked on two decades of social change. Revolutionary legislation wiping out high-interest collateral lending in 1914 was an early item on a radical agenda that included land reform and, later, the expropriation of natural resources. The directors of the Monte de Piedad shut the doors of the various installations at the first sign of revolutionary activity, successfully protecting material goods in their temporary custody. Private pawnbrokers also tried to protect their inventories from soldiers and angry credit customers but with very different results.

The Politics of Collateral Credit

Alliances between skilled and unskilled workers characterized political culture in the city in the first five years of the Mexican Revolution. Worker organizations joined forces with other sectors of society, especially when demands involved consumption issues. Revolutionary generals supported popular mobilizations in their bid to establish authority in newly constituted neighborhoods where respect for authority and wealth had waned. A pattern of radicalization had emerged in some neighborhoods, beginning with Madero's campaign for the presidency and stepped up after 1911.[5] In the material context of high inflation, chronic shortages of food, and worthless paper money, consumption needs and the desire to protect material investments in collateral goods led pawning customers down a revolutionary path of political action.

Not just proletarians put collateral credit on the revolutionary agenda. Much of the collateral in pawnshops sacked during the revolution represents consumption levels beyond the means of most factory workers—the desks and wardrobes the "superwomen" hauled through the streets, typewriters, bicycles. Moreover, some pawnshops sacked were in new middle-class areas of the city. Between 1905 and 1915, middle- and working-class residents suffered price inflation and stagnant wages. After 1913 incredible political instability made housekeeping from day to day even more challenging than usual. Petitions, collective action, and pawnshop sacking were strategies used to deal with this deteriorating situation. Acrimony between city residents and private pawnbrokers was not a simple class conflict between middle-class brokers and working-class clients, as middle-class residents were regular collateral-credit users. Conflict also involved ethnic hatred and nationalism. In the public mind brokers were Spanish and wealthy, both punishable offenses in the opinion of the mestizo Mexican public.[6] In concert with other nationalist manifestations of revolutionary fervor aimed at North Americans and the Chinese and continuing long-term ethnic hatred aimed at Spaniards, pawnshop customers protested against "los miserables gachupines."[7]

The newspapers in the Madero period regularly reported instances of abuse and fraud by pawnbrokers in their roles as purveyors of used goods and petty lenders, echoing earlier times. In December 1911 a crowd burned a pawnshop to the ground after its owner struck a client who had complained about the high interest rate.[8] A month later at a pawnshop located in the sixth block of Dr. Vertis, when Juana Rodríguez, with child in arms, tried to pawn a sarape, the clerk argued with her about the loan amount. When "el hispano" allegedly jumped over the counter and hit the woman, people in the neighborhood began to congregate and throw stones at the pawnshop. The police arrived and took the woman and the pawnbroker to the police station, where the clerk was detained for hitting the woman.[9] In another case Salvador Beltrán paid ten pesos for a walking stick with a gold tip at a downtown "empeño-bazar" on Jesús María near the Merced market. Soon after leaving the pawnshop, a neighboring watch repairman told Beltrán that the tip of the cane was only gold plate.[10] Shopping at the pawnshop like this suggests that some had only enough money to consume second-hand goods, a customary path of consumption in the city.

Porfirian pawning legislation remained in force in the city during the short reign of President Madero. The first step toward radical change in the legal structuring of pawnbroker-client relations came under the government of former Porfirian and then Maderista general Victoriano Huerta. Huerta emerged as military ruler after Madero's assassination in February 1913, ruling until his ouster by a coalition of revolutionary generals in August 1914. In March 1914 the city's newspapers brimmed with news of the impending changes in empeño regulations. Glowing reviews of this aspect of Huerta's "transcendental" social policy benefiting the middle class as well as workers must be read with a grain of salt, as there was rigorous press censorship for the duration of his dictatorship.[11]

On April 16, 1914, the Huerta government supplemented existing regulations for the pawning trade in a short five-article decree that aimed to decrease the loss of personal property by pawnshop customers due to the dire economic situation. The first article conferred the right of pawnshop clients to renew pawn contracts by paying only the interest accumulated to date, with the lender obliged to renew the same conditions as those in the old contract. The second, third, and fourth articles concerned installment payments and other flexible options for borrowers.[12] These changes reflected an increasing difficulty in putting together funds to recover collateral goods.

Back in 1912, when revolutionary fighting broke out in the city, the governing board of the Monte de Piedad had ordered the doors and walls reinforced, more security guards added, and the more expensive jewelry stored in strong boxes. Employees were to have pistols on hand. With the coup against Madero in early 1913, the main headquarters as well as branch offices of the Monte closed their doors. Consequently, they survived a ten-day siege that reduced sections of the city to rubble, while retail stores and other commercial establishments were looted. The government extended the pledge period for goods that were shut up in the Monte from six to nine months, resuming auctions for goods whose extended terms had expired in September 1913. Supposedly, when Pancho Villa brought his troops to Mexico City in November 1914, he said, "Don't touch the Monte de Piedad, it is the bank of the poor."[13] While the Monte in fact was not fundamentally for the poor, the discourse that had secured its reputation as such (witness the "Beneficio a Los Pobres" of the 1907 Juego de la Oca) apparently saved it from plunder. The institution remained closed until February 1915, when only branch offices reopened.[14] The main branch did not resume lending until January 1916. The Montepío Luz Saviñón apparently remained open during the revolutionary period, but it only had one installation, located near the main branch of the Monte de Piedad.[15]

In May 1914 a reform called for extending the existing requirement for bills of sale when automobiles, sewing machines, typewriters, and "tires, head lights [*farolas*], implements of furniture manufacturing, etc.," were pawned. New regulations in September 1914 added more luxury goods: there were to be no sizable loans secured by jewels, pianos, fine furniture, or their accessories without the presentation of a corresponding bill of sale or other guarantee of the honest origin of the good.[16] This provision, continuing the long-standing tradition of state attempts to curb patterns of theft and fencing in pawnshops through "forbidden collateral" lists, was to be expected given the chronic insecurity of homes and businesses during the revolutionary fighting.[17]

During the "ten tragic days" in February 1913, the pawnshop at the corner of Ancha and Victoria (three blocks south of the Alameda Park) owned by the Garcia brothers was sacked, apparently by Felix Díaz's troops, with a reported loss of thirty thousand pesos' worth of jewels.[18] This report and the almost four hundred goods in the transactions database from April 1915 show that middle-class clients turned to the private brokers for collateral loans when the Monte was closed. Almost half of the goods up for auction at the empeño owned by Silvio Calvo, located at the corner of Ancha and San Antonio (five blocks south of the Alameda), were held for loans over ten pesos. Among the more expensive goods hocked with Calvo were three sewing machines (securing loans worth fifty, thirty-five, and thirty pesos respectively) and a Monarch typewriter (forty pesos).[19] The average loan was only two and a half pesos at the pawnshop owned by José Escandón on Verdis. In contrast to Calvo's goods and in keeping with the nineteenth-century pattern, two-thirds of the collateral left by Escandón's customers at the end of 1914 was cloth (66 percent, including clothing, whole cloth, and linens), securing loans from between twelve centavos and five pesos.[20]

What impact would the disparate loans of twenty-five centavos and fifty pesos have on a household budget in the city at this tumultuous time? A 1913 Labor Department cost-of-living survey found that "almost all the women are occupied, in addition to domestic chores, in jobs such as seamstresses, sandal making, etc., bringing the sustenance of the family from 40 centavos to one or 1.4 pesos daily."[21] So just as the revolutionary turmoil began in the city, the need for multiple incomes for households to get by continued. But 1913 was only the beginning of the material crises brought to the city by revolution. If ever the traditional discourse about pawning's meeting "urgent daily needs to feed families" was relevant to the collateral credit process, it was during the years 1914–16. While wages and salaries in Mexico City since Bourbon times were rarely sufficient for the standards of living and need to keep up appearances of residents of the capital, the repeated emissions of quickly worthless paper currency exacerbated the usual interruptions in provisions and high inflation that war brings. While real wages for factory workers increased by 1913 following strikes and other worker agitation, with textile-factory workers throughout the country securing a minimum wage of one peso twenty-five centavos, multiple currencies and political instability conspired to keep price increases well above wage increases throughout 1914–16. In addition official wages applied to specific organized workers, not to the city's labor force generally, and certainly not for the many employed in domestic service and as day laborers.

The prolonged fiscal crisis for households began with Huerta's victory. Huerta forced loans from the major emission banks, lowering their reserve limits in the process. Residents rushed to change their paper money into hard currency, and on November 5, 1913, banks by law could stop exchanging paper money for coins. Price inflation only increased. Meanwhile, revolutionary groups throughout the country printed their own money.[22] Huerta's government suspended bank operations by decree from December 1913 until the end of March 1914, hoping to give time for new official paper currency issued by the Banco de Londres y México to take hold. Instead, the currency shortage intensified.[23] With the ouster of Huerta competing currency emissions continued, with paper-money values extremely volatile. The year 1915 was a deadly one, with long food lines and street demonstrations when Villista currency was invalidated. Starvation loomed as railroad supply lines were cut off. Conflict, first between Huerta and revolutionaries and then among revolutionaries from mid-1914 to early 1916, "left an indelible mark on the city's women," with many turning to prostitution to make ends meet.[24] With seemingly endless price increases, growing unemployment, and food scarcity, a collateral loan for one peso or five pesos would not go as far as it used to in covering housekeeping expenses, but it was not needed any less. If anything, the need for collateral credit increased across the board.

In contrast to the regulations of sexual commerce, the revolutionary pawning regulation did not see policy reversals each time power changed hands.[25] The different power contenders responded to union demands of unskilled workers (such as streetcar workers, electricians, seamstresses, and *cigarreras*) that included pawning issues. Union activity stepped up after Huerta's defeat in August 1914 by the short-lived alliance between the armies of Generals Carranza, Alvaro Obregón, Zapata, and Villa. New revolutionary leaders took control of city governance under the leadership of First Chief Carranza. City residents, including and sometimes led by women, contributed to the debate about the role of the state in mediating issues of daily life as they petitioned the government for relief from pawnbrokers, protested in front of closed provisioning arenas, and sacked pawnshops to recover their goods.

The infamous usury of pawnbrokers prompted authorities to consider interest-rate reductions.[26] In September 1914 regulations issued by the coalition imposed new interest rates. Pawnbrokers could charge only 3 percent a month, with a trade-off of a reduction in taxes levied against pawnbrokers, with tax rates lowest for those charging the lowest interest. This was a significant reduction in profits for brokers. Interest rates were as high as 16 percent monthly. At this rate customers would pay 64 percent interest on what they had borrowed to redeem goods when the four-month pledge period was up.[27] Under the revolutionary reforms brokers were guaranteed one month's interest, but after that they had to prorate interest should a good be redeemed before a month was up. If a good diminished in value due to negligence, the broker was responsible for the difference. When a pledge period passed and the owner of the good did not renew the pawn contract, the good was to go to auction, as had been customary, and any value above the legal interest and the cost of appraisal were still to be delivered to the owner of the good.[28]

Bureaucrats, workers, neighbors, and newspapers continued to debate the fate of pawnshops in the context of social revolution and diminished institutional pawning venues. A drastic proposal came in October 1914 from the Casa del Obrero. After a march of three thousand workers to the National Palace, they demanded that pawnshops, which they believed profited from their poverty, be closed permanently.[29] Other proposals followed. The consultant Torres called for separating the empeño business from the used goods business, as "bazares" only disguised illicit pawnbroker practices. Newspapers reported that Governor Heriberto Jara himself was considering closing the pawnshops altogether and expanding the services of the Monte de Piedad to take their place. Jara had the reputation of being one of the "anti-Spanish" elements among the Carrancistas.[30]

By November 1914 the uneasy alliances between Carranza and Obregón on the one hand and the more radical Villa and Zapata on the other hand fell apart as divisions among their delegates at the constitutional convention in Aguascalientes widened. Early that month Carranza's forces did a sweep of pawnshops in Mexico City to confiscate weapons and other goods pawned by ex-federal soldiers, hoping to keep them out of Zapatista hands.[31] Bystanders watching "celebrate[d] that the government took the army goods" because the brokers had profited from the sweat of the poor: "Three years ago the pawnshops were 'peciligas asquerosas' and now each one is a jewelry store or a luxurious warehouse."[32]

At the end of November 1914 the generals running the city for the newly victorious Conventionist forces (as Carranza and Obregón retreated to Veracruz) stepped up the attack on private pawnbroking. Governor Vicente Navarro ordered all private pawnbrokers to return within two months' time all collateral that had not been adjudicated to the ownership of the lenders up to that date, without charging interest on those with a loan value of less than five pesos.[33] How might these reforms affect individual participants in the pawning process? Of the almost 400 database goods still considered the property of the customer in April 1915, 14 percent were worth five pesos or more. The pawnbroker José Escandón would have lost the chance to charge interest on 92 percent of 341 pawned goods he had up for auction, while Salvio Calvo would have lost the interest on 42 percent of 53 goods his clients had not yet redeemed that were up for auction. For Calvo and Escandón's customers, of course, compliance with this decree would mean the return of their private property without the obligation to pay outstanding loans. Pawnbrokers refused to make collateral loans under these conditions, which meant that with the Monte de Piedad already closed, housekeepers with increasing needs for collateral credit would not be able to secure it.

"Does the Law Only Apply to the Poor?"

In the face of growing opposition to their business practices, pawnbrokers extended their long-standing collective petitioning strategy and organized a Unión de Casas de Préstamos, a lobbying strategy that other foreign entrepreneurs used as well. The "lenders' union" tried to negotiate with revolutionary governors to suspend the decree (especially the five-peso rule) and instead set up another commission to further study the problem. In a petition dated December 1, 1914, union leaders identified themselves as Spaniards—"the majority of those associated with us are of Spanish nationality"—and enlisted the help of the new Spanish Minister, José Caro, who had arrived in the capital in September. The International Committee of businessmen organized boycotts whenever a new army coming into town tried to impose their paper money, only reopening when allowed to do business exclusively in gold and silver coins. The Lenders' Union used the boycott strategy as well, hoping to affect policy, but with disastrous consequences for other players on the stage of everyday credit.[34]

One hundred and fifty two residents of the city, half of them women, petitioned the government after the brokers' petition "in exercise of our civil rights," urging the new governors not to back down.[35] Illustrating that they were informed "habitantes" of the city participating in its governance, the residents recapped the main points about limiting interest and abolishing the abuses of pawnbrokers as stated in the revolutionary decree, noting that they had read the law the day it was published in *La Nación*.[36] The petition, whose first two signers were Brígida Macias and Tisa Ayana, paints brokers as scofflaws: instead of complying with the decree, pawnbrokers shut their doors. It was bad enough that empeñeros got rich exploiting the proletariat, residents complained—they also thought they were above the law. The residents' petition analyzed the politics of usury using revolutionary rhetoric of class struggle:

> In effect, since remote times until today, philosophers and legislators have condemned usury, even if it is moderate; our Civil Code limits the profits earnable by interest; yet we see in the case which concerns us today, in this Capital such speculation occurs that reaches an interest of 14 percent monthly, even if the loan is repaid the following day, lent under extremely sure guarantees. We see that in the passing of a very short time the lenders have become rich on this exploitation of the proletariat, of those who suffer from hunger. Oh Señor! We can't help but admire, give a vote of thanks to the philanthropic government that would repress unmoderated usury and protect with justice its victims, far, very far from qualifying as hard or unjust the legal disposition that we have mentioned. But even if it were harsh, would it be the case that for this reason it would be legal to evade its compliance? . . . The law may be harsh, but it is the law, and this means that it must be complied with.[37]

El Correo Español reported that on December 3 pawning customers were parking themselves in front of the closed pawnshops, demanding the return of their goods in compliance with the law. The newspaper noted, "naturally, the discussions between owners of pawnshops and the public have been considerably bitter, and some scandal cannot be far off." The same day that customers were marching in front of shops, Cirilio López, owner of the empeño and bazaar on Avenida de la Paz in the far north of the city, wrote to the government in support of their measures against those he called "los miserables Gachupines." He was a "Mexican" broker, referring to "mi general Villa" and saying that only Felix Díaz supported empeñeros.[38] The anti-Spanish nature of the popular movement against pawnbrokers intensified. In their next petition to the governor dated December 4, organized pawnshop customers demanded that pawnshops be forced open and collateral returned to the thousands of clients camped out front of them "exercising their rights." Harking back to the days of conquest, they accused brokers of trying to repeat the abuses of that era and the colonial system: "It is about time, after more than a century since our political independence, that we energetically make them understand, that those times have already gone, and that Spaniards, like all foreigners, are obliged to respect and comply with the legal dispositions of the Public Authority of the Mexican Nation."[39] In this last aspect the petition supports scholarship concerning why anti-Spanish feeling was so strong: not only were Spaniards associated with the dominant class, they also were associated with a colonial past rejected by a century of liberalism.[40]

Revolutionary governors, who suspended the decree for a short time to reconsider the matter, entertained further broker pleas for a modification of the law. In response twenty women (no men signed this time) sent a letter on December 9 to the governor expressing their disappointment that he would give in to brokers. None of these women had signed the earlier petitions, yet they had a similar understanding of the rule of law and the injustice when it was not followed, asking: "Does the law only apply to the poor?" These women, self-identified "vecinos," a category that in the past applied only to well-to-do men, stated:

> When on December 2nd then Governor Vicente Navarro published a Decree referring to Pawnshops, this pueblo felt such immense satisfaction to receive such a great benefit after so many years of exploitation. But now we feel such deception when we see that the pawnbrokers laugh at what the decree calls for by closing their pawnshops. Even greater was the people's bitterness when we saw that you ordered that such a decree would not be enforced until further notice. The people interpreted this as a way to forget about the decree. Is it possible that even now the law only applies to the least valued, in its prejudice, and not to the rich as well, such that they always manage to get to laugh at us? It is only this poor Mexican pueblo that is obliged to comply with Government decrees: poor coal venders (we could cite a lot of examples of these) are obliged to immediately sell coal at the fixed price, and if they do not obey immediately they are taken to the Police Station where they are fined. In contrast the "señores gachupines" eagerly disobey all of the laws and, laughing in the face of those who govern, they close their pawnshops.

While the decree seemed beneficial, they said, instead it was harmful. When lenders occasionally reopened their shops after the long closure to take advantage of people's need for credit during such turbulent times, they would not return goods even if loans were repaid, with the excuse that while the shops were closed the pledge periods had expired so the goods now belonged to the brokers. When borrowers insisted that the law was on their side as they tried to redeem their goods, brokers "answer us with insults, saying that we are roving bandits just like those that govern today, whom they call a junta of thieves." These petitioning women, in a long line of women accustomed to provisioning their families through the strategic pawning and redeeming of household goods, ended by saying: "As you see Sr. Gobernador, the 'pueblo bajo' is always humiliated and is never listened to; perhaps now it will be different. For this reason we come to you asking that you resolve the matter of [compliance with] the decree as soon as possible so that we will know once and for all whether or not we have already lost our collateral goods."[41] Individual pleas complemented this collective defense of household economy. Ten days before Christmas, Felicitas and Luz Pagaza, seamstress sisters who occupied separate rooms in the same Estanco de Mujeres casa de vecindad, wrote to General Manuel Chao because they needed help recovering their sewing machines: "A while ago, since there was little work, some of us *compañeras* who have our own sewing machines had to pawn them. Now, since the first of December, we have work making military uniforms, but no machines. We have the money to redeem them, but with the Pawnshops closed, our interests are suffering."[42]

Continuing their dialogue with the Federal District in hopes of turning away the swelling tide against them, pawnbrokers represented by the union of lenders emphasized the hardships and sacrifices their trade entailed. In a petition signed by their president, Jorge Fernández, the union pointed out that they had to endure begging and needy clients. Their bad reputation stemmed from misunderstandings about their enormous operating costs: taxes were high, and brokers lost out when stolen goods were recovered. It cost them dearly when the armies of the south came into the city and pawnshops were sacked by the masses. Brokers argued that the revolutionary decrees were unconstitutional, that they were not reform but rather total suppression of their trade.[43] Villista general Chao, Conventionist governor of the Federal District, who had called for a "sane radicalism in pursuit of workers' interests," took into consideration the brokers' concerns and amended the pawnshop decree on December 29, 1914.[44] The new decree repeated that all goods pawned for over five pesos could be redeemed with the loan repaid plus 1 percent monthly interest "in the manner that the Nacional Monte de Piedad charges." All collateral pawned for under five pesos had to be returned upon repayment of the loan amount only (i.e., no interest could be charged). Article 7 stated that after ninety days pawnshops could only do business following the rules of the branches of the Monte de Piedad. As concessions to the brokers, goods not claimed within seventy days would be subject to the original pawning contract, and Article 8 exempted pawnshops from paying taxes for ninety days.[45]

Closed pawnshops continued to be targets of popular mobilizations of neighborhood women and men, with "a multitude" sacking the one at the corner of Lecumberri and Bravo in the eastern part of the city in early January 1915. Juan Fernández's store in the Avenida de la Paz in the north and Santos Sobrino's store at the corner of Peña and Peña were also sacked in January.[46] At the end of January the sacking scenes with which this chapter opened took place. Women took their stuff back from pawnbrokers who refused to give it back at a lower interest rate or, for those under five pesos, without interest. Just who were the "superwomen" sacking pawnshops and the women signing petitions urging the revolutionary government to hold pawnbrokers to the law? Were they working-class and poor "women of the people" as the press characterized them, echoing the historical and dominant discourse linking needy women to pawning? Were they seamstress businesswomen? Were they also middle-class household managers more likely to own and have pawned some of the collateral carried through the streets? In any case these sackings of Spanish pawnbroking businesses should be understood in the context of what at least some in the Spanish commercial community in general did during this turbulent time. A study by the Mexican army found that Spanish wholesale merchants enjoyed a huge profit (1,500 percent!) on the sale of sugar when the price hiked from fifty centavos a kilo to eight pesos. And in the capital, "the price of butter rose from one peso a kilo in January to eight pesos by August." Spanish merchants were accused of hoarding and speculating on scarce items and refusing to make transactions in the government's new official currency.[47]

Revolutionary Showdown

Constitutionalist forces led by Obregón reoccupied the city on January 30, 1915. Currency issued by Villistas was declared illegal, further exacerbating economic realities for the city's households. For two weeks, "large crowds of women" marched to insist that Villista money be accepted. Obregón responded to the women's demonstrations with a new Revolutionary Committee for the Relief of the Poor, which distributed new currency at relief stations to ten thousand people, overwhelmingly women.[48] The Obregón government proved to be no ally of small businessmen and instead fanned popular hatred of merchants and the long-standing xenophobia against Spaniards.[49] With speculation and scarcity of food and other staple goods continuing, women continued to take matters into their own hands. John Lear paints this picture of the first half of 1915: "Women, with empty baskets, went from market to market in the city only to find them closed; walking all day, from San Juan to La Merced, from La Lagunilla to Martínez de la Torre. Everywhere there appeared people willing to break down doors with hatchets and knives, in order to attack the businesses."[50] When Obregón left the city in March 1915 to pursue Villa for Carranza with newly formed Red Battalions of worker-soldiers, the local economy was in shambles. And attempts to redistribute the wealth of Spanish merchants had only pushed them to further withdraw their provisioning services.

Pawnbroker intransigence in the face of revolutionary decrees and popular mobilizations continued as Conventionist forces, dominated by Zapatistas, reoccupied Mexico City on March 10, staying through July 1915. These months saw constant organized-labor agitation and increasing mobilization at the neighborhood level as conditions continued to deteriorate. Individual residents took their problems with pawnbrokers directly to revolutionary authorities. At the end of March 1915, Señora María Rodríguez reported that pawnshops on Mina and Soto, a block to the north of the Alameda, charged her interest rates marked on old tickets instead of what the late-December decree allowed. The new government responded to Doña María's plea by sending an inspector to enforce the law.[51] In April 1915 Antonio Viña asked the governor to help him get his goods back from the pawnshop in the fifth block of Factor. "Señor," he said, "unfortunately we are the play things of foreigners, especially *los gachupines*, who see our laws and decrees and laugh at them."[52]

Some pawnbrokers attempted to avoid revolutionary regulations on pawning by closing legally, requesting permission to suspend operations, as was called for in Porfirian regulations. Some wanted to quit the collateral-credit business but keep bazaar operations running.[53] The lenders' union complained in April 1915 that instead of "clarifying" the revolutionary decrees and heeding any brokers' concerns, the Conventionist governor added new rules that would force shops that could not comply to go out of business completely.[54] At the end of April 1915, *La Convención* reported that given the dire economic situation, many people—"especially proletarians"—had been unable to redeem goods or pay to have pledges renewed. The newspaper called on the government to curb abuses of owners of bazaars who bought objects at ridiculously low prices and then sold them for great profits, "exploiting in this way the misery of the people that are obliged to turn to their establishments in order to get some money" for daily survival.[55]

On May 9, 1915, Zapatista general Gildardo Magaña, governor of the Federal District, issued another pawning decree. It confirmed a three-month moratorium on the sale of unredeemed goods, during which time (until July 16) pawnbrokers had to hold onto collateral goods to give owners more time to redeem them. It limited interest rates to 4 percent a month when goods were redeemed and set out regulations for appraisal and sale at public auction of goods not redeemed by July 17, with auctions having to take place by August 30.[56] In keeping with earlier rulings that bazaars were subject to empeño regulations, city treasury officials were sent out in June 1915 to inspect pawnshops that had converted to bazaars to see that they were paying appropriate taxes.[57] Dramatically, also in June, merchants fired on a group of women and children who had assaulted grocery stores owned by Spaniards, exacerbating the already tense relations between the city's population and the foreign business community.[58]

Newspaper editorials throughout 1915—the "year of hunger"—reinforced the nefarious image of pawnbrokers. An early 1915 editorial in *El Pueblo* highlighted similarities under the Díaz and Huerta regimes, especially in the way brokers manipulated the auctioning of unredeemed collateral goods.[59] An editorial in early October 1915 in the pro-Carranza *El Demócrata* showed ambivalence about who to blame for bad collateral-credit practices. The editorial, signed "Ejoff," pinned high interest rates in empeños on government regulation and taxation, which added costs to transactions that were passed on to customers. It chastised the public, who applauded regulations, "showing their scary ignorance of economic matters." Now usury laws were back in place, but taxes were still high. While this might seem bad for brokers, in the opinion of Ejoff it turned out to be worse for pawning customers. As more and more pawnbrokers got out of the lending business and instead bought goods outright, more people lost their property once and for all and therefore lost its collateral usage, which had yielded countless loans. The article outlined bad qualities of the "always Spanish" pawnbrokers: profiting from fencing stolen goods, stealing themselves when "they accept a diamond in hock and return a piece of glass . . . for a legitimate [painting by] Murillo they return a home-made copy, . . . a place setting from Sevres is switched for Ollivier porcelain, and a Chinese shawl is replaced with a commonplace one of ARTIFICIAL silk."[60]

Fig. 9. "En el Empeño." *El Demócrata*, October 24, 1915, 1.

The pawning process was so ingrained in Mexican culture that it had long served as metaphor for social and political commentary. This was no less true during revolution. A cartoon entitled "In the Pawnshop" appeared on the front page of the Carrancista *El Demócrata* in October 1915 (see figure 9). General Alvaro Obregón and U.S. president Woodrow Wilson are behind the counter, with pawned boots, sarapes, and hats behind them. The Villista Miguel Díaz Lombardo holds a pawn ticket that reads "Villista movement," saying he wants to extend the pledge period. Obregón replies that time is already up.[61]

The Demise of Private Pawnbroking

With Mexico City under the control of Carrancista general Pablo González, women demanding actions around consumption issues dominated Casa del Obrero meetings in August.[62] It is not clear how long pawnbrokers who had closed their doors back in early 1915 remained closed to making new loans. Announcements in August about the sale of goods pawned between July and November 1914 appeared in newspapers.[63] Some shops seem to have reopened by October 1915. By January bazaar owners were being warned to take down the word "empeño" from placards, and auction announcements ceased to appear in newspapers.[64] In general the long transition from pawnshop to used-goods bazaar accelerated rapidly, as these foreign businessmen sought ways to maintain profits in the face of revolutionary social policy, as if to answer that question of the militant women—"yes, the law only applies to the poor." Those pawnshops that had not changed their practices in keeping with new collateral-credit policies (i.e., charging only 5 percent interest) were to change their names to "bazares" and apply for a new license within fifteen days if they were going to continue to buy and sell jewels and furniture.[65]

Some newspapers could not suppress their glee at the demise of private pawnbroking as part of the revolutionary process. Witness this tongue-in-cheek imagery, at once positivist and revolutionary, from *El Pueblo*:

> To this Señora that they call the Revolution, and that which is the dry fruit [*el coco*] of more than four species and families of social octopi, the residents of this Metropolitan Urbe [Area] owe the extinguishing for forever of what have been called, due to the irony of language, "mountains of piety" ["montepíos"] but more appropriately should have been called "feather plucker of two-legged birds" ["desplumadero de bípedos implumes"]. Just as the Free Municipality has sparked the School of Democracy, the pawnshops came to become the School of Plutocracy, for to be a good "Científico" one had to be a good speculator [*agiotista*] and to be a good speculator one had to be a good pawnbroker. Certainly some stars in the art of Exploitation of the People had such natural talent that they could become master Científicos without passing by the classroom

> of the Pawnshop. Or better, luck smiled on them from the day they were wrapped in the finest diapers, and the honorable work of their dear fathers kept them from feeling anguish at amassing their fortune with the sweat of their victims. . . . What to do with a sick one in the house and no money in the box? Well, off to the pawnbroker with a sarape, a pair of irons, or the wall clock to meet the need [*para salir del apuro*]. . . . And pushed on by necessity, the client has to leave the collateral for whatever the "señores empeñeros" wanted to lend. And in three months minus one day, after saving the six reales through thousands of sacrifices in order to redeem the collateral, the client is obliged to pay another peso for the favor to cover "interests," as it was rare that pawn tickets did not stipulate 25 percent in favor of the house! . . . Goodbye, the beloved such-and-such [*tanto*] percent. . . . Goodbye, the fruitful pledge extension and the "honorable auctions." Haley's comet will return . . . but the pawnshops . . . will not.[66]

Despite this eulogy, casas de empeño were not abolished but instead limited to charging only 5 percent interest. This stipulation was enough, however, that pawnbrokers generally went out of the lending business and into the retail of used goods. But the disappearance of pawnshops was not matched by the disappearance of the need for collateral credit. Many of the problems of 1914–15 continued unabated. In June 1916, just after the decline in workers' purchasing power bottomed out to a seventh of what it had been in 1912, Carranza attempted to stabilize the monetary system through issuing of new paper currency in place of the myriad old ones, but this was unsuccessful. A bank seizure from September 1916 until the following January 21 created a further contraction in the supply of money. Despite monetary contraction, which theoretically should have led to a deflation of prices, prices increased enormously in 1917 due to decreased production caused by revolution, demand caused by World War I, damage to railroad supply lines, and bad weather that damaged crops. Increasing wages won by workers could not keep up with increasing costs of living. High prices did not hurt everyone, of course. The Casa Boker made record profits selling kitchen utensils and other imported hardware at triple the prerevolution prices, as the desire for these scarce status items in the context of civil and international war meant that they did not stay long on the shelf. How much older household hardware was pawned to purchase new imported goods?[67]

The transition from an empeño credit market to a bazaar buyer's market, where borrowers were permanently alienated from their investment goods, completed the decapitalization process that transaction costs and interest rates had started long ago. The permanence of sale transactions with bazaar owners was a blow to housekeepers, "who before went to pawn with the hope of redeeming their good some day." Now household budget managers, strapped for cash after the inconvenient hours kept by the montepíos, "had to give up the collateral forever" and sell their property outright to finance needs. Bazaars both symbolized and implemented property loss. They were "nothing more than disguised *empeños*, only that they managed to suppress the requirement of auctions and charge interest, so to speak, ahead of time, while making even lower appraisals than before."[68] Selling bedroom furniture instead of pawning it constituted an abdication of property rights, a transfer of property. For those who lost luxury goods chosen for their collateral value, the decapitalization could be substantial. But for those already at a minimal material level, the alienation of the kitchen table or the sewing machine was a bigger loss in terms of the hole left in the family's financial plan.

By November 1917 *El Pueblo*, which had so welcomed the demise of pawnshops, called for their reestablishment unless the Monte de Piedad was able to expand massively, make very small loans, and extend its business hours so that it would be open "from five or six in the morning and until nine or ten at night like the old pawnshops." This time, the editorial stressed pawnbrokers' public service—staying in business despite all the inconveniences of government inspections, bad reputations, poor treatment by customers, and exposure to disease from contaminated clothing. Even the interest rates that had been so shocking—13 percent each of the first two months, 25 percent each the third and fourth—no longer seemed unreasonable. Given the costs of overhead, taxes, rent on the building, salaries of clerks, and losses when auction sales did not meet the amount lent, brokers were lucky to earn 6 to 12 percent in the end. The editorial argued that the bazaar was no replacement for the pawnshop, as the needy customers were only losing their goods, while former brokers were making profits. The bazaar business was so profitable, without any of the hassle of pawnbroking, that the paper feared that if they were asked to return to pawnbroking, businessmen would flatly refuse.

In short, after all the sackings and petitions and regulations and revolutionary rhetoric, it appeared to these middle-class journalists that pawnbroking had been a necessary service in the political economy of Mexico City. In contrast another editorial a few weeks later in the same newspaper decried pawnbroking, as it inhibited Mexicans from learning to save. The editorial lamented, with a backhanded nationalist swipe at Spaniards: "From our Spanish ancestor we inherited the characteristic inability to plan and a lack of spirit for saving, [and] also the small affection for daily work, which we resist, and the love of adventure, which leads to gambling." But most of the editorial analyzes pawning from an "economic and psychological" standpoint, illustrating the continued influence of positivist scientific reasoning as well as classical economic liberalism in revolutionary context:

> Economic science teaches that no social advance is possible without capital, and this is formed principally through saving. He who uses everything that he produces will never be able to move up the social scale, and before he likely moves down a few rungs from the position he occupies, he will stop producing anything at all. It would not be so bad if the "empeño" loan was spent in meeting necessities. Most of the time it satisfies superfluous things, if not vices. The student who wants to go out on the town [*correr una juerga*] pawns his books; the store clerk or office worker who pawns the furniture wants to appear to have more than he really has; the artisan pawns tools when he has the urge to get drunk with his compadres.

Thus echoing traditional discourses about the evils of pawning, this editorial agreed that the bazaar was worse than the pawnshop and entertained the idea that either one or the other was a "necessary evil." But neither would be necessary if the government invested in real social-security programs such as savings incentives and insurance for workers, which would both alleviate poverty and make pawnshops obsolete. The paper argued that "all of our social classes would become accustomed little by little to not having pawnshops as an option," opting for the bazaar over the pawnshop during "these times of scarcity and monetary contraction" because it is better to sell goods once and for all and break the pawning habit.

El Pueblo thus identified the revolutionary agenda regarding collateral credit as one of reform and behavioral modification, linking modern middle-class values of sacrifice and thrift to the revolutionary theme of redemption: "No social reform is put in place without suffering, this is the law of humanity. The Revolution was not formed in the middle of a concert, but in the middle of combat, and nobody will be able to doubt its efficacy, without being ignorant of history and sociology. Tolerance in certain cases is equivalent to suicide, and Mexican society does not want to commit suicide, but rather wants to reform itself and live."[69] This version of the revolutionary agenda contrasts sharply with that proffered by customers of neighborhood pawnshops who pushed for protected access to inexpensive collateral lending.

In February 1920 a front-page editorial in the "official" *El Demócrata* resurrected the view that while empeños were bad, they were a necessary evil, and it called for abolition of the bazaar business and the return to pawnshops, which were operating outside the law anyway.[70] As things turned out, the entrepreneurial pawnbroking business did not reemerge on any sizable scale in the post-revolutionary city. Having reopened after the worst was over in the city, only two branches and the main office of the Monte de Piedad were in operation in 1917, with two more branches reopening in 1920. It would be another decade before the Monte expanded into new branches to meet constant demand for credit services in the pawning-services vacuum created by the revolutionary demise of pawnbroking.[71]

A Tarnished Monte de Piedad

As private pawnbroking disappeared and bazaars proliferated, the Monte was slow to fill the gap in collateral-credit coverage. It came under fire from the press during the revolutionary violence and afterward. *El Combate* characterized it in July 1915 as "the least pious Institution there is." Having been open again for a few months, the appraiser of Branch No. 2 was accused of "fitting the description of a cacique from the Porfirian era."[72] In an article from 1920, it is the guards overseeing "the thousand and one individuals who gather there daily to pawn or extend a pledge" whose character is impugned. The male guards are characterized as mean, speaking harshly to the women in line, calling them "viejas," and touching them inappropriately under the pretext of advancing the line. The "good women" in line tell the reporter they have been there for three hours, and "meanwhile, back at the house, the children have not had breakfast."[73] Sometimes children were in line, too. Photographs of the line from over the years show men and children, but mostly women, some with babies on their backs secured in rebozos. A photograph looking out the door of the main branch, circa 1930, pictures a long line of mostly women spilling into the street.[74]

The Monte de Piedad, repeatedly harangued to expand its services to poor neighborhoods, instead characteristically expanded the branch services to cater to more well-off clientele. In 1911 it had temporarily increased the loan amount available in branch offices from three hundred to five hundred pesos, anticipating that more middle-class residents with relatively valuable collateral needed its services. In the ugly year of 1915, the loan limit in the branches that were open was again raised, this time to two hundred pesos. By 1919 the maximum loan in the branch offices was back down to twenty pesos, but in 1920 it was raised again to three hundred pesos. Raising the limit not only restricted access for poor clients, it reserved the limited funds of the institution for a middle-class clientele, echoing the Bourbon concern with the material life-style of the middle class.[75]

In June 1917 the Monte made changes to the acceptable collateral they would take in deposit for loans. Until further notice they could no longer lend against furniture and sewing machines without special permission.[76] In August the Monte de Piedad announced that any goods pawned before November 1916 had to be redeemed by September, or they would go to auction. This announcement is unusual; auction announcements for unredeemed goods in the Monte had been published like clockwork for fifty years, with the only change in the ad being the date the goods had been pawned and the auction date. (See the Monte de Piedad auction announcement from 1886 in figure 8.) The August policy may mean that fewer people had been able to repay their loans than in the past, so unredeemed goods piled up. The institution had a storage problem stemming from the long time it had been closed, with some goods from before 1914 still on the shelves.[77] In 1920 one patron blamed the inability of people to redeem goods on increased transaction costs (the article noted that between the 3 percent monthly interest and other costs, including another 3 percent for storage, patrons were paying 44 percent annually).[78] The sale announcements detailed the items for sale and their cost, reflecting a reform of the auction system. To avoid fraud, with fake buyers pushing up the price well beyond the worth of the good, the institution no longer sold to the highest bidder but instead fixed "the going commercial value" of each item and sold it only at that price, announced in the paper.[79]

The hyperinflation as well as currency devaluations and annulments of 1914–16 must have driven housekeepers to the end of their patience. Currency problems continued to vex those merely trying to provision their households.[80] In July 1917 the customers of the Monte de Piedad complained to the government and to the press that they were having trouble getting the institution to accept repayment of loans in silver coins. The Monte clerks were under orders not to accept more than five pesos in silver coins, the rest having to be in gold coins. The secretary of Hacienda ordered the Monte's administration to follow the law, which called for any payment to be accepted in silver or gold coins.[81] Other complaints had to do with the *caja de ahorros* attached to the Monte, which limited the amount people could withdraw from their accounts or paid out cash in devalued currency instead of the silver and gold that they demanded from customers.[82]

Housekeeping and Everyday Life during Revolution

Whether the pawnshop-sacking and petition-writing women and men were poor, working class, or middle class, they had a history of everyday credit.[83] Many were long-term residents, who had long used pawning as a creative finance strategy. Some households likely had generations of experience with collateral credit. The city had been slowly industrializing, with its work force becoming proletarianized and the economy capitalized during the Porfiriato. At the household level at least some middle-class professionals employed servants, most supervised by a housewife, some allowing middle-class women to take teaching or office jobs. The revolutionary decade brought demographic changes evident in the next census, which was done in 1921. The female population in the city grew nearly twice as much as the male population between 1910 and 1921, and among the population aged twenty to twenty-four, there were three times as many women as men.[84] The published data for 1921 do not include occupational breakdowns, so there is no way to determine class breakdowns. The 1921 census did include ethnic identification. The breakdown of the "raza" category for the Federal District reveals that just over half the population was "mezclada," just under a quarter was considered "blanco" (compared to 50 percent of the 1811 population considered Spanish), almost a fifth were identified as "indígena," and only 3 percent were foreign born.[85] The revolution reintroduced ethnicity into bureaucratic categories, adapting a colonial practice for nationalist ends.

In 1921, six years after street mobilizations around credit and consumption issues, the same percentage of females in the city were minors as were married (27 percent), with an increase of 6 percent of those married from 1910. It may be that sharp economic crises lived during 1914–16 prompted couples to establish more committed relationships. The discourse about female domestic responsibility did not abate in the context of social upheaval. When Colonel David G. Berlanga, the new secretary of Gobernación, visited the Belén jail in September 1914, he convinced a dozen imprisoned unmarried mothers to get married "so that tomorrow their children will be protected from prejudice" by imposing lesser sentences on any who agreed to do so.[86] The widow population grew from 12 percent to 14 percent (73 percent of widowed persons were female), and a new population of the legally divorced made up 1 percent of women. While we do not know how many of the unmarried women headed their own households, more than two-thirds of twenty-something women who were widowed, divorced, or separated were also mothers.[87]

The gendered nature of the landlord market had changed by the end of the revolution. Females made up two-thirds of those residents who "lived from their rents" in 1910. By 1921 property holders were slightly more likely to be male than female.[88] Only 6.5 percent of the Federal District's population, however, owned real estate in 1921. Those without real property to mortgage still needed credit, of course, and as usual turned their movable property into collateral. The problem, however, was that the likelihood they would lose their stuff for good had increased.

While housekeepers in the city always faced challenges in meeting multiple demands on their labor and creativity in chronic contexts of inadequate incomes for necessary spending levels, the extreme years beginning with the Decena Trágica in early 1914 certainly raised the bar on the job's level of difficulty. In 1901 the positivist intellectual Julio Guerrero had defined the ideal Mexican wife thus: "The master and owner of her home: she watches over the expenses and calculates savings, and with her method and care she creates in abundance the fruits of the marital work. If she embellishes her house, she looks for art and simplicity as the basis of elegance; and in each deal, and each transaction, from the daily food purchases to the biggest of matrimonial transactions in which she intervenes, she manages to save some coins which go into the sacred deposit of the domestic reserve fund."[89] In January 1913 *El Diario* presented a picture of home economics under President Madero that was quite a contrast. A satirical rendition entitled "Por Poco Me La Saco," authored by "Fulano de Tal" (roughly, "any old so-and-so"), depicts less harmonious, even violent household relations and a housekeeping strategy that intertwines playing the lottery with pawning in a relentless play on words. In the "poor house" of the Delgado family (with the last name meaning thin or skinny), the following exchange takes place:

> Hey Pancho, you need to go and take out (*sacar*) the blue suit; the pawnshop is going to pass it over to the appraisers and we will lose it . . .
>
> Leave it be . . . I have a tenth of a share in a ticket for "the two hundred thousand" . . . which is sure to hit.

But what makes you believe that you can "hit"?

Woman . . . I have hit you many times . . . without reason.

Yes, you're good for that, but to hit the fat one [*pegarle al gordo*], for that you are useless.

Not so, your father is good and fat, and one day I hit him with two good punches . . . remember.

The Delgado family, every day thinner from hunger, had a budget planned for their twenty thousand pesos if their number won. The daughter drew up the plan: for medicine, one thousand pesos; for furniture and redeeming pawned goods, two thousand pesos; for a day in the country, one thousand pesos; for clothing and jewelry, six thousand pesos; for depositing in the bank, five thousand pesos; and to buy land, five thousand pesos. The story ends with them getting some medicine, but not with winnings from the lottery office on Montealegre (i.e., Happy Mountain). Instead, they take out another collateral loan from the "Sad Mountain" or "Montetriste (el Saviñón)," secured with a feather mattress.[90] The play on words in this satire, with the different kinds of "Montes," reminds us just how embedded in Mexican housekeeping routines was the collateral-lending institution. Middle-class and elite residents could see another cultural reflection of pawning on the stage in January 1918. The six-part play entitled "The Pawned Jewel" opened at the San Juan de Letrán Theater on Friday, January 4.[91]

While revolutionary activity in the city was perhaps hardest on women charged with maintaining livelihoods and status, the traditional collateral-credit structure they depended on was transformed, with one whole sector disappearing. Housekeeping roles continued to have a public profile, however. On Mother's Day 1916 the National School for Domestic Teaching opened in San Rafael *colonia* (planned neighborhood). The director, Elvira Espinosa, announced: "With the purpose of giving to women a new opportunity to practice household activities, in an absolutely practical setting, and provide the means with which to dutifully fulfill the transcendental role with which society has charged them, the school had organized complete courses for housewives and special short courses to prepare cooks, seamstresses, chambermaids, nannies, washerwomen, and ironers."[92] Domestic service staffs apparently continued to be thin with such prolonged economic troubles in the city. *El Demócrata* published a column called

"Femeninas" in 1919, with the lead article about "how to direct the household service when you only have one maid."[93]

The cult of domesticity may have continued, but some women needed to work outside the home, and other women stepped in to ease double burdens. Porfirian charitable institutions founded by elite women that both extended their motherhood roles into society and substituted them as mothers for working women were still to be found in the city. The Casa de Amiga de la Obrera, which had been founded by Diaz's wife in Colonia Indianilla, was still a part of Beneficencia Pública. Now under the direction of Sra. Alemán, the day-care center boasted "modern scholastic materials, excellent gymnastic equipment, a battery of kitchens, pots, pans, etc. allowing for instruction and sufficiently good subsistence to the little ones." This day-care center/school had a hundred students, who were provided free studies and meals. Certainly working women could also have used free help with the housekeeping after a long day's work.[94] And what did single mothers do with children and chores while studying for diplomas at a commercial night school such as the Academia Comercial Ignacio M. Altamirano in the city?[95]

These official and private efforts at shoring up the abilities of housekeepers and the discourse of domesticity occurred during major upheavals in the city's households and neighborhoods. The revolutionary population was fluid, with flexible household structures. Many *soldaderas* (camp followers and female soldiers) stayed on as troops moved out of the city. Jesusa Palancares, swept up into war in Oaxaca as a young *soldadera*, ended up living the rest of her life in Mexico City working every job imaginable, including servant, cardboard-box maker, cabaret dancer, and cabaret manager. She recalls going to the National Palace to secure her widow's pension: "The Palace . . . was full of women, a world of women such that one could not find where to leave or where to enter. All the doors jammed with petticoats, the palace was brimming with widows looking for pensions." None other than President Carranza denied Jesusa a pension because she was too young, and "someday you will get married again and the dead cannot maintain a new husband." The young migrant ripped up her papers and threw them in the president's face, exclaiming, "What does it matter to him if I am old or young. He had to pay me because it wasn't earned by his efforts; it was what death had left me to keep me alive. But Carranza kept my money, bad decision. He, of course, was maintained and continued to be by the revolutionaries that are living gloriously off of the efforts of my husband, my brother, my father, and all the rest who died because of him."

TABLE 7.1

Household Goods in Pawn, 1914–21
(354 transactions out of 1,043, or 33%)

Category	Empeños 1914–15	Monte de Piedad 1920–21	Total
Bedroom furniture	2	127	129
Other furnishings[a]	12	60	72
Living-room furniture	2	36	38
Pianos/organs		31	31
Linen	28	2	30
Dining-room furniture	4	18	22
Fabric, whole	12		12
Irons	9		9
Silver/ceramic table service	5		5
Kitchen/cooking[b]	6		6
Total	80	274	354

Source: AHCM, Gobierno del Distrito, Empeños, vol. 1429, exp. 442; *El Demócrata*, August 22, 1920, 3; October 12, 1920, 3; October 21, 1920, 10; November 12, 1920, 8; November 15, 1920, 7; November 22, 1920, 7; December 19, 1920, 7; January 18, 1921, 7; January 19, 1921, 7; February 20, 1921, 6; March 15, 1921, 10; April 24, 1921, 5.

[a] Includes twenty-two mirrors, eight rugs, eight desks, five bookshelves, five paintings, four safes, three garden furniture, and two each: bathtubs, commodes, sinks, statues, and lamps. Also, one each: flower vase, door bolt, washbasin with pitcher, chamber pot, and billiards table.

[b] Including a gas stove.

In a city bursting with refugees and other new arrivals, most young women had children to feed. Although women competed along with men for factory jobs, many ended up in domestic service in middle-class and elite households, restaurant or bar service, street vending, or prostitution in order to earn a living and maintain their households.[96]

The material goods used by housekeepers and servants to shape working- and middle-class culture had been transformed over the course of the nineteenth century. Collateral inventories from the revolutionary decade show that material contexts in which people lived continued to change, with goods that were more "modern" and more possessions generally. Table 7.1 gathers housekeeping goods on pawnshop shelves in the last half of the revolutionary decade. These goods represent a higher percentage than other categories of pawned goods and the highest percentage for the category compared to the other three period blocks in the database (see appendix 1, table F). The nature of household collateral goods changed, with less cloth and more furnishings and knickknacks than in earlier decades (see appendix 1, tables B–F for comparisons). The biggest change in household decoration in the early 1900s was the investment in quantity as well as quality of substantial pieces of furniture, expensive goods that replaced silver-service sets as the most durable for collateral purposes. Furniture became more prominent in neighborhood pawnshops in 1915—such as the pieces carried by the "super strong" women sacking pawnshops—because furniture had cultural value in shaping family status, the economic crunch in which people attempted to maintain that status increased, and the Monte de Piedad was closed for business for an extended period.

While most goods on hand in Escandón's pawnbroking business during the revolutionary turmoil were cloth goods worth only about a peso, the most valuable collateral was a bedroom set consisting of two armoires and two chests of drawers, securing a sixty-eight-peso loan to the Hernández household. The same customer had the next highest loan from Escandón: sixty-seven pesos for a bundle consisting of one typewriter and two sewing machines. The regular use of these goods was part of the day-to-day inconspicuous consumption of middle-class households, and as collateral, they financed more consumption. The published auction lists of the reopened Monte de Piedad in 1919 and 1920 show very high-ticket furniture items, with the average appraisal over three hundred pesos. How many of these pianos and wardrobes and living-room sets had been purchased on installment plans or outright during the Porfiriato?[97] How many times had these pieces of furniture been in the pawnshop, how many times had they changed hands—in short, how many lives had they had?

Furniture was necessary equipment for maintaining middle-class respectability.[98] The middle-class houses that Motts grew up in during the 1910s usually had a rug with a one-legged oval or round table sitting on it, sometimes with a marble top, then a lace runner, maybe a lamp, and "almost always an album with portraits of the family." If the family had a piano, it held center stage. The Monte de Piedad had more than two dozen unredeemed pianos for sale in 1920, suggesting that as important as they were for proper entertaining and the music education of girls, these expensive investments were more dispensable in their conventional sense and hence quite useful as collateral. Motts's descriptions of the tapestried and cane living-room sofa and chair sets echo descriptions of the same kinds of items in pawning inventories, both in the downtown empeño owned by Calvo in 1915 and the Monte de Piedad at the end of the decade. Other furnishings highlighted in the professor's description such as mirrors (of which there are more than twenty in the database), rocking chairs, and small statues sitting on corner tables all served as collateral in this period.[99] That eating utensils are missing from the data likely reflects the decrease in use of silver tableware, but it is also a reflection of a skewed sample of only the big-ticket items that were up for sale, without information on myriad other goods that Monte de Piedad customers were pawning and redeeming.

Indeed, most housekeeping collateral goods in table 7.1 would have come from houses with a relatively high level of comfort, even amid revolutionary turmoil. We can get a sense of what goods a modest middle-class home might store in and on all these furniture items—goods that could also be counted on for collateral—from a crime report from late 1915, a year of insecurity for many. José González was robbed by the "carrero" that drove the family luggage from the train station to the center of town on November 27. Owners of bazaars were to be on the lookout in case the thief tried to fence:

> Three trunks, one flat and two round, that contained six pillows; one man's suit; two women's suits; eleven pairs of sheer slippers; two women's *charol* shoes; two green hats; one case with aluminum spoon, knife and fork; two washbowls, one ceramic pitcher, kitchen tools, and buckets; two small feather mattresses (one flowered and one a light color); two children's dresses; kitchen pottery; flowered plates; a hot plate; photographs; a wallet; sheets, one blanket, and two curtains; one two-kilo Huachinango box with the address "Sr. D. José González, Capuchinas núm. 19"; one sugar bowl; coffee spoons; one tablecloth, six napkins, and two towels; two child's hats, one *estambre* the other *piqué*; women's and men's shirts; handkerchiefs, socks, ties and collars; underpants; two swaths of white filipina cloth; three pairs of pants, one white and two black; a child's gold jewelry set with two pearls, and one pair of women's earrings.[100]

As this is household property that can be moved in trunks, the furniture that the González family likely owned is not mentioned.

By 1920, when wages and prices were in better equilibrium, the poor in neighborhoods on Peralvillo Street, General Anaya, and around Tepito lived in crowded but simple conditions: "The 'furniture' in these cases constitutes a single chair, or a bench in which the head of the family sits. What other way do they have to distinguish themselves!"[101] Some factory workers lived in company dormitories or other housing that sprang up in industrial districts "with no more blanket for their sleep, nor bed on which to rest after a day's work, than the hard 'tepetate' on the floor." The high-end wage among male skilled weavers in San Angel was ten pesos a week, with which a wife made weekly purchases to feed herself, her husband, and her children. After buying staples not much was left for "the rest of the household expenses, for a child's illness, for the unemployment of the father, for clothes, for cigarettes . . . in these homes there is no meat."[102]

As was true for every other block of data analyzed in this book, more women's clothing than men's clothing was pawned in revolutionary years (see appendix 1, table E), though the ratio of female to male clothes was smaller than before. Enaguas and rebozos, once again, were the most common female articles, though the male *pantalón* came close to petticoats. Generally, there is less clothing in this portion of the sample; as a category, it comes in third behind jewelry and household goods. The "typical" Mexican sarape's appearance among collateral steadily diminished from its mid-nineteenth-century dominance among male clothing collateral, while the modern *pantalón*'s stature remained steady. In contrast, on the female side, the "typical" enagua and rebozo persisted, with more than ten times as many of these items as of the modern *vestido* (dress) in the middle of the nineteenth century, during the Porfiriato, and during the revolution.[103] Can we conclude by reading the "information system" of collateral goods that urban Mexicans moved through the modernizing era with women still wearing the traditional rebozo and enaguas (echoing Jesusa Palancares's image of the "palace full of skirts"), while the men literally wore the pants of modernity? While Western pants are prominent among the revolution-era collateral, there are fewer full suits, though there are relatively more than there were among Porfirian collateral. How to interpret this in light of the price as well as the cultural value that men's business and foppish attire had had? First, with the heightened economic crisis of revolutionary years, middle-class pawning practitioners had to reach deeper into household stock to get by. Second, with more women now working for business offices and schools of the city, the privileged position of male attire was waning, making it a more likely candidate for a turn as collateral. Third, an antifop movement was part of the Mexican Revolution, as a more working-class masculinity was promoted. In that climate pawning the fancy male attire of earlier decades could be a revolutionary statement.[104]

On May Day 1920 women in line at the Monte de Piedad pawned "un rebozo de bolita" acquired in better times on an installment plan; a silver spoon, "the only gift its owner ever received"; a guitar; fake diamond jewelry; an old burlap *tápalo*; an old colored tablecloth; silk flowers; a broken wristwatch; and a typewriter.[105] Aside from the typewriter, these are not unlike goods their grandmothers or even great-grandmothers might have pawned. In 1915 Calvo's pawnshop made loans of two and three pesos for electric irons, while other irons yielded one peso.[106] Other household goods, now electric, included a coffeepot, a lamp, a bell, and even an electric vertical piano. Traditional collateral included household linens. Some represented in table 7.1 likely came from relatively poor households, especially those at the Escandón pawnshop, where two-thirds of collateral was cloth. Motts remembered that some working poor had beds, usually with steel headboards painted bright colors, with the feather mattress and then the pillow sitting on wide wood tablets.[107] A handful of cotton and "gaucho" featherbeds secured loans from seventy-five centavos to five pesos. A cotton curtain yielded a loan of one peso, and sheets were hocked for fifty centavos up to two and a half pesos. Any of these small loans would have made a big difference for a factory weaver's wife, who was lucky to have ten pesos a week on which to manage her household.

Embroidering household linens still occupied middle-class and elite women, while servants cared for and cleaned sheets, blankets, bedspreads, tablecloths, and so forth, used day to day. In the tough political economy of the revolutionary 1910s, it may be that middle-class homes with just one or two servants let them go. Without paid help the housekeeping chores in a large middle-class home could take most of the day, with marketing in the morning, followed by cleaning bedrooms and cooking. In the afternoon checking over the clothes, mending where necessary, and making new articles of clothing from the household stock of fabrics kept women busy. The evenings were spent supervising children and knitting, tatting, and embroidering.[108]

Sewing machines continued to hold an important place among collateral goods and as a means for women who headed households to make a living. The Calvo pawnshop in 1915 had one hand machine, hocked by a client named Morales, while Esquivel, Romero, and Sánchez pawned Singer machines for between thirty and fifty pesos and Flores pawned a Damascus machine for a forty-peso loan. Might any of these customers have been among the seamstresses visited two years earlier by representatives of the Labor Department during an investigation into living and working conditions of seamstresses?[109] Gathering data for an upcoming Seamstress Convention, the Labor Department hoped to get firsthand testimony from seamstresses themselves about the "sad situation that this branch of work finds itself [in], the urgency to protect it, and the justification for the government to decide to give the aid which it has at hand." Remember the Pagaza sisters, the home-based seamstresses who needed their sewing machines from the closed-down pawnshops in 1915 so they could make military uniforms? In 1932 the government's interest in seamstresses' livelihood and the provision of collateral credit intersect again, when women who had pawned sewing machines in the new Tacubaya branch of the Monte de Piedad were allowed to keep using them in a large room of the establishment.[110]

Automobiles are not included in the housekeeping-goods count but nonetheless formed part of the material package that households used to shape public personas. For sale in the Monte de Piedad in 1921 were two automobiles, a six-cylinder 26/64 horsepower Studebaker for 2,000 pesos and a four-cylinder 10/16 horsepower Opel on sale for 1,800 pesos. The German Boker company sold "Studebaker steam cars." The Monte also had a motorcycle, car parts, and bicycles for sale.[111]

The growing function of the Monte de Piedad auction room as a clearing house for secondhand household furnishings paralleled the evolution of the pawnshops into bazaars. In the Porfirian era foreign visitors planning on a long stay lamented the dearth of furniture-shopping arenas and the need to order goods directly from European distributors. By the end of the revolutionary upheaval in the city, at least some imported furnishings were available to the general public, or at least to those who could afford them, in the Monte de Piedad and in bazaars selling furniture "de ocasión." The Monte's *almoneda* (auction) room thus competed with the many bazaars in the city as well as with furniture stores such as Mueblería Riestra, which specialized in "legitimate Austrian furniture."[112] A vigorous business in buying pawn tickets also emerged. Another business on the rise was the sale of jewels, used sewing machines, and typewriters.[113]

The Mexican Revolution has been interpreted as many things. Was it a popular revolution reacting to uneven economic development, either led by peasant resistance or caused by worker exploitation? Or a democratic revolt by middle-class aspirants shut out by Díaz's closed political system? Was it an anti-imperialist socialist revolution, or a primarily anticlerical and cultural revolution that forged the modern Mexican nation? Was it many revolutions taking place simultaneously? Was it not a revolution for women, even not a revolution at all, but instead a rebellion? Or was it a popular revolution "high-jacked" by big business?[114] The few studies of the revolution as it played out in the streets of Mexico City have been largely concerned with worker agency and/or the degree to which different revolutionary leaders manipulated workers in power struggles. The participation of "popular" classes is evident in the politics of collateral credit, though the writing and even signing of petitions implies a literacy level not characteristic of the poor. The whole series of events is filtered for us through the eyes of a professional middle-class media.[115] While generally ignored in studies of the revolutionary city, the middle classes certainly had a lot at stake in resolving the material crises in the 1910s. They had a longstanding dependence on collateral credit to keep up appearances, intensified since the economic downturn after 1905. They needed to recover pawned goods in order to avoid or prolong the slide down the status ladder, as the possession and display of luxury goods was still central to the construction and maintenance of their public reputations. They needed collateral credit in the difficult economic and social conditions of 1915 just to get by.

Clearly, revolution politicized daily life. Long challenged by inadequate wages and salaries and high costs of living, city residents took matters into their own hands as revolutionary factions paraded in and out of the city. The traditional two-tiered collateral-lending structure was tottering amid collective actions and policy changes, with the drama playing out in the newspapers and on the streets. The Porfiriato was the heyday of private pawnbroking in Mexico City. Although Madero did not directly challenge empeñeros, Huerta's regime might have done so had it lasted longer. As it turned out, it was the pawning policies of revolutionary generals that ended the lucrative profits gained through petty collateral lending. Successive rival revolutionary generals pushed radical reform along until the Spanish businessmen, accustomed to playing the role of "uncle" in neighborhoods, themselves said "uncle" and closed their doors. Revolution added another layer to the ongoing public discourse about the unfortunate national characteristic of an inability to save and a reliance instead on pawning for consumption beyond one's means.

The petitioning women are not unlike women in other social movements who mobilize community members around consumption and social-reproduction issues.[116] The visibility of women in the protests against pawnbrokers may have stemmed from their responsibilities in provisioning the home, the pawnshop being a major resource toward that end. But many women worked in multiple settings—on the streets, in other people's homes, in factories—and were not simply married housekeepers, widows, or single mothers. The Pagaza sisters, trying to get their sewing machines out of hock, made their living sewing for others. How many of their *compañeras* were among the women carrying sewing machines and furniture through the street? And women in the city were organizing unions in the same months that (perhaps some of the same?) women were organizing repossessions of their collateral goods from neighborhood pawnshops. Men mobilized around collateral credit, too, as they did around all contested issues. Yet in the antipawnshop movement there were women such as María Rodríguez and those in the petition collective who were rather unusual in that they left a written record of their cultural politics.[117] The December 2, 1914, petitioners spoke of "exercising civil rights" and the rule of law. Asking "Does the law only apply to the poor?" female charcoal vendors took part in a liberal political culture versed in the rule of law and the idea of "the people" as well as in the revolutionary political culture promoted by Obregón, who invoked the "sacred right" of crowds to popular justice.[118] Yet this revolution again bypassed women when rewarding full citizenship in the post-revolutionary nation, as had happened in the transition from colony to nation a century before, with female combatants denied pensions and young widows denied survivor benefits. Despite women's participation in military combat, in petitioning city leaders, in leading consumption protests and pawnshop sackings in Mexico City, the statesmen drafting the Constitution of 1917 again denied women the vote.[119] Women engaged the language of political liberalism and revolution in defense of their livelihoods, their ability to do their jobs as housekeepers, and their rights as Mexicans while remaining unenfranchised. Militant women and men also engaged liberal economic culture, moving to protect their investments in private property. Typically, Mexicans still considered collateral to be only temporarily in the custody of brokers and not given up for good. Indeed, the very actions of women and men pawning for cash to meet consumption needs occurred with such regularity precisely because of their participation in the market economy.

Long accustomed to creative financing, Mexican housekeepers charged with day-to-day survival as well as with the long-term reputation and cultural livelihood of families faced a huge challenge in revolutionary years, especially 1914–16. Pawning still financed housekeeping, and material goods acquired for private consumption continued to live additional lives as collateral, as they had throughout the nineteenth century. But the politics of collateral credit closed first the Monte de Piedad, in a defensive move of the institution's administrators, and then the pawnshops, as brokers offensively resisted drastic interest restrictions. While collateral in the revolutionary decade symbolized changes that modernity brought to daily life, the central traditions surrounding household finance through pawning represent fundamental continuity in this material history of Mexico City.

Conclusion

Housekeeping, Pawnbroking, and Politics

When pawnshops talk, what do they say? They tell us about the interlocking weave of social relationships and economic, political, and cultural strands of daily life. The pawning process constituted relations between and among state and society, the negotiation of governance, the intersection of patriarchy and capitalism, and links between politics, business, and the household. Gender relations, associations of brokers and customers, changes in cultural expression and material hierarchies, revolutionary protest—the pawnshop was an arena for all of these interconnected experiences. Material life was lived out in rich and poor households, workshops, bars, streets, and pawnshops. Access to and control of possessions and of collateral credit shaped the way everyday people of different genders, classes, and ethnicities kept house and the way they experienced colonialism, liberalism, capitalism, and ultimately revolution.

In the culture of everyday credit in Mexico City, housekeeping was integral to the larger economy, to cultural formation, and to society at large. Women running households included living-room furniture, clothes in the closets, and sheets off the beds as part of the capital resources that they managed in "keeping house" throughout the century. What women managed—whether elite wives with full domestic staffs, the women on those staffs, middle-class housekeepers doing more of the work themselves, or working-class wives and mothers squeezing the housekeeping between multiple paid jobs—was the everyday, mundane, inconspicuous social reproduction of Mexicans and their public personas at all levels of society. For those with the means to acquire status luxury goods, the use and display of those conspicuous goods in home entertaining and public presentation at theaters, at balls, and in visits to others were further manifestations of housework done by women. Shopping for suits, dresses, and jewels; decorating living and dining rooms; choosing china and silverware patterns; maintaining the family's clothing and housewares—all of these activities required work, work most often done in Mexico by women. One can conclude from this study that housekeeping involved a great number of management skills, that it did not just maintain a refuge for the middle-class men (and fewer women) from the world of business. Instead, managing a house was itself like managing a business. The management jobs grew when both businesses and households increased in capitalization as the century moved forward. Management of resources and investments in household goods continued to incorporate and yield rounds of collateral credit. Though it appears that more goods that left the household for this purpose did not find their way back home in the revolutionary 1910s, this departure from one of the distinct characteristics of Mexico City's culture of everyday credit was temporary. Today, the preponderance of pawned goods are recovered by their owners in Mexico City.

"Keeping house" meant different things depending on the status and material base one had to work with and the larger context in which one lived. The connections between housekeeping and pawning illuminate the shifting intersections between identities based on ethnicity and social class in the nineteenth century as well as highlighting what city residents of different positions had in common. As the Bourbon reforms saw more peninsular men taking government posts and challenging Creole hegemony in New Spain, it was important that widows who had sons with futures in the professions and daughters to either marry off or educate continued to groom their children in a way that distinguished them from the growing ethnically mixed population. Bourbon Creoles availed themselves of their privileged access to the Monte de Piedad to raise the financing necessary to maintain appearances, and white residents continued to draw on their investments in movable property through the pawning process in the transition to independent rule by "hombres de bien." Also, in this political transition, immigrant Spanish men in the bottom tier of the middle sector of commerce made a living as lenders. They met the steady demand of housekeepers for collateral credit, first as part of the grocery trade, then in freestanding collateral-lending establishments.

As status and social-class distinctions became less dependent on European ethnicity and aristocratic ties, the emerging mestizo and white middle class continued to use collateral credit to negotiate the material and political hierarchies in Mexico City. For some, pawning could be a strategy of social mobility, whether moving from lower-class to middle-class or from middle-class to elite status. Most of the evidence presented in this book, however, suggests that given the chronically challenging economic conditions in the city during most periods from the end of the eighteenth century through the early twentieth century, pawning was more of a strategy of prevention for middle groups. Collateral credit allowed people to use the inconspicuous and conspicuous material manifestations of status to stall the "declassing" that threatened that status. Pawning was a strategy of prevention for poorer collateral-credit borrowers as well. It staved off hunger when petticoats were exchanged for groceries in the early nineteenth century, it could prevent death when yielding money to pay the doctor, and it could prevent starvation during "years of hunger" amid the revolutionary fighting and currency havoc that devastated the city in 1915.

But regular access to collateral credit also allowed average folks to maintain the mundane and luxurious consumption levels attainable by those of their status and not just to subsist day to day. The Creole widow Ygnacia Ruiz, with four adult children (the eldest an attorney) and an indigenous servant in her household counting on her transactions with pulpero Miguel Dominguez to negotiate her family's status in 1811; the indigenous woman supplying Ambassador Thompson with fruit at midcentury who considered the pearls around her neck her soundest investment because of their collateral value at the Montepío; the Porfirian fops buying hardware on credit and then pawning them for more credit in order to keep consuming the latest styles; the self-employed seamstress Pagaza sisters stemming the tide until more job-market opportunities opened up by pawning their sewing machines during the revolution—all of these people managed daily lives in a culture of everyday credit.

As women made up more than half of the population throughout the nineteenth century, their numbers among the clientele are not surprising. However, given a growing liberal discourse of domesticity relegating women to the home as a "private" sphere, the numbers of women engaged in pawning transactions that took them into the streets and into business relationships is significant. All of these women left the home and visited commercial establishments in the public (and supposedly male) sector of business. Given women's insertion into capitalist structures—as domestic servants, as artisans, as seamstresses, as vendors, decreasingly as shopkeepers—low income was one factor that compelled women of various civil, economic, and social statuses to turn to collateral credit. Wives and mothers; women in free unions; single mothers and widows; small artisans and women producing products for the market at home, all were represented among pawnshop clientele. The state's representatives believed that it was mostly women who turned to pawnshops for credit and assumed that all were parents in need of cash and credit to provide for their families. This belief may have been the basis for steps taken by the colonial state to protect the welfare of "needy women," obligating corner grocers to provide credit services by accepting pawns from their customers. But not only the poor made use of popular credit mechanisms, as the public discourse emphasized—the middle-class also used pawnshops, especially the Monte de Piedad, perhaps also to stretch household budgets or to finance consumption of luxury goods and keep up with changing fashions. Provisioning takes on a different hue in middle-class households, where there are different standards for determining what was basic and what was luxury. Basic items such as cloth—the category of goods most often pawned—generally would have been of a different quality in these middling homes, representing a different level of investment and a larger line of credit. It would not always have been the mistress of a household who actually performed the pawning transaction. Certainly Indian, mestizo, and mulatta servants (and black and mulatta slaves in the colonial period) did the pawning for their Spanish, Creole, and mestizo employers. And children and husbands might be the ones visiting the broker with the table service or the linens in hand.

After the dramatic events of 1914–16, the press highlighted the plight of pawning customers, running feature stories about the people standing in line. At a Monte de Piedad branch on May 1, 1920, a reporter remarked that those in the long line waiting for assistance were "almost always women."[1] *El Demócrata* presented this testimony:

> "Sir, I have not always been so poor"—she declared, pushing a package back under her shawl, probably her last skirt. "Before, we got by more or less; but when I became a widow and found myself alone, I started to need to come to the Montepío. The Montepío has devoured everything. My house, furnished by sacrifice and economy, has been cheapened insensibly. First it was my half-set of matching jewelry, which had been a wedding gift; then, the necklace with the votive medallion; later, this piece of furniture; later still, that feather mattress, and in the end . . . what I have here are two of my children's outfits. Do you think they will take them?"[2]

A few months later, repeating a familiar refrain, many of the "humble women depositing their goods after waiting in the interminable daily line" were said to be descending little by little, like the characters in stories by Delgado and del Campo of decades before, "down the last rungs of the ladder into misery."[3] Whether this testimony of the woman in line at the Monte pawning her children's clothes is genuine, embellished, or even invented by the journalist, it reflects over a hundred years of discourse about pawning.

To some extent pawning may have served to mitigate patriarchal economic structures. The relegation of women to low-paying jobs coupled with husbands' control over a married woman's wages meant that women had less access to a generally cash-poor economy. Women heading and running households did have access to material goods, but with most pawnbrokers men throughout the nineteenth century, the broker-client relationship was still patriarchal. And liberal reform of patriarchal laws, beginning with the enlightened Bourbons and expanded to some extent under republican governments, were to make women more helpful to the family and the state, not to make women equal to men within the family and society. Mexico City's neighborhoods throughout this century and a half of change were full of unemployed women, widows, and female household heads. The safeguarding of public spaces so that these and other women could secure the cash to manage the private economies of their families fit the larger liberal project of empowering women as household managers and rearers of productive subjects and then citizens while extending patriarchal vigilance of women's honor into public businesses. By 1920 the revolutionary government banned women from working in places where liquor was consumed for reasons of morality and to protect women's honor (waitresses were described by one deputy as "live meat"). Both the Constitution of 1917 and the Work Law of 1919 contained provisions that protected women's health but at the same time restricted their economic activities.[4]

A few historiographical generations have passed since Fernand Braudel established the links between material life and capitalism. This study of the pawning process shows that the political companions to capitalism—liberalism and the growth of the republican state—are interwoven with material culture. Through its mediating and regulating role in material credit relations, the liberal state forged on the crumbling colonial edifice struggled to come to terms with popular economic and cultural concerns. Taking the long view, we find that by the revolutionary era, the state in some ways had come full circle, returning to colonial prohibitions on the right to earn profits through high interest rates and the colonial paternalism that aimed to guarantee popular access to credit and material wellbeing.

Embedded in the market economy, Spanish immigrant pawnbrokers were a constant, even ubiquitous, presence. While not literally kin to the pulpero, the first generation of empeñero, or even the Porfirian broker, the pawnbrokers who militantly resisted the changes wrought by revolutionary social policy nonetheless continued a tradition of political engagement in defense of their rights as businessmen when they organized their lender's association. Like their forebears and other Spanish merchants and in contrast to national businessmen, who might also have resented and resisted government interference in their business affairs, immigrant men such as Jorge Fernández and Santos Sobrino faced intense ethnic hatred embedded in Mexican public opinion. While engaging the economic liberal discourse about private property, the rights to profits, and noninterference by the government, they came up against a Mexican political liberalism that had developed throughout the nineteenth century with an antiforeign nationalist component. The Spanish, who had been out of political power for a full century, were more a target of this nationalism than other foreigners who had made bigger fortunes under the Porfirian development program—even the French, the last foreign power to rule Mexico. The story of pawning is part of the process of "imagining" a Mexican identity in terms of the negation of the colonial past. The persistent anti-gachupín political culture was a long process due to the continued presence of new Spaniards in an increasingly mestizo nation that, by the time of the revolution, had begun to reconsider the legacies of the conquest and the indigenous contribution to the nation.[5]

Liberal theories were rooted in conflicting tenets coming out of Enlightenment thought. On the one hand, the welfare strand within liberalism understood citizens as having the right to a dignified life and privileged "the public good" over the individual. On the other hand, beliefs that profits made by individuals unencumbered by the government paved the road to progress and beliefs about the sanctity of private property were in play. As the country worked through the political struggles of the nineteenth century, pawning regulation as welfare policy mixed with Santa Anna's and other statesmen's hatred of Spanish merchants. When more doctrinaire liberals were in power, liberal support for entrepreneurship obtained, as did protection of borrowers' private-property-turned-collateral.

Regulation of pawnbroking also continued as embattled governments needed the tax revenues. The major difference under liberal governance was that usury restrictions fell away, opening the door for an expansion of the collateral-lending business and the potential for high profits. Much of the nineteenth-century discourse played out in the print media (another liberal hallmark) about pawnbrokers had to do with their role in the capitalist development of Mexico. But welfare discourse did not disappear with economic liberals in power. Pawnbrokers themselves used the language of patriarchal protector of needy women in their negotiations with the government over pawning policy. On occasion newspaper editors grudgingly argued that pawnbroking provided a social service to the needy Mexican public that did not know how—or did not earn enough—to save money for a rainy day. Some economic liberals believed that pawnbroking infused cash into the consumer economy, while others believed that pawnbroking was bad for capitalism. Porfirio Díaz, as a liberal ruler, went the farthest in honoring the right of pawnbrokers to make a profit. At the same time he ensured that the state profited through taxation and safeguarded the public good through scientific regulation. Díaz also expanded the welfare apparatus in the city, including the Monte de Piedad, at the same time changing the explicitly public nature of charitable institutions and encouraging private benevolence. With the Mexican Revolution the state functioned as a mediator in everyday politics, as had colonial and liberal states. The revolutionary state, while in flux with armies and generals coming into and going out of the city, exercised a fairly steady mandate in response to workers' and women's demands regarding pawnbroking abuses. Century-long state attempts to counter abuses by empeñeros with the services of the Monte de Piedad had not been successful. The revolutionary state in the end held the private sector to the interest rates of the charitable institution.

Pawning policy and practice in Mexico City illuminate liberalism as a hegemonic process that had material manifestations. Middle-class pawnbrokers negotiated and contended with the state, through the liberal means of petitions and lobbying, for their right to share in the fruits of economic liberalism. Middle-class statesmen protected their movable goods through lists of forbidden collateral and servant regulations. It was not just political and economic power that was wielded in this negotiated process, but culture, too, as the strategic use of collateral resources for everyday credit attests. The cultural practices surrounding pawning saw women and men doing what they had to do. In defiance, city residents pawned solitary spoons—and even stole goods to pawn—despite regulations. In resignation, they yielded the last of their status goods in order to prolong their social descent. With deliberation, they invested in silver and other goods precisely because they were useful as collateral with which to maintain status and identities. In the revolution, liberal discourse and practices of collective action and petitioning provided the language for city residents to challenge liberalism itself, especially as manifested in the profits of Porfirian pawnbrokers. After 1905 liberal hegemony broke down, as middle-class material benefits and opportunities dwindled under economic pressures and revolutionary events in the city jeopardized the pawning avenue for maintaining middle- and working-class households while at the same time exacerbating the need for pawning.

Historians debate whether or not to "take the state out" of inquiries into the colonial past, because what mattered most to people were local community relations, not the state.[6] But at least in the case of pawning relations, both brokers and clients sought redress from the state and used it as an arena in which to debate broker-client relations as well as governance generally. Taking the long view on state-society relations calls for putting the state back in. The state increasingly engaged society, first as a mediator, then as a regulator, and finally as an enforcer, embedded in relations between brokers and clients over the trajectory of the long nineteenth century in Mexico. The state-run Monte de Piedad consciously operated as a safety net for whites. The regulation of credit mechanisms by the state played a stabilizing role, as different governments attempted to keep interest rates low enough for the poor to access credit; indeed, when the pawning structure broke down, revolutionary activity intensified. But control had its limits even in the absence of revolution. The pawning evidence suggests that who pawned what, where, and for how long was mostly determined by the pawning clientele, not by the state. The residents of the city disregarded state prohibitions on pawning artisans' tools, weapons, and other state goods up until the revolution.[7] Decisions made in the home about what was expendable and what was needed, decisions made by a wide variety of people about what to steal and where to fence it, and decisions by pawnbrokers to charge higher interest rates did more to shape pawning practice than did government regulation. Nonetheless, had pawning not existed as a regular recourse throughout the century, residents might have been more rebellious.

Much changed in the transition from colonial to republican rule, though many changes did not come precisely at the time of Independence in the early 1820s but instead occurred gradually beginning in the 1830s. The transition from liberal to revolutionary rule in the twentieth century brought more dramatic and immediate changes. Pawning legislation changed in the 1840s, when the nature of the businesses engaged in pawning was also transformed, and continued to change along with the state's role in the pawning process. When the new casa de empeño emerged, pawning was not a terribly lucrative business. With the elimination of anti-usury laws, however, profits skyrocketed along with soaring interest rates. The nature of state intervention paradoxically grew with the consolidation of the laissez-faire state. Conflict among brokers, clients, and the state increased, resulting in the ultimate demise of the empeños amid revolution. The middle class grew along with the population, and the working class became more proletarianized.

Also, much did not change. An important symbol of continuity since the colonial era is the Monte de Piedad itself. While the Monte underwent significant transformations, such as its expansion into branch offices in the 1860s, it was a steady institution through a long, tumultuous century, almost constantly open for business and often in financial trouble. The discourse about needy female clients and vice-ridden male clients continued, as did the unsavory reputation of the pawnbroker. The middle and lower classes shared a culture of everyday credit. Yet a segregation of the pawning clientele, with the working class pawning in private shops and the middle class pawning in public shops, continued for the most part, at least until the revolution brought extended closures of pawning venues. Both pawnbrokers and clients continued to disregard state efforts to regulate the movement of goods in and out of pawnshops. At the same time both brokers and clients continued to turn to the state to negotiate better terms for their end of the credit relationship. Business rhythms and patterns were other constants throughout the century. Pawnshops remained on the same corners for decades, while at the same time there was a steady turnover in their ownership. The history of pawning confirms that cultural change occurs slowly, though it sped up with industrialization at the end of the nineteenth century.

Everyday life in the city in the early years of the twentieth century, of course, was different from everyday life at the end of the Bourbon era a century before, and living conditions amid revolution were surely worse than they had ever been. Yet in other ways nothing more than time separated years such as 1815 or 1840 from 1915. All three years saw crises, in the face of political changes, hitting pocketbooks and household budgets; suspended salaries and scarce or worthless currencies; and the need to maintain one's social status in order to weather the political and economic crises. The pawnbroker's public identity as a "Spaniard" worked against him in the revolutionary context as it had in the early postindependence years. Perhaps the pawning clientele had experienced the most change by the revolutionary era. Collateral-credit customers—middle and working class—were more combative in the 1910s, petitioning the government both collectively and as individuals. Pawning clients took matters into their own hands when their access to pawnshops and the recovery of their property was threatened, demonstrating in the streets and sacking establishments to get their goods back. The material revolution in the city saw middle-class brokers pitted against middle- and working-class credit customers.

Women continued to be a visible group among pawning customers, especially among the politicized pawning patrons who were petitioning the government and taking to the streets to recover their goods in 1915, "the year of hunger." Indeed, female political participation grew as the economy worsened for householders during a time of political change and ideological passion about rights, liberty, justice, and nation. Given the demographic reality of so many women heading households in an economy that offered only low-income employment opportunities for women and not much better opportunities for men who might hope to keep their women out of the public work force, clearly housekeepers came to depend on the pawning process. During the economic crisis and political fervor of the 1910s, the traditions surrounding pawning, housekeeping, and consumption propelled neighborhood women, along with their men, into political action in Mexico City.

Epilogue

Still a Culture of Everyday Credit

In 1950 a feature film entitled *Monte de Piedad* told stories of people whose lives intersected with the charitable institution. Throughout the century before, investigative news pieces, poetry, novels, political satire, and even the theatrical stage had featured collateral credit. Now it became part of the golden age of Mexican cinema. The film was made during the heyday of the "economic miracle," a period as much heralded as the Porfirian progress of fifty years earlier, with just as unequal a distribution of the wealth generated.

In the film María walks away from the clerk's window with one hundred pesos, which means that she and her sick mother, Doña Lupita, will avoid eviction from her rooming house by the evil *casero*, Don Pedro, though her rent has been raised. Another story revolves around the "cabaret dancer" Margarita, who secures a loan for two hundred pesos, an amount that does not satisfy her "exploiter," René. Margarita ends up turning in René for killing Don Ruperto, whom the two of them have tried to fleece. The next tale concerns Mario, an old musician who pawns his beloved violin for three hundred pesos in order to pay his rent. Dejected when the Monte de Piedad refuses to let him pawn his equipment, a *bolero* (shoe shiner) bribes a police officer fifty centavos to not take away a little boy accused of stealing. He then buys medicine to save a girl's life after selling a valuable jewel of his mother's to a "coyote" at the Monte de Piedad. In the last story Marcos tries to pawn his watch because he is unemployed and his son is sick. An old priest, Gabriel, pawns a valuable crucifix for two thousand pesos, which he gives to Marcos. The child gets better without the need for medicine, but the priest dies shortly after his visit.[1] These cinematic vignettes, taking place in downtown Mexico City in the midst of an economic boom, demonstrate that in the mid-twentieth century Mexico still had a culture of everyday credit.

After the boom went to bust in the 1970s and early 1980s, credit cards were an alternative to pawning for awhile for those in the middle class. But with constant peso devaluations and rapidly rising bank interest rates, the line at the Monte de Piedad has gained even more adherents, as has the practice of pawning jewelry with neighbors. The institutionalization of the revolution during the boom years saw the establishment of other state credit institutions such as INFONAVIT, which builds apartment complexes and then makes fixed-interest housing loans to middle-class and working-class employees through employers or unions. The welfare apparatus also continued to evolve, with new institutions such as the national health-care system, family programs, and child development centers. The Monte de Piedad expanded into a multifaceted charitable institution, with new branches all over the city (some lending without interest) and the country. In addition the Monte established a mortgage lending service, built a housing project for Monte employees (called Colonia Romero de Terreros), a school lunch program, artisan workshops for carpenters and seamstresses, a rest home, a recreational center, and worker training centers. In 1990 the institution was transformed from its quasi-public character, becoming a completely private charitable institution.[2]

Wages improved steadily after 1920, and a legal industrial minimum wage was established in 1934. Women retreated from the paid labor force after the 1940s, despite the fact that the budget to meet basic needs in 1970 was almost twice the minimum wage, which only a minority of working people received. The "lost decades" of economic crisis in the 1980s and 1990s have only exacerbated this chronic inability of incomes to meet needed expenditures.[3] There is today an organized middle-class debtor's movement nationwide, which stages regular protests in front of government ministries in the city.[4] In this context the continued importance of the Monte de Piedad is easily understood, as is the establishment of new private pawning chains such as PrendaMex.

A hugely profitable consumer culture has taken hold in Mexico in the midst of a chronically troubled economy in terms of wages and salaries that would cover rising costs of living, and Mexico City's now 25 million people have led this cultural process. The Parián market, with its luxury clothing imports and jewelers along Plateros Street early in the nineteenth century, the Palacio de Hierro of the late nineteenth century, and Sears

Roebuck in the post–World War II era represent moments in a commercialization process that continues in Mexico.[5] Today enough people aspire to, or are able to afford one way or another to live at, a material and status level sufficient to support a tier of commercial retail chains, both domestic (Commercial Mexicana, Gigante, Liverpool) and foreign (Walmart, Kmart, Home Depot). This is in spite of the fact that the majority of people in Mexico City and other cities are struggling economically. Throughout the "miracle" years of the 1950s and 1960s, and especially during the crises and adjustments of the last three decades, most people have faced low salaries, environmental hazards, and multiple jobs. Many sell their gold jewelry downtown for a pittance, pawn their jacket or radio with the corner *pulquero*, or stand in line at the Monte de Piedad in order to make ends meet.

While doing research in Mexico City in 1996, I gained access to the Monte de Piedad's historical archive in order to sample the ledger books with the help of the then–public relations director. After an amiable interview with Luis Romero de Terreros, an engineer who holds the family's traditional seat on the Monte de Piedad's board of directors, I gained access to documents only from the early nineteenth century due to concerns about respecting the privacy of the institution's clientele. In two months I got through only a few boxes from an immense closet of records on the second floor, overlooking the patio of the Monte de Piedad's headquarters on the Zócalo.

Virtually every guidebook about Mexico City since the nineteenth century has included a description of the Monte de Piedad's imposing headquarters. Here is my contribution to that hallowed tradition of city chroniclers. Every day there was a brisk pace of pawning transactions, mostly of jewelry at this installation (transactions for appliances such as refrigerators, cars, and other large items are limited to the branch establishments). There is a jewelry showroom in the headquarters, where unredeemed gold necklaces, diamond rings, and other expensive items are for sale. The employees are expert at appraising jewelry and provide a formal appraisal service to those who want to assess the worth of antique jewelry for insurance or other purposes. Across the hall is a room with living-room knickknacks, fluted-glass lampshades, crystal decanters—a menagerie spanning decades of housekeeping style. A smaller room holds dictionary and encyclopedia sets, computer software, music amplifiers, VCRs, and a few musical instruments, both acoustic and electric. My stay overlapped with Mother's Day, which was acknowledged with a special rate on loans secured by kitchen appliances, announced on a banner at the entrances to the central hallway opening out to the National Cathedral on the Zócalo side and into the Palma plaza on the other side. Without fail every time I neared the building, a "coyote" interested in intercepting whatever it was I might be bringing to pawn approached me, promising a better deal than the institution would offer.

In the middle of new research for this book, the Employees' Union of the National Monte de Piedad shut the institution down for months with a strike over traditional labor issues—wage increases, benefits, and respect toward employees. The 1990s were watershed years in the political economy of pawning in Mexico, with changes under neoliberal policies of Carlos Salinas and then Ernesto Zedillo aimed at structural adjustment of the economy. The Monte de Piedad underwent structural adjustments of its own, with the appointment of a new director and cost-cutting measures. In an interview on May Day 1999 at a strike rally on the Zócalo, the union representative for the employees of the Casa Matriz answered questions about the union's agenda in economic, political, and cultural terms. The interview shows that historical legacies inform many of the practices surrounding collateral credit in the city today.[6] The foundational myth about the first principal of the Mexican Monte de Piedad's going to help the poor is alive and well, repeated by the delegate. The culture of paternalism also lives on, both in the relationship between the institution and the public and the institution and its staff. Employees today are "children of families that have worked in the Monte de Piedad by tradition, almost all of our grandfathers and uncles were our precursors." The link to housekeeping, the holiday rhythm of pawning cycles, the function of keeping the middle class and even the famous from slipping into bad times—all of these issues came to mind for the union delegate. According to the delegate, the typical client is still female: "Practically it is the housewife that comes to create 'el empeño,' to get the sustenance for her children, sent on the errand by the father." The busiest pawning times are La Cuesta de Enero before the gift giving of the Three Kings, Holy Week vacations, and August, when people need to buy school supplies for children. There is the story about a boxer who pawned his gold *esclava* (prize belt) that weighed almost a kilo. Indeed, "There are generations of people that today are alive—politicians, artists, professional people—thanks to the Monte de Piedad. They are indebted because in their years of studying, in the time it took them to gear up as functionaries, they had to turn to the Monte de Piedad in order to buy their books, take a trip, etc. All social classes economically speaking have turned to the Monte de Piedad."

Appendix 1

Collateral Transactions Data

TABLE A

Breakdown of Pawned-Good Database from Inventories by Business, 1787–1921

Doc. Date	Cloth	Noncloth[a]	Mixed[b]	Total	Business
Jan. 1787	1	1		2	Guarico
May 1787	683	66	2	751	Verdeja
Jan. 1788	105	19	1	125	Guarico
Sep. 1788	10	5	2	17	Quebrada
Sep. 1789	48	8	2	58	Fraile
Apr. 1792	42	6		48	Aguilita
Apr. 1792	13	12	1	26	San Juan
May 1792	4	5		9	Guadalupe
June 1792	58	3		62	Aguilita
Apr. 1793	3	1		4	San Juan
Dec. 1796	163	1		164	Coutiño
Oct. 1799	3	2	1	6	Monterilla
Jan. 1802	5	4		9	Sta. Gertrudis
Jan.–Mar. 1802	578	458	23	1,059	Monte de Piedad
Oct. 1804	34	13		47	Santísima
Jan. 1805	18	2		20	Santísima
Feb. 1805	6	4		10	Espirito Santo
Sep. 1805	10	3		13	Espirito Santo
Oct. 1805	10	17		27	Merced
Jan. 1808	6	8		14	Santo Domingo
May 1808	8	17		25	Santo Domingo
Jul. 1808	97	8		105	Manco
Jul. 1808	9	5		14	Montealegre
Dec. 1809	2	3		5	San Felipe
Feb. 1810	86	24		110	San Felipe
Dec. 1810	5	7		12	Coutiño
Jun. 1811	2	14		16	Portaceli
Nov. 1811	34	4		38	Aduana Vieja
Nov. 1814	2	6		8	Tarolito
Dec. 1817	71	3		74	Fraile
Jan. 1818	114	18		132	Cacaguate
April 1818	94	18		112	Cacaguate
May 1824	0	4		4	Victoria
Sep. 1825	1	2		3	La Luna
Jan. 1830	1	6		7	Monte de Piedad

TABLE A

Continued

Doc. Date	Cloth	Noncloth[a]	Mixed[b]	Total	Business
Jan. 1867	180	4		184	Cartagena
May 1868	257	18		275	Cartagena
Aug. 1868	225	27		252	Cartagena
1869	10	17		27	Monte branch
Feb. 1869	246	31	3	280	Cartagena
June 1868	311	39		350	Cartagena
Sep. 1871	67	15		82	Magdalena
June 1873	15	246		261	Monte de Piedad/ Montealegre
Mar. 1879	383	167		550	Constitución
Apr. 1880	590	197	5	792	Constitución
Feb. 1902	1	209		210	Monte de Piedad/ Relox No. 4a
Dec. 1902	5	4		9	Leguisamo
Dec. 1902	0	2		2	Palma
Dec. 1902	0	3		3	Portillo San Diego
Dec. 1902	91	64		155	Veronica No. 2a
Dec. 1902	49	104		153	Veronica No. 3a
Dec. 1902	39	77		116	Estampa Jesús
Jan. 1903	69	148		217	Veronica No. 3a
Apr. 1915	224	117		341	Verdis
Apr. 1915	2	51		53	Ancha No. 5a
1920–21	0	650		650	Monte de Piedad
Total	5,090	2,967	41	8,098	56 inventories

Source: AHNMP, Libros de Empeños, 1802; AGN, Consulado, vol. 11, exp. 43, fs. 388–93; vol. 24, exp. 13, fs. 302–6; vol. 25, exp. 13, fs. 310–12v; vol. 28, exp. 5, fs. 231–41; vol. 28, exp. 6, fs. 271–74; vol. 29, exp. 4, no. 3, fs. 1–6v; vol. 38, exp. 2, fs. 21–25v; vol. 38, exp. 2, fs. 35–38; vol. 38, exp. 5, fs. 292–98v; vol. 38, exp. 6, fs. 271–74; vol. 47, exp. 5, fs. 298–301; vol. 53, exp. 12, fs. 365–71; vol. 67, exp. 10, fs. 129–32; vol. 292, exp. 3, no. 3, fs. 1–4; vol. 292, exp. 3, no. 8, fs. 1–7; vol. 292, exp. 4, no. 3, fs. 1–6v; vol. 292, exp. 4, no. 5, fs. 1–4; vol. 292, exp. 4, no. 7, fs. 2–5; vol. 292, exp. 7, fs. 2–6; AGN, Gobernacion, leg. 873(7), exp. 1, fs. 6–73; leg. 1296(1), exp. 5, no. 7; leg. 2187(1), exp. 1, no. 9, fs. 4–6; leg. 1517(1), exp. 1, no. 5, fs. 1–12; CONDUMEX, Fondo CDLV-2; AHCM, Tacubaya, inv. 120, exp. 3, exp. 5, exp. 7, exp. 11; AHCM, Tlalpan, inv. 69, exp. 11, exp. 71; AHCM, Gobierno del Distrito, Empeños, vol. 1422, exp. 5, f. 17; vol. 1422, exp. 38; vol. 1429, exp. 442; AHCM, Gobierno del

TABLE A

Continued

Distrito, Empeños Ventas, no. 162, exps. 1, 7, 9, 14, 15, and 16. *El Demócrata*, August 22, 1920, 3; October 12, 1920, 3; October 21, 1920, 10; November 12, 1920, 8; November 15, 1920, 7; November 22, 1920, 7; December 19, 1920, 7; January 18, 1921, 7; February 15, 1921, 6; February 20, 1921, 6; March 15, 1921, 10; April 24, 1921, 5.

[a] Includes table-service items, accessories such as buckles and cigarette cases, and jewelry (mostly silver, also gold, copper, and precious stones) as well as weapons such as swords and pistols, tools, noncloth household goods, and other items.

[b] Includes loan transactions involving a bundle of at least one cloth and one noncloth item.

TABLE B

Categories of Goods in Pawning Transactions, 1787–1830

	Customers							
	Monte de Piedad			Retail				
Category	Female	Male	All	Female	Male	?[a]	All	Total
Clothing								
Female								
Enaguas	121	33	154	86	34	173	293	447
Rebozo	70	23	93	77	39	138	253	347
Enaguas w/rebozo	36	23	59			1	1	60
Huipil				1		2	3	3
Mantilla		2	2	1	1	3	5	7
Mantón	14	5	19			4	4	23
Saya	17	6	23	5	2	3	10	33
Túnico	14	6	20	5	6	12	23	43
Male								
Casaca		1	1	2	5	15	22	23
Frac					1		1	2
Pantalón				7	3	9	19	19
Sarape				2		1	3	3
Eccl. robe				1		1		1
Generic Clothing[b]	68	64	132	110	152	412	674	806
Subtotal	340	163	503	296	245	773	1,314	1,817
Household Goods								
Fabric	31	27	58	45	31	142	218	276
Linen	7	4	11	40	38	125	203	214
Silver service	100	84	184	6	7	16	29	213
Kitchen/cooking	4	1	5	1	2	3	6	11
Furniture					1	2	3	3
Subtotal	142	116	258	92	79	288	459	717
Jewelry								
Sole item, silver	12	10	22	16	9	39	64	86
With diamonds	31	25	56		1		1	57
With emeralds	5	5	10					10
Reliquary	14	6	20	5	3	13	21	41
Bundle/set[c]	62	27	89	4	1	10	15	105
String of pearls	38	12	50					50
Subtotal	162	85	247	25	14	62	101	349

TABLE B

Continued

	Customers							
	Monte de Piedad			Retail				
Category	Female	Male	All	Female	Male	?[a]	All	Total
Tools				8	16	50	74	74
Weapons								
Sword	1	4	5			8	8	13
Firearm					1	8	9	
Subtotal	1	4	5		1	16	17	22
Religious								
Rosary	3	5	8		4	5	9	17
Crucifix				1		3	4	4
Holy image					5	5	10	10
Subtotal	3	5	8	1	9	13	23	31
Watches					2	11	13	13
Other								
Silver accessory	13	7	20	2	9	17	28	48
Musical instrument					4	2	6	6
Piece/coin, silver/gold		2	2			3	3	5
Book				1	1	3	5	5
Umbrella						2	2	2
Lock				1	1		2	2
Saddle					2		2	2
Agricultural product						1	1	1
Eyeglasses						1	1	1
House title					1		1	1
Mixed bundle[d]	12	11	23	4	4	10	18	41
Subtotal	25	20	45	8	22	39	69	114
Total	673	393	1,066	430	387	1,252	2,069	3,135

Source: AHNMP, Libros de Empeños, 1802; AGN, Consulado, vol. 11, exp. 43, fs. 388–93; vol. 24, exp. 13, fs. 302–6; vol. 25, exp. 13, fs. 310–12v; vol. 28, exp. 5, fs. 231–41; vol. 28, exp. 6, fs. 271–74; vol. 29, exp. 4, no. 3, fs. 1–6v; vol. 38, exp. 2, fs. 21–25v; vol. 38, exp. 2, fs. 35–38; vol. 38, exp. 5, fs. 292–98v; vol. 38, exp. 6, fs. 271–74; vol. 47, exp. 5, fs. 298–301; vol. 53, exp. 12, fs. 365–71; vol. 67, exp. 10, fs. 129–32; vol. 292, exp. 3, no. 3, fs. 1–4; vol. 292, exp. 3, no. 8, fs. 1–7; vol. 292, exp. 4, no. 3, fs. 1–6v; vol. 292, exp. 4, no. 5, fs. 1–4; vol. 292, exp. 4, no. 7, fs. 2–5; vol. 292, exp. 7, fs. 2–6; CONDUMEX, Fondo CDLV-2.

[a] Customer either not named individually or named with last name only.

TABLE B
Continued

[b] Includes items that can be worn by a male or female, including shirts, capes, scarves, socks, belts, shoes, hats, and underclothes. This category also includes bundles of clothing that might contain male or female clothing articles but also a generic good such as a shirt or a cut of cloth.

[c] Includes matching sets of jewels as well as bundles of jewelry that include religious items such as crosses, reliquaries, and rosaries.

[d] Includes at least one cloth and one jewel item.

TABLE C

Categories of Goods in Pawning Transactions, 1867–80

	Customers							
	Monte de Piedad			Pawnshop				
Category	Female	Male	All	Female	Male	?[a]	All	Total
Clothing								
Female								
Enaguas	1		1	74	16	265	355	356
Rebozo	1	1	2	23	5	94	122	124
Vestido				11		30	41	41
Tápalo	3		3	11	2	25	38	41
Mantilla						1	1	1
Túnico	1	1	2			3	3	5
Other, female[b]				2		13	15	15
Male								
Sarape		1	1	13	10	213	236	237
Pantalón		1	1	8	26	42	76	77
Saco	1	1	2	2	1	19	22	24
Saco w/pantalón /traje						3	3	3
Men's shirt				2		2	4	4
Boy's outfit				1	1		2	2
Generic Clothing[c]	5	2	7	38	25	427	490	497
Subtotal	12	7	19	185	86	1,237	1,408	1,427
Household Goods								
Fabric whole	1	3	4	29	4	193	226	230
Fabric cut				4	3	49	56	56
Linen	1	1	2	79	37	319	435	437
Silver Service	4	10	14			55	55	69
Kitchen/cooking	1	1	2	3	1	32	36	38
Iron				10	4	69	83	83
Sewing instrument		1	1	1		8	9	10
Furnishing[d]	2	2	4			9	9	13
Subtotal	9	18	27	126	49	734	909	936
Jewelry								
Silver item		1	1	7	3	40	50	51
Gold item	14	29	43	5	1	25	31	74
Gold with diamonds	27	54	81	1			1	82

TABLE C

Continued

	Customers							
	Monte de Piedad			Pawnshop				
Category	Female	Male	All	Female	Male	?[a]	All	Total
Jewelry bundle/set[e]	9	24	33	6		17	23	56
Loose diamonds		6	6					6
String of pearls		10	10					10
Subtotal	50	124	174	19	4	82	105	279
Weapons								
Pistol	3	15	18			31	31	49
Rifle						4	4	4
Ammunition belt						2	2	2
Subtotal	3	15	18			37	37	55
Tools					4	71	75	75
Watches	9	35	44			9	9	53
Religious								
Rosary						3	3	3
Crucifix		1	1			4	4	5
Holy image						1	1	1
Subtotal		1	1			8	8	9
Other								
Silver accessory	1	3	4			18	18	22
Saddle/harness		1	1		2	19	21	22
Musical instrument				1	1	15	17	17
Pieces/coin, silver	1		1		2	3	5	6
Umbrella		1	1		1	2	3	4
Dolls						1	1	1
Eyeglasses						1	1	1
Theater glasses						1	1	1
Book				1			1	1
Mixed bundle[f]					1	9	10	10
Subtotal	2	5	7	2	7	69	78	85
Total	85	206	290	332	149	2,148	2,629	2,919

Source: AHCM, Inventario General de la Municipalidad de Tacubaya, inv. 120, exps. 3, 5, 7, and 11; Inventario General de la Municipalidad de Tlalpan, inv. 69, exps. 7, 11, and 71; AGN, Gobernación, 4th section, leg. 873(7), exp. 1, fs. 6–73v; leg. 1296(1), exp. 5, no. 6, f. 5, and no. 7; leg. 302, exp. 2, fs. 5–7; leg. 1517(1), exp. 1, no. 1, fs. 1–3v.

TABLE C

Continued

---

[a] Customer either not named individually or named with last name only.

[b] Includes *camisa de mujer*, *ropón*, *velo*, *calzones de mujer*, and *traje de mujer*.

[c] Includes items that can be worn by a male or female, including shirts, capes (most often *tilmas* in this sample), jackets, vests, aprons, scarves, belts, shoes, hats, and underpants. This category also includes bundles of clothing that might contain male or female clothing articles but also a generic good such as a shirt or a cut of cloth.

[d] This category includes boxes, furniture, table clocks, mirrors, lighting fixtures, and paintings.

[e] Includes matching sets of jewels as well as bundles of jewelry that include religious items such as crosses, reliquaries, and rosaries.

[f] Includes at least one cloth and one jewel item.

TABLE D

Categories of Goods in Pawning Transactions, 1902–9

Category	Monte de Piedad Customers	Pawnshop Customers: Female	Male	?[a]	Total	Total
Household Goods						
Table service	1	1		99	100	101
Linen		1		42	43	43
Furnishings[b]				28	28	28
Fabric, whole	1			23	23	24
Fabric, cut for clothing				5	5	5
Kitchen/cooking		1		5	6	6
Iron				11	11	11
Sewing instrument				2	2	2
Subtotal	2	3		215	218	220
Clothing						
Female						
Enaguas				38	38	38
Rebozo				20	20	20
Chal				8	8	8
Vestido				4	4	4
Male						
Sarape				5	5	5
Pantalón				17	17	17
Saco			1	7	8	8
Traje				6	6	6
Generic Clothing[c]		2	3	83	88	88
Subtotal		2	4	188	194	194
Jewelry						
Silver item	5			30	30	35
Gold item	39			44	44	83
Gold with diamonds	7			2	2	9
String, coral	1			4	4	5
Jewelry bundle/set[d]	58	1		4	5	63
Subtotal	110	1		84	85	195
Watches	77		3	67	70	144
Weapons						
Pistol	4			13	13	17
Rifle				1	1	1
Ammunition belt				3	3	3
Subtotal	4			17	17	21

TABLE D

Continued

Category	Monte de Piedad Customers	Pawnshop Customers				Total
		Female	Male	?[a]	Total	
Sewing Machines		1		11	12	12
Tools				8	8	8
Religious						
Rosary	1	1		2	3	4
Crucifix	1					1
Subtotal	2	1		2	3	5
Other						
Silver/gold accessory	3	1		8	9	12
Pieces/coin, silver	5					5
Umbrella				4	4	4
Doll/toy				2	2	2
Gold coins				3	3	3
Eyeglasses	3			2	2	5
Musical instrument				5	5	5
Saddle/harness				3	3	3
Bicycle				3	3	3
Pencil	1			1	1	2
Typewriter				1	1	1
"Copiador de cartas"				1	1	1
Theater glasses				1	1	1
Toothbrush		1			1	1
Billiard ball				1	1	1
Subtotal	15	2		32	34	49
Total	210	10	7	624	641	851

Source: AHCM, Gobierno del Distrito, Empeños, vol. 1422, exp. 5, f. 17, and exp. 38; Empeños Ventas, vol. 162, exps. 1, 7, 9, 14, 15, 16, 17, and 20.

[a] Customer either not named individually or named with last name only.

[b] This category includes electric appliances such as fans, telephones, and one "maquina para escuchar," one commode, table and alarm clocks, furniture, lighting fixtures, paintings, and "objetos varios."

[c] Includes items that can be worn by a male or female, including shirts, capes, jackets, vests, aprons, scarves, belts, shoes, and hats. This category also includes bundles of clothing that might contain male or female clothing articles but also a generic good such as a shirt or a cut of cloth.

[d] Includes matching sets of jewels as well as bundles of jewelry that include religious items such as crosses, reliquaries, and rosaries and accessories such as candle snuffers and cigarette cases.

TABLE E

Categories of Goods in Pawning Transactions, 1915–21

Category	Monte de Piedad	Pawnshops	Total
Jewelry			
Gold with diamonds	314		314
Gold item(s)	24	12	36
Pearls	16		16
Generic item	4	5	9
Silver item	3	2	5
Subtotal	361	19	380
Household Goods			
Bedroom furniture	127	2	129
Other furnishings[a]	60	11	71
Living-room furniture	32	2	34
Piano/organ	31		31
Linen	2	28	30
Dining-room furniture	17	4	21
Fabric whole		12	12
Iron		9	9
Silver/ceramic table service		5	5
Kitchen/cooking		6	6
Subtotal	269	79	348
Clothing			
Female			
Enaguas		29	29
Rebozo		17	17
Mantilla		3	3
Chal		4	4
Vestido		8	8
Other		4	4
Male			
Sarape		5	5
Pantalón		24	24
Saco		9	9
Saco pantalón		7	7
Traje		8	8
Generic Clothing[b]		70	70
Subtotal		188	188

TABLE E

Continued

Category	Monte de Piedad	Pawnshops	Total
Watches	11	25	36
Tools		28	28
Vehicles			
Bicycle		5	5
Auto parts		4	4
Automobile	2		2
Motorcycle	1		1
Subtotal	3	9	12
Sewing machines	2	7	9
Other			
Book[c]		6	6
Typewriter	1	3	4
Camera		3	3
Leather pouch		3	3
Musical instrument		3	3
Umbrella		2	2
Rifle		2	2
Rosary	1	1	2
Syringe		1	1
Shaving machine		1	1
Eyeglasses		1	1
Field glasses		1	1
Tent		1	1
Theater glasses		1	1
Victrola		1	1
Telescope	1		1
Fountain pen		1	1
Scale		1	1
Cigarette case, silver	1		1
Cigarette/matches case, gold	1		1
Teeth case		1	1
Wallet, leather		1	1
Handbag		1	1
Portable telephone		1	1

TABLE E

Continued

Category	Monte de Piedad	Pawnshops	Total
Skate		1	1
Doll		1	1
Subtotal	4	38	43
Total	650	393	1,043

Source: AHCM, Gobierno del Distrito, Empeños, vol. 1429, exp. 442; *El Demócrata*, August 22, 1920, 3; October 12, 1920, 3; October 21, 1920, 10; November 12, 1920, 8; November 15, 1920, 7; November 22, 1920, 7; December 19, 1920, 7; January 18, 1921, 7; January 19, 1921, 7; February 20, 1921, 6; March 15, 1921, 10; April 24, 1921, 5.

[a] Includes twenty-two mirrors, eight rugs, eight desks, five bookshelves, five paintings, four safes, three pieces garden furniture, and two each of bathtubs, commodes, statues, and lamps. Also one each of: flower vase, doorbolt, washbasin with pitcher, sink, chamberpot, and billiards table.

[b] Includes items that can be worn by a male or female, including shirts, capes, jackets, vests, aprons, scarves, belts, shoes, and hats. This category also includes bundles of clothing that might contain male or female clothing articles but also a generic good such as a shirt or a cut of cloth.

[c] Includes one dictionary, a single novel, a set of two novels, a set of three bibles, a set of three medical books, and a five-volume set of *Mexico atraves de los siglos*, all pawned by different customers.

TABLE F

Categories of Pawned Goods in Samples Compared
(percentage of samples)

	1787–1830			1867–80			1902–9				1914–21		
Category	M.P.	Retail	Total	M.P.	Emp.	Total	M.P.	Luz Saviñon	Emp.	Total	M.P.	Emp.	Total
Clothing	47	64	57	7	54	49	0		30	23	0	47	18
Household	24	22	23	9	35	32	1		36	27	41	20	34
Jewelry	23	5	11	60	4	10	52		13	23	55	5	36
Tools	0	4	2	0	3	3	0		1	>1	0	7	28
Sewing machines	0	0	0	0	0	0	0		2	1	>1	2	1
Weapons	>1	1	1	6	1	2	2		3	2	0	2	2
Watches	0	1	1	2	>1	2	37		11	17	2	6	3
Religious	1	1	1	>1	>1	>1	1		>1	>1	>1	>1	>1
Other	7	3	4	2	3	3	7		5	6	1	11	5
Undifferentiated:													
"Ropa"[a]								20	75	72			
"Muebles y objetos varios"[a]								39	20	21			
"Alhajas"[a]								41	5	7			
Individual goods	1,066	2,069	3,135	290	2,629	2,919	210		641	851	650	393	1,043
Undifferentiated goods								3,214	48,411	51,625			
Total	1,066	2,069	3,135	290	2,629	2,919	210	3,214	49,052	52,476	650	393	1,043

Source: See appendix 1 tables B–D; AHCM, Gobierno del Distrito, Empeños, vol 1420, exps. 109 and 322.

[a] The data for 1908–9 from the Montepío Luz Saviñon and four empeños are from summary reports, so "ropa" would include linen and whole or cut fabric (otherwise included in the household-good category) along with clothing. "Muebles y objetos varios" includes goods that would be included among household goods but underestimates the number of household goods, because fabric, linens, and silver table service are not likely to be included. "Alhajas" likely includes jewelry, watches,

TABLE G

Collateral Values of Goods in Retail Pawnshops, 1787–1825

	Total Lent on Prendas' Worth < 4 rs.[a]	Minimum[b] Prendas < 4 rs.	Value, "Menudas"/Value, All Prendas	Differentiated Prendas	Total Lent on Differentiated Prendas	Avg. Loan on Differentiated Prendas
Pulperías						
1788 Guarico	71 ps. 3 rs.	163	42%	123	97 ps. 7 rs.	6 rs.
1789 Rastro	29 ps. 2 rs.	67	36%	58	51 ps. 6 rs.	7 rs.
1792 Aguilita	44 ps. 3 rs.	101	52%	48	41 ps. 5 rs.	7 rs.
1805 Coliseo Viejo	15 ps. 6 rs.	36	70%	13	6 ps. 4 rs.	4 rs.
1808 Montealegre	21 ps. 3 rs.	49	68%	16	9 ps. 5 rs.	5 rs.
1810 Aduana Vieja	38 ps. 7 rs.	89	55%	38	31 ps. 1 r.	6 1/2 rs.
1817 Rastro	32 ps. 6 rs.	75	26%	74	91 ps. 2 rs.	1 p. 2 rs.
1822 Tesontlale Br.	34 ps. 7 rs.	80	71%	17	14 ps. 5 rs.	7 rs.
Tiendas						
1808 Santo Domingo	11 ps. 4 rs.	26	11%	33	88 ps. 6 rs.	2 ps. 5 rs.
1808 Santo Domingo	32 ps. 3 rs.	74	30%	14	76 ps. 5 rs.	5 ps. 3 rs.
Vinaterías						
1792 Rastro	19 ps. 6 rs.	45	64%	9	11 ps. 1 r.	1 p. 2 rs.
1804 Santísima	46 ps. 4 rs.	106	42%	47	64 ps. 2 rs.	1 p. 3 rs.
1810 Jesús Nazareno	20 ps. 2 rs.	46	14%	114	120 ps.	1 p.

Source: AGN, Consulado, vol. 11, exp. 43, fs. 388–93; vol. 24, exp. 13, fs. 302–6; vol. 25, exp. 13, fs. 310–12v; vol. 28, exp. 5, fs. 231–41; vol. 38, exp. 2, fs. 21–25v; vol. 38, exp. 2, fs. 35–38; vol. 38, exp. 5, fs. 292–98v; vol. 38, exp. 6, fs. 271–74; vol. 47, exp. 5, fs. 298–301; vol. 53, exp. 12, fs. 365–71; vol. 67, exp. 10, fs. 129–32; vol. 292, exp. 3, no. 3, fs. 1–4; vol. 292, exp. 3, no. 8, fs. 1–7; vol. 292, exp. 4, no. 3, fs. 1–6v; vol. 292, exp. 4, no. 5, fs. 1–4; vol. 292, exp. 4, no. 7, fs. 2–5.

[a] The most common notation for this category in the inventories reads "varias prendas menudas cuyos empeños no llegaron a 4 reales."

[b] This "minimum" number is calculated by converting the amount of the total value of prendas worth less than 4 rs. into reales [i.e., 71 ps. 3 rs. converted to 571 rs.] and then dividing by 3.5, to arrive at an approximation of the minimum number of prendas that the total might represent. There could be hundreds of goods worth 1 or 2 rs.

TABLE H

Repeat Pawning Customers by Gender

	Monte de Piedad						Cartegena Pawnshop						
	1802			1823–26			1869–73			1866–69			
Visits[a]	Female	Male	Total	Female	Male	Total	Female	Male	Total	Female	Male	?[b]	Total
2	57	34	91	212	197	409	7	8	15	35	8	49	92
34	36	20	56	147	107	254		1	1	11	2	13	26
5–10	12	1	13	108	43	151				4			4
11–20	1		1	26	7	33		3	3	1			1
20 plus				5		5		1	1				
Total	106	55	161	498	354	852	7	13	20	51	10	62	123

Source: AHNMP, Contaduria, Empeños en Contaduria, 1802, caja 1, vols. 1–3; AGN, Montepío, vol. 27, exps. 1–12; vol 28, exp. 2; AHCM, Inventario General de la Municipilidad de Tacubaya, vol. 120, exps. 5 and 7; AGN, Gobernación, leg. 1296(1), exp. 5, nos. 6 and 7; AGN, Gobernación, leg. 1517(1), exp. 1, no. 5.

[a] This number represents a minimum of visits. For 1802 the sample is a fraction of the transactions (every fifth page of the ledgers) for the first three months of the year. For 1823–26 only goods that were sold in 1824 and 1826 are captured in the data, so the majority of pawning transactions for those years, which resulted in goods' being redeemed, are not accounted for. For the Cartegena case only goods that were not redeemed from the pawnbroker are listed in the auction inventory. In both cases the majority of pawning transactions, which resulted in goods' being redeemed, are not accounted for.

[b] These clients were identified by a first initial and last name. Not included in the Cartagena tally above are cases where only the last name of the customer was given. Some of these customers surely are the same as the ones already accounted for in the table, and it is also likely that among customers only identified by their *apellido* are many repeat customers. Also not included are cases where the last name appeared alone only one time and with different first initials other times. Last names listed as the only identifier that appeared are most often Martínez (34 times), Campi (25), Hernández (23), and García (21). Also in this last-names-only group were another nine last names that appeared between ten and sixteen times, seventeen that appeared between five and nine times, thirty-two that appeared between three and four times, and forty that appeared two times. The total number of transactions for which the goods were going to auction (and therefore not redeemed) in the six Cartagena inventories from January 1867 to June 1869 is 1,362.

Appendix 1

TABLE I

Comparative Collateral Loans, 1818–1915

Pawnshop	Year	Avg. Value	Highest	Lowest
Cacahuate	1818	4 rs.	2 ps. 2 rs. *paño* jacket	1/2 r. sheet
Monte de Piedad Branch No. 4	1867	5 ps.	11 ps. 20 cs. watch w. top	56 cs. silver/copper spoon
Portal de Cartagena	1868	4 rs.	5 ps. 7 doz. half-silver buttons, 13 oz.	2 rs. tattered wool *tápalo*
Monte de Piedad Branch No. 3	1873	10.40 ps.	20 ps. 4 doz. ivory knives	25 cs. silver necklace
Plaza de la Constitución	1879	1 1/8 ps.	2 ps. Colt pistol/used metallic munitions belt	2 rs. No. 5 iron
Monte de Piedad Branch No. 2 Calle No. 4ª de Relox	1902	10.22 ps.	550 ps. 2 cuff links, 2 rings, 2 hairpins, diamond and turquoise	50 cs. silver chain
Estampa de Jesús María	1902	7.07 ps.	125 ps. gold necklaces	37 cs. 2 cuts fabric
Leguisamo No. 3	1902	11.44 ps.	45 ps. 4 china plates	25 cs. muslin petticoats
Verónica 2nd Block	1902	1.21 ps.	20 ps. half-set furniture	12 cs. undershirt
Verónica 3rd Block	1903	1.49 ps.	30 ps. sewing machine	12 cs. petticoats
Verdis No. 116 3rd Block	1915	2.54 ps.	68 ps. bedroom-set furniture	12 cs. apron
5th Ancha & San Antonio	1915	11.27 ps.	50 ps. Singer sewing machine	1 p. electric lamp
Monte de Piedad Main Branch	1920	367.61 ps.	4,500 ps. loose diamond 8 1/2 *quilates*, antique cut	120 ps. metal bed with wood headboard

TABLE I

Continued

Source: AGN, Ramo Consulado, vol. 47, exp. 6, fs.302–9; vol. 20, exp. 5, fs. 260–81; vol. 11, exp. 31, f. 321; Ramo Gobernación, leg. 2187 (1), exp. 1, no. 9(2), fs. 4–6; leg. 1517, exp. 1, no. 1, fs. 1–33v; leg. 1517, exp. 1, no. 5 fs. 1–12; leg. 1296(1), exp. 5, no. 7; 4th section, leg. 873(7), exp. 1, fs. 6–73; AHCM, Inventario General de la Municipalidad de Tacubaya, no. 120, exp. 5; Inventario General de la Municipalidad de Tlalpan, no. 69, exp. 71; Gobierno del Distrito, Empeños, Ventas, vol. 162, exps. 9, 14, 15, and 16; Gobierno del Distrito, Empeños, vol. 1429, exp. 442; *El Demócrata*, August 22, 1920, 3; October 12, 1920; October 21, 1920, 10; November 15, 1920, 7; November 21, 1920, 8; November 22, 1920, 7; and December 19, 1920, 7.

[a] The average values for these Monte de Piedad goods are the appraised value and that for which they are up for sale, not the amount that the original owner borrowed.

Appendix 2

Pawnbroker Data

Appendix 2

TABLE A

Store Profits, Net Worth, and Active Pawn Investment, 1785–1823

Store	Date	Net Worth (in pesos)	Store Average	Prendas (in pesos)	Store Average	Profit (in pesos)	Store Average
Pulperías							
López	Jun. 21, 1785	4,006		1,605		+1,600	
López	Nov. 8, 1786	5,651		1,524		+ 978	
López	Dec. 19, 1787	8,076		1,147		+2,425	
López	May 5, 1790	4,691	(5,463)	1,136	(892)	+ 875	(1,277)
López	May 3, 1791	3,625		822		+ 413	
López	Nov. 3, 1791	5,273		568		+1,373	
Frayle	Oct. 21, 1785	2,547		933		+1,254	
Frayle	Nov. 9, 1786	3,503		1,233		+1,957	
Frayle	Dec. 19, 1787	4,330		888		+ 947	
Frayle	Jan. 14, 1789	2,119		639		+1,110	
Frayle	Mar. 23, 1790	1,694		426		+ 538	
Frayle	Sep. 23, 1790	2,235	(3,508)	843	(929)	+ 709	(843)
Frayle	Mar. 23, 1791	2,818		1,022		+ 820	
Frayle	Nov. 4, 1791	3,157		1,168		+ 930	
Frayle	Jun. 20, 1792	2,848		975		- 308	
Frayle	Jan. 3, 1793	5,531		1,023		+ 349	
Frayle	Jul. 16, 1793	5,811		1,156		+1,315	
Frayle	Dec. 19, 1793	5,504		846		+ 498	
Aguilita	Nov. 10, 1786	1,013		269		+ 205	
Aguilita	Jan. 15, 1788	316	(655)	169	(179)	- 118	(101)
Aguilita	Jan. 17, 1789	810		171		+ 62	
Aguilita	Feb. 28, 1792	463		106		+ 20	
San Felipe	Dec. 23, 1787	3,647		25		- 702	
San Felipe	Nov. 27, 1789	5,671	(4,659)	1,284	(654)	+2,188	(743)
Victoria	Jan. 2, 1792	4,933		525		+1,365	
Victoria	Jul. 2, 1793	4,160		770		+ 260	
Victoria	Dec. 17, 1793	5,136	(4,783)	990	(818)	+ 938	(945)
Victoria	Jul. 10, 1793	4,905		988		+1,217	
Torito	Dec. 20, 1793	3,731		701		+ 787	
Callejuela	May 12, 1794	4,412		150		- 534	
Quartel	Oct. 21, 1802	568		200		- 532	
Manco	Jul. 14, 1808	1,041		212		+ 505	
Cacaguate	Apr. 16, 1818	263		79		- 119	

TABLE A

Continued

Store	Date	Net Worth (in pesos)	Store Average	Prendas (in pesos)	Store Average	Profit (in pesos)	Store Average
Tarolito	Nov. 4, 1818	314		58		- 880	
Academia	Dec. 10, 1823	2,091		524		-1,909	
Viñaterías							
Monterilla	Oct. 15, 1799	2,460		74		- 6	
Santísima	Oct. 25, 1804	675		110		+ 1	
Santísima	Jan. 26, 1805	424	(550)	46	(78)	- 178	(-354)
Herradura	Oct. 8, 1805	4,824		101		- 220	
San Felipe	Dec 1, 1809	4,041		241		- 179	

Source: AGN, Consulado, vol. 11, exp. 43, fs. 388–93; vol. 24, exp. 13, fs. 302–6; vol. 25, exp. 13, fs. 310–12v; vol. 28, exp. 5, fs. 231–41; vol. 28, exp. 6, fs. 271–74; vol. 29, exp. 4, no. 3, fs. 1–6v; vol. 38, exp. 2, fs. 21–25v; vol. 38, exp. 2, fs. 35–38; vol. 38, exp. 5, fs. 292–98v; vol. 38, exp. 6, fs. 271–74; vol. 47, exp. 5, fs. 298–301; vol. 53, exp. 12, fs. 365–71; vol. 67, exp. 10, fs. 129–32; vol. 292, exp. 3, no. 3, fs. 1–4; vol. 292, exp. 3, no. 8, fs. 1–7; vol. 292, exp. 4, no. 3, fs. 1–6v; vol. 292, exp. 4, no. 5, fs. 1–4; vol. 292, exp. 4, no. 7, fs. 2–5; vol. 292, exp. 7, fs. 2–6.

TABLE B

Retail Stores in Continuous Operation with Continuous or Changing Ownership, 1781–1843

Dates in Business	Total Years	Number Establishments
1781–1843	62 years	54 stores
1803–43	40 years	10 stores
1806–43	37 years	15 stores
1808–43	35 years	3 stores
1781–1815	34 years	29 stores
1815–43	28 years	11 stores
1781–1808	27 years	17 stores
1781–1806	25 years	12 stores
1781–1893	22 years	4 stores
1803–15	12 years	10 stores
1806–15	9 years	73 stores
1808–15	7 years	2 stores
1803–8	5 years	7 stores
1803–6	3 years	3 stores

Source: AGN, Consulado, vol. 11, exp. 43, fs. 388–93; vol. 24, exp. 13, fs. 302–6; vol. 25, exp. 13, fs. 310–12v; vol. 28, exp. 5, fs. 231–41; vol. 28, exp. 6, fs. 271–74; vol. 29, exp. 4, no. 3, fs. 1–6v; vol. 38, exp. 2, fs. 21–25v; vol. 38, exp. 2, fs. 35–38; vol. 38, exp. 5, fs. 292–98v; vol. 38, exp. 6, fs. 271–74; vol. 47, exp. 5, fs. 298–301; vol. 53, exp. 12, fs. 365–71; vol. 67, exp. 10, fs. 129–32; vol. 292, exp. 3, no. 3, fs. 1–4; vol. 292, exp. 3, no. 8, fs. 1–7; vol. 292, exp. 4, no. 3, fs. 1–6v; vol. 292, exp. 4, no. 5, fs. 1–4; vol. 292, exp. 4, no. 7, fs. 2–5; vol. 292, exp. 7, fs. 2–6; AGNCM, Calapiz, vols. 1053 and 1054; AGNCM, Ferriz, vol. 1477; AGN, Gobernación, vol. 2167(1), exp. 2, no. 20(1), fs. 5–7; AHCM, Empeños, vol. 885, exps. 18, 24, 35, and 37; AHCM, Mercados, leg. 4, exp. 192.

TABLE C

Census Stores with Continuous Ownership in the Family

lperías		*Tiendas Mixtas*	
hiquis & Colegio de Santos		Arquito, in front of Arcos de Belem	
D. José Rodríguez	1806	D. Justo Udias	1803
D. Antonio Rodríguez	1815	D. Justo Udias	1806
		D. Justo Udias	1808
rtega, corner Bustamante & Damas		"Da. Monica, hija de Don Justo Udias"	1815
D. Domingo Gil Toboada	1781	Cruz Vidriada & Las Mochas	
D. Bernando Gil	1806	D. Manuel Fuentes	1781
D. Bernando Gil	1808	D. Antonio Fuentes	1803
D. Bernando Gil	1815	D. Antonio Fuentes	1806
ovincia		D. Antonio Fuentes	1808
D. Josef Morales	1781	Las Moras	
D. Rafael Morales	1806	D. Bartholome Rivas	1781
D. Rafael Morales	1815	D. José Rivas	1803
nto Domingo & Medinas		D. José Rivas	1806
D. Venancio Estanillo	1815	D. José Rivas	1808
Da. Carmen Estanillo	1843	Parroquia de la Palma	
(a.k.a. Da. María del Carmen Cacho)		Da. Francisca Torres	1806
la de Sota & San Fernando		Da. Teresa Torres	1815
D. José Quixano	1803	Santo Domingo, Letra A, No. 4	
D. Ygnacio Quixano	1806	D. Lorenzo Torices	1806
D. Mariano Quixano	1808	D. Hypólito Torices	1815
D. Ygnacio Quixano	1815		
azuela del Factor & Puerta Falsa		*Viñaterías*	
D. Domingo Gil Taboada	1781	Gigante, corner of Puente Blanco	
D. Bernardo Gil	1806	Da. Jacinta Cordova	1806
D. Bernardo Gil	1808	D. Antonio Cordova	1843
n Agustín		*Tiendas/Viñaterías*	
D. José Montes de Oca	1803	Puente de Tesontlale	
D. José Montes de Oca	1806	Don Luis Rivera	1815
D. Agustín Montes de Oca	1815	Don José Rivera	1843

urce: AGN, Consulado, vol. 267, exp. 8, fs. 1–18; AHCM, Panaderías y Pulperías, leg. 1, exp. 32, f. 29; leg. 2, exp. 78, f. 6; GN, Padrones, vol. 54, f. 326.

TABLE D

Salary Increase, Monte de Piedad Employees, 1826

Employee	Actual Salary	New Salary
Director	2,000	3,000
Four Ministers, @ 1,200 pesos	4,800	7,200
Controller	600	900
Three officials with most seniority, @ 400 pesos	1,200	2,400
Three junior officials, @ 400 pesos	1,200	2,100
"Oficial ultimo"	400	600
Jewelry Appraiser	400	700
Clothing Appraiser	400	600
Three "meritorios," @ 100 pesos	300	450
Two guards, @ 182 pesos 4 reales	365	547
Doorman	250	400
Total	11,915	18,897

Source: AGN, Gobernación, leg. 2187(1), exp. 1, no. 5(1), fs. 1v–2.

TABLE E

Volume of Pawning and Redeeming at Monte de Piedad, 1775–1887

Date	Number of Clients Pawning	Amount Loaned (in pesos)	Average Loan (in pesos)	Number of Clients Redeeming	Amount Repaid (in pesos)	Average Repaid (in pesos)
1775–76	24,728	501,489	20	12,290	254,751	21
1777	24,163	439,106	18	20,985	380,670	18
1783	33,098	672,772	20	30,939	624,037	20
1802	29,029	446,320	15	—	—	—
1815	30,551	305,551	10	21,002	197,105	9
1821	35,989	365,225	10	37,400	346,213	9
1822	40,316	407,117	10	35,982	360,783	10
1823	47,400	413,119	9	41,049	374,320	9
1824	42,719	433,236	10	42,925	402,174	9
1825	45,344	465,349	10	42,650	446,965	10
1826	52,034	614,694	12	48,708	559,417	11
1827	49,882	542,751	11	45,630	493,379	11
1828	47,464	510,228	11	45,127	477,722	11
1829	40,053	504,741	13	41,595	469,930	11
1830	40,845	547,019	13	37,654	487,601	13
1831	41,956	578,706	14	39,209	544,127	14
1832	48,787	583,820	12	44,212	561,645	13
1833	40,061	592,984	15	41,352	541,453	13
1834	38,908	624,878	16	36,320	572,917	16
1835	37,283	562,587	15	35,213	543,253	15
1836	29,629	477,772	16	31,641	483,435	15
1837	33,646	572,917	17	27,560	483,103	18
1838	35,883	572,917	16	32,733	528,512	16
1839	31,526	500,804	16	31,046	488,228	16
1840	30,416	533,384	18	29,908	515,647	17
1841	28,191	491,438	17	25,825	447,427	17
1842	52,428	510,277	10	42,511	496,552	12
1843	42,707	502,350	12	41,428	477,942	12
1844	41,916	504,942	12	39,325	479,656	12
1845	44,045	500,669	11	39,606	480,437	12
1846	47,555	471,687	10	43,399	457,041	11
1847	25,448	245,426	10	26,788	256,767	10
1848	38,427	411,598	11	36,573	381,874	10

TABLE E

Continued

Date	Number of Clients Pawning	Amount Loaned (in pesos)	Average Loan (in pesos)	Number of Clients Redeeming	Amount Repaid (in pesos)	Average Repaid (in pesos)
1849	42,500	511,188	12	38,381	452,267	12
1850	47,333	652,815	14	40,521	554,563	14
1851	50,507	670,614	13	46,028	622,006	14
1874	321,505	1,636,543	5	290,474	1,499,700	5
1875	329,260	1,582,708	5	303,272	1,473,051	5
1886	206,169	1,112,887	5			
1887	193,122	1,021,813	5			
1917	400,000	2,000,000	5			

Source: AGN, Montepío, vol. 17, exp. 10, f. 168; AGN, Montepío, vol. 28, exp. 2; Felipe de Zuñiga y Ontiveros, *Guía de forasteros para el año de 1777* (México: Oficina de Zuñiga y Ontiveros, n.f.); Felipe de Zuñiga y Ontiveros, *Calendario manual y guía de forasteros para el año de 1784* (México: Oficina de Zuñiga y Ontiveros, 1783); AHNMP, Contaduria, Empeños en Contaduria, caja 1, vols. 1–3; caja 2, vols. 4–6; caja 3, vols. 7–9, caja 4, vols. 10–12; Mariano Zuñiga y Ontiveros, *Calendario manual y guía de forasteros en México, para el año de 1816 bisiesto* (México: Zuñiga y Ontiveros, n.f.), 218–19; Mariano Galvan Rivera, *Calendario manual y guía de forasteros de Mejico para el año de 1832* (México: Mariano Arévalo, 1832), 246–47; Juan Nepomuceno Almonte, *Guía de forasteros, y repertorio de conocimientos útiles* (México: Imprenta de I. Complido, 1852), 131; and AGN, Gobernación, leg. 2187(1), exp. 2, f. 16; AGN, Gobernación, leg. 2187(2), exp. 1, no. 21(8); AGN, Gobernación, leg. 2187(2), exp. 1, no. 23; AGN, Gobernación, leg. 2187(2), exp. 1, no. 27(3), f.2; AGN, Gobernación, 4th section, leg. 875(1), exp. 1, no. 30; Pérez, *Almanaque estadistico*, 457; *El Siglo XIX*, January 12, 1887; January 10, 1888; González Navarro, *La pobreza*, 173.

TABLE F

Limosnas and Loans at the Monte de Piedad, 1802

Month	Customers	Limosnas Received	Capital Loaned	Loan Average	Limosna Average	Interest (six-month %)
January	2,679	1,273 ps. 1 3/4 rs.	50,737 ps.	19 ps.	4 3/4 rs.	3.1
February	2,290	1,132 ps. 6 1/4 rs.	45,677 ps.	20 ps.	4 rs.	2.5
March	2,734	1,315 ps. 1 r.	52,392 ps.	19 ps.	7/8 rs.	3.2
April	2,495	1,048 ps. 1/4 r.	41,753 ps.	17 ps.	3 3/8 rs.	2.4
May	2,714	949 ps. 6 1/2 rs.	37,881 ps.	14 ps.	2 3/4 rs.	2.5
June	2,665	928 ps. 7 rs.	37,097 ps.	14 ps.	2 3/4 rs.	2.5
July	2,250	728 ps. 4 1/2 rs.	29,113 ps.	13 ps.	2 3/4 rs.	2.7
August	2,046	1,129 ps. 4 3/4 rs.	25,151 ps.	12 ps.	4 3/8 rs.	4.6
September	2,080	1,000 ps. 7 1/2 rs.	39,994 ps.	19 ps.	5 rs.	3.3
October	2,881	1,040 ps.	41,826 ps.	14.5 ps.		2.5
November	2,405	843 ps. 6 3/4 rs.	24,304 ps.			3.5
December	1,811	755 ps. 2 1/2 rs.	20,395 ps.			3.7
Total	29,050	12,146 ps. 3/4 r.	446,320 ps.			2.7

Source: AHNMP, Libros de Empeños, 1802.

TABLE G

Disposition of *Prendas Cumplidas* at the Monte de Piedad, 1802

Item(s)	Customer Gender	Date Pawned	Date Sold	Loan Amount (in pesos)	Sale Price	*Sobrante*	Paid to Customer
2 pearl bracelets/diamond necklace	M	Jan. 4	May 25	250	300 ps.	50 ps.	Jul. 30, 1803
Gold cigarette case w/diamond	F	Jan. 4	Sep. 9	45	60 ps.	15 ps.	Sep. 18, 1802
12 spoons/12 forks	M	Jan. 4	Oct. 9	70	74 ps.	4 ps.	Nov, 11, 1802
Linen petticoats/white shawl	F	Jan. 8	Aug. 12	6	7.5 ps.	1.5 ps.	Sep. 23, 1802
New rebozo	F	Jan. 11	Aug. 17	2	4 ps.	2 ps.	
Reliquary and gold chain	F	Jan. 11	Sep. 5	7	7 ps.		
Diamond earrings/hat twist	M	Jan. 15	Sep. 9	75	120 ps.	45 ps.	Sep. 9, 1802
2 emerald & diamond hat twists	M	Jan. 15	Oct. 9	8	8 ps.		
String of pearls/pearl & diamond earrings	M	Jan. 2	Oct. 16	113	150 ps.	37 ps.	Oct. 16, 1802
String of pearls/pearl & diamond earrings	F	Jan. 29	Nov. 23	20	50 ps.	30 ps.	Dec. 18, 1802
2 plates	F	Feb. 8	Sep. 9	34	34 ps. 6 rs.	6 rs.	Apr. 24, 1804
2 plates	F	Feb. 15	Dec. 14	34	34 ps.		
Waistcoat	M	Feb. 22	Oct. 9	3	3.5 ps.	4 rs.	Jun. 23, 1803
Cotton petticoat	F	Feb. 26	Oct. 9	3	4 ps.	1 p.	Oct. 20, 1802
Child's poncho/2 rebozos	F	Mar. 1	Oct. 23	8	12 ps.	4 ps.	Oct. 23, 1802
Piece of *cavo* cloth	F	Mar. 3	Nov. 23	6	7 ps.	1 p.	
3 spoons/2 forks	M	Mar. 5	Nov. 9	12	13 ps. 6 rs.	1 p. 6 rs.	Nov. 11, 1802
Overcoat/silk lapel	F	Mar. 26	Oct. 23	6	7 ps.	1 p.	Nov. 6, 1802
Cotton-print tunic	F	Mar. 29	Nov 23	8	10 ps.	2 ps.	Oct. 26, 1803

Source: AHNMP, Libros de Empeños, 1802.

TABLE H

Casas de Empeño in Locations Formerly Retail, 1840–78

Address	Earliest Date as Empeño	Former Business
Esclavo & La Aguila	Dec. 15, 1840	Tienda, viñatería
Cuervo Bridge	Aug. 12, 1843	Tienda, viñatería
Plazuela Concepción	May 11, 1854	Viñatería
Rastro & San Miguel	May 11, 1854	Tienda mixta
Santiago Corner	May 11, 1854	Pulpería
Medina & Pila Seca	Oct. 16, 1854	Tienda mixta
San Lorenzo	Oct. 27, 1854	Viñatería
Verdeja	Oct. 27, 1854	Pulpería
Puesto Nuevo	Mar. 6, 1855	Tienda, viñatería
Zapo Corner	June 4, 1858	Tienda, viñatería
Peredo & San Juan	July 28, 1858	Tienda, viñatería
Venero	Nov. 20, 1867	Tienda mixta
San Dimas	Feb. 6, 1868	Tienda, viñatería
Santo Domingo No. 6	Jan. 29, 1878	Tienda mixta
Manzanares No. 12	Feb. 12, 1878	Tienda mixta
Monzón Bridge	Feb. 12, 1878	Pulpería
Necatitlán No. 11	Feb. 12, 1878	Tienda mixta
Palma & Cornejas	Feb. 12, 1878	Tienda mixta
Pila Seca	Feb. 14, 1879	Pulpería
Santo Tomás, 2ª Calle	Feb. 12, 1878	Pulpería

Source: El Siglo XIX, May 11, 1854; March 6, 1865; Oct. 16, 1854; July 28, 1858; AGNCM, Calapiz, vol. 1053, f. 69v; AHCM, Empeños, exps. 35, 37; AGN, Padrones, vol. 85(1), fs. 20–28.

Appendix 2

TABLE I

Casa de Empeño Database, 1836–1915

Year	Number Documented	Year	Number Documented
1836	5	1880	25
1840	2	1881	30
1841	1	1882	24
1842	102	1884	6
1843	35	1885	22
1844	3	1886	22
1845	1	1887	4
1846	8	1891	10
1854	138	1895	37
1855	13	1898	21
1856	3	1901	21
1858	4	1902	156
1866	2	1903	27
1867	95	1906	9
1868	10	1907	106
1871	23	1908	2
1872	5	1909	3
1874	105	1912	38
1875	2	1913	21
1877	31	1914	28
1878	45	1915	29
1879	89		
Total			1,373

Source: *El Siglo XIX*, 1854–68; *Diario del Imperio*, June 20, 1866; AGNCM, Calapiz, vols. 1053 and 1054; AGNCM, Ferriz, vol. 1477; AGN, Gobernación, vol. 2167(1), exp. 2, no. 20(1), fs. 5–7; AHCM, Empeños, vol. 885, exps. 18, 24, 35, and 37; AHCM, Mercados, leg. 4, exp. 192; AHCM, Actas de Cabildo, vol. 166–A; Galvan Rivera, *Guía de forasteros*, 330–32; and Pérez, *Almanaque*, 238–41; *El Diario*, 1912–13; *El Imparcial*, June 22, 1906; *El Pueblo*, 1914–15.

TABLE J

Retail Establishments Complying with the 1842 Casa de Empeño Bond Requirement

Address	Date of *Fianza*	Business Type
Arcos de Belem	June 30, 1846	Tienda, viñatería, prendas
Ave María & Santa Cruz	July 29, 1842	Tienda mixta
Cadena & Pajaritos	July 6, 1842	Tienda, prendas
"Calavera" Sto. Tomás & Palma	July 7, 1842	Pulpería
Callejón de Camarones	June 30, 1846	*Tendajón*, viñatería, prendas
"La Cruz" Los Gallos	July 11, 1842	Pulpería
Moscas & Maravillas	July 6, 1842	Tienda mixta
Portal de Tejada No. 9	April 18, 1843	Tienda, viñatería, prendas
Quemada & Jurado	July 6, 1842	Tienda, viñatería
Santísima	July 28, 1842	Tienda

Source: AHCM, Mercados, leg. 4, exp. 192; AGNCM, Calapiz, v. 1053, f. 47, v. 1054, fs. 75–76, f. 89.

TABLE K

Entrepreneurs in Both Retail and Pawning, 1854

Broker	Retail Business	Pawn Business(es)
Antonio Acuña	Ciegos	Gallos
Amado Aguilar	Quemada & Ciegos	Curtidores
Mariano Amaya	Portaceli	Candelaria
Manuel Campuzano	Jardín Plazuela	Verdeja Montero Plazuela
José Domínguez	Niño Perdido	Rábano Plazuela
Joaquín Espinosa	Sto. Tomás 2nd Bl.	Santo Tomás 3rd Bl.
Jesús González	Jardín	San Andrés
Ramón Moctezuma	Sotano Bridge	Palma
Agustín Ordáz	Niño Perdido	Rábano Plazuela
José María Ortega	Rastro 1st Bl.	Relox 5th Bl.
Cesario Sanchez	Don Toribio	Ancha

Source: Nepomuceno Almonte, *Guia de forasteros*, 307–13, 329–30.

TABLE L

National Monte de Piedad Directors, 1775–1924

Vicente Trebuesto	1775–1796
Manuel Gamboa	1796–1814
Manuel Antonio Cuoto	1815–36
Francisco Manuel Sánchez de Tagle	1836–47
Manuel Gómez Pedraza	1848–51
José Joaquín de Herrera	1851–53
Antonio María Lazpita	1853–61
Francisco de Paula Cendejas	1861–63
Antonio María Lazpita	1863–67
Francisco de Paula Cochicoa	1867–68
Francisco de Paula Cendejas	1868–76
Mariano Riva Palacio	1877–80
Trinidad García	1880–84
José Fuentes Núñez	1884–95
Antonio Villamil	1895–1905
Manuel Campos	1905–11
Luis Martínez del Campo	1911–14
Eugenio Baorousse	1914–15
Luis Martínez del Campo	1915
Eugenio Baorousse	1915–20
Daniel Ríos Zertuche	1920–22
Epigmenio Ibarra	1922–24

Source: Cabrera Siles and Escandón, *Historia*, 35.

TABLE M

Porfirian Empeños in Traditional Retail or Pawning Locations

Location	Documented Years of Operation
Aduana Vieja 2nd block	1806, 1843, 1878, 1881, 1886, 1902, 1907
Candelaria	1781, 1803, 1815, 1843, 1878
Colegio de Niñas No. 2	1781, 1803, 1815, 1878, 1902, 1907
Coliseo Viejo	1781, 1806, 1815, 1843, 1878
Damas Corner 2nd block	1781, 1806, 1843, 1895, 1902, 1907
Don Toribio	1781, 1815, 1843, 1902
Hospital Real & Victoria	1846, 1854, 1886, 1903
Indio Triste	1806, 1815, 1872, 1879, 1882
Juan Carbonero No. 6	1815, 1843, 1898, 1902, 1907
Leguízamo Bridge No. 3	1781, 1843, 1886, 1902, 1907
Leña Bridge	1781, 1803, 1815, 1879, 1898, 1902, 1907
León	1808, 1815, 1854, 1872, 1880
Medina & Pila Seca	1781, 1806, 1815, 1842, 1854, 1877, 1882
Misericordia Bridge	1781, 1815, 1842, 1902
Monzón Bridge	1781, 1815, 1843, 1879, 1902
Nahuatlato & Ratas	1843, 1878, 1886, 1898, 1902, 1907
Necatitlán	1803, 1815, 1843, 1878
Niño Perdido No. 28	1854, 1874, 1902
Pipis & Concepción	1781, 1815, 1878
Puesto Nuevo	1781, 1803, 1843, 1855, 1879
Rastro & Buena Muerte	1806, 1815, 1902
Salto del Agua	1842, 1872, 1907
San Andrés No. 8	1854, 1880, 1901
San Juan & Peredo	1806, 1815, 1858, 1877, 1882, 1895, 1902
Santa María Bridge	1781, 1806, 1898, 1902, 1907, 1909
Santísima Plazuela	1781, 1803, 1815, 1842, 1887, 1903
Santo Domingo Bridge No. 6	1806, 1815, 1879, 1902, 1907
Tezontlale Bridge	1781, 1806, 1815, 1843, 1854, 1886, 1902
Verdeja	1787, 1803, 1806, 1843, 1854, 1878, 1903

Source: AGN, Consulado vols. 11, 24, 25, 28, 29, 38, 47, 67, 292. AHCM, Empeños, vol. 885; Gobierno del Distrito Empeños, vols. 8, 9, 1422, 1429, and 1430; Gobierno del Distrito Empeños Ventas, vol. 162; *El Siglo XIX*, 1885–95; Pérez, *Almanaque estadístico*, 238–41; and AGN Gobernación, 2nd section, vol. 811.

TABLE N

New Empeño Locations, 1870s–1910

Location	First Date Documented	Location	First Date Documented
Aduana Vieja & San Gerónimo	Jan. 1902	Ortega No. 22	Feb. 1882
Alegría No. 2	Jan. 1878	Ortega No. 29	Mar. 1872
Alfaro No. 4	July 1886	Paz Avenue No. 7	Jan. 1902
Alfaro No. 12	Feb. 1878	Peñon 2nd Bl. No. 6	Apr. 1907
Artes 3rd Bl. No. 1	Jan. 1902	Peralvillo 1st Bl. No. 4	Apr. 1907
Ascension No. 4	Jan. 1902	Rastro & Buena Muerte No. 4	Jan. 1902
Degollado 3rd Bl. No. 2	Apr. 1907	Rastro Nuevo No. 3	Jan. 1903
Degollado 3rd Bl. No. 37	Jan. 1903	San Antonio & Callejon S.A.	Jan. 1907
Escondida No. 4	June 1906	San Cosme Rivera No. 1	Dec. 1901
Guerrero 2nd Bl. No. 10	Jan. 1902	San Cosme Rivera No. 31	Jan. 1902
Guerrero 3rd Bl. No. 49	Jan. 1903	San Diego Portillo No. 10 1/2	June 1879
Guerrero 4th Bl. No. 53	June 1898	San Hipólito No. 10	Dec. 1895
Guerrero 7th Bl. No. 39	June 1901	San Hipólito No. 19	Nov. 1886
Guerrero & Delgollado	Jan. 1902	San Juan & Plaza Madrid	Jan. 1902
Guerrero & Luna	Apr. 1907	San Juan & Polilla	Jan. 1902
Guillermo Prieto 3rd Bl. No. 45	Jan. 1907	San Juan Plaza No. 5	Feb. 1886
Hidalgo & Galeana	Jan. 1902	San Juan Plaza No. 6	Dec. 1895
Jesús Estampa F	May 1885	San Pedro & San Pablo No. 14	June 1879
Jesús Estampa G	June 1886	San Pedro & San Pablo Chiconautla	Jan. 1902
Lecumberri & Bravo	Apr. 1907	Santa Ana & Matamoros	Apr. 1901
Lerdo, 3rd Bl. No. 5	Jun. 1901	Santa María Bridge No. 4	Aug. 1898
Lerdo & Moctezuma	Jan. 1902	Santa María Bridge No. 5	Jan. 1902
Lerdo & Mosqueta	Jan. 1902	Santa María Redonda No. 71	Apr. 1907
Manrique No. 2	Apr. 1877	Santa María Ribera & Colonia	Apr. 1907
Manzanares & Veas	Jan. 1902	Soto 4th Bl. No. 38	May 1898
Merced No. 3 1/2	Dec. 1895	Soto & Madrid	Dec. 1895
Merced No. 4	Feb. 1879	Soto & Magnolia	Jan. 1902
Merced No. 12	June 1879	Trapana No. 1	Jan. 1902
Merced No. 13	Aug. 1898	Verdeja & Miguel Lopez	Jan. 1902
Merced No. 22	Dec. 1895	Verdeja & Salitreros	Feb. 1902
Merced No. 28	Jan. 1877	Vergara No. 9	Aug. 1880
Merced No. 31	Feb. 1878	Vergara No. 10	Jan. 1895
Merced & Jesús María Bridge	Jan. 1902	Vergara No. 11	Jan. 1901
Niño Perdido 2nd Bl. No. 22	Apr. 1907	Veronica & Fraternidad	Jan. 1903

TABLE N

Continued

Location	First Date Documented	Location	First Date Documented
Niño Perdido 2nd Bl. No. 25	Apr. 1907	Veronica & Coyote	Jan. 1907
Niño Perdido 2nd Bl. No. 33	June 1906		

Source: AHCM, Empeños, vol. 885, exps. 10, 12, 14, 18, 19, 22, 23, 24, 35, 37, 39, 46, 57, 95, and 113; Gobierno del Distrito Empeños, vols. 8, 9, 1422, 1429, and 1430; Gobierno del Distrito Empeños Ventas, vol. 162; *El Siglo XIX*, 1885–95; Pérez, *Almanaque estadístico*, 238–41; and AGN, Gobernación, 2nd section, vol. 811.

TABLE O

Changes in Ownership of Porfirian Pawnshops

Location	Owner	Date
Aduana Vieja & San Geronimo	Raymundo Alvarez	Jan. 1902
	Gaspar Dosal	Jan. 1907
Alegría No. 2	Juan B. Perea	Jan. 1878
	Goni Wenceslas	Jun. 1879
Alfaro No. 12	Jacinto Donesteve	Feb. 1878
	Manuel Escalante & Co.	Jun. 1879
	Wencesclao Goni	Oct. 1886
Amargura 1st Bl. No. 10	T. Lavenant	Dec. 1874
	Bonifacio Azcué	Jan. 1878
	Guillermo N. Triay	Jan. 1903
	Ruiz and Costa	Feb. 1903
Ancha & San Antonio	Francisco Pérez Fernández	Feb. 1869
	José Yglesias	May 1898
	Alberto C. Díaz	Jan. 1902
Artes 3rd Bl. No.1	Alipio Vega	Jan. 1902
	Manuel Alonso	Jan. 1903
	Vicente García	Feb. 1903
Asencion No. 4	Tomás Gavidia	Jan. 1902
	Luengas Hermanos	Jan. 1903
Blanco Bridge 2nd Bl. No. 6	Martinez Hermanos	Jun. 1898
	Tamés & López	Jan. 1902
Colegio de Niñas No. 1	S. Bustillos	Dec. 1874
	F. Bridal	Jan. 1878
	Rámon Bustillo	Aug. 1880
	Francisco Bustillo	Dec. 1884
Colegio de Niñas No. 2	P. Lobrado	Dec. 1874
	Diego Bustillo	Jun. 1879
	Julián Gutiérrez	Jan. 1902
	Francisco Bustillo	Jan. 1903
Damas 2nd Bl. No. 2	Manuel González	Dec. 1895
	B. Quintana & Co.	Jan. 1902
Don Toribio	C. Becerril	Dec. 1874
	José Gorraéz	Feb. 1902

TABLE O

Continued

Location	Owner	Date
Factor No. 1	Manuel Arratia	Jun. 1879
	Blas Truchuelo	Aug. 1880
	Manuel Arratia	Feb. 1882
	Antonio Solarín	Jul. 1898
Guerrero 7th Bl. No. 99	Crespo & Co.	Jan. 1902
	José Gómez	Jun. 1906
Hidalgo & Galeana	Eulogio del Caso	Jan. 1902
	Martínez & Co.	Jan. 1907
Hoacalco & Pelota	Federico Donesteves	May 1886
	Francisco Pérez Fernández	Jan. 1878
	Cornelius Pérez Fernández	Jun. 1879
	Demetrio Pérez Fernández	Aug. 1880
	J. Pérez Fernández	Feb. 1882
Hospital Real & Victoria	Domingo Verdeja	Jul. 1885
	Gómez Hermanos	Jan. 1903
Indio Triste	Perea & Zarandona	Dec. 1872
	Francisco Zarandona	Feb. 1878
	Laureano Zarandona	Jun. 1879
	Joaquín Poo	Feb. 1882
Jesús Bridge & Corazón	Francisco Bastierra	Feb. 1878
	Diego Candamo	Aug. 1880
	J. Pérez	Apr. 1886
	Juan Díaz	Dec. 1901
	V. Dosal	Jan. 1902
Jesús Estampa E	Juan B. Perea	Jan. 1878
	Federico Cevallos	Mar. 1885
	Juan Gutiérrez & Manuel González	May 1895
	León Alvarez	Jan. 1902
Juan Carbonero Plaza No. 6	B. Rivera	Apr. 1898
	G. Carrandi	Jan. 1902
	Ramón Noriega	Jan. 1907
Leña Puente No. 3	J. Galindez	Dec. 1875
	Santiago Barquin	Jun. 1879
	H. Díaz	Jan. 1902

TABLE O

Continued

Location	Owner	Date
León No. 8	Huerdo & González	Jan. 1879
	Rafael González	Jun. 1879
	Julia Treissiuier	Aug. 1880
Manrique No. 2	Wenseslao Quintana	Apr. 1877
	Altuna & Co.	Feb. 1879
	Girón & Co.	Mar. 1881
Medinas & Pila Seca	Fernández & Co.	Dec. 1874
	Cirilio Manrique	Jan. 1878
	Estéban Becerril	Jun. 1879
Merced No. 4	José del Torno	Feb. 1879
	Manuel Gavito	Aug. 1880
	Juan Río	Sep. 1885
	José del Torno	Jun. 1886
	Santo Sobrino	Dec. 1901
Nahuatlato & Ratas	Juan Gutiérrez	Feb. 1878
	José Zabalbozo	Dec. 1886
	Pria Hermanos	Jul. 1898
	J. Pria	Jan. 1902
Palma Plazuela No. 1	Teodoro Hermosa	Jan. 1902
	Fidel Pria	Apr. 1907
Paz Avenida No. 7	M. Molleda	Jan. 1902
	M. Borgolla	Jan. 1903
	Gumersindo Tamez	Jan. 1903
	Tamez & López	Jan. 1903
	Fernando Tomas Tamez	Jan. 1907
Peredo & San Juan	Manuel Uriarte	Feb. 1879
	Mateo Mejía & Co.	Jun. 1879
	Matías González	Jan. 1887
	Gómez Hermanos	Jan. 1895
	Gorraéz Hermanos	Jan. 1902
San Andrés No. 8	Lugarda García	Feb. 1879
	Antonio J. Portillo	Jun. 1901

TABLE O

Continued

Location	Owner	Date
San Diego Portillo No. 10 1/2	J. Lezameta	Dec. 1875
	Alejandro Villar	Jun. 1879
	Manuel Peres	Jul. 1879
	Angel Villar	May 1989
	Bustillo Villar	Dec. 1901
	Ygnacio Dosal	Jan. 1902
San Hipólito No. 19	Domingo Ugarte	Dun. 1885
	Altuna Hermanos	Nov. 1886
	Yarto & Co.	Dec. 1895
	Felix Nieto	Jan. 1902
San Pedro y San Pablo No. 14	Ramón Torel	Jun. 1879
	Juan del Llano	Mar. 1881
	Osada & Porrúa	Dec. 1901
	Porrúa Hermanos	Jan. 1903
	Diego Laro	Apr. 1907
San Pedro y San Pablo & Chiconautla	Manuel Molleda	Jan. 1902
	Manuela Molleda y Escandon	Jan. 1903
	Manuel Borbolla	Jan. 1903
	Manuel Garay & Co.	Feb. 1903
	Taméz Hermanos	Jun. 1906
Santa María Bridge No. 4	M. Marcos	Feb. 1885
	F. Sobrino	Aug. 1898
	M. & T. Sobrino	Jan. 1903
	Eduardo Noriega Sordo	Apr. 1907
Santísima & Victoria	F. Piedras	Dec. 1874
	J. Pérez	Feb. 1879
	M. Posada y Porrúa	Dec. 1895
	Sorena Hermanos	Oct. 1903
	José Porrúa	Jan. 1907
Santísima Plazuela No. 3	Estanislao Hermosa	Jan. 1887
	Taméz & Lopéz	Jan. 1902
	Lucas Yraztorza	Jan. 1902
	Taméz & Lopéz	Jan. 1903

TABLE O

Continued

Location	Owner	Date
Santo Domingo Sepulcros No. 6	J. Lezameta	Jan. 1875
	Diego González	Jan. 1878
	Manuel González	Aug. 1880
	R. del Rio	Feb. 1882
Tezontlale Bridge 2nd Bl. No. 7	J. Lezameta	Jul. 1886
	José de Abiega	Aug. 1886
	S. Alvarez	Jan. 1902
Vanegas 2nd Bl. No. 1	Emilio Fernández	Dec. 1895
	A. Mestras	Feb. 1902
	Alfredo Fernández	Jan. 1903
	Alfonso Fernández	Jan. 1907
Verdeja & Miguel López	Joaquín Alvarez	Dec. 1895
	Salvador Alvarez	Dec. 1902
	José Mendoza	Jan. 1903
Vergara No. 10	Altuna Hermanos	Dec. 1895
	Antonio Portillo	Jun. 1901
	Angel Mijares	Dec. 1902
Veronica & Coyote	Francisco Sanchez	Dec. 1901
	Ricardo Sanchez	Jan. 1903
	Somohano & Dosal	Jan. 1903
	Alvarez & Risco	Jan. 1907

Source: AHCM, Empeños, vol. 885, exps. 10, 12, 14, 18, 19, 22, 23, 24, 35, 37, 39, 46, 57, 95, and 113; Gobierno del Distrito Empeños, vols. 8, 9, 1422, 1429, and 1430; Gobierno del Distrito Empeños Ventas, vol. 162; *El Siglo XIX*, 1885–95; Pérez, *Almanaque estadístico*, 238–41; and AGN, Gobernación, 2nd section, vol. 811.

TABLE P

Demasías Deposited by Pawnbrokers, 1877–79

Broker	Pawnshop	Pesos Deposited 1877	1878	1879
Victor Aldama	Santo Domingo Sepulcros No. 1	70.55		
Altuna & Co.	Manrique No. 2		12.22	
Manuel Arratia	Factor No. 1	12.67		
Pontifical Ascend.	Amargura 1st Bl.	2.63		
Estéban Becerril	Pila Seca		37.65	
Felipe Bridal	Colegio de Niñas No. 1	132.09		
Diego Bustillo	Colegio de Niñas No. 12	79.25	12.44	110.71
Fidencio Cortés	Santa Ana		22.10	
Ignacio Chavarrí	Santo Domingo		53.82	128.68
Lugarda García	San Andrés No. 8		24.90	
Antonio Gómez	Juan Carbonero & San Juan N.	52.30		229.16
Winceslao Goni	Alegría No. 2	53.59		228.15
Diego González	Santo Domingo Sepulcros No. 6	42.45	24.32	310.52
Manuel González	Relox No. 1		34.38	
Angel Guaso	Plaza Zaragoza		7.91	45.15
Eduardo Hermosillo	Arcos de Belem & Chiquihiteras	9.32		
Huerdo y González	León No. 18	173.00		147.75
Eduardo Lara	Merced 1st Bl. No. 12	167.33		
Pedro Lobrado	Arguillo & Cazuela	34.91		100.91
Bernardo López	Puesto Nuevo		12.99	
Cirilio Manrique	Medinas & Pila Seca	43.70		504.29
José Peres	Santísimo & Victoria		34.89	209.05
Francisco Pérez	Hoacalco & Pelota	24.13	20.75	65.89
Francisco Pérez	Ancha & San Antonio		22.75	40.96
Joaquín Poo	Merced No. 31		24.19	4.73
Manuel Pérez	San Diego Bridge		30.75	
Eligio Rendón	San Cosme & Col. Santa María	6.39		
Ramón Toral	San Pedro y San Pablo		14.26	85.38
José del Torno	Merced No. 4		28.30	168.54
Blas Trachuelo	Factor		15.10	138.26
Manuel Uriarte	Nevedo Bridge		78.89	12.87
Alejandro Villar	San Diego		10.10	
Villola y Quintana	Arquillo		24.15	130.04

Source: AHCM, Empeños, exp. 37.

TABLE Q

Collateral-Credit Interest Rates Compared, 1758–1920

Establishment	Year	Legal Interest Rate
Pulperías	1758	Nothing specified
	1790	1/8 real/peso
		6% annually if redeemed in 6th month
	1810	No limit specified
Empeños	1842	9 to 19% annually, depending on when redeemed
	1850s–60s	Juárez and Maximilian, no usury limits
	1871	No limit
	1914	5% monthly (60% annual)
	1915	4% monthly (48% annual)
Monte de Piedad	1775	Voluntary contribution, no set amount
	1782	1/4 real/peso over six months
		12% annually if redeemed in 6th month
	1818	12.5%
	1841	9 to 19% annually, depending on when redeemed
	1867	8 to 12% annually, depending on when redeemed in Main Branch
		24% annually, depending on when redeemed in branches for loans over 1/2 peso
		8 to 48% annually, depending on when redeemed in branches for loans under 1/2 peso
	1871	12 to 48% annually, depending on when redeemed
	May 1873	6 to 12% annually, depending on when redeemed
	1874	12% annually
	1881	Branches 1–4, 12 to 48% annually, depending on month redeemed
		Branches 5–8, 16 to 48% annually
	1916	3% monthly (36% annually)
	1920	2% monthly (24% annually)

Appendix 3

Census Data

TABLE A

Mexico City's Population

Year	Population	Year	Population	Year	Population
1772	112,462[a]	1824	114,084[b]	1869	225,000
1790	113,240	1838	205,430	1880	250,000
1803	137,000	1842	200,000	1895	329,774
1811	168,846	1856	185,000	1900	344,721
1820	179,830	1865	200,000	1910	471,066[c]
				1921	615,367[c]

Source: From a list culled from various sources, some of them estimates, in *Estadísticas históricas de México*, tomo 1 (México: Instituto Nacional de Estadística e Informática/Instituto Nacional de Antropología e Historia, 1986), 24, except where otherwise noted.

[a] John Kizca, *Colonial Entrepreneurs: Families and Business in Mexico City*, (Albuquerque: University of New Mexico Press, 1983), 2.

[b] AHCM, Censos, vol. 1, s.f.

[c] The Federal District population was 720,753 in 1910 and 906,063 in 1921. Estados Unidos Mexicanos, Departamento de la Estadistica Nacional, *Censo general de habitantes 30 de noviembre de 1921: Distrito Federal* (México: Talleres Gráficos de la Nación "Diario Oficial," 1925).

TABLE B

Cuartel 9, Mexico City, 1811 Census

	Single	Married	Widow	Total	Census
Spanish men	886	384	44	1,314	24,734
Spanish women	638	353	255	1,246	31,481
Subtotal	1,524	737	299	2,560	56,215
Casta men	122	55	7	184	6,666
Casta women	132	58	69	259	9,880
Subtotal	254	113	76	443	16,546
Indian men	138	71	8	217	11,359
Indian women	231	71	89	391	14,893
Subtotal	369	142	97	608	26,252
Total men	1,146	510	59	1,715	42,759
Total women	1,001	482	413	1,896	56,254
Total	2,147	992	472	3,611	99,013

Source: AGN, Padrones, vol. 55, f. 121 has totals by category for Cuartel 9. For totals by category for most of the census, see Herbert J. Klein, "The Demographic Structure of Mexico City in 1811," *Journal of Urban History*, 23, no. 1 (1996): 66–94.

TABLE C

Cuartel 9 Sample, Mexico City, 1811 Census
(1,132 individuals = 31% of cuartel population)

	Sample	Percent Sample	Cuartel	Percent Cuartel	Census	Percent Census
Spanish men[a]	404	36	1,314	36	24,734	24
Spanish women[a]	394	35	1,246	35	31,481	33
Subtotal	798	71	2,560	71	56,215	57
Casta men	57	5	184	5	6,666	7
Casta women	86	8	259	7	9,880	10
Subtotal	143	13	443	12	16,546	17
Indian men	8	7	217	6	11,359	11
Indian women	111	10	391	11	14,893	15
Subtotal	191	17	608	17	26,252	26
Total men	541	48	1,715	47	42,759	43
Total women	591	52	1,896	53	56,254	57
Total	1,132		3,611		99,013	

Source: AGN, Padrones, vol. 55, Cuartel 9 totals on p. 121. For totals by category for most of the census, see Klein, "Demographic Structure."

[a] For 305 of the 404 men and 322 of the 394 women, the "Spanish" identification can be further broken down into "peninsular" and "Creole." For men 28 percent of the "españoles" have Iberian birthplaces listed, while 72 percent have American birthplaces. For women 97 percent of the "españolas" have American birthplaces.

TABLE D

Widows in Cuartel 9 Sample, Mexico City, 1811 Census

	Cuartel Total	Sample Total	Household Heads	Guest in Household	Live-in Servants
Creole	255	75	34	36	5
Casta	69	24	7	6	11
India	89	16	2	4	10
Total	413	114	43	46	25

Source: AGN, Padrones, vol. 55.

TABLE E

Household Heads in Cuartel 9 Sample
(183 households)

	Married	Single	Widow/er	Total
Male Household Heads				
Sample	96	17	9	122
Entire census	3,066	590	367	4,023
Female Household Heads				
Sample				
Spanish	6	9	34	49
Casta	3	0	7	10
India	0	0	2	2
Subtotal	9	9	43	61
Entire census	228	429	1,268[a]	1,925
Sample total, household heads	105	26	52	183
Census total, household heads	3,294	1,019	1,635	5,948

Source: Cuartel 9 figures are in AGN, Padrones, vol. 55. For totals for most of the census, see Klein, "Demographic Structure."

[a] According to Klein's analysis of the 1811 census, 64 percent of Spanish female household heads, 76 percent of casta female household heads, and 68 percent of Indian female household heads were widows.

TABLE F

Servants Living in Cuartel 9 Sample Households, Mexico City, 1811 Census

	Female		Male		Total		Percent Sample		
Category	No.	%	No.	%	No.	%	Female	Male	Total
Creole	28	15	9	5	37	20	7	2	5
Casta	44	23	14	7	58	30	51	25	40
India	69	37	25	13	94	50	62	31	49
Total	141	75	48	25	189		24	9	17

Source: AGN, Padrones, vol. 55.

TABLE G

Households with Servants in Cuartel 9 Sample, Mexico City, 1811 Census
(75 of 183 households in sample)

Number Servants	Household Heads					
	Peninsular	Creole		Casta	Indian	
in Household	Male	Male	Female	Female	Female	Total
1	9	10	6	1	1	27
2	6	7	2			15
3	9	4				13
4	6	1	1			8
5	3					3
7	1	1				2
8	1					1
9	1					1
11	2					2
13	1	1				2
16	1					1
Totals	40	24	9	1	1	75

Source: AGN, Padrones, vol. 55.

TABLE H

Ethnicity and Marital Status of Male Merchants, Mexico City, 1811 Census

	Married	Single	Widower	Total
Peninsulars				
Merchants	12	19	3	34
Clerks		15		15
Cashiers		7		7
Creoles				
Merchants	2	6		8
Clerks		9		9
Traveling traders		1		1
Mestizos				
Merchants		1		1
Total	14	58	3	75

Source: AGN, Padrones, vols. 53 and 55.

TABLE I

Distribution of Middle-Class Occupations,[a] Federal District, 1895 Census

	Commerce[b]			Public Admin./Police, Military Officers			Professions, Arts and Sciences[c]			Total		
	F	M	Total	F	M	Total	F	M	Total	F	M	Total
Mexico City	6,403	18,149	24,552	106	4,749	4,855	2,524	14,108	16,632	9,033	36,081	46,039
Gpe. Hidalgo	183	632	815	3	186	189	40	203	243	226	1,021	1,247
Tacubaya	554	1,499	2,053	6	515	521	3	644	647	563	2,658	3,221
Tlálpan	358	1,151	1,509	3	231	234	3	216	219	364	1,598	1,962
Xóchimilco	113	726	839		49	49		176	176	113	951	1,064
Total	7,611	22,157	29,768	118	5,730	5,848	2,570	15,347	17,917	10,299	42,309	53,533

Source: México, Ministerio de Fomento, Dirección General de Estadistica, *Censo general* . . . 1895, 62–64.

[a] This table is only an approximation of the middle-class working population. Included are certainly individuals who live on an income well beyond the middle class (for example, wealthy hacendados and bankers). Not included are others who live on a middle-class income (some among the bakers, butchers, shoemakers, tailors, silversmiths, watchmakers, modistes, seamstresses, etc.), but their category is not broken down into owners and employers in the census tables.

[b] Includes bankers, merchants, store employees, *canteros*, landlords, and acrobats. Does not include itinerant vendors.

[c] Includes hacienda, mine, and factory administrators and clerks; priests; medical professionals; engineers and architects; lawyers, accountants, and notaries; actors, artists, and musicians; writers, journalists, and instructors; telegraph and telephone operators; photographers and engravers.

TABLE J

Distribution of Middle-Class Occupations,[a] Federal District, 1910 Census

	Commerce[b]			Public Admin./Police, Military Officers			Professions, Arts and Sciences[c]			Total		
	F	M	Total	F	M	Total	F	M	Total	F	M	Total
Mexico City	11,406	25,933	37,339	707	6,226	6,933	8,029	27,507	35,536	20,142	59,666	79,808
Atzcapotzalco	311	581	892		57	57	85	387	472	396	1,025	1,421
Coyoacán	126	508	634	21	243	264	48	212	260	195	963	1,158
Cuajimalpa	16	82	98		49	49	10	1	11	26	132	158
Gpe. Hidalgo	406	728	1,134	12	270	282	184	576	760	602	1,574	2,176
Ixtapalapa	163	460	623		42	42	15	154	169	178	656	834
Mixcoac	400	788	1,188	7	69	76	228	790	1,018	635	1,647	2,282
Milpa Alta	207	370	577		36	36	41	104	145	248	510	758
San Angel	154	359	513	15	134	149	43	169	212	212	662	874
Tacubaya	706	1,438	2,144	7	180	187	423	1,806	2,229	1,309	3,424	4,733
Tacuba	538	1,411	1,949	6	163	169	256	1,226	1,482	800	2,800	3,600
Tlálpan	90	345	435	5	360	365	58	274	332	143	979	1,122
Xóchimilco	172	574	746		17	17	65	250	315	237	841	1,078
Total	14,695	33,577	48,272	780	7,846	8,626	9,485	33,456	42,941	25,123	74,879	100,002

Source: Tercer censo, vol. 2, 387–428.

[a] This table is only an approximation of the middle-class working population. Included are certainly individuals who live on an income well beyond the middle class (for example, wealthy hacendados and bankers). Not included are others who live on a middle-class income (bakers, butchers, shoemakers, tailors, silversmiths, watchmakers, modistas, etc.), but their category is not broken down into owners and employers in the census tables.

TABLE K

Distribution of Working-Class Occupations, Federal District, 1895 Census

	Mining/Agriculture/ Fishing[a]			Petty Commerce[b]			Artisan/Crafts[c]		
	F	M	Total	F	M	Total	F	M	Tota
Mexico City	14	6,264	6,278	3,246	1,818	5,064	11,093	42,498	53,5
Gpe. Hidalgo		2,704	2,704	71	17	88	91	715	80
Tacubaya		3,316	3,316	233	187	420	237	1,783	2,02
Tlálpan		8,878	8,878	124	6	130	100	1,976	2,07
Xóchimilco		10,220	10,220	15	41	56	52	265	3
Total	14	31,382	31,396	3,689	2,069	5,758	11,573	47,237	58,8

Source: Censo general . . . 1895, 62–64.

[a] Includes peons, orchard workers, miners, "obreros" in mining and refinery establishments, fishermen, a hunters.

[b] Includes ambulent vendors, water vendors, florists, lottery-ticket vendors, butchers, and *tortilleras.*

[c] Includes *aceiteros,* masons (*albañiles*), potters, cobblers, biscuit makers, embroiderers, carpenters (including *carp teros, ebanistas,* and *fusteros*), coach makers and detailers, wax makers, brewers, cigarette and cigar makers, co persmiths, firework makers, leathersmiths, gold leafers, candymakers, bookmakers, matchmakers, welders, sa and rope makers, glove makers, metalsmiths (including *afiladores, armeros, herraduras, herreros, hojalateros, latone*

Industrial Workers			Service Sector[d]			Total		
F	M	Total	F	M	Total	F	M	Total
732	1,544	2,276	32,649	20,299	52,948	47,734	72,423	120,157
	1	1	690	512	1,303	852	3,949	4,801
	193	193	2,036	1,331	3,367	2,506	6,810	9,316
	731	731	1,166	745	1,911	1,390	12,336	13,726
	2	2	446	690	1,136	513	11,218	11,731
732	2,471	3,203	36,987	22,577	60,564	52,995	106,736	159,731

and *plomeros*), mold makers, soap makers, brick makers, stonecutters, modistes, tailors, seamstresses, bread and cake bakers, thread spinners, silversmiths, watchmakers, hat makers, mattress makers, weavers, dyers, typographers, coopers, *torneros*, candlemakers, glassmakers, cast makers, and hand millers (*molenderas*).

[d] Includes barbers, carriage drivers, mule drivers, load bearers (including *cargadores* and *carretoneros*), domestic servants, gardeners, launderers, prostitutes (*mesalinas*), door persons, soldiers, and mechanics.

TABLE L

Distribution of Working-Class Occupations, Federal District, 1910 Census

	Mining/Agriculture/ Fishing[a]			Petty Commerce[b]			Artisan/Crafts[c]		
	F	M	Total	F	M	Total	F	M	Total
Mexico City	491	13,145	13,636	1,938	2,411	4,349	11,846	42,097	53,94
Atzcapotzalco	37	2,354	2,291	16	20	36	49	661	71
Coyoacán		1,610	1,610	3	266	269	63	530	59
Cuajimalpa	2	1,356	1,358		3	3		18	1
Gpe. Hidalgo	60	2,157	2,217	80	25	105	24	1,083	1,10
Ixtapalapa	145	6,226	6,371	18	2	20	10	232	24
Mixcoac	52	2,103	2,155	70	125	195	101	1,107	1,20
Milpa Alta	404	3,947	4,351	4	2	6	105	108	21
San Angel	4	2,271	2,275	37	122	159	115	460	57
Tacubaya	123	2,212	2,335	100	71	171	401	2,668	3,06
Tacuba	23	2,605	2,628	98	84	182	193	3,533	3,72
Tlálpan	98	2,874	2,972	23	48	71	54	823	87
Xóchimilco	29	7,928	7,957	20	17	37	8	349	35
Total	1,468	50,788	52,156	2,407	3,196	5,603	12,969	53,669	66,63

Source: *Tercer censo . . . 1910*, vol. 2, 387–428.

[a] Includes peons, orchard workers, miners, "obreros" in mining and refinery establishments, fishermen, hunter and quarry workers.

[b] Includes ambulent vendors, florists, lottery-ticket vendors, water vendors, butchers, and *tortilleras*.

[c] Includes *aceiteros*, masons (*albañiles*), potters, cobblers, biscuit makers, embroiderers, carpenters (including *carpi teros, ebanistas*, and *fusteros*), coach makers and detailers, wax makers, brewers, cigarette and cigar makers, co persmiths, firework makers, leathersmiths, gold leafers, candymakers, bookmakers, matchmakers, welders, sas and rope makers, glove makers, metalsmiths (including *afiladores, armeros, herraduras, herreros, hojalateros, latonerc plomeros*), mold makers, soap makers, brick makers, stonecutters, modistes, bread and cake bakers, thread spinner

Industrial Workers			Service Sector[d]			Total		
F	M	Total	F	M	Total	F	M	Total
3,335	7,133	10,468	41,988	20,742	62,730	59,598	85,528	145,126
3	65	68	597	312	909	702	3,412	4,114
108	154	262	654	302	956	828	2,862	3,690
			41	21	62	43	1,398	1,441
9	92	101	914	355	1,269	1,087	3,712	4,799
4	87	91	315	266	581	492	6,813	7,305
14	127	141	1,549	877	2,426	1,786	4,339	6,125
4	44	48	185	212	397	702	4,313	5,015
224	1,327	1,551	539	324	863	919	4,504	5,423
97	377	474	3,467	1,237	4,704	4,188	6,565	10,753
55	378	433	2,195	1,019	3,214	2,564	7,619	10,183
21	110	131	492	324	816	688	4,179	4,867
7	51	58	211	201	412	275	8,546	8,821
3,881	9,945	13,826	53,147	26,192	79,339	73,872	143,790	217,662

silversmiths, watchmakers, tailors, hat makers, mattress makers, weavers, dyers, typographers, coopers, *torneros*, candlemakers, glassmakers, cast makers, hand millers (*molenderas*), electricians, and machinists.

[d] Included are those who were paid for providing services: domestic servants, launderers and ironers, door persons, barbers, manicurists, carriage drivers, mule drivers, load carriers (including *cargadores* and *carretoneros*), gardeners, prostitutes (*mesalinas*), and mechanics. Not included in this category are housewives (*quehaceres dómesticos*), some of whom lived and worked without pay in working-class households.

TABLE M

Females in Federal District, 1895 Census

Census Category	Mexico City F	Mexico City %[b]	Tacubaya F	Tacubaya %[b]	Tlálpan F	Tlálpan %[b]	D.F. Total[a] F	D.F. Total[a] %[b]
Diverse Occupations								
Maids/servants	25,129	74	1,754	76	1,044	75		
Washers/ironers	5,673	98	253	96	117	88		
Seamstresses	5,505	100	146	100	44	100		
"Tortilleras"	2,701	100	148	100	50	100		
Door women	1,431	59	28	54	5	33		
Corn grinders	1,051	100	62	100	47	100		
Private employees	794	12	51	22	3	2		
Prostitutes	416	100	1	100				
Lottery vendors	86	36						
Water carriers	2	>1						
Sector subtotal	42,788	66	2,443	78	1,310	41	47,875	63
Industries, Fine Artists, Artisans, and "Oficios"								
Cigarette makers	1,709	100			2	100		
Weavers	1,150	33	1	7	150	14		
Modistes	773	100	24	100	7	100		
Industrial workers	732	32	35	15	223	23		
Industrial admin.	451	44						
Shoe "aparadores"	264	45						
Candymakers	202	31						
Embroiderers	159	76	4	100				
Book binders	118	22						
"Pasamaneros"	115	39						
Florists	100	62	78	37	21	25		
Musicians	76	7	2	6				
Mattress makers	68	18	1	7				
Hat makers	59	5	1	17				
Matchmakers	47	26		7				
Actors	47	33						
Singers	36	55						
Cigar makers	26	8						
Dyers	26	17						
Wax makers	20	13						

TABLE M

Continued

Census Category	Mexico City F	Mexico City %[b]	Tacubaya F	Tacubaya %[b]	Tlálpan F	Tlálpan %[b]	D.F. Total[a] F	D.F. Total[a] %[b]
Sketch artists	19	26						
Sash/belt makers	18	22	3	43				
Pastry bakers	17	7						
Artistic painters	15	8	1	4				
Gold leafers	12	7						
Writers	7	5			3	100		
Glove makers	4	44						
Acrobats	4	16						
Watchmakers	1	>1						
Telegraph operators	7	5						
Sector subtotal	6,282	12	157	6	406	13	6,918	12
Commerce								
Merchants	5,199	28	312	21	291	26		
Clerks	324	13	6	4				
Street vendors	357	41	15	68	4	40		
Sector subtotal	5,880	26	333	20	295	24	6,770	25
Professions								
Teachers	1,067	65	75	58	44	68		
Dentists	3	>1						
Doctors	2	>1						
Midwives	183	100	10	100	4	100		
Sector subtotal	1,255	23	85	22	48	25	1,455	24
Miscellaneous								
Unemployed adults	72,287	97	3,783	94	4,065	80		
Unemployed minors	22,177	51	4,115	50	5,213	93		
Pupils	18,733	50	410	51	1,421	47		
Students	1,613	26	116	17	6	10		
Landlords	1,496	63	236	77	65	47	1,839	64
Public admin.	106	4	6	2	3	3	118	3
Mining	14	24	5	45				
Professions unknown	2,217	62	5,213	93	9,050	96	16,480	89

TABLE M

Continued

Census Category	Mexico City F	Mexico City %[b]	Tacubaya F	Tacubaya %[b]	Tlálpan F	Tlálpan %[b]	D.F. Total[a] F	D.F. Total[a] %[b]
Total								
Females employed[c]	60,038	45	8,478	65	11,172	63	82,464	54
		32		46		44		36
Female population	174,848	54	16,902	53	21,882	47	247,481	53
Female adults	132,325		13,119		17,871		151,638	

Source: Censo general . . . 1895.

[a] Includes all 5 municipalities (total populations in parenthesis): Mexico City (325,707), Guadalupe Hidalgo (15,928), Tacubaya (32,152), Tlálpam (46,360), and Xóchimilco (48,558). Total population for the Federal District: 468,705.

[b] Percentage of females in the census category.

[c] Includes totals by sector, miscellaneous professions (including those living by rents, i.e., landlords, where women make up a majority), and "professions unknown." This figure does not include students, unemployed adults, or unemployed minors. It also does not include women who work in their own homes as housekeepers (unless they were included in the "profession unknown" category, which may be the case for Tacubaya and Tlálpan, where this category is relatively large), as they were not counted as such in the census. It is likely that housekeeping women are among the "unemployed," especially for Mexico City, where the number is relatively large. The first percentage indicates women employed in paid work out of all adult females. The second percentage indicates working women out of all employed adults, male and female.

TABLE N

Females in Federal District, 1910 Census

Census Category	Mexico City		Tacubaya		Tlálpan		D.F. Total[a]	
	F	%[b]	F	%[b]	F	%[b]	F	%[b]
Domestic Work								
"Porteras"	1,752	64	58	73	3	43		
Housekeepers[c]	89,346	100	7,399	100	3,997	100		
Subtotal	124,612	93	10,439	95	4,432	96	196,126	94
Clothing/Toilette								
Shoe repairers	1	>1	1	33				
Embroiderers	127	78	22	100				
Seamstresses	7,387	100	293	100	52	100		
Florists	100	67	2	100				
Washers/ironers	5,982	90	419	96	57	100		
Modistes	2,132	100	63	100	1	100		
Hair stylists	123	9						
Hat makers	127	19	1	14				
Cobblers	5	>1						
Manicurists	2	40						
Subtotal	15,986	62	801	61	110	53	18,272	61
Commerce								
Merchants	8,062	26	403	23	61	15		
"Corredores"	2	1	1	8				
Street vendors	310	29	14	78				
Lottery vendors	64	32						
Paper vendors	3	20						
Acrobats	21	30						
Subtotal	8,462	26	418	24	61	15	10,807	26
Arts and Sciences								
Actors	183	71	1	20				
Singers	53	47						
Sketch artists	12	8	2	25				
Writers/journalists	12	6	1	8				
Photographers	17	6						
Engravers	4	2						
Musicians	79	8	11	21				
Artistic painters	28	10	3	14				
Instructors	2,230	71	163	71	36	55		

TABLE N

Continued

Census Category	Mexico City F	Mexico City %[b]	Tacubaya F	Tacubaya %[b]	Tlálpan F	Tlálpan %[b]	D.F. Total[a] F	D.F. Total[a] %[b]
"Taquigrafos"	223	53	12	40				
"Mecanógrafos"	13	87						
Subtotal	2,854	37	193	40	36	41	3,582	38
Food Industry								
"Bizcocheras"	22	5						
Cigarette makers	512	75						
Candymakers	196	27	11	35				
Millers	10	18	3	38				
Bread bakers	17	1	1	1				
Pastry bakers	43	17	3	16				
Cigar makers	11	8						
Corn Grinders	349	100			1	100		
Tortilla makers	1,464	100	94	100	23	100		
Subtotal	2,624	35	112	35	24	13	3,170	35
Textiles								
"Galoneras"/"tiradoras"	2	29						
"Pasamaneros"	82	63						
Weavers	213	15						
"Empuntadores"	287	100	2	100				
"Reboceras"	15	5						
Subtotal	599	24	2	2			668	23
Agriculture								
Farmers	37	6			9	3		
"Hacendadas"	4	9						
Gardeners/horticulturists	2	>1	7	3				
Peons/"jornaleras"	451	4	122	6	89	3		
Carbon makers	13	8	1	2				
Fiber "talladoras"	3	13						
Firewood sellers	1	100						
Subtotal	510	4	130	5	98	3	1,515	3
Chemical Products								
Wax makers	11	22						
Matchmakers	11	31						
Soap maker	1	>1						

TABLE N

Continued

Census Category	Mexico City F	Mexico City %[b]	Tacubaya F	Tacubaya %[b]	Tlálpan F	Tlálpan %[b]	D.F. Total[a] F	D.F. Total[a] %[b]
Dyers	7	7	1	100				
Candlemakers	14	13						
Subtotal	44	8	1	4			45	6
Communications								
Telephone operators	25	66	2	100				
Telegraph operators	41	14	2	16				
Subtotal	66	20	4	29			76	19
Furniture industry								
Furniture makers	1	>1						
Mattress makers	49	14						
Subtotal	50	6					50	6
Artisans/luxury production								
Gold leafers	6	6						
Bookbinders	135	24	1	25				
Typographers	29	2						
Lithographers	11	1						
Subtotal	182	5	1	2			183	5
Medicine								
Dentists	6	5	1	13				
Pharmacists	28	9						
Doctors	11	2	1	2				
Midwives	181	100	11	100	5	100		
Nurses	261	97	8	100				
Subtotal	487	30	21	23	5	29	575	29
"Unproductive/Minors"								
Pupils	12,405	48	1,060	52	169	37		
Students	2,521	37	123	22	7	16		
Prostitutes	602	100	1	100				
Unempl. adults	18,274	84	1,724	76	40	31		
Unempl. minors	46,493	51	4,300	49	2,176	47		
Subtotal	80,295	55	7,208	53	2,392	45	125,772	53
Miscellaneous								
Personal assistants	4,014	18	195	14	16	8		
"Other" industrial	3,335	32	97	20	21	16	10,807	26

TABLE N

Continued

	Mexico City		Tacubaya		Tlálpan		D.F. Total[a]	
Census Category	F	%[b]	F	%[b]	F	%[b]	F	%[b]
Landlords	3,125	68	302	76	29	59	4,082	67
Public admin.	707	13	7	7	5	8	781	13
Clerks	671	21	10	11	1	7		
Potters	13	7						
Miners	7	>1						
Basket makers	6	20						
Decorative painters	3	>1						
Business agents	2	>1						
Electricians	1	>1						
Attorneys	1	>1						
Unknown	3,636	46	40	52	57	56	4,244	44
Total females								
"Occupied"[d]	172,599		12,774		4,900		254,025	
"Paid"[e]	83,253	44	5,373	37	903	18	103,027	37
		33		23		9		31
Population	252,292	54	19,981	53	7,287	47	379,195	53
Adults	190,873		14,498		4,935		277,411	

Source: Tercer Censo . . . 1910, vol. 2, 387–428.

[a] Includes all 13 municipalities of Federal District (total populations in parenthesis): Mexico City (471,066), Atzcapotzalco (14,419), Coyoacán (13,230), Cuajimalpa (5,193), Guadalupe Hidalgo (18,344), Ixtapalapa (24,507), Mixcoac (21,812), Milpa Alta (16,268), San Angel (16,734), Tacubaya (37,552), Tacuba (36,087), Tlálpan (15,448), Xóchimilco (30,093). Total population for the Federal District: 720,753.

[b] Percentage of females in the census category.

[c] Identified in the census as "quehaceres domésticos." These females are distinct from other "occupied" females, as their labor would not have been remunerated.

[d] Includes total by sector (with domestic sector including housekeepers), "mesalinas" (i.e., prostitutes), and miscellaneous professions (including those living by rents, i.e., landlords, where females make up a majority). Figure does not include students, unemployed adults, or unemployed minors.

[e] Excludes females engaged in unremunerated "quehaceres domésticos." First percentage indicates women employed in paid work out of all adult females. Second percentage indicates working women out of all employed adults male and female.

NOTES

Introduction

1. For the 1802 case see AHNMP, Libros de Empeños, 1802. For the 1902 case see AHCM, Gobierno del Distrito, Empeños, Ventas, num. 162, exp. 9. "Morena" indicates a dark-skinned woman.

2. A major contribution of the French *Annales* journal and school has been the examination of historical processes over the *longue dureé*. For discussions of slow cultural and economic change, see Fernand Braudel, *Capitalism and Material Life, 1400–1800*, trans. Miriam Kochan (New York: Harper & Row, 1967). For the long view on Latin America generally, see Mark D. Szuchman, ed., *The Middle Period in Latin America* (Boulder: Lynne Rienner, 1989). For the Mexican case see William H. Beezley, Cheryl English Martin, and William E. French, eds., *Rituals of Rule, Rituals of Resistance: Public Celebrations and Popular Culture in Mexico* (Wilmington DE: Scholarly Resources, 1994). See also Solange Alberro and Serge Gruzinski, *Introducción a la historia de las mentalidades* (México: Seminario de Historia de las Mentalidades y Religión en el México Colonial, INAH, 1979). For a recent survey of material culture that preserves traditional period breaks, see Arnold J. Bauer, *Goods, Power, History: Latin America's Material Culture* (Cambridge: Cambridge University Press, 2001).

3. For a discussion of restricted money circulation, see Ruggiero Romano, *Monedas, seudomonedas, y circulación monetaria en las economías de México* (México: Fondo de Cultura Económica, 1998), 116, 133, 135–37, 148. For pawning practice in the seventeenth century, see R. Douglas Cope, *The Limits of Racial Domination: Plebeian Society in Colonial Mexico City, 1660–1720* (Madison: University of Wisconsin Press, 1994), 110–12.

4. This work continues an emerging trend in "everyday" Mexican history, much of it inspired by James C. Scott, *Weapons of the Weak: Everyday Forms of Peasant Resistance* (New Haven: Yale University Press, 1985). See Gilbert M. Joseph and Daniel Nugent, eds., *Everyday Forms of State Formation: Revolution and the Negotiation of Rule in Modern Mexico* (Durham: Duke University Press, 1994); Richard Boyer, "Negotiating Calidad: The Everyday Struggle for Status in Mexico," *Historical Archeology* 31, no. 1 (1997): 64–72; Mark Wasserman, *Everyday Life and Politics in Nineteenth-Century Mexico* (Albuquerque: University of New Mexico Press, 2000). See also María Odila Silva Dias, *Power and Everyday Life: The Lives of Working Women in Nineteenth-Century Brazil* (Rutgers: Rutgers University Press, 1995).

5. "El Camino del Curato o Sea La Oca de la Orquesta," reproduced in *Artes de Mexico: El Arte de la Suerte* 13 (1991): 42. The Juego de la Oca likely came to Mexico with the Spaniards. The origins of the game are disputed. Whether created during the siege of Troy or by the Knights Templars much later in Jerusalem during the Crusades, it was known in medieval Florence. For the modern Mexican version, the board usually has a spiral of sixty-three squares depicting everyday life, with a goose (*oca*) at regular intervals. When landing on a goose, the player places a wager before rolling the die to determine the next move. Some squares are traps—a well, a labyrinth, the grim reaper (*la muerte*), a jail—where a player must remain until, freed by another player's arriving on the square, the player returns to square one. If the roll takes one

past square sixty-three, one completes the turn by moving backward. The player who rolls a number that lands him or her exactly on square sixty-three wins the game.

6. D. S. Parker, *The Idea of the Middle Class: White-Collar Workers and Peruvian Society, 1900–1950* (University Park: Pennsylvania State University Press, 1998). Recent scholarship has disassembled stereotypes about and elite labels for nonelites—"léperos," "vagos," "populacho." Pablo Piccato, *City of Suspects: Crime in Mexico City, 1900–1931* (Durham: Duke University Press, 2001); Robert Buffington, *Criminal and Citizen in Modern Mexico* (Lincoln: University of Nebraska Press, 2000); and Silvia Arrom, *Containing the Poor: The Mexico City Poor House, 1774–1871* (Durham: Duke University Press, 2000).

7. Patricia Seed, "Social Dimensions of Race: Mexico City, 1753," *Hispanic American Historical Review* 62, no. 4 (November 1982): 569–606; and Michael Scardaville, "Crime and the Urban Poor in the Late Colonial Period" (PhD diss., University of Florida, 1977).

8. Timothy Anna, *The Fall of the Royal Government in Mexico City* (Lincoln: University of Nebraska Press, 1994), 22. "Mestizo" refers to Indian and European parentage; "mulatto" refers to African and European parentage.

9. Silvia Arrom, *The Women of Mexico City, 1790–1857* (Stanford: Stanford University Press, 1985), 101. For the relationship between race and class in the colonial period, see John K. Chance and William B. Taylor, "Estate and Class in a Colonial City: Oaxaca in 1792," *Comparative Studies in Society and History* 19 (Oct. 1977): 454–87; Robert McCaa, Stuart B. Schwartz, and Arturo Grubessich, "Race and Class in Colonial Latin America: A Critique," *Comparative Studies in Society and History* 21, no. 3 (July 1979): 421–33; Seed, "Social Dimensions of Race"; Magnus Mörner, "Economic Factors and Stratification in Colonial Spanish America with Special Regard to Elites," *Hispanic American Historical Review* 63, no. 2 (May 1983): 335–69; and Cope, *Limits*, 9–26, 49–67. On mobility at the end of the eighteenth century of individuals between ethnic categories, including mobility from nonwhite into white categories, see Bruce A. Castelman, "Social Climbers in a Colonial Mexican City: Individual Mobility within the Sistema de Castas in Orizaba, 1777–1791," *Colonial Latin American Review* 10, no. 2 (2001): 229–49; Steve J. Stern, *The Secret History of Gender: Women, Men and Power in Late Colonial Mexico* (Chapel Hill: University of North Carolina Press, 1995), 26, 35; and Anna, *Fall*, 9, 12–13.

10. Herbert J. Klein, "The Demographic Structure of Mexico City in 1811," *Journal of Urban History* 23, no. 1 (1996): 66–94. The 1921 census does not break down by occupation. By 1910 those with middle-class occupations made up 30 percent of the population. Secretaría de Agricultura y Fomento, Dirección de Estadística, *Tercer censo de población de los Estados Unidos Mexicanos: Verificado el 27 de Octubre de 1910* (México: Departamento de Aprovisionamientos Generales, 1918), 2:387–428. By 1921 another three hundred thousand people lived in outlying areas of the Federal District. Estados Unidos Mexicanos, Departamento de la Estadistica Nacional, *Censo general de habitatantes: 30 de Noviembre de 1921; Distrito Federal* (México: Talleres Gráficos de la Nación, 1925). See appendix 3, table A, for general population over the long term.

11. Frederick John Shaw Jr. "Poverty and Politics in Mexico City, 1824–1854" (PhD diss., University of Florida, 1975), 49.

12. "Ciclo Histórico. 1907. Juego para Niños. Dispuesto por el Señor Profesor Don Andrés Oscoy," reproduced in *Artes de Mexico: El Arte de la Suerte* 13 (1991): 43.

13. Historically, the "middle" has represented only a fraction of society and has played a small role in stories of political and economic power that have interested scholars. Consistent census manuscripts for measuring occupational categories and analyzing household com-

positions across time are not available. Mexico City—viceregal and then national political capital as well as commercial hub—has had a sizable bureaucratic and commercial apparatus run by a middle sector throughout its history. On middle-class culture see Arrom, *Women* and *Containing the Poor*; Donald Fithian Stevens, *Origins of Instability in Early Republican Mexico* (Durham: Duke University Press, 1991); and Michael P. Costeloe, *The Central Republic in Mexico, 1835–46: Hombres de Bien in the Age of Santa Anna* (Cambridge: Cambridge University Press, 1993).

14. Indeed, throughout Latin America and the Caribbean, middle-class households today still pay for some aspect of household chores, in contrast to North America and Europe, where middle-class women do most such work themselves with assistance from modern appliances, whether they are housewives or are employed in white- or pink-collar jobs. See Ruth Schwartz Cowan, *More Work for Mother: The Ironies of Household Technology from the Open Hearth to the Microwave* (New York: Basic Books, 1983).

15. My understanding of the broad scope of housekeeping comes from a synthesis of a wide literature. Feminist scholars such as Laura Balbo, Rayna Rapp, and Christine Stansell and historians of gender in Latin America such as Asunción Lavrín, Silvia Arrom, Donna Guy, Steve Stern, and Ann Blum have examined interdomestic relations (conflictual or consensual) and gendered divisions of labor and roles within the family. See Laura Balbo, "The Servicing Work of Women and the Capitalist State," *Political Power and Social Theory* 3 (1982): 251–70; Rayna Rapp, "Family and Class in Contemporary America," in *Rethinking the Family: Some Feminist Questions*, ed. Barrie Thorne and Marilyn Yalom, 47–70 (New York: Longman, 1982); Christine Stansell, *City of Women: Sex and Class in New York, 1789–1860* (Urbana: University of Illinois Press, 1987); Asunción Lavrin, "Lo femenino: Women in Colonial Historical Sources," in *Coded Encounters: Writing, Gender, and Ethnicity in Colonial Latin America*, ed. Francisco Cevallos-Candau, Jeffrey A. Cole, Nina M. Scott, and Nicomedes Suárez-Araúz, 153–76 (Amherst: University of Massachusetts Press, 1994); Arrom, *Women*; Donna J. Guy, "Women, Peonage and Industrialization: Argentina, 1810–1914," *Latin American Research Review* 16, no. 3 (1981): 65–89, and "Lower-Class Families, Women, and the Law in Nineteenth Century Argentina," *Journal of Family History* 10, no. 3 (1985): 318–31; Stern, *Secret History*; and Ann S. Blum, "Cleaning the Revolutionary Household: Domestic Servants and Public Welfare in Mexico City, 1900–1935," *Journal of Women's History* 15, no. 4 (2004): 67–90. See also Richard R. Wilk, "Decision Making and Resource Flows within the Household: Beyond the Black Box," in *The Household Economy: Reconsidering the Domestic Mode of Production*, ed. Richard Wilk, 23–52 (Boulder: Westview Press, 1989); Sarah Chambers, *From Subjects to Citizens: Honor, Gender, and Politics in Arequipa, Peru, 1780–1854* (University Park: Pennsylvania State University Press, 1999), esp. 189–216; Eileen Boris, "The Home as Workplace: Deconstructing Dichotomies," *International Review of Social History* 39 (1994): 415–28; Diana diZerega Wall, "Family Meals and Evening Parties: Constructing Domesticity in Nineteenth-Century Middle-Class New York," in *Lines That Divide: Historical Archaeologies of Race, Class, and Gender*, ed. James A. Delle, Stephen A. Mrozowski, and Robert Paynter, 111–12 (Knoxville: University of Tennessee Press, 2000); and Mary Ryan, *Cradle of the Middle Class: The Family in Oneida County, New York 1790–1865* (Cambridge: Cambridge University Press, 1981). On "presentation" as a structure of consumption that includes the work of domestic servants, see Pierre Bourdieu, *Distinction: A Social Critique of the Judgment of Taste*, trans. Richard Nice (Cambridge: Harvard University Press, 1984), 184.

16. Bourdieu says nothing explicit about pawnbroking or its place in middle-class household economics. He does argue that "social class is not defined solely by a position in the relations of production, but by the class habitus which is 'normally' . . . associated with that position." Bourdieu, *Distinction*, 372; on class fractions see 102; see also 101–11, 147–51, 163–64, 170–73. For further discussion of the relationship between class and habitus, see Pierre Bourdieu, *Outline of a Theory of Practice*, transl. Richard Nice (Cambridge UK: Cambridge University Press, 1977), 85–86. Habitus "is the dynamic intersection of structure and action, society and the individual." Moishe Postone, Edward LiPuma, and Craig Calhous, eds. *Bourdieu: Critical Perspectives* (Chicago: University of Chicago Press, 1993), 4. For a dynamic study of habitus in twentieth-century Colombia, see Ann Farnsworth-Alvear, *Dulcinea in the Factory: Myths, Morals, Men and Women in Colombia's Industrial Experiment, 1905–1960* (Durham: Duke University Press, 2000).

17. E. P. Thomson, *The Making of the English Working Class* (New York: Vintage, 1963). For discussion of how to define the English "middle station," see Peter Earle, *The Making of the English Middle Class* (Berkeley: University of California Press, 1989).

18. Brian Owensby applies Michel de Certeau's concept of "making do" to Brazil in *Intimate Ironies: Modernity and the Making of Middle-Class Lives in Brazil* (Stanford: Stanford University Press, 1999), 3; Michel de Certeau, *The Practice of Everyday Life*, trans. Steven F. Rendall (Berkeley: University of California Press, 1984); Parker, *Idea*, 7.

19. In contrast, classic cultural history of the "Porfirian persuasion" portrays Mexican society as split in two, with a small elite and largely undifferentiated pueblo during the rule of Porfirio Díaz. William H. Beezley, *Judas at the Jockey Club and Other Episodes of Porfirian Mexico* (Lincoln: University of Nebraska Press, 1987).

20. Manuel Gutierrez Najera, "La historia de un peso falso," in *Antología de la literatura mexicana*, ed. Carlos Castillo, 294–302 (Chicago: University of Chicago Press, 1944), quotes on 294–95.

21. Irene Elena Motts, *La vida en la ciudad de México en las primeras décadas del siglo* (México: Editorial Porrúa, 1973), 7.

22. Middle-class rank-and-file protagonists in the revolution beginning in 1910, in the capital or elsewhere, have not been a focus of historiography. For recent studies of urban revolutionary activity that emphasize working classes, see John Lear, *Workers, Neighbors, and Citizens: The Revolution in Mexico City* (Lincoln: University of Nebraska Press, 2001); and Andrew Grant Wood, *Revolution in the Street: Women, Workers, and Urban Protest in Veracruz, 1870–1927* (Wilmington DE: Scholarly Resources, 2001).

23. Barbara Tenenbaum, *The Politics of Penury: Debts and Taxes in Mexico, 1821–1856* (Albuquerque: University of New Mexico Press, 1986).

24. Though commonly told in textbook narratives about the conquest, this story is likely myth. If true, Isabella was not the only monarch to hock royal jewels. Queen Anne of England, in the early seventeenth century, was known to borrow against jewels and then not be able to pay back loans, which got her London jewelers in trouble. See Bruce P. Lenman, "Jacobean Goldsmith-Jewelers as Credit-Creators: The Cases of James Mossman, James Cockie and George Heriot," *Scottish Historical Review* 74, no. 2 (1995): 159–77.

25. Eric R. Wolf, *Europe and the People without History* (Berkeley: University of California Press, 1982), 109, 113. Looking back at the history of credit from today's postmodern world of consumer and national debts, a recent study argues that modern nations rest on fictitious treasuries, a subterfuge that has put them on the road to cultural and financial bankruptcy,

and that nationalism and national identity are passing commodities bought on credit. Patrick Brantlinger, *Fictions of State: Culture and Credit in Britain, 1694–1994* (Ithaca: Cornell University Press, 1996).

26. The next most common was the *censo*, or real-estate mortgage given by the church. See María de Pilar Martínez López-Cano, *El crédito a largo plazo en el siglo XVI, Ciudad de Mexico (1550–1620)* (México: Universidad Nacional Autónoma de México, 1995). Despite the ubiquity of pawnbroking, only top tiers of credit networks have been studied historically for Mexico. See María del Pilar Martínez López-Cano and Guillermina del Valle Pavón, eds., *El Crédito en Nueva España* (México: Instituto de Investigaciones Dr. José María Luis Mora, 1998). On ecclesiastical lending see Gisela von Wobeser, "Las fundaciones piadosas como fuentes de crédito en la época colonial," *Historia Mexicana* 38, no. 4 (April–June 1989): 779–92; "La inquisición como institución crediticia en el siglo XVIII," *Historia Mexicana* 39, no. 4 (April–June 1990): 849–79, and *El crédito eclesiástico en la Nueva España, siglo XVIII* (México: Universidad Nacional Autónoma de México, 1994). See also John Frederick Schwaller, *Origins of Church Wealth in Mexico: Ecclesiastical Revenues and Church Finances, 1523–1600* (Albuquerque: University of New Mexico Press, 1985); Susan A. Soeiro, "The Social and Economic Role of the Convent: Women and Nuns in Colonial Bahia, 1677–1800," *Hispanic American Historical Review* 54, no. 2 (1974): 209–32; Asunción Lavrin, "El capital eclesiastico y las elites sociales en Nueva España a fines del siglo XVIII," *Mexican Studies/Estudios Mexicanos* 1, no. 1 (1985): 1–28; A. J. Bauer, *La iglesia en la economía de América Latina* (México: INAH, 1986); Agueda Jiménez-Pelayo, "El impacto del crédito en la economía rural del norte de Nueva Galicia," *Hispanic American Historical Review* 71, no. 3 (1991): 501–29; and Kathryn Burns, *Colonial Habits: Convents and the Spiritual Economy of Cuzco, Peru* (Durham: Duke University Press, 1999). On business lenders see John Kicza, *Colonial Entrepreneurs: Families and Business in Bourbon Mexico City* (Albuquerque: University of New Mexico Press, 1983); David Brading, *Miners and Merchants in Bourbon Mexico, 1763–1810* (Cambridge: Cambridge University Press, 1971); Linda L. Greenow, *Credit and Socioeconomic Change in Colonial Mexico: Loans and Mortgages in Guadalajara, 1720–1820* (Boulder: Westview Press, 1983); and Tenenbaum, *Politics of Penury*. Banks were slow to develop in the nineteenth century. See Leonor Ludlow and Carlos Marichal, eds., *Banca y poder en México, 1800–1925* (México: Grijalbo, 1986). In contrast to European charitable collateral-lending institutions, the only studies of the Mexican Monte de Piedad have been published by the institution itself and by a few detractors. Esperanza Cabrera Siles and Patricia Escandón, *Historia del Nacional Monte de Piedad, 1775–1993* (Nacional Monte de Piedad, 1993); J. M. Villela, *El Monte de Piedad, 1775–1877* (Imprenta de Jens y Sapiain, 1877); and Rubio Dario, *El Nacional Monte de Piedad* (Talleres Gráficos de la Cía. Editora, 1949). See also Edith Couturier, "The Philanthropic Activities of Pedro Romero de Terreros: First Count of Regla (1753–1781)," *The Americas* 32 (July 1975): 13–30. For the European literature see José López Yepes, *Historia de los Montes de Piedad en España*, 2 vols. (Confederación Española de Cajas de Ahorros, 1971); Brian Pullan, *Rich and Poor in Renaissance Venice* (Harvard University Press, 1971); Carol Bresnahan Menning, *Charity and State in Late Renaissance Italy* (Ithaca: Cornell University Press, 1993); and Cheryl L. Danieri, *Credit Where Credit Is Due: The Mont-de-Piété of Paris, 1777–1851* (New York: Garland, 1991). On Mexican retail merchants who doubled as pawnbrokers, see Kicza, *Colonial Entrepreneurs*; Jay Kinsbruner, *Petty Capitalism in Spanish America: The Pulperos of Puebla, Mexico City, Caracas, and Buenos Aires* (Boulder: Westview Press, 1987); Stanley J. Stein, "Tending the Store: Trade and Silver at the Real de Huautla, 1778–1781," *Hispanic American Historical Review* 77, no. 3 (1977): 377–407; and Cheryl English Martin, *Governance and Society in Colonial Mexico: Chihua-*

hua in the Eighteenth Century (Palo Alto CA: Stanford University Press, 1996), 135–39. For comparative perspectives on private pawnbroking, see Melanie Tebbutt, *Making Ends Meet: Pawnbroking and Working-Class Credit* (New York: Leicester University Press / St. Martin's Press, 1983); William R. Simpson and Florence K. Simpson, with Charles Samuels, *Hockshop* (New York: Random House, 1954); and Avram Taylor, *Working Class Credit and Community since 1918* (Hampshire UK: Palmgrave Macmillan, 2002).

27. William Chester Jordan, *Women and Credit in Pre-Industrial and Developing Societies* (Philadelphia: University of Pennsylvania Press, 1993), 125. See also Grethe Jacobsen, "Women's Work and Women's Role: Ideology and Reality in Danish Urban Society, 1300–1550," *The Scandinavian Economic History Review and Economy and History* 30 (1983): 3–20.

28. Greenow, *Credit and Socioeconomic Change*; Asunción Lavrin and Edith Couturier, "Dowries and Wills: A View of Women's Socioeconomic Role in Colonial Guadalajara and Puebla, 1640–1790," *Hispanic American Historical Review* 59, no. 2 (May 1979): 280–304.

29. One-fourth of individuals holding privately owned property (as distinguished from the large holdings of the church) in 1813 were female. By the Porfiriato 68 percent of those making a living from rental property were female. By 1921 the female percentage of landlords was down to 48 percent, with only 4 percent of the total population living off rental property. The history of Mexican women as private lenders remains largely unexplored and is beyond the reach of this study. Arrom, *Women*, 172; *Tercer censo de 1910*, 2:390.

30. Carlos G. Vélez-Ibañez, *Bonds of Mutual Trust: The Cultural Systems of Rotating Credit Associations among Urban Mexicans and Chicanos* (New Brunswick: Rutgers University Press, 1983). A number of historical studies mention pawning systems in Spanish America, though none provide systematic analysis. See Donald Chipman, "The Will of Nuño de Guzmán: President, Governor and Captain General of New Spain and the Province of Pánuco, 1558," *The Americas* 35, no. 2 (1978): 238–48; Cuauhtemoc Velasco Avila, "Labour Relations in Mining: Real de Monte and Pachuca, 1824–74," in *Miners and Mining in the Americas*, ed. Thomas Greaves and William Culver, 47–67 (Manchester UK: Manchester University Press, 1985), 61; Frank Solomon, "Indian Women of Early Colonial Quito as Seen through Their Testaments," *The Americas* 44, no. 3 (1988): 325–41; Bianca Premo, "From the Pockets of Women: The Gendering of the Mita, Migration and Tribute in Colonial Chuchito, Peru," *The Americas* 57, no. 1 (July 2000): 63–94; Jane Erin Mangan, "Enterprise in the Shadow of Silver: Colonial Andeans and the Culture of Trade in Potosí, 1570–1700" (PhD diss., Duke University, 1999), esp. chap. 4; Christine Hunefeldt, *Liberalism in the Bedroom: Quarreling Spouses in Nineteenth-Century Lima* (University Park: Pennsylvania State University Press, 2000), 276–84; Teresa González de Fanning, "Concerning the Education of Women," in *Confronting Change, Challenging Tradition: Women in Latin American History*, ed. Gertrude M. Yeager, 38 (Wilmington DE: Scholarly Resources, 1994); and Leonidas García, *Montes de Piedad: Lectura para el pueblo* (Quito: Imprenta de la Universidad, 1913), 8–15.

31. In general middle-class borrowers have been left out of European and North American historiography of pawning, maybe because they in fact were not there, more likely because their presence was made invisible by concerns of honor, shame, and image.

32. Villela, *El Monte*, 25.

33. Witness this memory from 1920s England: "There was a penny pawn shop, you could put your frying-pan in to get your kettle out! Mind you a penny went a lot further in them days." Taylor, *Working Class Credit*, 1.

34. See Jordan, *Women and Credit*; Tebbutt, *Making Ends Meet*; Ellen Ross, "Survival Networks: Women's Neighborhood Sharing in London before World War One," *History Workshop* 15 (Spring 1983): 4–27; and Stansell, *City of Women*.

35. Martha Judith Sánchez Gómez, "Consideraciones teórico-metodológicas en el estudio del trabajo doméstico en México," in *Trabajo, poder y sexualidad*, ed. Orlandina de Oliveira, 60 (México: El Colegio de México, 1989); Lourdes Benería, "The Mexican Debt Crisis: Restructuring the Economy and the Household," in *Unequal Burden: Economic Crises, Persistent Poverty, and Women's Work*, ed. Lourdes Benería and Shelley Feldman, 83–104 (Boulder: Westview Press, 1992). It is not simply natural that women do housework, but rather the case that housekeeping has been historically constructed in Mexico as the responsibility of women. In eighteenth-century Europe, 1870s Peru, and 1890s Havana, the majority of domestic servants were men. See Peru, Dirección General de Estadística, *Censo general de la Republica de Peru formado en 1876* (Lima: Imp. Del Teatro, 1878); Cuba, Oficina del Censo, *Censo de la República de Cuba bajo la Administración Provisional de Los Estados Unidos 1907* (Washington: Oficino [*sic*] del Censo de los Estados de Unidos, 1908). Multiple studies of domestic service in colonial Africa show housekeeping gendered male. See Karen Tranberg Hansen, ed., *African Encounters with Domesticity* (New Brunswick: Rutgers, 1992); Gertrude Mianda, "Colonialism, Education, and Gender Relations in the Belgian Congo: The Évolué Case," in *Women in African Colonial Histories*, ed. Jean Allman, Susan Geiger, and Nakanyike Musisi, 144–63 (Bloomington: Indiana University Press, 2002); and Margaret Strobel, "Gender, Sex and Empire," in *Islamic and European Expansion: The Forging of a Global Empire*, ed. Michael Adas, 345–75 (Philadelphia: Temple University Press, 1993).

36. Balbo, "Servicing Work of Women"; Rapp, "Family and Class."

37. Beverly Lemire, "Petty Pawns and Informal Lending: Gender and the Transformation of Small-Scale Credit in England, circa 1600–1800," in *From Family Firms to Corporate Capitalism: Essays in Business and Industrial History in Honor of Peter Mathias*, ed. Kristine Bruland and Patrick O'Brien, 112–38 (Oxford: Clarendon Press, 1998). See also Jordan, *Women and Credit*; Jacobsen, "Women's Work"; and Ross, "Survival Networks."

38. Leonore Davidoff and Catherine Hall, *Family Fortunes: Men and Women of the English Middle Class, 1780–1850* (Chicago: University of Chicago Press, 1987), 30. On female consumption in Mexico, see Steven B. Bunker, " 'Consumers of Good Taste': Marketing Modernity in Northern Mexico, 1890–1910," *Mexican Studies/Estudios Mexicanos* 12, no. 2 (Summer 1997): 227–69. On masculine consumption tied to status, see Victor M. Macías-González, "The Largatijo at The High Life: Masculine Consumption, Race, Nation, and Homosexuality in Porfirian Mexico," in *The Famous 41: Sexuality and Social Control in Mexico, 1901*, ed. Robert McKee Irwin, Edward J. McCaughan, and Michelle Rocío Nasser, 227–50 (New York: Palgrave Macmillan, 2003). See also Susan Porter Benson, *Countercultures: Saleswomen, Managers, and Customers in American Department Stores, 1890–1940* (Urbana: University of Illinois Press, 1986); Erika Diane Rappaport, *Shopping for Pleasure: Women in the Making of London's East End* (Princeton: Princeton University Press, 2000); and Lisa Tiersten, *Marianne in the Market: Envisioning Consumer Society in Fin-de-Siécle France* (Berkeley: University of California Press, 2001).

39. Amanda Vickery, "Women and the World of Goods: A Lancashire Consumer and Her Possessions, 1751–81," in *Consumption and the World of Goods*, ed. John Brewer and Roy Porter, 274–301 (London: Routledge, 1993), 279.

40. Caracas, Santiago, São Paulo, Belo Horizonte, and Iguape also had levels of female headship from 24 to 45 percent. These numbers are higher than those in eighteenth-century

England, where 16 percent of households were headed by women. Elizabeth Kuznesof, "Gender Ideology, Race, and Female-Headed Households in Urban Mexico, 1750–1850," in *State and Society in Spanish America during the Age of Revolution*, ed. Victor M. Uribe-Uran, 161–65 (Wilmington DE: Scholarly Resources, 2001); Shaw, "Poverty and Politics," 38; Arrom, *Women*, 120, 132, 166, 186, 197; and Lorna Weatherill, "The Meaning of Consumer Behavior in Late Seventeenth- and Early Eighteenth-Century England," in Brewer and Porter, *Consumption*, 211.

41. Studies of other historical settings and of modern Mexico reveal sharing networks, informal lending, and even the lending of pledge goods from neighbor to neighbor. See Taylor, *Working Class Credit*; Sarah Levine, *Dolor y Alegría: Women and Social Change in Urban Mexico* (Madison: University of Wisconsin Press, 1993). Gutmann argues that men in Mexico City have been slow to take up housekeeping in the late twentieth century even as the stress of their women's *doble jornada* has increased. Matthew C. Gutmann, *The Meanings of Macho: Being a Man in Mexico City* (Berkeley: University of California Press, 1996), 146–72.

42. Guillermo Prieto, cited by Wasserman, *Everyday Life and Politics*, 148.

43. In Porfirian Mexico City, "a bourgeois search for social identity created a desire to consume foreign-made items, and an individual's claims to 'modernity' rested on the consumption of imported goods." Jurgen Buchenau, *Tools of Progress* (Albuquerque: University of New Mexico Press, 2004).

44. Paul Johnson argues that for twentieth-century England, "the role of goods in the budget management of households was a crucial one . . . goods were important because, given the extent of the pawnbroking market, they had the status of near-money." Paul Johnson, "Credit and Thrift and the British Working Class," in *The Working Class in Modern British History*, ed. Jay Winter, 147–70 (Cambridge: Cambridge University Press, 1983), quote on 157.

45. In the last half of the nineteenth century, there were "conflicting interests" among liberals, with no one version of liberalism winning out; instead, Mexican liberalism was "an accumulation of ideas, programs, and groups." Alan Knight, "El Liberalismo desde la reforma hasta la revolución (una intepretación)," *Historia Mexicana* 35, no. 1 (1985): 59–91. For a sampling of the huge literature on liberalism in Mexico, see David Brading, *The First America: The Spanish Monarchy, Creole Patriots, and the Liberal State, 1492–1867* (Cambridge: Cambridge University Press, 1991); Carlos Marichal and Daniela Marino, comps., *De colonia a nación: Impuestos y política en México, 1750–1860* (México: El Colegio de México, 2001); Vincent C. Peloso and Barbara Tenenbaum, eds. *Liberals, Politics, and Power: State Formation in Nineteenth-Century Latin America* (Athens: University of Georgia Press, 1996); Victor M. Uribe-Uran, ed., *State and Society in Spanish America during the Age of Revolution* (Wilmington DE: Scholarly Resources, 2001); Jaime E. Rodríguez O., ed. *The Independence of Mexico and the Creation of the New Nation* (Los Angeles: University of California Press, 1989); Charles A. Hale, *Mexican Liberalism in the Age of Mora, 1821–1853* (New Haven: Yale University Press, 1968); Costeloe, *Central Republic*; Stevens, *Origins of Instability*; Martin, *Governance and Society*; William E. French, *A Peaceful and Working People* (Albuquerque: University of New Mexico Press, 1996); Margaret Chowning, *Wealth and Power in Provincial Mexico* (Stanford: Stanford University Press, 1999); and Florencia Mallon, *Peasant and Nation: The Making of Postcolonial Peru and Mexico* (Berkeley: University of California Press, 1995). See also Chambers, *From Subjects to Citizens*; and Hunefeldt, *Liberalism in the Bedroom*. E. P. Thompson's idea that class "happens" is easily adapted to social, political, economic, and cultural transformations brought with evolving liberalism in Mexico. See E. P. Thompson, *The Making*, 9–10.

46. In addition to works already cited, see Pilar Gonzalbo Aizpuru, *Las mujeres en la Nueva España* (El Colegio de México, 1987); and D. S. Chandler, *Social Assistance and Bureaucratic Politics: The Montepíos of Colonial Mexico, 1767–1821* (Albuquerque: University of New Mexico Press, 1991).

47. It has been argued that in seventeenth- and eighteenth-century New Spain women's property rights were protected and that in cases of malfeasance women used legal recourse to recover their property. Lavrin and Couturier, "Dowries and Wills." In contrast English common law held that all of a woman's liquid assets became the property of her husband upon marriage. English women lost the guarantee of a third of a deceased husband's estate in 1833, and a widow might only inherit in the form of trust in the hands of a male relative or other male executor. Davidoff and Hall, *Family Fortunes*, 210, 276. See also Vickery, "Women and the World of Goods," 294.

48. Valuable clothing, jewels, and furniture dominated eighteenth-century dowries in Mexico City, with less valuable "ollas, trapos, canastos" (pots, cloth, baskets) no longer mentioned as they had been earlier. Pilar Gonzalbo Aizpuru, "Ajuar doméstico y vida familiar," in *El arte y la vida cotidiana*, coord. Elena Estrada de Gerlero, 125–37 (México: Universidad Nacional Autónoma de México, 1994).

49. Mallon argues that nineteenth-century Latin America saw "profound social, economic, and political transformations associated with the transition to capitalism." Florencia Mallon, "Introduction," *Latin American Perspectives* 48 (Winter 1986): 3–17, quote on 3.

50. The term "relations of forces" is from Antonio Gramsci, *The Modern Prince and Other Writings* (New York: International Publishers, 1957), 164–73; "bundles of relationships" is from William B. Taylor, "Between Global Processes and Local Knowledge: An Inquiry into Early Latin American Social History, 1500–1900," in *Reliving the Past: The Worlds of Social History*, ed. Olivier Zunz, 140–66 (Chapel Hill: University of North Carolina Press, 1985); "multiplicity of force relations" is from Michel Foucault, *The History of Sexuality*, vol. 1, *An Introduction*, trans. R. Hurley (Harmondsworth UK: Penguin, 1978), 92. For state power as "a cluster of relations," see C. Gordon, ed., *Michel Foucault: Power/Knowledge: Selected Interviews and Other Writings, 1972–1977* (London: Harvester Wheatsheaf, 1980), 199.

51. On hegemony see Gramsci, *The Modern Prince*, 153–55, 186–88. On the colonial state see Linda Arnold, *Bureaucracy and Bureaucrats in Mexico City, 1742–1835* (Tucson: University of Arizona, 1988); and Chandler, *Social Assistance*.

52. Foucault argued that resistance through discourse can turn legislation from "an instrument and effect of power" into a "starting point for opposing strategy." Foucault, *History of Sexuality*, 1:101. On the "rhetoric of practice" and "tactics of the weak," see de Certeau, *The Practice*, 39–42.

53. Phyllis L. Smith, "Contentious Voices Amid the Order: The Opposition Press in Mexico City, 1876–1911," *Journalism History* 22, no. 4 (1997): 138–45; and Castillo, *Antología de la literatura mexicana*.

54. Cope, *Limits*, 7.

55. Mary Douglas and Baron Isherwood, *The World of Goods: Towards an Anthropology of Consumption* (New York: Basic Books, 1968), 39; Bourdieu, *Distinction* and *Outline*; Victoria de Grazia and Ellen Furlough, eds., *The Sex of Things: Gender and Consumption in Historical Perspective* (Berkeley: University of California Press, 1996); and Arjun Appadurai, "Introduction: Commodities and the Politics of Value," *The Social Life of Things: Commodities in Cultural Perspective*, ed. Arjun Appadurai, 3–63 (Cambridge: Cambridge University Press, 1986).

56. For Mexican studies of material culture using wills and dowries, see Lavrin and Couturier, "Dowries and Wills"; Gonzalbo Aizpuru, "Ajuar doméstico"; and Amanda P. Angel, "Spanish Women in the New World: The Transmission of a Model Polity to New Spain, 1521–1570" (PhD diss., University of California Davis, 1997). For English probate inventories, see Weatherill, "Meaning of Consumer Behavior," in Brewer and Porter, *Consumption*, 206–26. For a focus on mundane and inconspicuous consumption, see Vickery, "Women and the World of Goods." For a rare examination of the property inventories of poor women in São Paulo, see Silva Dias, *Power and Everyday Life*, 139–67. See also John Storey, *Cultural Consumption and Everyday Life* (London and New York: Oxford University Press, 1999), 1–17, 36–51.

57. Problems with the inventories include their lack of uniformity and their spotty temporal coverage. Some record all pawned goods in a business on a given day, others record only those whose pledge time has expired. Other issues include identifying collateral owners in terms of gender and "class," or even at all. Tebbutt's study of English working-class pawning practices found that the shame of needing the pawnshop created a business opportunity for runners who would do people's pawning for them. While it is clear that servants regularly ran the pawning errand for those who had them, it is not clear to what extent this independent "pawnshop runner" occupation obtained in Mexico. If it was very common, a problem in interpreting the sources arises. Who is recorded as the owner of an item when the servant is doing the pawning or when anyone other than the goods owner is sent to make the transaction? Taylor finds that Tebbutt's nineteenth-century pattern continued to obtain among his twentieth-century informants. Tebbutt, *Making Ends Meet*; Taylor, *Working Class Credit*.

58. In addition to Mexicanists already cited, these include Carlos Illades and Ariel Rodríguez, comp., *Ciudad de México: Instituciones, actores sociales, y conflicto político, 1774–1931* (México: El Colegio de Michoacán and the Universidad Autónoma Metropolitana, 1996); Isabel Tovar de Arechederra and Magdalena Mas, eds., *El corazón de una nación independiente*, 3 vols. (México: Gobierno del Distrito Federal, 1994); Regina Hernández Franyuti, ed., *La Ciudad de México en la primera mitad del siglo XIX*, 2 vols. (México: Instituto Mora, 1994); Juan José Pescador, *De bautizos a fieles difuntos* (El Colegio de México, 1992); Susan Deans-Smith, *Bureaucrats, Planters, and Workers: The Making of the Tobacco Monopoly in Bourbon Mexico* (Austin: University of Texas Press, 1992); Richard Warren, *Vagrants and Citizens: Politics and the Masses in Mexico City from Colony to Republic* (Wilmington DE: Scholarly Resources, 2001); Katherine Elaine Bliss, *Compromised Positions: Prostitution, Public Health, and Gender Politics in Revolutionary Mexico City* (University Park: Pennsylvania State University Press, 2001); and Lanny Thompson, "Households and the Reproduction of Labor in Mexico, 1876–1970" (PhD diss., State University of New York at Binghamton, 1989). On material culture and identity, see Jeffrey M. Pilcher, *¡Que vivan los tamales!* (New Mexico, 1998); Benjamin Orlove, ed., *The Allure of the Foreign* (Ann Arbor: University of Michigan Press, 1997); and Delle, Mrozowski, and Paynter, *Lines That Divide*. For comparative perspectives on material culture, see Douglas and Isherwood, *World of Goods*; and Braudel, *Capitalism and Material Life*. On honor, ethnicity, and identity, see Ann Twinam, *Public Lives, Private Secrets: Gender, Honor, Sexuality, and Illegitimacy in Colonial Spanish America* (Stanford: University of California Press, 1999); Verena Martínez-Adlier, *Marriage, Class and Colour in Nineteenth-Century Cuba* (Cambridge: Cambridge University Press, 1974); and Lyman L. Johnson and Sonya Lipsett-Rivera, eds., *The Faces of Honor* (Albuquerque: University of New Mexico Press, 1998).

59. Eric Van Young, "Material Life," in *The Countryside in Colonial Latin America*, ed. Louisa Schell Hobermann and Susan Migden Socolow, 49–74 (Albuquerque: University of New Mexico Press, 1996), 52.

60. Douglas and Isherwood, *World of Goods*, 112, 118. See also Appadurai, *Social Life of Things*, 15.

61. Bourdieu, de Certeau, and Foucault all offer theoretical conceptualizations of everyday cultural practices that have informed my reading of pawning practices in Mexico City. See Bourdieu, *Outline*; De Certeau, *The Practice*; and Foucault, *History of Sexuality*, vol. 1. De Certeau argues that "what interests Bourdieu is the genesis, 'the mode of generation of practices'; not, as in Foucault, what they produce, but what produces them." De Certeau, *The Practice*, 58. My study of pawning practice explores both, as well as what goes on in between—that is, pawning as process, negotiated and contested among pawning customers, credit providers, and state regulators.

1. Hocking the Private in Public

1. The October 1811 inventory for the pulpería at the corner of Aduana Vieja Bridge and Calle San Felipe de Jesús in downtown Mexico City, which includes the pawned-goods list, is found in merchant guild records at the AGN. The inventory was taken at the request of the store's creditors, Don Domingo Ortiz and Doña Juana Miranda. AGN, Consulado, vol. 67, exp. 10, fs. 129–32. The 1811 census records for neighboring Cuartels 9 and 11 are in AGN, Padrones, vols. 55 and 57 respectively. Doña María Gertrudis is listed in vol. 55, f. 32; Ygnacia Escorcia is listed in vol. 55, f. 80; María Rosales is listed in vol. 57, f. 153; and Ygnacia Ruiz is listed in vol. 57, f. 154. In archival documents the use of diacritical marks, especially in first and last names, is inconsistent. I have modernized accentuation throughout the text, except where quoting directly.

2. Jorge Silva Riquer, "Precios y mercancías menudas en las pulperías de la ciudad de México, 1784–1794," in *Cincuenta años de historia de México: En el cincuentenario del Centro de Estudios Historicos*, vol. 1, coord. Alicia Hernández Chávez and Manuel Miño Grijalva, 407 (México: El Colegio de México, 1991).

3. On honor in Mexico see Stern, *Secret History*, 13–16, 301–2; Martin, *Governance and Society*, 123–83; Arrom, *Women*; and Robert McCaa, "Calidad, Class and Marriage in Colonial Mexico: The Case of Parral, 1778–1790," *Hispanic American Historical Review* 64, no. 3 (August 1984): 477–501. For Latin American colonial settings, see Twinam, *Public Lives*; Martínez-Adlier, *Marriage, Class and Colour*; Susan M. Socolow, "Women and Crime: Buenos Aires, 1757–97," *Journal of Latin American Studies* 12, no. 1 (May 1980): 39–45; and Johnson and Lipsett-Rivera, *Faces of Honor*, which includes three articles on Mexico. For the relationship of honor to patriarchy and liberalism, see Chambers, *From Subjects to Citizens*.

4. "Ordenanzas para el regimen, y goveirno de los tenderos y tiendas de pulpería, dadas por la muy noble, leal, insigne, e imperial Ciudad de Mexico, cabeza de los reynos, y provincias de esta Nueva-España," December 3, 1758, reproduced in Miguel L. Muñoz, *Tlacos y pilones: La moneda del pueblo de México* (México: Fomento Cultural Banamex, A.C., 1976). For verbal assault on a Creole woman by a Creole man in Chihuahua in the 1750s, see Martin, *Governance and Society*, 168–69.

5. The law only stated that whatever the fee, it had to be noted on the pawn ticket. BN, Mexico City. Colección Especial, Manuscript no. 1320, "Reglamento para el gobierno y dirección de las tiendas de pulpería," Febrero 1810; AGN, Bandos, vol. 7, exp. 51, f. 188. This safety-valve function of the pawning process also has been noted for the English context. Tebbutt, *Making Ends Meet*, 116. A comparative study of pulperos in different Latin American settings argues that the obligation to accept pawns was unique to Mexican businesses. Kinsbruner, *Petty Capitalism*.

6. The specific situation involves gendering the legal profession: "it is neither proper nor honorable for a women to assume masculine duties, mingling publicly with men in order to argue cases for others"; Partida 3, Title 6, Article 3, cited in Arrom, *Women*, 61.

7. "Reglamento para . . . las tiendas de pulpería," 1810, Article 18.

8. J. A. P., "Dolores del parto" (México: Oficina de D. J. M. Benavente y Socios, 1820), 2.

9. The birth metaphor continues in a second pamphlet defending collateral lenders but with a more negative connotation. Pawning transactions are "little infants that are born every day, breeding like mice" and "abortions." A. S., "Defensa de los tenderos" (México: Oficina de D. J. M. Benavente y Sócios, 1820), 4, 6.

10. For the institutional history of the Monte de Piedad, see Couturier, "Philanthropic Activities"; Edith Boorstein Couturier, *The Silver King: The Remarkable Life of the Count of Regla in Colonial Mexico* (Albuquerque: University of New Mexico Press, 2003), 128, 130, 137, 143–47; Cabrera Siles and Escandón, *Historia del Nacional Monte de Piedad*; and Marie Francois, "When Pawnshops Talk: Popular Credit and Material Culture in Mexico City, 1775–1916" (PhD diss., University of Arizona, 1998), chap. 3. For discussion of the Monte de Piedad as part of a safety net that mitigated urban unrest, see Michael Scardaville, "(Habsburg) Law and (Bourbon) Order: State Authority, Popular Unrest, and the Criminal Justice System in Bourbon Mexico City," *The Americas* 50, no. 4 (April 1994): 501–25. While this argument would have more weight if the colonial Monte de Piedad catered to the poor, which it did not (though the corner stores did), one might consider the extent to which dissatisfaction with colonial governance among middle groups and even elites was mitigated by privileged access to inexpensive collateral credit.

11. For the Bando establishing the Monte de Piedad, see AGN, Bandos, vol. 9, exp. 4, f. 6. For the statutes see AGN, Bandos, vol. 10, exp. 35, fs. 122–289.

12. AHNMP, Libros de Empeños, 1802.

13. The macro-level political and economic restructuring that took place throughout Spanish colonies in the eighteenth century has been well studied by historians, but only recently have they investigated cultural and more micro-level political-economy issues. For the social impact of Bourbon reforms in Mexico, see Patricia Seed, *To Love, Honor, and Obey in Colonial Mexico: Conflicts over Marriage Choice, 1574–1821* (Stanford: Stanford University Press, 1988); Arrom, *Women* and *Containing the Poor*; and Juan Pedro Viqueira Alba, *Propriety and Permissiveness in Bourbon Mexico*, trans. Sonya Lipsett Rivera and Sergio Rivera Ayala (Wilmington DE: Scholarly Resources, 1997). For Peru see Chambers, *From Subjects to Citizens*. For elite gender and family relations throughout Bourbon Spanish America, see Twinam, *Public Lives*.

14. Bernard E. Bobb, *The Viceregency of Antonio María Bucareli in New Spain, 1771–1779* (Austin: University of Texas Press, 1962), 14–15; Virginia Guedea, "Ignacio Adalid, un equilibrista novohispano," in *Patterns of Contention in Mexican History*, ed. Jaime Rodríguez O. (Wilmington DE: Scholarly Resources, 1992), 77. The Spanish Constitution of 1812 introduced republican government and division of powers to empire and was the model for the Mexican Constitution in 1824. Linda Arnold, "La administración, la adjudicación y la política en la rama judicial en México, 1825 a 1835," in *Memoria del IV Congreso de Historia del Derecho Mexicano (1986)*, coord. Beatriz Bernal (México: UNAM, 1988), 1:60.

15. For the decline of institutions for seclusion of women, or "casas de recogimientos," and legal distinctions between "decent" and "loose" women, see Arrom, *Women*, 47 and 55. For patriarchal subjection of women, children, and servants to male household heads and the link between honor and female sexuality, see Martin, *Governance and Society*, 151–60. See also

Lee M. Penyak, "Safe Harbors and Compulsory Custody: *Casas de Depósito* in Mexico, 1750–1865," *Hispanic American Historical Review* 79, no. 1 (1999): 83–99.

16. This decree required that parents give permission for "white" children to marry, an idea that challenged the Catholic ideal concerning freedom to choose one's spouse. The crown sought to counter rising incidence of "unequal" marriages, or marriages that crossed ethnic, class, and status groups, throughout Spanish American colonies in the late colonial period. The permission requirement was extended in 1807 to include mixed-race children. Susan M. Socolow, "Acceptable Partners: Marriage Choice in Colonial Argentina, 1778–1810," in *Sexuality and Marriage in Colonial Latin America*, ed. Asunción Lavrin, 209–51 (Lincoln: University of Nebraska Press, 1989); Arrom, *Women*, 69, 77; Seed, *Love, Honor, and Obey*.

17. Throughout colonial Latin America the state allowed a few hundred spinster mothers, almost-married mothers, or married women who had children fathered by men other than husbands to legitimize their adult children. Twinam, *Public Lives*, 70–71. On the pension system for white widows, see Chandler, *Social Assistance*; Gary M. Miller, "Bourbon Social Engineering: Women and Conditions of Marriage in Eighteenth-Century Venezuela," *The Americas* 46, no. 3 (1990): 261–90; and Ann S. Blum, "Public Welfare and Child Circulation, Mexico City, 1877 to 1925," *Journal of Family History* 23, no. 3 (July 1998): 240–71.

18. For the Hapsburg state's inability to "protect" rural indigenous women in sixteenth- and seventeenth-century Peru, see Premo, "From the Pockets of Women."

19. Indian girls at the nuns' school La Enseñanza Nueva learned only basic literacy and concentrated on housekeeping skills such as washing and ironing. By the 1790s new waves of migration from the countryside prompted the city to establish public schools and encouraged charitable institutions to provide education to arriving youth, with three thousand girls enrolled by 1802. See Arrom, *Women*, 17; See also Sonya Lipsett-Rivera, "Bourbons and Mothers: The Mother of All Papers," paper presented to Rocky Mountain Council on Latin American Studies, 1998.

20. By 1795 over three thousand women represented 45 percent of the workforce. In 1809 almost four thousand women made up 71 percent of the workforce. Deans-Smith, *Bureaucrats, Planters, and Workers*, 13, 176, 212. Workers in royal enterprises—such as the tobacco factory and the Casa de Moneda—had to conform to a dress code to keep their jobs. For women a white muslin skirt, sleeveless hemp jacket, wool rebozo, socks, and shoes were required; for men, white muslin underpants, blue wool trousers, shirt, wool *chupa* (waistcoat), cape of domestic wool, hat, socks, and shoes. Norman Martin, "La desnudez en la Nueva España del siglo XVIII," *Anuario de Estudios Americanos* 29 (1972): 261–94.

21. A royal decree in 1784 that abolished guild restrictions against women in Spain, on which Viceroy de Anzana drew in his 1798 decision in the colony, argued that barring women on the one hand stifled production and on the other discouraged men from more robust work in "Agriculture, Arms, and the Marine" as they worked at tasks better suited to women. Arrom, *Women*, 28.

22. Jorge González Angulo, "Los gremios de artesanos y la estructura urbana," in *Ciudad de Mexico: Ensayo de construcción de una historia*, ed. A. Moreno Toscano, 30–36 (México: INAH, 1978).

23. Ana Lidia García Peña, "El impacto popular de las reformas fiscales borbónicas en la Ciudad de México (1780–1820)," in Marichal and Marino, *De colonia a nación*, 85–113. See also Marcella M. Litle, "Sales Taxes and Internal Commerce in Bourbon Mexico, 1754–1821," (PhD diss., Duke University, 1985).

24. See Richard Garner, "Price Trends in Eighteenth Century Mexico," *Hispanic American Historical Review* 65, no. 2 (1985): 279–326; and Enrique Florescano, *Precios de maiz y crisis agrícolas en México, 1708–1810: Ensayo sobre el movimiento de los precios y sus consecuencias económicas y sociales* (México: El Colegio de México, 1969).

25. The colonial monetary system was based on an octavate system, with eight reales equaling one peso. After Independence the system remained the same until 1861, when the metric decimal system was adopted, with ten centavos equaling one peso. Diego G. López Rosado, *Curso de historia económica de México* (México: Universidad Nacional Autónoma de México, 1963), 243. For wage discussions see Scardaville, "Crime and the Urban Poor," 67–68. Laborers and artisans employed full time in private workshops or royal enterprises in 1791 earned between sixty and three hundred pesos annually. García Peña, "El impacto," 97; Anna, *Fall*, 23–24.

26. Many others simply continued on with what they could manage, in effect evading the law. Martin, "La desnudez."

27. Flora Salazar, "Los sirvientes domésticos," in Toscano, *Ciudad de México*, 124–32; María Gayón Córdova, *Condiciones de vida y de trabajo en la ciudad de México en el siglo XIX* (México: Instituto Nacional de Antropologia e Historia, 1988), 58.

28. This large "catch-all" category of pawned goods is not included in the transaction database, because there is no information available on the individual pawning client, the pawned good, or the exact amount loaned. Appendix 1, table G, approximates the number of pawned goods that fit this category from inventories used for this book.

29. "Reglamento para . . . las tiendas de pulpería," 1810, Article 12; J. A. P., "Dolores del parto," 3.

30. Torcuato S. di Tella, *National Popular Politics in Early Independent Mexico: 1820–1847* (Albuquerque: University of New Mexico Press, 1996), 6. For examples and analysis of client nicknames, most associated with occupations and a few related to appearance (i.e., "morena") or status (i.e., "Don"), see Marie Francois, "*Prendas* and *Pulperías*: The Fabric of the Neighborhood Credit Business in Mexico City, 1780s–1830s," *Estudios de Historia Novohispana*, 20 (1999): 67–110. See appendix 1, table G, for relative worth of pawned goods in corner stores.

31. García Peña, "El impacto," 103.

32. Spanish subjects in the metropole had more arenas for collateral credit in the late eighteenth century. In addition to Montes de Piedad, *cofradías* (religious brotherhoods) also provided pawning services. New Spain had fewer *cofradías*, and none seem to have provided pawning services.

33. The Montepíos provided pensions to only two hundred individuals (paid out four times a year), the Hospicio de Pobres housed and fed about two hundred people at a time, and the tobacco factory employed from five thousand to nine thousand working-class people between 1771 and 1809. See Chandler, *Social Assistance*; Arrom, *Containing the Poor*; and Deans-Smith, *Bureaucrats, Planters, and Workers*. Even institutions aimed at poorer city residents were part of the safety net for the better off. Arrom argues that despite the institution's stated purpose of rehabilitating the worthy poor and disciplining vagrants, middle-class Creoles made use of the Poor House for their own family purposes in response to declining economic positions.

34. I interpret Bucareli's use of "naturales" as refering to Spaniards "native" to New Spain—that is, Creoles—and not the indigenous population, which was small in the city and certainly not prominent among those with sufficient collateral to secure loans of up to one

thousand pesos. Manuel Romero de Terreros, *El Conde de Regla: Creso de la Nueva España* (México: Ediciones Xochitl, 1943), 123–25.

35. For statutes of the Madrid Monte de Piedad, see Lopez Yepes, *Historia de Los Montes*, vol. 2, 160–80. The loan maximum of one hundred *doblones* is in Statute 16.

36. Bureaucrats observing but not taking part in daily operations of the institution recognized that the Monte clientele included more than the poor. A 1789 report from the Real Tribunal de Cuentas to the Real Hacienda discussing business methods characterized clients as "every class of women coming for the favor" of a loan. Report dated October 23, 1789, AGN, Montepío, vol. 17, exp. 13, f. 267.

37. AGN, Montepío, vol. 17, exp. 13, fs. 243, 254, 281v, 345. Whether clientele were poor or better-off, they did not always act with decorum. Shortly after the Monte opened, customers' behavior was so scandalous while they waited in line that men were separated from women and stocks were put in to punish those guilty of misconduct such as insulting employees. Cabrera Siles and Escandón, *Historia*, 231; Dario, *El Nacional Monte de Piedad*, 13.

38. Anna, *Fall*, 19; Di Tella, *National Popular Politics*, 5.

39. For salary tables of colonial governmental departments from 1771, 1781, 1794, and 1825, see Arnold, *Bureaucracy and Bureaucrats*, 131–49; for deductions from salaries to support war efforts, see 21, 63–65, 100.

40. Josefina Zoraida Vázquez and Pilar Gonzalbo Aizpuru, *Guía de protocolos: Archivo General de Notarías de la Ciudad de México, año de 1839* (México: El Colegio de México, 1987), 370.

41. Official salaries were paid quarterly throughout the year. On the richest Creole families maintaining their status through economic and social strategies, see John K. Kicza, "The Great Families of Mexico: Elite Maintenance and Business Practices in Late Colonial Mexico City," *Hispanic American Historical Review* 62, no. 3 (1982): 429–57.

42. Chandler, *Social Assistance*, 165.

43. AHNMP, Libros de Empeños, Contaduria, caja 1, vol. 2, f. 166v, 1802.

44. Julia Tuñon, ed., *El álbum de la mujer: Antología ilustrada de las mexicanas* (México: INAH, 1991), 3:214.

45. Marie Francois, "Cloth and Silver: Pawning and Material Life in Mexico City at the Turn of the Nineteenth Century," *The Americas* 60, no. 3 (January 2004): 325–62.

46. José Joaquín Fernández de Lizardi, *Don Catrín de la Fachenda y Noches tristes y día alegre* (1832l; repr., México: Editorial Porrúa, 1978), 87.

47. Storekeepers' petition quoted in Aida Castilleja, "Asignación del espacio urbano: El gremio de los panaderos, 1770–1793," in Toscano, *Ciudad de México*, 42–43.

48. AGN, Bandos, vol. 20, exp. 100, f. 209.

49. Rebecca Haidt, "A Well-Dressed Woman Who Will Not Work: Petimetras, Economics, and Eighteenth-Century Fashion Plates," *Revista Canadiense de Estudios Hispánicos* 28, no. 1 (Autumn 2003): 137–57, and "Luxury, Consumption and Desire: Theorizing the Petimetra," *Arizona Journal of Hispanic Cultural Studies* 3 (1999): 33–50. On this antifashion discourse in New Spain, see Jean Franco, "Women, Fashion and the Moralists in Early Nineteenth-Century Mexico," in *Homenaje a Ana María Barenechea*, ed. Lía Schwartz Lerner and Isaías Lerner, 421–30 (Madrid: Editorial Castalia, 1984).

50. Torcuato S. di Tella, "The Dangerous Classes in Early Nineteenth Century Mexico," *Journal of Latin American Studies* 5, no. 1 (1973): 79–105.

51. AGN, Gobernación, leg. 2187(1), exp. 1, no. 7, fs. 3–5; exp. 1, no. 4; AGN, Montepios, vol. 17, ex. 13, f. 293v.

52. In Spain a critique of overly consumptive women sometimes included pawning in order to purchase attire. Here, female pawning activity was cast as vice instead of virtuous womanly duty. Haidt, "Luxury, Consumption," 43, 45.

53. Viceroy Revillagigedo (Juan Vicente de Güemes Pacheco y Padilla, second Count Revillagigedo) also highlighted persistent pawning practices of vice-driven men in instructions to his successor in 1794. AGN, Bandos, vol. 11, exp. 101, f. 297; Shaw, "Poverty and Politics," 131.

54. Scardaville, "Crime and the Urban Poor," 71.

55. The distinction in welfare policy between deserving and undeserving poor is persistent. See Arrom, *Containing the Poor*; and Karin Alejandra Rosemblatt, "Charity, Rights, and Entitlement: Gender, Labor, and Welfare in Early Twentieth-Century Chile," *Hispanic American Historical Review* 81, no. 2–4 (2001): 555–86. On drinking vices See William Taylor, *Drinking, Homicide and Rebellion in Colonial Mexican Villages* (Stanford: Stanford University Press, 1979); John E. Kicza, "The Pulque Trade of Late Colonial Mexico," *The Americas* 37, no. 2 (1980): 193–221; and Michael C. Scardaville, "Alcohol Abuse and Tavern Reform in Late Colonial Mexico," *Hispanic American Historical Review* 60, no. 4 (1980): 643–71.

56. AGN, Padrones, vol. 52, f. 283.

57. Quote from Martin, "La desnudez," 262; Shaw, "Poverty and Politics," 131; Scardaville, "Crime and the Urban Poor," 157.

58. José Joaquín Fernández de Lizardi, *El periquillo sarniento* (1816; repr., México: Editorial Porrúa, 1987), 198, 201, 214, 236, 276, 278, 282, 291, 297.

59. AGN, Criminal, vol. 87, exp. 10, fs. 275–80. Scardaville reports an instance in 1801 of complicated but no doubt common reasoning rooted in poverty: "Juan Baptista, an unemployed coachman, pawned some personal belongings for betting money in the hopes of winning needed money for his starving family. Why use the loan money for food . . . when, with the help of luck, he could convert it into large sums of cash?" Scardaville, "Crime and the Urban Poor," 99.

60. For the 1781 order see AGN, Bandos, vol. 11, exp. 101, f. 297.

61. Scholarship has shown how this self-interest of Creole statesmen or their privileging of concern for their peers manifested itself in policy at the local and later the national level. González Angulo argues that when the colonial cabildo of Mexico City fixed maximum prices for guild products, it was "trying without doubt to protect the interests of these social groups that were dominant in colonial society and that came face to face with artisans as consumers." Guedea finds that many Creoles with position and influence "promoted their own interests" working within the colonial system of governance, and did so as well within movements for independence in the early nineteenth century. According to Archer, within urban cabildos at the end of the colonial period, Creoles sought "to protect their political powers." For Tenenbaum, the first federalist Constitution in 1824 appeased the wealthy by not taxing elites to support the republic, instead counting on taxes from foreign trade. González Angulo, "Los gremios," 31; Guedea, "Ignacio Adalid," 71–96; Christopher I. Archer, "What Goes Around Comes Around: Political Change and Continuity in Mexico, 1750–1850," in *Mexico in the Age of Democratic Revolutions, 1750–1850*, ed. Jaime Rodríguez O., 267 (Boulder: Lynne Rienner, 1994); Barbara A. Tenenbaum, "They Went Thataway": The Evolution of the Pronunciamiento, 1821–1856," in Rodríguez, *Patterns of Contention in Mexican History*, 190.

62. The city got whiter as the eighteenth century came to a close. In 1790, 50 percent were Spaniards, 25 percent castas, and 25 percent Indians. By 1811, 57 percent were Spaniards, 27

percent castas, and 11 percent Indians. Herbert J. Klein, "Demographic Structure," 66–94. See also Castelman, "Social Climbers."

63. Kuznesof, "Gender Ideology."

64. I sampled one household from each of 121 pages of the volume that constitutes the census for Cuartel 9 and then filled in all households on one side of the following streets in the southern portion of the cuartel: San Felipe de Jesús (the southern perimeter), Puente de Aduana (the southwestern perimeter), Puente de Jesús, and Venero. Mine is not a completely random sample of the more than three thousand residents of this cuartel. Instead, I attempted to get a sense of who lived next to whom. The sample thus captures casas de vecindades, divided into dwellings for multiple households of artisans, alongside large households in separate houses where European merchants lived with their Creole wives, children, and servants. As comparison of statistical tables shows, this cuartel was whiter than the population overall, which was true generally for central neighborhoods, with outlying districts having larger Indian populations. But by other measures this sample is fairly representative of Cuartel 9 and of the city's population generally. The sample population is 53 percent women, compared to 53 percent and 57 percent respectively for Cuartel 9 as a whole and for the city, while 33 percent of the households in the sample were headed by women, compared to 32 percent for the city overall in 1811. See appendix 3, table C.

65. Arrom, *Women*, 78–81; Gonzalbo Aizpuru, *Las mujeres*, 114.

66. Stern, *Secret History*, 255–56; Anne Staples, "Policia y Buen Gobierno: Municipal Efforts to Regulate Public Behavior, 1821–1857," in Beezley, Martin, and French, *Rituals of Rule*, 116. Twinam notes that especially in Mexico, "unmarried women formed significant social groupings within colonial cities," including elite women who were secretly mothers, widows, and nonelites. Twinam, *Public Lives*, 81.

67. Arrom, *Women*, 140. Arrom also found the same likelihood that widows would be taken in by a relative or friend in her sample of the 1811 census.

68. Quoted in Arrom, *Women*, 139.

69. Quoted in Arrom, *Women*, 201, see also 55, 185–86; John E. Kizca, "La mujer y la vida comercial en la ciudad de México a finales de la colonia," A *"Analisis Histórico y Sociedad Mexicana) Revista de la División de Ciencias Sociales y Humanidades* UAM-A 2 (1981): 39–59. On the vagaries of widowhood see Robert McCaa, "La viuda viva del México Borbónico: Sus voces, variedades y vejaciones," in *Familias novohispanas: Siglos XVI al XIX*, ed. Pilar Gonzalbo Aizpuru, 299–324 (México: El Colegio de México, 1991).

70. Arrom, *Women*, 161.

71. Prostitutes are invisible in census data. The Bourbon state prosecuted women for selling sex in Mexico City. Gonzalez and her housemates returned to court at least once for suspicion of prostitution. AGN, Criminal, vol. 89, exp. 1, fs. 14–19.

72. Gonzalbo Aizpuru, *Las mujeres*, 125.

73. Kicza, "La mujer," 44–45, 55–57; Arrom, *Women*, 168–71, 174, 176.

74. Stern notes that in the city, "age, ethnicity, and property could more easily crosscut rank by gender" and men could be dominated by their wives. Stern, *Secret History*, 255–57, quote on 257. See also Gonzalbo Aizpuru, *Las mujeres*, 206–7; Arrom, *Women*, 180.

75. AGN, Padrones, vol. 53, fs. 13, 14, and 18; vol. 54, f. 241.

76. AGN, Padrones, vol. 55, fs. 6, 8, 32. In Arrom's 1811 sample, *The Women*, 75 percent of servants were women.

77. Miller, "Bourbon Social Engineering," 287–88.

78. On the role of clothing, other cloth goods, and silver in material culture in Mexico City from the 1770s to 1830s and the prevalence of cloth and silver in pawning transactions, see Francois, "Cloth and Silver."

79. See Laura Fair, "Dressing Up: Clothing, Class and Gender in Post-Abolition Zanzibar," *Journal of African History* 39, no. 1 (1998): 63–94.

80. Shaw, "Poverty and Politics," 134.

81. In the sample from Monte de Piedad ledgers for 1802, less than 1 percent of goods pawned went unredeemed and sold at auction. The low transaction costs that had to be paid when loans were repaid no doubt account to some extent for this high redemption rate. AHNMP, Contaduria, Empeños en Contaduria, caja 1, vols. 1–3; caja 2, vols. 4–6; caja 3, vols. 7–9, caja 4, vols. 10–12. For discussion of "the money invested in women's jewelry by the elite" in colonial and republican Peru and "the prominence of silver tablewares in colonial inventories of elite houses due to their great economic value, and the fact that they were portable and could be priced accurately on weight," see Ross W. Jaimeson, "Doña Julia and Her Two Houses," in Delle, Mrozowski, and Paynter, *Lines That Divide*, 157–58. For a comparative perspective on clothing as investment in the same period, see Stana Nedadic, "Middle-Rank Consumers and Domestic Culture in Edinburgh and Glasgow, 1720–1840," *Past and Present* 145 (1994): 122–54.

82. I thank an anonymous reviewer of my article in *The Americas* for this observation about the impact of repeated high-interest lending on the same item, or "petty decapitalization." See chapter 2 for discussion of the changes in interest rates.

83. The database used for this chapter consists of 3,135 transactions for which pawned item and loan value are known, with 1,059 transactions at the Monte de Piedad in the first quarter of 1802, 7 transactions at the Monte from archival sources for 1830, and 2,069 transactions from thirty-three retail pawnshop inventories between 1787 and 1825. See appendix 1, table A, for a breakdown of cloth and noncloth goods in each pawnshop's inventory. See appendix 1, table B, for a more detailed breakdown of pawned goods in this block of data according to category of goods and client gender. The 1802 Monte transactions list loan value and sale value for the less than 1 percent of goods that were sold.

84. Half the pawned goods in the database from private pawning arenas and the Monte de Piedad are articles of clothing. Of the Monte sample for January–March 1802, 15 percent of transactions involved bundles of goods that included articles of cloth or clothing, but because the value for each good in the bundle is not listed individually, bundled goods are not counted in this tally.

85. A third of petticoats in pulperías have no descriptions listed, but for those that do, *indianilla* is again the great favorite, followed by *angaripola* (stamped linen), *cambaya* (Madras style), *carmin* (crimson colored), *chapaneco*, *pintado* (multicolored), and silk.

86. The exact degree is difficult to determine, because so many articles of clothing might be worn by either sex and because of the practice of bundling multiple items together as one collateral package. Appendix 1, table B, gives a breakdown of goods by category, with each loan transaction counted only once, though there may have been more than one good held as collateral. Hence enaguas are underrepresented in this table, because often at the Monte two petticoats were pawned in one transaction. Other enaguas that are not captured by these totals are those that were bundled with other garments, cloth, jewelry, or tools, listed in appendix 1, table A, as "mixed."

87. Sonya Lipsett-Rivera, "Clothes in Late-Colonial Mexico: A Most Anxious Topic," paper presented to Rocky Mountain Council on Latin American Studies, Santa Fe, February 1996, 13.

88. Quotes from Gonzalbo Aizpuru, "Ajuar doméstico," 128–29, 135; see also Tuñon, *El album*, 3:30–31, 136. In her study of probate inventories, Lorna Weatherill argues that for eighteenth-century England, "women were traditionally responsible for the household linen, and it is recorded more often in their inventories." Weatherill, "Meaning," 211.

89. Gonzalbo Aizpuru, "Ajuar doméstico," 136. For wealthy households "the reinvestment of profits in luxury goods and not in production permitted keeping a large number of servants." Salazar, "Los sirvientes domésticos," 126. Weatherill notes the importance of meals as social events and the fact that table-service goods in eighteenth-century English households were overwhelmingly pewter and earthenware (stoneware and porcelain) and not silver. Weatherill, "Meaning," 212–16. See also Vickery, "Women and the World of Goods," 285. On the importance of table service to middle-class respectability in nineteenth-century New York, see Wall, "Family Meals," 109–41.

90. Independence heroine Doña Leona Vicario paid 420 pesos to silversmith Don Mariano de la Torre in January 1808 for two dozen spoons, two dozen forks, one dozen knives, one *bracerito* (small grill), three candleholders, a salt shaker, a vinegar bottle, and two crystal decanters. "Cuenta de mi sobrina Da. María Leona Martin Vicario, desde el dia de la muerte de su madre Da. Camila Fernandez de San Salvador acaecida la noche del 9 de Septiembre de 1807," in *Documentos historicos mexicanos*, vol. 5, ed. Genaro García, 112–13 (México: Instituto Nacional de Estudios Históricos de la Revolución Mexicana, 1985).

91. AHNMP, Libros de Empeños, 1802, caja 1, vol. 1, f. 14. There is a notation that the silver was appraised at 110 pesos, meaning that the loan represented two-thirds the value of the good, which follows Monte de Piedad statutes.

92. AHNMP, Libros de Empeños, 1802, caja 1, vol. 1, f. 20.

93. Ley LXV Recopilación de las Indias, lib. IX, title XLVI, in Juan N. Rodríguez de San Miguel, *Pandectas hispano-mexicanas* (México: Universidad Nacional Autónoma de México, 1980), 2:365.

94. Silva Riquer, "Precios y mercancías," 410–12.

95. AGN, Judicial, vol. 58, exp. 10, fs. 148–49; Archivo Histórico de la Ciudad de México, Juzgados Criminales, vol. 3, exp. 3.

96. Couturier, "Philanthropic Activities," 26. Goods stolen from one pawning establishment might turn up in another, including the Monte de Piedad. Repawning goods may have been what Don Ramón Garrido planned to do before he was arrested in March 1787 for stealing goods from the pawnshop that he ran for Don Cristóval Rodríguez. AGN, Consulado, vol. 56, exp. 1, fs. 5–9v. For other examples, see AGN, Criminal, vol. 87, exp. 2, fs. 60–69v; Fernández de Lizardi, *El periquillo sarniento*, 197. For further discussion and examples of pawning stolen goods, see Francois, "Cloth and Silver," 348–49.

97. Among pawned goods in several corner stores from 1802 to 1818 were metalworker's tools such as iron pincers, gilders, anvils, and silver-leaf scissors; the fuses and parchments of fireworks manufacture; chair arms, hammers, drills, and picks of carpenters; bolts of lace, tailor's scissors, skeins of thread, and thimbles of seamstresses and tailors; and combs and shuttles of weavers. For fuller discussion of pawned work tools, see Francois, "Cloth and Silver," and "When Pawnshops Talk," chap. 6.

98. Again, this is likely an underestimation of female pawning, as the unknown category is sizable. Women in the retail-pawning database were less likely to pawn at general stores (52 percent) and wine shops (26 percent). Francois, "*Prendas* and *Pulperías*," 81; see 78–84 for discussion of gender identification through names and nicknames.

99. For Eusavia and La Robago, see Francois, "Cloth and Silver," 332–36. For La Robago and other repeat customers, see Francois, "*Prendas* and *Pulperías*," 84–88.

100. Tuñon, *El album*, 3:135.

101. CONDUMEX, Fondo CDLV-2, 1796.

102. Observers noted a similar high level of material consumption, especially extravagant clothing styles, in Lima in the eighteenth century. Jorge Juan and Antonio de Ulloa, *Voyage to South America* (London: L. Davis and C. Reymers, 1758), 2:54–65. Another way to interpret this evidence, though there is little to directly support it, is that people used collateral goods to fund social climbing through the use of attire and accessories commensurate with the next level.

103. CONDUMEX, Fondo CDLV-2, 1796; AHNMP, Contaduria, Empeños en Contaduria, 1802; AGN, Montepío, vol. 27, exp. 12; AGN, Montepío, vol. 28, exp. 2. See appendix 2, table E, for average loans by year at the Monte de Piedad.

104. The Monte de Piedad sample consists of 1,057 transactions taken from ledger books for January, February, and March of 1802, compiled with data from every fifth page of the ledgers. The total number of transactions for those three months from which the sample is taken was 7,682. AHNMP, Contaduria, Empeños en Contaduria, caja 1, vols. 1–3. For a table breaking down repeat customers at the Monte, see Francois, "Cloth and Silver," 340.

105. For a table laying out Mariana Ruiz's twenty-six transactions and discussion of this client, see Francois, "Cloth and Silver," 339–42.

106. In the database the value of fewer jewels pawned by men was substantially higher than the value of more numerous jewels pawned by women, especially strings of pearls. For a fuller discussion and tables breaking down pawned jewelry by type, loan amount, and gender, see Francois, "Cloth and Silver."

107. Chandler, *Social Assistance*, 108. Creole widows are among the clients of the Monte de Piedad. For three widows cross-referenced in Monte ledgers and census manuscripts, see Francois, "Cloth and Silver," 343.

108. Arrom, *Women*, 199–201.

2. Collateral Lending

1. J. A. P., "Dolores del parto," 2. Pamphlet literature proliferated in 1820, when the Spanish Constitution of 1812, which called for a free press, was reinstated.

2. A. S., "Defensa de los tenderos," 1.

3. Those with their pawning business located in their homes or lending over pledges informally, and therefore beyond oversight of the Consulado or Gobernación, are not included in this study.

4. On pulperías and pawning beyond the urban realm, see Stein, "Tending the Store"; and Martin, *Governance and Society*, 135–39.

5. The fifteenth-century Ordenanzas de Bilbao were incorporated into book nine, title four of the *Novísima Recopilación*. These laws were superseded by Ordenanzas del Consulado de Mégico in 1636, 1772, and 1816. Rodríguez, *Pandectas hispano-mexicanas*, 2:353–60. For a review of Spanish laws regarding retail commerce and ownership and transfer of goods and governance, see Francois, "*Prendas* and *Pulperías*," 71–74.

6. Warren, *Vagrants and Citizens*, 34–55. The municipal council had been a center of elite Creole power, Creole families having purchased seats long ago. The Bourbon reforms brought appointed peninsulars to the council, as the crown attempted to check Creole elite

control. In elections under the Constitution of 1812, loyalists were largely defeated and Creoles retained control of the council.

7. "Ordenanzas de tenderos, 1757," in *Ordenanzas de gremios de la Nueva España*, comp. Francisco del Barrio Lorenzot (México: n.p., 1920); Kicza, *Colonial Entrepreneurs*, 51–55; "Decreto de 16 de Octubre de 1824," in Rodríguez, *Pandectas*, 2:366. After independence, governance in the city was complicated by overlapping jurisdictions created with the Federal District in 1824. See Rodríguez Kuri, "Política e institucionalidad: El ayuntamiento de México y la evolución del conflicto jurisdiccional, 1808–1850," in Hernández Franyuti, *La Ciudad*, 2:51–94; and Jorge Silva Riquer, "El abasto al mercado urbano de la Ciudad de México, 1830–1860," in Hernández Franyuti, *La Ciudad*, 1:68. Suffrage became increasingly limited in the 1830s as politicians played on class fears. See Warren, *Vagrants and Citizens*, 87–120.

8. In 1809 Viceroy Pedro Garibay republished a Bando from his predecessor Revillagigedo in 1791, which in turn reiterated a Bando from 1764 outlining responsibilities of notaries associated with the Consulado. Rodríguez, *Pandectas*, 2:369–70. Notaries were attended by a scribe and two witnesses, who were merchant guild members. Audits usually included an inventory of all goods, store equipment, and pawned goods as well as an accounting of all debts and credits.

9. Quote from AGN, Bandos, vol. 7, exp. 51, f. 188; Article 18, "Reglamento para . . . las tiendas de pulpería," Febrero 1810.

10. The state's efforts to control commercial space went beyond pulperías. Wine retailers were chided in 1822 for not getting the counter ready immediately after opening doors, which the law called for. Vinateros were to be sure that their counter was no more than three-quarters of a yard from the doorway, so that no one other than the customer would fit inside, and that the counter was secured, so that no one but employees got behind it. Restricting the physical space in which business transactions occurred also meant that no one could congregate with others to drink his or her purchases. Enough small businessmen were not complying with the law, refusing to do business in this very structured way, that the city council discussed it. AHCM, Actas de Cabildo, vol. 140-A, f. 230v.

11. Attempts at altering popular practices of selling and drinking alcoholic beverages were unsuccessful, as tavern owners selling pulque continued to circumvent the law by accepting pawns, women continued to set up illegal bars, and the populace continued to drink as often as and wherever they wanted. From the colonial period there were contradictions in governance of the pulque trade. The state was concerned with drinking by lower classes and talked about it in terms of vice and illicit activity, yet elites with pulque haciendas and pulquerías profited from the trade, so supply of the intoxicant was never threatened or made illegal. In 1816 new pulque stands were allowed in central plazas. Those already holding licenses complained that these plazas were disorderly. During the Independence era, some Creole elites, such as Don Ignacio Adalid y Gómez, held multiple pulquerías and haciendas. In September 1821, in the midst of Independence turmoil, police reported that "suddenly" there had been an increase in the number of pulque and *tepache* (alcoholic pineapple beverege) outlets, along with tables for game playing and a disturbing increase of men and women mixing together. The city council called for the enforcement of an 1813 Bando prohibiting the sale of pulque outside specified outlets. Regulations for *casillas* promulgated by Emperor Iturbide in October 1822 included a ban on pawning as well as the obligation of pulqueros to obstruct the view through the door from the street; prohibition of music, dancing, or game playing; and keeping the same hours that pulquerías had to keep. Pulqueros were also not to

mix pulque with noxious substances nor to let customers litter on sidewalks and streets contiguous to their taverns and *casillas*. AGN, Padrones, vol. 52, f. 283. AGN, Gobernación, no section, caja 31, exp. 6, no. 14. AHCM, Actas de Cabildo, vol. 140-A, fs. 186v–87. AGN, Gobernación, no section, caja 115, exp. 16, fs. 9–10, caja 140, exp. 5, f. 1; caja 345, exp. 1, f. 37. Scardaville, "Alcohol Abuse"; Di Tella, "Dangerous Classes," 96; Guedea, "Ignacio Adalid," 74; Francois, "*Prendas* and *Pulperías*," 77.

12. A large literature on popular defiance of social legislation from the late Bourbon era has shown that many in society had their own preferences and agendas in their daily lives. See Beezley, Martin, and French, *Rituals of Rule*.

13. AGN, Bandos, vol. 11, exp. 101, f. 297; AGN, Bandos, vol. 15, exp. 58, f. 162. For examples of broker noncompliance, see Francois, "*Prendas* and *Pulperías*," 74–75.

14. Tebbutt notes that in the early nineteenth century in England, certain goods were forbidden for pawning: military and naval equipment and clothing; military pay and pension papers; police clothing; rifles and pistols; property that belonged to the Guardians of the Poor; unfinished goods and washing entrusted to another person to wash, scour, iron, mend, or make up; savings bank books and goods from children or intoxicated pledgers. Tebbutt, *Making Ends Meet*, 72.

15. A 1790 decree (repeating earlier ones from 1762 and 1766) expressed the state's disgust with noncompliance in acceptance by businessmen of forbidden collateral goods in stores and bars. The viceroy reiterated the prohibition against buying, selling, trading, bartering, or receiving weapons, ammunition, and items pertaining to military uniforms and lamented that "far from complying with such just determinations, owners of *pulperías*, *vinaterías* and *pulquerías* repeatedly infringe the law." The decree went on to postulate consequences of traffic in these forbidden goods, such as soldiers who pawned said goods risking desertion for fear of punishment when they could not redeem the good in question in time. Brokers accepting military goods had to answer to military courts, turning over the good, losing the amount lent, and paying more than a fifty-peso fine for the first offense. Quote from AGN, Bandos, vol. 15, exp. 58, f. 162.

16. "Ordenanzas de tenderos," 1790. *Tlacos* were often made of wood or soap.

17. "Ordenanzas de tenderos," 1757; AGN, Bando, Viceroy Revillagigedo, 19 enero 1790; "Reglamento para . . . las tiendas de pulpería," 1810.

18. AGN, Bandos, vol. 7, exp. 51, f. 188.

19. The 1758 law set the pledge period at one year. A 1781 Bando changed the redemption period to six months, and the new Reglamento in 1810 ratified the change.

20. See CONDUMEX, Fondo CDLV-2, 1796, for an example of auction list for the Coutiño store. For details on *sobrantes* see "Ordenanzas de tenderos de pulpería," in Lorenzot, *Ordenanzas de gremios*, 167–73.

21. In New York City in the nineteenth and early twentieth centuries, "the pawnbrokers who were uninformed lost money because they could not tell a gem-fine stone from the mediocre or even imitations. When asked for a loan on a piece of jewelry set with colored stones they hesitated about giving the customer the benefit of the doubt. They would offer only what the mounting justified—and this was never much—plus a nominal amount for the jewels." Simpson and Simpson, *Hockshop*, 123.

22. A. S., "Defensa de los tenderos," 4–5. See also Beverly Lemire, "The Theft of Clothes and Popular Consumerism in Early Modern England," *Journal of Social History* 24, no. 2 (1990): 255–75.

23. This change was incorporated into the 1810 Reglamento. "Ordenanza," 1757; "Reglamento," 1810; Kinsbruner, *Petty Capitalism*, 26. Storekeepers also actively sought to shape retail policy of the national government. In response to an 1836 law calling for a license fee for merchants and artisans, retail merchants were among nearly four hundred merchants and artisans who published a pamphlet complaining of onerous charges at a time of declining profits for "the humble shops of the working poor and the ruined workshops of unhappy artisans." *Exposición dirigida al gobierno supremo de la República, por los comerciantes de México, reclamando la observancia de la ley de 7 de julio de 1836* (México: Ignacio Cumplido, 1837).

24. Kicza, *Colonial Entrepreneurs*, 3–4.

25. While the ethnicity of storekeepers is not clear from inventories or retail censuses, the 1811 residential census listed Manuel Trejo, a mestizo boarder in the home of merchant Don Vicente Montes de Oca, as a *comerciante*, though at what level he operated or how many others were like him is unknown. AGN, Padrones, vol. 55, f. 8.

26. We cannot know how many merchants in the 1811 sample were engaged in retail (only vinateros were named specifically, and not uniformly), though cross-referencing them with retail censuses identifies some as owners of corner and general stores. The 1790 census listed 1,502 "comerciantes," a catchall category that would have included large import-export merchants, wholesalers in the domestic market, itinerant traders moving back and forth between city and small towns, and the variety of retail-business people discussed in this chapter. Kicza, *Colonial Entrepreneurs*, 50 and passim.

27. A. S., "Defensa de tenderos," 7.

28. Garrido is found in AGN, Padrones, vol 57, f. 60; Rivera and Montes de Oca in AGN, Padrones, vol. 55, f. 8; AGN, Consulado, vol. 67, exp. 19, fs. 381–86.

29. Don Francisco Montes de Oca, a twenty-year-old Creole vinatero, shared his household with merchant Don Manuel Marroquin y Trebuesto, a fifty-year-old married *peninsular*, and his Creole wife and two Indian servant women. In the first block of Calle de Jesús, Don José Estrada, a *peninsular* from Asturias married to a Creole, shared his house with six bachelor merchants, ranging in age from sixteen to thirty-two, all also from Asturias, only one obviously a relative. One apparently was Estrada's *caxero* (cashier) and the rest were perhaps in business independently or with him, all listed as *comerciantes*. AGN, Padrones, vol. 53, f. 120; vol. 55, f. 58.

30. Don Antonio was a forty-year-old Spaniard who had recently immigrated from Andalusia with his wife, Doña Ysabel Marroquin, and their young daughter. Also living with them was another Spaniard, Don Ygnacio Tres Palacios, who was an unmarried *dependiente* (clerk), likely working at the store. In addition the residence housed María Josefa Suares, a twenty-two-year-old Spanish seamstress who was single; Viviana Vera, a Creole widow who was a servant; and José Agustín Ximenez, a twenty-year-old single Indian, also a servant. AGN, Padrones, vol. 53, f. 121.

31. On ownership of multiple businesses and the prevalence of administrators in colonial Mexico City, see Kicza, *Colonial Entrepreneurs*, 103, 223. See also Kinsbruner, *Petty Capitalism*, 59–60. For discussion of Antonio Mariano Maldonado, a multiple shop owner with a variety of administrator arrangements, see Francois, "*Prendas* and *Pulperías*," 91–93.

32. In seventeenth-century Potosí in the Viceroyalty of Peru, women were much more commonly retailers, and in the Scandanavian city of Milo in the sixteenth century, women outnumbered men five to one in retail merchant trade, which included pawning activity. See Mangan, "Enterprise in the Shadow of Silver"; and Jacobsen, "Women's Work." In the

English context in the nineteenth century, Tebbutt found that 45 percent of shopkeepers and over half the total members of the family employed in small businesses were women. Tebbutt, *Making Ends Meet*, 63.

33. AGN, Consulado, vol. 20, exp. 3, fs. 206, 212, 221, 223, 229, 235–38v.

34. Kinsbruner, *Petty Capitalism*, 28–29; Lugar, "Merchants," 55.

35. Will Fowler, *Tornel and Santa Anna: The Writer and the Caudillo, Mexico, 1795–1853* (Westport CT: Greenwood Press, 2000), 6; see also Florescano, *Precios de maiz*.

36. Fowler, *Tornel and Santa Anna*, 7.

37. Archer, "What Goes Around," 267–80.

38. J. A. P., "Dolores del parto," 2.

39. David M. Quinlan, "Issues and Factions in the Constituent Congress, 1823–1824," in Rodríguez, *Patterns of Contention in Mexican History*, 196. For discussion of *capitulados*, see Archer, "What Goes Around," 271, 276.

40. It is unclear from available documentation whether the expelled included pulperos and pawnbrokers. An 1827 bill to expel Spaniards excluded those *peninsulares* who had loaned cash to the government. Tenenbaum, "They Went Thataway," 192; Harold Dana Sims, *The Expulsion of Mexico's Spaniards, 1821–1836* (Pittsburgh: University of Pittsburgh Press, 1990); Romeo Flores Caballero, *Counterrevolution: The Role of the Spaniards in the Independence of Mexico, 1804–1838*, trans. Jaime E. Rodríquez O. (Lincoln: University of Nebraska Press, 1974), 110.

41. Elaborate agreements were made between kings and Jewish businessmen to handle money-lending operations in Christian kingdoms. In the mid-sixteenth century, King Charles I reprimanded merchants who abused "workers and miserable persons," whom they compelled to accept onerous interest arrangements on credit that customers obtained in stores. Pope Benedict XIV addressed where the line was drawn between usurious behavior and sound business practice in 1745, when he reiterated that it was immoral to earn money by lending money. Rodríguez, *Pandectas*, 3:563–70; Walter P. Zenner, *Minorities in the Middle: A Cross-Cultural Analysis* (New York: State University of New York Press, 1991), 32.

42. For example, customers redeeming collateral goods in the third month under the 1790 decree faced a 6 percent interest rate in their repayment, and early redemption in the first month would mean a 19 percent annual rate.

43. Carrera Stampa reported "2,000 *tiendas* of various types; more than 98 clothing warehouses; 330 warehouses of notions and household goods; more than 410 *vinaterías*; nearly 40 *cererías* [notions stores]; more than 90 bakeries; about 50 pig butchers; 40 *boticas* [drug stores]; more than 55 *platerías* [silver jewelers]; 120 tailor shops; 220 *pulquerías*, and more than 50 *cacahuaterías* [small grocery stores]. Carrera Stampa, "La ciudad," 308–15. See also Kinsbrunner, *Petty Capitalism*, passim.

44. Kicza, *Colonial Entrepreneurs*; and Kinsbruner, *Petty Capitalism*.

45. Using inventories of goods taken at the time of sale as sources for the examination of business practices has limitations. These inventories might only represent businesses in crisis, providing a picture of the end of an unsuccessful endeavor. We do not know what percentage of a store's business volume escaped documentation. Healthy businesses may be underrepresented in the sample of store inventories. Other problems stem from the nature of the prendas category of inventories. The inventories capture the contents of a store at a particular moment, and the prendas listed are "active," meaning that their pledge period has not expired. While these goods were not the storekeeper's property and therefore not usable capital, they did represent the merchant's investment, and as such were listed as assets in

inventories. The assumption of existing obligations by new owners was a stipulation of 1757 and 1810 regulations.

46. Francois, "*Prendas* and *Pulperías*," 96–98.

47. Kinsbruner interprets auction lists from stores as meaning that brokers were stuck with hundreds of goods to auction off (*prendas cumplidas*) and argues that this was the biggest drain on business. Unknown, however, is how many of those goods were sold at auction, perhaps earning enough to reimburse storekeepers for their loans as well as to meet real costs and provide profit. And *prendas cumplidas* were not mentioned, as either assets or debits, in sale- and business arrangement–inspired inventories. It may be that this controversy results from the nature of documentation, where all costs and profits are not accounted for. Kinsbruner, *Petty Capitalism*, 56–61. The pamphlet "Defensa de tenderos" also supports the idea that unsellable goods were a burden and that brokers suffered even when they could resell them. A. S., "Defensa de tenderos," 7. Zenner argues that in other settings, "the net profit of the licensed pawnbroker is low, despite the high interest rate which he charges. His administrative costs are high, including the often extortionate license fees of medieval cities, rent on a suitable house, the wages of servants and employees, commissions of canvassers seeking business, interest on till money, and the sale of forfeited pledges, often at a loss. His opportunity costs include the idleness of his money while holding a pledge. His risks include loss through theft, insolvency, and the loss-in-value of unredeemed pledges." Zenner, *Minorities in the Middle*, 36.

48. For examples, see Francois, "*Prendas* and *Pulperías*," 99.

49. Francois, "*Prendas* and *Pulperías*," 100.

50. AHCM, Panaderias y Pulperias, leg. 1, exp. 32, f. 29. The 1757 and 1810 regulations of corner stores required that pulperos register with the government and be bonded up to five hundred pesos to insure the value of prendas they took in. This practice goes back to at least 1602, when the crown demanded that moneylenders put up *fianzas* (bonds) in order to protect the public from problems arising from bankruptcies of lenders. The 1757 law called for a sliding scale for taxation, depending on class of establishment. This system changed with the 1810 law, where all pulperías, regardless of capital, were to pay a flat rate. Ley 5, Nov. Rec. Lib. 9, Tit. 3, in Rodríguez, *Pandectas*, 2:350.

51. In the English context in the 1860s, rates of redemption were high: in Leeds "low" shops, 66 percent redeemed within one week, 82 percent within one month, and 92 percent within six months; in "medium" shops [with more valuable goods], 33 percent, 62 percent, and 80 percent, respectively. See Tebbutt, *Making Ends Meet*, 9.

52. For the pulpería on the corner of Calles Coliseo Viejo and Espíritu Santo, inventories were taken on April 2 and then on July 9, 1805. The April inventory lists thirteen individual pawning transactions for goods (three rosaries, two pairs of underpants, tablecloths, bedspreads, one shawl) all pawned for under a peso. None of these goods are listed in the July inventory, three months later, when ten different collaterals and different clients are listed. For this store pawning traffic under each owner was light, and goods were redeemed before the six-month loan period expired. AGN, Consulado, vol. 28, exp. 2, fs. 21–25v and fs. 35–38.

53. AGN, Consulado, vol. 25, exp. 13, fs. 302–6 and fs. 310–12v.

54. For consideration of the limitation of retail censuses on which this section draws, see Francois, "*Prendas* and *Pulperías*," 100 and 108.

55. In addition to wives identified as "viuda de," Doña María Rendón took over the liquor store at the corner of San Felipe in December of 1809 "to stand in for her sick husband."

AGN, Consulado, vol. 53, exp. 12, f. 396. See AGN, Consulado, vol. 94, exp. 22, fs. 139–42v for another example of wives replacing husbands in a business capacity.

56. High turnover has been attributed to terms of sale for pulperías in Mexico City, with credit available for capital to purchase businesses. Sometimes no initial payment was required, with the purchaser paying a monthly installment instead. With such agreeable terms, store administrators were sometimes able to acquire businesses for themselves. Kinsbruner, *Petty Capitalism*, 35.

57. Such was the case for the store owned by Don Manuel Rivera on Portaceli, who in June of 1811 took a loss of over eight hundred pesos and went out of business. AGN, Consulado, vol. 67. Kicza characterizes the commercial climate, apparently especially at higher levels, as "cutthroat rivalry." Kicza, *Colonial Entrepreneurs*, 51. For customers shopping for the best deal, see Tebbutt, *Making Ends Meet*, 78–79.

58. AGN, Bandos, vol. 9, exp. 4, f. 6.

59. The prohibition about wet clothing is not surprising given the repeated flooding that Mexico City suffered. The contaminated clothing is surely in reference to epidemics, which city residents also repeatedly faced. This connection between sanitation and pawned goods reemerged periodically in the nineteenth and early twentieth centuries, especially during public-health programs hoping to stem the spread of diseases.

60. Emphasis in the original. For discussion of the insistance of the founder, Romero de Terrero, that the service be free, see Couturier, *Silver King*, 146.

61. Pullan, *Rich and Poor*, 432, 451. Plans to establish funds for lending to the poor at no interest in order to combat usurers were proposed by bishops in England in 1326 and 1361 as well as by French burghers in Salins in the fourteenth century. The first Montes de Piedad that targeted the poor were founded in 1462 in Perugia, Italy, by Franciscan priests. The Italian institutions, called Monti di Pietá, were public loan banks, set up as part of poor-relief policies established in the context of bad harvests, fluctuating food prices, and growing tax demands. The Montis de Pietá were run by communes of town residents in their first years, supervised by a combination of municipal officials and representatives of local churches. Later, "rich residents" were charged with administration of funds. The name "monti de pietá" referred to both a sum of money with pious and charitable ends and the Virgin of Piety, whose convent was in Perugia. See also Carlos Romero Giordano, *Las casas viejas de Moctezuma: Historia de una institución* (México: Banco "Nacional Monte de Piedad," 1969), 37. For lending by Jews and usury debates in the Italian context, see Pullan, *Rich and Poor*, 433–42; and Menning, *Charity and State*.

62. Juan A. Martínez de la Fe, *Cajas de ahorros y Montes de Piedad (Provincia de las Palmas)* (Sevilla: Las Palmas de Gran Canaria, 1980), 8–11; López Yepes, *Historia de los Montes*, 1:4–6.

63. Cuoto noted that there had been a lot of robberies in the area, and the Depository had more than half a million pesos' worth of jewels in custody, "consisting for the most part of small pieces which could be easily sold and altered, which combination of circumstances could lead thieves to attempt a new robbery." AGN, Montepíos, vol. 17, exp. 13, f. 305.

64. Cabrera Siles and Escandón, *Historia*, 237–38.

65. The Bourbon Junta General was made up of the viceroy's representative, the Oidor Decano of the Real Audiencia (who also held the post of judge protector of the Monte), the Fiscal Civil of the Real Hacienda, a representative of the archbishop, the canon of the Metropolitan Cathedral, a representative of the consulado, the director of the Monte de Piedad, and founder Conde de Regla or his descendant. Other Monte officials also attended Junta General

meetings. The junta's duties were to review and approve acts of the Junta Particular, review the Monte accounts, undertake audits and visits to the institution when necessary, and approve junior staff appointments. The board was to meet annually, though this requirement was not always met.

66. The republican Junta General was composed of the minister of Relaciones and Gobernación, an ecclesiastical judge (it is unclear if this person was appointed by the archbishop canon from the metropolitan church or chosen by the government), the governor of the Federal District, the president of the Ayuntamiento, the director of the Monte de Piedad, and one of the direct descendants of the founder, Romero de Terreros. The Junta Particular, which supervised day-to-day operations, consisted of director and officers, including the heads of the four sections. In the colonial period two Interventors (controllers) also sat on the board. This body was to review accounts monthly, examine employment applications, vote on proposals made by the director, oversee compliance with statutes, and ensure the integrity of the lending principal. The Junta Particular was to meet monthly and at other times deemed appropriate by the director. AGN, Montepíos, vol. 17, exp. 13, f. 230; Villela, *El Monte*, 15–21; Cabrera Siles and Escandón, *Historia*, 245–46; Antonio Villamil, *Memoria histórica del Nacional Monte de Piedad que por orden del C. Director Mariano Riva Palacio ha formado el Contado* (México: Imprenta de Ignacio Escalante, 1877), 17.

67. First quote from AGN, Montepíos, vol. 17, exp. 13, f. 283; second quote from BN, "Reglamento para . . . las tiendas de pulpería."

68. AGN, Gobernación, leg. 2187(1), exp. 1, no. 1, fs. 8–9v.

69. The architect José Torres inspected the Monte's facilities in the San Pedro and San Pablo building in October 1796. The downstairs offices, which used to be the Jesuits' theology classroom and now housed the Depository office, had storage shelves packed beyond capacity with jewels and clothes. Upon one's entering the warehouse humid vapors were manifest, a problem for the public, whose "*alahas* got wet and all the clothes disintegrated." Another inspector suggested to the viceroy that a new building was necessary, one that was "secure, in good condition, and equipped with ventilation, to avoid the rotting caused by moths and dampness." Employees had to air out in the sun moldy goods whose redemption time approached. AGN, Montepíos, vol. 7, exp. 4, fs. 123–26.

70. While direct family relations are not always clear, surnames of Monte de Piedad officers are the same as those of some city notables. In 1823 the Monte director was Don Antonio Manual Couto, while José Bernardo Couto was an adviser to Gómez Farias and later a liberal senator. Warren notes that Francisco Manuel Sanchez de Tagle was a prominent Creole and a member of the secret antiroyal Guadalupe society and was elected to the municipal council in 1812. Costeloe points out that Manuel Sanchez de Tagle and José Berruecos were recurring power brokers in national politics. Both surnames appear in the lists of early nineteenth-century Monte staff. Warren, *Vagrants and Citizens*, 40; Costeloe, *Central Republic*, 44.

71. AGN, Montepíos, vol. 7, exp. 7, fs. 177–209; vol. 7, exp. 16, fs. 318, 320; vol. 17, exp. 4, f. 57; vol. 17, exp. 5, f. 55.

72. Article 2, Chapter 14, of the statutes, cited in Rubio, *El Nacional*, 8.

73. AGN, Montepíos, vol. 7, exp. 16, f. 318; vol. 17, exp. 8, f. 88; vol. 17, exp. 9, fs. 128–128v; vol. 17, exp. 13, f. 290. Figueroa's census information is found in AGN, Padrones, vol. 55, f. 24. Most documents in the Montepíos ramo at the National Archive do not distinguish between *peninsular* and Creole, using the notation "español."

74. AGN, Montepíos, vol. 17, exp. 6, f. 70, first quote; f. 68, second quote.

75. AGN, Montepíos, vol. 17, exp. 5, fs. 53–55; vol. 17, exp. 4, fs. 45–47.

76. In 1806 the jewelry appraiser position was open again, and Director Gamboa recommended to Juez Protector Mier that Don José Roman fill the job. Roman agreed to serve for four hundred pesos annually and to arrange a bond of one thousand pesos, as required in the statutes. AGN, Montepíos, vol. 7, exp. 5, f. 154; vol. 7, exp. 10, fl. 238; vol. 7, exp. 11, fs. 242–245, 250–51.

77. The director informed the president of this personnel problem before disciplining the employee according to the statutes, because he wanted to be sure that the "new form of government" did not mean administrative change at the Monte as well. AGN, Gobernación, leg. 2187(1), exp. 1, no. 4(3), fs. 1–4v.

78. AGN, Gobernación, leg. 2187(1), exp. 1, no. 8(2), fs. 1–1v.

79. AGN, Montepíos, vol. 17, exp. 8, f. 88; Anna, *Fall*, 159.

80. AGN, Montepíos, vol. 17, exp. 9, fs. 126–28v. Quote from AGN, Montepíos, vol. 17, exp. 5, f. 54; Cabrera Siles and Escandón, *Historia*, 247.

81. Rubio, *El Nacional*, 9.

82. The new uniform consisted of a blue military-style overcoat, pants with a silver trim, short blue or white jacket with three silver stars, silver buttons, boots, and a hat. The title of the department in which one worked was to be visible on jacket and hat. All signs of rank did not disappear, however, as those higher up had stars embroidered in silver and those at entry level had plain uniforms with no decoration. Cabrera Siles and Escandón, *Historia*, 58.

83. AGN, Montepíos, vol. 17, exp. 13, f. 193v.

84. AGN, Gobernación, leg. 2187(1), exp. 1, no. 7(7), fs. 3–5.

85. AGN, Montepíos, vol. 7, exp. 14, fs. 269, 296–99; AGN, Gobernacíon, leg. 2187(1), exp. 1, no. 13(1), fs. 1–2v; leg. 2187(1), exp. 1, no. 13(1), fs. 1–3v.

86. First quote from AGN, Gobernación, leg. 2187(1), exp. 1, no. 3, f. 2; second quote from AGN, Gobernación, leg. 2187(1), exp. 1, no. 3, f. 3v.

87. Cabrera Siles and Escandón, *Historia*, 231, 233; Rubio, *El Nacional*, 15.

88. AGN, Montepíos, vol. 17, exp. 9, f. 124.

89. Rubio, *El Nacional*, 17, 14.

90. AGN, Montepíos, vol. 17, exp. 13, f. 268.

91. In 1805 Don José Cruces, a Monte Treasury official, faced four years in prison for having falsified Monte tickets nine years earlier. AGN, Montepíos, vol. 17, exp. 3, f. 24. For the case of Candamo see AGN, Montepíos, vol. 17, exp. 1, f. 6; for Esquivel see AGN, Montepíos, vol. 17, exp. 10, f. 166; for Cruces see AGN, Montepíos, vol. 17, exp. 6, f. 77.

92. For Ossoro's case see AGN, Montepíos, vol. 17, exp. 3, fs. 22–24; vol. 17, exp. 9, f. 141. For Gerardi's case see AGN, Montepíos, vol. 17, exp. 7, f. 81. For the Centenac case see AGN, Montepíos, vol. 17, exp. 6, fs. 69–70, 74–76; vol. 17, exp. 2, fs. 18–19. Doña Francisca Antonia was not successful, as the only document she could produce regarding the relationship of her property to her husband was a receipt for four thousand pesos, the value of assorted clothing, jewels, and cash, dated February 23, 1792, after the date of their marriage. The court held that these were not the goods embargoed.

93. In the case of Don Centenac's crimes, it appears that goods were listed in Contaduría record books as having been *prendas cumplidas* available for sale but did not appear in auction section reports. Other discrepancies included goods whose redemption was noted in auction-room records but did not show up in general accounting books, indicating that money received for the goods never made it to the Treasury. AGN, Montepíos, vol. 17, exp. 11, fs. 207, 209, 202; vol. 17, exp. 6, fs. 72–73.

94. Cabrera Siles and Escandón, *Historia*, 239–40.

95. AGN, Gobernación, leg. 2187(1), exp. 1, no. 3, fs. 1–3v.

96. The Monte de Piedad was not the only public institution that operated in the red, had poor accounting practices, and faced the scrutiny of royal auditors at the turn of the nineteenth century. Royal accountants repeatedly asked to review cabildo records from 1786 up to 1817. In 1788 auditors accused the city of arbitrary procedures, a lack of formal accounting structures, and abuses in management of city funds. Among those cabildo members accused of corruption was none other than Manuel Gamboa, who had been replaced as Monte director in 1814 for misusing public funds. When he returned to the city council in 1817, he was barred from financial operations. Cabildo officials refused to cooperate with royal audit efforts in 1817. Anna, *Fall*, 159.

97. First quote from AGN, Montepíos, vol. 17, exp. 13, fs. 281v–282; second quote from AGN, Montepíos, vol. 17., exp. 13, f. 294v.

98. For the employees' perspective, see AGN, Montepíos, vol. 17, exp. 13, fs. 288–89v; for the Hacienda view, see AGN, Montepíos, vol. 17, exp. 13, f. 271.

99. This was not the first time that Monte employees faced discounted salaries. In 1782 the Junta General favored an increase in salaries as recognition that "work has increased considerably." Four years later individual manager and subaltern salaries were halved upon promotion. In 1795, when new employees were named to posts, a discount of 4 percent was applied to the salaries of the director, the *contador*, the treasurer, and the heads of Depository and Auction. The funds thus generated went to the king to fund his conflict with France. AGN, Gobernación, leg. 2187(1), exp. 1, no. 5(1), f. 2.

100. AGN, Montepíos, vol. 17, exp. 1, f. 3.

101. Monte employees were bonded through a *fiador*. The *fianzas* for department heads were six hundred pesos, for controllers six hundred pesos, for officials four hundred pesos, and for the jewelry appraiser one thousand pesos. AGN, Gobernación, leg. 2187(1), exp. 1, no. 5(1), fs. 1v–4.

102. Cabrera Siles and Escandón, *Historia*, 248, 255.

103. For figures for the first forty years, see AGN, Montepíos, vol. 7, exp. 14, f. 272. See also Francois, "Cloth and Silver," 337.

104. AGN, Gobernación, vol. 2187(1), exp. 1, no. 1, fs. 8–9v.

105. In 1802 less than 1 percent of goods pawned were left beyond their pledge term and sold at auction. AHNMP, Contaduria, Empeños en Contaduria, caja 1, vols. 1–3; caja 2, vols. 4–6; caja 3, vols. 7–9; caja 4, vols. 10–12. The years 1821, 1824, 1829, 1833, 1836, and 1847 were all years in which more redemptions took place than loans were made. See appendix 2, table E.

106. AGN, Gobernación, leg. 2187(1), exp. 1, no. 1, fs. 8–9v; leg. 2187(1), exp. 1, no. 4, fs. 1–2v, 7–14v, 18–21v.

107. Villela identifies different nineteenth-century Monte directors with political factions: Trebuesto, Couto, and Lazpita as Conservatives, and Sanchez de Tagle, Pedraza, Herera, Gochicoa, and Cendejas as Liberals. Villela, *El Monte*, 7.

108. AGN, Gobernacíon, leg. 2187(1), exp. 1, no. 7(7), fs. 3–5; Cabrera Siles and Escandón, *Historia*, 237, 247, 252.

109. Report by Junta General to Viceroy Branciforte on precarious financial health of Monte de Piedad in 1797. AGN, Montepíos, vol. 7, exp. 8, fs. 212–13; Cabrera Siles and Escandón, *Historia*, 232–33. In July 1804 the governing board renewed the annual charge of 6.25 percent. AGN, Gobernación, leg. 2187(1), exp. 1, no. 5(1), f. 4.

110. AGN, Montepíos, vol. 17, exp. 13, fs. 253–66; vol. 17, exp. 13, f. 291.

111. AGN, Gobernación, leg. 2187(1), exp. 1, no. 13(1), fs. 2–2v; AGN, Montepíos, vol. 7, exp. 10, f. 233; vol. 17, exp. 13, f. 267v.

112. In sum 66 percent of the goods that sold for more than the value of the loan that they secured garnered under five pesos for their owners.

113. AGN, Gobernación, leg. 2187(1), exp. 1, no. 1, f. 8v.

114. AGN, Gobernación, leg. 2187(1), exp. 1, no. 14 (3), fs. 2–6.

115. AGN, Montepíos, vol. 17, exp. 7, f. 81.

116. Villela, *El Monte*, 9.

117. AGN, Gobernación, leg. 2187(1), exp. 1, no. 1, f. 8v; leg. 2187(1), exp. 1, no. 13(1), fs. 1–3v.

118. AGN, Montepíos, vol. 17, exp. 13, fs. 282–282v.

3. Collateral Living

1. María was probably an even more frequent customer. These inventories only represent goods that she and others were unable to redeem and that therefore went to auction. And even among auctioned goods, there are an additional six transactions by a client named Robledo, but no first name is given. AHCM, Inventario General de la Municipalidad de Tacubaya, no. 120, exp. 5.

2. See chapter 4 on the changing pawning trade.

3. AGN, Gobernación, leg. 2187(1), exp. 2, no. 20(2), f. 31. For an overview of the pace with which governments changed hands and the dominance of a military caste in government in the 1820s–1850s, see Costeloe, *Central Republic*, 2–15. See also Gayón Córdova, *Condiciones de vida*, 53.

4. Warren, *Vagrants and Citizens*; Costeloe, *Central Republic*, 33–45.

5. Costeloe, *Central Republic*, 218.

6. Mora is quoted in Costeloe, *Central Republic*, 17–18. Political office was limited to those with an annual income of at least 500 pesos in the 1820s and 1830s. To be a deputy to congress in 1836 one needed an income of annual 1,500 pesos. An income of 2,500 pesos made a man eligible to be a senator. Presidents could only come from those native-born men over forty years of age with an annual income of at least 4,000 pesos. Costeloe, *Central Republic*, 18, 100–102.

7. Juan Nepomuceno Almonte, *Guía de forasteros y repertorio de conocimientos útiles* (México: Imprenta de I. Cumplido, 1852), population chart inset following p. 524.

8. About 4 percent of households were upper class in 1811, 18 percent middle class (gente decente with one or two servants), and the remaining 88 percent lower class. Arrom, *Women*, 5–7; Shaw, "Poverty and Politics," 373–76. See also Warren, *Vagrants and Citizens*, 11.

9. Costeloe, *Central Republic*, 19. For a study of the gendered nature of "keeping up appearances" in early twentieth-century Brazil, see Owensby, *Intimate Ironies*.

10. Stevens, *Origins of Instability*, 101–2. Stevens's main concern in chapter seven is to show that living conditions of the political elite (whether conservative, moderate, or radical) shaped their ideological positions. See Costeloe, *Central Republic*, 33–35, for the radical program, and 109–10, for the Siete Leyes.

11. What had been a relatively small discount of 5 or 6 percent for copper coins rose to more than 70 percent in 1835. In response to the copper-currency crisis in 1835, tenants in Mexico City refused to pay rents except in copper, since that was what they were paid in, and

retailers petitioned for tax relief, because they were receiving no silver from their customers. When a new bank authorized to redeem existing copper coins opened in 1837, public confidence hit bottom and rumors of further devaluations of copper led producers to stay out of the capital and shopkeepers to close their doors, while high prices brought the poor into the streets in protest. Costeloe, *Central Republic*, quote on 4; 80–81, 93.

12. Cabrera Siles and Escandón, *Historia*, 62. This situation lasted for twelve years.

13. For the 1839 and 1840 events in the city, see Costeloe, *Central Republic*, 162, 177–79; for the decree calling for resumption of business, see AGN, Gobernación, no section, caja 244, exp. 18(3), fs. 2; for 1841 currency protests, see Costeloe, *Central Republic*, 191.

14. The empeño law is found in AGN, Gobernación, leg. 2187(1), exp. 2, no. 20(9), fs. 1–3v.

15. The Monte discontinued the practice of deducting the now-mandatory *limosna* from the loan amount and instead began collecting the fee when the loan was repaid and collateral redeemed or when the good sold at auction. *Diario Oficial*, January 15, 1842. In 1836 jewels could be repawned, but not clothing or furniture, because their condition was more likely to deteriorate. Cabrera Siles and Escandón, *Historia*, 58, 252.

16. Article 3 reads, "Waiters and waitresses, people serving in inns, in billiard halls, in ice cream parlors, in bath houses and pulque saloons, pages from convents and monasteries, those working in horse stables, cowboys, wagoneers and cart drivers, truck drivers, and public and private chauffeurs and taxi drivers, are included in this category of domestic servants." "Reglamento para criados domesticos," 323–29, in Almonte, *Guía de forasteros*; statistics on numbers of servants at midcentury, 487. The percentage of employed women working as *criados* and *sirvientes* decreased from 54 percent in 1811 to 30 percent in 1848. Arrom, *Women*, 164. See also Flora Salazar, "Los sirvientes domésticos."

17. While it appears that the *libreta* requirement was new for Mexico City in 1852, this was a requirement in a servant law passed by the congress of the state of Sonora in 1831 though apparently not put into effect until Santa Anna's administration in 1843. "Ley de sirvientes, espedida por el Congreso Constituyente de Sonora, y nuevamente adoptada y adicionada por la Exma. Junta Departmental de Sonora," Guaymas 6 de Julio de 1843.

18. Anyone without a notebook or without employment for six months was defined as a vagrant and punished with sentences of labor on forced work projects. Clothing-storage requirements are in Articles 14 and 15.

19. Arrom, *Women*, 165; Piccato, *City of Suspects*, 153–55.

20. *Decreto exceptuando del pago del derecho de capitación a las clases que se espresan, dado en 3 de julio de 1843* (México: Imprenta de J. M. Lara, 1843).

21. Costeloe, *Central Republic*, 132–33, 163, 204, 223–24, 236, 244–46. Government agents confiscated goods of middle-class residents who refused to pay taxes.

22. A recent study has found that Reform laws that took property out of church hands facilitated the purchase of property by those who had been renting from the church in Michoacán. Many lower and middle-class residents bought property but, not able to keep up with payments, lost it to creditors. It is not clear to what extent this process also occurred in Mexico City. Chowning, *Wealth and Power*, 272–73.

23. Costeloe, *Central Republic*, 82, 129, 133, 244; Tenenbaum, "They Went Thataway," 195; María Dolores Morales, "Estructura urbana y distribución de la propiedad de la ciudad de México en 1813," in Moreno Toscano, *Ciudad de México*, 79.

24. Edith Couturier suggests that "women became property owners in far greater numbers in the nineteenth century" based on notarial records from 1800 to 1878. Edith Couturier,

"Women and the Family in Eighteenth-Century Mexico: Law and Practice," *Journal of Family History* 10, no. 3 (1985): 294–304, quote on 303.

25. AGN, Ramo Gobernación, no section, caja 505, exp. 14, no. 1, f. 5.

26. The colonial system that controlled New Spain consisted of corporate groups of nobility, clergy, military, and Indians, with internal hierarchies in terms of power, rights, and functions. The nuclear family was the building block for this corporate structure, "with men governing their wives and children just as they were in turn governed by the state." Silvia Arrom, "Changes in Mexican Family Law in the XIXth Century: The Civil Codes of 1870 and 1884," *Journal of Family History* 10 (Fall 1985): 309–22.

27. Quinlan, "Issues and Factions," 204.

28. Ignacio Ramírez, delegate to the constitutional convention, criticized his colleagues for having forgotten about social rights for women within marriage. He thought that within marriage women were equal to men and had the right to legal recourse that should be guaranteed by law. Writing in the 1890s, jurist Genaro García believed that the Constitution of 1857 opened the possibility of careers to women, but in practice women did not exercise the right to work because of "juridical irresponsibility" on the part of the state. Marcia Muñoz de Alba M., "La condición jurídica de la mujer en la doctrina mexicana del siglo XIX," 815–19 in Bernal, *Memoria del IV Congreso.*

29. For the failure of promised schools to materialize, see Muñoz de Alba, "La condición jurídica," 811–12; Arrom, *Women*, 201. For discussions of republican gender ideologies and legal status in Mexico, see Muñoz de Alba, "La condición jurídica," 811–22; Arrom, *Women*, 82–97. For other areas of Latin America, see Chambers, *From Subjects to Citizens*; Hunefeldt, *Liberalism in the Bedroom*; Elizabeth Dore, "One Step Forward, Two Steps Back: Gender and the State in the Long Nineteenth Century," in *Hidden Histories of Gender and the State in Latin America*, ed. Elizabeth Dore and Maxine Molyneaux, 3–32 (Durham: Duke University Press, 2000).

30. Kuznesof, "Gender Ideology," 161–65; Shaw, "Poverty and Politics," 38; Arrom, *Women*, 120, 132, 166, 186, 197.

31. Along with sons, daughters were released from their fathers' authority at age twenty-one, when they could control their personal acts such as choosing a career, entering into contracts, and choosing marriage partners. Twenty-one-year-olds also could control their property. But a daughter had to have her father's permission to move out of the family home to live as an unmarried woman on her own before the age of thirty, in order to protect her reputation (and therefore the family's honor). A single daughter did not need permission to leave if her widowed parent remarried and brought a stepparent into the home. Overall, these changes "augmented individual freedom at the expense of parental authority, [and] reflect the ongoing weakening of patriarchy over the last few centuries." Arrom, "Changes in Mexican Family Law," 307.

32. Arrom, "Changes in Mexican Family Law," 308; see also 208, 310.

33. Shaw, "Poverty and Politics," 208.

34. The Banco de Avío operated from 1830 to 1843, lending only to industrialists. The Banco Nacional de Amortizacíon was created in 1837 to stabilize copper money, but it was poorly administered and was closed in 1841 by Santa Anna. From the 1840s to the 1870s, a savings bank was attached to the Monte de Piedad, but it was not in the business of making loans. In 1846 the Banco de Londres y México opened its doors in Mexico City and was the first to issue bank notes in the country. While lending to the government through the turn of the twentieth century, this bank and others that soon emerged did not engage in small-scale

lending. Rosa María Meyer Cosío, "La ciudad como centro comercial e industrial," in Tovar and Mas, *El corazón de una nación*, 62; López Rosado, *Curso de historia*, 243; M. Gayón Córdova, "Guerra, dictadura y cobre: Crónica de una ciudad asediada (agosto–diciembre 1841)," *Historias* 5 (1984): 53–65; and Costeloe, *Central Republic*, 81. On the Banco de Avío see Robert Potash, *Mexican Government and Industrial Development in the Early Republic: The Banco de Avío* (Amherst: University of Massachusetts Press, 1983); López Rosado, *Curso de historia*, 250; and O. Ernest Moore, *Evolución de las instituciones financieras en México* (México: Centro de Estudios Monetarios Latinoamericanos, 1963), 15.

35. For Monte de Piedad banking operations, see AGN, Gobernación, leg. 2187(2), exp. 1, no. 33(3), f. 19; and no section, caja 567, exp. 4. On the Banco de Londres y México, see López Rosado, *Curso de historia*, 248–51; see also Moore, *Evolución de las instituciones*, 11.

36. Waddy Thompson, *Recollection of Mexico* (New York: Wiley and Putnam, 1846), 129–30; see also Sonya Lipsett-Rivera, "Clothes in Late-Colonial Mexico," 20. Prieto also commented on working women adorned with elaborate jewelry, such as the enchilada vendor who stationed herself in front of a church wearing "necklaces and *relicarios* (religious lockets), silver rings on her hands and earrings with *calabacillas de corales* [little gourds of coral]." Jewelry such as this often found its way to the pawnshop shelves. Guillermo Prieto, *Memorias de mis tiempos* (1848; repr., México: Editorial Porrúa, 1996), 149.

37. See chapter 4.

38. Costeloe, *Central Republic*, 24–25. On the discourse of vagrancy see Arrom, *Containing the Poor*; and Warren, *Vagrants and Citizens*.

39. Salazar, "Los sirvientes domésticos," 125, 131; Arrom, *Women*, 198–200; Baltasar Dromundo, *La metrópoli mexicana* (México: Baltasar Dromundo, 1957), 80–81. See the illustration of the *recamarera*, or chambermaid, in Juan de Arias et al., *Los mexicanos pintados por sí mismos: Tipos y costumbres nacionales por varios autores* (1854; facsimile, México: Centro de Estudios de Historia de México CONDUMEX, 1989), 100, quote on 232; Shaw, "Poverty and Politics," 147.

40. Arrom, *Women*, 164.

41. In legislation calling for a census in advance of voter registration in 1834, census takers were to make note of houses of prostitution that they encountered, along with gambling establishments and other "houses of scandal," so that respective police authorities could arrest and jail "the delinquents . . . according to the law." Beginning with Maximilian in 1865 and continuing during the Restored Republic and the Porfiriato, houses of prostitution were regulated instead of banned, and prostitutes registered with public-health authorities. Prostitutes attached to a brothel were taxed by liberals less than prostitutes working on their own, with the latter facing more severe treatment from authorities. In the *Reglamento de la prostitución* in 1871, these "prostitutas aisladas" had to pay a monthly tax that was equal to what they paid in rent, while those in brothels were not obliged to pay the personal tax. "Circular relativa al padron para elección de diputados y prevenciones en cuanto á vagos, casas de prostitución, de juego ó escándalo, y acerca de la educación de la juventud," 8 de agosto de 1834, 53–56, in *Legislación electoral mexicana, 1812–1973* (México: Secretaría de Gobernación, 1973). For the nineteenth century see Katherine Elaine Bliss, "Guided by an Imperious, Moral Need": Prostitutes, Motherhood, and Nationalism in Revolutionary Mexico," in *Reconstructing Criminality in Latin America*, ed. Carlos A. Aguire and Robert Buffington, 167–94 (Wilmington DE: Scholarly Resources, 2001), 160; and Elisa Speckman Guerra, "Las flores del mal: Mujeres criminals en el Porfiriato," *Historia Mexicana* 47, no. 1 (1997): 183–229.

42. Shaw, "Poverty and Politics," 147, quote on 120.

43. Shaw, "Poverty and Politics," 145. See pages 146–48 for a description of poor living conditions in casas de vecindad at midcentury.

44. Arias, *Los mexicanos*, 231.

45. Richard Warren found these smaller downstairs quarters of rooming houses rented for between two and five pesos a month, which represented most of or even more than a working-class salary. Even more humble *jacales*, or huts, rented for one to three pesos a month. Warren, *Vagrants and Citizens*, 50; Shaw, "Poverty and Politics," 148.

46. AGN, Gobernación, leg. 2187(1), exp. 2 no. 20(9), fs. 24–41; for Barrera, see AGN, Gobernación, leg. 2187(1), exp. 2 no. 8, fs. 3–3v; for Ramírez y Rojas, see AGN, Gobernación, no section, caja 505, exp. 14.

47. AGN, Gobernación, leg. 2187(1), exp. 2, no. 20(9), fs. 25, 28.

48. Shaw, "Poverty and Politics," 138.

49. AGN, Gobernación, leg. 1517(1), exp. 1, no. 1, fs.1–3v.

50. Shaw, "Poverty and Politics," 101; Prieto, *Memorias*, 242.

51. Fernández de Lizardi, *Noches triste y dia alegre*, 207.

52. Vicente Riva Palacio, *Calvario y Tabor* (1868; repr., México: Editorial Porrúa, 1985), first quote on 222, second quote on 194.

53. Arias, *Los mexicanos*, 94, 178, 234.

54. The portals "were full of *tiendas*, cafes, peddlers, used clothing sellers, toy stores, florists, sweet shops, book stores, used goods stalls, antiques (real and spurious), and the customary throng of idlers and the curious." Brantz Mayer, *México, lo que fue y lo que es*, ed. Juan Ortega y Medina (México, 1953), 80–81.

55. AHCM, Mercados, vol. 3730, leg. 3, exp. 161, f. 11; Shaw, "Poverty and Politics," 13–14.

56. Quote from Prieto, *Memorias*, 118–19; Shaw, "Poverty and Politics," 132.

57. Manuel Rivera Cambas, *México pintoresco artístico y monumental* (México: Editora Nacional, 1880), 177; AHCM, Tacubaya, inventory 120, exp. 11; AHCM, Tlalpan, inventory 69, exp. 71.

58. Almonte, *Guía de forasteros*, 458–59.

59. See chapter 5 for a statistical analysis of middle-class professions in 1895. See also Michael C. Meyer and William L. Sherman, *The Course of Mexican History*, 4th ed. (New York: Oxford University Press, 1991), 422, 472; Shaw, "Poverty and Politics," 373. For the middle class in other Latin American settings in the early twentieth century, see Parker, *Idea*, and Owensby, *Intimate Ironies*.

60. Shaw, "Poverty and Politics," 145; Warren, *Vagrants and Citizens*, 50; Stevens, *Origins of Instability*, 99–101.

61. Donald Stevens has analyzed data from the 1848 census to get a sense of living situations of fifty-two statesmen in Mexico City. He argues that "the greater a family's wealth, the more they would spend on housing to enjoy the comforts of money, to entertain friends, and to impress acquaintances." Stevens, *Origins of Instability*, 89, quote on 99.

62. Prieto describes this experience of a young newly hired commercial clerk: "Proud to be guarding the keys to the business in his handkerchief pocket, he lived with his employers to whom he turned over 8 pesos a month. He ate in his employer's house, said his rosary during the family prayers, and retired to the landing to sleep." Prieto, *Memorias*, 235.

63. El Siglo XIX, April 30, 1845, cited by Costeloe, *Central Republic*, 21; José Benítez, *El traje y el adorno en México, 1500–1910* (Guadalajara, 1946), 162; Arias, *Los mexicanos*, 57.

64. Josefina Zoraida Vázquez and Pilar Gonzalbo Aizpuru, *Guía de protocolos: Archivo General de Notarías de la Ciudad de México, año de 1855* (México: El Colegio de México, 2000), 369. See also Couturier, "Women and the Family."

65. John Kicza found that among the elite this practice was already on the wane in the eighteenth century. See Kicza, *Colonial Entrepreneurs*, 161, and 163, table summarizing dowry values in twenty-one merchants' marriages between 1782 and 1815.

66. Vázquez and Gonzalbo Aizpuru, *Guía de protocolos, 1855*, 307.

67. Costeloe, *Central Republic*, 20.

68. "Tarifa de precios a los coches del sitio," in Luis G. Saldivar, *Diccionario de la legislación mexicana* (México: Imprenta de "La Constitución Social," 1868), 149.

69. Meyer Cosío, "La ciudad," 55. See also Silvia Arrom, "Popular Politics in Mexico City: The Parián Riot, 1828," *Hispanic American Historical Review* 68 (1988): 245–67; María del Carmen Ruiz Castañeda, *La ciudad de México en el siglo XIX* (México: Departamento del Distrito Federal, 1974), 59; and Shaw, "Poverty and Politics," 10–11.

70. Manuel Carrera Stampa, "La ciudad de Mexico a principios del siglo XIX," in *Planos de la Ciudad de México* (México: Boletín de la Sociedad Mexicana de Geografía y Estadística, 1949), 308–18, quote on 315; Gonzalbo Aizpuru, *Las mujeres*, 266.

71. Quote from Marcos Arroníz, *Manual del viajero en México* (Paris: Librería de Rosa y Bouret, 1858), 42; Shaw, "Poverty and Politics," 10.

72. Carlos Illades, "Composición de la fuerza de trabajo y de las unidades productivas en la ciudad de México, 1788–1873," in Hernández Franyuti, *La Ciudad*, 2:259–60; Frances Calderón de la Barca, *Life in Mexico* (1843; repr., London: J. M. Dent & Sons, 1954), 65.

73. William Bullock, *Seis meses de residencia y viajes en México* (México: Banco de México, 1983), 136; Prieto, *Memorias*, 118. The 1850 description is from Shaw, "Poverty and Politics," 130.

74. *Diario del Gobierno de la República Mexicana*, 16 de febrero de 1842, 188. For other examples of clothing establishments and prices, see Marie Francois, "Vivir de prestado: El empeño en la ciudad de México," in *Bienes y vivencias: El siglo XIX mexicano*, vol. 4, ed. Anne Staples, *Historia de la vida cotidiana en México*, series ed., Pilar Gonzalbo (México: El Colegio de México / Fondo de Cultura Económica, 2004).

75. Juan E. Pérez, *Almanaque estadístico de las oficinas y guía de forasteros y del comercio de la república para 1875* (México: Imprenta del Gobierno, 1874), 564, 567. There is debate about relative costs of clothing across time, especially in terms of the impact of tariffs and industrialization. According to Lucas Alamán, the price of clothing and cloth decreased after Independence due to industrialization of textile production. Others note that it was foreign competition that lowered prices, as even with tarriffs the foreign cloth "was sold below the price of Mexican cloth." Laws in 1821, 1836, 1837, and 1845 intended to prohibit the importation of cotton thread or cloth as well as manufactured cotton clothing in order to protect the Mexican textile industry, but it is unclear how effective they were. Carlos Illades, "Política arancelaria y desarrollo de la industria textil mexicana, 1821–1846," *El Economista Mexicano* 20, nos. 4, 1 (1988–89): 177, 183; Costeloe, *Central Republic*, 91; Shaw, "Poverty and Politics," 132; Almonte, *Guía de forasteros*, 478–80.

76. The first description is from Gonzalbo Aizpuru, *Las mujeres*, 279; the second, from Calderón de la Barca, *Life in Mexico*, 80–84; and the third, from Shaw, "Poverty and Politics," 130. On the tunic as a new and disturbing fashion, see Franco, "Women, Fashion and the Moralists," 421.

77. Reform-era laws led to changes in lending abilities of mercantile houses in Morelia, a traditional source of credit for provincial gente decente, which led to the establishment of other "more specialized businessmen" in casas de empeños in the 1870s to take up the slack. "The public horror" over interest rates of 12.5 percent a month "led to the establishment of the Monte de Piedad, which performed essentially the same service, lending small amounts in Morelia beginning in 1881 at the 'reasonable' annual rate of 12 percent, though this institution did not entirely supplant the pawnshops." Chowning, *Wealth and Power*, 281–82.

78. Edith O'Shaughnessy, *Intimate Pages of Mexican History* (New York: George H. Doran, 1920), 56.

79. Arias, *Los mexicanos*, 229–30.

80. Villela, *El Monte*, 26.

81. AHCM, Inventario General de la Municipalidad de Tacubaya, no. 120, exp. 5.

82. AHCM, Tacubya, Empeños 1853–1903, exp. 3.

83. See Francois, "Cloth and Silver", 337–38, for analysis of the rhythm of pawning at the Monte de Piedad. Though the connection between the two is not clear, it is interesting that the remarkable near doubling of the number of transactions from 1841 to 1842 occurred as the first law regulating casas de empeño was promulgated. The year 1847 stands out, with a marked decline in both pawning and redemptions. It is unclear whether the institution actually closed its doors during the occupation of the city by U.S. troops that year. During this tumultuous time there arose "serious fears among the population" that kept them from continuing their "assiduous habit" of visiting the offices of the Monte. American troops occupied part of the building in 1847. Cabrera Siles and Escandón, *Historia*, 60, 255.

84. The Cacahuate inventory was taken when the business sold, so pawned goods in it represent those whose pledge period was still ongoing and that might be redeemed by their owners. In contrast the Cartegena inventories are reports by pawnbrokers to the city about unredeemed goods going to auction. AGN, Consulado, vol. 47, exp. 6, fs. 302–9; AHCM, Tacubaya, Inventario General de la Municipiladid de Tacubaya, no. 120, exps. 3, 5, and 7.

85. AHCM, Justicia, Juzgados Criminales, vol. 2, exp. 2; Juzgados Criminales, vol. 2, exp. 3; Juzgados Criminales, vol. 1, exp. 1.

86. Sometimes victims only wanted their belongings back. In April 1856 a J. López published a plea in *El Siglo XIX* asking that anyone who recently had been sold or had received in pawn a new rug with big flowers on it deliver it to the house at Escalleras Street No. 9, where he "would satisfy what had been paid for it with no questions asked." *El Siglo XIX*, May 14, 1856.

87. It is difficult to separate some articles by gender, especially *calzones*. This term refers to both knee britches and long pants made of muslin that men wore as well as underpants worn by both sexes. In this analysis "calzones" are counted as men's pants, which were likely more commonly used and pawned than underpants.

88. Prieto, *Memorias*, 126; Benítez, *El traje*, 176.

89. Prieto, *Memorias*, 65.

90. Arias, *Los mexicanos*, 241. For comparative discussion of the transformation of household linens and clothing into successive articles and garments, see Vickery, "Women and the World of Goods," 282.

91. For another example, somebody with the last name Ayala (it might have been María de Jesús or Manuela, both regulars at the Cartagena shop) visited Cortes's twice in one day (July 22, 1868), first pawning two and a half varas of calico cloth for 87 ½ centavos and then

returning with four more varas of the same cloth for a loan of 1 peso 37 ½ centavos. In the Cartagena inventories from 1867–69, "Ayala" is also listed for pawning cuts of *hamburgo*, *manta*, and *indiana* and pieces of marino cut to make petticoats, finished men's clothing, and women's dresses, along with two irons. AHCM, Tacubaya, Inventario General de la Municipiladid de Tacubaya, no. 120, exps. 3, 5, and 7. Inventories for 1868 list loan values in pesos and reales, while the 1869 inventories list values in pesos and centavos.

92. Arrom, *Women*, 165.

93. This liberal project began with the Bourbons and continued to be modified by liberals in the republican era. Arrom, *Women*, 17–30, 82–99, and passim; Raquel Barceló, "Hegemonía y conflicto en la ideología porfiriana sobre el papel de la mujer y la familia," in *Familias y mujeres en México*, comp. Soledad González Montes y Soledad and Julia Tuñon, 73–110 (México: El Colegio de México, 1997); Carmen Ramos Escandón, "The Social Construction of Wife and Mother: Women in Porfirian Mexico, 1880–1917," in *Gender, Kinship, Power: A Comparative and Interdisciplinary History*, ed. Mary Jo Maynes et al., 275–85 (New York: Routledge, 1996); French, *Peaceful and Working People*, 87–107.

94. AGN, Ramo Consulado, vol. 47, exp. 6, fs. 306–9; AHCM, Inventario General de la Municipalidad de Tacubaya, no. 120, exp. 5.

95. Emma Cosío Villegas, "La vida cotidiana," in *Historia moderna de México: La Republica Restaurada; La vida social*, ed. Luis Gonzálezy González, Emma Cosío Villegas, and Guadalupe Monroy, 463 (México: Hermes, 1955).

96. Prieto, *Memorias*, 20–25, 66, 183, 202, 302–3; Arias, *Los mexicanos*, 234.

97. Some totals by category here are greater than those in appendix 1, table C, because table 3.2 includes household goods that were included in a mixed bundle of collateral.

98. Arias, *Los mexicanos*, 91.

99. Arias, *Los mexicanos*, 230. For the *mestizaje* of cuisine, see Pilcher, *¡Que vivan los tamales!*

100. Prieto, *Memorias*, 183, 302. For discussion of material goods as projecting status in Peru, see Jaimeson, "Doña Julia and Her Two Houses," 157–58. For England see Vickery, "Women and the World of Goods." For New York see Wall, "Family Meals," 110–14. For description of poor homes see Arias, *Los mexicanos*, 231.

101. For an example of inherited pawn tickets, see AGNCM, notario Antonio Pintos, vol. 3566, fs. 49–60, Testamento de doña María Josefa Romero y Huerta, 12 de abril de 1836.

102. First quote from Arias, *Los mexicanos*, 101; second quote on 230. In the photograph of the *molendera* in figure 2, a *petate* is in the corner. While this photograph is certainly posed, it is likely that elements are typical of a middling kitchen. The mat might indicate that this space was both the *tortillera*'s work space and where she slept.

103. Prieto, *Memorias*, 54.

104. AGN, Ramo Criminal, vol. 84, exp. 16, f. 255. See also Arias, *Los mexicanos*, 59.

105. AGN, Gobernación, leg. 2187(1), exp. 2, no. 20(9), fs. 1–3v; Bancroft Library, University of California–Berkeley, "Reglamento de las casas de empeño," July 27, 1871, manuscript, fs. 3–14. Ornaments from churches also continued to be banned from pawning in 1842 legislation. When a silver decoration from the baptismal font was stolen from the cathedral in 1845, the city government ordered police to inform casas de empeño and retail outlets, especially in "los Barrios," or popular neighborhoods, in case the thief tried to pawn or sell the silver.

106. "Orden de la Secretaría de Estado, 6 de diciembre de 1868," Saldivar, *Diccionario*, 510; AHCM, Inventario General de la Municipalidad de Tlalpan, inv. 69, exp. 71, March 1879.

107. For goods stolen and pawned by servants in 1852, see AHCM, Justicia, Juzgados Criminales, vol. 3, exp. 3. See also Prieto, *Memorias*, 128; and Arias, *Los mexicanos*, 107.

108. AGNCM, Antonio Pintos, vol. 3544, f. 164.

109. Arias, *Los mexicanos*, 100.

110. Calderón de la Barca, *Life in Mexico*, 139–40; Benítez, *El traje*, 183.

111. First quote from AGN, Gobernación, no section, caja 505, exp. 14, no. 1, f. 3v; second quote from AGN, Gobernación, leg. 2187(1), exp. 2, no. 20(9), f. 26.

112. The bulk of these goods (262) came from a document detailing goods stolen from the Monte in 1873. Other documents list 1 good from 1868, 27 goods from 1869, and 1 good from 1879. AGN, Gobernación, Leg. 1517(1), exp. 1, no. 1, fs. 1–3v; Leg. 1517(1), exp. 1, no. 5, fs. 1–12; Leg. 1296(1) exp. 5, no. 6, f. 5; Leg. 1296(1), exp. 5, no. 7; 4 sección, Leg. 873(7), exp. 1, fs. 6–73v. In 1875 the average loan at the main branch of the Monte was twenty-three and one-half pesos. Ramo Gobernación, leg. 2187(2), exp. 1, no. 27.

113. Cabrera Siles and Escandón, *Historia*, 73.

114. Photograph reproduced in Cabrera Siles and Escandón, *Historia*, 72. Quote from AHNMP, *Juntas Menores*, 6 de marzo de 1848 a 29 de junio 1875, quoted in Cabrera Siles and Escandón, *Historia*, 72.

4. Brokering Interests

1. For 1842 petition see AGN, Gobernación, leg. 2187(1), exp. 2, no. 20(9), fs. 24–41; for Ramírez y Rojas's views see AGN, Gobernación, no section, caja 505, exp. 14, no. 1, f. 3; and for Galindez's argument see AGN, Gobernación, 2nd section, leg. 873 (7), exp. 2, no. 3, fs. 4–8v.

2. Hale, *Mexican Liberalism*, 249–57.

3. Arrom, *Containing the Poor*, 178, 187, 193, 205–7, 214, 220–21, 226–27, 240–41.

4. The latest reference to a tienda engaging in pawning activity in my documents is 1868. *El Siglo XIX*, March 8, 1868. The earliest reference to a business as a "casa de empeño" is 1831. AGN, Gobernación, leg. 2187(1), exp. 2, no. 18, f. 3.

5. A comparison of 1842 notary records of new empeño businesses and the list of "tiendas y vinaterías" in the 1854 *Guía de forasteros* yields more than two dozen names of businessmen who appear in both lists. Mariano Galvan Rivera, *Guía de forasteros en la Ciudad de México, para el año de 1854* (México: Imprenta de Santiago Perez y Cia., 1854).

6. The life cycle of particular commercial establishments or real estate is not easily traced from the early nineteenth century onward, with spotty census data and street names changing as development projects and expansion changed the city map. The database for this chapter is compiled from documents from the Empeños ramo at the Archivo Histórico de la Ciudad de México and the Archivo General de Notarías de la Ciudad de México as well as from announcements published in the daily newspapers and city guidebooks. This is a subset of the larger database of 1,373 nonretail pawnshop addresses used for the book, covering the years 1836–1915. See appendix 2, table I, which summarizes the breakdown of number of pawnshops by years, though there is no way of knowing what percentage of existing pawnshops in any given year this sampling represents. The exceptions to this may be numbers for 1854, 1874, and 1902, which come from more complete official registers.

7. AHCM, Panaderías y Pulperías, leg. 1, exp. 33, fs. 9–14v; AHCM, Empeños, exps. 35, 37, and 46.

8. AGN, Padrones, vol. 85(1), fs. 20–28; *El Siglo XIX*, October 16, 1854.

9. AGN, Gobernación, leg. 2167(1), exp. 2, no. 20(1), fs. 5–7; *El Siglo XIX*, October 27, 1854.

10. AHCM, Panaderias y Pulperías, leg. 1, exp. 33, fs. 9–14v; *El Siglo XIX*, February 28, 1868; AHCM, Empeños, exp. 19.

11. It appears that not all retail establishments were expected to come into compliance. A list compiled of "empeñeros" in April 1842 by district authorities noted with perhaps some exaggeration that "all the small retail stores that exist in the diverse *cuarteles* receive *prendas*" but did not list stores individually. Other tiendas had stopped accepting collateral goods and only remained in the pawning business long enough for goods they already held to be redeemed. AGN, Gobernación, leg. 2167(1), exp. 2, no. 20(1), fs. 3–7.

12. While the 1842 documentation does not give the address, this pawnshop may be the same one that he was operating on the corner of Santa Ana and Santiago in May 1854.

13. AGN, Padrones, vol. 85(1), fs. 20–28; *El Siglo XIX*, May 11, 1854; AGNCM, Calapiz, vol. 1054, f. 109; AGN, Gobernación, leg. 2187(1), exp. 2 no. 20(9), fs. 1–3v.

14. AGNCM, Calapiz, vol. 1054, fs. 87, 89.

15. AGNCM, Calapiz, vol. 1054, f. 54, fs. 88–88v, 99v; vol. 1953, f. 47. For the cross-reference of Juan Acosta in the retail census and bond documents, see AGN, Padrones, vol. 85(1), fs. 20–28; AGNCM, Calapiz, vol. 1054, f. 88.

16. AGN, Gobernación, leg. 2167(1), exp. 2, no. 20(1), fs. 3–7.

17. AGNCM, Calapiz, vol. 1054, 57v and 91v.

18. In addition to the ten listed here, there were another fifty-six newly established pawnshops in the documents, but there were no addresses identified in the documents, which do list the owners, bondholders, and amount of bond. AGNCM, Calapiz, vols. 1053 and 1054, passim.

19. Decree dated "septiembre 23 de 1843," Ministerio de Hacienda, Sección Primera.

20. Almonte, *Guía de forasteros*, 307–13, 329–30. See Francois, "*Prendas* and *Pulperías*," for analysis of business patterns in retail pawning in the Bourbon era.

21. Costeloe, *Central Republic*, 13, 16; see also Rosa María Meyer Cosio, "Empresarios españoles después de la independencia," in *El poder y el dinero: Grupos y regiones mexicanos en El Siglo XIX*, coord. Beatriz Rojas, 218–25 (Mexico: Instituto Mora, 1994).

22. In another case Juan de la Serna y Echarte's will was recorded in October 1838. Was he related to Joaquin Serna, who owned a casa de empeño on the Palma Pazuela around the corner from the Monte de Piedad in 1854? María Dolores de la Vega is one of only a handful of Spanish women in the 1838 notary index, having completed her will in June 1838. Might she have been related to Manuel de la Vega, who owned a casa de empeño on the Plazuela de Santa Cruz in April 1842, or Joaquina de la Vega, who announced the auction of pawned goods in her empeño on the corner of Ave María in June of 1855 in the newspaper? For the Villarutias see Josefina Zoraida Vázquez and Pilar Gonzalbo Aizpuru, *Guía de protocolos: Archivo General de Notarías de la Ciudad de México; Año de 1838* (México: El Colegio de México, 1986), 319; and AGNCM, 170 Calapiz, vol. 1054, f. 10. For the Sernas see Vázquez and Gonzalbo Aizpuru, *Guía de protocolos, 1838*, 319; and Galvan Rivera, *Guía de forasteros*, 320. For de la Vega see Vázquez and Gonzalbo Aizpuru, eds., *Guía de protocolos, 1838*, 319; AGN, Gobernación, vol. 2167(1), exp. 2, no. 20(1), fs. 5–7; and *El Siglo XIX*, January 12, 1855.

23. Josefina Zoraida Vázquez and Pilar Gonzalbo Aizpuru, eds., *Guía de protocolos: Archivo General de Notarías de la Ciudad de México; Año de 1841* (México: El Colegio de México, 1989), 230–31; AHCM, Empeños, exp. 37; *El Siglo XIX*, January 24, 1855; AGNCM, Calapiz, v. 1053, f. 58v; Galvan Rivera, *Guía de forasteros*, 332; AGN, Gobernación, vol. 2167(1), exp. 2, no. 2(1), fs. 5–7; and Pérez, *Almanaque estadístico*, 241.

24. Josefina Zoraida Vázquez and Pilar Gonzalbo Aizpuru, eds., *Guía de protocolos: Archivo General de Notarías de la Ciudad de México; Año de 1850* (México: El Colegio de México, 1996), 271; and Galvan Rivera, *Guía de forasteros*, 330.

25. Josefina Zoraida Vázquez and Pilar Gonzalbo Aizpuru, eds., *Guía de protocolos: Archivo General de Notarías de la Ciudad de México; Año de 1853* (México: El Colegio de México, 1998), 264–65, 270, and *Guía de protocolos*, 1855, 267–75; AGNCM, Calapiz, vol. 1053, f. 39v; Galvan Rivera, *Guía de forasteros*, 331; Pérez, *Almanaque estadístico*, 240; *El Siglo XIX*, October 16, 1854, January 21, 1855, January 24, 1855, May 6, 1855, and May 11, 1855; AHCM, Empeños, vol. 885, exps. 35 and 37; AHCM, Gobierno del Distrito, Empeños, vol. 1415; and vol. 1429, exp. 39, f. 2. For Doña María, see Galvan Rivera, *Guía de forasteros*, 331; and *El Siglo XIX*, April 12, 1855.

26. José Fernández Huergo, Manuel García Arrendondo, José Gutierrez Pelaez, José Lézameta, Manuel María de Palacios, Antonio Perez, José Pontones, Joaquín Poo, José María Revuelta, Manuel Ruiz, and Laureano Zarandona appear in *Guías de forasteros* and archival records as pawnbrokers and can be cross-identified as Spanish in credit, mortgage, marriage, and power-of-attorney documents indexed for 1875. Robert A. Potash, Jan Bazant, and Josefina Zoraida Vázquez, eds., *Guía de protocolos notariales del Archivo General de Notarías, México, D.F., año 1875* (México: El Colegio de México, 1984), 581–82; Galvan Rivera, *Guía de forasteros*, 330–31; Pérez, *Almanaque estadístico*, 240; AGN, Gobernación, leg. 2167(1), exp. 2, no. 20(1), fs. 5–7; and *El Siglo XIX*, October 16, 1854, and October 27, 1854. For Lezameta see Pérez, *Almanaque estadístico*, 239; *El Siglo XIX*, May 22, 1886, and July 28, 1886; AHCM, Empeños, no. 885, exps. 57 and 58; and AGN, Gobernación, leg. 1489(1), exp. 2, fs. 9–11. For Poo see AHCM, Empeños, no. 885, exps. 35, 37, 46, and 58.

27. AHCM, Actas de Cabildo, no. 166–A.

28. Other pawnbrokers who were likely foreigners judging by their surnames include Antonio Bonhomme in 1854, Pedro Arillaud in 1855, Pedro Strittmater in 1868, and H. Steyer and Hortensia Stiges in 1874. Pawnbroker Leon Arnaut, identified as "Francés," is listed in notary documents from 1855, as is Antonio Meyer, who owned a pawnshop in 1875. Vázquez and Gonzalbo Aizpuru, *Guía de protocolos*, 1855, 276, 279; Galvan Rivera, *Guía de forasteros*, 330; *El Siglo XIX*, January 17, 1855, January 13, 1868; Pérez, *Almanaque estadístico*, 240; AGN, Gobernación, leg. 1489(1), exp. 2, fs. 9–11v; and AHCM, Empeños, vol. 885, exp. 70.

29. In November 1838 Manuela Alonso de Caso, identified as a Spaniard, visited a notary to draw up paperwork concerning business investments. It is unclear whether she was related to these pawnbroking Casos. AGN, Padrones, vol. 85(1), fs. 20–28; AGNCM, Calapiz, vol 1054, f. 188; Vázquez and Gonzalbo Aizpuru, *Guía de protocolos*, 1839, 319. Another example is the pawnshop on Verdeja operated by Don Manuel Campuzano in October 1854, which was owned by León Campuzano in February 1878. *El Siglo XIX*, October 27, 1854; AHCM, Empeños, exp. 35.

30. The percentage depends on the documents used. In the tally from retail censuses, women are listed as owning 10 percent. Using the 1854 *Guía de forasteros*, women are only 8 of 103 pawnbrokers listed, or 7 percent. In an 1867 tax document, women owned 15 percent of 102 pawnshops listed.

31. That women had fewer employment opportunities after Independence is one of the conclusions of Arrom's seminal study of women in Mexico City. See Arrom, *Women*, 266–67. Women of the emergent middle class were to be in charge of the "moral world" and the dignified work of domestic chores, to be "exclusively occupied in making happy all those that destiny has placed at her side." See Angela Grassi, "La misión de la mujer," in *La illustración:*

Semanario de las señoritas, 1859, vol. 1, cited in *El album de la mujer: Antología ilustrada de las mexicanas*, ed. Marcela Tostado Gutiérrez (México: Instituto Nacional de Antropología e Historia, 1991), 3:77.

32. At midcentury women constituted 60 percent of 143 silk merchants, while in 1874 they constituted only 42 percent of 38 listed. One branch of business where women held on over these twenty years is pasta making; they owned 43 percent of more than a dozen pasta-making businesses in 1854 and 1874.

33. While there were only seven auction houses listed in the 1852 *Guía de forasteros*, all of them run by men with Spanish surnames, foreign women seemed to suddenly dominate the auctioneer trade, owning 20 of 26 auction houses listed in the 1854 *Guía de forasteros*. Doña Virginia Gourgues, who is listed in 1854 as the owner of an auction house in the second block of Plateros, may be related to pawnbroker Mademoiselle María Goungues, noted above, whose pawnshop was on the same block nine years earlier. There is only one auctioneer listed in the 1874 guide, a man. Almonte, *Guía de forasteros*, 457; Galvan Rivera, *Guía de forasteros*, 320. The 1854 female auctioneers include Doñas N. Barenur, N. Berthier, Coral Deveaux, Ester Doral, Juana Dostugue, Patricia Echeonti, Virginia Fortoni, Carlota Got, Virginia Gourges, Lucia Guillet, Josefa Larroche, Margarita Mansberg, Rosalia Mesciera, Eugenia Ouvrard, Juana Pinsou, Rita Rayard, Margarita Sans, Faustina Totie, and Clara Wiel.

34. For the bazaar list that includes Poo, see Pérez, *Almanaque estadístico*, 231. His empeño is registered in the tax records found in AHCM, Empeños, exp. 37.

35. AGN, Gobernación, leg. 2187(1), exp. 2, no. 20(9), fs. 24–41.

36. The Spanish advertisement reads "recibirá prendas en clase de empeño, ofreciéndole que será considerado con la equidad que las circunstancias demandan." Almonte, *Guía de forasteros*, 430.

37. For pawnbroker characterization of clientele and their self-characterization as social workers, see chapter 3. The widow language is from AGN, Gobernación, leg. 2187(1), exp. 2 no. 8, fs. 3–3v. Luther N. Steward Jr., "Spanish Journalism in Mexico, 1867–1879," *Hispanic American Historical Review* 45, no. 3 (1965): 422–33.

38. Hale, *Mexican Liberalism*, 95–98, 176–79, 249–51, 298–303. For discussion of leading ideologues and major tenets of economic liberalism, see Moisés González Navarro, *La pobreza en México* (México: El Colegio de México, 1985), 39–42.

39. AGN, Gobernación, leg. 2187(1), exp. 2, no. 18, f. 5.

40. Silvia Arrom has recently argued that the "much maligned" Santa Anna's reputation might be due for rehabilitation, given improvements in the Poor House under his administrations. His professed concern for the poor in the empeño law supports that assertion, though the law also served other agendas of the mercurial statesman. See Arrom, *Containing the Poor*, 186–87. On war taxes see Meyer and Sherman, *Course*, 330. On Santa Anna's relationship with Spanish merchants see Quinlan, "Issues and Factions," 177–207.

41. If redeemed in the first or second month, the owner would pay one-eighth real per peso loaned; in the third or fourth month, interest would be one-quarter real per peso; in the fifth or sixth month, it would be three-eighths real per peso; and in the seventh or eighth month, after the six-month pledge time expired, the owner would be charged one-half real per peso.

42. AGN, Gobernación, leg. 2187(1), exp. 2, no. 20(9), fs. 1–3v.

43. A loan of one real paid back at one and one-eighth reales represented 12.5 percent interest over one month (150 percent at annual rate) but 2.25 percent a month over six months (or 4.5 percent annually). The low rates that brokers touted went to those with seven-real

loans, where paying back seven and one-eighth reales in the first month constituted 1.8 percent (or 21.6 percent annually) but in the sixth month meant only 0.3 percent a month, or 3.6 percent annually. AGN, Gobernación, leg. 2187(1), exp. 2 no. 20(9), f. 1v.

44. AGN, Gobernación, leg. 2187(1), exp. 2, no. 20(9), fs. 24–41.

45. In keeping with the law, he was ordered to register and pay for his license, give back all goods he had accepted in pawn, and, in the future, not exceed the legal interest rate. *El Siglo XIX*, January 12, 1855, 1. For more cases of charging high interest, see *El Siglo XIX*, January 24, 1855, 4; February 7, 1855, 4; and February 15, 1855, 3. For Arillaud, see *El Siglo XIX*, January 17, 1855, 4. For Gómez, see *El Siglo XIX*, January 21, 1855, 2.

46. *El Siglo XIX*, January 22, 1855, 3.

47. AGN, Gobernación, no section, caja 505, exp. 14, no. 1, f. 3. For usury laws, see Rodríguez, *Pandectas*, 2:561–70. See also Clara García Ayluardo, "El comerciante y el crédito durante la época borbónica en la Nueva España," in Ludlow and Marichal, *Banca y poder en México*, 28–30.

48. *Diario del Imperio*, July 20, 1866, 2.

49. Bancroft Library, University of California–Berkeley, "Reglamento de las casas de empeños," July 22, 1871, manuscript, fs. 3–14. The complaint about receiving stolen goods is in Article 12.

50. *Diario Oficial*, December 4, 1867, 1.

51. AHCM, Empeños, vol. 885, exp. 35.

52. Many of these bureaucratic articles outlining duties of state inspectors are similar to a reglamento published in Juárez's last months before being deposed by the French. AGN, Gobernación, no section, caja 505, exp. 14, no. 1 fs. 9–10. The new law reflects the growth of the regulatory bureaucracy, calling for filing documents in triplicate and outlining the duties of the six inspectors, who would be paid fifty pesos a month. It also suggests a shift in regulatory authority from the ministry of Gobernación to the government of the Federal District (which itself was under Gobernación), or at least shared jurisdiction in pawning matters, with the Ayuntamiento, the Federal District's governor, and the ministry of Gobernación all involved.

53. Pawnbrokers expressed concern that the law called for the employment of only four government appraisers, not nearly enough to avoid practices of favoritism and of a few individual brokers' monopolizing their time to the detriment of the public. The brokers wanted twelve or even fifteen appraisers, to ease tensions that they thought would result from current provisions. AGN, Gobernación, leg. 611, exp. 3, fs. 29–33.

54. The brokers also seemed to resent the revenue that the state would earn from their business. They calculated that at least twenty establishments would have more than 1,000 pesos' worth of salable goods appraised each month, which would result in the government appraisers' earning 1,200 pesos monthly just from those brokers with larger volumes. The rest of the seventy or eighty establishments would probably yield 600 pesos monthly for government agents.

55. And, brokers argued, the regularly scheduled visits of inspectors called for by the law would have to last two weeks to thoroughly review all books and shelves in the larger shops. AGN, Gobernación, leg. 611, exp. 3, fs. 1–37v.

56. AGN, Gobernación, 2nd section, leg. 873(7), exp. 2, no. 3, fs. 1–3v. For the government's point-by-point response to the brokers' petition, see AGN, Gobernación, leg. 611, exp. 3, fs. 18–25 and 39–42v. Other changes included a reduction in the fee paid to the appraiser

by the broker from 6 percent to 2 percent (an issue the brokers had addressed), but also an increase in the salary of inspectors from fifty pesos to sixty-six pesos sixty-six centavos a month and the elimination of bonding requirement of inspectors for five hundred pesos.

57. This provision is difficult to translate. Article 44 states that goods left over from two auctions "serán adjudicadas al prestamista en la cantidad en que hubieren sido empeñadas, mas el premio y los gastos." In this sense "adjudicar" seems to mean appropriated by the lender for the pawned price plus interest and expenses. The definition of "adjudicar" is "to declare that a thing pertains to a person or to attribute something to satisfy a right." See *Diccionario enciclopédico abreviado*, vol. 1, 7th ed. (Madrid: Espasa-Calpe, 1957), 152.

58. AGN, Gobernación, leg. 611, exp. 3, fs. 1–7.

59. AGN, Gobernación, 2nd section, leg. 873(7), exp. 2, no. 3, fs. 4–16v.

60. *El Distrito Federal*, August 16, 1874, 3.

61. AGN, Gobernación, 2nd section, leg. 873 (7), exp. 2, no. 3, fs. 4–8v.

62. AGN, Gobernación, 2nd section, leg. 873(7), exp. 2, no. 3, fs. 9–13v.

63. AGN, Gobernación, leg. 611, exp. 3, fs. 18–25.

64. In the colonial period, when most pawning took place in retail establishments, inspections were done by courts. In June 1813 that changed, and the Ayuntamiento became responsible for them. In November 1813 the city's districts were divided among four commissioners. AHCM, Actas de Cabildo, vol. 132–A, fs. 144v, 326.

65. In February 1844 the councilmen told the commission responsible for the visits to consult with Don Francisco Calapiz, the notary who had produced the many bond and license documents discussed earlier, as he had knowledge of where the newest establishments were. AHCM, Actas de Cabildo, 1844.

66. First-class business, with a capital of 1,000 to 8,000 pesos, had to pay the inspector 10 pesos. Those in the next class, with a capital of 500 to 1,600, paid 5 pesos; those with capital of 100 to 498 paid 20 reales; and those with a capital of 24 to 99 pesos paid 10 reales. AGN, Gobernación, no section, caja 505, exp. 14 no. 4, fs. 9–10.

67. AGN, Gobernación, leg. 1489(1), exp. 2, fs. 1–15.

68. The owner of the pawnshop on the corner of Estampa de Jesús María and Vanegas complained to the police inspector that Don Guillermo Arteaga and another individual, identifying themselves as inspectors of empeños, were in a drunken state when they came to inspect the shop in April 1872. AGN, Gobernación, 2nd section, vol. 872(5), exp. 4, no. 1, fs. 1–4.

69. AGN, Gobernación, 2nd section, vol. 873(7), exp. 2, no. 2, fs. 1–9.

70. For the Ortiz case see AGNCM, Calapiz, vol. 1054, f. 54. For a bond of one hundred pesos for a business operating with one hundred pesos capital, see AGNCM, Calapiz, vol. 1054, f. 60. For a bond and capitalization of two hundred pesos, see AGNCM, Calapiz, vol. 1054, f. 65.

71. AGNCM, Calapiz, vol. 1054, fs. 73 and 40; *Diario Oficial*, December 4, 1867, 1.

72. AGN, Gobernación, leg. 2167(1), exp. 2, no. 20(1), fs. 3–7.

73. AHCM, Empeños, exps. 35, 37, 46, 57, 58; *El Siglo XIX*, January 29, 1885, March 14, 1885, July 5, 1886. The authorities compiling a list of empeños in April 1842 noted that were none in Cuartels 17 through 22. AGN, Gobernación, leg. 2167(1), exp. 2 no. 20(1), fs. 3–7.

74. Don Miguel Azcarate also held two in 1842, one on the corner of Esclavo and El Aguila and another at No. 12 in the first block of San Lorenzo. For Ortiz see AGNCM, Calapiz, vol. 1054, f. 84; *El Siglo XIX*, May 11, 1854. For Chávarri see Galvan Rivera, *Guía de forasteros*, 330; and

Pérez, *Almanaque estadístico*, 238. For Andrade see AGN, Gobernación, leg. 2167(1), exp. 2, no. 20(1), fs. 5–7; AGNCM, Calapiz, vol. 1054, f. 60. For Azcarate see AGN, Gobernación, leg. 2167(1), exp. 2, no. 20(1), fs. 5–7.

75. These inventories list unredeemed goods up for sale by their item number and date of transaction, so these averages are "at least," because we cannot know how many more goods before the first and after the last item number listed in the *cumplida* inventories for a given month were pawned and redeemed. AHCM, Inventario General de la Municipalidad de Tacubaya, no. 120, exps. 5 and 7; AHCM, Inventario General de la Municipalidad de Tlalpan, no. 69, exps. 11 and 71. These suburban pawnshops may not be representative of more numerous and longer-standing establishments in neighborhoods of Mexico City, for which there are no comparable records for these years.

76. AHCM, Inventario General de la Municipalidad de Tacubaya, no. 120, exp. 7.

77. For the first three: 62 percent in January 1867, 65 percent in May 1868, and 63 percent in February 1969. For the remaining two: 68 percent in August 1868 and 69 percent in June 1869.

78. "Armas" include pistols, rifles, and a solitary machete. "Varios objetos" include musical instruments, an umbrella, hats, pots and pans, eyeglasses, needles and cuts of fabric, artisan's tools, boots, agricultural tools, many irons, a table clock, a few saddles, some mattresses, and many ceramic dishes.

79. Four other watches were pawned in multiple-goods transactions, with the loan value listed for the bundle, but the appraisal value not broken out by individual item and therefore left out of this discussion.

80. AGN, Gobernación, leg. 2187(1), exp. 2, no. 20(9), fs. 24–41.

81. AGN, Gobernación, no section, caja 505, exp. 14, no. 1, f. 6.

82. Other pawnbrokers among the Monte branch clientele included Francisco Herrera, José Pérez, and José Velázquez. AGN, Gobernación, 4th section, vol. 873(7), exp. 1, fs. 6–73v.

83. Cabrera Siles and Escandón, *Historia*, 243–44, 246, 250–55; Rubio, *El Nacional*, 19. The Italian Montis di Pietá were also expected to lend to governments in times of extraordinary need. See Pullan, *Rich and Poor*, 604–6.

84. Cabrera Siles and Escandón, *Historia*, 259, 261, 265.

85. Cabrera Siles and Escandón, *Historia*, 55.

86. In 1841 interim president Santa Anna had tried to protect and augment the Monte's capital by ordering that any *depósitos judiciales* ordered by court authorities be deposited in the Monte de Piedad, where 4 percent interest would be charged monthly, but only for the first year the money was held. In 1853 Santa Anna again attempted to increase the Monte's coffers when he included the institution in his conflicts with the press, ordering that journalists deposit money in the Monte de Piedad as a guarantee against fines that would eventually be levied as punishment for "abusing the freedom of the press." Cabrera Siles and Escandón, *Historia*, 252–57. Villela dates the court change to 1851; Villela, *El Monte*, 8.

87. Cabrera Siles and Escandón, *Historia*, 255–57.

88. AGN, Gobernación, leg. 2187(2), exp. 1, no. 33(3), f. 19.

89. By 1867 the Monte was charging at its Casa Matriz (to differentiate the downtown branch from new neighborhood branches opened the same year) a rate of between 8 and 12 percent annually, depending on what month redemption took place. In 1871 adjustments to the interest rate boosted it to 12 to 48 percent depending on the month, and then that rate was halved in May 1873. Cabrera Siles and Escandón, *Historia*, 252, 269, 271–73; Villela, *El Monte*, 11. See also AGN, Gobernación, no section, caja 505, exp. 14, no. 1, f. 4.

90. AGN, Gobernación, no section, caja 505, exp. 14, no. 1, fs. 6–8.

91. Director Lazpita suggested that alarm and panic would be easily triggered if the staff had to leave their posts to secure more cash for transactions, which they would have to do if the Monte's treasury was tapped to fund new branches instead of the government's treasury. AGN, Gobernación, no section, caja 505, exp. 14, no. 1, fs. 3–5–8v.

92. Parallel to the Monte's growth in the city was the establishment of Montes de Piedad in other cities in Mexico, including Puebla, Guadalajara, Oaxaca, and San Luis Potosí.

93. *Diario del Imperio*, July 10, 1866, p. 1.

94. Cabrera Siles and Escandón, *Historia*, 70.

95. Arrom, *Containing the Poor*, 228.

96. AGN, Gobernación, no section, caja 505, exp. 14, no. 1, f. 5.

97. The charge would be two centavos per peso loaned for the first month, four for the second month, six for the third, eight for the fourth, ten for the fifth, and twelve for the sixth.

98. *Diario del Imperio*, October 31, 1866, 2; AHNMP, Legislación, Leyes y Decretos, caja 1. The decree refers to both reales and centavos, suggesting a complex transition to the new monetary system.

99. *Diario del Imperio*, October 30, 1866, 2.

100. Villamil, *El Monte*, 145, 150.

101. The administrator needed a two-thousand-peso *fianza*, the appraiser a one-thousand-peso *fianza*, and each of the scribes a five-hundred-peso *fianza*. *Diario del Imperio*, October 31, 1866, 2; *Diario del Imperio*, October 30, 1866, 3. For a comparison of these salaries with those of the Poor House, see Arrom, *Containing the Poor*, 215. Maximilian's plan to turn the Monte toward assisting the poor included a provision limiting deposits in the savings bank to less than ten pesos. It is not clear if this measure was implemented, or how it would have aided the poor. The laws confirming the expansion by Juárez and Lerdo de Tejada make no mention of the savings bank. *Diario del Imperio*, July 10, 1866, 1.

102. AGN, Gobernación, no section, caja 505, exp. 14, no. 1, f. 4.

103. AGN, Gobernación, no section, caja 505, exp. 14, no. 1, fs. 6–8v.

104. AGN, Gobernación, leg. 1517(1), exp. 1, no. 5, fs. 1–12.

105. Butrón y Pereda explained that he immediately signed in when he arrived to expedite his duties. Director Cendejas claimed the supporting documents Butrón y Pereda submitted showing that this behavior was customary of many Monte employees were fraudulent and that the employees were in a conspiracy to hide sloppy behavior. AGN, Gobernación, 4th section, leg. 872(2), exp. 1, no. 19(20). For the Olmedo case see AGN, Gobernación, 4th section, leg. 872(3), exp. 3, no. 6, f. 1.

106. AGN, Gobernación, 4th section, leg. 872(3), exp. 3, no. 2, fs. 100–6.

107. AGN, Gobernación, leg. 2187(1), exp. 2, no. 20(9), fs. 26–27.

108. Jaime E. Rodríguez O., "Introduction," in Rodríguez, *Patterns of Contention*, 2–5.

109. John Tutino, "Agrarian Social Change and Peasant Rebellion in Nineteenth-Century Mexico: The Example of Chalco," in *Riot, Rebellion, and Revolution: Rural Social Conflict in Mexico*, ed. Friedrich Katz, 95–140 (Princeton: Princeton University Press, 1988).

110. Tenenbaum, *Politics of Penury*.

5. Positivist Housekeeping

1. Fanny Gooch Chambers, *Face to Face with the Mexicans*, 1887, ed. and with an introduction by C. Harvey Gardiner (Carbondale IL: Southern Illinois University Press, 1966), 84.

2. Julio Sesto, *El México de Porfirio Díaz: Estudios sobre el desenvolvimiento general de la República Mexicana despues de diez años de permanencia en ella; Observaciones hechas en el terreno oficial y en el particular* (Valencia: F. Sempere, 1909), 210.

3. For a recent study of Mexican domestic servants, see Blum, "Cleaning the Revolutionary Household."

4. First quote from Gooch Chambers, *Face to Face*, 107; second quote from *El Monitor Republicano*, November 12, 1886.

5. This separation of property could favor some women but represented a loss of security for most. The only situation where the woman would clearly benefit is that of the working-class married woman, who would gain control over her own income, especially when the joint estate was small. But "the woman of modest means who neither earned a salary nor owned property (or whose property was less than her husband might earn), the separation of property system represented a loss of protection, for she could be left penniless if separated or widowed." Arrom, "Changes in Mexican Family Law," 314.

6. Carmen Diana Deere and Magdalena León, *Empowering Women: Land and Property Rights in Latin America* (Pittsburgh: University of Pittsburgh Press, 2001), 57.

7. After 1870 parents of means no longer had to endow their daughters upon marriage. And after 1884 children were no longer guaranteed to inherit an equal share of their parents' property. Daughters in middle-class and elite families might receive neither dowry nor inheritance, and they were more vulnerable than their brothers because they were less likely to secure a job that paid well.

8. On the one hand the abolition of the *legítima*, or equal share of the parent's property guaranteed to each female and male child, threatened the institution of the family by no longer protecting each of its members and by providing the chance for legitimate children to lose out to illegitimate ones. On the other hand, and this was the lawmakers' chief purpose, it promoted economic development by enhancing the ability to accumulate capital and free up the flow of property. Arrom, "Changes in Mexican Family Law," 313–15.

9. *Tercer censo de 1910*, 2:390.

10. Deere and León, *Empowering Women*, 58.

11. For gendered positivism see Carmen Ramos, "Mujeres trabajadores en el México porfiriano: Género e ideología del trabajo femenino, 1876–1911," *Revista Europea de Estudios Latinoamericanos y del Caribe* 48 (June 1990): 27–44, and "Señoritas porfirianas: Mujeres y ideología en el México Progresista, 1880–1910," in *Presencia y transparencia: La mujer en la historia de México* (México: El Colegio de México, 1987), 143–61; Verena Radkau, *"Por la debilidad de nuestro ser": Mujeres del pueblo en la paz porfiriana* (México: Centro de Investigaciones y Estudios Superiores en Antropología Social, 1989); and Susana Vidales, "Ni madres abnegadas, ni Adelitas," *Criticas de la Economia Política* 14/15 (April–June 1980): 241–81. On gendered discourses in Mexico, see Jean Franco, *Plotting Women: Gender Representation in Mexico* (New York: Columbia University Press, 1988).

12. In the words of intellectual Andrés Molina Enríquez: "The two primordial functions of life are existence and reproduction. It is logical that the organic division of labor . . . has divided these functions between the two sexes. . . . The separation of the sexes is the division of one organism into two exclusive but complementary functions. A man is not complete, because he lacks the ability to procreate; the woman is not complete either, because she lacks the ability to prevail in the unequal struggle of work among men." Quoted in Radkau, *Por la debilidad*, 15.

13. Margaret Towner, "Monopoly Capitalism and Women's Work during the Porfiriato," *Latin American Perspectives* 4, nos. 1–2 (1977): 90–105, quote on 97; Horacio Barreda, *El siglo XIX ante el femenismo: Una interpretación positivista* (1909; repr., México: Universidad Nacional Autónoma de México, 1991); L. Josefina Reyes, *La mujer en el hogar y en la sociedad* (Puebla, 1903); M. A. Sanz, *La mujer mexicana en el santuario del hogar* (México, 1907).

14. These included *La Mujer*, *El Correo de las Señoras*, and *Violetas de Anahuac*. With the new century *La Mujer Mexicana: Revista mensual científico-literaria consagrada a la evolución, progreso y perfeccionamiento de la mujer mexicana* began publication.

15. In an article in the ninth issue of *La Mujer Mexicana*, published in 1902, it is clear that it is not just wives and mothers who have a domestic role to play. "The Mission of the Señorita in the Home" primed daughters—"the centerpiece of the family"—to understand that they were "like the flowers that beautified the park, like the ray of sunlight that gives heat," and that "our mission in the home is one of peace, sweetness, condescension, abnegation, and we should always be disposed to sacrifice of ourselves, if with that those around us will be gratified." *La Mujer Mexicana: Publicación mensual dedicada al bello sexo, escrita por Mariano de Jesus Torres*, entregas 1–10 (Morelia, 1901–2). The article entitled "Rights of the Woman" is on p. 15 in entrega 2. The article "The Mission of the Señorita in the Home" is on p. 73 in entrega 9.

16. While these calculations should be "easy according to the Arithmetic that our ladies have learned in school," the tables "save them the effort" by calculating fractions of a monthly fifty-centavo wage so the employer knows what to pay should a servant leave before the month is out. After nine days the employer would owe the departing domestic servant fifteen centavos, after fifteen days twenty-five centavos, and so on.

17. Quote from *La mujer*, cited in Radkau, *Por la debilidad*, 32.

18. The reality that many women had to work outside their own homes was recognized by some positivists, such as reformer Luis Lara y Pardo, who investigated the women working as prostitutes in the city, lamenting that 120 of every 1,000 women worked in the commercial sex trade. The 1910 census data for the Federal District lists only 601 "mesalinas," or prostitutes, as much an underestimate as Lara y Pardo's number of over 20,000 is an overestimate. Luis Lara y Pardo, *La prostitución en México* (México: Librería de la Viuda de Ch. Bouret, 1908), 252–53. On prostitution in Mexico City during the Porfiriato, see Bliss, *Compromised Positions*, 23–61.

19. Images of women in late nineteenth-century mainstream culture were often reduced to that of either sanctified mother and wife or degraded whore, reflecting the extent to which the Porfirian gender ideology pervaded society, with contradictions of class intertwined with contradictions of gender in the dominant popular culture. See Radkau, *Por la debilidad*, 28–34.

20. Lanny Thompson, "Artisans, Marginals, and Proletarians: The Households of the Popular Classes in Mexico City, 1876–1950," in *Five Centuries of Mexican History*, ed. Virginia Guedea and Jaime E. Rodríguez O., 310 (México and Irvine: Instituto Mora / University of California, 1992). This was true at the beginning of the century as well. Silvia Arrom found in the 1811 census that "the most employed group [of women] were also the most married." Arrom, *Women*, 202.

21. Muñoz de Alba, "La condición jurídica," 814–15. For discussion of women's role in the Porfirian education project, see Mary Kay Vaughan, "Women, Class and Education in Mexico, 1880–1910," *Latin American Perspectives* 12/13 (1977): 135–52.

22. Jesús Galindo y Villa, "Educación de la mujer mexicana," quoted in Muñoz, "La condición jurídica de la mujer," 821.

23. Under the Civil Code a single woman was not really free until the age of thirty, before which time she could not move out of her father's house. This violated the constitutional freedom of movement. García also considered unconstitutional the requirement that a married woman have her husband's permission in order to appear in court, do business, administer, or acquire property, because it violated the article that proclaimed all those born in the Republic to be free. Muñoz, "La condición jurídica," 819.

24. García, whose own education was positivist, again disagreed with his coreligionists, arguing that female suffrage would benefit the progress and modernity of the country. García linked education and suffrage, arguing that equal access to education was the solution to any supposed deficiencies in female voters. Muñoz, "La condición jurídica de la mujer," 820.

25. Carmen Romero Rubio, the president's wife, founded the Casa Amiga de la Obrera, a day-care center for working mothers, with other women establishing and running institutions aiding poor women and children, including shelters, orphanages, and mothers' clubs. Ann S. Blum, "Conspicuous Benevolence: Liberalism, Public Welfare, and Private Charity in Porfirian Mexico City, 1877–1910," *The Americas* 58, no. 1 (2001): 7–38, quote on 20–22.

26. Gutierrez Najera, "La historia de un peso falso," 297.

27. In the 1882 municipal census of Mexico City, "little physical or social distance" separated skilled artisans, unskilled laborers, small merchants, vendors, and domestic servants. All still lived side by side in casas de vecindad. By the end of the Porfirian years, workers lived in recently constructed tenement housing as well as casas de vecindad, now notoriously slumlike both upstairs and down. The rooms were "true caves [with] poor artisan families of women and young children and orphans inside, who live from a thousand small industries, making sweets, making toys, embroidering shawls, sewing uniforms, making shoes, the apprentice carpenter' wife, the mother of the domestic servant, or the humble seamstress of fashions." Ruiz Castañeda, *La ciudad*, 47; Tony Morgan, "Proletarians, Politicos, and Patriarchs: The Use and Abuse of Cultural Customs in the Early Industrialization of Mexico City," in *Rituals of Rule*, ed. Beezley, Martin, and French, 151–71, quote on 157.

28. Motts, *La vida*, 36–38; Berta Tello Peón, "Intención decorativa en los objetos de uso cotidiano de los interiores domésticos del Porfiriato," in Estrada de Gerlero, *El arte y la vida*, 140; Michael Johns, *The City of Mexico in the Age of Díaz* (Austin: University of Texas Press, 1997), 7–41.

29. The number of native speakers is the same as the number of residents speaking a foreign language, though here there was a gender imbalance, with more males speaking a foreign language. A dependence on language statistics undercounts foreigners in the city at the end of the Porfiriato, as the more than twelve thousand Spanish residents spoke the same language as most Mexicans. The Spanish dominated retail, and the French, English, and German had run the big trading houses since the mid-nineteenth century. The American colony in the city, not more than three hundred people in the early Porfirian years and by the end ten times that big, invested in development projects, banking, and business. Next to Spaniards, those from the United States of America were the most numerous foreign population, with just over three thousand, followed by the French colony of about two thousand, and then the Chinese and German populations, each over one thousand, with the English just short of that total. México, Secretaría de Agricultura y Fomento, Dirección de Estadistica, *Tercer censo de 1910*, 2:150–52, 156–65; Francisco López Cámara, *La estructura económica y social de México en la época de la Reforma* (México: Siglo XXI Editores, 1967), 87. For a study of the German Casa Boker, see Buchenau, *Tools of Progress*. For a study of the American colony, see

William Schell Jr. *Integral Outsiders: The American Colony in Mexico City, 1876–1911* (Wilmington DE: Scholarly Resources, 2001).

30. In 1895, 63 percent of the 2,357 landlords were women, while in 1910 women made up 68 percent of the 4,586 rental-property owners in Mexico City. This increase in female property ownership may be the result of the testamentary freedom instituted in 1884, with more women—whether widows or daughters—now inheriting the family home or business outright, though there is no way to determine the status of these proprietors from the published census statistics. Ministerio de Fomento, Dirección General de Estadistica, *Censo general de la Republica Mexicana verificado el 20 de Octubre de 1895: Censo del Distrito Federal* (México: Oficina Tip. de la Secretaría de Fomento, 1898), 387–428; *Tercer censo de 1910*, 2:390. For an analysis of the Porfirian and subsequent censuses, as well as a critique of studies based on them, see Donald B. Keesing, "Structural Change Early in Development: Mexico's Changing Industrial and Occupational Strucure from 1895–1950," *Journal of Economic History* 29 (1969): 716–37.

31. The different numbers of married men and women might mean that more wives than husbands were absent from the city when the census data were gathered, especially for the earlier period, or that people living together reported their civil status differently. One problem with interpreting what these numbers mean is the ambiguity of terms such as "casado" and "soltera." We do not know, for example, how many in either category are in long-term consensual relationships that have not been formalized through marriage. Robert McCaa, "Marriageways in Mexico and Spain," *Continuity and Change* 9, no. 1 (1994): 11–43; Blum, "Public Welfare," 252.

32. Thompson, "Artisans, Marginals, and Proletarians," 316.

33. Blum suggests that earlier female-headed household patterns continued (if we cannot say they increased). Many of the women using the Casa de Cuna to temporarily place their children (especially if taking live-in servant jobs) during the Porfiriato were household heads and "self-supporting mothers." Blum also points out that the Casa de Maternidad, a charitable maternity hospital, promoted child abandonment by poor women. To what extent this policy was aimed at stemming the numbers of female-headed households, protecting children from poverty, or providing servants for the Casa de Cuna to place out is unclear. Porter notes that most of the ambulant vendors resisting regulations in the Porfirian era self-identified as single mothers and widows with children. And despite a century of family legislation aimed at regularizing the nuclear family, high rates of illegitimacy continued into the twentieth century, with 70 percent of all births in the country illegitimate in 1908. Blum, "Public Welfare," 243–49, 254–55; Susie S. Porter, "'And That It Is Custom Makes It Law': Class Conflict and Gender Ideology in the Public Sphere, Mexico City, 1880–1910," *Social Science History* 24, no. 1 (2000): 111–48, 129–42. For illegitimacy rates see Ramos Escandón, "Social Construction," 280.

34. A study of the 1895 census divided the urban population nationwide into three basic classes: upper class (2 percent), middle class (30 percent), and the popular class (68 percent). Iturriaga, *La estructura social y cultural de México*, calculated from table on p. 28.

35. The apparent decrease in population of Tlalpan and Xochimilco over fifteen years represented in table 5.2 is likely because districts were divided into new municipalities by 1910, with San Angel separated from Tlalpan and Milpa Alta separated from Xochimilco. The population of Mexico City itself grew substantially but at a somewhat slower pace, with 325,707 people in 1895 and 471,066 residents in 1910, a 45 percent increase.

36. Based on the published summaries and not on manuscript census entries, table 5.2 is not a perfect measure of class distinctions. The narrow occupational criteria certainly fall short in terms of defining social and cultural elements of class identifications and groupings. Determining the makeup of specific classes is problematic, because of divisions within job categories, whether between owners and employees, masters and journeyman, or skilled and unskilled, middle or working class. There are also no data on how employed people reported in the census configure into households (i.e., how many workers per household), which makes comparison with manuscript census studies for earlier in the nineteenth century difficult. On balance my census analysis likely underestimates small-business owners in the middle class, an undercount certainly larger than the overcount represented by the inclusion of elite businessmen and high-level bureaucrats. The biggest problem is that except for "maestros de obras" in the 1895 data, none of the artisans and craftsmen and women are distinguished by skill level or ownership of workshops. The same problem obtains for measuring the commercial sector, though there is a clearer indication of the distinction between counter clerks and presumed business owners. Thus, perhaps lower middle-class small-business owners are missing from middle-class data. On the other end of the economic scale, data in the tables surely capture individuals who live well beyond a middle-class lifestyle—military generals, high-level bureaucrats, and successful large-scale businessmen and industrialists who are likewise lumped in with the more humble.

37. Already by 1865 the number of textile shops had dropped to 310 from the 400 that the city had counted in 1794. Between 1895 and 1900 the total number of textile workers in the country diminished from 63,000 to 52,000. The nation's artisan textile sector fell from 44,000 to 26,000, while the textile factory sector increased from 19,000 to 26,000 jobs. Other industries had similar impact on artisans of earlier times, bankrupting small shops and forcing masters and journeymen to find work in the new industrial sector, where conditions and wages got worse in Pofirian boom-and-bust cycles. Factories absorbed formally skilled artisans in now "unskilled" mechanical tasks and construction jobs. Illades, "Composición de la fuerza," 264; Carmen Ramos Escandón, "Working Class Formation and the Mexican Textile Industry: 1880–1912" (PhD diss., State University of New York, Stonybrook, 1981), 111–14; Morgan, "Proletarians, Políticos," 56.

38. For the Federal District the industrial sector increased from just over three thousand in 1895 to almost fourteen thousand in 1910 (compare appendix 3, table K, with appendix 3, table L). On the industrializing city see Rodney Anderson, *Outcasts in Their Own Land: Mexican Industrial Workers, 1906–1911* (DeKalb: Northern Illinois University Press, 1976), 59; Dawn Keremetsis, "Development of the Cotton Textile Industry in Nineteenth Century Mexico" (PhD diss., University of California–Berkeley, 1971); Gayón Córdova, *Condiciones de vida*, 96.

39. Lummis believed these wages were sufficient and that workers were "far from suffering." He also noted that Mexican mechanics earned two to three pesos a day, while American mechanics earned four to almost six pesos a day, supposedly because of a difference in skill level. Mexicans "are not, in our sense, mechanics, but 'helpers' and 'handy-men.' " Charles F. Lummis, *The Awakening of a Nation: Mexico of Today* (New York: Harper and Brothers, 1899), 75; Thompson, "Households," 73.

40. The full list Thompson gives is: seamstress, fifty centavos; common tailor, one peso twenty-five centavos; skilled shoemaker, two pesos fifty centavos; unskilled shoemaker, one

peso twenty-five centavos; carpentry foreman, five pesos; common carpenter, one peso fifty centavos; bricklayers, one peso fifty centavos; common day laborers, sixty-seven centavos; unskilled male operatives, fifty centavos; spinners and weavers, one peso; mechanics, five pesos; silversmiths, three pesos fifty centavos. Thompson, "Households," 103. He lists both low and high—these are the high end.

41. Almost half of the households in Thompson's sample were composed of two or more earners, even though the average household was only 3.6 members. Thompson, "Artisans, Marginals, and Proletarians," 308–10, and "Households," 72–73.

42. Gutierrez Najera, "La historia de un peso falso," 300–302.

43. Gooch Chambers tells us that "as the streetcar lines have their second- and third-class lines, with prices to correspond, so also is the cab system regulated. The distinction in prices is indicated by flags. Carriages bearing a blue flag are first class, and may be had for one peso an hour, while a red flag is second class and costs 75 cents; a white flag shows a third class coach, price 50 cents an hour." Reflecting the growth of the city, "rápidos," or express trains, from the center to the outlying neighborhoods were inaugurated in 1906 along existing electric train lines, "arriving . . . at the Zócalo a little before 8 and 9 o'clock in the morning, with the object being that employees could arrive on time at work." The express left again from the Zócalo at one o'clock, returning two hours later so that office employees could go home for the midday meal and return promptly to the office. The express fare cost between ten and thirty centavos, depending on distance traveled. Gooch Chambers, *Face to Face*, 77; Motts, *La vida*, 38.

44. Ramos Escandón, "Working Class," 42; López Rosado, *Curso de historia*, 238. In Veracruz, where wages for factory work were likely higher than in Mexico City, in the first decade of the new century nominal wages rose substantially (41 percent), but real wages declined 3.8 percent overall. There was a marked decline of 18 percent from 1907 to 1911, due to "enormous increase in prices" between 1909 and 1910. Aurora Gómez-Galvarriato, "The Evolution of Prices and Real Wages in Mexico from the Porfiriato to the Revolution," in *Latin America and the World Economy since 1800*, ed. John H. Coatsworth and Alan M. Taylor, 347–81 (Cambridge: Harvard University / David Rockefeller Center for Latin American Studies, 1998), 351. The author provides an appendix describing her index method as well as charts that lay out conflicting findings using different indices.

45. As world silver prices fell relative to gold in the last two decades of the nineteenth century, the peso depreciated. In 1891 the exchange against the U.S. dollar was 1.27 Mexican pesos, and by 1902 it was 2.39, with conversion to the gold standard coinciding with a stabilization of the peso. Edward Beatty, "Commercial Policy in Porfirian Mexico: The Structure of Protection," in *The Mexican Economy, 1870–1930: Essays on the Economic History of Institutions, Revolution, and Growth*, ed. Jeffrey L. Bortz and Stephen Haber, 205–52 (Palo Alto: Stanford, 2002), quote on 211. Gómez finds that inflation for 1900 to 1910 overall was either 41 percent or 52 percent, depending on which index is used, but the average comes out to 4 percent a year, compared to 2.4 percent for the United States. Gómez-Galvarriato, "Evolution of Prices," 349. Beatty cites a lower average inflation, 3.4 percent.

46. Ruiz Castañeda, *La ciudad*, 48. On public and private charities for the poor see Blum, "Conspicuous Benevolence," 35; "Por qué had subido los precios?" *El Imparcial*, September 25, 1906, 1. See also Eugenio Sancho Riba, "Las condiciones económicas en los últimos años del Porfiriato y la clase media," *Revista de Historia* 5, no. 9/10 (1980): 9–32; Gayón Córdova, *Condiciones de vida*, 92–94.

47. First quote from María García Castillo, "La sociedad porfiriana: Una lectura de *Los parientes ricos*, de Rafael Delgado," *Historias* 38 (1997): 89; second quote from *El Monitor Republicano*, November 12, 1886.

48. "Fiesta de aniversario: El Centro Nacional de Empleados de Comercio, velado en el Renacimiento," *El Imparcial*, June 12, 1906, 2. On the rise of the Mexican "bourgeoisie" in this period, see Moisés González Navarro, "El Porfiriato: La vida social," in *Historia moderna de México*, ed. Daniel Cosío Villegas, 387–93 (México: Editorial Hermes, 1970).

49. Already in the 1880s newspapers were decrying that businesses, the government, and the Monte de Piedad itself employed too many people "now accustomed to the idea that it is only on the [government] budget that one can live." *El Monitor Republicano*, November 12, 1886.

50. Molina Enríquez, cited in Sancho Riba, "Las condiciones económicas," 11, 17.

51. Rafael Delgado, *Los parientes ricos* (1903; repr., México: Editorial Porrúa, 1974). See also García Castillo, "La sociedad," 83–91.

52. Rafael Delgado, *Angelina* (1893; repr., México: Editorial Porrúa, 1964), 77.

53. Delgado, *Angelina*, 174.

54. Gooch Chambers, *Face to Face*, 86.

55. Meyer and Sherman, *Course*, 472.

56. See Sancho Riba, "Las condiciones económicas," 16, for statistical tables.

57. Motts, *La vida*, 48.

58. Delgado, *Angelina*, 176.

59. Sancho Riba, "Las condiciones económicas," 12–14.

60. In 1895 over sixty thousand females accounted for 32 percent of the population identified in Mexico City as working for wages or salaries, with a little over eighty-two thousand females making up 33 percent of the Federal District's labor force. Females dominated the 1895 census category "Diverse Occupations," representing over 60 percent, which included servant, laundry, sewing, corn-milling, and tortilla-making jobs—all poorly paid occupations. The female cohort in the "Industries, Fine Arts, Artisans and Oficios" category was only 12 percent. All of the cigarette makers and modistes and most of the textile workers were female, while they were absent from the construction, woodworking, and metalworking trades. Females had a stronger showing among the city's commercial sector (26 percent), especially the ambulatory vendor level and even the professional level (23 percent), owing mostly to their dominance of the teaching profession. In 1900 about twenty-five thousand females were employed in domestic service, compared to over five thousand employed as laundresses and seamstresses, fewer than two thousand employed as cigar makers and concierges, and others in the new industrial sector.

61. Blum, "Conspicuous Benevolence," 22.

62. Tobacco factories were adopting machinery that according to *La Convención Obrera* in 1889 "will leave five thousand unlucky women workers that earn their living making cigarettes without a job." Quoted in Towner, "Monopoly Capitalism," 91.

63. First quote from Gooch Chambers, *Face to Face*, 103; García Castillo, "La sociedad," 84; second quote from Mrs. Alec Tweedie, *Mexico As I Saw It* (London: Horst and Blacket, 1901), 220.

64. Thompson, "Households," 130.

65. Women who provided unpaid housekeeping services in their own homes in 1895 instead are likely among the categories of "unemployed" (which includes 95,843 females) and "profession unknown" (which includes 16,480 females; see appendix 3, table M).

66. Porter, "And That It Is Custom," 111–48.

67. Gooch Chambers reports that in 1887 the well-appointed household of General Vicente Riva Palacio had no less than thirty-five servants to serve the family of six. Mrs. Tweedie believed that "millionaires" like the two Escandón families, with houses situated on either side of the Jockey Club, had forty or fifty servants for each household. Gooch Chambers, *Face to Face*, 112; Tweedie, *Mexico*, 220, 231; Wasserman, *Everyday Life and Politics*, 39.

68. Porter, "And That It Is Custom," 139.

69. Manuel Payno, *Bandidos del Río Frio* (México: Ediciones México Moderno, 1919), 60–72, 77, 93, 97.

70. Angel del Campo, *Cosas vistas y cartones*, 3rd ed. (México: Editorial Porrúa, 1974), 107.

71. Del Campo, *Cosas vistas*, 121–29.

72. *El Monitor Republicano*, November 27, 1866, 1.

73. First quote from *El Monitor Republicano*, January 12, 1887, 1; second quote, January 6, 1887. See also "Los empeñeros y el público," *El Partido Liberal*, January 6, 1887.

74. Frederick A. Ober, *Travels in Mexico and Life among the Mexicans* (Boston: Estes and Lauriat, 1884), 252, 283; Tweedie, *Mexico*, 203, 223.

75. Emphasis in the original. López de Mendoza, *Los empeñeros en México: Cuadros de costumbres escritos en verso por el general Rafael López de Mendoza* (México: Librería "La Ilustración de Rafael B. Ortega," n.d.), 7.

76. Ober, *Travels in Mexico*, 252; Del Campo, *Cosas vistas*, 157–58.

77. Tweedie, *Mexico*, 237. Mrs. Tweedie points out that the gambling tables frequented by the middle and upper classes are "the property of, or licensed by, the State, and large revenues are annually received from them."

78. See chapter 6.

79. Quoted in Gayón Córdova, *Condiciones de vida*, 57. For a similar characterization of clientele, see AHCM, Gobierno del Distrito, Empeños, vol. 1429, exp. 382.

80. *El Siglo XIX*, January 16, 1885.

81. Ober, *Travels in Mexico*, 251.

82. *El Monitor Republicano*, January 22, 1887, 3.

83. Villela, *El Monte*, 25.

84. Payno, *Bandidos*, 33. Might "showing a friend" be the Mexican equivalent of the American "going to see Uncle"?

85. Quoted in Jonathan Kandell, *La Capital: The Biography of Mexico City* (New York: Random House, 1988), 384.

86. The first model Profesora Motts saw as a child in the early years of the century was "very cumbersome, hanging on the wall; to place a call through 'la Central,' one had to move a crank." The Mexican Telephone Company inaugurated telephone service in the city in 1878 and changed its name to The Mexican Telephone and Telegraph Company in 1905. In 1907 the Swiss firm "Ericcson" intiated services. Motts, *La vida*, 15.

87. AHCM, Gobierno del Distrito, Ventas, no. 162, exps. 15 and 17.

88. Ober, *Travels in Mexico*, 251. It could be that "gods" should read "goods," but the published work says "gods."

89. Gooch Chambers, *Face to Face*, 96, 106–7.

90. Julio Guerrero, *La génesis del crimen en México* (Paris: Viuda de Ch. Bouret, 1901), 162. On the department stores see Meyer Cosío, "La ciudad," 59–60; Bernardo García Díaz, *Un pueblo fabril del Porfiriato: Santa Rosa, Veracruz* (México: Secretaría de Educación Pública, 1981), 16–19; and Buchenau, *Tools of Progress*, 51–54.

91. Quote from Porter, "And That It Is Custom," 125; AHCM, Gobierno del Distrito, Empeños, vol. 1422, exp. 5, f. 17; and exp. 38.

92. Tweedie, *Mexico*, 145–50.

93. The data for this time period are thinner in terms of information about specific pledge items than for those periods analyzed in chapters 1 and 3, as the only available records for the Monte are from a list of goods stolen from the Branch No. 2 office located on Relox, which consists mostly of jewels and watches, both valuable and inexpensive.

94. AHCM, Gobierno del Distrito, Empeños, vol. 1420, exp. 322.

95. In 1867 there had been three categories of "loza" recognized in the municipal tax index: "fine," "from Tonalá, Puebla and other factories," and "common, from Cuatitlán and the rest." The tariff for the first group was five times as high as that for the third group. "Tarifa de los derechos municipales que deben pagarse," in Saldivar, *Diccionario*, 61.

96. *La Mujer Mexicana*, entrega 18 (1905), 142.

97. Gooch Chambers, *Face to Face*, 107.

98. Tweedie, *Mexico*, 151.

99. Tablada's story turns out badly, as the family member left in charge of keeping the pledge contracts up to date spent the money drinking, and the family lost their antiques. José Juan Tablada, *La feria de la vida*, 2nd ed. (1937; México: Conaculta, 1990), 242. I thank Victor Macías for passing along this reference.

100. Tello Peón, "Intención decorativa," 140. Photographs of chandeliers and lighting fixtures appear on 140, 143, 150–51; on *quinquines*, see Delgado, *Angelina*, 121. Motts says that *quinquines* were used by "the comfortable classes" in the early twentieth century, while poorer homes used candles or cheaper oil lamps.

101. AHCM, Gobierno del Distrito, Empeños, Ventas, vol. 162, exps. 1, 7, 9, 14, 15, 16, and 20. For photographs of Porfirian commodes as well as furniture for foyers, living rooms, and dining rooms, see Tello Peón, "Intención decorativa," 144–48.

102. Gooch Chambers, *Face to Face*, 107; Tweedie, *Mexico*, 208.

103. Gutierrez Najera, "La historia de un peso falso," 301; Delgado, *Angelina*, 29, 31, 75–76, 132.

104. Delgado, *Angelina*, 39–40.

105. Tweedie, *Mexico*, 196. Motts mentions *La Moda Elegante* and *El Hogar*, edited by Obdulia Enríquez de Rivera. I have translated "tejidos con gancho o con agujas" as crochet and knitting. Motts, *La vida*, 44.

106. The poem is unattributed. "La Aguja," in *La Mujer Mexicana*, entrega 9 (1902), 73–74; Mariano de Jesús Torres, "Manualito de La Costurera," in *La Mujer Mexicana*, entrega 18 (1905), 148–49.

107. AHCM, Gobierno del Distrito, Empeños, vol. 1422, exp. 42; Empeños, vol. 1422, exp. 43. See Francois, "Vivir de prestado," for discussion of two examples.

108. Sesto, *El México de Porfirio Díaz*, 136, 210; "Estuafas en los empeños," *El Imparcial*, August 1, 1904, 6.

109. Arias, *Los mexicanos*, 54. See also Fernández de Lizardi, *Don Catrín*, 207.

110. Quote from Prieto, *Memorias*, 199. Motts's father got his suits from a French tailor named Charrier, on Avenida de San Francisco, who charged fifty pesos for an English cashmere suit. Motts, *La vida*, 49.

111. Tweedie, *Mexico*, 146. For women wearing mantillas to mass along with Parisian fashions, see Ober, *Travels in Mexico*, 279.

112. Cosío Villegas, "La vida cotidiana," 476.

113. Ober, *Travels in Mexico*, 280; for examples from Delgado, see *Angelina*, 85, 182; hurricane quote from Delgado, *Angelina*, 151.

114. Macías-González, "Largatijo at the High Life"; Robert McKee Irwin, *Mexican Masculinities* (Minneapolis: University of Minnesota Press, 2003), xxxii.

115. In the Independence era most petticoats were made of cotton *manta*, coarse *jerguetilla*, or *angaripola* (a kind of stamped linen), and a few were made of *cambaya*, stamped *indiana*, and *muselina*. Statesman and poet Guillermo Prieto had noted at midcentury that women from the humble classes wore the *jerguetilla* and *indiana*, while the *muselina* was identified with the middle class and the *gró*, silk, and velvet were worn by the wealthiest. In the last years of the French intervention, there was a greater variety in the fabric used to make petticoats. In the data from the late 1860s, most of them are of *muselina*, wool, and *manta*, although *hamburgo* and *indiana* come close and *percal*, *varé*, *gró*, calico, *cambaya*, linen, and silk also appear. Prieto, *Memorias*, 27, 52; Arias, *Los mexicanos*, 51.

116. Motts reports prices of fabric per meter in the first decade of the twentieth century: *camabaya*, ten centavos; *calicot*, from twenty centavos depending on the width; *organdí*, fifteen centavos; natural silk, one peso; and wool, a peso and a half. Motts, *La vida*, 29.

117. Mariano de Jesús Torres, "La lavandera," in *La Mujer Mexicana*, entrega 18 (1905), 143–44.

118. Ober, *Travels in Mexico*, 283. Pawning other people's laundry was also reported by the English press. "Pawning Linen," *The Times*, July 21, 1847, 6.

119. An 1852 advertisement for three models of sewing machines made by Elías Howe Junior is in Almonte, *Guía de forasteros*, inside cover. For discussion of the impact of the sewing machine on the manufacturing of clothing, see Francois, "Vivir de prestado."

120. In another case a "White" sewing machine was hocked for fifty pesos in the empeño on the corner of Jesús Bridge and Corazón de Jesús, a few blocks south of the Zócalo, soon after the machine had left the agency on an installment plan. The agency was only able to recover its machine after paying the amount of the loan to the broker. AHCM, Gobierno del Distrito, Empeños, vol. 1422, exp. 37. Buchenau found that sewing machines were only affordable to city residents because of these installment plans and that agencies had a hard time getting their customers to make payments in a timely manner. Buchenau, *Tools of Progress*, 28–29.

121. Pérez, *Almanaque estadístico*, 11. For examples of watch vendors and pawned watches in the early Porfiriato, see Francios, "Vivir de prestado."

122. AHCM, Inventario General de la Municipalidad de Tlalpan, inv. 69, exp. 71, March 1879; AHCM, Gobierno del Distrito, Empeños, vol. 1422, exp. 38; Ventas, vol. 162, exps. 9 and 16.

123. AHCM, Gobierno del Distrito, Empeños, vol. 1422, exp. 29. For pawned bicycles and the meaning of bicycles in Mexico, see Francois, "Vivir de prestado." See also Beezley, *Judas at the Jockey Club*, 41–52. The first bicycle repair shop in the city opened on Dolores in 1896.

124. This may reflect the downtown location of the shops, where office work now dominated. It may also reflect the fact that artisan tools now had little resale value, so former artisans trying to use them as collateral had a harder time getting brokers to secure loans with them. For discussion of pawned tools early in the Porfiriato, see Francois, "Vivir de prestado."

125. Both items were pawned by a client identified as "García." One of the items stolen from the Monte de Piedad Branch in the fourth block of Relox in 1902 was a gold mechanical pencil, pawned for twelve pesos. AHCM, Gobierno del Distrito, Empeños, Ventas, vol. 162, exp. 15; Empeños, vol. 1422, exp. 5, f. 17.

6. Porfirian Paradoxes

1. Tweedie, *Mexico*, 207.

2. Ober, *Travels in Mexico*, 251. For discussion of the larger welfare network of asylums, hospitals, and orphanages in the Porfirian era, see Blum, "Public Welfare," 252–55.

3. "Los empeñeros y el público," *El Partido Liberal*, January 6, 1887.

4. For example, see AHCM, Gobierno del Distrito, Empeños, vol. 1429, exp. 385, f. 9.

5. *El Siglo XIX*, January 13, 1887.

6. Thomas John McMahon, "The Spanish Immigrant Community in Mexico City during the Porfiriato, 1876–1911" (PhD diss., University of Notre Dame, 1974), 7, 44–52, 73–77, 88–89, 91–136.

7. McMahon, "Spanish Immigrant Community," 43–44, 157. Quote from "Disposición Necesaria," *El Partido Liberal*, December 8, 1866, 3.

8. Gutierrez Najera, "La historia de un peso falso," 302. Not all portrayals of "gachupines" were acrimonious, though they were usually associated with commercial occupations. Rafael Delgado's description of "some young Spaniards [*gachupinillos*], clothing merchants, or employees of El Puerto de Vigo [a store], innocent youngsters, recently arrived, rudely standing around, looking at everyone with a protective air" is perhaps condescending and satiric but not vitriolic. Delgado, *Angelina*, 151.

9. Thomas McMahon notes that many of the Spanish pawnbrokers in the city were actually Cuban, with Cuba being the last colonial holding of Spain. It is not clear whether these Spanish Cubans were recent immigrants, arriving as the island achieved its independence amid the Spanish-American War at the end of the century. See *El Siglo XIX*, September 6, 1887; González Navarro, *La pobreza*, 118. Quote from McMahan, "Spanish Immigrant Community," 49.

10. Published in *El Partido Liberal: Diario de Politica, Literatura, Comercio y Anuncios*, November 30, 1886, 1.

11. *El Monitor Republicano*, October 31, 1890, 1.

12. *El Centinela*, June 26, 1881, 2; and *El Correo de España*, May 2, 1899, 1, cited in McMahon, "Spanish Immigrant Community," 116 and 149 respectively.

13. McMahon, "Spanish Immigrant Community," 150–52.

14. Sesto, *El México de Porfirio Díaz*, 196.

15. AHCM, Gobierno del Distrito, Empeños, vol. 1433, exp. 25.

16. A document that divvied up the pawnshops in the city among four officials searching for goods stolen from a branch of the Monte de Piedad suggests that there were only 64 pawnshops in the city in 1902. The discrepancy between this number and the 137 culled from other official documents and auction announcements in *El Siglo XIX* may be due to some of the latter being located outside the city limits, or it may be that the 64 shops to be searched had a history of accepting stolen goods. AHCM, Gobierno del Distrito, Empeños, vol. 1422, exp. 5. González Navarro presents different numbers of pawnshops, suggesting there were only 60 in 1885 and 70 in 1902. González Navarro, *La pobreza*, 117–18.

17. There were also businesses not registered as pawnshops that nonetheless engaged in the pawning trade; clandestine shops were often discovered by state inspectors on their rounds. AHCM, Gobierno del Distrito, Empeños, vol. 1422, exp. 6; vol. 8, exp. 3; Empeños Indiferentes, 1902–15, vol. 8, exp. 19.

18. Conversely, some long-term retail and later pawning locations apparently disappeared. Examples include the Amaya Bridge location, the corner of the Fierro Bridge and Puerta Falsa de Merced, and the corner of Cobacho and Niño Perdido. Notably absent from lists of pawnshops after the 1850s was Portacoeli near the Zócalo, which had had many retail and pawning establishments early in the century.

19. Of the seventy-one new pawnshop locations, 62 percent began operations in the first decade of the twentieth century. Fourteen percent opened in the 1870s, 10 percent in the 1880s, and 14 percent in the 1890s.

20. Jorge H. Jimenez Muñoz, *La traza de poder: Historia de la política y los negocios urbanos en el Distrito Federal de sus orígenes a la desaparición del Ayuntamiento (1824–1928)* (México: Codex, 1993); Johns, *City of Mexico*, 28–29, 34–38.

21. It is difficult to determine from the available data how many of these stores were owned at the same time (with the exception of those with identical dates), how many represent an owner's moving from one to another, or how many pawnbrokers went in and out of business.

22. Similarly, the pawnshop at the corner of Hoacalco and Pelota was owned by the Pérez Fernández family between 1879 and 1882, represented by Francisco, Demetrio, and Cornelius Pérez Fernández.

23. The entire sample for the Porfirian years is composed of 175 different stores, with 292 different brokers. AHCM, Empeños, vol. 885; Gobierno del Distrito, Empeños, vol. 1422, 1430.

24. AHCM, Empeños, vol. 885, exp. 10.

25. AHCM, Empeños, vol. 885, exp. 19.

26. AHCM, Gobierno del Distrito, Empeños, vol. 1422, exp. 24.

27. This is what happened to Don Antonio Gómez, who failed to pay on time the fifty-two pesos thirty-two centavos he owed in leftover profits for his shop on the corner of Juan Carbonero and San Juan Nepomuceno. AHCM, Empeños, vol. 885, exp. 12.

28. AHCM, Empeños, vol. 885, exp. 21.

29. AHCM, Empeños, vol. 885, exp. 35. Brokers Bastierra, Lobrado, Urrutia, Ugarte, Donesteve, Sarandona, and Poo collectively deposited their share in the Monte de Piedad in 1877.

30. *El Siglo XIX*, October 29, 1888. At the end of September 1888, the Monte de Piedad held a total of 2,524 pesos deposited by empeñeros. *El Siglo XIX*, November 21, 1886; AHCM, Empeños, vol. 885, exp. 37.

31. AHCM, Gobierno del Distrito, Empeños, vol. 1430, exp. 1.

32. Cabrera Siles and Escandón, *Historia*, 74.

33. AHCM, Empeños, vol. 885, exp. 70.

34. AHCM, Gobierno del Distrito, Empeños, vol. 1422, exps. 4 and 21.

35. The Damas pawnshop loaned an average of 8,050 pesos per month in the ten months between December 1901 and November 1902 for which data are available. AHCM, Gobierno del Distrito, Empeños, vol. 1422, exp. 21.

36. Collectively, the goods went for 2,950 pesos, with the average price upon sale of the goods over four pesos, although some went for almost nine. Without knowing what these

brokers (Santos Sobrino, Posada y Porrua, B. Trespalacios, Veronica Dosal, Francisco M. Sanchez, and Juan Dias) had originally lent against this specific collateral, of course, we cannot determine to what extent these sales represent profits. From another perspective, the fact that only 3 percent of the goods generated a return for the person who had pledged them might suggest that the sale price did not meet the sum of the loan amount, costs, and interest, in which case the pawnbrokers, too, lost potential profit. AHCM, Empeños Indiferentes, vol. 14, exp. 4.

37. *El Monitor Republicano*, October 31, 1890, 1.

38. González Navarro, *La pobreza*, 117–18. According to *El Siglo XIX*, empeñeros charged at least 25 percent interest for a four-month term in 1887, the equivalent of 75 percent annual interest. *El Siglo XIX*, September 13, 1887, September 14, 1887.

39. *El Siglo XIX*, September 13, 1887.

40. The council cites "Instituciones de Crédito," by Lic. D. Joaquin D. Casasús. "Dictamen sobre impuestos á casas de empeño," Biblioteca de Mexico, Memorias del Ayuntamiento, 1900, vol. 2, doc. 11; González Navarro, *La pobreza*, 117–18.

41. AHCM, Gobierno del Distrito, Empeños, vol. 1422, exp. 21, capitalized emphasis in the original. On illiteracy see González Navarro, *La pobreza*, 118.

42. AHCM, Gobierno del Distrito, Empeños 1906–15, vol. 13, exp. 3.

43. *El Monitor Republicano*, October 31, 1890, 1; "Dictamen sobre impuestos," vol. 2, doc. 11.

44. This was not the first time that the Monte was tapped by governments. During the wars of the Reform, conservative governments taxed the Monte, and the church forced a loan of twenty-five thousand pesos to support the conservative cause. Cabrera Siles and Escandón, *Historia*, 68–69, 73–74.

45. Cabrera Siles and Escandón, *Historia*, 75–76.

46. Juan de D. Peza, *La beneficencia en Mexico* (México: Imprenta de Francisco Diaz de Leon, 1881), 184.

47. Cabrera Siles and Escandón, *Historia*, 76.

48. *El Siglo XIX*, January 28, 1885; Cabrera Siles and Escandón, *Historia*, 76.

49. *El Siglo XIX*, January 16, 1885, February 6, 1885, August 10, 1886; Cabrera Siles and Escandón, *Historia*, 76.

50. "Venta de Prendas," *El hijo del Ahuizote*, December 23, 1888, 62.

51. *El Monitor Republicano*, January 20, 1887, 1.

52. *El Monitor Republicano*, January 26, 1887, 1; January 28, 1887.

53. "Visita al Monte de Piedad," *Diario del Hogar*, August 29, 1890.

54. *El Monitor Republicano*, September 9, 1890, 3.

55. Ann Blum argues that "by encouraging private benevolence, the Díaz regime substantially broadened and in certain circumstances improved services available to the working poor and unemployed in the capital." Blum, "Private Benevolence," 35.

56. Secretary of Gobernación Manuel Romero Rubio declared that private charity was the most secure and natural means of aiding the needy. On privatization of charity see González Navarro, *La pobreza*, 121–22; and Cabrera Siles and Escandón, *Historia*, 76–78. For discussion of the debate among Porfirian liberals about the state's responsibility to the poor, see González Navarro, *La pobreza*, 46–50. On the tensions between laissez-faire positions and the role of welfare, see Blum, "Public Welfare," 253, and "Conspicuous Benevolence," 8–17.

57. John Robert Lear, "Workers, Vecinos and Citizens: The Revolution in Mexico City, 1909–1917" (PhD diss., University of California–Berkeley, 1993), 71; Thompson, "Artisans, Marginals, and Proletarians," 308.

58. El Economista Mexicano, July 23, 1904, 370.

59. AGN, Gobernación, 1st section, leg. 917(1), exp. 2, fs. 8–17v; González Navarro, La pobreza, 118.

60. We cannot know how many unredeemed yet unsold goods remained in the Luz Saviñón auction room, effectively tying up the establishment's lending capital.

61. "La ley de beneficencia privada: Sus buenos efectos," El Imparcial, August 24, 1904, 1.

62. Reproduced in Artemio de Valle Arizpe, "Las loterías del Sacristán," Artes de México 13 (1997): 43.

63. Cabrera Siles and Escandón, Historia, 78.

64. The brokers argued that the municipal president did not have the authority to promulgate laws that would govern their trade and that instead this authority lay with the Federal District and the ministry of Gobernación. Pawnbrokers also resented an increase in the number of and reasons for on-site inspectors and repeatedly complained that the government inspectors were incompetent at best and abusive at worst. Pedro Lobrado, Laureano Zarandona, Francisco Basterra, Juan Urrutia, P. Donesteve, Domingo Ugarte, and Joaquín Poo were all parties in the lawsuit. AHCM, Empeños, vol. 885, exp. 11, 27.

65. AGN, Gobernación, 2nd section, leg. 881(9), exp. 5, no. 3, f. 3.

66. AHCM, Empeños, vol. 885, exps. 11 and 19.

67. For cases from 1902 see AHCM, Gobierno del Distrito, Empeños, vol. 1422, exp. 1.

68. AHCM, Empeños, vol. 885, exp. 38.

69. AHCM, Empeños, vol. 885, exp. 35.

70. El Monitor Republicano, January 12, 1887, 1.

71. El Siglo XIX, November 21, 1886. For discussion of the reforms aimed at markets and vendors, see Porter, "And That It Is Custom."

72. El Partido Liberal, January 18, 1887.

73. For example, an 1854 law regarding licensing procedures and municipal tax laws from 1864 and 1867 still governed the industry in the 1880s. AHCM, Empeños, vol. 885, exps. 30, 35, and 70.

74. The brokers' petition also questioned the governor of the Federal District's right to fine brokers from ten to five hundred pesos for noncompliance at his discretion, as called for in Article 65. The governor replied that his jurisdiction in this matter derived from the administrative authority granted his office in the Constitution of 1857. El Siglo XIX, January 13, 1887.

75. El Siglo XIX, January 6, 1887.

76. El Siglo XIX, January 13, 1887.

77. El Siglo XIX, January 13, 1887.

78. El Siglo XIX, January 13, 1887.

79. El Siglo XIX, January 15, 1887; El Monitor Republicano, January 14, 1887, 3.

80. El Siglo XIX, January 19, 1887; January 25, 1887; September 8, 1887. The idea of a pawning charity funded by private capitalists was taken up by other newspapers in the city, such as El Monitor Republicano, La Patria, and La Semana Mercantil. Similar proposals surfaced again after the turn of the century. José del Castillo Velasco proposed the establishment of a chain of eight charitable pawnshops, which would be exempt from taxes, but the government declined, arguing that they would unnecessarily duplicate the Monte de Piedad. AHCM, Empeños, vol. 885, exp. 124.

81. El Siglo XIX, January 18, 1887; La Federación and La Convención Radical, cited in El Monitor Republicano, January 25, 1887, 3.

82. El *Monitor Republicano*, January 28, 1877, 1, September 5, 1890.

83. El *Monitor Republicano*, October 29, 1890, 1.

84. El *Siglo XIX*, June 21, 1888. Margaret Chowning notes, however, that the establishment of a Porfirian Monte de Piedad in Michoacán was not successful in stamping out the private pawning sector. Chowning, *Wealth and Power*, 282.

85. El *Siglo XIX*, September 6, 1887. The editors argued that the branches of the Monte were not effective, because they were "palaces where the employees lived in splendor" rather than establishments where only the poor would benefit.

86. El *Siglo XIX*, September 13, 1887.

87. The brokers suggested that maybe they had not gotten their money back because the Administrador de Rentas was ignorant of the court's decision, and they enclosed a copy. AHCM, Empeños, vol. 885, exp. 84. The brokers signing the November 1891 petition were the Altuna brothers, Julian Gutiérrez, A. del Villar y Barbolla, Pedro Biestra, the Trastoza brothers, Rafael Canpullo, Manuel Molleda and Co., Gemerino Jamis and Co., Pedro Lobrado, and Antonio Solarín.

88. The city argued that the auditor position was an additional post and in no way altered the regulations that had been in place since 1886.

89. AHCM, Empeños, vol. 885, exp. 95. The brokers signing the October 1895 petition were M. M. Molleda, A. Dosal, Jesús Crespo, S. Alvarez, E. Torrez, E. Fernández, M. Fernández y Durán, Y. Villar and Co., the Altuna brothers, Pedro Biestra, and Posada and Porruas.

90. AHCM, Empeños, vol. 885, exp. 101.

91. AHCM, Empeños, vol. 885, exp. 94.

92. The Gómez brothers, with an empeño on the corner of San Juan and Peredo Bridge, withheld over 2,500 pesos' worth of pawned goods. The Pria brothers withheld over 3,000 pesos' worth of goods up for auction in their shop on the corner of Nahuatlato and Ratas streets. AHCM, Empeños, vol. 885, exp. 113.

93. William D. Raat, "Ideas and Society in Don Porfirio's Mexico," *The Americas* 30 (1973): 32–53, quote on 46.

94. "Dictamen sobre impuestos," vol. 2, doc. 11.

95. Brokers signing the September 1908 petition were: B. Quintana and Co., Silvio Calvo, Pablo Gándara, Manuel Nieto, Manuel Alonso, Domingo Campollo and Co., Noriega and Corral, Franco M. Puente and Co., Vicente García, V. G. del Collado, Amadeo Velar, Gustamante and Brother, Luengas Brothers, Ramón Turanzas Ien C., J. Corral Villar, Porrua Brothers, Antonio H. Portilla, P. P. Francisco Bustillo, Santos Z. Bustillo, Napoleon C. Mendiola, José Simon Alonso, Bernardo Rivera, Noriega and Quintana, Gregorio Via, Fernando Tames, E. Fuentevilla, Santiago Fernández, Basilio Trespalacios, and B. Trespalacios and Co. AHCM, Gobierno del Distrito, Empeños, vol. 1420, exp. 332.

96. AHCM, Gobierno del Distrito, Empeños, vol. 1420, exp. 332.

7. A Material Revolution

1. "Los zapatistas saquearon las casas de préstamos y azuzaron al populacho para que los imitara," El *Demócrata*, February 8, 1915, 1. For discussion of the "journalistic hacks" spinning a bad image of Zapatistas at the service of Venustiano Carranza, see Alan Knight, *The Mexican Revolution* (Cambridge: Cambridge University Press, 1986), 2:213.

2. On the *decena trágica*, see Michael C. Meyer, *Huerta: A Political Portrait* (Lincoln: University of Nebraska Press, 1972), 45–63; Bliss, *Compromised Positions*, 70–71; and Knight, *Mexican Revolution*, 2:484–90.

3. Wasserman, *Everyday Life and Politics*, 136.

4. There is a huge literature on the roots and repercussions of the Mexican Revolution. For a review of historiography of the revolution, see Mary Kay Vaughan, "Cultural Approaches to Peasant Politics in the Mexican Revolution," *Hispanic American Historical Review* 9, no. 2 (1999): 269–305. For revolutionary activity in the city, see Lear, *Workers*; and Meyer, *Huerta*. For the policy phase of the revolution in terms of the regulation of sexuality, see Bliss, *Compromised Positions*.

5. Lear, *Workers*, 192–214, 361–62.

6. Carlos Illades suggests that the resentment against Spanish usurers was strongest among people of "few economic resources." Carlos Illades, *Presencia española en la Revolución Mexicana (1910–1915)* (México: Instituto Mora, 1991), 56. Josefina MacGregor points out that Spanish immigrants not only were merchants but were fanned out throughout society, including the leadership of organized workers, teachers, and priests. Josefina MacGregor, *México y España del Porfiriato a la Revolución* (México: INEHRM, 1992), 61–67. See also Douglas W. Richmond, "Confrontation and Reconciliation: Mexicans and Spaniards during the Mexican Revolution, 1910–1920," *The Americas* 43, no. 3 (1984): 215–28.

7. Knight points out that targets of urban mobs throughout the country after the fall of Díaz were "uniformly consistent—the goals and government buildings, officers and officials, moneylenders, pawnbrokers and the small shopkeepers who supplied the urban poor with basic essentials. Many were Spaniards, some (in the north and northwest) were Chinese: hence the popular xenophobia which bypassed the real agents of economic imperialism, the American and British company managers." Knight, *Mexican Revolution*, 1:208. MacGregor, on the other hand, argues that revolutionary activity in Mexico City was not xenophobic, because in attacks against Spanish merchants in Mexico City, "this hatred did not manifest itself violently during the revolution" as it did in Chihuahua or Puebla. MacGregor, *México y España*, 56. Nonetheless, Lear, Illades, and others document numerous and frequent attacks on commercial establishments when the impact of revolutionary activity took its toll in the city.

8. Lear, *Workers*, 303.

9. That night the owner of the pawnshop arrived, asking that his clerk be freed. When officials refused, the pawnbroker left, furious, saying that "they'd see whether or not he'd get out." "Fué golpeada por un empeñero," El Diario, January 29, 1912, 8.

10. "Empeñero acusado por estafa," *El Diario*, January 29, 1912, 8.

11. *El Imparcial*, which had been a bastion of Porfirismo, commended Huerta's minister of Gobernación, Ignacio Alcocer, for the "great improvement that will bring noted benefits to the *clase menesterosa*, that which feels the greatest harms from the abuses to which some pawnbrokers make them victims." This "transcendental reform" would "guarantee the interests of the public who frequent, because of misfortune, these places." "Será reformado el reglamento de empeños," *El Imparcial*, March 24, 1914, 1. *El Diario* published an editorial heralding the "hugely important" changes: "The matter is transcendental for the middle and popular classes because it will cut at the root the great abuses that have been committed in this area. The work of the Minister of Gobernación deserves all kinds of lucky congratulations, as it exclusively watches over the interests of the working classes, and surely it will cause an excellent impression on the public when it is known." "Cuales son las reformas que

se van a introducir en el reglamento de empeños," *El Diario*, March 27, 1914, 1. *El Imparcial* received a government subsidy under Huerta, as it had under Porfirio Díaz. Meyer, *Huerta*, 132–34. On the militarization of Mexico City under Huerta, see Meyer, *Huerta*, 96–100.

12. The second article ordered that the debtor had the right to make installment payments of at least 25 percent of the amount loaned, with the lender obliged to record the payment on the pawn ticket and in his books so that they would be duly taken into account at the time of redemption of the collateral. The third article stated that when installments had been made to a debtor account, the pledge period was automatically extended for the period of time that the installments could cover as renewal interest. The fourth article built in even more flexibility for the customer, stating that the installments could be returned to the customer interest free at the expiration of the extended pledge period if the customer was unable to muster the rest of the loan payment in order to redeem the good, declaring that he or she would "dejarla perdida." The final article established a fine of fifty to two hundred pesos against brokers who defied these regulations. "Reformas utiles al reglamento de empeños y bazares," *El Diario*, April 18, 1914, 1. The office of General García Cuéllar, who governed the Federal District under Huerta, had in the works a more comprehensive reform project that would radically alter other provisions of the Porfirian empeño regulations for the city, including the establishment of a city-run centralized auction house for the sale of expired pledges. This Huertista reformist trend regarding collateral credit lends credence to historian Michael Meyer's questioning of the blanket "counterrevolutionary" label often applied to Huerta. AHCM, Gobierno del Distrito, Empeños, vol. 1429, exp. 365. See Meyer, *Huerta*, 156–77, for the argument that Huerta's government spent more on social programs such as education than did Madero before him or Venustiano Carranza after him. Huerta's government undertook factory safety inspections, established labor-mediation mechanisms and policies to combat unemployment, and supported minimum-wage and maximum-hour legislation. Meyer concludes that while the Huerta government's social policy was not counterrevolutionary, neither was it revolutionary: "Many of the ministers spotted the critical areas for reform but none of them were thinking in terms of a fundamental social upheaval designed to alter the nature of society from the top to the bottom," 176. For a counterargument, see Knight, *Mexican Revolution*, 2:94–104.

13. Quote from Cabrera Siles and Escandón, *Historia*, 83–84; Meyer, *Huerta*, 50–51. For a concise narrative of the events of November 1914, see Meyer and Sherman, *Course*, 518–19.

14. See the published announcement of auction times separated by the category of goods (clothing sold one week; furniture, watches and "various objects" sold the next; and jewelry going to auction last) and by establishment (main office and branches, all on different days) in *El Diario*, September 10, 1913, 3.

15. This charitable lender's image was tarnished in 1913 and 1914, as an investigation of an embezzlement of over one hundred thousand pesos made the headlines. "El robo al Montepio Luz Saviñón por un grupo de altos empleados," *El Imparcial*, June 7, 1913, 1; "La voz del público: El asunto del Montepío Saviñón," *El Imparcial*, January 9, 1914, 6; "Montepío Luz Saviñón," *El Imparcial*, June 21, 1914, 6; "El robo al Montepío Saviñón," *El Diario*, February 11, 1914, 8; "El asunto del Saviñón," *El Imparcial*, March 20, 1914, 7.

16. "Reformas al reglamento de empeños," *El Imparcial*, May 7, 1914, 7; "La reglamentación de las casas de empeños se llevara a cabo," *El Demócrata*, September 20, 1914, 1.

17. Old patterns of servants stealing from employers and pawning the loot continued. For example, the coachman Dionisio Urrutia found himself in the Belén jail for stealing and

pawning a watch and ring worth 140 pesos, in addition to other valuable objects totaling 200 pesos stolen from his employer, engineer Palbo Ruíz. "Vendía boletos de empeño falsos," *El Diario*, June 9, 1913, 7. Emilio Villegas's pawnshop on Soto north of the Alameda Park was the victim of a robbery, when Mariano González and Amparo Sánchez purchased a silk mantilla for seventy pesos but also stole three other mantillas, a Tulancingo rebozo, and an overcoat. And María Asunción Tejada got herself in trouble the next year pawning seven dresses that she stole from her employer, Carmen Garnica, for forty pesos in a pawnshop on Santa María Redonda. "Compraron y robaron en una casa de préstamos," *El Diario*, September 11, 1912, 7; "María Asunción está confesa," *El Diario*, June 9, 1913, 7. After the "decena trágica" of February 1913, a group of *soldaderas* was arrested with more than twenty-five thousand pesos of stolen jewels taken from elite homes abandoned during the siege of the Ciudadela, and their associates in the federal army were also detained after "various diamonds that had been dismounted from jewels were found rolled in their socks." "Los saqueos de Huertistas y Felixistas en la Decena Trágica," *El Demócrata*, September 28, 1914, 1.

18. "Los saqueos de Huertistas y Felixistas," 1.

19. Calvo also was auctioning a five-volume set of history books entitled *Mexico atraves de los siglos*, an Opal bicycle, a wooden bed with its *tambor*, and a framed painting, each of which secured loans of twenty-five pesos. Because of the attraction of a much lower interest rate, the customers who pawned these relatively expensive items might rather have taken their business to the recently reopened Monte de Piedad's two branch offices. Maybe the late opening and early closing hours at the two open branches made that impossible. Or the line at the Monte branch might have been too long the day the customers needed the cash, or the staff might have already loaned their limit for the day. It was the usual custom for the Monte de Piedad to lend only so much on a given day, though the amount changed. See *El Demócrata*, May 1, 1920, 1.

20. Two hundred and one of the 341 goods were either clothing or whole cloth, with another 25 household linen items. Artisan tools were the next largest category (though only 9 percent). Thirty-one tools secured loans of between fifty centavos and eight pesos. There were also twenty-five watches securing loans of from one to five pesos, jewelry securing nineteen loans from fifty centavos to thirty-five pesos, and a handful of loans over fifty pesos made for furniture, typewriters, and sewing machines.

21. Lear, *Workers*, 80.

22. Gómez-Galvarriato, "Evolution of Prices," 355.

23. One sector that boomed in this crisis was that of private mortgage lending, which became more expensive when Huerta assessed a 1 percent tax on mortgages operations, passed on to the borrower. Jorge H. Jiménez Muñoz, *La traza del poder: Historia de la política y los negocios urbanos en el Distrito Federal* (México: CODEX Editores, 1993), 118–20.

24. Bliss, *Compromised Positions*, 70–71. For a stark picture of starvation and scavenging, see Francisco Ramírez Plancarte, *La ciudad de México durante la revolución constitucionalista* (México: Ediciones Botas, 1941), 366–67; Knight, *Mexican Revolution*, 2:317.

25. Bliss finds that "whenever it occupied the capital, each army sought to establish its presence by dictating new rules governing urban social morals." Bliss, *Compromised Positions*, 66–80, quote on 74.

26. Back in September 1913 a proposal by Deputy José Carrión (never implemented) called for all private pawnshops to come under direct government control and be held to interest fixed by the authorities, not to exceed 5 percent a month. González Navarro, *La pobreza*, 156.

Lear, in *Workers*, identifies the author of this proposal as the brother of Emiliano Zapata, Eufemio.

27. Reported by Professor Ramón Torres, hired by Huerta's Federal District government to study the pawnshop trade. There were other reports of up to 32 percent monthly interest. AHCM, Gobierno del Distrito, Empeños, vol. 1429, exp. 365.

28. Other provisions of the September 1914 regulation included reduced lending periods for clothing and other perishable objects to four months, while sturdier goods could be held for six to eight months. Pawnbrokers would be obliged to accept installment payments on loans and make proportional deductions in the interest charged. They were also obliged to disinfect clothing or other objects that needed it, to maintain an insurance policy against fire, and to not accept pawns from minors. "La reglamentacion de las casas de empeños se llevara a cabo," *El Demócrata*, September 20, 1914, 1. In the regulations drafted by Huerta's last Federal District governor, the interest was apparently limited to 10 percent, but tax incentives were in place to lower them. For example, a lender charging from 8 to 10 percent monthly interest would be taxed at a rate of 7 percent, one charging from 6 to 8 percent would be taxed at 4 percent, one charging from 4 to 6 percent would be taxed at 2 percent, and one charging from 2 to 4 percent would be taxed at 1 percent. Brokers who charged less than 2 percent interest would be exempted from taxation altogether. AHCM, Gobierno del Distrito, Empeños, vol. 1429, exp. 365.

29. The petition also called for lower staple prices. "La Casa de Obrero pide el cierre de empeños y la abolición de la pena de muerte en el país," *El Pueblo*, October 5, 1914, 1. See also Lear, "Workers, Vecinos," 297. In a petition a few days earlier, workers had demanded a minimum wage of 1.50 pesos and a decrease of 33 percent in rents. "Peticiones de la Casa del Obrero Mundial," *El Demócrata*, October 3, 1914, 3.

30. AHCM, Gobierno del Distrito, Empeños, vol. 1429, exps. 365 and 382; "Desaparecerán las casas de empeños," *El Pueblo*, October 8, 1914, 4; José Fuentes Mares, *Historia de dos orgullos* (México: Oceano, 1984), 59.

31. "Armas y parque en los empeños," *El Pueblo*, November 11, 1914, 3. The strategy of supplying the troops through requisitioning pawned goods was apparently as common as soldiers' pawning military goods. In October 1914 the Mexico City pawnshops were combed for saddles to "alleviate the difficulties that the cavalry has in outfitting its columns of horsemen in the new organization that they are putting in place." "Seran recogidas las monturas de los empeños," *El Pueblo*, October 11, 1914, 4. On the rising tensions among revolutionary leaders, see Lear, *Workers*, 255. The Monte de Piedad suspended the pawning of pistols in 1911. While weapons are conspicuously absent from the database for the revolutionary period, in June 1913, 104 pawnshops were reported as having arms among their collateral. AHCM, Gobierno del Distrito, Empeños, vol. 1421, exp. 349. The Madero government ordered that the weapons were not to be redeemed unless the owner filled out a form attesting to the honor of the pawnee or wrote a letter explaining why the gun owners needed it "to protect their house" or to comply with military service. Cabrera Siles and Escandón, *Historia*, 289; AHCM, Gobierno del Distrito, Empeños, vol. 1421.

32. Bystanders told reporters that brokers allegedly lent only five pesos for an overcoat that was worth seventy and then claimed there was no *demasías* to be claimed after it had been sold. Others refused to accept paper money as loan repayment but instead demanded only silver, thus acquiring high-quality goods by making their redemption impossible. "Seran recogidas las prendas de ex-federales," *El Demócrata*, November 11, 1914, 1.

33. González Navarro, *La pobreza*, 157. Ramírez Plancarte characterizes this move against the lending businesses as "arbitrary." Ramírez Plancarte, *La ciudad*, 256. Lear notes that the switch from civilian to military rule in the city, beginning with Carranza's appointment of General Heriberto Jara, meant a switch to rule by decree. The pawning decrees of the conventionist generals, beginning with General Manual Chao, continued this pattern while also leaving the civilian city council to legislate other issues. In other ways the revolutionary pawning policy of the conventionists is a departure from what Lear finds in his study of working people during the revolution. He argues that when the conventionist forces occupied the city from November 1914 to January 1915, they "were less than decisive in forging close ties with the city's poor and working people. Neither Zapata nor Villa proved particularly concerned with the affairs of urban workers or the well-being of the population of Mexico City." See Lear, *Workers*, 252–53; quote on 268.

34. The petitioned is signed by two attorneys representing the union (Lic. Ramón Alvarez de Toledo and Lic. Rafael Ramos), not the brokers themselves. AHCM, Gobierno del Distrito, Empeños, vol. 1429, exp. 385, fs. 6–7. MacGregor chronicles the arrival of the new ambassador and his negotiations with potential heads of the state concerning diplomatic recognition of a new government in Mexico and, principally, the protection of Spanish interests in Mexico but makes no mention of the pawnbroking issues. MacGregor, *México y España*, 183–89. German merchants joined other foreign entrepreneurs in an International Committee that represented foreign business interests to revolutionary leaders. Buchenau, *Tools of Progress*, 76.

35. These petitioners followed the path blazed by female ambulatory vendors who resisted efforts to relocate them or eliminate them altogether in the Porfirian era through repeated petitions and collective letters to the city. Of the 138 full names on the petition, 68 are female. AHCM, Gobierno del Distrito, Empeños, no. 1429, exp. 385, f. 12. For vendor petitions see Porter, "And That It Is Custom," 134–36.

36. According to the 1910 census, 64 percent of the Federal District population over twelve years old could read and write, another 2 percent could only read, while 33 percent were unable to read or write.

37. AHCM, Gobierno del Distrito, Empeños, vol. 1429, exp. 385, f. 12. It is interesting that the petition cites 14 percent monthly interest, whereas other reports put it much higher. Still, 14 percent a month represents 168 percent annual interest.

38. AHCM, Gobierno del Distrito, Empeños, vol. 1429, exp. 385, fs. 11 and 17.

39. AHCM, Gobierno del Distrito, Empeños, vol. 1429, exp. 385, f. 9. Twenty-two of the forty-five signers of this second petition also signed the first: A. Alarcón, Dominga B., Mateo C. de Vaca, Enrique Delgado, Modesta Domínguez, Manuel Fernández, Domingo Flores, Ernesto Guzmán, Antonio Hernández, A. Juarez, M. Llerena, Ezequiel López, Fabian Olvera, Alfredo Paniagua, Manuel Paniagua, Ygnacio Pérez, Francisco Rivera, H. Rivera, Alfredo Robledo, Jesús Torres, Angel Urquiza, José Yslas. Ten women signed their full names. The exact number of women is unknown, because some signers only gave a first initial.

40. Illades, *Presencia española*, 57–58.

41. The petition is signed: "Somos a Ud. Afectísima y servidoras. María Garnica, Angela Cuevas, Arcadia Frias, Matilde Aguila, Onésima Llagado, Abrana Santos, Teofila Pérez, Ynes Cantú, Yincrita Santiago, Margarita Tierros, Juana Péres, Francisca Sólis, Concha García, Lola Llaños, Carlota Aguirre, Basilia Quiros, Benita Juárez, Paula Antonia, Paulina Celso, Elodia Carpio." AHCM, Gobierno del Distrito, Empeños, vol. 1429, exp. 385, f. 19. On the suspen-

sion of the decree, see Ramírez Plancarte. He says that General Manuel Chao repealed the decree immediately after being named governor of the Federal District on December 5. There was no documentation found in the archives regarding this outright repeal. Ramírez Plancarte, *La ciudad de Mexico*, 262.

42. AHCM, Gobierno del Distrito, Empeños, vol. 1429, exp. 407.

43. AHCM, Gobierno del Distrito, Empeños, vol. 1429, exp. 385, f. 24.

44. Knight identifies General Chao as a northern "schoolmaster-revolutionary" and an "educated, respectable figure" who was first in the Carranza camp, was revolutionary governor of Chihuahua in 1914, and was then a chief ally of Pancho Villa, who was prone to expropriate property from Spaniards and expel them from territory under his control. Knight, *Mexican Revolution*, 2:109, 120, 316; quote on 316.

45. AHCM, Gobierno del Distrito, Empeños, vol. 1429, exp. 385, f. 29.

46. AHCM, Gobierno del Distrito, Empeños, vol. 1429, exp. 419, fs. 1–2.

47. Richmond, "Confrontation and Reconciliation," 222–23.

48. Lear describes how women "holding worthless Villista money in their hands marched to Obregón's headquarters and then on [to] the monument to Juárez, demanding that Convention currencies be accepted and that the water supply, restricted throughout early February to one hour a day, be restored." Lear cites an estimate that 85 percent of the ten thousand people who accepted relief were women. Lear, *Workers*, 271–73.

49. Merchants in the city now had to face the requisitioning of 10 percent of their stock for poor relief, prompting shopkeepers to close their doors and turn to the Spanish consulate for their own relief from this attack on their business rights and then a direct tax on capital investments.

50. Alejandra Moreno Toscano, "Del porvenir de los recuerdos," *Nexos* 86 (1985): 5.

51. She had pawned a black petticoat for sixty-two centavos and three scarves for seventy-five centavos, and the Mina broker charged her 32 percent interest. On a transaction where she pawned six cotton napkins for two pesos and a piece of cotton cloth for fifty centavos, the Soto broker charged her 26 percent interest. AHCM, Gobierno del Distrito, Empeños, vol. 1429, exp. 427.

52. AHCM, Gobierno del Distrito, Empeños, vol. 1429, exp. 385, f. 51.

53. AHCM, Gobierno del Distrito, Empeños, vol. 1429, exps. 392, 393, 394, 395, 399, 400.

54. AHCM, Gobierno del Distrito, Empeños, vol. 1429, exp. 442.

55. "Se evitarán los abusos de los empeñeros," *La Convención*, April 29, 1915, 1.

56. The decree called for turning over windfall profits to original owners of collateral goods or to charity if owners did not come to collect the money, and it limited any future pawning business to 4 percent monthly interest. "El decreto sobre los empeños," *El Combate*, July 8, 1915, 3. Knight says that Magaña was "one of that breed of secretaries, advisers, brokers and polemicists which habitually surrounded successful caudillos. But unlike many of that breed, Magaña placed peace, conciliation and principle before personal ambition. Emerging as Zapata's key adviser after 1916, he was designated leader of the movement in the crisis following Zapata's death." Knight, *Mexican Revolution*, 2:372.

57. AHCM, Empeños, vol. 885, exp. 131.

58. Fuentes Mares, *Historia de dos orgullos*, 55. In 1911 the foreign minister had authorized foreigners to defend themselves and their property. Illades, *Presencia española*, 62.

59. The editorial described a fictional scenario of pawning a gold diamond ring worth 100 or 150 pesos that the pawnbroker "appraised" at about 10 percent of its value, or 15 pesos,

giving the client a loan of 12 or 13 pesos. This injustice was compounded by "the ramble of insults that it was necessary to suffer in order to secure the loan" in the first place. The owner of the diamond ring would be unable to put together the money to repay the loan, plus 25 percent monthly interest, 10 percent of the amount loaned for the cost of the appraisal, and "who knows what other charges." If the broker had not cut a deal with the government inspector and was thus unable to claim the good outright, "which was a rare instance indeed," the ring would go to auction, where more fraud would occur. Then "the auction takes place, which on many occasions no one attends; if this happens, the broker acquires the good by paying the amount of the debt; and if there is an audience, he still gets the goods with the help of his 'puleros' [planted buyers] and never, in any case, do the *demasías* get turned over to the owners of the goods, [the broker] always committing a great robbery." "Las vendutas en los empeños," *El Pueblo*, January 17, 1915, 6.

60. Other abuses include excluding collateral that they want from the record books, colluding with government officials to make faulty appraisal or avoid announcing the sale of goods in the newspapers, and providing "their agents" with false pawn tickets that then get sold, with the buyer hoping to get a deal on a watch or some other item. "El monopolio de estado de los empeños," *El Demócrata*, October 4, 1915, 3. Emphasis in original.

61. Díaz Lombardo was a Maderista from the north who joined the Villista camp, serving as minister of Foreign Affairs after Villa split from the Convention in January 1915. Obregón was not actually in Mexico City in October 1915, though Díaz Lombardo may have been. Obregón had recently defeated Villa at the battle of Aguascalientes in the north. President Wilson had recognized the Carranza government that Obregón represented, a change in U.S. policy, as earlier it was Villa who had U.S. support. That October, Villa's plan was to force Wilson to reconsider his support for Carranza by taking control of Chihuahua and Sonora, two border states that were important to American business. Wilson instead supported the Constitutionalists. "En el empeño," *El Demócrata*, October 24, 1915, 1; Knight, *Mexican Revolution*, 2:292; Michael J. Gonzalez, *The Mexican Revolution*, 1910–1940 (Albuquerque: University of New Mexico Press, 2002), 150–51.

62. By November the Casa was facilitating stepped-up unionization of the sectors in which women were employed: clothing, hats, corsets, cigarettes, bottle caps, boxes, candy, and flour. These female unions and unions in male sectors continued to make both short-term demands concerning wages to alleviate the dire economic situation in the city as well as long-term demands about workplace safety, union recognition, and job protection. Lear, *Workers*, 319–25.

63. "Venta de prendas," *El Demócrata*, August 16, 1915, 4; August 30, 1915, 4.

64. In October 1915 Governor César López de Lara informed pawnshop owners that establishments not operating under the new regulations would be closed by the government, suggesting that by that time some pawnbrokers had reopened. "Si los dueños de empeños no se sujetan a lo dispuesto se les cerraron sus establecimientos," *El Demócrata*, October 17, 1915, 1; "Los dueños de bazares haran borrar de sus comercios la palabra 'empeño,'" *El Pueblo*, January 5, 1916, 2.

65. "Reglamento de bazares," *El Demócrata*, January 28, 1916, 1, 7.

66. "Los empeños," *El Pueblo*, January 27, 1916.

67. Knight, *Mexican Revolution*, 2:317; Gómez-Galvarriato, "Evolution of Prices," 355–56, 360–65; Buchenau, *Tools of Progress*, 76–77.

68. "Comentarios breves: Los empeños y los bazares," *El Pueblo*, October 13, 1917, 3.

69. "Casas, empeños, Montes de Piedad, bazares, agencias de inhumaciones," *El Pueblo*, November 19, 1917, 4. For more on the themes of necessary evil, redemption, and revolution in the city, see Bliss, *Compromised Positions*, and "The Science of Redemption: Syphilis, Sexuality and Reformism in Revolutionary Mexico City," *Hispanic American Historic Review* 79, no. 1 (1999): 1–40.

70. "La vuelta de los empeños," *El Demócrata*, February 10, 1920.

71. *El Pueblo*, October 4, 1917, 6. In response to the world depression's impact in Mexico, in 1933 the Monte de Piedad expanded to ten branches in the Federal District. Their addresses were: Mesones No. 14, La Merced No. 3, Justo Sierra No. 31, Tacubaya No. 7, Puente de Jesús No. 12, Brasil No. 8, Hidalgo No. 3, San Juan No. 13, Puente de Alvarado No. 62, and Totoquihuatzin No. 8. González Navarro, *La pobreza*, 229.

72. Loaning what he pleased, he allegedly refused to accept pawns whenever he felt like it: "This confirms the vulgar saying, 'from a stick you get splinters.' Almost all of the appraisers of the branches are of the same wood as the director, who, in addition to his huge salary [*sueldazo*] and living regally in the palace on Empedradillo, is the owner of half of Mexico. Not to mention the fact that he also does business on the side and speculates with [other people's] poverty." "El Monte de Piedad," *El Combate*, July 2, 1915, 2. It is not clear who was director at this time, as 1915 saw three turnovers in the position: Eugenio Barousse, Luis Martínez del Campo, and then again Eugenio Barouuse. Cabrera Siles and Escandón, *Historia*, 35. The institution's management took a paternalistic stance toward the behavior of their customers. When the governing board proposed to close on Sundays (they had been open from 8 to 10 A.M.) and extend Saturday hours until 8:30 P.M. instead of 7 P.M., the logic was that if the hours on Saturday, which was usually payday, were expanded, it would be easier for workers ("generally the people who visit the branches") to redeem their goods before they spent the money on "unfortunate" choices.

73. The "thousand and one" description and the length of the wait is from "El Monte de Piedad, al descubierto," *El Demócrata*, April 30, 1920, 1. The behavior of the guards is noted in "Por que una atormentada teoria," *El Demócrata*, May 1, 1920, 1.

74. For a photograph from 1915, see Fondo Casasola, Fototeca Nacional del Institutio Nacional de Historia, no. 88457. For the 1920s, see Cabrera Siles and Escandón, *Historia*, 94, 107, and 113. For the circa 1930 photograph, see Fototeca no. 88473 For two others from the 1930s featuring women, see nos. 86903 and 86905.

75. A reporter believed that if the institution really wanted, as claimed, to help more of the "people in the middle class or the lower needy class" and not run out of money in a few hours, then the maximum loan should be lowered by one half or one third. "Por que una atormentada teoria," *El Demócrata*, May 1, 1920, 3; Cabrera Siles and Escandón, *Historia*, 288, 292.

76. In 1920 beds with *tambours* that were not metal were eliminated altogether, as was furniture that was well worn or damaged. Weapons, however, could again be pawned. Cabrera Siles and Escandón, *Historia*, 296–300.

77. *El Pueblo*, August 6, 1917, 9.

78. "El Monte de Piedad al descubierto," *El Demócrata*, April 30, 1920, 4.

79. *El Demócrata*, July 28, 1920, 5. For an example of the new Monte advertisement format listing large furniture items and pianos individually with set prices, see *El Demócrata*, August 22, 1920, 3.

80. Carranza's first attempts to stabilize paper currency failed, and the establishment of a National Bank was under study through the first part of 1917.

81. Motts, *La vida*, 45; "Verdades económicas y financieras," *El Pueblo*, July 23, 1917, 7; "Una irregularidad en el Nacional Monte de Piedad," *El Pueblo*, July 25, 1917, 5; "Recibirá a la par los tostones y el oro el Nacional Monte de Piedad," *El Pueblo*, July 28, 1917, 1.

82. "Por qué una atormentada teoría," *El Demócrata*, May 1, 1920, 4.

83. Some were new arrivals, as the revolutionary activity increased the factors that pushed people out of the countryside, providing a constant stream of refugees into the city. But those women not versed in the culture of collateral credit would have quickly learned from neighbors which pawnbroker would give the best deal when the pinch of the disastrous economy of 1914–16 hit them. New arrivals may have been regular collateral-credit borrowers, as hocking with individuals, retail businesses, and pawnshops was common throughout the country.

84. The historic female majority continued to obtain, with 496,325 females (55 percent) and 409,738 males, for a total population in the Federal District in 1921 of 906,063. In some parts of the city the ratio of females to males was higher. Mexico City's Cuartel 8, for example, was 60 percent female. But in three municipalities (Cuajimalpa, Tlalpan, and Xochimilco), there were slightly more males than females. Females made up 55 percent of the "mixed" population, 56 percent of the white population, 54 percent of the indigenous population, and only 36 percent of the foreign immigrant population.

85. This reinclusion of ethnic categorization in the census gathering is interesting in light of historical debates about a periodization for Mexican identity. Back in 1811, when Creoles were emerging nationalists, colonial bureaucrats counted inhabitants according to a tripartite ethnic code: "español," "casta," and "indio." In the nineteenth century, when Charles Hale argues "Creole" identity took hold, the census categories became generic. Though Creole nationalism emphasized the European-American legacies that shaped the new country, the liberal government counted people in terms of sex, civil status, employment status, and age, but not race. The Porfirian censuses did count indigenous-language speakers as well as foreign-language speakers, but this is not a sufficient measure of ethnicity. In the twentieth century, when a "mestizo" identity emerged validating both the indigenous past and the benefits of a "cosmic race," there was a return to a tripartite count, but the specific "Spanish" was exchanged for a more general "white," "caste" becomes "mixed," and "Indian" becomes "indigenous." Charles Hale, "Los mitos políticos de la nación mexicana: El liberalismo y la revolución," *Historia Mexicana* 46, no. 4 (1997): 821–37; Brading, *First America*; José Vasconcelos, *La raza cosmica: Misión de la raza Iberoamericana, Argentina y Brasil* (México: Espasa-Calpe, 1966).

86. "Por la moralidad de los hogares," *El Demócrata*, September 28, 1914, 1.

87. The percentage of single females decreased significantly from 1910 to 1921, from 40 percent to 30 percent, even more than the married population grew. Estados Unidos Mexicanos, Departamento de la Estadistica Nacional, *Censo General de Habitantes, 30 de Noviembre de 1921, Distrito Federal* (México: Talleres Graficos de la Nación, 1925). Ann Blum found that "of the women age twenty to twenty-nine who had been married but were widowed, divorced or separated in 1921 (14.6 percent of married women aged twenty to thirty), almost 82 percent had at least one child." Blum, "Public Welfare," 259.

88. The degree to which this divesting of female real-estate owners is due to a generation of changes in inheritance law stemming from the Porfirian civil codes or other factors is unclear.

89. Cited in Thompson, "Households," 153.

90. "El gordo" is a common euphemism for a lottery jackpot still used today. Fulano de Tal, "Por poco me la saco," *El Diario*, January 4, 1913, 3.

91. Balcony seats went for twenty-five pesos, while those in the gallery cost ten pesos. *El Demócrata*, January 4, 1918, 7.

92. "Inscripciones en la Escuela N. de Enseñanza Doméstica," *El Demócrata*, May 10, 1916, 5.

93. "Los Criados," *El Demócrata*, August 2, 1919, 2.

94. "La Casa Amiga de la Obrera," *El Pueblo*, January 4, 1917, 2. It is not known how many other day-care facilities there were in the city or how many households they served.

95. "Reparto de certificados a las alumnas de la Academia Comercial Nocturna Ignacio M. Altamirano," *El Pueblo*, January 4, 1917.

96. Elena Poniatowsa, *Hasta no verte Jesús Mío*. 22nd ed. (México: Era, 1983), 136; Bliss, *Compromised Positions*; Blum, "Public Welfare."

97. Two other sewing machines, furnishings such as mirrors, electric coffeemakers, kitchen utensils, table-service items, a rifle, two bicycles, and accessories such as eyeglasses and umbrellas were also in the Escandón collateral inventory. The owners of the forty-five-piece table-service set, another framed painting, and two portable telephones, each pawned for a twenty-peso loan, were certainly middle-class residents. On the purchase of Singer sewing machines on installment, see Bucheanau, *Tools of Progress*, 28–29.

98. Appadurai, *Social Life of Things*. On the relationship between furniture and class, see Patricia Vega Jiménez, "From Benches to Sofas: Diversification of Patterns of Consumption in San José (1857–1930)," in Orlove, *Allure of the Foreign*, 67–92; and Leora Auslander, *Taste and Power: Furnishing Modern France* (Berkeley: University of California Press).

99. Remembering Mrs. Tweedie's imagery of the bulky wardrobe suspended on poles in the crowded streets, one wonders what it cost the borrower to transfer such heavy goods to the lending establishment. Motts, *La vida*, 57–58,

100. "A los señores propietarios o encargados de los bazares," *El Pueblo*, December 4, 1915, 5.

101. "Como viven los pobres," *El Demócrata*, May 8, 1920, 3.

102. The weekly expenses consisted of: seven kilos of cornmeal, seventy centavos; one kilo of rice, forty-eight centavos; one kilo of lard, one peso eighty centavos; three liters of milk, ninety centavos; half a kilo of coffee, fifty centavos; half a kilo of sugar, seventy centavos; two bars of soap, forty centavos; two kilos of beans, sixty-four centavos; seven candles, twenty-one centavos; coal or kindling, fifty centavos; and finally, chiles, fifty centavos. "Huelga general de los obreros de San Angel," *El Demócrata*, April 10, 1920, 5.

103. This dichotomy suggests an interesting parallel with what Greg Grandin found for nineteenth-century Guatemala, although he dealt there with an overwhelmingly indigenous population. Photographs show that while K'iche elite men adopted Western clothing as they developed an alternative nationalism to the acculturation-based liberal one, women continued to wear indigenous dress, thus combining in K'iche nationalism elements of white and indigenous symbols. Greg Grandin, *Blood of Guatemala: A History of Race and Nation* (Durham: Duke University Press, 2000), 174–96.

104. Irwin, *Mexican Masculinities*.

105. "Por que una atormentada teoria," *El Demócrata*, May 1, 1920, 1.

106. Pawning a pair of irons when one was in need of cash to buy medicine was a scenario featured by the press in their indictment of private pawnbroking during the revolution. Indeed, irons were often pawned in pairs. Motts reports that at the turn of the century irons were made of steel, and electric irons were not available until 1906. Motts, *La vida*, 55.

107. Motts, *La vida*, 57.

108. Motts, *La vida*, 64.

109. Businesses were inspected for compliance with the Sanitary Code, and for women who sewed at home, the investigators wanted to "verify the conditions in which they do so, what kind of finances they have, work orders, . . . whether or not there is work constantly throughout the year and how it is distributed and remunerated." "Visitas preparatorias a la Convención de Costureras," *El Diario*, December 31, 1913, 5.

110. González Navarro, *La pobreza*, 228. During the government of Avila Camacho in the 1940s, almost 7,500 sewing machines that had been pawned for loans totaling more than 786,811 pesos and fees totally 62,000 pesos in the Monte de Piedad and the Montepío Saviñón were returned to their owners without their having to repay the loans. González Navarro, *La pobreza*, 260.

111. *El Demócrata*, March 15, 1921, 10. González Navarro argues that the Monte did not accept automobiles until the 1930s, "when the crisis also reached those of high economic position." González Navarro, *La pobreza*, 229; Buchenau, *Tools of Progress*.

112. For the classified section with dozens of used-furniture ads, see *El Demócrata*, April 26, 1920, 9; for the Riestra ad, see *El Demócrata*, April 30, 1920, 10.

113. While not a new practice, the number of businesses advertising their desire to purchase Monte de Piedad pawn tickets is notable in the newspapers. To what extent these businesses overlapped with the more traditional bazaars, as well as to what extent pawnbrokers turned into second-hand jewelers, is not clear. See, for example, "Boletos Nacional Monte de Piedad," and "Ventas varios," *El Demócrata*, October 23, 1915, 4.

114. Study of the Mexican Revolution constitutes a cottage industry for historians, with works too numerous to cite. For overviews of the vast literature and positions on particular interpretations, see the works cited in chapter 7, note 3, above. See also Keith A. Haynes, "Dependency, Postimperialism, and the Mexican Revolution: An Historiographic Review," *Mexican Studies/Estudios Mexicanos* 7, no. 2 (1991): 225–51; Anna Macias, *Against All Odds: The Feminist Movement in Mexico to 1940* (Westport CT: Greenwood Press, 1982); Sancho Riba, "Las condiciones económicas"; Ramona Falcon, "Los origenes populares de la revolución de 1910: El caso de San Luis Potosí," *Historia Mexicana* 29, no. 2 (1979): 197–240; Cole Blaiser, "Studies of Social Revolutions: Origins, in Mexico, Bolivia, and Cuba," *Latin American Research Review* 2, no. 3 (1967): 28–64; Frank Brandenburg, *The Making of Modern Mexico* (Prentice Hall, 1964).

115. On newspapers as middle-class cultural productions, see Bourdieu, *Distinction*.

116. For discussion of female motives in collective actions, see Porter, "And That It Is Custom." See also Temma Kaplan, "Female Consciousness and Collective Action," *Signs: Journal of Women in Culture and Society* 31 (1982): 545–66; Lear, *Workers*; Sonia E. Alvarez, *Engendering Democracy in Brazil: Women's Movements in Transition Politics* (Princeton: Princeton University Press, 1990).

117. Lear depends on descriptions of consumption riots, because "rioters themselves apparently left no written record." Lear, *Workers*, 305–10. The revolution is not the first time that women engaged the government over policy issues. Susie Porter analyses a number of petitions from female ambulant vendors in the last years of the Porfiriato.

118. Obregón is quoted by Lear, *Workers*, 306. Charles Hale has explored the relationship of liberalism and revolution as two unifying political myths for Mexico. Hale, "Los mitos políticos," 821–37.

119. Enriqueta Tuñon, "El otorgamiento del sufragio femenino," *Historias* 41 (1998): 91–111; Macias, *Against All Odds*; Elizabeth Salas, *Soldaderas in the Mexican Military* (Austin: University of Texas Press, 1990).

Conclusion

1. "Por que una atormentada teoria de mujeres forma 'cola' a las puertas del los Montepios," *El Demócrata*, May 1, 1920, 1.

2. "El Monte de Piedad al descubierto," *El Demócrata*, April 30, 1920, 4.

3. *El Demócrata*, July 28, 1920, 5.

4. Some deputies dissented on this part of Article 9 of the Ley de Trabajo, arguing that it was against the constitution to prevent anyone from exercising their right to work wherever they wanted to do so. Waitresses defended their right to make a living by striking and shutting down fancy restaurants. "Otros tres artículos de la Ley del Trabajo son aprobados," *El Demócrata*, May 11, 1919, 6; "Aprobada la Ley de Trabajo, no habrá más mujeres en las tabernas de la República," *El Demócrata*, May 13, 1919, 3; "Huelga de meseras," *El Demócrata*, January 9, 1920, 7. For regulation of the sex trade in the city in the 1920s and 1930s, see Bliss, *Compromised Positions*.

5. Benedict Anderson, *Imagined Communities: Reflections on the Origins and Spread of Nationalism* (London: Verso, 1983).

6. Eric Van Young, "The Raw and the Cooked: Elite and Popular Ideology in Mexico, 1800–1821," in Szuchman, *Middle Period*, 75–102; Cope argues that patron-client relationships were more important than the state in colonial urban daily life. Cope, *Limits*. See also Susan Deans-Smith, "Culture, Power, and Society in Colonial Mexico," *Latin American Research Review* 31, no. 1 (1998): 257–77.

7. Literature on popular defiance of social legislation from the late Bourbon era has shown that the popular sectors of society long had their own preferences and agendas in living their daily lives. See the essays in Beezley, Martin, and French, *Rituals of Rule*. See also Viqueira Alba, *Propriety and Permissiveness*; Silvia Arrom, "Vagos y mendigos en la legislación mexicana, 1745–1845," in *Memoria del IV Congreso de Historia del Derecho Mexicano* (México, Universidad Nacional Autónoma de México, 1986), 1:71–87; Pamela Voekel, "Peeing on the Palace: Bodily Resistance to Bourbon Reforms in Mexico City," *Journal of Historical Sociology* 5, no. 2 (1992): 183–208; *Del dicho al hecho . . . Transgresiones y pautas culturales en la Nueva España* (México: Instituto Nacional de Antropología e Historia, 1989); and González Angulo, "Los gremios," 25–36. In summing up the lessons of this social and cultural history scholarship, Arrom states that "the popular classes contested the state for control of their daily lives, and they often won." Silvia Arrom, "Introduction," in *Riots in the Cities: Popular Politics and the Urban Poor in Latin America 1765–1910*, ed. Silvia M. Arrom and Servando Ortoll, 9 (Wilmington DE: Scholarly Resources, 1996).

Epilogue

1. Emilio García Riera, *Historia documental del cine mexicana, 1949–50* (Guadalajara: Universidad de Guadalajara, 1992), 349–50. On post-1940s culture see Gilbert Joseph, Anne Rubenstein, and Eric Zolov, eds. *Fragments of a Golden Age: The Politics of Culture in Mexico since 1940* (Durham: Duke University Press, 2001); Eric Zolov, *Refried Elvis: The Rise of the Mexican Counterculture* (Berkeley: University of California Press, 1999); and Anne Rubenstein, *Bad Lan-*

guage, Naked Ladies, and Other Threats to the Nation: A Political History of Comic Books in Mexico (Durham: Duke University Press, 1998).

2. Cabrera Siles and Escandón, *Historia.*

3. Thompson, "Households," 66, 76–77.

4. Heather L. Williams, *Planting Trouble: The Barzón Debtors' Movement in Mexico* (San Diego: Center for U.S.–Mexican Studies, 1996).

5. Julio Moreno, *Yankee Don't Go Home! Mexican Nationalism, American Business Culture, and the Shaping of Modern Mexico, 1920–1950* (Chapel Hill: University of North Carolina Press, 2003).

6. Raul Daniel García López, delegate of the Employees Union of the National Monte de Piedad, May 1, 1997, interview by Juan Rodríguez Buendía, Mexico City.

INDEX

Page numbers in italics refer to illustrations.

Acordada, Revolution of the, 98
agiotistas, 7, 216, 239
Aladama, Juan de, 54
Alemán, Lucas, 81
Amarillas, Viceroy Marqués de, 19
American occupation (of Mexico), 120, 128, 141
appraisal (of pawned goods), 27, 58, 63, 67–68, 74–75, 129, 130, 136–38, 145, 211, 215
Arrom, Silvia, 143
artisans, 23, 30, 42, 90
auctions, 65, 67–68, 73–75, 122, 129, 131, 211, 215, 230, 239, 244, 254
automobiles, 254
Azanza, Viceroy Miguel Joseph de, 23

bakers, 27
bank: Porfirian, 206, 229; savings, at Monte de Piedad, 141–42, 245; seizures, 240
baratillo, 93–94
Bases Orgánicas, 140
bazaars, 122, 220, 230, 236, 237, 238–41, 254
Beneficencia Pública, 75, 248
benevolence, 155
Berrenguer de Marquina, Viceroy Felix, 28
bicycles, 185
Bourbon Reforms, 10, 18, 21–23, 45–46, 48
Bourdieu, Pierre, 5, 13
boycotts, 231
Braudel, Fernand, 262
Bucareli, Viceroy Antonio María de, 21, 25–26, 61
bureaucrats, 26, 31, 61, 81
Bustamante, Carlos María, 54
Bustamante, President Anastasio, 55, 82, 83

Calderón de la Barca, Fanny, 98, 176
Calleja, Viceroy Félix María, 69
capitalism, 7, 12, 15, 131–32, 190, 258, 260, 262
Carlota, Empress, 142
Caro, José, 231
Carranza, Venustiano, 229, 236, 240, 248
Carranzistas, 230, 238, 239
carriages, 30, 97
Casa Boker, 240
Casa de Amiga de la Obrera, 248
Casa del Obrero, 230, 239
Casa de Niños Expósitos, 22
casas de empeño. *See* pawnshops
casas de vecindad, 31, 34, 90–91
castas, 31–32
Cendejas, Francisco de Paula, 10
census, 18, 80–81; of 1811, 31–35; of 1843, 54; of 1844, 86; of 1882, 154; Porfirian, 155–57, 163–64; of 1921, 245
Chandler, D. S., 26
charity, 4, 7, 14, 21, 75, 140, 161, 211
Charles III, King, 25
Chao, General Manuel, 234
Chavero, Alfredo, 128
church divestment, 84
citizenship, 80–81, 256
cloth, 11, 17, 38, 102, 203, 250
clothing: cost of, 29, 94, 98, 99, 182; in dowries, 11; dress codes, 24; pawned, 1, 12, 17, 20, 36–38, 59, 102–3, 182, 203, 250–52; sewing of, 42, 103–4, 180–82, 253; style of, 10, 80, 88, 94, 97, 99, 182–83, 252
Cofradías, 91
collective action, 226, 231, 255–56
Company of Mary, 22
conflict: between merchants and customers, 237; between pawnbrokers and customers, 226, 233–34
Congress, 10, 55, 85
conservatives, 15, 80, 61, 112, 124, 140
consignment of goods, 192, 215–16, 217
Constitution of 1812 (Spanish), 49
Constitution of 1824, 60
Constitution of 1857, 85
Constitution of 1917, 256, 262
Consulado, 49, 50, 60–61
consumption, 4, 6–9, 13–14, 18, 28, 43, 92–100, 111–13; in Porfiratio, 150, 173, 176, 187; during revolution, 225, 239, 250, 260; today, 269–70

Conventionists, 231
corner stores: 4, 17, 19, 21, 22, 24–25, 29, 31; and business trends, 56–58; capital investment in, 57; as family enterprises, 57–58; pawning clientele in, 24, 42
corn grinders, 88, 89, 104, 164
Cortes de Cádiz, 10, 48
Costeloe, Michael, 97
cost of living, 24, 36, 80, 90, 94–101, 160–61, 228, 240, 252, 255
Couto, Antonio Manuel, 63, 70, 75
Creoles, 2, 13, 17, 21, 26–28, 31–32, 36, 44, 50, 55, 259
Croix, Viceroy Carlos Francisco de, 50
currency: copper, 81–82; issues at Monte de Piedad, 71–72; paper, 206, 225, 229, 231, 240

daughters, 11, 22, 23, 152, 259
decapitalization, 240–41
Decena Trágica, 224, 228
Del Campo, Angel, 170–71
Delgado, Rafael, 162
department stores, 176, 270
Diario del Hogar, 186, 208, 209
Diario Oficial, 214
Díaz, Felix, 228
Díaz, President Porfirio, 100, 150, 175, 189, 209, 225, 264
discourse: about domesticity; 18, 104, 151–55, 245; about liberalism, 123, 213; about pawning, 7, 18, 20, 24, 28–31, 45, 91, 112, 150, 170–76, 242, 262, 271; about vice, 20, 28–29
domesticity, 9, 121, 151–55, 187, 248, 260
Dominguez, Miguel, 54
Douglas, Mary, 13
dowries, 11, 13, 23, 35, 96–97
drinking, 28–29, 50

education of women, 22–23, 154
El Correo Español, 190, 192, 232
El Demócrata, 224, 238, 238, 243, 247, 261
El Diario, 246
El Distrito Federal, 131
El Hijo de Ahuizote, 208
El Hogar, 181
El Imparcial, 163, 211
El Monitor Republicano, 171, 174
El Nacional, 215
El Obrero Mexicano, 174
El Pabellón Español, 190
El Partido Liberal, 215
El Pueblo, 241
El Siglo XIX, 97, 216
embroidery, 23, 104, 179, 253
empeñeros. *See* pawnbrokers
Employees' Union of the National Monte de Piedad, 271
employment, informal, 33–34
enaguas. *See* petticoats
Enlightenment, The, 11, 18, 21, 22, 263
entrepreneurs, 4, 53, 123, 147, 213; female, 53–54, 121–22, 197
ethnicity, 14, 18, 21, 31, 34, 44, 47, 80, 156, 245, 259, 261

Fagoaga, Francisco, 124
Farnsworth-Alvear, Ann, 5
fashion, 97–99, 126, 151, 252
fathers, 22, 31, 86
Federal District, 128, 130, 132, 157–59, 164–65
Feijóo y Montenegro, Benito Gerónimo, 22
Fernández de Lizardi, José Joaquín, 27, 29, 93
fondas, 95, 121
French Intervention, 10, 120, 140
Fuentes Nuñez, José, 206
furniture, 9–11, 15, 84, 171, 179–80, 180, 224, 227, 239, 241, 250, 254

Gachupìn. *See* Spanish immigrant
Gálvez, Viceroy José de, 21
gambling, 173–74, 242
Gamboa, Manuel de, 61, 65, 68
gender, 13, 181; and goods 101–3, 252; and labor market 223, 88, 164; and policy, 18
gente de bien, 1, 36, 95
gente decente, 1, 3, 36, 80; employed at Monte de Piedad, 61
Gobernación, 12, 60, 82, 116, 146, 213
González, General Pablo, 239
González, President Manuel, 206
Gooch Chambers, Fanny, 150, 162, 165, 176, 179
goods: collateral, in *empeños*, 25, 78–79, 82, 101–7, 138–39, 175–86, 203–5, 227, 228, 240, 250–54; —, items forbidden as, 29–30, 108, 112, 125, 128, 148, 228; —, as investment, 42, 44, 46, 87–88, 225, 259; —, in Monte de Piedad, 38–41, 58–59, 73–74, 77, 85, 143, 146, 244–45, 250–54; —, in *pulperías*, 4, 7, 11, 14, 15, 19, 21, 27, 28–29, 36–42; —, redeemed, 8, 37, 66, 73–75, 124,

211; —, unredeemed, 66, 73, 75, 124, 128–29, 130–31, 135, 136, 200, 237; household, 4, 10, 11, 19, 36, 38, 79, 101–7, 176–86, 188, 189, 249, 254, 270–71; luxury, 28, 83, 108, 176, 255, 258; pawned, 4, 8, 25; secondhand, 93–94, 226, 240 (see also *baratillo*; bazaars); stolen, 30, 92, 102–3, 127, 128. *See also* redemption
government: of city Ayuntamiento, 27, 50, 93, 116, 198, 214, 221; colonial, 12, 18–19; Federal District, 72, 116, 123, 132, 214; national, 12, 81
grocers, 17, 19
Guías de forasteros, 99, 119, 120, 123
guilds, 23, 24
Gutierrez Najera, Manuel, 6, 160, 180, 191

Hacienda, Real, 26, 60, 66, 67
hegemony, 12, 13, 78, 111, 147, 259, 264–65
holidays, 63, 93, 271
hombres de bien, 36, 78, 80, 95–101, 112
honor, 5, 18–22, 28, 86, 262
households: female-headed, 8–9, 30, 31–33, 41, 79, 86, 156, 267
housekeeping, 5, 8, 10, 18, 19, 23, 34, 36, 43–44, 79, 81, 101, 150–88, 226, 245–54, 258–59; in statistics, 165–69
housing, 31, 34, 90–91, 95, 252
Huerta, Victoriano, 226, 229
husbands, 9, 11, 31, 32, 152, 261

identity, 2, 5, 6, 14, 28, 36, 43, 44, 161, 259
immigrants, 17, 49, 53, 118–21. *See also* Spanish immigrants
imports, 10, 28, 183, 240, 254
Independence, 21, 24, 50, 55, 60
Indians, 17, 31–32, 34, 156
industrialization, 115, 245
inflation, 24, 161, 205, 225, 229, 244
inheritance, 96, 108, 152
inspections (of pawnshops), 132–33
interest rates: at corner stores, 20, 55–56; at Monte de Piedad, 26, 72; at pawnshops, 82, 114–15, 124–27, 129–30, 142, 148–49, 198, 202–3, 206, 222, 230, 236–37, 239, 241, 263
International Committee, 231
inventories, 12–14, 37, 135–38, 177–86
irons, 106, 107, 177
Isabella, Queen, 7
Isherwood, Baron, 13
Iturrigaray, Viceroy José de, 54

Jara, Heriberto, 230
jewelry, 1, 11, 17, 19, 27, 36, 87–88, 93, 110, 228, 239, 254
Juárez, President Benito, 10, 124, 128, 132, 140, 143
Juego de la Oca, 1–6, 9–12, 80, 213
Junta de Beneficencia, 209

labor, gendered division of, 9, 23, 88, 151, 164–65
La Colonia Española, 190
La Familia, 154
La Federación, 217
laissez-faire economics, 79, 114, 130
La Mujer Mexicana, 153, 181
La Nación, 232
landlords, 83, 84, 152, 156, 246
laundresses, 12, 90, 107–8, 109, 154, 167, 170, 177, 183, 184–85
laundry, 33
La Voz de España, 190
Lazpita, Antonio María, 142–43
Lear, John, 236
legislation: and Civil Codes, 86, 152; family, 151; pawning, 12, 19, 82, 108, 112, 116–18, 123–33, 146, 189, 266; property, 152; Siete Partidas, 20
lenders: in factories, 87, 161; married women and widows as, 7
Lender's Union, 231, 234
Lerdo de Tejada, President Sebastián, 10, 124
Liberalism, 3, 10–12, 15, 21, 79–86, 114–15, 123–33, 146–48, 151–55, 213–18, 221, 223, 242, 256, 262–65
liberals, 15, 55, 80, 81, 82, 90, 123, 128, 263–64
lifestyle: middle-class, 3, 6, 9, 23, 25–27, 36, 47, 48, 80, 92, 146, 151, 162–64, 170, 177, 252–54; working-class, 3, 13, 25, 92, 94, 161, 253
lighting, 179
linens, 5, 11, 14, 38, 107, 177–78, 251
Lizana y Beaumont, Viceroy Francisco Javier, 60
loan values, 26, 27, 37, 40, 43–44, 75, 78, 84, 94, 102, 110, 136–37, 140, 143, 145, 179, 185–86, 203, 205, 243–44
lottery, 12, 67

Madero, President Francisco, 224–25, 226
Magaña, General Gildardo, 237, 402n56
marriage, 19, 22, 245
married women. *See* wives
Maximilian, 78, 84, 124, 128, 142–43
Mejía, General Ignacio, 10
merchants, 26, 31, 34, 52–55, 237

mestizo/mestiza, 3, 31, 34, 36, 81, 156, 259
Mexican Revolution, 6, 15, 224–57, 264
middle class, 1–8, 12, 16, 26, 79, 80, 95–101, 146, 156–59, 173, 187, 190, 250–55
Miramón, Miguel, 140
mobilizations, popular, 15, 231–32, 235, 236
molenderas. *See* corn grinders
Molina Enríquez, Andres, 162
Monte de Piedad: archive, 12, 14, 270; balance, 66, 69, 75, 141, 205; branch offices, 16, 84, 142–46, 189, 205–8, 269; business operations, 68–75, 140–47; business volume, 70–71, 209–10; clientele, 21, 26, 28, 43–44, 110–11, 243, 253, 261–62; colonial period, 17, 19, 25–27, 45, 48; founding, 4, 12, 21, 31; fraud, 66, 68, 145; governance of, 58–70; location of, 61, 140; in Madrid, 35–36; mismanagement, 66–69, 145, 205; national period, 6, 8, 15–16, 139–47, 174–75, 205–12; pawned goods at, 38–40, 102, 253; precursors of, 58; public image, 48, 189, 209; relation to pawnshops, 139, 149, 214, 219; relations with government, 60, 76–77, 139–40, 206; during revolution, 227, 243–45; statutes, 62–63
Monte de Piedad (film), 268–69
Montepío (state pension institution), 22
Montepío Luz Saviñon, 209, 211–12, 227
montepíos. *See* pawnshops
Montiel, Tiburcio, 130, 132
Mora, José María Luis, 80
mothers, 18, 21, 22, 86–87, 245, 248, 261
Motts, Irene Elena, 6, 163, 250
mujeres de bien, 36, 79

nationalism, 226, 263
Navarro, Vicente, 231
newspapers, 13, 190, 208, 226, 237, 239

Ober, Frederick, 172, 185, 189
Obregón, Alvaro, 229, 235, 236, 256

Palancares, Jesusa, 248
pamphlets, 20, 24, 48
Paredes y Arrillagam Mariano, 80
Parián market, 33, 55, 98, 124
patriarchy, 18, 21, 23, 31–32, 44–46, 79, 85, 147, 262
pawnbrokers: 9, 12, 14, 15, 91, 100, 114–38; public image of, 122–23, 149; resistance of, 125–27, 214–15, 217–20
pawning: transaction costs of, 37, 130, 142, 244
pawnshops: business operations, 134–38, 189, 192–204; capitalization of, 134–35, 200–202; *casas de empeño*, 4, 14, 101–7, 114–38, 231; classification of, 116, 134–35, 200; clientele of, 101–7; closures of, 217, 231–33, 235; as family enterprises, 121, 196; locations of, 116–17, 134, 193; *montepíos*, 3, 4; multiple ownership of, 192–96; regulation of, 12, 124–33, 213–15, 226–37; as retail arena, 92, 226; sackings of, 224, 230, 235; turnover of, 196–97
pawn tickets, 126–27, 131, 139, 202, 236, 240
Payno, Manuel, 170
pensions, 4, 22, 35, 86, 248, 256. *See also* Montepío
petitions, 12, 124–27, 215, 221, 226, 229, 231–35, 255
petticoats, 17, 36–38, 94, 99, 102–3, 252
Philip IV, King, 41
Plan de Iguala, 60
pledge periods, 39, 59, 124, 143, 227, 230
policy, 13, 14, 17, 18, 19, 30, 32, 36, 47
population: of Mexico City, 3, 31, 80–81, 155–57, 164, 245
Porfiriato, The, 6, 11, 150–223, 255
Porrua, José, 192
positivism, 150–54, 189, 223
poverty, 5, 7, 24–25, 45, 91–92, 209, 235; and relief from, 90, 111, 235, 242
prendas. *See* collateral goods
prendas cumplidas. *See* collateral goods, unredeemed
Prieto, Guillermo, 9, 96, 104
profits: for owner of pawned good, 129, 132, 147, 198, 230; pawnbroker, 15, 51, 56–57, 115, 123, 189, 230, 255, 263
property: and statesmen, 81, 83, 112, 148, 152; and women, 7, 11, 42, 44–45, 96, 152, 246
prostitution, 33, 90, 249
protest, 230, 235, 255
pulperías. *See* corner stores
pulpero. *See* grocers; pawnbrokers; storekeepers
pulquería, 50, 189

rebozos, 17, 37, 38, 93, 99, 183, 252
Red Batallions, 236
redemption (of pawned goods), 8, 37, 66, 72, 74, 211, 236, 241, 259
Reform, The, 10, 84, 112, 128, 151
regulation: of commerce, 79, 123–33; of domestic servants, 82, 108; of pawning, 12, 20, 22, 29, 124–33, 191, 213–15, 226–37, 230, 233, 234–35, 237; of *pulperías*, 19, 24, 29–30, 45, 48–53, 56. *See also* legislation

rent, 84, 91, 95–96, 160
repawning, 82, 170
reproduction: cultural, 2, 5; social, 2, 8–9, 18, 20, 46, 81, 92, 258
respectability, 2, 5, 40, 250
Restored Republic, 10, 128, 143
retail, 14, 18, 19, 21, 49–58, 116–19, 190; shopping at pawnshops, 93, 226; of used goods, 240
Revillagigedo, Second Count of, Viceroy, 19, 56
Revolutionary Committee for the Relief of the Poor, 235
Riva Palacio, Mariano, 205
Riva Palacio, Vicente, 93
Romero de Terreros, Pedro, Conde de Regla, 21
Royal Pragmatic on Marriage, 22

Salinas de Gortari, President Carolos, 271
Santa Anna, President Antonio López de, 54, 82, 83, 112, 116, 118, 124–25, 141
satire, 2, 184–85, 208, 246–47
saving, 240–42, 255
seamstresses, 34, 35, 90, 93, 154, 160, 164, 181, 234, 253–54
Second Empire, 143
servants: in Bourbon era, 5, 9, 12, 17, 24, 30, 32, 34, 35, 36, 41; at mid-century, 79, 80, 82–83, 88, 90, 107–10, 112; in Porfiriato, 153, 160, 163–64, 166; during revolution, 247–48, 249, 253
Sesto, Julio, 150, 192
sewing, 23, 42, 93, 103–4, 180–82, 253
sewing machines, 180, 185, 186, 224, 228, 234, 253–54
shopping, 8, 83, 98, 176, 226
Siete Leyes, 81
Siete Partidas, 20
silver: as collateral, 7; jewelry, 11, 14, 27; tableware, 11, 14, 30, 38–40, 105–6, 108, 138, 177
single men, 91, 154, 156
single women, 9, 31, 86–89, 154, 156, 245–46
social class, 2, 5, 18, 21, 23, 259
social mobility: downward, 19, 25, 27, 41, 46, 79, 100, 242, 260, 262; upward, 171, 260
social welfare, 12, 19, 51–52, 79, 82, 112, 114–15, 189, 209, 263–64, 269
Spanish immigrants: in commerce, 118–20, 190–92, 231, 235, 237; prejudice against, 4, 52–56, 76, 118–19, 190–91, 232–33, 263; public image of, 122–23, 226, 237
storekeepers, 17, 19, 24, 27, 48–58
street vending, 33, 98, 167, 176
subsistence, 47, 48, 92, 111
suburbs, 150, 186
Supreme Court, 10

table-service items, 105, 177
taxes, 12, 23, 24, 83–84, 128, 148, 200, 205, 220
Thompson, E. P., 5
Thompson, Waddy, 87–88
tiendas de raya, 7
tobacco monopoly, 23, 34
tortilleras, 91, 94, 164, 193
transportation, 97–98, 160–61
Treasury, 4, 6, 145
Tresbuestos, Vicente, 61, 68
Tutino, John, 148
Tweedie, Mrs. Alec, 165, 172, 173, 176, 179, 189

unions, 229, 256
usury, 55, 114, 123, 216, 218, 230, 237

Venegas, Viceroy Javier, 60
Verrúa, Manuel, 104
Victoria, President Guadalupe, 63
Villa, General Francisco "Pancho," 227, 229, 236
Villistas, 235, 239

wages and salaries, 9, 24, 26, 88–90, 96, 127, 160–61, 165, 228–29, 252, 255, 269; at the Monte de Piedad, 68–70, 96, 144
watches, 111, 138, 175, 185
weapons, 111, 230
whiteness, 18, 22, 259
widows: in Bourbon era, 4, 7, 8, 9, 17, 20–21, 24, 31–32, 44, 198; at mid-century, 86; in Porfiriato, 152, 156; during revolution, 246, 256, 261
wives, 7, 17, 21–22, 26, 31, 34, 44, 86, 150, 151–52, 154, 261
worker organizations, 2, 4, 225, 236
workers, 24, 81
working class, 3, 6, 15–16, 156, 160–61, 187, 251–52
working women, 22–23, 152–53, 157, 165–67, 187, 248

Zapata, General Emiliano, 224
Zapatistas, 224, 230, 236
Zedillo Ponce de Leon, President Ernesto, 271

In the Engendering Latin America series

Sex and Danger in Buenos Aires: Prostitution, Family, and Nation in Argentina
Donna J. Guy

Between Civilization and Barbarism: Women, Nation, and Literary Culture in Modern Argentina
Francine Masiello

Women, Feminism, and Social Change in Argentina, Chile, and Uruguay, 1890–1940
Asunción Lavrin

I'm Going to Have a Little House: The Second Diary of Carolina Maria de Jesus
Carolina Maria de Jesus
Translated by Melvin S. Arrington Jr. and Robert M. Levine

White Slavery and Mothers Alive and Dead: The Troubled Meeting of Sex, Gender, Public Health, and Progress in Latin America
Donna J. Guy

Class Mates: Male Student Culture and the Making of a Political Class in Nineteenth-Century Brazil
Andrew J. Kirkendall

Female Citizens, Patriarchs, and the Law in Venezuela, 1786–1904
Arlene J. Díaz

False Mystics: Deviant Orthodoxy in Colonial Mexico
Nora E. Jaffary

Mexican Karismata: The Baroque Vocation of Francisca de los Ángeles, 1674–1744
Ellen Gunnarsdóttir

The Case of the Ugly Suitor and Other Histories of Love, Gender, and Nation in Buenos Aires, 1776–1870
Jeffrey M. Shumway

A Culture of Everyday Credit: Housekeeping, Pawnbroking, and Governance in Mexico City, 1750–1920
Marie Eileen Francois

CPSIA information can be obtained at www.ICGtesting.com
Printed in the USA
LVOW10s1758160813

348130LV00013B/345/A

9 780803 269231